W9-CNK-686

No Experience Required

Jackie Sherrill and Texas A&M's 12th Man Kickoff Team

Text: Caleb Pirtle III • **Design: Jutta Medina**

The Story That's Ne'er Been Told

Copyright© 2008 by the 12th MKOT Foundation.

All rights reserved. No part of this book can be reproduced, stored in a retrieval program, or transmitted in any form or by an means, electronic or mechanical, including photocopying, recording, or otherwise except as may be expressly permitted by the applicable copyright statues or in writing by the publishers and by the 12thMKOT Foundation.

ISBN: 978-0-9626682-0-3

12thMKOT Foundation Officers:

> Robert Crouch, President
> David Coolidge, Vice President
> R. Sean Page, Secretary
> Dennis Mudd, Treasurer

12thMKOT Board Members

David Coolidge	Mark Wurzbach
Robert Crouch	Tom Arthur
Dennis Mudd	Ike Liles
Barry Stevens	Billy Pickard
R. Sean Page	Ray Barrett
Ronnie Glenn	Steve Stevens
Dean Berry	Jackie Sherrill
Dana Batiste	Dr. John J. Koldus

No Experience Required: Jackie Sherrill and Texas A&M's 12th Man Kickoff Team
has been developed and produced by
Dockery House Publishing,
1221 Chateau Lane, Lindale, Texas 75771.
Phone: 903-882-6230.

Rodney L. Dockery, Publisher
Caleb Pirtle III, Editorial Director
Kim Dockery, Vice President of Marketing
Jutta Medina, Art Director

Cover Painting by Rick Rush: "Heart of the Twelfth"
Rick Rush of Tuscaloosa, Alabama, has been acclaimed as America's Sports Artist. Rush is recognized nationally and internationally for his ability to capture a single moment of time with an exuberance of style that reflects the power of the moment and the quiet solitude or sudden impact of the time. His brush has become the unequaled recorder of sports history.

Printed in the United States of America

First Edition

Tribute to James Barrett

In 1983, students at Texas A&M were not plugged in to cell phones, text messages, or internet. We typed our papers with the long forgotten typewriter. We stood in lines to receive our class schedules, picture ID's, and sports passes. The lines were so long we called them a tradition in Aggieland. At Northgate, the crowd at the Dixie Chicken spilled over onto the street on Thursday nights. We enjoyed Blue Bell ice cream at Charlie's. We scraped up two dollars for a Cow Pie, fries, and a coke at the Cow Hop. There were three male students to every female student. The Battalion newspaper was everyone's study break. And most students were related to a former Old Ag who had planted the Aggie seed deep in their souls. The question for these young people was not: "Where are you going to school?" but "What will be your class year at Texas A&M?"

James Barrett was a proud member of the Texas A&M Fightin' Class of '85. He was the son of Ray Barrett, Jr., a former Junction Boy and successful farmer and rancher. He played football on a small Class A football team in Rankin, Texas, and during his senior season, he played in the State Championship game with that team. James was even chosen to play in the Texas High School All Star game in Dallas. He desperately wanted to continue to play football, but only if it could be at Texas A&M. The seed his father planted many years earlier was maroon and white. He felt he was too small to ever step on Kyle Field wearing the maroon and white jersey, so he decided that being a student at Texas A&M was better than being a student athlete anywhere else.

It was just a small advertisement in The Battalion, but James was on an infamous study break when he spotted it. As students, we heard Coach Sherrill had been on the Bonfire stack, and that he was having try-outs for a kick off team. When James saw the ad, his eyes lit up, and he made me promise I would not tell another living soul. He did not want to disappoint his mom and dad if he didn't make it.

I will never forget when he came back after the first day of try-outs. He said there were a couple of hundred guys. He told me he wasn't the fastest, but he thought he could hold his own. It was going to be a battle, he would have to stay focused and work hard, but he was determined to make it. He told me he was going to wear that jersey.

The first home game of the 1983 season when he walked out on Kyle Field wearing Number 16, he was so proud. He was just a regular guy lucky enough to make the team. He had tried out for his own personal reasons, but when the student body reacted to the kick off team, he was humbled. He could not believe he was so fortunate to stand in the middle of Kyle Field playing the game he so passionate about for the school he loved. He happily went before practice and stayed after practice to be a part of the team. For the 1983 and 1984 football seasons, James Barrett was a proud member of the Fightin' Texas Aggie 12th man kickoff team.

On February 20, 1999, James was faced with a new battle. He was diagnosed with Amyotrophic Lateral Sclerosis (ALS), known to most as Lou Gehrig's Disease. The doctors told him to get his affairs in order; his life expectancy was two to five years. It was a devastating blow. He was a 35-year-old man with a wife and four young children. Yet somehow that same determination that I had seen nearly sixteen years earlier came back to him. He would do whatever it took to beat this wretched disease.

He went to California, Canada, Houston, and China looking for his miracle. He took vitamins, tried different diets, and drank herbal teas. The herbal teas were hard to smell. I will never know how he drank them. But he was willing to do whatever it took to win and be here to help raise his children.

Six and half years later, James Barrett's battle ended on May 20, 2005. As the disease weakened every muscle in his body, his faith grew stronger. He chose to fight the battle with courage and humor. He had a spirit that captivated everyone he came into contact with.

James literally impacted people all across the world through his illness. James loved his God and his family above all else, and he loved being on the 12th man kickoff team. He loved his fellow teammates. He loved joking with them and running downfield with them. He loved and respected Coach Sherrill. He loved Texas A&M University.

During their twenty-year reunion in 2003, the Original 12th man team gathered at our house. It was their first time to see James since his diagnosis. After the initial shock of seeing their buddy in a wheelchair, it was amazing to see these guys interact like no time had been lost. They were relentless in giving each other a hard time. They were telling stories and laughing. At that very moment, I realized the reason why the 12th man kickoff team worked. Coach Sherrill found a bunch of regular guys with heart and a zest for life. They loved football, and they loved Texas A&M. These guys worked toward a common goal – they just clicked. And the ordinary became extraordinary.

A Special Tribute

The 12th man kickoff team respectfully honors and pays tribute to

those 12th man teammates who have also gone before us:

12th Man Jeff Blair

and

12th Man Ashley Eddington

Their hard work and dedication on the practice field and

on game day provided an inspiration for us all.

Acknowledgements

First and foremost, Dockery House Publishing wants to acknowledge the long hours and many interviews allowed us by Coach Jackie Sherrill, who invented the 12th man kickoff team in 1983 to connect the Texas A&M student body with the football team. It was daring. It was criticized. It worked. Without the total dedication and determination of Coach Sherrill, the book on the exploits and the triumph of the 12th man team could have never been written.

Dockery House Publishing also acknowledges:

• The untiring efforts, support, and hard work of the 12th MKOT Foundation's officers for making the book a reality: Robert Crouch, Sean Page, David Coolidge, and Dennis Mudd.

• The members of the 12th man kickoff team, from 1983 through 1989, for the time they gave us: interviews and both reading and editing the manuscript to authenticate the accuracy of the events, the emotions, and the dialogue – although everyone admits that memories may have dimmed since they last raced onto Kyle Field more than two decades ago. So many of their personal photographs in the book depict better than words the impact they had on Aggie football. We also thank their wives and their families for allowing them the long hours it took to create No Experience Required. Also recognized are Vince Palasota for overseeing the design of the 12th man kickoff team Website and who, along with Ronnie Glenn and Rick Tankersley, was so instrumental in promoting and marketing the book. We appreciate Larry "Butch" Motley, Dennis Mudd, Dean Berry, Bubba Hillje, and Garry Sorrell for tracking down so many lost members of the 12th man teams and providing their own insights in countless revisions of the manuscript.

• The 12th man kickoff team coaches – David Beal, Roy Kokemoor, Burnis Simon, and Chris Massey ¬– for the memories they gave us in interviews. And we greatly appreciate the interviews provided by Coach R. C. Slocum, the defensive genius of Texas A&M, and Billy Pickard, the equipment manager, who made life miserable for members of the 12th man unit but worked diligently with Coach Sherrill to mold the players into the hard-nosed team they became.

• The sports writers and columnists for the campus newspaper, The Battalion, the Bryan Eagle, the Houston Post, and the Houston Chronicle who all provided day-to-day exploits of the 12th man kickoff team and Texas A&M football under the guidance of Coaches Jackie Sherrill and R. C. Slocum.

• Three fine books on Texas A&M, which provided us with a better understanding of Bear Bryant's days at Texas A&M, as well as the era and the Aggie players of the 1980s: The Junction Boys, written by Jim Dent for Thomas Dunn Books in 1999, Game of My Life, written by Brent Zwerneman in 2003 for Sports Publishing L.L.C., and Where Have You Gone, written by Rusty Burson in 2004 for Sports Publishing L.L.C.

• Cathy Capps, director, Texas A&M University Letterman's Association and Museum for the information and photographs she provided. Her devotion to the project went above and beyond the call of duty.

• The staff of the Cushing Library and Archives on the Texas A&M campus, who supplied old files that covered all aspects of Aggie football during the 1980s.

• Alan Cannon, sports information director, at Texas A&M who kept pointing us in the right direction when we reached a major new crossroad.

• Glenn Johnson of Johnson Photography in Bryan, whose brilliant photographs chronicled the glory days of the 12th man kickoff team.

• Carol Barrett, who supplied wonderful stories and photographs concerning Sherrill's first 12th man kickoff team.

• The Red Pots who traditionally supervised the building of Bonfire, in particular James Fuqua and Michael Guerra who remembered those nights on the stack with Coach Sherrill. Fuqua was there when the idea of a 12th man kickoff team was first envisioned around a domino game within the confines of an old shack known as the Bonfire Hilton.

• Dr. John J. Koldus for his sage wisdom and guidance in the development of the book.

Caleb Pirtle III acknowledges:

• Linda, my wife, for her strength and encouragement during the development of the book, and for the countless hours she spent editing, revising, and correcting the manuscript.

Sean Page acknowledges:

• Michael Paul, esq., of Gunn & Lee PC – Legal

• The law firm of Thornton, Biechlin, Segrato, Reynolds & Guerra for its legal work on the project:
    J.J. Trevino, esq.
    Randall Hutton, esq.
    Tim Singley, esq.
    Roger Howerton, certified paralegal

• Ed Mainz, esq., a former partner of Thornton, Biechlin, Segrato, Reynolds & Guerra, who provided edits and an invaluable life lesson in courage in the face of ALS.

• Jennifer Mainz, head tennis coach at the University of Alabama, who flew to Dallas to recite the entire manuscript to her father because of his health condition.

• Paul Uptmore and Johnny Stallings – two true 12th Men.

• James R. Page, '49, my hero.

• Mary Strauss-Page, my best friend

David Coolidge acknowledges:

• John Madden a true Aggie, who selflessly donated his time and expertise in creating the first 12th man kickoff team Website.

• Ashley Coolidge, my wife, the greatest thing in my life and who has made all of my dreams come true.

Dennis Mudd acknowledges:

• Awards and Engraving of Baytown, Texas, and Michelle Bitterly for her tireless efforts and assistance in designing the 12thMKOT logo.

• Wife Jamie and children, Galen, Shannon, Mary, and Brandon, for the sacrifices they made when I had to dedicate my time to completing reviews and edits of the manuscript.

• The many good friends from Yoakum and my High School coaches and teachers who helped continue to kindle the fire within me to reach for and attempt to do what most said could not be done, and my brothers and sisters and their families forr all of their encouragement during those tough teenage years, and finally to my parents J. E. and Tillie Mudd, who paved the way for my chance "to try."

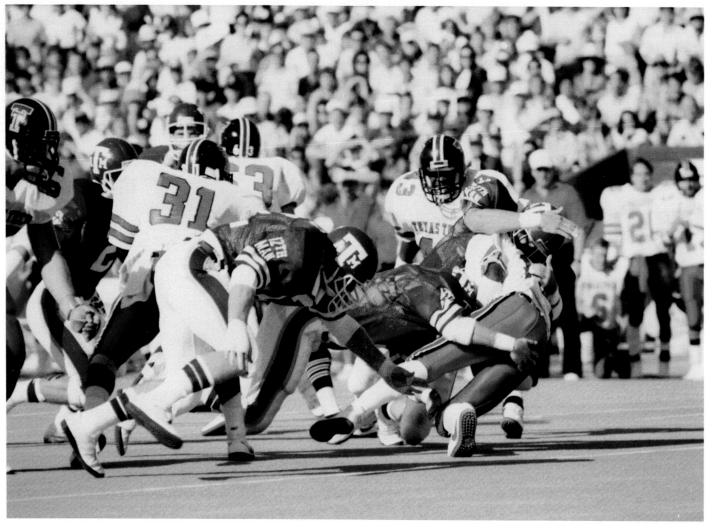

They came downfield with reckless abandon, did the 12th man, with one mission in mind. Find the man with the ball, especially if he were wearing a Texas Tech jersey, and bury him beneath an avalanche of maroon and white.

Prologue

They were crazy.

Wild.

And reckless.

A bunch of good old boys who had hung up their cleats as soon as the last strains of a high school band had faded into the night.

For years, they had been Friday night heroes.

But the last whistle had blown.

They had spit the last blade of grass from their teeth.

The last cheerleader had walked off the field.

The last patch of sweat and blood had dried on their faces.

They had kissed their last homecoming queen.

That's what they thought.

That was the cold, harsh reality facing them all.

No more wins.

No more losses.

At least, not personally.

For them all, the memories might grow brighter by the day, but the glory of it all had dimmed.

And now it was gone.

A few smaller colleges, a handful of junior colleges, might have wanted them, might have given them a chance to play again, might have promised to resurrect the bare remnants of a fading dream.

But, to a man, they wanted Texas A&M and the academic hope that the university offered them. For so many, the maroon and white tradition was a family inheritance. They could go to any college they wanted, but dad's money was going to Texas A&M.

Life was no longer measured in yard lines and hash marks.

The future lay at the end of four, maybe five years, not a mere hundred yards and a cloud of dust away.

With few exceptions, none of them had any right to even hope of wearing a Texas A&M football uniform.

Division One football, in all of its collective wit and wisdom, glanced haphazardly at each of these players and, with prejudiced eyes, quickly made up its mind.

They were a little too slow.

They were a little too short.

They didn't weigh quite enough.

They weighed a little too much.

And they jumped like they had lead weights or far too many hamburgers in their shoes.

They were out of shape, generally hadn't lifted serious weights for a long time, were better at chasing girls than running backs, never expected to come any closer to an on-field collision than their seats in the third deck of the twenty yard line, and, most often, suffered bodily injury only when they slipped off the barstool or found themselves face to face with a wayward fist at the Dixie Chicken.

They simply didn't have the speed, quickness, agility, strength, or muscle to play big-time college football.

That's what Division One Football thought.

But Division One Football didn't see what I saw, know what I knew about Texas A&M, its traditions, its legacy, and the never-say-die, never-say-quit, never-back-down spirit that dwelled deep within the hearts of a student body that would run through a brick wall or tear the sonuvabitch down with their bare hands if and whenever the maroon and white asked them to.

They were the builders of bonfire.

They were the keepers of the flame.

Individually and collectively, they were the heartbeat of everything so special about Texas A&M.

Like E. King Gill, the original 12th Man, they were ready to come down out of the stands if the football team needed them.

Unlike E. King Gill, they did take the field, time and again, year after year, a handful of them becoming my notorious 12th Man Kickoff Team, a motley collection of nondescript walk-ons with more courage than sense, a wild bunch with eyes peeled back and ears laid flat, charging hell-bent-for-leather toward the promised land like a runaway freight train with its boiler exploding, ready to hit or be hit, break a wedge or break a neck, with one undeniable thought in mind, and that was find the man with the football and tear his helmet off, preferably with his head still inside it.

Nobody, from one end of the country to the other, believed they could take the place of scholarship athletes and successfully accomplish what they had been assigned to do.

Most high-dollar, big-time, buttoned-up college football coaches thought I was as crazy, maybe even crazier, than those madcap renegades and mavericks who formed the 12th Man Kickoff Team.

Jackie's lost it, I heard them say.

He's mad.

He's naïve.

He's a little touched in the head.

Don't worry. It's just a publicity stunt.

He'll never pull it off.

It'll never happen.

But they didn't see what I saw or know what I knew about a special time and a special place at Texas A&M.

They had never looked into the eyes of that kickoff team and stared into the depth of a raging wildfire burning deep in their souls.

They were walk-ons, all right.

Well, maybe they weren't.

They were run-ons.

They were running hard wherever they went, on the field, off the field, in practice, in games, in unison, even when they knew that some six-five, 290-pound, All-State, All-American Defensive End was only a step away from taking the hundred and eighty pounds that God had given them and slamming them ground-level flat on dirt, on grass, on turf, on their back.

They didn't flinch.

They never hesitated.

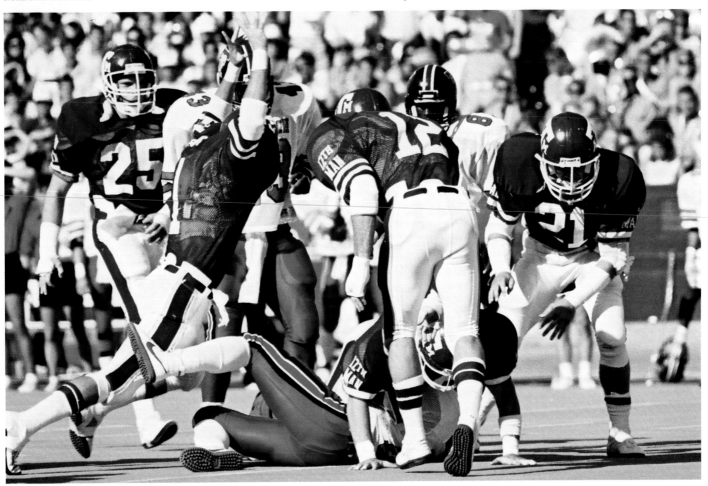

Whichever member of the 12th man made the tackle, he always knew that help was on the way, closing in with the furious intensity of a jailbreak. Butch Motley (25), Chad Adair (12), Dean Berry (1) and Mark Wurzbach (21) enthusiastically look over the aftermath of another collision. For the wild and crazy 12th man unit, it was just another day on the job.

The intensity and the dedication of the 12th man kickoff team helped propel Jackie Sherrill and the Texas Aggies to their second consecutive Cotton Bowl appearance against Ohio State. Sometimes, it took a swarm to stop a kickoff. Sometimes, it only took one, particularly if the one was Rick Tankersley.

Knock them down, and you knew you had to stand up one more time and do it again.

They were tackling dummies in practice.

They were cannon fodder and dared those high-profile, highly-recruited, well-publicized varsity players to take their best shot.

They left their blood on the field.

They left their skin on the turf.

They went home at night battered.

And bruised.

A day without pain was a day that simply no longer existed for any of them.

But they stood tall and defiant, did the members of those 12th Man Kickoff Teams, and they never stayed down no matter how many times they were hammered to the ground.

They played with broken bones.

They played with twisted ankles.

They played when they would have been better off in an emergency room. They played hurt because they were afraid that an injury, regardless of how serious it might be, could well keep them off the team.

It didn't.

But there was always that nagging fear digging ragged holes deep inside their chests.

Most were high school stars with All-District patches on their back-home letter jackets.

All-district didn't count anymore.

A few had played on Friday nights before thirty or forty thousand screaming fans. Others had even experienced the glory of Kyle Field during an autumn run of playoff games. And some only knew the agony and ecstasy of grinding it out beneath the dim glare of packed stadiums that barely held four hundred on a good night.

One played six-man football.

And two had never even played a down of high school football. One came from the Fightin' Texas Aggie Band, although he had been on the golf and tennis teams back home, and another had to choose between football and a cello in the high school orchestra. He selected the cello.

But they were all athletes.

They were tough.

They loved to compete.

And while running with the scout teams during practice, they were willing to get battered play after play, day after day, hour after hour, for just one clean, open shot at a starter.

Eyes open.

Jaws clenched.

Muscles tight.

Bones jarred.

Impact.

God, how they loved impact.

In practice, my scholarship players were preparing for Saturday.

For the 12th Man Kickoff Team, every day was game day.

They came with everything they had.

I could count on it.

They made my varsity players better.

I could depend on it.

In practice and in games, they showed no mercy.

They gave no quarter.

They had no idea what the word quit meant.

On kickoffs at home and away from Kyle Field, they had only one goal, and it kept their engine running even when the gas was low. They wanted to keep the kickoff returner inside the twenty yard line, not a yard farther, not a step better, and they faced the best that college football could throw their way, including All-Americans and a Heisman Trophy winner.

During my years as head coach at Texas A&M, no one ever returned a kickoff for a touchdown. Only a couple ever reached the fifty. Every yard came with a price, and it was paid for with stitches and blood.

It was commonplace for the 12th Man Kickoff Team to lead the nation with the fewest return yards allowed, or at least be in the top three. It wasn't unusual at all for them to have a better average in the kickoffs they covered at home than my varsity return team had on the road.

I would have proudly taken them to every game.

I would have lined them up on every kickoff.

I had that much confidence in them.

But NCAA rules limited our travel squad to sixty players, and, except for the last road game of the year when that restriction was eliminated, I had no alternative but to keep my 12th Man Team at home.

Kyle Field has traditionally been recognized as one of the loudest and most frenzied venues in the nation for college football.

But when those towel-waving members of the 12th Man Kickoff Team bolted out of the tunnel, Kyle Field exploded.

The noise was deafening. The decibel level touched nerves that hadn't been touched in years. You could scream, but there was no way you could hear the words you were screaming.

I had All-Americans playing for Texas A&M. Many would go on to have great careers in the NFL playing on Sunday.

But those members of the 12th Man Kickoff Team weren't just a hand-me-down collection of small-time, small-town football players.

On campus, they were rock stars.

They were the Aggie connection with the student body.

And, amidst the tumult and the shouting, they brought the hopes and aspirations of the entire student body down onto the revered turf of Kyle Field with them.

I believed in the 12th Man.

They never let me down, and I never doubted they would.

But then, from the very beginning, nobody else was able to see what I saw or know what I knew about them and the indomitable spirit that drove them so hard.

Individually they may not have belonged on a college football field.

But collectively, they would fight until there was no one left standing, and no one was ever able to get them all.

They had a job to do, and no one did it better.

They were the 12th Man.

They were Texas A&M.

They became a legend.

JACKIE SHERRILL

Head Football Coach
Athletic Director
Texas A&M University
1982-1988

Bobby Middleton (18) and the the 12th man mob storm Ohio State. A&M may have lost the game that day, but the 12th man unit left the Cotton Bowl turf littered with wreckage on kickoffs.

Chapter 1

Robert Crouch knelt on the thirty-five yard line and stared at the scoreboard. The numbers had faded to zero. They lingered only for a moment or two, flickered for a final time, then went dark. A few players brushed past him on their way to the dressing room, and the parking lot was filled with headlights, all headed toward the open road, all headed home or down to the Dairy Queen, which was always on the way, whichever way a car happened to be traveling. Crouch had suffered through a few bad nights before. A flat tire in a fast car in a race he could have won if the tire had a few more treads on it and one less nail in it. A fight he may or may not have started. He couldn't remember. The breakup with his latest heartthrob. It may or may not have been her idea. He couldn't remember that either. But none of the nights had ended as badly as this one. There would always be another race, another fight, another girl or two. But on a chilled night in Poteet, Texas, football had just slipped away from his grasp forever.

Crouch had been one of fourteen seniors who took the field for the Poteet Aggies. Their mission had been simple enough. Win and move on into the playoffs. Lose and go home. Crouch had not even considered losing. For forty-seven minutes and twenty-eight seconds, he had played the game of his life. A touchdown on offense. An interception on defense. But with the final seconds ticking off the clock, Crouch could do nothing but watch as a desperate field goal attempt for the win drifted to the left. Maybe it was the wind. Maybe the kicker just missed it. He felt bad for both. Poteet had not been to the playoffs in years, and now his last chance of advancing into a bi-district game had sailed a foot wide. The difference between winning and losing had been about the length of a football. The energy drained out of his body long before

the football bounced harmlessly off the turf and into the fence. He tried to move, but couldn't. He felt numb, all except the hurt, and it stabbed him in the gut as deeply as a hunting knife. Crouch stared hard at the ground, then closed his eyes. He could still see the kick in the air. And, try as he might, he could not will the ball between the goal posts. Finally, Crouch pulled himself to his feet, walked into the dressing room, and removed his cleats and shoulder pads for the last time. The pain did not spread to the rest of his body until he tried to roll out of bed the next morning.

Dennis Mudd sat on the grass beside the driveway of his home in Yoakum, Texas, and looked down the long, narrow road that wound its way toward a glow of bright lights, barely visible in the haze and shadows that hovered over the farm fields of an early Friday night. He was only five years old, and he clutched a ragged leather football. His black cocker/beagle sat beside him. If Dennis listened hard enough, he could make out the distant words of the announcer, and he would know who was winning and who was losing by the size of the roar from the crowd. For hours, he would sit quietly as the shades of evening settled around his shoulders, and his eyes never left the glow of the lights. His vision went no farther, nor did it need to. That's where I'll be some day, he told his dog. Down there. Down where the lights are bright and they're playing football, and I'll be playing football with them. The stadium sat at the end of the road on the edge of the world. Once a boy reached the football field, there was no reason to go any farther or anywhere else. He had gone as far as he could go.

On Saturday afternoon, and sometimes at night, Dennis Mudd would steal away to the family's hay barn where he had an old plug-in radio hanging haphazardly on the wall. And he would listen, without fail, to every football game played by the Texas A&M Aggies during the middle years of the 1970s. He would yell in the darkness of a secret place where no one could hear him and throw his football from one end of the barn to the other. There was never a pass he did not complete or a game he did not win. Dennis Mudd knew every player by name and by number. He saw every touchdown, witnessed every tackle, cried when A&M won, and cried when A&M lost. He saw it all on the radio. When the final sounds of the game faded into static, he would return to his room and carefully write down the score onto the shade of a lamp beside his bed.

As the years passed, Dennis Mudd fed cows and took care of the farm animals with his dad before breakfast, and on those days when frost lay upon the ground, the cold hurt. He chased down twelve-week-old coyotes and caught them by hand. He shot raccoons with a .22 rifle, skinned them, and earned fifteen dollars a hide. With an old shotgun, he would hunt skunks and armadillos until midnight. No hides. No money. Just a boy in the woods beyond the hay fields.

The day came when he finally walked down that long, winding road and into the bright lights of Yoakum's football stadium. His world began on the fifty-yard line, and it ended just ten yards shy of the goal posts. The end zone was holy ground. A boy could become a hero just by falling into its clutches. Everyone in Yoakum knew his name when he walked the downtown sidewalks.

He and his friends hauled coastal hay to Houston on Saturday mornings just so they could hear the radio replay the high school game from the evening before. They listened for his name, they knew when the play was coming. And Mudd heard his name often. He glanced out the truck's window and, from farm to farm, saw small boys, who, like him, had been looking down that long, narrow road that wound its way toward the glow of bright lights, barely visible in the shadows and haze that hovered over the farm fields of an early Friday night.

Dennis Mudd left the footprints that others would follow, and he would never know their names.

David Coolidge played big-time football at a big-time high school in Texas. As a strong safety, he had earned All-City, All-District, and All-Greater Houston honors. He was pretty fast, and he hit with the ferocity of a sledgehammer. Well, maybe it was more like a chainsaw than a sledgehammer. But, Lord, he was small. Coolidge was 5-11 and weighed in on good days at 165 pounds, but that was before the heat, humidity, and sweat of Houston melted away any excess weight from his bones. After a game, he was nothing more than a sack of bones, laced together with grit and gristle.

He could play at the college level. Coolidge knew he could. But only the small colleges were interested in someone his size, a player who was pretty quick for high school but probably a step too slow for any Division 1 program. A few coaches had sent him some scholarship or financial aid offers. He glanced them over but took none of them seriously.

He had left his heart on the football field, but his body was on its way to Texas A&M. There had never been any doubt about it. An older sister had gone to A&M, and Coolidge, by the time he was thirteen, would visit her on Saturday just so he could watch the Aggies play football. The afternoons may be hot as hell, but he didn't care or hardly ever noticed. He often had to sit in the end zone, but that didn't trouble him either. He was high above a big-time college football field, watching, merely watching, and wondering how he would feel racing down the turf of Kyle Field. College football didn't have tackles. It had collisions. He could feel the sudden shocks of impact and pain fifty rows up.

That's where I'm going to be someday, he told himself, but, down deep inside, he knew it would never happen. He wanted to believe. But David Coolidge never lied to himself or anyone else.

James Barrett had grown to manhood in the shadow of a Junction Boy, and his heart bled Maroon. His father had boarded one of Bear Bryant's buses in 1954 and headed out toward parts unknown. It was an era when a 5-9, 190-pound guard had a chance to play, and Ray Barrett was as tough as nails. Two buses rolled away from College Station, filled with 103 Texas A&M football players. Ten days later, only one bus came back to town, and it carried only twenty-seven players, lean and haggard, beaten, battered, and thirsty. One was Ray Barrett. The others had walked away from the hard-scrabble earth surrounding Junction, most of them leaving during the dead of night, escaping practice held beneath an unforgiving August sun that seared a rock patch generally referred to as hell's little acre.

James Barrett remembered, I've heard some chilling tales from my dad. It was one of those barracks-type places. At night you went to bed, and, in the morning, you woke up and the bed next to you was empty. It was always dusty. There were always snakes.

My father said you'd work out in the morning, take a great big jug of milk down by the river and rest until the afternoon workout.

There were cactus, sandspurs, goat head thorns, a stifling heat, broken bones, heat strokes, and concussions, but no water, never any water. A doctor had told Coach Bryant, a stomach full of water can cause the blood flow to increase to the

James Barrett and his father Ray symbolized the Texas A&M tradition. James became a member of the 12th man kickoff team, and his father was one of Bear Bryant's famous Junction Boys. Both helped build a standard of excellence.

spleen, causing it to rupture. And Bryant's trainer explained it this way: Hell, you never pour ice water into a car's radiator, so why pour ice water into a hot and burning boy. At Junction, no one did.

A sports writer would describe the two-a-days at Junction as the toughest and most brutal fall camp ever, but Bryant believed that, in the fierce heat of battle, he had found a team that would form the backbone of Texas A&M's football fortunes. As he said, in life, you'll have your back up against the wall many times. You might as well get used to it. Ray Barrett did. And the 1954 Aggie football team would be revered and respected for all time.

No one revered or respected it more than James Barrett. James Barrett had helped propel the Rankin Red Devils to a state championship. But he had heard the whistle blow for the last time, and he packed away a football that had spent so much time in his hands. It was, as the Good Book said, time to put away childish things, and football was, after all, a childish game. If he wasn't big enough or fast enough to play on the field where his father played, then Barrett was satisfied to simply move on with the rest of his life. You need to walk on at A&M, his friends told him. But James Barrett laughed at them. Only one Barrett was good enough to wear an Aggie uniform, and it had already been worn. James Barrett was proud of his heritage and his lineage. He could say what only a very few could say and mean it. He was the son of a Junction Boy.

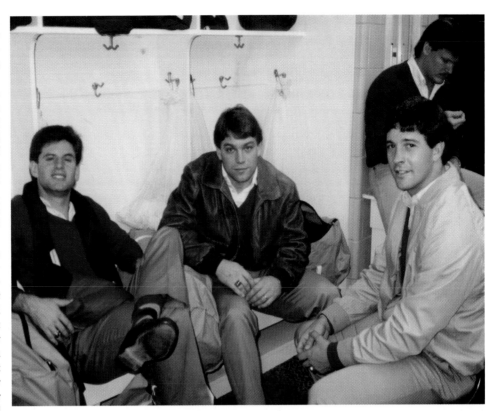

In the locker room, blessed with the chance to continue playing football are, left to right, Sean Page, Warren Barhorst, and Harold Huggins. In the background is Brian Edwards.

Sean Page felt like a champion. He was only a junior, and already his San Antonio Churchill High School football team had fought its way to the State Semi-finals. His quarterback, Cody Carlson, had a golden arm and was virtually unstoppable. And Page? Well, he believed he could run with the best of them. He had played with two of his teammates, Harold Huggins and Dan Pollard, since the third grade, and they had all swaggered into a high school football program where only the strong survived. The weak didn't make it. The cowards didn't bother to try out.

As a junior, only one game separated Sean Page from playing for the state championship. He confidently took the field at Rice Stadium and lined up against Houston Yates. He didn't fear the threat of losing. Hell, his team hadn't lost enough to even know how to lose. San Antonio Churchill was a rich, all-white school that wore black. Houston Yates came from the Fifth Ward, a team comprised mostly of African American players, and it raced out of the dressing room wearing white. It was a curious comparison of styles, strategies, and status. Churchill did not back down from any team, anytime, anywhere. Churchill would have stopped Yates dead in its tracks, but the tracks didn't stay in one place quite long enough. A step, a stride, a fake, a feint, and somebody was gone. Just like that. Here one minute. Gone the next.

On that humid Houston afternoon, Sean Page got his first fleeting glimpse of what Division 1 talent was all about. As he said, they were bigger, stronger, and faster. I had always heard that speed kills. It almost killed me.

Before the day ended, a ragged thread of doubt began to weave its way through Sean Page's troubled psyche. Perhaps, he thought, my days of playing football just might be numbered. One more year of high school. One more season. A few playoff games simply because we always went to the playoffs. Then it would be over.

He looked across the line of scrimmage at Houston Yates. He studied their faces and mentally measured the width of their shoulders. A bunch of those guys, he decided, would be playing big-time football somewhere. They probably already had a ton of scholarship offers tucked into their uniforms. Today just might be his first and probably his last taste of big-time football. The bruises took a long time to heal.

Ike Liles could have been a Junction Boy. Even a good day on the practice field of Stamford, Texas, was like a hotter-than-usual day on the backside of hell. The coach walked the sidelines, wiping the sweat off his face, telling his players when they dropped to their knees that a little hard work never hurt anybody. And he worked them hard. His sole purpose in life was to turn those boys into men. Wins were all right. He could live with a few losses. But, by gawd, when they walked away from that the hard-rock field of Stamford, they would face the world as men. They could endure and survive any calamity or damnation that might confront them. Didn't matter what it was. Nothing in life would ever be worse than Stamford football. He made sure of it.

When the team was given a break during two-a-days, Ike Liles remembered, we drank water out of pipe like cows. Temperatures would be nudging the high side of 108 degrees and threatening to go higher, especially when a cloud left the sun and the shade was brushed away from the cracks in the field. The coach had hooked up a long PVC pipe to a water hose, then punched a few holes in the pipe. Little spurts of water shot out of the pipe, and the boys fought each other, sucking down every drop before it hit the ground. Lord, life out on a sun-baked prairie was water, and water was as precious as life itself. Liles had been a tailback,

Vince Palasota defied the odds. He was probably too small to play football for Mexia, but he was fast, had a chip on his shoulder, and was determined to play for Texas A&M as well.

a tight end, a safety. He was long and lanky, built like the slender blade of a dagger and almost as deadly, and the coach simply plugged him in wherever there was a hole that needed to be filled. If a first down could be made, Liles would snake his way past the chains. If a tackle could be made, Liles would find a way to get there. He stormed over, around, and through people, and when the field finally went dark his senior year, Ike Liles had only one thought racing though his mind. They won't treat me like cannon fodder ever again, he said. I'll never have to drink water through a damn PVC pipe. By now, the holes had more dirt than water.

On a high school football field, with the heat of the lights stabbing him between his shoulder blades, Vince Palasota felt as big as he knew he would ever be. He was a wiry, 138-pound cornerback, leading a Mexia Blackcat squad that never went to the playoffs and possessed no illusions about moving on after the last whistle ended the last game of the year. No tears. No regrets. Come Monday, Palasota would be sprinting down a cinder track and back on the diamond, throwing a baseball.

The seasons all ran together and piled on top of each other at Mexia. Vince Palasota didn't mind. By the time the footballs were bagged up and thrown into the far corner of the locker room, he was ready for something else, for anything else. He was small. That was his plight in life. He could not eat enough or drink enough to gain weight. Bones and sinew. That's all he was. But Vince Palasota was a fighter. He had a chip

on his shoulder. He had a lot to prove, he was determined to prove it, and time was running out for him.

On Friday nights, Palasota may have been the lone Blackcat player who never bothered to glance toward the bleachers and check out where his father might be sitting. He knew his father wasn't there and wouldn't be coming. Not tonight. Not any night. Life has many roads and many turns, and people sometimes take the wrong one, or at least a different one.

His father's road did not lead to the Mexia football field. Years later, as he lay dying, however, a gentle man with a lot of regrets sadly lamented the fact that he had never seen his son don a Blackcat uniform and play. Deep regrets. Proud moments he had missed and would like to live again. But time had passed them by. They, like life itself, had come and gone. It did not really matter. Vince Palasota had at last become a son and a friend. He looked into his father's eyes and forgave him.

Rick Tankersley sighed and turned his back to the wind as it came boiling up out of Palo Duro Canyon in far west Texas and blasting its way savagely through the stadium. It was tough enough to score against another team, but a strong head wind made it virtually impossible. A single question kept running through Tankersley's mind. If this was organized high school football, then why was the team in such utter disarray? Canyon had a handful of pretty good players, more than most teams, but there were no great athletes among them. Now they were fighting for their worthless lives, and only a mere eighteen seconds stood between them and another defeat. Losing was bad enough. Losing at Homecoming was criminal. If the coach had any weapons left in his arsenal, then why had he chosen to keep them locked up in his playbook?

Tankersley glanced angrily at the scoreboard. Canyon trailed by thirteen points. His stomach was in knots. What, he wondered, could they do in eighteen seconds? He trotted into the offensive huddle with the play his coach had called on the sidelines. It was a running play. Hell, he thought, we don't have anybody who can run a hundred yards in eighteen seconds, much less go the distance twice with time running out. He looked at his quarterback. His quarterback waited. And Rick Tankersley, for reasons known only to him and God, changed the play.

Throw it, he said.

Where, his quarterback wanted to know.

As far as you can, Tankersley said.

Who's the receiver?

Tankersley grinned. Throw it long enough and high enough, he said, and I'll go get it.

I can't throw it that high or that far.

You've got the wind at your back. Give it your best shot.

He did,

Tankersley went deep, and a fluttering football was waiting on him when he finally arrived. Canyon found itself only six points behind with a little more than ten seconds remaining on the clock.

An on-side kick.

A wild scrum.

Canyon lay on top of the football.

One more chance.

One last chance.

And now Tankersley was again running into the offensive huddle with the play his coach had called.

Run it, the coach said.

We don't have time.

It'll surprise them, the coach said.

Tankersley looked at his quarterback. His quarterback waited. And Rick Tankersley changed the play. Throw it, he said, then he knelt and drew up the play in the dirt. One thing about a West Texas football field.

There was plenty of dirt.

A long pass.

A receiver running free.

A catch.

A touchdown.

A homecoming to remember.

The coach glared at Tankersley as the receiver ran down the sidelines past him. His eyes were ablaze. His chin was quivering. Tankersley was in trouble. He knew damn well he was in trouble. He wondered why it felt so good. The coach grabbed his jersey.

Who took it upon himself to change my plays, the coach demanded to know.

I did, said the quarterback.

I did, said Tankersley. He turned and walked away. What was the coach going to do? Throw them off the team? Another few Friday nights, and he would be off the team for good anyway. That was just about all seniors had to look forward to.

For Scarborough High School in Houston, Ronnie Glenn had been a star. He was a quarterback, but colleges must not be looking for quarterbacks, he figured. No coach was knocking on his door. No big-time coach was making any promises or offering him any illusions, grand or otherwise. But then again, Ronnie Glenn had always been able to punt the ball farther than he could throw it, forty-three yards on average. He received a single letter from a single university stuck somewhere out in West Texas, and the coach thought Ronnie Glenn just might be able to kick the ball for the Sul Ross Lobos.

Where's Sul Ross, Glenn wanted to know.

In Alpine.

How far is Alpine from Houston?

About eleven hours on a good day.

Is that still in Texas?

It is.

No thanks.

Mike Tolleson had one love. Football. He was only a freshman, but he was a freshman for the Celina Bobcats, a small school in a small Texas town that needed every player, every body, it could find. Big. Little. Fast. Slow. It didn't matter. Given a little time, Coach G. A. Moore could turn them into winners. Tolleson had to square his shoulders and stretch on the balls of his feet to reach 5-8 on the height chart. He weighed in at about 220 pounds, but that was before Coach started running the team, and Coach strongly believed in speed, endurance, and stamina. And, oh yes, G. A. Moore hammered his number one rule into the heart of every player on every team he ever coached. Boys, he said, if you play football for me, you don't have a girlfriend. At Celina, it's all about football. Girls get in your way, keep you confused. I don't want a season to go bad on me because some girl broke up with you when we've got a game to play.

No questions. No arguments. No exceptions.

When the boys of Celina happened to hear about a good-looking little blonde whose family had moved to the country outside of town, they headed down toward her house as fast as their cars could take them. Mike Tolleson suddenly had a new star in his eyes. She was blonde, all right, and she was as beautiful as the rumors had said she was. And when the rest of the boys of Celina drove away, he stayed for awhile. He now had a second love, and it had nothing to do with football. Her name was Jenny Oaks.

Tolleson knew Coach's rules. He knew them well. But as the days passed, he would grab his motorbike, stay far off the main roads, and cut his own trail through the back fields toward Jenny's house. Coach Moore may know football, and few would ever know it better, Tolleson thought, but Coach Moore had never met the lovely Jenny Oaks.

During the summer between his junior and senior year, Tolleson was on a downtown Celina Street when Coach Moore walked around the corner and stopped him. Mike, he said, getting right to the point, I hear you've been seeing that little Oaks girl.

Tolleson did not hesitate nor back down. He looked Coach G. A. Moore dead in the eyes and said, as boldly as he could, no, sir. I've been running this summer, running a lot. I have my focus on football and my senior year. We're gonna win it again this year, Coach. We're gonna win it again.

Coach Moore was not impressed. Every little town had its secrets. In Celina, few were still secret by the time the sun hit the football field the next morning. Mike, he said, I don't want you to see her anymore this summer. You understand?

Yes, sir.

No ifs, ands, or buts. Just a direct order.

By nightfall, Mike Tolleson had cranked up his motorbike, cut through the back country once more, and was sitting beside Jenny Oaks on the family front porch long after the stars had begun to dance across the tree tops.

During Tolleson's four years in high school, Celina lost two games. The last came in the last game he would ever play for the Bobcats. Archrival Pottsboro, at 9-0, defeated Celina, 9-0, for the district championship. Only one team could advance to the playoffs in those days. It would not be Celina. The final touchdown came late, and the Bobcats had bitten the dust, 14-13. Tolleson was devastated. The whole town was devastated. As far as Celina was concerned, he said, we might as well have gone 0-10. One loss for Coach Moore meant we had a losing season. No. Not winning the state championship meant we had a losing

David Coolidge (7), Mike Tolleson (32) and Spencer Baum (5) found Coach Jackie Sherrill willing to give them a second chance to play football at A&M after high school.

season. Mike Tolleson, however, had one saving grace. After four years of dating on the sly and in secret, he could actually take Jenny Oaks out in public, and, if he did that, he decided, he might as well marry her. So he did.

Butch Motley wasn't sure he would ever play football again, but he wasn't telling a living soul. He doubted if anyone would miss him. He had taken his first snap at Novice High School in a town that had a population of 193, give or take a few old soreheads, and, by the time he was a junior, there weren't enough boys left in class to field a decent six-man football team. The eighth grade had flat run out of boys, and few others were on the way. As a freshman, Motley hadn't won a game. When he was a sophomore, Novice drop-kicked all of its extra points, and the team went 7-2-1 even though it practiced on a field littered with red ant beds, goat head thorns, grass burrs, and an occasional cactus. Novice may not have been on top of the world, but it had certainly crawled out from beneath the bottom. On his six-man team, Motley had played linebacker, tight end, running back, kick returner, and even quarterback. When we substituted, he said, that only meant we changed positions on the field. As a junior, he became the new kid on the block at Jim Ned, a 2-A high school in Tuscola. What do you play, his coach asked.

Quarterback, said Motley. Hell, why not?

Taking his first snap as a JV signal caller, he wondered, where did all of these people come from? Never faced that many before. He didn't have time to think, much less react.

Three sacks later, the coach said, son, I think we'll try you someplace else. Motley, spitting dirt and grass from his mouth, said, that sounds good to me.

Butch Motley might have done all right if he just hadn't kept riding those bulls on the summer rodeo circuit. It was a hell of an adrenaline rush, just he and the bulls, one kicking for dear life, and the other holding on for the same reason. There was nothing quite like it. A bull ride lasted eight seconds. A football game could go on all night, or so it seemed. At Ranger, Texas, Motley climbed atop the chutes, eased onto

the back of a big Brahma, and tried a brand new wrap he had heard about. Gives you better balance, someone said. A stronger grip. Keeps you from falling off, he was told. Motley was always looking for any edge he could find. He rode the bull all right. Eight seconds came at just about the right time, but when he jumped off, the wrap kept holding him tight. The bull headed for the fence, and Motley was being dragged along, going wherever the bull had decided to take him. He heard the sickening pop when the bone shattered in his arm. The rodeo clowns carried him to an ambulance, but Motley didn't want to pay for the ride. He ended up talking a friend into driving him in a pickup truck to a little hospital down by the side of the road that, looked for all the world like a veterinarian's clinic. At least, that's what Motley thought.

The doctor studied the X-ray and only shook his head. I'll put a cast on it, he said, but you'll need to have that arm seen by a specialist.

There's a pretty good one in Abilene.

Motley nodded, wandered out to the friend's car, and headed home. He tossed the pain pills away because they hadn't dulled the pain. He waited around until he knew his mother had left for work the next morning before heading home. He didn't want to worry her. Motley slipped into the kitchen. His father mentioned that he was going into Abilene to buy some new tires for the car, and Motley asked him, do you think we can possibly run by the hospital while we're there?

Why, his father wanted to know.

I got a little bone in this arm that needs to be set, Motley told him. Probably broke.

You get in a fight?

With a bull, I did.

It took a metal rod to hold the bone in place. The surgery cost ten thousand dollars, and, Motley said, I didn't even get a good hamburger out of the bull.

In reality, he probably should have lost interest in bulls a month earlier when a gate hatch punched a hole in his right shin as it slid out of the chute. Instead of finding some doctor to stitch it up, Motley went home, took a razor, shaved the hair around the wound, stuffed a towel in his mouth so his parents wouldn't hear him scream, and proceeded to douse the wound with hydrogen peroxide and iodine. A childhood friend had already refused to travel to any more rodeos with him. You're gonna get yourself killed, the friend said, and I don't want to be the one to tell your parents.

It might be awhile before he crawled on a bull again. Butch Motley had absolutely no unreasonable thoughts about ever seeing another football field up close and personal. He had always thought a linebacker would end his career. The bull came out of nowhere.

Dean Berry had never felt more frustrated in his life. His father had been a defensive captain for Texas A&M. His brother Greg had been a defensive captain for Texas A&M. His brother Ray would become a defensive captain for Baylor. Now the mantle had fallen on his shoulders. He was the last son, the last Berry. He was looking tradition squarely in the face, and tradition had turned its back on him. There was a time when he thought that he just might be the greatest Berry of them all. Dean Berry had been a super athlete in the fifth and sixth grades. He was quarterback and an genuine offensive machine. If a touchdown was scored, chances were good he had bolted, probably untouched, into the end zone. It was so easy, and he was a natural. But then came junior high. Dean Berry walked out onto the football field and saw a sight that startled him. Over the summer, everyone else had grown. He hadn't. He was still 5-2 and ninety-nine pounds, and the coach said, son, I'm afraid you can't play quarterback anymore. Without another word, he was moved to cornerback, someplace out of the way, someplace where

Butch Motley was a high school and college bull rider from the little West Texas town of Novice, which meant he was certainly tough enough to play for the 12th man unit.

Dean Berry had a storied football tradition staring him in the face. His father Powell and brother Greg, at Texas A&M, and another brother Ray, at Baylor, had all been captains of their college teams. And Dean didn't have a scholarship offer.

he might not get hurt. Dean Berry was already hurting. The dream of becoming the greatest Berry of them all was fading like a mist that had been rudely stepped on by a summer sun.

High school was no better. Maybe it was even worse. He had grown to 140 pounds by the time he was a junior but could not escape the humility of playing on JV. Lord, he thought, he was almost a senior and here he was, still playing with the scrubs on the wrong day of the week. Matchstick thin, and scrawny, Berry covered receivers, he covered kickoffs, and there were days when he cursed the day he had ever been born. He didn't know it, but, after the ninth grade, his coach met with his father after practice one day and said, I think you should talk Dean out of playing football. He's liable to get hurt.

His father only shook his head. No, he said, if he wants to play, I'll let him play. It's good to be part of a team. You learn a lot that way.

Just before his senior year, Dean Berry's body suddenly went haywire. He grew eight inches, and his weight climbed to 160 pounds. Unfortunately, his feet didn't keep up with his height. His body headed in one direction, and his feet moved in another. As he said, if I could catch them, I could hit them. But I couldn't run out of sight if it took me all day and half the night. Dean Berry lost his last high school game. His storied Abilene Cooper team was beaten by archrival Abilene High, and it was the most heart-wrenching night of his life. There had been no letters from college coaches. No one wanted him or even knew his name. Dean Berry had watched the tumult and the shouting when Greg was being recruited to Texas A&M and Ray was signing to play at Baylor. He had long heard tales of his father's exploits on the football field at Aggieland. But no team, large or small, had any interest in him. No coach had even bothered to come watch him play. Dean Berry drove home after the game, sat down in the bathtub, turned on the hot water, and cried for two hours. It was over before it ever began, and he knew he had

let his family down.

So it was in 5-A schools and beneath the Friday night lights shining down on six-man football teams. Hope springs eternal until the last game is played and the last bruise turns purple, then green, and finally washes away with time. The competition of high school football rarely translated to a Division 1 playing field. Only those blessed with the right height, the right weight, and the right time in the forty-yard dash would ever play on Saturday.

For so many of them, their time had come, then run out. The grass of a football field would now be growing under someone else's feet. They could look back with pride but never forward. They could sit in the bleachers but never on the bench again. While those enduring two-a-days would be begging for water, they would be raising a cold beer. The beer would grow stale but not the memories, never the memories.

Cheerleaders, older and wiser, would be searching for another hero to hug, and it would take a holy miracle for any of the players to ever pull on a pair of shoulder pads again, the kind of miracle that usually leads to sainthood.

They would have to be attending the right school. The team would have to be under the leadership of the right coach. The coach would have to be possessed with the right attitude and be able to measure the size of the heart in a body far too small and, most assuredly, too slow. The coach would need a plan and a premonition. Even that might not be enough. It would take a perfect alignment of the planets, a confluence of fate, time, and circumstance, and a coach who didn't give a damn what anybody thought.

Among the Aggie faithful, football reigns supreme at Texas A&M. Kyle Field becomes their Saturday temple every autumn.

Chapter 2

It was growing late on a wintry January night in Dallas, and darkness had begun falling heavily around his shoulders like an oppressive shadow. The plush, well-appointed twenty-sixth floor office of high-dollar attorney William A. McKenzie had the smell of stale cigarette smoke and the bitter aftertaste of day-old coffee. He glanced at the clock. It was fourteen minutes before nine o'clock, and he had a phone call to make.

Frankly, McKenzie wasn't looking forward to dialing Bum Bright's number. He would rather have waited until the light of morning, after he had time to collect his thoughts, clear the confusion from his mind, and develop a new strategy for approaching the unexpected set of circumstance that suddenly confronted them. The urgency of the situation, arising amidst the din of chaos and criticism within the past twenty-four hours, had gotten a little too far out of hand. Decisions had to be made, and they had to be made now. The ugly spectre of time was falling like quicksilver from their grasp.

Normally, as an attorney, McKenzie did not particularly mind being the bearer of bad news. It was an accountability that came with the job and the territory. In the courtroom, however, it was hardly ever personal. His call to Bright would be extremely personal, and he knew the wealthy Dallas oil magnate would be smitten with the feelings of anger and betrayal gnawing at his gut. McKenzie was mired in a rotten mood himself. The burning sensation in his chest and throat felt like the seared end of a branding iron and tasted like bile, and he felt as alone as he had ever been.

For more than a month, William McKenzie and Harvey R. (Bum) Bright had been working quietly and surreptitiously behind the scenes to find and hire a new football coach at Texas A&M University. The trouble was, Texas A&M already had a head football coach, Tom Wilson, who had led the Aggies to the Independence Bowl in Shreveport, Louisiana, only a few weeks earlier. But, my lord, McKenzie thought, it was, of all things, the Independence Bowl, best known to too many of the diehard faithful as the Leftover Bowl, which almost always looked at the nation's array of football teams and invited the best two leftovers that nobody else wanted.

McKenzie shuddered. The "haves" were out harvesting cotton or roses or oranges or sugar on New Year's Day. The "have-nots" were doomed to play in nondescript bowl games at nondescript hours on nondescript nights, being rewarded with small, insignificant, one-column stories, often set in agate type and wedged into the back pages of the national press.

A final score.

A few statistics.

A winner.

A loser.

The name of the Most Valuable Player.

And that was about all.

Texas A&M, McKenzie knew, deserved better, far better. But the football program, he realized, would forever be looked on nationally as the orphan stepchild of the Southwest Conference until it became a big-time winner.

A few wins here or there didn't count.

Not really.

Neither did a winning season if all it brought the Aggies was a chance to play for a few thousand dollars in some second-rate, down-the-road Leftover Bowl.

William McKenzie and Bum Bright wanted championships.

Cotton would do fine.

But, Lord, it had been a long and long-suffering fourteen years since Texas A&M had rolled into Dallas after a championship season and swaggered onto the field of the storied Cotton Bowl. In fact, the Aggies had played for Cotton only once in the past forty years. It had been a long dry spell for a proud institution in a state that knew all too well about disasters, famines, and droughts.

Some Aggie alumni had simply decided that Texas A&M was jinxed, or maybe even cursed. That was the only explanation they had for it.

They didn't like losing, they never would, but, over the miserable years, they had grown accustomed to the dastardly fate each football season brought them.

Each loss had a different excuse.

Bad calls.

Bad injuries.

Bad coaching.

And, after awhile, the losses didn't quite hurt nearly as badly nor as deeply as they once did.

Some Aggies had embraced the short, happy coaching years of Emory Bellard, the godfather of the high-powered, high-octane wishbone attack that, in some corners, had left defenses cowering in shock and awe. While at The University of Texas, Bellard sat down with Darrell Royal and drew up an innovative new running formation he had invented during his high school coaching days, and the Longhorn rode the sleight-of-hand strength of the triple option wishbone to thirty straight victories and a National Championship.

In 1972, Emory Bellard arrived on the Texas A&M campus with the secrets and the nuances of the wishbone locked away in his brain, and he immediately began to revive a program that hadn't quite yet died but was definitely wasting away on life support. For too long, Aggies had endured an offense so dull, so predictable, so unimaginative that three yards and a cloud of dust would have felt like a wide-open attack. As one alumnus said, during most of the sixties, it looked as though our coach's game plan was to go out, kick a field goal early, then try and let the defense hold it.

Touchdowns were rare. Wins in a year could generally be counted on one hand. And Aggies had grown tired of having to kiss their dates on first downs. Low-scoring games had simply taken the romance out of Kyle Field.

Bellard appeared to be the savior. After two tough, back-breaking years, the Aggies bolted to an impressive 8-3 record. In 1975, they raced undefeated through the first ten games, even knocking off Texas and being splashed, for their first and only time, in living color across the cover of *Sports Illustrated*.

Like the mythical Phoenix of old, Texas A&M had risen from the ashes. Its football team was being likened to a runaway freight-liner on a downhill run. The triple option had been a godsend. Nothing could stop it. Nobody had even been able to slow it down. But then, once again, the jinx – or maybe it was the curse – raised its ugly and damnable head.

The Aggies lost badly and unexpectedly to Arkansas, 31-6, and the dream of a conference championship died before anyone heard the death rattle. The loss hung like a burr in their throats, and a Southern California Trojan team, wrapped in the uninspired throes of mediocrity, stopped Texas A&M in the Liberty Bowl, 20-0.

Again, there had been no Cotton.

No Oranges.

No Sugar.

Nothing more than another loss in another second-rate, down-the-road, take-what-you-can-and-be-proud-of-it Leftover Bowl.

A year later, the Aggies marched valiantly to a 10-2 record, but the season ended abruptly without a title. Texas A&M kept grabbing for the gold ring. It might just as well have been an illusion. Texas A&M wanted it badly, but the championship ring always lay just beyond its grasp.

For Emory Bellard, the relentless pressure to win it all began to

William McKenzie helped spearhead the behind-the-scene search for a football coach that he strongly believed would lead Texas A&M back to the top of the Southwest Conference – where it always deserved to be.

take a devastating toll, both mentally and emotionally. He suddenly lost back-to-back games in 1978, one to high-riding Houston and the other to Baylor at Kyle Field. The Bears didn't scare anyone. The Bears should have been little more than another notch on the Aggie belt. But the Bears, under the brilliant whip of head coach Grant Teaff, rose up and left College Station wallowing in the sackcloth and ashes of a 24-6 defeat. There was weeping and wailing and the gnashing of teeth on Kyle Field, and Bellard immediately met with A&M President Jarvis Miller, privately asking for a vote of confidence in a last-ditch effort to silence those who were calling for his head and sending him maps marked with the roads out of town.

Bellard wanted and desperately needed the President's support. And he wanted it now.

When Miller hesitated, Emory Bellard took a deep breath, resigned, and promptly walked off the Texas A&M campus. There had been neither threat nor bluff. Bellard had been playing for keeps, and he simply had all he could take. The stress and uncertainty had grown stifling, then suffocating. He was a good man who had done a commendable job, but it had not been good enough. The wishbone at Aggieland would limp away and die in the tracks Bellard left behind on his way out of town.

Jarvis Miller and the Texas A&M athletic department, without any delay, turned to offensive coordinator Tom Wilson and anointed him to lead the Aggies through the rest of the season. Wilson wasted little time in placing his own personal brand on Aggie football. He had

been a college quarterback, a passing quarterback, who had grown weary of running the fullback up the middle or tossing the ball to a trailing back on the sweep. Tom Wilson was a high-flying aerial gunner who was determined to run a high-flying circus. He wanted his quarterbacks to plant their fingers firmly on the trigger. Fire and keep firing as long as the bullets lasted. Wilson introduced his offense by throwing the ball downfield on his first play as head coach.

Forget the cloud and the dust.

The Aggies were going skyward.

Tom Wilson had been both confident and ambitious. But then, that was what you expected from a big time quarterback who had his eyes set on becoming a big-time coach for a big-time football program. Wilson was convinced he had the ability to direct the Aggies to far greater heights than they had been able to climb under the tactical leadership of Emory Bellard. His offense, Wilson swore, could score at any time from anywhere on the field. It could go the distance as easily as it could go three yards, and the deep passing game would never find itself bogged down and choking in a cloud of dust.

Tom Wilson kept on winning more than he was losing at Texas A&M, had the interim tag removed, and settled down in the office reserved for the head football coach. He beat Texas twice, thank God, and took the Aggies to a couple of Leftover Bowl games. That didn't concern him. One was the Independence Bowl, where his Aggies defeated Jimmy Johnson and Oklahoma State just before Johnston bolted to Miami. To Wilson, Cotton would have been nice, but a bowl was a bowl. He viewed any of them, big or small, as the ultimate reward for a job well done.

Wilson, however, was young – only thirty-four years old – and unprepared for the back-room, hard-nosed politics of College football, especially Texas A&M football. He made one strategic mistake from which he would never be able to recover.

It was shortly before noon on an autumn Monday afternoon in 1981, November twenty-third to be exact, when Wilson strode into the dining room of Cain Hall, Texas A&M's athletic dormitory, and searched the room until he found Wally Groff, the university's business manager and interim athletic director. Groff had just sat down with his plate of food when Wilson leaned across the table and told him urgently, I need to see you. No, it won't wait. I need to see you now.

What's the problem?

I'm ready to quit as head football coach, Wilson said sternly.

You can't.

Why not.

We play Texas in three days.

Don't worry. I'm not leaving the team until after the game, Wilson said, his crisp tone softening somewhat. What I'm asking for you to do is deliver my resignation to A&M President Frank Vandiver at halftime of the game. I'll break the news to the team as soon as the game is over.

Tom Wilson, by most standards, had a successful coaching career at Texas A&M. He had winning seasons, beat Texas twice, and had taken the Aggies to bowl games – even defeating Jimmy Johnson and Oklahoma State – before being unexpectedly replaced by Jackie Sherrill.

Wally Groff was stunned. He didn't quite know what to say. First, Emory Bellard had unexpectedly quit, and now Tom Wilson was apparently ready to walk out as well. Was Wilson bluffing, or was he serious? Groff was in no position to gamble.

In reality, Tom Wilson had no intention of quitting.

What he really wanted was an extension of his contract. Like Emory Bellard before him, he was beginning to hear rumblings and rumors that Aggie alumni were losing faith in him and his football program. Maybe it was time for Wilson to leave, the gossip said in no uncertain terms.

The season had started badly and now it was gradually starting to deteriorate. The aerial game had begun to sputter, and his high-flying circus was having trouble getting back off the ground. Perhaps Tom Wilson's idea of success and A&M's idea of winning a championship were being measured justly or unjustly on two distinctly different levels. For Wilson, the scattered bits and pieces of acrimonious dissension being intertwined within the heart, soul, and telephone lines of Aggieland were no longer sounding like rumors. They had a frightening ring of truth to them.

Tom Wilson's contract as head coach only had a year remaining, and he was feeling a reasonable doubt cracking his confidence. He had enough wins to give him the leverage he needed, he figured. Besides, he said, the rumors were negatively affecting his recruiting. Other coaches were telling recruits, don't go to A&M to play for Tom Wilson. He may not be there after you get there. He has no guarantees. Tom Wilson simply wanted a guarantee. He wanted a contract extension. He believed he deserved it.

After all, he had beaten the Longhorns and could damn well do it again. A win over Texas was, in some minds, as good as a bowl game, and no one even dared harbor the thought of A&M going to battle with its most hated rival without a genuine, big-time head coach strolling the sidelines, keeping the ball in the air and downfield. Tom Wilson didn't hold all of the cards, but he was bold enough to believe he held the most important ones.

I want our discussion held in the strictest confidence, he told Wally Groff. I don't want you to tell anyone.

I can't do that, Groff argued. I'm an employee of the university, and I really don't feel comfortable keeping your request a secret from my superiors.

Tom Wilson thought it over, and finally he relented. Well, Wilson said at last, I really don't have any objection if you go ahead and tell President Vandiver of my plans before we play Texas. I guess he has a right to know.

Groff said he would. He felt relieved. Wilson's proposed resignation was not a terrible burden he wanted to carry alone. He didn't like secrets, especially not when his university was trapped unwittingly in the middle.

Wally Groff walked straight to the president's office.

A new wave of gossip and speculation immediately began to make their circuitous way from the fields and farms to the boardrooms and twenty-sixth floor offices that held the Aggie faithful. In Dallas, Harvey R. (Bum) Bright caught wind of Tom Wilson's unscrupulous demands, and he was livid. What Bright heard, whether true or not, was that the head coach, behind closed doors, had threatened to walk out of the Texas game at halftime if he were not given an immediate contract extension. Without new money, the rumor said, Wilson had no intention of even leading his team back on the field for the second half. Such a deed,

H. R. "Bum" Bright engineered the hiring of Jackie Sherrill as Texas A&M's new million-dollar football coach. He was convinced that President Frank Vandiver could run the university. But he and the Board of Regents at Texas A&M were responsible for the football program.

Bright decided, was absolutely unthinkable and unforgivable.

The rumor, however, was wild, fictitious, and unfounded. Wilson said, I would have never walked out on my team at halftime. I was too much of a professional to even contemplate such a thing. I respected A&M and my players too much.

The rumor crucified him. Fact or fiction, Bum Bright was livid. Wilson's trying to blackmail me, he bellowed. If I had been there, I would have fired him on the spot.

Bright served as the ranking chairman of the powerful Texas A&M Board of Regents, and he knew how to play hardball. He would defiantly call a man's bluff no matter how much money it might cost him in the long run. He desperately wanted a winner at Texas A&M. Bum Bright was smoldering in his own misplaced anger.

Texas A&M, during the decade of the 1970s, had been in the midst of constant turmoil. The University had hired three presidents in the past five years, one acting president, three athletic directors, and three head football coaches. The athletic director under Tom Wilson's regime was no longer around, primarily because of the athletic department's mediocre record in a variety of sports. The alumni were growing restless, and A&M, like all universities, lived and died – both academically and athletically – on the financial generosity of its alumni. *Sports Illustrated* once described Texas A&M as "a very ambitious and rich university with a powerful board of regents that runs it more or less like a banana republic." If the school did have a dictator with an iron hand, the ruler's name was definitely Bum Bright.

Frank Vandiver took a firm diplomatic and bureaucratic approach to solving the sudden and potentially explosive problem confronting the Aggie football program. He decided it would be best to hold a meeting and, along with a representative or two from the Board of Regents, attempt to dissuade Tom Wilson from quitting his job as head football coach. He made a single, yet urgent, phone call on the afternoon of November 24, and reached Joe Richardson, Jr., an independent oil and gas man from Amarillo, who was on his way out of the ornate wing that housed the regents offices. He was with his close friend, Keith Lang-

his closest allies on the A&M Board of Regents, attorney William McKenzie. Neither had been in College Station that day, and neither had any idea that Tom Wilson, at that very moment, was in the midst of eloquently presenting his case for a contract extension to Vandiver and Joe Richardson. They had no interest in hearing the coach's pleas. All they wanted was Tom Wilson's head. As rumors have it, Bright was saying that, if Tom Wilson had the audacity to walk out of the Texas game, he would personally make sure that Wilson never again coached in Texas. No one doubted that Bum Bright was powerful enough and rich enough to make his rant a reality.

In the quiet solitude of Frank Vandiver's home on the Texas A&M campus, Tom Wilson, obviously stressed and distraught, carefully outlined the reasons why he feared for his job. He argued that a vote of confidence and a long-term contract extension would keep the dreaded alumni off his back and give him the freedom he needed to build a win-

Even on those days when its stands are empty, Kyle Field holds a place of sacred importance for students and alumni of Texas A&M. Upon its turf have been fought battles with everlasting memories for those who come watch the Aggies play.

ford, a board member of the Aggie Club, and Richardson assured the university president that both men would gladly meet with Tom Wilson at Vandiver's home. The sooner, the better.

When they walked in, they found the football coach already seated along with the president, Wally Groff, and Charles Samson, chairman of Texas A&M's athletic council. As Vandiver remembered, the meeting and the discussions that transpired were calm and controlled.

There were no angry outbursts. Nobody stomped. Nobody yelled. It was nothing more than a group of gentlemen conducting a gentlemen's meeting in a genteel manner.

In Dallas, Bum Bright was seething and on the phone with one of

ning football program without constantly looking over his shoulder, wondering who would be the next angry Aggie trying to jerk his job out from under him. His confidence was eroding, and Wilson's demeanor was anything but arrogant. However, Wilson once again vowed to resign if a vote of confidence was not promptly forthcoming.

Joe Richardson, speaking on behalf of the Board of Regents, did his best to allay any fears dogging Wilson. A majority of the board, he pointed out, was in fact firmly positioned on the coach's side. In a closed session that afternoon, Richardson said, the regents discussed Wilson's future at A&M, and all had agreed they supported him and wanted him to continue coaching the Aggies for the life of his contract. He should not be worried or concerned about a few scattered rumors and a little gossip. The regents certainly had no interest in firing him.

Living in the crosshair and crossfire of an unforgiving, restless, and critical alumni was simply part of the job that all A&M football coaches had to endure. Some withered and some survived the storm. It was the nature of the beast. Wilson's job, his future, his contract were, after all, a university matter that would be properly, efficiently, and effectively handled by the university president.

Frank Vandiver, however, had only been president of Texas A&M for a mere six months, and, as a distinguished historian, did not feel comfortable at all being in the middle of an athletic squabble, especially one that had the potential of blowing up in his face. In his heart, he genuinely wanted Tom Wilson to remain as the A&M football coach. The man's record was solid if not spectacular, and much could be said in his favor about the wins over Texas.

Sure, athletics were important. Vandiver was quickly learning that the strength of the Aggie pulse depended a great deal on the strength of its football season, but he was more concerned with watching new buildings dominate the campus, instituting new research programs developed to add stature and prestige to A&M, hiring the best and the brightest of the top educators in the nation and the world, and making sure the university remained as one of the country's wealthiest institutions of higher learning. In recent years, Texas A&M had doubled its enrollment, raised its admission standards, and improved its faculty in part by establishing endowments of professorial chairs. In the broad scope of Texas A&M and its quest to achieve global prominence and preeminence, Frank Vandiver was convinced that Tom Wilson's so-called pressing contract problem seemed a bit trivial.

Wilson listened to Vandiver's calm assurances that he did indeed have a coaching job for the life of his contract. Win a few big games, and there was a good chance he might never leave Texas A&M. Well, he didn't quite hear those exact words, but Wilson thought he had. He nodded while Groff and Langford and Samson all pleaded with him not to resign, and, for the first time in a long time, he felt like A&M actually wanted him to stay. Wilson could sense some of that old confidence beginning to course once again through his veins.

Less than an hour later, he walked out of the president's home, and Wilson was greatly relieved. He had, he reasoned, gambled and won. He couldn't wait to feel the dimpled leather of a football in his hands again. In his mind, Tom Wilson had his guarantee.

As soon as practice was completed that afternoon, Wilson met with a *Bryan Eagle* sports reporter and reported, without any hesitation, that he had been given a personal vote of confidence by no less than the president of Texas A&M himself.

As night descended on College Station, Wilson announced to the Quarterback Club that he would indeed be back on Kyle Field and at the controls of the Texas Aggie football program in 1982. What he didn't say, although he no doubt thought it, was: *if anybody out there has any criticisms about me or my team, you might as well as keep those animosities and that dissension to yourself. Tom Wilson is not going anywhere.*

When he returned home, Wilson found Keith Langford waiting for him on the porch. He was not surprised. Langford was a good friend and had endured the grueling and somewhat humiliating afternoon at Vandiver's place. He must be wondering if Wilson had reached any conclusions about football, about Texas A&M, about his own future. After all, Wilson had indeed been a troubled man when the two had parted ways earlier in the day.

Wilson smiled broadly. I've decided to stay, he said.

What made you change your mind?

I wanted to go to Palm Springs and play golf again.

Langford laughed. For years now, he had faithfully taken Wilson to the California resort every Memorial Day for a golf excursion.

Tom Wilson felt as good as he had in a long time, and he was feeling even better the next morning when he read the personal statement that Frank Vandiver had released to the press. It said, "I'm delighted that the coaching situation has been resolved. The fact is, there wasn't actually anything to resolve, because Coach Wilson has a contract that extends through next year ... This should put all the rumors to rest. I am pleased that Coach Wilson has publicly stated that he looks forward to next year ... Next year looks like a winner for the Aggies, and I know that all of us will support Coach Wilson and his team to the utmost."

In his office, Frank Vandiver was wondering exactly how his official statement would be received. Had his words been strong enough, or had they had been too vague? He was feeling a little vague himself. Maybe it would have been a wiser move not to say anything at all about the turmoil surrounding the coaching situation. Simply put, Vandiver had been urged by all of those concerned to go on record and say something that would help the team and calm the uncertainty revolving around the growing rumors targeting Tom Wilson's promised return or possible demise. Whether the alumni liked it or agreed with the decision, the issue could officially be placed at rest.

Nothing out of the ordinary was going to happen at Texas A&M. Tom Wilson's team would again be throwing the ball downfield in 1982 and, who knows, maybe for years thereafter. For the next few weeks, the grumblings did not cease, but they weren't quite as loud or as disconcerting as they had been.

In Dallas, behind closed doors, Bum Bright and William McKenzie had begun their late-night, highly secretive search for a new football coach at Texas A&M.

Frank Vandiver be damned.

The Board of Regents be damned.

Frank Vandiver could run the academic, gift-giving, and expansion programs at the university any way he wanted to operate them. He was damn good at it. But Bum Bright was determined to run the football program. If a man was willing to duel or dare bluff Bum Bright for a contract extension, then he had better be ready and able to bite the dust, no matter how bad it might taste. Tom Wilson only thought he had a coaching job. Tom Wilson was already fired. It would, however, take another seven weeks before anybody ever got around to letting him know.

The culture at Texas A&M was perched on the threshold of change. Bum Bright and William McKenzie were aware of it, even if no one else was. For too long, they believed, Texas A&M football had been regarded as the outsider looking in, the ugly little sister of the Southwest Conference, the waifs no one ever invited to the dance, a second-class citizen on the football field, always chasing but never quite catching the teams on top.

It had been different when Bear Bryant was roaming the sidelines during the late 1950s, but the Bear was gone, and so was the legacy. Gene Stallings, who had played with the Bear, who had coached with the Bear, who had been a survivor of the Bear's notorious and legendary shootout at Junction, had flirted with glory in 1967 and even led the Aggies to their first Cotton Bowl appearance since 1942. On a cold New Year's Day in Dallas, Stallings had even beaten the Bear, and the A&M faithful believed that the good times had returned and might just last

Billy Pickard had already reached legendary status within the confines of Texas A&M football when Jackie Sherrill arrived. He had been with Bear Bryant in Junction, and he believed it was his duty to toughen up members of the 12th man team and make sure they understood what Aggie football was all about.

make it talk as loudly as any coach was inclined to hear.

John Blocker, a Houston oilman who owned his own drilling firm and who had donated more than a million dollars to Texas A&M, headed up the search committee. He pointed out, the only one we thought we couldn't get was Bear Bryant.

Sure, College Station was a nice, friendly, unassuming little hamlet perched just beyond the banks of the Brazos River. It didn't have the bright, beckoning, neon lights of a Dallas, a Houston, a Fort Worth, or an Austin. But Bum Bright and William McKenzie were convinced that A&M had the tradition and the power to turn heads and make any coach worth his salt listen to their offer, even those who were widely regarded as football icons. They had money, lots of money, and they could get more if necessary. Castoffs need not apply. Only the best coaches were good enough, coaches with glowing track records and championship skins on the wall. And, across the nation, there were only a handful of those.

By December, Bright and McKenzie had flirted with Florida State's Bobby Bowden, but settled on Bo Schembechler, the head coach of the Michigan Wolverines. Bo coached a remorseless and punishing brand of football. He had never posted a losing season, and, during the 1970s, his record at Michigan had been 96-16-3. He knew what it was like to win championships. He had won so many of them in the Big Ten that it was embarrassing. Bo had been the National Coach of the Year, and he, as much as anyone, understood the science of recruiting the kind of top-echelon players it took to build championship programs. At A&M, Bo Schembechler would not only win the Southwest Conference, he would own it. Year after year, he would own it. Bright and McKenzie were sure of it.

The die was cast. William McKenzie made the call. Schembechler was definitely interested, or so he said, but he placed an array of demands on the table that stunned the search committee.

He wanted to be head coach, as well as athletic director.

That was all right. Bright and McKenzie would have had it no other way.

Bo Schembechler asked for a ten-year contract at $225,000 a year. He might as well. After all, A&M had approached him, and he knew McKenzie damn well wouldn't be calling a coach of his national stature with empty pockets.

Bum Bright shook his head. From what he had been able to learn from an investigation or two, Schembechler was only earning sixty-five thousand dollars a year at Michigan. Of course, he had a few lucrative deals on the side, and they always added up. Rumors hinted that Bo was raking in close to $200,000 annually.

But a salary of $225,000 a year?

For ten years?

Before all of those additional lucrative deals had been signed?

No coach in America was making that kind of money. Or, Bum Bright wondered, had coaching finally become as financially glamorous as the oil business?

Bo Schembechler was also demanding guaranteed ten-year contracts with those companies, as many as possible, that would be rounded up by Texas A&M to sponsor his television and radio programs. That part of the fine print might be a little more difficult to achieve. Neither

forever. Once again, the Aggies were at the summit. But the climb had taken far longer than the fall from grace. Gene Stallings had given them all hope, but, since New Year's Day in 1968, the road no longer ran from College Station to Dallas and the Cotton Bowl.

As far as Bum Bright was concerned, it was time for A&M to quit looking for a heavily decorated assistant football coach or even some up-and-coming coordinator to command its football team. Kyle Field didn't need to be a training ground or the place where young coaches came to die. He and William McKenzie were convinced that Texas A&M had the power, the finances, and the prestige to go boldly out and hire one of the pre-eminent head football coaches in America. Gil Brandt, the vice president of player development for the Dallas Cowboys, had once shared an office with McKenzie's law firm, and he bluntly warned them, boys, you can't go elephant hunting with a popgun.

On the surface, they set up a search committee to find a new athletic director. But in reality, and during the dead hours of night when no one happened to be standing behind them and looking over their shoulders, Bright and McKenzie were eyeballs deep in the names of great coaches who just might be persuaded to make the break to Texas A&M. Money talked, and they were tied in to the resources that could

Bright nor McKenzie could envision anybody, no matter how good an Aggie they might be, agreeing to invest ten guaranteed years' worth of money to sponsor a series of radio and TV programs that did not yet exist. Bo even envisioned, he said, "a stem-winding television program," running the name of every supporter at the end of each episode – A&M loyalists who had the wisdom and foresight to give two thousand dollars apiece to the venture every week. Bo might be a football coach, Bum Bright thought, but he certainly understood television, and he did know a thing or two about business.

The inference was quite clear. If, perchance, any of the sponsors or donors bailed at any time, then A&M would be committed to dig deeply into its own pockets to make up the difference. Bo thought he was worth it. Bright did, too. McKenzie didn't doubt it for a minute. The legendary Bo Schembechler, all decked out in maroon and white, would cement A&M's football reputation on a national stage, and, over time, the ultimate value of a university's reputation could not be measured in mere dollars and cents.

Bo Schembechler was driving a hard bargain, but he just might be worth the risk.

McKenzie continued the negotiations. A little give here. A little take there. Some compromising along the way. He thought he had a better than average chance of working it all out. Maybe, just maybe, Bo was merely shooting high in an effort to strike the best deal possible. However, if anyone had the God-given ability to find a crack or a weakness in the Michigan coach's demands, McKenzie was the odds on favorite to ferret it out. His courtroom sense could indeed come in handy. William McKenzie knew how to read a man and locate the secret pages that were almost always missing.

Bo Schembechler could not be read.

He had brought his Michigan Wolverines to the Bluebonnet Bowl in Houston a few days after Christmas, then flown on to Dallas to meet with Bright and McKenzie. Much to his dismay, Frank Vandiver, under the cloak of anonymity, was asked to drive up from his home and join the discussions.

For him, it was an awkward, uncomfortable afternoon. He did the best he could to remain presidential and hospitable in the finest A&M tradition. But Vandiver knew he had already given his word to Tom Wilson, told the coach that he would remain at Texas A&M for the life of his contract, and now, God forbid, the great Bo Schembechler himself was being actively courted to take Tom Wilson's job. Vandiver did have one saving grace, however.

Never in his wildest dreams could he imagine that someone of Schembechler's obvious status within the coaching profession would ever leave Michigan for Texas A&M. The thought gave him a measure of solace, if nothing else, during the Christmas holidays.

Now it was the night of January 15, 1982. Shortly after eight o'clock, McKenzie, sitting alone in his office, spoke with the Michigan coach, and it would be for the last time.

I've decided to remain at Michigan, Bo said.

I thought we had a deal.

We only had discussions.

I thought we had a deal, McKenzie repeated.

Silence.

I'm a Wolverine at heart, Bo finally answered, and I guess there's no need for me to tell you that Michigan has sweetened my deal up here a little.

How much?

I'm not at liberty to say.

Do we have a chance to make a competing offer, McKenzie wanted to know. He felt as though Schembechler had kicked him in the gut.

I'm afraid not.

Thanks, Bo had said.

But no thanks.

William McKenzie sighed, glanced at the clock again, dialed Bum Bright, and broke the bad news.

Silence.

Then Bright said, You think Bo was only using us.

Probably.

Any chance of him changing his mind?

Bo's not coming to A&M. He's off the list for good.

Bum Bright hung up the phone and stared at the wall.

Time was running short for him and McKenzie both. Maybe time had already run out. There was a new and growing sense of urgency gnawing at his innards. His cloak and dagger search for a new football coach wasn't much of a secret anymore.

Within the past twenty-four hours, news about the closed-door negotiations with Bo Schembechler had leaked out and was beginning to run rampant throughout the state and the nation. The story was being transferred from the sports pages to the front page and even to the editorial pages of the country's press.

Bum Bright knew that he and McKenzie had to move and move quickly in order to restore some sense of decency, credibility, and order to the search. Fail now, and they would be buried beneath an avalanche of ridicule, scorn, and criticism, which was already headed in their general direction.

Bum Bright didn't particularly care what happened to him personally. He had weathered worse storms before. He only dreaded the thought of reading about any censure or blame that might be leveled at his beloved university. The press could be pretty insensitive sometimes. No. The press could be downright mean.

He sat back in his stuffed chair and closed his eyes. At the moment, he was dead set on hiring any big-name, big-time, high-profile college football coach he could find not named Tom Wilson.

Damn the cost.

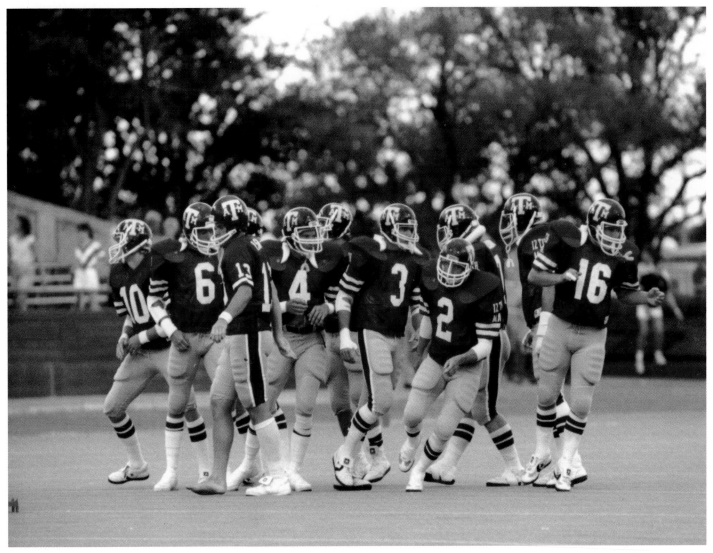

As strong-legged, barefoot kicker Alan Smith lines up for another kickoff, the 12th man team is ready to rock and roll: Dennis Burns (10), Leroy Hallman (6), Tom Arthur (4), Tom Christner (3), and James Barrett (16).

Chapter 3

It was an odd touch of irony. If two schools had ever been created with an instant dislike for each other, it was Texas A&M and The University of Texas. From their battles on the football field had grown one of the nation's great, often bitter, rivalries, and Aggies were in the stands, singing goodbye to texas university and sawing off horns, regardless of which team they might be playing. Behind closed doors, however, the rivalry was not nearly so heated.

In 1956, when Bear Bryant held the reins of Texas A&M's football program, he received a telephone call from a young coach at the University of Washington. Bryant had watched him for a long time and knew him better for his guts and glory days as the quarterback at Oklahoma. He had been a leader then. He was a leader now.

Coach, I have a favor to ask, said Darrell Royal.

Shoot.

I hear the head coaching job's open over at Texas.

It is.

I'm thinking about throwing my name in the hat, Darrell Royal told him, and, Coach, I would appreciate any good word you could put in for me.

Are you crazy, Bear Bryant asked.

What do you mean?

Why in the world would I want to help you get a job at Texas when all it means is that you'll be down here kicking my ass every year, Bear Bryant said with a hint of venom dripping off his tongue.

Darrell Royal waited for him to laugh.

Bear Bryant hung up the phone.

He waited less than a minute, then placed a call to the athletic director at the University of Texas. For some ungodly reason, Bear Bryant said in that deep, graveled voice of his, there's a young man named Darrell Royal who wants to coach over there in Austin. He's a hell of a competitor. If you don't hire him, it'll be biggest mistake you ever make.

Within weeks, Darrell Royal, unaware that Bryant had given Texas his personal endorsement and recommendation, pulled up stakes in Washington and was on the road, heading toward Austin and a football stadium that would one day bear his name.

Bear Bryant never mentioned it again.

Now, twenty-six years later, Bum Bright and William McKenzie were searching for a football coach, and Darrell Royal, over at Texas, was as high as anyone could rise on their list of most despised individuals. Since God had looked down after the sixth day and decided to go ahead and invent football, those bastards in Austin had been A&M's most fierce rival. Bright and McKenzie loved to hate Royal and would aggressively root for any team playing against him. But they also had an unwavering respect for Darrell Royal. He was as much a gentleman as he was a competitor. Even before the negotiations had gotten underway with Bo Schembechler, Bright had called and asked for the names of any coaching candidates Royal thought they should pursue.

The Texas coach didn't hesitate. You need to talk with Jackie Sherrill, he said. Wherever Jackie goes, he wins. He knows how to recruit. He knows how to graduate players. You can go out there, dig around a little, and track down anybody you want, but you won't find yourself a better coach than the one they have up at Pittsburgh. Jackie Sherrill is one of the Bear's boys.

But then, that opinion was pretty much what the Bear himself had told them.

And so had Gil Brandt from his inner sanctum within the Dallas Cowboys. Brandt had a grand reputation for knowing talent.

While their internal discussions had been primarily focused on Bo Schembechler, neither Bright nor McKenzie ever lost sight of Jackie Sherrill on their radar. A few weeks earlier, they asked Brandt, an inter-mediary far removed from any connection to A&M, to quietly approach the Pittsburgh coach and determine what interest, if any, he might have in the Texas A&M job. Few thought Jackie Sherrill would ever have any thoughts about leaving the football dynasty he had built in a land long ruled by the Nittany Lions of Joe Paterno's Penn State.

Paterno, however, was no longer the man sitting alone at the top of football supremacy in Pennsylvania. His legend had a little tarnish on it. For the past three years, Sherrill's Panthers had gone 11-1, 11-1, and 11-1, and the fiery, feisty Joe Paterno was being outsmarted, out-re-cruited, and, more often than not, out-coached by the aggressive, show-no-mercy and take-no-prisoner tactics of the University of Pittsburgh coach. Sherrill had shoved the heel of his shoe in Paterno's throat and never eased up on the pressure. He had not come to Pittsburgh to win friends. He had come to win football games, which, he believed, was what a coach's mission in life should be. Their rivalry was as fierce off the field as it was on the field.

Sherrill had been able to bring in a young running back, then give Tony Dorsett the offense, the game plan, and the ball often enough for him to carry home the Heisman Trophy. Dorsett, in time, would be just as good, if not better, with the Dallas Cowboys, which was another reason why Gil Brandt had such a strong appreciation for the obvious coaching ability of Jackie Sherrill.

Sherrill did not merely recruit Pennsylvania. He recruited the nation. He found a defensive end in an historic little Mississippi town perched on a bluff overlooking the Mississippi River when few even knew someone as talented and explosive as Hugh Green even existed.

When Alan Smith (13) kicked off, the 12th man unit bolted with reckless abandon downfield, praying that he would place the ball short of the goal line and give them a chance to take their frustrations out on some unsuspecting ball carrier.

The behind-closed-doors secret search for a new football coach led A&M to Jackie Sherrill, who had become one of the top five names in the coaching profession. He had just completed three straight seasons of 11-1, 11-1, and 11-1 at the University of Pittsburgh.

And Hugh Green was destined to become one of the most feared and dominant defensive players of his generation. Sherrill's strong-armed quarterback, Dan Marino, was in the midst of assaulting every college passing record in the books, and he was only a junior. Five other Pitt players were destined to become first-round NFL draft choices. Pittsburgh, from all accounts, had the talent to make a legitimate run at the

National Championship in 1982, and Jackie Sherrill was no longer a long shot to get there. The odds makers liked him a lot and would be ranking the Panthers No. 1 in the national pre-season polls.

Sherrill had a better-than-average financial arrangement at Pittsburgh but was suffering from a malady that often struck successful coaches. He simply felt as though Pittsburgh, at least the hierarchy within the institution, did not appreciate him or the job he was doing. Little things, which in time became big things, kept happening to his program without his knowledge. Late one afternoon, for example, he learned in an elevator ride that a new opponent had been added to the Pitt schedule, and no one had bothered to tell him. He had to prepare for a team and had no idea who the team was. Jackie Sherrill was a man who liked to be in charge, and, at Pittsburgh, he was, day after day, at someone else's mercy. He frankly did not like the idea of always being obliged to follow someone else's rules. Jackie Sherrill was his own rules maker.

The head football coach's job at Pitt, when Sherrill joined Johnny Majors' staff in 1973, was widely considered to be the worst college job in the country. The program had sunk dreadfully to unfathomable depths, had not produced a winning record in a decade, was staggering off a 1-10 record, had been outscored the year before, 350-193, and had been beaten by Penn State for the past eight years. Majors had told his coaches, bring in anybody who can help us win, and Sherrill promptly began tracking down and hounding players from Georgia, Florida, Maryland, Ohio, and, of course, Western Pennsylvania.

Sherrill returned to head the program in 1977 and discovered that, even after a national championship, the political landscape of Pittsburgh sports remained unaltered. He made some immediate changes, worked hard, traveled night and day on the recruiting trail, and faced a constant struggle against the corporate structure of the university, one governed by too many regulations established at too many board meetings, and drawn up by too many self-appointed dignitaries who wanted to meddle with his football program. Sherrill had to fight to secure pay increases for his assistants. He had to fight to buy new socks for his football team. It was a never-ending fight from daylight to dark, and the pressure from outside sources was beginning to smother him. He led the Panthers to a 9-2 record, and the Pittsburgh press blatantly called him the worst coach in America. Even when his team went 11-1 for three consecutive years, Pittsburgh had not been able to sell out the stadium, and newspapers were continuing to criticize the job he had done. At Pitt, Sherrill realized that he was trapped in a no-win situation.

Sherrill listened to Brandt's unofficial overture from Bright and McKenzie, then said, sure, I'm interested in Texas A&M.

Would you really leave Pittsburgh?

For Texas A&M, I would.

You know that Bo Schembechler is their first choice, Brandt carefully explained.

Sherrill shrugged nonchalantly. Bo would certainly be my first choice, he replied.

Before the East-West Shrine game, Sherrill sought out Schembechler and urged him to make the move from Michigan. The job at A&M, Sherrill said, is the greatest opportunity in college coaching today.

Bo smiled.

Maybe it was.

Maybe not.

Jackie Sherrill was about to find out.

As soon as Bo Schembechler had firmly declined the offer, William McKenzie was on the phone to Pittsburgh. I'd like to talk to you more about Texas A&M, he told Sherrill. Is there a chance we can get

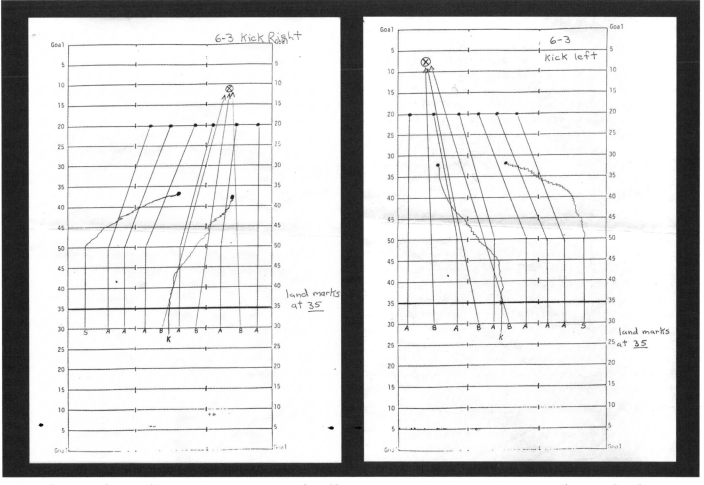

By the time Jackie Sherrill created the 12th man kickoff team, he had already scratched out a diagram for his coverage scheme. To the players, it was known as 63 Right and 63 Left, and it was an all-out, aggressive, attacking scheme.

together and talk it over?

I don't know, Sherrill replied. First, I'll have to clear it with my athletic director. He believed in honesty and protocol above all else.

If he has no objections, McKenzie said, feeling his way through the conversation, let me know when I can be there.

How soon can you come?

Tomorrow.

Tomorrow worked out fine.

McKenzie asked Frank Vandiver to make the journey to Pittsburgh with him. They were not on a fact-finding trip, the attorney said. Already, the committee knew virtually everything there was to know about Jackie Sherrill. He had played seven positions for two of Bear Bryant's National Championship teams at Alabama. He had worked under the famed Frank Broyles at Arkansas and Johnny Majors at both Iowa State and Pittsburgh. In five years as head coach at Pitt, Sherrill had compiled an enviable 50-9-1 record. He was only thirty-eight years old and was known as a masterful recruiter and brilliant tactician. He understood X's and O's like a mathematician understood the square root of numbers, any number to any power.

Jackie Sherrill, McKenzie said without any hesitation, had the youth, the drive, and the stamina to build a first-class athletic program at A&M. He could provide the stability and the leadership that the Aggies had been sorely missing. No, McKenzie reiterated to the president, they would not be on a fact-finding mission. He and the regents were ready to make Jackie Sherrill an offer they didn't think he could refuse. Vandiver assumed that McKenzie was referring to the athletic director's job, which happened to be the only position open in the athletic department. Texas A&M already had a football coach, and the coach still had a year remaining on his contract. Vandiver had been worried about Schembechler, but, with Bo taking himself out of the coaching picture, the president's greatest concern had been alleviated, if not entirely eliminated. He certainly had not been looking forward to telling Tom Wilson that his services were no longer desired or needed at Texas A&M.

Frank Vandiver certainly wanted to make the trip to meet with Sherrill. He thought it was important, perhaps even necessary, for him to go. After all, the new athletic director would be making the calls on all A&M sports, and selecting the right one was historically the kind of decision that a university president had been hired to make.

Unfortunately, Vandiver had awakened that morning to a nightmare that only another administrator could understand. A morass of unexpected problems had arisen suddenly as students besieged the campus for spring registration. Long lines snaked their way across campus. Confusion was elbow-to-elbow and shoulder-to-shoulder. Everything that could possibly go wrong was in the process of going wrong. His office was being inundated with phone calls from angry students and disappointed parents. Since Vandiver had a growing and snarled crisis on his hands, he asked James Bond, A&M's general counsel, to take his place on the flight to Pittsburgh.

An Aggie Yell Leader takes charge of the crowd at Kyle Field.

do with football. It was all about business. But then, somewhere down through the years, football had become as big a business as there was in the country.

When Sherrill returned, the talks, during the next three hours, gradually took on a more serious form of negotiations. McKenzie refused to leave without making an offer. Sherrill had no intention of letting anyone on the committee leave before an offer was placed on the table. Sherrill was quite willing to play hardball and hard to get. After all, he had a potential National Championship team waiting for him in Pittsburgh. What exactly did Texas A&M have to propose that was any better?

The A&M representatives walked away in the darkness of night. No one had seen them arrive, seen them depart, or had any idea who they were or why they happened to be in Pittsburgh on such a brutally cold night. A fresh layer of snow blanketed the ground. The temperature had fallen on the south side of zero. Sherrill had not given them a final decision. He wanted to meet with Frank Vandiver first, but McKenzie wondered privately if that would be such a good idea.

Vandiver was not particularly concerned about the circumstances on campus. With a little time, they could all be easily solved. Off campus was an entirely different matter. Vandiver didn't know why, but already he had a foreboding dread about the weeks to come.

Bond hooked up with McKenzie and John Blocker at Love Field in Dallas. As the clock ticked toward the afternoon side of noon, the three men headed north by northeast on one of Blocker's private planes. By five-thirty, they were knocking on the front door of Sherrill's large, two-story home. He and his wife had plans to host a dinner buffet that evening, but, don't worry, Sherrill told them all, we have a couple of hours before any of the guests arrive. He was as jovial and as hospitable as a genteel country gentleman, although those dark, deep-set, smoldering eyes of his were absolutely hypnotic. When he walked into the room, Jackie Sherrill was definitely in charge. No one doubted it for a minute. The three representatives from A&M followed him into his study, heard the door close behind them, and opened their briefcases. The men only thought they had been prepared. Jackie Sherrill had every detail outlined and underlined, and he answered almost every question before it could be asked. He knew how to run a football team, a business, and certainly the study of his own home.

For two hours, the talk was mixed with a little supper, and the A&M hiring committee waited together in secrecy while Sherrill left to play the gracious host for awhile. On the far side of the door, among the Panther faithful, no one was harboring any foggiest of ideas that Jackie Sherrill just might be a negotiation point or two, a dollar or two away from leaving Pittsburgh as abruptly as he had arrived. It had nothing to

The next morning, early on Sunday, McKenzie called the A&M president and reported that Jackie Sherrill had not yet taken the job and would not take the job without meeting personally with Vandiver to discuss, among other things, the recruitment of a new staff.

Vandiver frowned. He did not quite understand the unspoken message being cloaked by McKenzie's words. He paused a moment, then asked, what does an athletic director need with a staff?

It's a little more complicated than that, the attorney told him.

What do you mean?

Jackie will only come to A&M if he's hired as both athletic director and head football coach.

Vandiver felt as though he had taken a sudden shot to the midsection. He realized that the decision to hire a football coach had been made behind his back – neither Bright nor McKenzie had bothered to consult with him – and he knew that Tom Wilson's pride would be taking a serious beating. The man was being treated shabbily and probably unfairly. A coach was losing his job and didn't know a thing about it. No. He had already lost his job, was out on the road recruiting somewhere, and still in the dark as far as his future at A&M or anywhere else, for that matter, was concerned.

Vandiver did not have any reason to fault Jackie Sherrill, but he certainly did not like the way the search had been handled. Controversy would be only one step behind. Although the president was upset, he would not stand in the way or create any friction or furor when Jackie Sherrill came to College Station to hammer out the details of his contract. Frank Vandiver was and would remain the consummate professional. It was his nature. If anything derailed or disrupted the negotiations, his hands would be clean. But breaking his word to Tom Wilson would haunt him for a long time.

Jackie Sherrill's plane touched down on Monday, January 18, and he, along with Gil Brandt, met briefly with the A&M athletic council before sitting down to business in Vandiver's office. The discussions were formal, low key, and cordial. The president had the authority to make it all official, but he had already been given his orders and the key to the bank by Bum Bright. Whatever Jackie Sherrill wanted, within reason, and almost every request was within reason, he would receive.

The new Aggie head football coach and athletic director walked out with a five-year rollover contract, meaning that it would be automatically renewed at the end of every year and always have five years remaining on the ultimate life of the agreement. Sherrill's base salary, paid from athletic department funds, totaled $95,000, which was five thousand dollars more than Vandiver received each year. The ship was righted a month later when the president's salary was increased to $100,000. The regents were able to guarantee another $130,000 a year from television and radio programming, as well as from board memberships and a few assorted endorsement deals. Using private donations to the athletic program, the university managed to subsidize half the purchase price of a new home, with Sherrill paying the other half. The coach received an insurance policy valued at close to $200,000, two cars, and a paid membership to the prestigious Briarcrest Country Club.

Bum Bright had been right.

The earnings of a big-time, college football coach had indeed become as glamorous and almost as lucrative as the oil business.
Jackie Sherrill and Frank Vandiver signed on the dotted line. They stood and shook hands. No criticism. No dispute. No disagreements. No second thoughts, at least not on the surface.

The deal had been struck.

The ink had not yet dried on the contract.

And even as he watched Sherrill leave, Vandiver was reaching for the phone to call Tom Wilson. His efforts to save the coach's job had failed miserably and ended badly, he said, but A&M would financially honor the final year of Wilson's contract. Good luck and Godspeed.

Tom Wilson, at the moment was in Austin – in enemy territory of all places – preaching the gospel of A&M and trying to recruit a hot new football player. He walked out of the young man's house and called his wife. She told him, A&M has hired Jackie Sherrill. You've been fired. I just saw it on television news.

It was the first Wilson had heard of his coaching demise with the Aggies. He would talk to Frank Vandiver, but the conversation took place long after the knife had been placed in his back.

Wilson had no choice but to accept the offer. He had threatened to resign. His bluff had been called, then trumped. Now he was being shoved rather rudely out the door. He said, A&M wanted to make a coaching change and made it. I was caught in the middle. He offered up one bitter and public tirade against what he considered to be the unethical tactics of Bum Bright before quietly making preparations to leave College Station. It had been a good run, he thought, but a short run, and he still had a year's worth of salary, which gave him time to decide what he should do next. College was too political, he decided, so he turned his attention to the Friday night lights of high school football in Texas.

Somewhere out there, he knew, was some wiry, teenage quarterback just waiting for Tom Wilson to show him how to throw the ball often and downfield.

Frank Vandiver was deeply wounded and left feeling somewhat humiliated. He would say, we looked as though we put the cart before the horse, that we had decided to become a great football power and

Jackie Sherrill met with students and players and even sampled the food, when he came to College Station to hammer out details of a new contract. Sherrill had turned his back on a successful career coaching the University of Pittsburgh to accept the A&M job. Some said Pitt had the makings of a National Championship, but Sherrill preferred the promise in Aggieland.

thus we brought down some ridicule upon ourselves.

He promptly called A&M Chancellor Frank Hubert to discuss the strong possibility of submitting his own resignation. Maybe A&M did not need him anymore. Maybe he should have never taken the job in the first place. Maybe he should have fought the Board of Regents harder. But how do you ever fight the regents and win?

Let everything cool down, Vandiver was told, and, sooner than later, it will. Don't do anything you'll regret. Just take care of the university. Nobody can do it better. And let football take care of itself. This is, after all, Texas A&M.

Bum Bright realized that the search could have probably been handled in a more fortuitous manner, but he had the coach he wanted and, at long last, he believed, Texas A&M football was headed in the right direction. His only fear was that he would expect too much too soon. But he was an Aggie, and that was an affliction that affected them all.

Jim Uptmore, a former student and successful building contractor in San Antonio, had worked hard with Gene Stallings during the late

James Barrett (16) came out of the small West Texas high school in Rankin and carried on his father's tradition of walking on an Aggie football team that was in the midst of building something special.

1960s to build the Aggie network of alumni clubs throughout the state and around the nation. He was typical of those who had been disgruntled with the misery that had historically surrounded the A&M football team. He watched Darrell Royal take over a weak and struggling program at Texas and turn it into a national powerhouse. The Aggies had been left behind. Too far behind.

The phone rang, and Uptmore answered. He heard the unmistakable voice of Gene Stallings on the line. I want to give you a heads up, Stalling said.

About what?

Somebody's coming in who'll make things happen at A&M.

Who?

Jackie Sherrill.

What's so special about Sherrill?

Once you meet him, you'll know.

That became the mantra all across the Aggie landscape. Once you met Jackie Sherrill, you'd know.

On a Tuesday, Texas A&M announced the signing of Jackie Sherrill. When he called Bear Bryant to tell him he had accepted the job, his old coach told him, well, boy, there's one thing you have to understand. You won't be able to sneak up on anybody. Those Aggies like to brag. And they'll be telling the whole world that you're better than you are before you ever take the field. That'll make you mad and make everybody else mad as well.

The Bear laughed. He felt almost as close to A&M as he did to Alabama.

The day Sherrill walked on campus, Jim Uptmore, said, was the day that changed Texas A&M football. The team began to believe in itself. Sure, there would be a hard road ahead. But no longer would the Aggies simply be forced to take those recruits that Texas and Oklahoma didn't want. Sherrill stood toe-to-toe with the big boys. He didn't back down. Great players were coming to A&M simply because Sherrill asked them. They believed he was a coach who would make something happen, and they wanted to be around when it did.

On a Wednesday, Sherrill sat down at a press conference and again expressed his conviction that Texas A&M represented the greatest opportunity in college coaching. He leaned close to the microphone and drawled softly, the tradition here is unreal: the tradition of the corps, the tradition of the students, the tradition of the school. It's probably the closest-knit football family in the whole United States. When you look at the Texas A&M job, it's the plum you want to pick. I know a lot of football coaches across this country who would walk to Texas to take this job.

By week's end, Sherrill had hired most of his staff and written each of the high school football players he had recruited to play for Pittsburgh, urging them honor their commitment to the university. He did not encourage any of them to follow him to Texas A&M, although there might have been an All-American or two in the bunch. That, he decided, would be unethical and out of the question. They should stay home and play their football in Pennsylvania. That's what he believed, and that's what he told them.

By Monday, he was on the road recruiting, flying from city to city across Texas and across the nation, heading down backroads that were missing from some maps and knocking on doors in places some coaches couldn't find or pronounce.

As he always pointed out, I have one leg in one pair of pants and the other leg in another pair. I'll change in the air.

The cupboard certainly wasn't bare at Texas A&M, but the cupboard always needed to be restocked. If a kid could play, Sherrill would track him down. If the kid could play well, Sherrill would sign him. It was the beginning of a brand new day at Texas A&M, but some days, Aggies would find out, might take as many as three years before the dawn broke. On the road and out of the limelight, however, Jackie Sherrill was finding a distant measure of peace and contentment.

Back in College Station, all hell was busting loose.

The A&M faculty was outraged. One disgruntled professor simply shook his head and said, it will take ten years to recover from this. The university, some wrote, had been exposed as an institution seemingly willing to pay any price for a national championship in football, and the price, for some, had been exorbitant. The *Washington Post* reported that the events transpiring at Texas A&M were characterized by a quality of rawness and insensitivity that shocked even those people who had grown accustomed to big money in college football. As the newspaper said, Texas A&M was not, after all, Michigan or Notre Dame, searching to replace a legend. It was a university with a mediocre reputation in athletics grasping for greatness.

Bum Bright threw the newspaper to the floor. That's the point, he said to anyone who happened to be eavesdropping or listening to him. We aren't Michigan or Notre Dame, but there is absolutely no reason why Texas A&M can't become the next Michigan or Notre Dame. No, we weren't searching to replace a legend. We were searching to find a legend. And we may just have found ourselves one.

Jackie Sherrill had learned long ago in his coaching career that critics, like sharks in shallow waters, without reason or provocation, would always be searching for the smell of blood, particularly his blood. However, he had about as much concern for the national uprising as Bum Bright did. He drove wearily back into College Station about one o'clock on a chilled January morning after a day-long recruiting trip had carried him by plane from Houston to San Antonio and finally across the vast West Texas landscape to Midland. His shoulders were aching, and the long hours were beginning to take their toll. He said simply, I didn't create this situation. I'm here to rectify it. Wins, he knew, would make the difference.

According to card-carrying members of the national media, who had pieced together every dollar and cent scattered throughout the fine print of Sherrill's contract, the new Aggie coach was earning $267,000 a year. For the five-year length of its terms, the salary totaled a little more than $1.3 million, which, the press claimed, made Jackie Sherrill America's first million-dollar coach. True or not, repeated twice and printed once, the label stuck.

Even college football coaches expressed hypocritical shock at the dollar amount associated with Sherrill's contract. Up in Arkansas, Lou Holtz was saying, this is over emphasis on football at its height, but so what? I just hope our fans, as broad minded as they are, don't expect a poor, old forty-thousand-dollar-a-year coach like me to be able to beat

When Jackie Sherrill made the decision to implement his notorious 12th man kick-off team, Tom Arthur (4) quickly became one of his key players.

a two million-dollar coach like Sherrill. Holtz could always play fast and loose with the numbers. Back in Pennsylvania, Joe Paterno was pointing out, heck, you know how naïve I am, but I would be shocked if there is any other coach even making two hundred thousand dollars. Tell Jackie I'm proud of him and that if he could send a couple of thousand dollars a month up here to help a poor Italian boy, I'd be grateful. In Michigan, athletic director Don Canham, who had almost lost Bo Schembechler to Texas A&M, said the Aggies had gone financially berserk, explaining, I'm afraid this will start an escalation in bidding I don't like to see. Suddenly money doesn't mean anything. It becomes plastic. Everything is out of whack.

So the weeping and the wailing had begun.

What the leering press did not bother to uncover, however, was that Alabama's Paul "Bear" Bryant reigned as the highest wage earner in all of collegiate sports, earning salary and benefits that totaled $450,000 annually. When the Bear retired, Ray Perkins would be given a six-figure shoe deal that, along with income generated by the potato chip and soft drink sponsors of his television show, virtually doubled the coach's salary. Oklahoma's Barry Switzer was banking $270,000 a year. You name a deal, said one Oklahoma insider, and Barry has it. Lou Holtz, who billed himself as a poor old forty-thousand-dollar-a-year coach, was taking home $226,000 and probably more when the endorsement deals were added to his pay. Chuck Fairbanks, lured from professional football to the University of Colorado, was receiving at least $200,000 a year, including fringe benefits. In Kentucky, Jerry Claiborne had been hired for $152,000, and Kentucky had not fielded a big winner since Bear Bryant left the school in 1954 for his legendary, almost mythical, journey to Texas A&M. To keep Pat Dye at Auburn, the alumni chipped in and bought his family a home valued at $412,000. If he won enough to remain a War Eagle for fourteen years, they would give him the deed.

Bo Schembechler, whose athletic director had complained long and hard about the so-called ridiculous amount of money being heaped upon Jackie Sherrill by A&M, was being paid $147,000 a year. Quietly, and on the side, he had been given a major interest in a Columbus pizza parlor that was, if nothing else, a virtual money machine, running non-stop in Ohio of all places, the home of Schembechler's biggest rival. Nobody, other than the IRS, had even the foggiest notion of how large Bo Schembechler's home-grown fortune, double the cheese and cut the anchovies, was continuing to grow.

Yet, the leering press swarmed like frenzied locusts around Texas A&M and Jackie Sherrill, the million-dollar coach. Investigative reporters had been taught long ago that scandals were front-page news, and since none of them wanted their stories bottled up at the bottom of page 43-G, they kept searching for something bad to say and someone angry enough or envious enough to say it.

Frank Vandiver stepped forward to finally place the issue clouding Sherrill's salary in its proper perspective. Given an ideal world, he said, I'd rather see this kind of money go for faculty salaries or scholarships for the library. Unfortunately, the disparity between what a distinguished professor of chemistry earns compared with salary of a football coach can allow you to get bent out of shape. The professor might win a Nobel Prize and change the course of human affairs. But maybe we have to realize that football brings in the money necessary to keep the professor's laboratories open. We need football here because of the support and interest it affords our institution. Our people want and need a major football program.

Even Lou Holtz at Arkansas, in a more somber moment, admitted that the salary for hiring Jackie Sherrill wasn't particularly exorbitant. The money simply tells people all over the country how important Texas A&M thinks football is, he said. Besides, when it's all said and done, you'll find out that Jackie is worth it.

Sherrill never doubted it. The salary is not out of reason, he would say. After all, they're paying me to do two jobs, one as head football coach and the other as athletic director. He realized, however, that the

leering press had absolutely no use and a great distaste for logic.

Faculty members rose up in unison to call Sherrill's financial package out of line, outrageous, and even a sad sidelight on American society. But the nation, as a whole, was beginning to understand what many universities had known all along: Winning football programs brought the institutions a whole package of such intangible benefits as prestige, attention, and increased alumni support. *Sports Illustrated* would explain that the money to make the hiring possible had been generously donated by Aggies who genuinely loved football. And, as Douglas Looney wrote, should Congress ever pass a law outlawing football, those same people weren't about to turn around and give to the chemistry department. One old sports pundit always declared that athletics and academics would never be placed on an equal playing field until a school could persuade fifty thousand screaming fans to buy tickets to a geometry test.

Jackie Sherrill did not ignore the controversy, nor did he hide from it, which was not, nor had ever been, his style. He met the issue head on, and during the next few months, he would make nearly forty trips throughout the state. He shuttled from major metropolitan areas to small town communities, often flying his own propeller-driven plane like a crop duster just above the tree lines. He spoke to Texas A&M alumni groups, stressing the university's academic achievements and preaching the importance and the necessity of an athlete leaving A&M with both a degree and an education.

All the while, Sherrill was working to balance the athletic budget, market the football team, handle the promotions, supervise the personnel, sell the program, and recruit the kinds of players it would take to move A&M a little higher and into the winner's circle. As he said, we may not be able to recruit the super players, but we'll find some damn good ones. He did have quite a compelling story to tell those players who sat down to talk with him. All they had to do was look at his track record at Pitt. Sherrill had pieced together the nation's top defense six years hand running. His starting receivers were each averaging forty catches a year, and an array of running backs were all racing for eight hundred yards or more a season. Sherrill, it sometimes seemed, had a direct line to the NFL since fifty-four of his players at Washington State and Pittsburgh had gone on to the professional ranks. And, he could proudly proclaim to mama, more than eighty percent of his players had graduated.

Back at Texas A&M, Sherrill knew that Kyle Field held 73,000 fans, yet, in spite of Aggie pride and tradition, it was selling only 58,000 tickets a game. He did some quick math and realized that if his presence and his team could increase attendance by only five thousand more fans a game, the university could net $385,000, which would more than pay for his salary and his benefits. Another five thousand tickets were a paltry number, he thought. Easily printed. Easily sold. Sherrill would not be satisfied until every seat was filled and a team of architects, who was no doubt earning larger salaries than his, were down on the field, drawing up sketches to add more sections and build more bleachers. It could be done, he reasoned. After all, this was Texas A&M.

On campus, Sherrill had personally written a letter of assurance to each member of the faculty, vowing that – during his tenure as Aggie head football coach and athletic director – education would never rank second to athletics. He was making a firm commitment that his players would go to class and graduate. He also established a faculty committee on admissions and eligibility, giving representatives the power to

With Tom Christner (3) only a step away, Robert Crouch (14) explodes into a UTEP blocker, opening the way for his team-mates to make the ball carrier suffer. The unit proved the critics wrong. The 12th man unit would not be a novelty act or public relations ploy. It was made up of hard-nosed football players who probably played better than they really were.

reject any player he recruited to A&M and did not measure up to their academic standards.

You're crazy, coaches across the country told him. You're turning athletics over to the academic people, and they'll make life miserable for you. Those highbrows in academics, frankly, don't like athletics. How do you expect to survive?

Sherrill wasn't worried. He had always prided himself in being a careful and demanding recruiter. As he said, I like to be around the kids' parents. I can tell more by seeing a kid with his mother for five minutes than I can by watching him play football for thirty hours. He had once driven two hundred miles to recruit an outstanding football player. But during the early evening, mother and son had a sudden disagreement, and the conversation began to turn sour.

The boy's eyes glared as he told his mother to shut up. Sherrill didn't say another word. He promptly closed his briefcase, picked up his jacket, walked out the door, and drove those four long and lonely hours back to Pittsburgh. He never considered recruiting the young man again. Mama came first. If a kid did not respect his mama, he wouldn't respect his school, his coaches, or his team. The Panthers needed players, but they could get along just fine without this one.

The tension around Texas A&M had not mellowed. Out in the hinterland, however, there was a growing belief that Jackie Sherrill was far different from the man who had been castigated and blasphemed in the press. He was a gentleman above all else, soft-spoken and polite. He would look a people squarely in the eyes when he talked to them. He had been shot at, hit on occasion, and missed a few times, but he had not flinched. He never flinched. At times, he said, it felt like a billion people were all pointing their fingers at him, all raising their voices against him. It had not been easy mentally or emotionally, but he had endured. The press, the critics, had taken their best shots, and Jackie Sherrill was still standing.

He was a private, no-nonsense kind of guy with a subtle, genteel air of deep Southern sophistication. He was shy, and that surprised a lot of people, especially those who mistook his shyness for being aloof or possibly even arrogant. Sherrill arrived at A&M as a driven, independent, and complex man, fiercely motivated and persistently battling to exceed his own high expectations. He was decisive, possessed a silent determination, and spoke with the stern, unwavering voice of authority. His one shortcoming, he said, was his lack of patience. I wish I could be patient, he said, but I can be pretty hard-headed. He always had a plan, left nothing to chance, and stuck to his guns regardless of the obstacles confronting him. Bear Bryant had taught him that, if nothing else. Sherrill was his own man. No one ever disputed it. But the shadow of the Bear was never far away.

Sherrill was extremely image conscious. As Neil Landsman reported in the *Bryan Eagle*, he's a rugged-looking guy … He dresses Ivy League style and admits he has a weakness for clothes. Vidal Sassoon would envy his blow-dried look. In fact, his spiffy, slick image suggests he can change the image of the ridiculed Aggie. Such an accomplishment would merit a raise without a whimper of protest.

Another reporter wrote that if the Southwest Conference concocted a best-dressed list, Sherrill would make first team. Knute Rockne probably would have mistaken him for a Wall Street analyst. Pop Warner might have thought of him as a C.P.A. He may be the only college coach in America who will go to the trouble of skipping lunch to meet his tailor for an early fitting.

Jackie Sherrill was straight off Madison Avenue, and he viewed himself as a corporate CEO, who ran a big business, rather than as a coach who simply directed a football team. That's my job, he said. Man-

agement. Putting people together, organizing thoughts, putting ideas into practice. Being able to compete. Hiring the right people and keeping them all happy. His strength, in fact, was to bring in great coaches, then move out of their way and let them coach. Sherrill was a strict disciplinarian and believed he had taken the best traits, the most valuable teachings, from the three great bosses who had tutored him along the way: Bear Bryant, Frank Broyles, and Johnny Majors. The Bear, he said, was mentally and physically tough, yet he could be a very compassionate person. Broyles had the best head for business he had ever seen in a head coach. And Majors was an absolute genius when it came to public relations. They were winners all. And he had been quite willing to walk in their shadows until the time came to walk on his own and cast his own shadow.

Most of the nation in 1982 had a warped vision of Texas A&M, knowing it primarily as a university that had started as an agricultural school. According to Charlie Thornton, the associate athletic director, people thought of our students as guys who drove pickups and had dirt under their nails. Plus, for many years, it had been strictly a military school with an all-male enrollment. When Sherrill left Pittsburgh, some across the country were laughing and saying that airplanes landing in College Station were equipped with sweepers in order to clear the cows off the runway.

Few were aware that A&M had become the fastest-growing university in the nation with a student body exceeding thirty-seven thousand. Aggies were no longer an assortment of country boys and girls straight of the farms, and Sherrill knew the difference.

He felt like he belonged.

There was a lot about Sherrill that he didn't let anybody see. He had an inner self permanently veiled behind his own intimidating stare. It was part of the mystery and the mystique that surrounded him. Sherrill would admit, some people are saying I don't fit the Aggie image. I am definitely not a good old boy. But that's not the Aggie mold anymore. Discipline, mental toughness, and strong work habits, that's what defines the real Aggie these days. If so, Jackie Sherrill had been possessed with the Aggie Spirit the day he arrived on campus.

Jack Gallagher at the *Houston Post* pointed out that even if the timing had been wretched and Tom Wilson had indeed received a raw deal, hiring Jackie Sherrill could well have been one of Bum Bright's few bright moves.

Even President Frank Vandiver was beginning to experience a new respect and admiration for Sherrill, enough so that he was willing to rewrite a piece of recent history. He would say, when we were looking for a coach, we were kind of at a crossroads. We were either going to continue trying to field a winning team, or we were going to actually get there. I liked Jackie Sherrill and his great attitude from the start. And the board was all for his hefty contract, looking on it as corporate decision for the future. Like them, I thought, if we get the right man, then let's keep him. I thought we'd come out all right, and we did.

Texas Monthly presented its opinion in a typical *Texas Monthly* manner: For its $1.3 million investment, Sherrill should give A&M winning football, stunning upsets, stoic determination, daring gambles, strategic genius, and hope for the future.

Jackie Sherrill read the story and smiled.

He would have it no other way.

The first class of the 12th man team in 1983, with the statue of E. King Gill as their focal point of the 12th Man tradition at Texas A&M, are, first row, Jeff Blair (15), Tom Bumgardner (9), Leroy Hallman (6), Ron Reynolds (1), Barry Stevens (12), James Barrett (16). Second row: Tom Christner (3), Tom Bevans (8), Coach David Beal, Les Asel (11), Larry Johnson (5), Head Coach Jackie Sherrill, Tom Arthur (4), Ike Liles (3), Robert Crouch (14), Keith Newton (17), Dennis Burns (10).

Chapter 4

Jackie Sherrill had never been afraid of hard work. As he said, I was raised in Duncan, Oklahoma. I grew up behind a plow. I've had a lot of dirt between my toes. Physical exhaustion could often be a relief from the mental anguish of a workaday world. But emotional exhaustion was a killer.

He only had thirty-eight years of living behind him, but the distant miles, the long days, and the uncompromising hours were all beginning to wear him down like water on limestone. In one hectic week alone, Sherrill had broken bread with the A&M faithful in Austin, New Orleans, Lafayette, Tulsa, and Little Rock. Airports were becoming as familiar as football fields, and there was one constant that did not change from city to city. Aggies were ready for a change, and Aggies, especially those who wanted wins for their donations to the university, did not suffer silently. For them, tolerance was not recognized as a virtue.

The football faithful had experienced brief periods of fleeting success, but nothing permanent. Long suffering had already gone on far too long for them. Aggie teams did not always win, but they were always expected to play with rabid fanaticism. And the faithful, win or lose, always kept coming back for more. They had their hearts broken game after game, year after year, but they never broke ranks. Tomorrow would be a better day, they believed, or at least not as bad nor as disappointing as the last one had been. Their spirit was not only indomitable but also infectious. They were quick to criticize and even quicker to give their hard-earned dollars. The Aggie Club, for example, had two hundred and

fifty members, each donating two grand a year, and another three hundred were lined up to join the elite organization as soon as there was room for them.

To the Aggie faithful, Jackie Sherrill had the look and the attitude of a winner. But he also had a stern message for them all, delivered either in person or in print. I have been told that this is a great job except you can't control the alumni, he said. I don't believe that. You can't buy me. You don't own me. And you never will. You can call me on the phone, and I will call you back. You can write me, and I will answer you. But if you come into my office, you'd better have some size on you.

Years earlier, Sherrill had been offered a head coaching job, and, in an effort to cinch the deal, a wealthy alumnus promised him a $75,000 stipend at the end of each year.

No thanks, said Sherrill. I'd rather have $75,000 worth of stock in your company.

How come, the executive wanted to know.

Sherrill grinned. I'd rather win a piece of you than have you own a piece of me, he said.

A man was valued by his character, he said, not by his bank account or the price on his head.

When Jackie Sherrill spoke, people listened. His very presence cast a hypnotic spell. His voice was soft. His eyes cut like a dagger. He had been a disciple of Bear Bryant, and some said Sherrill had as much fire in the belly, as much grit and gumption as the Bear, and no one at A&M

had forgotten those ten grueling days when Bryant took 103 football players to the sun-seared, rock-scarred, goat head thorn practice field of Junction and came back with only twenty-seven.

No one knew exactly what it would take for Jackie Sherrill to build a winner in the image of Bear Bryant, but the faithful were willing to sit back and wait as long as they didn't have to wait too long. A year should be plenty of time, they thought, and some doubted it would even take that long. In a world short on patience, they wanted instant success. After all, they whispered among themselves, Tom Wilson had gone 7-5 during his last season and, with a little luck, could have easily wound up 10-2. Even though the noose had already been dropped around his neck, he beat Oklahoma State in the Independence Bowl. Jackie Sherrill was a million-dollar coach. He should already be making reservations for the Cotton Bowl. It had been such a long, long time.

Jackie Sherrill had not grown up with any intentions or aspirations of becoming a football coach. Oh, he had the ability to play the game all right, and, in grade school, no one in Duncan, Oklahoma, was tough enough or strong enough to tackle him. He was that big and that good. Down at the drug store, his friends would tell him, someday you're gonna play college football, and Jackie, the boy, would simply laugh. Small town boys from Duncan, Oklahoma, did not play college football. They had fields to plow and too much dirt between their toes to run very far or very fast.

Jackie, the last of eight children, had been only four months old when his father, William, a bright but restless soul, left home and took a job in the shipyards in California. William Sherrill never came back home, and, other than a faded photograph or two, Jackie hardly ever saw the face of his father. I met him, he said, but I never knew him. It was an empty space in his life he had never been able to fill. When his divorced mother, Dovie, remarried in 1959, Jackie moved to Biloxi, Mississippi, to live with his brother John's family, which included a wife and three children. I moved, he said, because I had always had my mother to myself, and I didn't want to share her with anyone else. Dovie let her son go because she was working nights at the hospital and feared that Jackie, out running the mean streets on his own, might be led astray and into trouble by some of the older and more worldly of his friends.

Sherrill has never been able to remember a day when he didn't have a job. Hard work was as natural as breathing for him. By the time he was seven, Jackie was earning thirty-five dollars a week, setting up pins in a bowling alley. Throughout his boyhood years, he sold newspapers, either door to door or on street corners, worked in concession stands at sporting events, swept the gym floor during the halftime of basketball games, and Jackie once talked his way into being hired as a safety patrolman at a school crossing. He was free. He was independent. He was shoving his own money in his pockets, and he had control of his life. As soon as he settled down in Biloxi, Jackie began doing odd jobs on his brother's chicken farm. He would later look around the Southwest Conference and say, I've probably shoveled more manure than any coach in this league.

Jackie's early life on the streets had not been an easy one. He found temptation waiting for him on every corner, and a little beer for someone his age was not particularly difficult to track down. Bootlegging was almost a respectable profession. Any time he wandered back to his house by midnight, he was home early. Football, however, kept Jackie on the straight and narrow. All of his aggression, all of his drive, all of his anger, all of his energy were channeled toward the inexact science of hitting somebody or being hit, as long as it was between the lines and sometimes when it wasn't. He did not talk a lot, he did not back down from anything or anyone, and he played with both tenacity and intensity, which was the only way Jackie knew how to play, whether the game happened to be football, baseball, basketball, or track.

Jackie was an unstoppable force in Mighty Mite Football during those elementary school years. Unfortunately, the league did not permit anyone to be a running back if he weighed more than a 105 pounds. Jackie was 5-11 and already tipping the scales at a 161 pounds by the time he had reached the seventh grade. He lined up at center. There was no way any of the coaches would allow him to run the ball. Pain and punishment on the field would come later. His mother remembered, Jackie used to bring in every old football uniform they

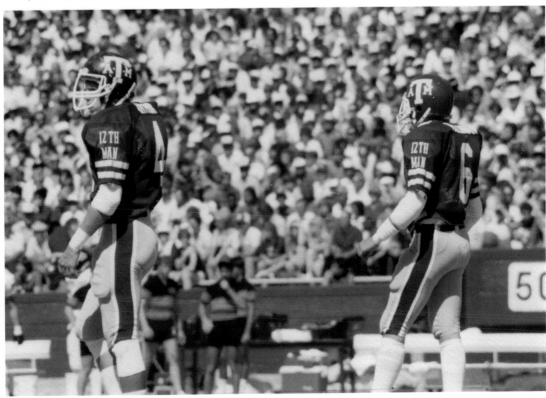

Tom Arthur (4) and Leroy Hallman (6) have one goal. Find the ball, go to the ball, and level the ball carrier. The 12th man team knew every play could well be its last, and no one dared let a kick returner break free. The team's reputation was always on the line.

Coaches make last-minute adjustments before sending the Aggies back into battle. In close games, a victory most often went to the team that could make the last critical adjustment in is offense, its defense, or its kickoff schemes.

had over at the school and say, momma, wash these. All we've got to play in are these dirty uniforms. So I'd wash them, and he'd go right out and get them dirty again. Jackie didn't come up the easy way. He did it the hard way.

After moving to Biloxi, Jackie became one of two sophomores to earn a starting position on the varsity team. Said W. D. Wiles, Biloxi's high school coach, the day he walked into the back door of my house with his brother, I knew that Jackie was something special. He came in and looked me straight in the eye when he talked. He said "yes, sir" and "no, sir." I knew that here was a winner.

Jackie's boyhood friends, coaches, and teachers said he was always burning with desire, was mature for his age, fiercely competitive, and yet he tempered his toughness and aggression with a healthy respect for the person in charge. He understood authority. His high school coach pointed out, Jackie was never a discipline problem. In fact, he would handle the team's discipline problems for me. He'd go to a guy and say, look, we're not gonna have that kind of stuff on this team. Now, that's called leadership.

His teammate, Harold Breal, recalled, Jackie had guts. He fit right in and became a team leader even as a sophomore. He was quiet about it, didn't push himself off on anybody, but he always worked extra hard after practice. He always seemed to be in better shape than everybody else on the team, and I don't think I ever saw him breathe hard, even after we finished our wind sprints on the first day of practice.

Jackie ran the ball as a fullback and stopped the ball as a linebacker. He was as good – as hard-nosed an athlete – as anyone in Biloxi had ever seen. Beneath his photograph in the 1962 high school yearbook was written, "Combining qualities of athletic prowess, dependability, and friendliness, Jackie Sherrill is Mr. Biloxi High School." Years later, when Sherrill's Pitt team was training for the Sugar Bowl in Biloxi, he learned that his brother's former wife was having car trouble. He didn't offer to fix the automobile or even send out a mechanic. When she awoke the next morning, she found a new car sitting in her driveway. That's the way Jackie is, a friend said. He takes care of his own.

As a high-school All-American, Sherrill was beginning to believe he might indeed have a chance to play college football somewhere. He had always harbored a dream of going back to the fields of his birth as an Oklahoma Sooner. He was also smitten with the rambling wrecks of Georgia Tech.

Then he met Bear Bryant.

Coach is what Sherrill called him then.

Coach is still the way Sherrill refers to Bear Bryant.

The Bear sat down with Jackie, and the two talked in a rambling, mostly one-sided conversation for a couple of hours. Bear did not mind talking, and Jackie hung onto every word he said. .Not once did Bryant offer him a scholarship to Alabama. Not once did he even ask Jackie to consider playing football at Alabama. Not once did he make any promises that the Biloxi fullback and linebacker might ever have a chance to start or even take the field in a Crimson Tide uniform. No promises. No pressure. Long before the Bear left town, Jackie Sherrill had forgotten all about Oklahoma and Georgia Tech. In Bryant, he had found a man he could trust. In Bryant, he had found a coach whose wisdom and philosophies about football and life after football would become a profound influence on his own life.

Sixty-seven wide-eyed freshman football players were given uniforms on the first day of practice at Alabama, Sherrill said. During a wild, catch-as-catch-can era of unlimited scholarships, the policy was simple: recruit everybody you think has even the faintest chance of making your team a little better. If they can't play for you, then, at least, they won't be playing for anybody else or playing against you. Jackie was just another face in the crowd. By the time we were seniors, he remembered, only six of us were still with the team. And the ones who left were better than the ones who stayed.

Some dropped out. Some were run off. Some just couldn't take the tough, harsh, discipline handed out by the Bear and his staff. As one player said, the coaches were mean sonuvaguns. They put pressure on you just to see how you'd react. They tried to break us, and some of us broke.

Jackie Sherrill did not bend or crack.

Alabama's notorious off-season drills were sheer torture and bordered on cruelty. During the spring, players attended a special so-called class three times a week, although there was no classroom involved. They lifted weights until their muscles ached and sometimes refused to respond, forced themselves through hard and demanding agility drills, and finally finished up with a conditioning workout on the mat. It was a bitter taste of hell boiled down into a span of forty-five minutes. Dying would have been the easy way out.

None of them would ever forget the morning when one of Bear's assistant coaches, Howard Schnellenberger, kept relentlessly pushing the team until the players reached the point of physical exhaustion. He yelled at them. He harangued them. He was in their face, cursing them, his own face the color of a bad fever. Sweat and spit were flying savagely around the room, the strain was debilitating, and all but one dropped from sheer fatigue. Schnellenberger looked around, and only he and Jackie Sherrill were still on their feet. Sherrill might be whipped from time to time, but he could not be beaten.

For Bear Bryant, Jackie Sherrill lined up, when the occasion called

for it, as a 195-pound center, linebacker, fullback, defensive end, tight end, nose guard, and tailback. He learned early about the unforgiving ways of the Bear. I wasn't good enough to hold down one position, Sherrill remembered. I was what they called the utility man. Find a hole, plug him in. Find a need, let Jackie fill it.

Two days prior to one game, Bryant walked over and, in a gravel-pitched voice, asked him, can you play tight end?

I think I can, Coach, Jackie answered.

Hell, son, I didn't ask you if you thought you could, the Bear snapped. I asked you if you could.

Yes, sir. I can do it.

It ain't all glory, son.

None of it is, Jackie thought.

Only the scoreboard counted.

In a game against Miami, Jackie watched nervously from the sidelines as Hurricane quarterback Georgia Mira methodically marched his offense down the field. The game was tight. Alabama has hanging on by a thread, and it had begun to unravel. Time was running out. Jackie couldn't take it any longer. He turned to the Bear and said, Coach, put me back in, and I'll get one of his passes for you.

Bryant studied the face of his young linebacker. He knew X's and O's all right, but he made his crucial decisions from his gut. He could read a man's heart through his eyes. The bear nodded.

Mira's march ended. Jackie, watching the quarterback's eyes, always the eyes, intercepted the last pass that the multi-talented George Mira ever threw at Miami.

The Bear only shrugged. That's Jackie, he said. He always finds a way to win.

At Alabama, his aggressive, no-holds-barred style of play helped lead the Crimson Tide to two National Championships. Of course, Jackie said with a grim smile, having quarterbacks Steve Sloan, Joe Namath, and Kenny Stabler around to pull the trigger on offense hadn't hurt any. The Bear preferred that his defense manufacture shutouts

Sherrill's family had encouraged him to become a doctor. He had the grades and was the only freshman football player at Alabama not required to go to study hall. But then he took a course in Biology and realized that he might not be as academically prepared for college as he thought. His professor grinned and said, I knew what Jackie was feeling. I felt the same way when I took my first college test.

Jackie promptly switched to a business degree, deciding that, in the long run, he might be better off as a Certified Public Accountant. After a class in Cost and Theory, however, he decided that he would rather become a business executive than a C.P.A. The corporate world lost a good soldier in the boardroom. Once again, Bear Bryant changed Jackie's life forever. The Bear, offering up no promises and no illusions, persuaded him to stay on at Alabama as a graduate assistant coach. The money wasn't particularly good. In fact, the money was downright pitiful. The experience he gained from shadowing Bryant's every move would, as time passed, become invaluable. Jackie Sherrill had a business degree. However, he was earning a doctorate degree in coaching from the master himself.

Sherrill married his college sweetheart, the daughter of a Decatur, Alabama, cotton broker, and moved to the University of Arkansas, with the Bear's blessing, to begin his graduate studies, working for a hundred dollars a month as a graduate assistant for the most remarkable of all Razorbacks, Frank Broyles.

At the time, there were those who saw a striking facial resemblance between Sherrill and Dallas Cowboy quarterback Don Meredith. However, one major difference separated the two. Meredith was already

James Barrett (16) brought a special brand of tenacity and toughness to the field, emerging as one of the quiet leaders of the 12th man kickoff team. When he slammed into an opposing kick returner, it was lights out.

famous. Sherrill was the unknown.

Sherrill was hurrying through the Dallas airport one night on a recruiting trip for Arkansas when a young boy awkwardly approached him and asked for his autograph.

I was in a hurry, Sherrill said.

He followed me across the terminal.

I liked his persistence, if nothing else.

Sherrill finally stopped and knelt down to face him. Do you know who I am, he asked.

Yes, sir. The boy grinned. His little heart was pounding.

He thought he did.

He didn't.

Sherrill said, I didn't have the heart to sign Jackie Sherrill. I signed "Don Meredith."

After the birth of his daughter Elizabeth, however, Sherrill decided the time had come to forge his way into the great American work force and find a legitimate, steady paying job. Suddenly,

financial security had become more important to Sherrill than football. He hit the streets and began selling insurance, hoping to bring home at least twelve grand a year, live in suburbia, have two automobiles in the garage, and enjoy the social status of a country club membership.

Coaching, however, kept getting in the way. When one of Broyles' assistants, Johnny Majors, left to take over the head job at Iowa State, he began assembling a hot-shot staff of top gunners that included Jimmy Johnson, Larry Lacewell, Joe Avezzano, Bobby Roper, and, of course, Jackie Sherrill. Insurance, left on the backside of the Red River, lost a hell of a salesman. When Majors moved to Pittsburgh, Sherrill packed up and dutifully followed, finding himself in charge of the staff, the recruiting, the budgets, the discipline. Sherrill would say, I was prepared to be a head coach at a very young age.

A head coaching position at a major university like Texas A&M was an elixir that gave some men strength and suffocated others. With it came power, but the rigors and pressure of big-time football could just as easily destroy the powerful. Jackie Sherrill was finally where he wanted to be, a college that lived and breathed tradition. He kept his perspective in sharp focus as he walked across a tree-shaded campus whose football program had long been surrounded by the quiet desperation of College Station. He was an intense man who had cursed himself with ambitious goals, timetables, and aspirations from which he could not escape. Even when he commanded himself to relax, which was never often enough, Sherrill admitted that peace of mind did not come easily. He strongly believed, my players are always first, my coaches second, and I'm third.

Sherrill immediately hired the coaches he wanted and needed to begin the unenviable task of revitalizing Texas A&M's stagnant football fortunes. They were good coaches all right, but, more importantly, they were great recruiters. To run his defense, Sherrill hired R. C. Slocum away from the University of Southern California, bringing back a man who had spent eight years coaching with the Maroon and White. He turned the machinations of his varied but balanced offense over to Pat Ruel and hired Jerry Pettibone to head up his national recruiting blitz. In earlier years, Pettibone had received acclaim for his work as recruiting coordinators at both Oklahoma and Nebraska. Sherrill persuaded George Pugh, who had been a star tight end at Alabama, to make the trek down with him from Pitt. And he rounded out his staff with Greg Davis, Paul Register, Bobby Roper, Dan LaGrasta, Jim Helms, and Curley Hallman, who would always be remembered, with a stoic reverence, as the Aggie defensive back who came out of nowhere to make the critical interception against Alabama, ensuring a victory in A&M's last Cotton Bowl appearance. Lord, little Curley Hallman was just a kid then, the Aggie faithful remembered, and now he was old enough to coach the big boys. They shuddered. A lot of time had passed them by since a journey to Dallas had anything to do with the Cotton Bowl.

Those ten coaches had quite a pedigree. Between them, they had been on the sidelines for thirty conference titles and ten National Championships. The big game certainly wouldn't scare them, and, as far as the Aggie faithful were concerned, the Aggies did not play any little games. And, by golly, a million-dollar coach ought to know how to win them. That was the feeling anyway, and Jackie Sherrill wondered if there were any immediate miracles left in Kyle Field. He wasn't worried about the long haul. He knew how to build a winner. But would A&M give him time? Would A&M give anyone time?

Jackie Sherrill lived in the dark abyss of the film room. Game after game, play after play, kept flickering on the screen before him. Pause. Stop. Back it up. Play it again. Once more. Play it again. Pause. Stop. No. Never stop. The flickering frames rolled past his burning eyes. Weariness began to knife its way between his shoulder blades. His head hurt. Back it up. Play it again. And again. Always again.

The Aggies definitely had some impressive talent. No doubt about it. Gary Kubiak had the arm, the poise, and the promise of a great quarterback. Johnny Hector, Thomas Sanders, and Earnest Jackson could carry the ball on anybody's team in anybody's conference. Mark Lewis was a force to be reckoned with at tight end. Greg Berry was the strong, solid anchor of the linebacking corps. And Ray Childress was an absolute monster. He could bow up and dominate the line of scrimmage as well as any defensive end Sherrill had ever seen, and Sherrill had coached Hugh Green.

No, the cupboard wasn't bare, but the depth of talent concerned him a great deal. A torn knee here. A pulled muscle there. A concussion. A sprain. A separated shoulder. And then what would happen? They were all facts of life on a football field, where nightmares never took a day or a play off.

Somewhere lurking out there in Texas and beyond, Sherrill knew, were football players who could make a difference at Texas A&M. All he and his staff had to do was find them and convince them that the night lights at College Station were as bright as anywhere else. Sherrill only wanted one kind of recruit. If he wasn't hell bent on playing for a cham-

pionship, then he could go somewhere else. Austin would be fine. Burnt orange would probably look better on him anyway.

Jackie Sherrill was considered the consummate recruiter. He was not merely peddling the opportunity to play football. He was on the road selling the university, its academics, its traditions, and its promise. For him, the emphasis on education was not a hat full of empty words. There was a right way and a wrong way, he said. The whole academic process was important to me. Others talked about it. I did something about it. Football only goes so far. Knowledge stayed with them for the rest of their lives.

In the selling of Texas A&M, the miles were no longer important. Neither was distance. Time had stopped being of any consequence. All Sherrill cared about were height, weight, speed, strength, grades, and how a young man treated his mama. Road miles. Air miles. City limit signs. State lines. After awhile, they all began to run together.

While at Pitt, he swerved his car off to the side of the road one night, found a pay telephone, and called one of his best friends, Lynn Patterson. Sherrill was out of breath. He sounded somewhat akin to a kid at Christmas. Lynn, he said, without taking the time to say hello, I've just signed the best athlete in the South, maybe the best damn athlete in the country.

That's great, Patterson replied. Who is it?

Hugh Green. He's from a little school down in Mississippi.

Well, I'm happy for you, Patterson said. But, Jackie, do you have any idea what time it is?

No.

It's two in the morning. The rest of the world is asleep.

Jackie Sherrill could not afford to sleep. There might be another Hugh Green out there in the hinterlands waiting for him.

Jackie couldn't sit still, Patterson said. When he was recruiting, he lost all sense of time.

I love recruiting, Sherrill said as he walked across the runway toward his plane. Recruiting is the one thing I can do for sure. And you know what's the best thing about being here in Texas? It's so flat that if you have plane trouble, you can land on any of those fields out there without any problem. It's not that way in Pennsylvania.

In Pennsylvania, the clouds had mountaintops in them.

Jackie Sherrill only took four days off during the next eleven months. No weekends. No vacations. No holidays. Nothing but recruiting and coaching and late night sessions in the film room. Nothing but searching his soul and the inner reaches of his mind, trying to piece together a formula that would ease the pain of losing and unlock the secret of whatever it took to bring Texas A&M a winner.

He was not merely driven. He was a man obsessed.

But, as Sherrill said, I've always had the ability to do more than one thing at the same time. Other people have a lower tolerance to work than I do. Work is therapy for me. I can't get enough of it. The work, the hours, the days on the road, the nights away from home had already cost him one marriage. A coach's wife, he said, never had a chance to lead a normal life or have an existence of her own.

She mostly lived alone. She raised the children alone. She saw her husband mostly from some seat on the fifty-yard line. For most coaches, it was a career of broken promises, broken plans, and broken hearts. The business of coaching was an insatiable fire that, sooner or later, consumed them all.

Sherrill gathered his staff together and told them, don't try to keep my pace. Don't try to do what I do. I don't expect you to. You guys have to be fresh at all times because I won't be.

He sighed, walked out the door, and headed wearily toward the airport again. It was a new day, and it didn't look a lot different from the last one.

During a game, Jackie Sherrill was a study in concentration, always thinking one or more plays ahead, always searching for psychological or motivational edge. He was viewed at the C.E.O. of Texas A&M football. He was definitely the man in charge.

Chapter 5

Jackie Sherrill had preached a message of patience, not miracles, but no one paid much attention to him or believed him if they did. The Aggie faithful had heard it all before, and their patience had run out somewhere between Stallings and Sherrill. *Where was the Bear when they needed him most?* There was even talk among a few that it just might do the Aggies some good to take another trek down to the hardscrabble fields of Junction, as long as they weren't the ones who had to go. Jackie Sherrill, they reasoned, could well be the re-incarnation of Bear Bryant. He was, after all, a no-nonsense, tough-as-boot-leather disciple of the Bear. He knew how the Bear coached. He knew how the Bear won. He had the Bear's same go-for-the-throat mentality. And, suddenly, a new jolt of energy began working its way like an electric current throughout the near and far corners of the Aggie nation. Expectations for a championship season had never been more acute. No longer would A&M be playing second fiddle to those bastards in Austin. Jackie Sherrill had arrived on campus. Happy days were here again.

Jackie Sherrill, however, was a realist. Sure, it took great players to win, and, yes, the Aggies had some damn good football players. But the Aggies needed a few more. No. The Aggies needed a lot more. There were some who could help a lot of teams in a lot of places in a lot of conferences, but, if their services were ever needed at Kyle Field, A&M was in a world of trouble. The coaches before him had recruited some quality players, yet too many of them were given scholarships for the simple reason they happened to be the sons or grandsons of Aggies, or maybe the sons of men who happened to be influential donors to A&M.

A championship team needed a foundation with a few less cracks. Sherrill, from day one, made the trek to College Station with the intention of grabbing the top players away from LSU in Louisiana, OU in Oklahoma, Miami in Florida, Southern Cal in California, Penn State in Pennsylvania, and, of course, Texas in Texas. Nothing to it. He had done it before. Sherrill realized that a championship team needed depth and maturity, and the Aggie were sorely lacking in both. He said, when the players reach the point where they know who they are, why they are playing, and how they are playing, then you have a team that can win. We coach. But make no mistake about it. Players win. And often they have to learn what it takes to win, which is a lot more difficult and takes a lot more time than learning how to pass, catch, run, block, and tackle.

Sherrill only grinned when those who turned out copy for the leering press said he had descended from the *old school.* If winning is from the old school, he said, then that's okay. There are a lot of people who throw the ball around the park half a hundred times, but they don't win games, not the big games anyway. These days, you have to be flexible enough to win. If you ask your players to do something they can't do, and they lose, then it's not their fault. Sherrill looked for balance. He wanted to throw the ball. He wanted to run it down somebody's throat. The few players capable of executing Sherrill's complex offensive scheme were already wearing Maroon and White. The rest were playing on Friday nights.

Sherrill had personally inspected every inch of the facilities at Texas A&M, and it galled him to find some ragged holes being haphazardly torn in the artificial turf by the members of the Fightin' Texas Aggie Band when they practiced each day. He did not want his field unraveling at the seams, and there was only one way to stop it. He called in Billy Pickard, his equipment manager, who it sometimes seemed, had been at the university ever since Texas A&M got the M. He had been with the Bear in Junction.

Billy, he said, get out there and tell Colonel Haney that his band can't practice on my field anymore.

Coach, Pickard replied, I don't think you want to do that.

Sherrill thought it over and said, Billy, if you're afraid to deal with the Colonel, I'll go tell him myself.

He marched defiantly out of his office and headed straight to the field, Pickard moving with slumped shoulders right behind him. Sherrill walked out into the sunlight and watched a few moments as the band went smartly through a series of exact, precise, complicated movements that computer models said were impossible to make.

Pickard nudged Sherrill with his elbow and asked, you gonna talk to the Colonel?

No.

Why not?

Billy, the coach said as he turned and walked back inside, when our football team can execute as well as that band, we'll win the Southwest Conference.

Jackie Sherrill had always been a competitor and a motivator. At Pitt, he had shown up before the Notre Dame game dressed as a leprechaun. On the Friday leading up to the clash with West Point, he came riding onto the field astride a mule and dressed in full Army gear. He could definitely light a fire under his players. He could make them laugh. If necessary, he could make them cry or even curse him. He could give them a reason to win and a way to do it. He could turn them into believers. And he demanded the best, even though he was convinced that their best was never good enough. You have to take it one game at a time, he said. You have to go out, do your job, and take care of business. You play strictly on emotion, not with emotion. If players get revved up too high for a game, he said, and something goes dreadfully wrong, the score can get out of hand before you can either fire up or calm down your players again. Personally, I relate to those players who have an inner strength. I can count on them to come through when its fourth and one, and in football, not unlike life, it's always fourth and one.

Bob Smizik, a writer with the *Pittsburgh Press*, always said, Sherrill has a real knack for keeping his players happy. He doesn't crowd them. He gives them room to breathe.

One of his old coaches, Joe Avezzano, pointed out, Jackie can relate to a good, committed, hard-nosed football player in a way that will allow the player to be his best. However, he's going to have trouble with a spoiled individual. He'll go a long way if the player goes with him. That kind of loyalty will come through in a tough situation.

As one of his players recalled, Jackie always energized me. He got himself fired up more than the players did, and that was inspiring for all of us. That really got me to play because I knew he wanted to get out there and play as much as I did. I guess he was just a little too old, a little too slow, and his eligibility had run out.

A new attitude began to pervade the practice field. As defensive end Paul Pender said, we still work hard and have the same goal. But there is a difference in atmosphere because the coaching staff makes it possible for us to be completely confident in those things we're taught. There is more of a subtle enthusiasm because everyone's goal has become the Cotton Bowl. Nothing else. The Cotton Bowl or bust. These guys yell at you a little more, but they also pat you on the back when you've done something well.

Tight end Mark Lewis pointed out, I've learned more football in two weeks than all of my other time here. The techniques are a lot different, which changes the whole program. It is a serious mood. The coaches are constantly on our backs, but it's because they know we can do the things they want. They are urging us to do them and won't be satisfied until we do.

Quarterback Gary Kubiak, if anyone cared to ask him, and almost everyone did, said he had grown to believe that Sherrill was the best, assuredly one of the best, coaches in the country. As he pointed out, Coach exudes an electricity of confidence among his players.

Jackie Sherrill knew the fundamentals.

He had mastered the techniques.

He could draw up X's and O's in places they had seldom been before and generally make them work.

He preached the gospel according to Bryant, Broyles, Majors, and himself, especially those scriptures about commitment, discipline, character, perseverance, and toughness.

But did Jackie Sherrill have the magic?

A&M was ready for the magic.

Sherrill wandered Kyle Field in the shadows of an approaching night and alone in his thoughts. He believed in hard work. He believed in putting the right building blocks in place. He believed in recruiting the right kinds of players, and that meant finding them nationally, not necessarily in some 2-A hamlet down the road. He believed in finding a weakness and exploiting it. He believed in looking for an edge, climbing inside the head of an opposing coach and leaving him confused and bewildered when Sherrill finally climbed back out.

What Jackie Sherrill did not believe in was magic.

The leering press knew what to expect and blazed it in sixty point headlines just so the Aggie faithful would have a better understanding of the dramatic changes that would no doubt be made beneath the skies above Kyle Field. At Pittsburgh, Sherrill's defense had placed the clamps on Heisman Trophy winner George Rogers of South Carolina in the 1980 Gator Bowl, then came back two years later to shackle Georgia All-American Herschel Walker in the Sugar Bowl. Stop the run. Stop it dead in its tracks. Then stop the pass. Attack and punish. Make a team suffer, and chances were, it would lose heart. Don't worry about a Sherrill team. That was the consensus. A Sherrill team would never lose heart as long as the heart kept beating.

The faithful crowded into Kyle Field when Boston College rolled into town to open the 1982 season. The Aggies were in a wild and uncontrolled frenzy. They couldn't wait to find out exactly what a million dollars had bought them. They stood up, sawed a few horns, and waited for the magic.

Jackie Sherrill was exactly as advertised. He strode confidently and briskly out of the tunnel as though he had been peeled from the front cover of *Gentleman's Quarterly*. His rugged face was stern, maybe even grim, and almost always seemed to be masked with a shadow that hid his piercing eyes, prominent chin, and nose that only a middle linebacker could love. He had experienced head-on collisions and been at the bottom of pileups before. Sherrill roamed the sidelines, wearing a crisp dress shirt and tie. He was the businessman, the CEO with a whistle hanging around his neck. He would have looked just as comfortable in a company boardroom. He was the poised strategist, a man who may have carried a clipboard but kept the game plan in his head.

Nobody expected Boston College Quarterback Doug Flutie to do what he did on that hot and humid September night. He was so small it looked as though he should have bought a ticket and sat in the end zone bleachers with the rest of the runts. But his passing wizardry cut out A&M's beating heart and left it on public display in the middle of Kyle Field. The final score, 31-16, was not that important, but the loss was devastating to the Aggie faithful, to Jackie Sherrill, and to Bum Bright, the man who had engineered the million-dollar deal.

It was only the beginning.

It was an omen of things to come.

Sherrill sat alone in Kyle Field, sweat masking his face, his eyes shifting slowly from one end zone to the other. The season was beginning to wear on him. He was losing as many as he won, and that was simply not good enough for him or for Texas A&M. He could hear the whispers, the grumbling, the disappointment, the disenchantment growing throughout the vast reaches of the Aggie nation. Some were saying that hiring him had been a grave, a tactical, and an expensive mistake. One of the faithful complained in the press that a million dollars just didn't buy what it used to buy.

Sherrill remained stoic and undaunted. Anyone who expected him to crack or panic would be sorely disappointed. He had a plan, and he had faith in his plan regardless of what the faithful believed. The losses hurt. Lord, how they hurt. But he kept the pain buried deep inside him. Sherrill had squared his shoulders and said, after a loss you might see

me kick a hole in the wall, but you won't see me cry. You'll never see me cry. I don't feel comfortable around people who feel sorry for themselves.

When discussing the teams in the Southwest Conference, he told the leering press, these boys better get their licks in while they can. He grinned. It was not a playful grin. When the tide did turn, and it surely would, there would be a war, in the trenches and in the air, from which the SWC could not evade nor avoid. His day was coming. He had no doubt about it. He firmly believed, he said, that the seniors on his football team would look back years from now and say, we didn't win it all that year, but we certainly started it.

The leering press turned a deaf ear.

The injuries kept mounting, and so did the losses. A lot had been expected of tight end Mark Lewis. He was good, damn good, but he was out for the year. Gary Kubiak had gone down for two and a half games, and the offense began sputtering, unable to gain any traction, without its number one quarterback at the controls. At various times, and always at the wrong time, running backs Thomas Sanders, Johnny Hector, and Earnest Jackson were all afflicted with assorted aches and pains, tweaks and tears. A few heady beat writers for Texas newspapers began spreading rumors, in and out of context, that maybe, just maybe, it was time for Jackie Sherrill to begin looking for employment at some school not named Texas A&M in some town other than College Station, preferably in some state on the other side of the Texas borderline. A million-dollar coach, columnists wrote, shouldn't need a full year to prove his worth.

On the surface, Sherrill brushed the criticism aside. He had nerves of iron and a confidence that could neither be shaken nor stirred. But inside, the harsh words, written simply because sports writers had nothing better to do than take scattered pot shots and use him as their nearest and easiest target, began to grow wearisome. The words were little more than catcalls, absurd, ridiculous, and without justification, fired from the big guns of the fourth estate, a self-righteous band of journalistic brothers who thought they knew but had no idea of what was going on.

For Sherrill, the pressure was stifling. He draped a steel curtain between himself and the leering press. He seldom talked to them, and, when he did, a simple yes, no, or maybe were the only answers they pried out of him. He stoically refused to be their quote machine. And the less that Sherrill spoke with the writers, the more angry they became. As mad as hell was the conventional wisdom. Their barbs and diatribes sold newspapers, he knew, but they sold Texas A&M short, and that's what upset Jackie Sherrill the most. He could weather the storm. Had done it before. Could do it again. But Texas A&M deserved better, and even if it sucked the last breath from his lungs, Sherrill vowed to bring the Aggies a championship. He was the only one who believed it could be done.

It would take a few games, but ultimately the Aggie varsity players coming on the field began to slowly appreciate and respect the 12th man team as it left after a kickoff. They realized that members of the special forces unit refused to back down from any team.

Jackie Sherrill was deeply impressed and touched by the hard work and long hours spent by students building Bonfire in the glow of night-time torches. It gave him an understanding that Texas A&M's culture and its traditions were far different from any other university in the nation. Within the blurred nights, Aggie students were creating a special bond.

Chapter 6

James Fuqua was headed across campus, looking like a wayward vagabond who had gone too many hours without sleep. He had. He was bone tired, hungry, had the day-old taste of cheap whiskey lingering on his tongue, and his wrinkled clothes smelled like suet from burning wood smoke. James Fuqua had long been a rebel either with or without a cause. His friends had been calling him Fumes since those days in a Corpus Christi high school when he founded a club referred to as the PNIVVW, the Psycho Neurotic Institute for the Very, Very Weird. And that was on one of his less neurotic days.

Out on a sacred piece of ground just across the road from Frank Vandiver's presidential mansion, he was called **Boss.** Fumes Fuqua was a Red Pot charged with cutting, hauling, and wiring together as many as six thousand logs that would send the flames of Bonfire climbing into the chilled skies draped across the Texas A&M campus. It was his duty to make the hard decisions and fix whatever had broken, and something was always coming apart. If not, he was tearing it apart. For weeks he had not bothered to bathe, shave, change clothes, or even comb his hair. When a man had a Red Pot covering his head, the state of his hair was the least of his worries. Being a Red Pot, he always said, was a lot like drinking from a fire hose, although he could never quite figure out why he said it.

Fuqua turned into the athletic building and stormed into Jackie Sherrill's outer office. The secretary looked up and frowned. No one dared burst that way into the inner most world of Texas A&M football.

It was akin to trespassing. I'm here to see Coach Sherrill, Fuqua said.

I'm afraid he's too busy to talk to you, she replied as politely as possible. She turned back to her work, expecting the unkempt, haggard, and disruptive student, if he was a student, to leave.

Fuqua walked past her and opened the door to Jackie Sherrill's private office. No problem, he thought. He certainly wasn't upset with the coach's secretary. She was just a nice lady doing what a good gatekeeper had been hired to do. He stepped inside the office as the coach looked up and jolted him with a glare from those intimidating eyes.

Sherrill had always said, if you come in my office without an invitation, you'd better have some size on you. The young man standing before him had very little size at all. He probably wouldn't be 5-7 if he weren't wearing boots. He was about as big as someone who had been living on cigarettes and grease for the last semester. But there was something about the young man's bold, daring attitude that could make a junkyard dog cower in the corner.

Fuqua leaned across the desk, his eyes doing their best to be just as intimidating. If you're gonna be the coach of our football team, he said, you need to be an Aggie.

Sherrill wasn't for sure what to say, so he stayed quiet.

If you don't know what being an Aggie is all about, Fuqua went on, I'm here to educate you.

Go ahead.

Let's take a walk.

Jackie Sherrill watched dedicated Aggie students devote long hours, day after day, night after night, to cutting logs by axe in the forest, hauling them to campus, and wiring them together to create the Bonfire stack. He believed those students were the "toughest sonuvaguns" he had ever seen, he said, and they inspired his idea to create the 12th man kickoff team.

To Fuqua's surprise, Sherrill was on his feet in an instant.

Let's go, Sherrill said.

If Fumes Fuqua had enough guts to bolt into his office, Sherrill decided, then he needed to hear what the young man had to say. Sherrill knew about the Red Pots. They had a reputation for being as tough as they were resourceful, and the student body looked on them as demigods. They had a job to do, and they got it done. Rules may not be made to be broken, but Red Pots were known to bend them into submission. They had two basic, unwritten rules. If you're not making dust, you're eating it. And, if you cause a problem, it's easier to correct the situation promptly and personally than wait for somebody else to make a decision. Red Pots were responsible. They knew their jobs. They were tolerated on and off campus solely because they had the innate ability to build the stack for Bonfire with the finesse of an architect and the technological skills of an engineer.

They scrounged up hundreds of rolls of baling wire and found fuel in the oddest places for their old hauling trucks, usually donated because the aging, decrepit vehicles couldn't pass inspection anymore. Can't sell it. Want to get rid of it. Give it to a Red Pot. Hell, they'll take anything. The trucks were junk, but they could flat haul logs, and the trick was to keep them rolling on tread, even if the rubber was gone, until the last log had been reverently placed against the Bonfire stack.

One of the trucks spit, sputtered, and broke down in the middle of a small town on the near side of the cut site, and a highway patrolman pulled up alongside. He looked it over and told Fuqua, I guess you know the tag's out of date. It's been out of date for a long time now.

Fuqua nodded. He wasn't worried. If he had carried enough money in his pocket to pay the fine, he would have already bought lunch. And he hadn't eaten since Monday. He just couldn't remember which Monday it had been.

We'll block traffic until you figure out how to move the truck, the patrolman said, but please do me a favor.

Fuqua nodded again.

It'd be a lot better for all of us if you'd just take the license plates completely off the truck and throw 'em away so it won't embarrass the state of Texas. Maybe the folks passing by will think you're from someplace else. The patrolman shrugged and grinned. Even the law had a measure of patience for the Red Pots hauling logs to Bonfire.

So many people did. There were, in fact, so many unseen and unheard who, year after year, made Bonfire possible. Colonel Parson and the campus police force worked hand in hand with the Red Pots and never attempted to enter their domain unless a situation arose that demanded their presence. Red Pots tried hard to never give them a reason. Of course, sometimes it couldn't be helped.

When Fuqua was a sophomore, the Rice band parked its bus near the stack after a game, and a handful of members began loading up anything they could steal from the Bonfire site. The Red Pots came running with their axe handles. Band members had one avenue of escape, but the Red Pots stood in their way. The headlights of a police car were coming nearer by the moment. The siren pierced the night. Band members had no real interest in the standoff. They simply thought that a little vandalism on the hallowed grounds of Bonfire would become the stuff of great lore when they returned to Houston. Now they had no interest in keeping whatever they had stolen. Now they were ready to leave, on the run if necessary. The Red Pots had not budged.

What's going on, a policeman asked sternly as he stepped out of the darkness.

This is our problem, a Red Pot said.

The policeman glanced over at the rolls of wire and pulley lying on the ground in front of the band members.

They're not taking anything that matters, he said.

It matters to us, the Red Pot said.

Then go ahead and deal with it, the policeman told him.

The band bus had loaded up and left before the police car drove out of sight. The rolls of wire and pulley still lay clustered on the ground behind them.

Police never made unnecessary demands. They were respectful. The Red Pots knew their limits. And if the problem could be worked out, the police let them deal with it. In reality, the police preferred that they deal with it.

Bonfire had become a community as well as a campus event that crossed all ages, schools, and economic boundaries. Engineer and Technology professors, time and again, helped repair parts that had broken on trucks, chainsaws, and generators. The work and dedication of the Red Pots were admired, even appreciated, by the powers that be.

But, Lord, Red Pots were a pain in the ass.

Jackie Sherrill felt a kinship with them.

As Red Pot Mark Thurmond said, we probably came off as a bunch of rogue, irreverent, incorrigible heathens and misfits, but more than anyone, we understood and valued what it was like to be an Aggie.

Fuqua led Sherrill to the Drill Field where fifty-five flags had been placed beside fifty-five live oak, cypress, and cedar elm trees, all looking out from the campus and on toward Kyle Field. When A&M was a military school, Fuqua said, this was where the infantry and horse-drawn artillery held their exercises.

Now, the trees stand tall as a living memorial to the fifty-five Aggies who died during the fighting in World War I.

Sherrill nodded. He was impressed.

They walked to the site of Yell Practice and the Fish Pond. Every time we win, Fuqua said, the freshmen fish rush out on the field, grab the yell leaders, carry them over here, and throw them in the pond. They come up splashing and kicking, and it does us all good to see our yell leaders get wet as often as possible. Sherrill did not miss the meaning of his message.

The education of Jackie Sherrill went on non-stop. He learned about the Aggie ring, muster, silver taps, loyalty, unity, and the spirit of the 12th Man. It all started back in the twenties, Fuqua said. The Aggies had a big bowl game up in Dallas, I think, and they found themselves running short of players. The coach called a student named E. King Gill to come down out of the stands and suit up in case the team needed him. It never did. But he was ready, and that's all that mattered. Now, regardless of what happens, Aggies are always ready.

The shadows of night were beginning to wrap themselves around the skeletal stack of great logs by the time Fuqua and Sherrill reached the Bonfire Field. For the coach, the spectacle unfolding before him was an unbelievable collision of the senses. Smoke from the parameter fires was thick and acrid. Flickers of flame cast strands of strange shadows on a rain-soaked ground layered with sawdust and pine bark.

A mass of humanity drifted aimlessly, but with a purpose, across the field. Truck engines labored beneath their loads, and engines backfired. It sounded like gunfire. They had worked from can till can't, and can't had passed them by several hours ago. Classes had been skipped and meals missed. A light mist hung in the trees. A deep chill began working its way into the bones of the weary and the wicked alike.

Those students who passed Sherrill said, howdy.

Everyone said, howdy.

Red pot Mike Cotton had issued the edict early on day one. If you see a stranger on the field, he had said, make sure you speak to him.

Why?

Hell, he might be a donor, Cotton said, and we're fifty thousand dollars short of having fifty thousand dollars.

Music blared from loud speakers, dangling from light poles, and worn cassette tapes ran the gamut from the Aggie Band to country to hard rock and to a few illicit and probably illegal songs snatched from small-town, hometown bands playing in roadside, hometown beer joints. Most had an assortment of ribald lyrics, comical and wry, dealing primarily with love lost, love found, love thrown away, love at the bottom of a bottle, and the temptations derived from gazing on or partaking of various parts of the female anatomy.

Mike Cotton looked up in the early-morning hours of one night and saw a lady, her nightgown flowing in the wind, standing on the edge of the field, almost in tears with shame and anger, and demanding that the music's volume be toned down, turned down, or, more appropriately, turned off. The songs were too loud, she said, too crude and much too offensive for her delicate ears. It's not funny, she said when she heard a stifled laugh. I don't like it. I want you to cut the music off. Now. This instant.

Cotton thought she might be the president's wife. Didn't know for sure. Thought it could be. After all, the Vandivers did live across the street. We'll do what we can, he said. No promises. No guarantees. Just a simple, we'll do what we can, which, when broadly interpreted by a Red Pot, meant, don't worry about it, lady, we've got ourselves a Bonfire to build.

The Red Pots changed the song, which was ready to change anyway, but did not touch the volume. Fuqua never realized before how loud and how far good music could carry on a chilled November night.

Less than thirty minutes later, the Colonel in charge of the Corps of Cadets drove up at a speed somewhat greater than the legal limit, parked, and marched out across the field in full uniform. He was obviously upset, probably because someone had awakened him at such an ungodly hour.

What brings you out so late? Fuqua asked him.

Turn that music off, he snapped.

Now why should we do that?

Because the President of Texas A&M called me and ordered me to tell you to turn the music off.

Fumes Fuqua should have been nervous standing in the face of conflict and the most omnipotent of all authorities on the A&M campus. He respected the Colonel. He really did. And he felt a pang of sympathy for a good man who had been confronted with an impossible task. The Colonel wasn't talking to an average, run-of-the-mill student, or a mere mortal. Fumes Fuqua was a Red Pot. His grin was full of irony. You mean to tell me that you actually let somebody who graduated from Rice University wake you up in the middle of the night to be his errand boy, Fuqua asked. The president just lives across the street. If he doesn't like what's going on, then why doesn't he just get himself over here and tell us himself?

The music goes, the Colonel said as he turned and walked away.

Duty done.

But the mission had not been accomplished.

The music stayed.

Fuqua regretted he couldn't make the volume any louder. It was already rocking as high as it could go. He did, however, wrestle the speakers away from the President's Mansion and point them in another direction just to prove he wasn't the absolute barbarian that everyone in administration thought him to be. The song still proclaimed that *Lucy breaks down like a shotgun,* but the words were mostly garbled by the night, and, perhaps, the lady across the street would not be so offended anymore. The Red Pots, being Southern gentlemen, did respect the ladies, if no one else. And they did have a growing respect for Mrs. Vandiver. She did, after all, have the courage, in the face of crisis, to make her request in person.

The center pole is rising above campus, and the first logs for Bonfire are in place. The building of Bonfire linked students together and forever endowed them with the traditions of Texas A&M.

The gauntlet had been thrown rather haphazardly at Fuqua's feet. The next move was his, and it was a move he relished. He recalled, we thought about having a pig for a mascot for the sole purpose of raising our own Thanksgiving dinner. We couldn't get a pig, so we went with a goat, since we decided that cabrito probably wasn't bad when grilled over an open fire. And someone, Lord knows who, staked the poor old goat in the president's front yard. He ate the grass. He ate the flowers. But what do you expect? He was a goat.

The message this time was delivered from Frank Vandiver himself. He was no longer making any demands. He simply wanted to know, what will it take to keep that goat out of my yard?

Just come on over and visit us sometime, the Red Pots said.

They walked in unison across the street, carrying a White Pot, the beginner's pot, to present personally and proudly to the president. It

was the least they could do, a sign of truce, if nothing else. Al Link rang the doorbell.

We came to meet with the president, he said.

The president is not available.

The door closed.

This is not going to work, Mike Cotton said.

So the Red Pots walked back to Bonfire and went back to wor

They waited and knew they probably wouldn't have to wait long.

They left the goat behind. The grass was good, the flowers plentiful, and the goat didn't really care where he was staked.

When the yard began to look bare in places, and the flowers had lost their blooms, the Red Pots were invited to walk once more across the street. They rang the bell. The door opened. Out came a hand holding a fifth of Jack Daniel whiskey. Now take the bottle and go away, came a voice from inside the mansion.

The Red Pots did.

And, this time, they took their goat with them.

Jackie Sherrill knew about Bonfire, understood its historic importance to Texas A&M, and realized that on the Thursday night before the Texas game, he would be asked to climb atop a wooden platform wedged against the stack and talk to the multitude that had assembled to hear how he and his Aggies, regardless of what their record might be, were planning to dismantle those bastards from Austin. Emory Bellard had managed it. So had Tom Wilson. And, by comparison, they were penny ante coaches.

Rains had hammered the ground. Mud was a black gumbo and ankle deep. A cold November wind assaulted the field, and it felt as though the air around them had attached itself to icicles. Fuqua marched toward the stack of logs, shaped a lot like a wedding cake, and Sherrill followed without hesitation or complaint even though he wore dress slacks and fine leather shoes that kept bogging down in the quagmire. As many as a thousand students, maybe more, were hard at work, hauling in logs and attaching them to a chain, watching as a crane carried them up into a black abyss devoid of stars.

They had been working around the clock. Collectively, they would spend more than a hundred and twenty-five thousand work hours on Bonfire, sharing backaches and blisters that remained painful and raw long after their handiwork lay in embers and ashes. Their muscles were tired and sore. Their skin had become a patchwork of scars, torn by splinters and grazed by axe blades, their shoulders bruised by carrying around six-hundred-pound trees taken from the land of farmers and ranchers who wanted their pastures cleared. Texas Municipal Power Authority had simply told them, take all the trees you want. We'll bulldoze what you don't get.

The hide on their hands was long gone. They had left the tattered edges of their fingerprints on the bark of old pine trees. None of them wore gloves. With gloves, they couldn't feel the baling wire. Their thumbs had been mashed, their toes flattened. Bones had been fractured. Band-aids worked when there was no time for splints or stitches. Bonfire was a rite of passage. Sure, it represented a burning desire to beat the hell out of a university that A&M preferred to call t.u., but it also bonded together those who left their skin and their blood permanently embedded on the logs. Bonfire was and had always been camaraderie at its best.

Fuqua and his Red Pots had been authorized to precisely stack the logs no higher than fifty-five feet. The restriction was established by the fire marshal and A&M officials after the 1969 stack reached a hundred and nine feet in height, sending up flames that could be seen in communities throughout the Brazos Valley. The university feared that flames from a stack that high might get out of hand, blown by unpredictable winds, and consume those grand old buildings surrounding it, the president's mansion among them. Residents who had homes lining the campus were just as worried.

Sherrill looked up. How tall is it, he asked.

Tall enough for Cotton. He rides the outhouse up and places it on top of the pile.

Cotton must be crazy.

Cotton's afraid of heights.

Why does he do it?

Because we expect him to do it.

Looks dangerous to me, Sherrill said.

So are two football players colliding at full speed.

They have helmets.

Fuqua shrugged and tapped the top of his Red Pot. So do we, he said. He paused, then asked the coach, you want to go out wire some of the logs together?

Sure.

The logs were about forty feet in length, six to thirty-six inches in diameter, cut with an axe, trimmed by a chainsaw, and moved out of the woodlands by hand. It's all a giant puzzle, Fuqua said. You have to sort out the logs, then find the right one to fit the right spot, and they all have to fit before it burns.

Sherrill had never been content to be a spectator, not when there was work to be done. It wasn't his nature. He rolled up the sleeves of his dress shirt and reached for the baling wire, an odd fellow who looked a little too old, a little too well dressed, and a little too clean shaven to be traipsing around in the mud and mire working on Bonfire. He was obviously someone of importance, and no one of any real importance had ever before bothered to bless Bonfire with his presence. Jackie Sherrill felt right at home. His was just another face in the crowd, and only a scattered few stopped long enough to notice or pay any attention to who he was, which was pretty much the way he preferred it.

Who's that, someone wanted to know.

Jackie Sherrill.

The football coach?

The flames of the torches cast an odd array of shadows upon the field leading toward Bonfire.

The flames from Bonfire symbolized a burning desire to beat t.u. Thousands of students and alumni circled the burning stack to acknowledge their undying love and support for the school. The t.u. outhouse is perched proudly at the top.

That's him.

The student shrugged. I didn't recognize him without his headset, he said.

The hierarchy was designated by the color of protective helmets the students wore. Red Pots were in charge. They were the decision makers and fund raisers who had to come up with fifty thousand dollars to cover the cost of Bonfire. Brown Pots handled equipment safety and site logistics. Yellow Pots coordinated all workers from the dorms, and that meant for everyone living in a dorm to drag himself out to the Bonfire and work when his time came. No crying. No bitching. No excuses. No absences allowed.

Yellow Pot Jerry London had a student studying to be an aerospace engineer in his dorm, and the young man refused to leave his room. Bonfire meant nothing to him, he said. He didn't have time for it. The first week of work ended, and still he had not gone out to either the cut site or the stack. Can't, he said. Too busy. I'm studying for a test. Can't afford to fail it.

London, with a wry grin on his face, simply began walking across the Bonfire field, taking up a collection.

How much?

A quarter apiece.

What's it for?

London grinned. The door, of course, he said.

By the time Jerry London cut his way through the dorm door with a chainsaw, the aerospace engineer was dressed and ready to volunteer for Bonfire anytime he happened to be needed. Day. Or night. He was delighted to volunteer. To hell with the test. Can't pass it anyway. Just turn that damn chainsaw off, he said.

London did, then drove downtown, gathered up the quarters he had collected, and bought a new door for the dorm.

Pink Pots were female students who did what they could any time they could, most notably smuggling food out of Duncan Hall and out to the Bonfire site. The ladies in the kitchen always cooked a pot or two too much just so they would have leftovers ready when the Pink Pots came knocking on their back door. If the Red Pots had anything to eat at all, it was generally what the Pink Pots brought them. Stale bread, mashed potatoes, with or without lumps, cold pizza, fried chicken wrapped in grease, day-old doughnuts, and a pot of crusted gravy were gratefully accepted and acknowledged as a feast.

Sometime during the week, they could count on the school registrar to bring down a pot of her steaming, home-made chili, sometimes made of deer, sometimes beef. One was as good as the other, and it all tasted the same on an empty stomach. It was hot no matter how cold the nights became, and it kept their innards warm.

For some reason, Fuqua said, it became quite social for sorority committees to want a Red Pot in attendance. Bonfire was approaching, and those comely young ladies liked to show us off. It gave them prestige to have a Red Pot milling around a collection of socialites. One sorority president made her way out to the Bonfire site to invite me to join her committee, which meant I got to go to all the parties, and I was happy to go any place that might have an extra plate or two of food and an extra girl or two looking for a way home.

I was down to my last thirty-nine cents, Fuqua said. Our Pink Pot, Kathy Seaburg, had brought us some bags of stale potato chips, and, since I hadn't eaten much in seventy-two hours, I tore into them, accidentally splitting the bag open and spilling most of the chips on the ground. A famished man will do fooling things like that.

I was on my knees, picking potato chips out of the mud with both hands and shoving them into my mouth when I suddenly became aware of these two, long, and shapely legs about a lick or two away from my face. I casually looked up to see this beautiful girl, dressed all prim and proper, and she was holding an umbrella to keep the dirty rain out of her lovely face.

I did what any gentleman ought to do, Fuqua said. I offered her a potato chip.

She turned abruptly and walked away. If she had worn a smile, it was gone. I could hear her feet sloshing in the mud and the rain pounding down on her umbrella. I was so used to bad weather by this time that I hadn't even realized it was raining.

She left without a word, he said. Didn't say hello or goodbye, and I never did get an invitation to her party.

The freshmen wore white stripes, fashioned from athletic tape and wrapped around their legs, high up on their thighs. They were the beginners, the gophers, the lowest of the low. A white stripe signified that the wearer had never worked on Bonfire before. Be careful. He has no idea what he's doing or how to do it, and he damn sure needs all of the help he can get. Keep an eye out for them. Jackie Sherrill had a white stripe taped around the thigh of his dress slacks. That's the way it was done. He had no trouble with it. On the football field, his word was law. At Bonfire, he, like everyone else, was at the mercy of the Red Pots.

Sherrill didn't merely show up, hang around on the periphery for a few minutes, shake a few hands, make sure he was seen, and then leave. He stayed for hours, wearing a white pot to protect his head from God knows what, and, around Bonfire, anything might happen, usually did, and a pot was his last line of defense. He ignored the aches and the pain, acting as if the cuts, scratches, bruises, and busted knuckles didn't bother him at all. One thing did trouble him, however. He worried that, when he finally went home about daylight, his wife would smell the smoke on his clothes and think he had been at a bar all night.

Want to go up on the fourth stack, Fuqua asked.

Hell, no, I don't want to go up on the fourth stack was what Sherrill told himself. But only Red Pots were allowed to climb the logs that high. Standing there with them would be an honor he could not refuse. Sherrill nodded and forced a grin. How do we get there, was all he wanted to know.

A crane, on loan from the H. B. Zachry Construction Company in San Antonio, carried the logs by chain up the side of the stack. It would carry Fuqua and Sherrill to a walkway on the fourth stack. Zachry's personal crane operator watched the Red Pot and the Coach grab the chain and place their feet into a narrow loop. Fuqua's foot was on bottom, Sherrill's foot on top.

Rook, the crane operator, had no intention of taking it easy. The chain whined, groaned, and jerked its way upward. Gentle was not a word in Rook's vocabulary. As far as he was concerned, it was just another moment in another day's work, and he might as well be swinging logs toward the top. He had no idea what these clowns were doing in the chain, even if one did wear a Red Pot.

Red Pots never waited for the chain. They just hauled themselves up side of the stack until they had gone as high as they wanted to go. When it was time to leave the logs, they took the same way down.

They called it taking the Red Pot Express.

The crane operator slowly pulled the chain about twenty feet off the ground, then suddenly, without warning, dropped it five feet, caught it with a jerk, and began lifting it back up again. He yawned and stifled a laugh. Up and down Sherrill and Fuqua went, mostly up, hanging on desperately when an occasional, convulsive drop, marked by a sudden stop, left them slowly twisting and turning in the wind as the ground fell away far beneath them. They were swinging alongside the platform of logs, the old chain bitching and lamenting every inch of the way.

Sherrill looked down and could see the students, all grouped together and watching them. He strained to hear what they were yelling, but a cold wind blew away their words as easily as it stirred the sawdust. A deadly silence surrounded him. But he knew they must be laughing at a dumb football coach, wearing a White Pot, who was out of place and probably out of his mind. It wasn't until the chain finally reached the fourth stack, dangling high above the good earth, that Sherrill dared to take a breath. He shouldn't have bothered.

The crane operator had not finished with them. He slowly turned Fuqua and Sherrill a hundred and eighty degrees away from the growing stack of logs, crawled out of the cab with a sardonic laugh hung in his throat, and went on a fifteen-minute coffee break. He left the Red Pot and the million-dollar coach swinging in the wind, the sharp cold biting into their lungs, slowly spinning around above the mud that caked the Bonfire Field.

Fuqua never thought he would cry and had no intention of dying. But he would recall, there was Coach Sherrill standing on my foot, and he was a pretty good-sized man compared to me. His weight cut off the blood in my foot, and it would take me most of the night to get any feeling back. There for a minute, I thought I might be walking around numb for the rest of my life. But numb's not bad compared to pain.

Word had quickly spread through the students that Jackie Sherrill himself had come to work on Bonfire. For hours, he had been wiring logs together, and, as he looked down from his perch on the fourth stack, Sherrill heard some of the Red Pots yelling for him to go home. At least, that's what he thought they were saying. He looked at Fumes Fuqua. I'm not ready to leave, he said.

You don't have to leave.

They're yelling for me to go home.

Out here, Fuqua explained with a wry grin on his face, going home means sliding down the logs to the ground. They want to see you get down like the Red Pots do.

You mean slide down on the soles of my shoes, on my back, or on my backside?

Whatever it takes to get down.

They're out of their minds.

I won't argue that.

It's gonna hurt.

You'll get used to it after awhile.

What stops the pain?

The calluses on your ass.

Sherrill shrugged. He had faced and met challenges before, but seldom on a stack of logs above the ground. It can't be as bad as riding that damn chain up here, he said.

You'll lose a little hide, Fuqua told him, but, in time, it'll grow back. Always does.

Sherrill was on the logs and going down, slowly at first, then picking up speed whether he wanted to or not.

He could hear the students but no longer see them. Everything was a blur.

And he couldn't tell whether they were laughing or cheering or a little of both. He waited for the ground to come up, and it reached him far faster than he thought or hoped it would. Jackie Sherrill still wore his White Pot, but he had gone where only Red Pots had gone before.

For the Aggie football coach, Bonfire would not be a one-night stand. Time and again, he tramped through the mud, fought off the rain, and spent hours at a time tying logs together on the stack. He brought his football players to the field so they could hoist logs on their burly shoulders and find out what being an Aggie was all about. He painted white virgin stripes on their pants and scattered the players with other members of the student body. You know each other, he told them. Now get out there and meet some kids you don't know. They're not as big, and they don't have full-ride scholarships, but it looks to me like they may be as tough as you are.

Nothing escaped Sherrill. He watched the Red Pots eat road kill. They had been out hog hunting with a rifle one night, Mike Cotton was driving a little too fast, and a tire blew out on their truck. It pitched forward, rolled over, and killed three wild hogs running for their lives down the ditch beside an empty country road. Fuqua crawled out of the wreckage and stared in disbelief, wondering how someone could tear up a brand new Ford so fast. The sticker was still in the window. But

Cotton hadn't panicked nor gotten upset. He never saw the dark side of anything. All in all, Cotton said, it was a pretty good hunt.

Sherrill saw Pots of all color play smudge-pot soccer in the dark. Their only light was the fire still burning in the smudge pot they kept kicking from one end of the field to the other.

No rules.

Nobody won.

Nobody lost.

Sherrill heard that someone from a Corps unit, swinging an axe out at the cut site, had virtually sliced his foot in half. Fuqua wrapped a wad of duct tape around the gash to hold his boot and his foot in place, and the student continued working, leaving bloody tracks behind him, until the Red Pots hauled him to the emergency room in the bed of a pickup truck. A doctor stitched up the wound. And, by the time the day turned dark again, the student was back working on Bonfire.

Night after night, Sherrill caught a glimpse of professors trudging out to the field after dark to tutor those who no longer had time to study or even show up in their classrooms. The professors did not want the time and effort they had invested in those students going to waste. Said Dr. Curtis Laird, Dean of the College of Agriculture, I'm thinking about putting a neon sign on my wall that says: *If Fuqua graduated, you can, too.* From his perch on the fourth stack, Sherrill saw it all.

He was there, long after football practice, wiring logs in place and donating what little hide he had left on his fingers to the Bonfire logs, when Dr. J. Malon Sutherland, assistant vice president of student affairs, drove to the site. Sutherland had heard that his football coach was working into the late hours and wanted to shake Sherrill's hand, he said, for taking such an active role in the lives of A&M students. Of course, the photographer trailing after him would be there to catch it all on film. Photo ops were precious in any kind of public life.

There's only one way to get up there to Coach, Sutherland was told. Ride the chain.

Sutherland looked up.

Sherrill was barely visible on the fourth stack.

That's really high, Sutherland said.

You'll get used to it.

Sutherland knew he probably wouldn't. A man can't become accustomed to something until he does it more than once, and the Aggie overseer of student affairs was convinced that this would be his only and his last time. Craig Barker, a junior Red Pot, said he would ride with him to the top, and, to his credit, Sutherland agreed, but he never quite made it off the chain. That final step from chain to logs was too severe and too far away for a sane man to risk it. Dangling in the air, Sutherland had such a tight grip around Barker's neck that it felt, the Red Pot thought, more like a chokehold.

If he wants to shake my hand, Sherrill said, then they can lower Dr. Sutherland to the ground. Take him on back down before he chokes Barker to death. Sherrill took the Red Pot Express to the ground. The first time down the logs was suicidal. The second time was painful. From then on, it was as easy as an elevator. At least, it was headed in the same general direction. Dr. J. Malon Sutherland smiled apologetically. His hand was cold and a bit unsteady when Sherrill shook it. A flash. A second shot. One picture. Then two. And Sutherland was gone. Only Sutherland had felt like smiling for the camera.

Only two Pots were ever given to anyone. One went to the president of Texas A&M, Frank Vandiver. The other was handed to Jackie Sherrill. The president wore his only once in public, and he wore it backwards. Sherrill never came to Bonfire without his Pot.

On cold nights, when a cold and reckless wind got out of hand and rain hammered the logs without mercy, the Red Pots allowed Jackie Sherrill into the sanctuary of an old shack, hastily thrown together near the stack, and called, with a certain amount of reverence, the Bonfire Hilton. Sherrill was no longer an outsider. The shack was small and cramped, but it was dry. Piles of grease-stained pizza boxes and dried, weeks-old pizza lay in piles in the corner. A potbelly stove worked overtime on the far side of the room, throwing out what heat it could before the wind and rain forced their way through the cracks and washed the heat back inside.

The Red Pots and Sherrill played dominoes. Far into the night, they rattled the top of an old card table with misdemeanor games of forty-two. On one night, the damp chill had overpowered the little stove, and it lay as cold as the gray ashes inside. Paul Tomaso said he would restart the fire, and no one questioned him. He had done it plenty of times in the past. Outside sat a can of gas and a can of diesel. Tomaso would always swear that he picked up the right can and threw diesel into the little stove.

No one else ever knew for sure.

The stove exploded.

Sparks showered the Bonfire Hilton.

Flames were splinters in the night, shooting toward the ceiling, then quickly dying in the darkness.

Shrapnel rattled the windows.

Around the old card table, sitting on logs for chairs, nobody moved or blinked. James Starr turned to Sherrill and asked, what's your bid?

Smoke hung thick in the shack.

Someone coughed.

The smell of gasoline was rancid.

I pass. Sherrill shrugged. I like my partner's hand better.

The shack was cold again, but nobody cared. The Red Pots remained cold, and Cotton shivered as the damp crawled under his skin. But no one ever asked Tomaso to throw fuel on the embers again.

Rumor said that somebody reached for the fifth of Jack Daniel whiskey down under the cot, but nobody who left the shack that night ever confirmed it.

They were all sitting around the Bonfire Hilton when the mention was made that Texas A&M had always cherished the tradition of the 12th Man but had never really done much to embrace it, other than remain standing at football games. Fuqua popped off and said, you know, the worst fear college football players have is that they'll get hurt and never make it to the NF of L.

Everyone nodded.

He continued, it might be a psychological boost to our football team if we have a bunch of Aggie headhunters out there, and their sole purpose is to take somebody's head off at the shoulder pads. The runner. The blocker. It doesn't make any difference. Give the other team something to worry about. Let 'em know in advance that, by gawd, we got ourselves a suicide squad, and if you mess with 'em, somebody's gonna wind up hurt and hurt bad. This ain't no gentleman's duel, and we may take a leg with us when we go back to the bench. Let 'em think about

Jackie Sherrill in his White Pot came to Bonfire in the early morning hours to work high on the stack, wiring logs together. He brought his football teams to work on Bonfire. It was, he said, a vital and integral part of them all becoming Aggies.

that when they think about the NF of L. Fuqua laughed. Jackie Sherrill didn't. He began mulling those thoughts over in the back recesses of his mind. He had been searching for a way to connect the entire student body with his football team, and maybe this was it. What if he invited a bunch of students, let's say from the Corps of Cadets, to come out of the stands and suit up for every home game? What if he sent them down on kick-offs? Nothing but kickoffs. What if they turned out to be a bunch of kamikaze players who were willing to sacrifice their bodies simply for the love of the game, for the love and devotion they had for Texas A&M, for the chance to nail somebody on a football field one more time?

Surely, within a student body of more than thirty-five thousand, he would be able to find at least ten or eleven old high school football players who could still run sixty yards without wearing out and deliver a hit as hard as an axe handle on a Bonfire tree. Wild? Maybe. Out of control? Probably. Feared? No doubt about it. But were they tough enough? That was the question. College football was an entirely different game played at an entirely different level. You had to be tough or die. Somehow, in a curious way, the idea made sense, Sherrill thought, or was it the long hours on the fourth stack and lack of decent sleep that had him thinking as oddly as Fumes Fuqua? He didn't know, but the idea certainly did intrigue him.

The push for Bonfire had reached its final, frantic hours. The last of the seventy-nine truckloads of logs had arrived at the site. Jackie Sherrill was looking out across a field that had grown surreal in those unnatural hours approaching midnight. All around him was a cacophony of sights and sounds that might well be emanating from another world, or maybe even from the innards of hell itself. The crowd of bone-weary students formed a strange collection of dark shadows, and around them burned the flames of crude, homemade torches. The night smelled of sweat and smoke. Drums were beating a harsh and rhythmic cadence as axe handles hammered against logs or trash cans or anything else that might echo the sound of a person's own heartbeat.

It was the holiest of all nights at Bonfire.

Although he had known nothing about it, Sherrill was witnessing the Passing of the Pots. The torch of leadership was being handed down to the next generation of Red Pots, standing atop the stack, their faces painted red and black by shadows cast up from the flaming torches. Their yells were not unlike the screams of a banshee in the face of a good fight, usually one to the death.

It was their night. And, Lord, they would endure so much and suffer beyond belief before the sun of a new day cast its light on the campus again. Being a Red Pot was not, however, a rank freely given. The juniors had to earn it. A Red Pot had personally chosen each of them, and now, before God and anyone else who had the stomach to watch, it was time to prove themselves worthy of the selection.

The Passing of the Pots was never held in secret. It was staged out in plain sight of whomever might want to stand among the crowd and represent the hierarchy of students at Texas A&M.

The Red Pots gathered in a tight huddle and gazed out across the shadows: James Fuqua, James Starr, Mark Thurmond, Al Link, Mike Cotton, Joe Lee, Walter Benadof, and Thomas Mayfield. The laughter had long faded away. They knew what was coming. They had been there before. Tonight, they would inflict pain in the damndest rite of passage that Jackie Sherrill had ever observed.

He saw the juniors, perched on the end of the crossties atop the fourth stack, begin doing a class set of pushups. It was a strain. It began to drain the energy from their bodies. He could almost see the steam rising up from the sweat that cloaked their faces.

The end was near, and everyone was aware of it. Sherrill watched them take the time-honored Red Pot Express down from the stack, walk stiffly out of the crowd like condemned men, and make their way toward the Red Pots, eyes wide, nostrils quivering, faces empty of any emotion. Each of the Chosen Ones marched boldly forward. No one ever hesitated. No one's legs failed him. Each took a hasty breath, bent over, grabbed his jewels with both hands, squeezed hard to protect his manhood, clenched his jaws, and waited for the Red Pots, one by one, to slam an axe handle against his buttocks. No padding.

It was not a gentle swing.

Theirs was not a bloodless ritual, full of empty pomp and worthless circumstance.

Each Red Pot took a baseball swing and drove the axe handle as hard as he could into the backside of the Chosen One.

A grunt.

Thunder.

That's what it sounded like. A sharp, sudden clap of thunder.

Feet came up off the ground.

But no sound came from the throat or passed the lips of the Chosen One.

Wham!

Again.

Wham!

Fuqua said, you get hit until you can't sit down. No. That's not true. You can sit down, but you can't get back up. You move around slow for days like you've been in a car wreck. You and Milk of Magnesia became real good friends. Red Pots believed that pain bonded us together. It forged a friendship like no other. We were above and beyond any hardship that might confront us. We had faced the worst, and still the sun rose the next morning.

As much as anyone, Jackie Sherrill understood the abuse that the Red Pots were dishing out to their replacements.

As a freshman at the University of Alabama, he had been given slats as a formal introduction to big-time college football. Someone had hit him once, and, before the next swat came, Sherrill walked across the room and toward the door.

You can't leave now, somebody said.

Why the hell not?

You've got another slat coming.

Sherrill had turned, his glaring eyes moving slowly from one player to another. He squared his shoulders and said defiantly, I don't think there's a wretched soul in here tough enough to give me another slat.

No one stepped forward to try.

But Sherrill later relented.

For the good and the unity of the team, even though it was against his better judgment, he went back into the locker room, bent over, grabbed his jewels, squeezed hard, and took his second and last swat. With pain came bonding. That's what they said anyway. Pain forever changed the shape of a man's psyche. Hurt badly enough, and he was never afraid of hurting again. Fear was no longer part of the equation. The man had already endured and survived the worse that could possibly ever happen to him.

Sherrill realized how much those slats hurt, and he had only been inflicted with two of them. The juniors, bending over within a ring of students, were taking at least six or eight without ever flinching. Maybe ten. Maybe more. He had stopped counting.

On the juniors came, and now Mark Hackfeld, bright, intelligent, a straight A student chosen personally by Al Link, was bending over. He had been waiting long enough. His time had come.

The Red Pots had an unwritten rule.

If an axe handle broke at any time, the beating started again from the beginning. It was as though the first set of slats never happened. They certainly did not count.

Hackfeld took seven swats.

On the eighth swing, the axe handle broke.

A hush fell over the crowd.

Eyes stared in disbelief.

Some were afraid they might get sick.

Someone did.

No one fainted.

But a few thought about it.

Only one pair of eyes remained calm. Mark Hackfeld had complete control of himself, his ordeal, the pain that had been inflicted, the pain yet to come. His breathing was slow and easy. His eyes were focused on the night. This, too, he knew would pass.

And here they came, another eight slats, as hard as the first ones, maybe even harder. To let up would show disrespect, and no ever dared to disrespect a Red Pot.

The punishment, the pain must be unbearable, Sherrill knew.

But Hackfeld did not reveal any hint of pain or emotion.

His expression was made of stone.

Hackfeld held his ground and took it.

My God, he's tough, Sherrill thought.

They're all tough.

He would say, *I've never seen a defensive end as tough as a Red Pot*, and Sherrill had coached Ray Childress and Hugh Green.

The idea to create an all-volunteer suicide squad straight from the Aggie student body had been gnawing at him for days. A kickoff team was the perfect answer. It did not require a lot of finesse. Just run as hard as you can and hit anybody who gets in your way.

But Sherrill had worried that he might not be able to find ten or more who were tough enough to run downfield like David, collide head on with Goliath, and knock the giant clear to the backside of eternity.

All doubts were erased when he saw Mark Hackfeld tolerate the fifteen slats he suffered. There was no quit in him. Aggies were far dif-ferent from anyone else. They were a rare and special breed. There was no quit in any of them. They were, Sherrill believed, the toughest, strongest, sons-of-guns he had ever seen.

Sherrill grinned.

There in the shadows, amidst flaming torches, with handmade drums disturbing the silence of night, with Red Pots being passed from one to another like a red badge of courage and honor, was formed a confluence of fate, time, and circumstance.

Jackie Sherrill turned and walked into the darkness, leaving the Red Pots and the rain to clean up the mess. The torches smoldered. The drums were beating with the rhythm of his own pulse.

A&M had no idea what lay in store for its football team.

Jackie Sherrill had made up his mind.

During the passing of the pots, Joe Lee, in 1981, was given his slats by other members of the Red Pots, who believed that pain bonded them together. By the time Jackie Sherrill arrived a year later, Lee was one of the Red Pots supervising the building of Bonfire. He said that he had never seen a defensive end as tough as a Red Pot. He should know. He worked with them both.

There was no place to run and no way to escape for the ball carrier when the 12th man team, led by James Barrett (16) came roaring downfield. Each member had a specific assignment, and the team kept its kickoff coverage wall strong and solid.

Chapter 7

Jackie Sherrill strode briskly into the meeting room deep beneath the bowels of Kyle Field. A chilled morning sun had barely broken the December horizon, and the loss to Texas was fresh on his mind. The final score cut him like a knife, but that game was past him, and he could not change the outcome no matter how hard he tried. It was time to regroup, make whatever changes needed to be made on and off the field, focus on a new season that lay waiting nine months way, and move on. A foundation was in place, but Sherrill knew where all the cracks had been hidden. They weren't hidden anymore. He had been going to war with too many players he had not recruited, and it was time to bring in the kind of raw talent that could win championships. The search for the Cotton Bowl had simply taken too many wrong turns down too many bad roads. Before he was through, Sherrill believed, the road to Dallas on New Year's Day would travel through College Station, and Kyle Field would become the most feared and dreaded venue for football in the nation. Give him time, he thought. Just give him time.

The coaches looked up and studied his face. Jackie Sherrill was not smiling, but then he hardly ever smiled. The weight of a losing season lay heavy on his shoulders. It was a day no different from any other. A report. An update. Recruiting data. A running back who could run through walls. A quarterback who carried a rifle for an arm. The arm might be more lethal. A linebacker who could crush cement blocks with his bare hand. A defensive end who should be kept in a cage. Get out there and find them. The sooner, the better. The 1983 season had already begun,

and, for the coaches, it was time to hit that long, winding road again. They already had Texas maps stashed in the dashboards of their automobiles. One yawned, and another reached for his third cup of coffee. The silence was so thick it felt oppressive.

Jackie Sherrill dropped his bombshell.

Gentlemen, he said, this is what I'm going to do.

They waited. The yawn was stifled. The coffee lost its taste.

Gentlemen, he said, come next season, we are going to have a 12th man kickoff team for home games. It's never been done before. Don't think it could be done any place but Texas A&M. I believe it will work.

A frown. A raised eyebrow. No more yawning. The coffee became too bitter to drink. R. C. Slocum leaned forward on his chair. He had no idea what the head coach was about to say, but already he was trying to figure out how to make it work.

That was his job on the defensive side of the ball. For a long time, he had known that Sherrill was an innovator when it came to football, but maybe it was time he quit innovating and stuck to coaching. Another losing season or two, and Coach might be leaving. And, if Sherrill was shown the road out of town, well, he no doubt would be out of a job as well.

Gentlemen, Sherrill continued, we are going out and recruit players from the Corps of Cadets. I've seen the kind of regimen they are forced to endure. The Corps is definitely not for the weak. We'll work them out and find ourselves at least ten good kids who happen to be crazy enough, tough enough, and fast enough to run hell-bent-for-leather downfield on a kickoff and make somebody pay for the privilege of tucking a football under his arm. This is a big state, gentlemen, and it's a state that loves its football. We have a bunch of former high school football players running around campus every day, and a lot of them are in the Corps. A few of them would kill for another chance to play football. I've been to Bonfire. I've watched them crawl up and down those stacks of logs. They are fearless. I've seen them work day and night until they are so tired they can hardly walk, but they keep on going until the last log is shoved in place.

They are so devoted to Texas A&M they're willing to risk it all for the good of this university. All they'll have to do is come out for thirty minutes or so on Thursday and Friday, practice with the kickoff team over and over until they get it right, and, after awhile, I'm betting they'll get to be pretty good at it. I think they'll go down on coverage like a bunch of swarming torpedoes. They will be the 12th man this university always talks about. They will be our connection to the student body.

Silence.

Someone shifted uncomfortably in his seat.

Someone coughed.

Too damn many cigarettes.

Jackie Sherrill folded his arms, set his jaw, and waited. He could tell from the silence pervading the room that his idea was not gaining a lot of support. Only Bobby Roper was, more or less, possibly willing to somewhat back him up on the creation of a 12th man kickoff team. But that was only because Sherrill had sought him out earlier that morning and persuaded Roper to admit that the idea might not be nearly as ludicrous or as crazy as it sounded. I didn't want to go in without at least one coach standing behind me, Sherrill said. Roper wasn't sold, but, at least, he was willing to say he was.

R. C. Slocum was the first one to voice an opinion. Did you fall off those logs out there and hit your head on something, he asked. A kickoff team made up of kids who don't have any size or speed just flat wouldn't work, he thought. Couldn't work. If those kids could play football, they would have been given scholarships somewhere. Sherrill was taking a risk, a big risk, and Slocum wasn't sure it was a very smart one. In fact, it might well have been the craziest damn thing he had ever heard of. Slocum frowned, looked at Sherrill, and asked, are you sure that's what you want to do?

Jackie Sherrill nodded. His face was a mask, hard, stoic, and devoid of any emotion. The first volley had been fired, and it was not nearly as bad as he had feared it would be. He had no problem forgiving Slocum's outburst. He could only imagine the sudden, unexpected concern working through the mind of his assistant head coach and defensive coordinator. Slocum, he believed, was on the borderline of being a defensive genius. He just might possess the most inventive mind in the country when it came to developing some out-of-the-box game plan designed to shut down an offensive scheme, anybody's offensive scheme, new or old, dead in its tracks. Slocum had the ability to move players around like marbles on a Chinese Checkers board from one play to the next and make it all work.

On the ground. Through the air. It didn't matter. Just give Slocum a few assorted game films, and you could begin hearing the mechanisms grinding in the back corners of Slocum's brain. His week-to-week game plans, Slocum always said, were simply preliminary game plans, based on the schemes that teams had used in the past. On game day, however, opponents almost always had a tendency to suddenly introduce a different scheme, add a few new wrinkles, and it was his job to make adjustments on the fly. He couldn't afford to hesitate. In the heat of the action,

often with the final score hanging in the balance, he had to make split decisions and spontaneous changes on his own. There was no time for committee meetings, and no one in the country could make those moment-to-moment modifications to a defense better than R. C. Slocum. More than once, he marched into the second half of a game with a new tactical scheme his team had never run before, a scheme he had never used before. And, time and again, it worked. R. C. Slocum would have been a master at chess.

However, Slocum had every right to be concerned about the 12th man kickoff team, no matter how ingenious the idea might be. What if a bunch of walk-ons weren't quite as good as Sherrill thought they would be? What if they were just a little too slow or too intimidated to be the force he had envisioned them to be? What if they were just a bunch of high school Harrys who didn't belong in a football stadium that held more than a thousand or two on Friday night? What if they did allow too many long runbacks, no matter how hard they might be trying? What if a porous kickoff team left Slocum's defense with its back to the wall and the opponent's offense only a first down or two out of field goal range? A short field. A quick score. And no would ever criticize the kickoff team. Not that bunch of clean-shaven kids. The blame would be heaped on the defense and probably on Slocum himself.

As Slocum said, our primary mission on kickoffs had always been to keep teams as far away from our goal line as possible, preferably down inside their 20-yard line. Make them go a long way. Give them a chance to make a lot of mistakes, and their chances of scoring dropped dramatically. I knew Sherrill's idea had better work.

If our opponents were always starting on the 40-yard line, then we were in trouble. Those extra twenty yards could be killers and usually made the difference between a touchdown, a field goal, or a punt. I had my concerns, but Sherrill and I never had any arguments or confrontations about football or about the 12th man. I respected his ideas. He respected my suggestions. We made our critical decisions in a professional atmosphere and moved forward. He knew what he wanted to do, and it was my duty to help him make his all-volunteer kickoff team work. Winning football games at Texas A&M might depend on it.

Sherrill could almost feel the disappointment, the dread, the apprehension that gripped Slocum's better judgment, and, frankly, Sherrill did not blame him. But he knew he could depend on Slocum.

The reality was, his coaches did not know or even suspect what he knew about Texas A&M and the students who proudly called themselves Aggies. As General George S. Patton had once said, give me an army of West Point graduates, and I'll win a battle. Give me a handful of Texas Aggies, and I'll win a war. Jackie Sherrill wore a wry grin. He was gearing up for an all-out assault. He was determined to win a war.

That evening Jackie Sherrill walked into Duncan Dining Hall where the Corps of Cadets was eating dinner. Sherrill explained that he had asked squadron leaders to pick out the best athletes in their outfits who wanted to be on a special 12th man kickoff team. As Al Carter of the *Houston Chronicle* wrote, his announcement sparked dinner-hour pandemonium. When Sherrill said the 12th man would work out with the team and earn varsity letters, the dining hall erupted in "whoops" and impromptu yells of approval known among Aggies as "wildcatting."

Tom Joseph, a senior cadet and the school's head yell leader said, it's good bull. It's excellent bull! Nobody in the nation is doing this. It's great. Coach Sherrill wants to utilize everything A&M has to offer. He realizes there's a reservoir here that other schools don't have, and he's going to use it.

Sherrill said, I simply want to endorse what the students are doing.

E. King Gill gained mythical fame when he became the symbolic 12th Man during the 1922 Dixie Classic between Texas A&M and Centre College. Injuries had taken their toll. A&M had no subs left. And Gill came down out of the stands to stay ready in case his coach needed him to play.

They have been standing ready a long time. It won't be long now before they'll be helping us out.

Corps Commander Mike Holes was almost overwhelmed. It's like letting us be the original 12th Man, he said.

That was certainly what Jackie Sherrill had in mind.

The tradition of the 12th Man had been birthed out of necessity by a young coach named Dana X. Bible, the X standing for Xenophon. In 1916, he arrived at Texas A&M at the age of twenty-five, not much older than the players themselves, and was asked to coach the freshman team. His squad regularly beat the varsity during scrimmages, and, after awhile, LSU hired him away to become head coach of the Tigers. After Bible defeated Texas A&M by 13-10, the Aggies brought him back home where he proceeded to lead the Maroon and White to five Southwest Conference championships.

Bible's first Aggie team in 1917 was undefeated, and no one crossed its goal line. The young coach lost a year, fighting in the trenches of France during the final, deadly-but-triumphant days of World War I, before returning to again take the throttle of A&M's football machine. His Aggies would not surrender a point nor suffer a defeat until the last game of 1930. Texas won 7-3, and A&M knew that it would never again have any love or respect for those bastards in Austin.

Dana X. Bible had his own ideas about coaching football, and even though many raised their eyebrows at his curious strategies, no one dared question him. Winners can do whatever it takes as long as the wins keep outnumbering the losses, and for Bible, they always did. It was not unusual at all for him to punt the ball away on first down, always preferring to play field position until his opponent made a mistake, and, sooner or later, his opponents always did. As he said, kicking was a big part of the game even up until well after the first World War. The punt formation was our basic formation on offense, and we always worked the ball until we got well into the opposing team's territory. We used to kick on first down when we were within twenty yards of our own goal. We didn't pass until we got past our forty. As Joel Hunt, a former player, said of Bible, he was as confident as a banker, astute as a schoolmaster, and as expressive as a salesman.

A blue norther had ripped across Dallas on January 2, 1922, and the Aggies came marching into a rickety old football stadium at Fair Park to battle Coach Charlie Moran's legendary Praying Colonels of Centre College in the Dixie Classic.

Texas A&M had won the Southwest Conference, but there was not yet a Cotton Bowl, and the Praying Colonels were regarded far and wide as the most feared college football team in the nation. Quite frankly, to anyone who happened to gaze across the field, the players suited up for Centre College were bigger and appeared to be a good deal faster than the Aggies.

There were certainly a lot more of them. The Praying Colonels had become one of the most fabled powers in College football. They were undefeated, had dealt Harvard its first loss in two years, and warmed up for the Dixie Classic by taking a passenger train from their campus in Danville, Kentucky, to San Diego, where they kicked the University of Arizona from one end of California to the other.

Their quarterback, Alvin "Bo" McMillan, looked a little chunky, but he had been named to Walter Camp's All-American team for three straight years. When he passed, the ball usually headed in the direction of Red Roberts, another three-time All-American. He may have lined up as a wide receiver, but Camp had named him to the team as a center. The passing tandem of McMillan to Roberts was a lethal combination regardless of their positions.

Dana X. Bible stood on the sidelines of Fair Park Stadium and carefully studied the Praying Colonels, wondering if he could give them a reason to keep praying before the day had ended. Big. Fast. Impressive. Bible shrugged and grinned. He had never seen a team he didn't think he could beat. The trouble was, the Aggies had only managed to reach town with seventeen able-bodied players. Of course, they would have had eighteen, but Bible's fullback had broken a leg.

Up in the press box, high above the wooden bleachers, sports writer Jinx Tucker decided quickly that the Aggies might well be the best the Southwest Conference had to offer, but they would be no match for the formidable Praying Colonels of Centre College.

An article in the *Houston Chronicle* expressed a little more optimism. It said, in their workouts, the Aggies have exhibited a remarkable spirit of pep that has done much to convince spectators that the squad will quite possibly surprise anyone looking for a top-heavy score.

But most newspapers, especially those with a national audience, looked upon Texas A&M as simply an orphan stepchild on a remote corner of the football world, a team with little significance and no real importance, nothing more than another isolated pothole in Centre College's march to another undefeated season.

Ben Beesley, a player for A&M, would remember, we were all just a bunch of old country boys who didn't read the newspapers because we were too busy getting ready for the game. If we had, we probably would have been scared to death

adet E. King Gill was a young Aggie that Tucker had recruited to sit with him in the press box during the game. The sports writer needed a good spotter, and Gill knew every player at a glance. He would be an absolute godsend. Gill was tall, wiry, and had played football for Bible during his sophomore year before deciding to concentrate on basketball and baseball. He might never have left football, but the basketball coach said he desperately needed him, and Gill always went wherever he was needed most.

As the game exploded into the first quarter, here came the Aggies with their famed punt formation. No run. No pass. A punt, and the ball sailed into the end zone. Centre College's returner, having little if any respect for A&M, caught the wobbling punt, and Puny Wilson nailed him where he stood. A safety. The Aggies had struck first blood. The score stood 2-0, and the crowd breathed a sigh of relief. At least the Aggies wouldn't get shut out. The Praying Colonels were not particularly concerned. Two points were easy enough to make up. But they found out in

Jackie Sherrill, from his first day on campus, involved himself with the special culture and traditions of Texas A&M. For him, "sawing horns" along with members of the 12th man kickoff team was as normal and as natural as breathing.

a hurry that Dana X. Bible did not always just punt. He could coach a little defense as well. Once, twice, three times, Centre College was stopped inside the Aggie five-yard line. But they were paying a high price.

As one writer remembered, wounded Aggies were being hauled off the field like cord wood. Quarterback Bugs Morris was knocked cold. Halfback Heinie Weir went down with a broken leg. His replacement, Bill Johnson, was carried to the sideline and then to a treatment room on the far side of the chilled stadium. Two more players were dragged away with injuries, and Texas A&M found itself working with a patchwork team that even had one beefy linemen, then another, operating out of the backfield.

Beesley had been a benchwarmer for most of the season, but he was called on to play for fifty-seven minutes against the fiercest team in the land, sometimes lining up under center, even though he had never been a quarterback or thrown a ball that counted.

Through all of the adversity, the Aggies kept clinging precariously to its two-point lead. Beesley hit Red Roberts hard, and the All-American end's head bounced off the ground. Beesley, with a certain amount of pride, said, Roberts played sick the rest of the day.

A fumble. A Centre College recovery. A quick touchdown. And, as A&M found itself trailing for the first time in the game, Sammy Sanders was carted off the field on a stretcher, knocked unconscious while covering a punt. Dana X. Bible grimaced and looked around him and found one of the strangest situations to ever confront a big-time college coach.

He was sitting all alone on the bench.

There were no subs beside him. The only players he had left were still on the field, and he only had eleven healthy enough to stand.

Another injury, and A&M would be wandering into territory best described as ridiculous.

Bible stood, turned toward the press box, and motioned for E. King Gill to come down out of the stands. The coach met him as Gill climbed across the fence separating the bleachers from the field. It doesn't look like I'm going to have enough players to finish the game, Bible said. You may have to go in there for us. I know you don't know the plays, but you can stand around and fill a hole.

Gill nodded.

The stadium had no dressing room, so Gill slipped without hesitation beneath the bleachers. The players, during a timeout, grouped together and held a blanket around him, and he stuffed himself into Heinie Weir's uniform. It was spotless, and Gill was nervous. What if someone else did get hurt? Would he run left when everyone else was going right? Would he do A&M more harm than good? Did he have enough stamina? It had been a long time since he ran either up or down a football field, and there were almost two quarters left to be played.

The Aggies may have been riddled with injuries.

The Aggies may have had players in the wrong position and, more likely than not, running the wrong plays.

But the Aggies suddenly caught fire.

With an intercepted pass, a recovered fumble, and one of Bible's patented strokes of genius, a forty-yard, triple pass play, Texas A&M built up a 22-7 lead.

Not even a desperate, end-of-the-line, end-of-the-day seventy-yard drive by Centre College with time running out troubled them. Worn out? No doubt. Ready to crumble? Not on your life.

A Dallas newspaper wrote that the Aggies fought every inch of the way – a thin line of battling players, aware that there was no reserve strength on the bench to replace them. The great Bo McMillan only completed three passes, and just one of them to the great Red Roberts.

The defenders of Eastern football blamed the bad weather, the long train ride, the excessive celebrations that erupted on New Year's Eve, the fact that McMillan had been married the night before. But the *Bryan Eagle* retorted, if those Praying Colonels were wobbling over the gridiron, it wasn't from too much moonshine, it was from too much A&M.

As the final whistle blew, the president of Texas A&M, Dr. W. B. Bizzell, tore his hat in pieces. And when the bruised and battered team returned to College Station, they discovered a 430-pound cake, decorated in eight shades of Maroon and White and topped by a football, waiting for them.

Almost overlooked on the field was E. King Gill.

He had stood nervously the entire second half beside Dana X. Bible, feeling both a little awkward and uncomfortable, but ready to play if needed or called upon.

Most people at the time didn't pay much attention to him at all.

However, the *Dallas-Galveston News* wrote, the sought-after player, whether he be professional or not, tends to regard himself as bigger than the necessity of loyalty to the athletic interests of his school. On the other hand, the player chosen from the ranks of students in schools for a serious purpose feels an overwhelming sense of gratitude and love for his school which no non-collegian can estimate, and which no football coach can call upon in vain.

The difference that lies between the solicited 'star' with whom his college is an incident and the volunteer player with whom his college is an epoch in his life – this is the difference that still holds out against the commercialization of college sport and against the reduction of it to a mere trail of bone and sinew.

E. King Gill had been the volunteer, the student from the stands. He would point out later in life, I wish I could say that I went in and ran for the winning touchdown, but I did not. I simply stood by in case my team needed me.

His spirit of readiness for service, however, his desire to support his coach and his team, his enthusiasm for the university he loved kindled a flaming spirit that only grew brighter and hotter as the decades passed.

He had not played.

But he would never be forgotten.

E. King Gill became the 12th Man.

And tradition followed where he had walked.

Jackie Sherrill's original plan had been to choose his 12th man kickoff team from the Corps of Cadets. It made sense to him. It would be a harmonious blending of two of Texas A&M's most cherished and storied traditions. Some outside the Corps, however, began expressing a strong interest in trying out for the team, and Student Body President Pat Pearson wrote the head coach, asking him to give every student attending A&M the opportunity to become a part of a team unlike any other in the country. Even Sherrill's coaches, who were continuing to look at the 12th man kickoff team with a certain amount of suspicion, fear, and trepidation, suggested he broaden his search to include the whole student body. Increase the odds of finding a handful of football players flying far under the radar, they said. Jackie Sherrill, as he seldom does, changed his mind. The spring tryouts of 1983, he announced, would be open to everyone who had the guts to play. He was simply looking for a few good men, and when spring rolled around, he had two hundred and fifty-two students walk out onto the turf of Kyle Field in shorts, T-shirts, and tennis shoes.

Two of them were women. They weren't around long.

12th Man Kickoff Team

Persons interested in trying out for the 1984 12th Man Kickoff Team should report to the Kyle Field Dressing Room on Monday, January 30th at 5:30 pm for General Meeting. No prior experience is required.

An advertisement running in the campus newspaper, the Battalion, announced the formation of the 12th man kickoff team, explaining that no experience was required to play. It may not have been entirely truthful.

As equipment manager Billy Pickard explained to them as gently as possible, they had various and sundry places on their bodies that his pads and gear wouldn't be able to adequately or properly protect. Well, Billy Pickard may not have actually explained it in those particular terms, but the girls got the idea. He didn't have a place for them to take a shower. He didn't have a place for them to

change clothes. He didn't want them hurt. He didn't want them around. Then again, Billy Pickard didn't particularly want any of the 12th man kickoff team around. They would be a nuisance and probably a hindrance. They had no idea what they were doing and would get in his way.

He didn't have time for them. He didn't have equipment for them, so he unpacked a box or two of hand-me-downs – pads and practice uniforms that no one wore anymore and should have been thrown away long ago. But this so-called glorified kickoff team was Sherrill's idea, and Sherrill was still the boss. Pickard bitched and complained to everyone but Sherrill and did his best to be a loyal soldier. Chances were, the hard work and tougher practices would run a few of them off. Besides, he had been with the Bear in Junction.

He had seen the master run kids off. Make it tough. Make it unbearable. Make it insufferable. And a bunch of fool kids would wilt every time. Billy Pickard was sure of it.

Skeptics were raising their ugly heads and standing in line to condemn the team before it had ever covered a kickoff, run out onto the field, allowed a runback, had a practice, or even been chosen. Baylor Coach Grant Teaff called the idea absolutely ridiculous. Other coaches laboring throughout the Southwest Conference could not believe Jackie Sherrill would do such a foolhardy thing. At A&M, football coaches were merely holding their breath and their tongues.

Even columnist John Wagner sat down at his desk in the *Battalion* office and wrote that the kickoff team might well become the greatest embarrassment of Sherrill's existence. It was born in November, he wrote, the product of a coach getting involved with the student body. It was announced a short time later and caused a slight uproar, if there is such a thing. And now, as it moves toward reality, there is a concern that the 12th man kickoff team may be a mistake. Maybe those guys can run and tackle and hit. Maybe Sherrill is right when he says the team will work out just fine. Maybe the Aggies will finish the season in November without one kickoff being run back for a touchdown.

But what if they don't? What if the whole idea backfires? What if the cute story suddenly goes sour? Is there a way to back out in midseason, to save face, and protect pride if a tradition-come-to-life falls apart right in front of our eyes? The idea of a 12th man kickoff team – regular students taking part in a game normally reserved for highly recruited, mostly-pampered athlete-students – is a good one, if it works. But how great are the odds? Texas A&M students are tired of the football season being something they have to suffer through. They are tired of seeing their school laughed at and ridiculed. They are tired of athletes in a fishbowl – the Aggies struggle on as the media and the nation look in and snicker. It doesn't matter that the idea of the kickoff team was conceived innocently, or that there are good intentions behind it. It still poses a threat. And it would be a shame if the Texas A&M student body – after all these years of standing at football games – had to ask the 12th man kickoff team to sit down.

John Wagner had learned well from the professionals of the leering press. When in doubt, go ahead and criticize. Stir the pot. If the kickoff team doesn't work, you can always say, I told you so. If it does, you never have to say you're sorry. The leering press never does. Then again, Sherrill knew, Wagner's skepticism just might be right on target.

Yet, over on the *Bryan Eagle,* Glenn Dromgoole, who had once written for the *Battalion* himself, was thoroughly intrigued with idea lodged in Sherrill's mind. He wrote in his Editor's Notebook, conventional wisdom is conventional, but not always wise. The off-the-wall idea often turns out to be the inspiration of genius. Sure, I snickered, too, when I first read about Jackie Sherrill's idea of recruiting members of the Corps of Cadets to serve as A&M's kickoff team at all home games next season.

Had Jackie gotten beaned by one of those logs when he was working on the Aggie Bonfire? Has he sung the Aggie War Hymn one too many times?

Has he lost his ever-loving mind? Everyone knows that college football is a tough sport, best left to the super-athletes-for-hire. The idea of recruiting a bunch of students to come out for football and take an active role on the team is crazy. It just isn't done that way. Leave athletics to the semi-pros who get paid room and board for playing … Sherrill's idea might prove to be a real flop.

Maybe the opposition will take the first kickoff from the Corps and run it back for a touchdown, and Jackie – and A&M – will be the laughingstock of college football.

Or maybe, just maybe, his idea is so crazy it just might work.

There is, of course, a practical benefit to Sherrill's plan that should not be overlooked; he wouldn't run the risk of having any of his regulars injured on kickoffs, where there is a high risk of injury. Practicality aside, I like the idea because it's so different and because it's so appropriate.

A&M has a unique type of spirit. A good many students probably stand at the football games because that's the tradition, and that's what all the other Aggies do. But there are some who really would come out of the stands and help out if called on. And I suspect that there are a good many who have the speed, size, and athletic experience to be of valuable assistance. As Sherrill put it, you couldn't do something like this at any other place in the country. That's what makes it so unique. Indeed. That's why it's worth the risk that Jackie Sherrill is willing to take.

The die was cast.

Win, lose, or draw, Sherrill was going forward with his plan, and, as always, he ignored any hint of criticism, ridicule, or disdain being thrown on his shoulders by either foes or the leering press. As Dromgoole had written, the 12th man kickoff team could be the most publicized special unit since LSU's Chinese Bandits back in the '50s. It would make the 12th Man tradition a reality.

Well, as far as Sherrill was concerned, the 12th Man was already a reality, and so was his kickoff team.

He picked up the phone and called David Beal to his office. Beal was a young graduate assistant with an eye on someday coaching, and Sherrill knew him well. He had heart. He could stand up to pressure. And he was pretty damn smart. David Beal had originally been recruited out of Russellville, Arkansas, by Tom Wilson to quarterback the Aggies. Beal soon learned the cold, hard facts about the illusions and veracity of college football. I came to Texas A&M with the promise that I would run the offense, he said, and, when I arrived, I discovered that the coaching staff had gone out and signed seven high school quarterbacks. I thought I had heard some kind of faint promise about me being the heir apparent. When my time came, I would be the man in charge. The rest of the quarterbacks all came to College Station with the same faint promise tucked away in their pockets. One-on-one competition. To the victor went the spoils.

The Aggie coaches let it be known early that they would probably keep only two or three of the freshmen signal callers. David Beal stayed. He was bright, athletic, and he probably would have played more if, as he said, some quarterback named Gary Kubiak had not shown up on campus. Kubiak was the man. Watch him throw the ball, and you knew.

Kubiak was destined to play professional football. So Beal stood on the sidelines, backed him up, started when Kubiak went down with injuries, threw a few touchdown passes of his own, and watched A&M make its awkward transition from Tom Wilson to Jackie Sherrill. Wilson, he said, was a hands-on coach with the offense.

Sherrill kept an eye on the defense. And Sherrill was not afraid to surround himself with great coaches, then step out of their way and let them do their jobs. If something needed to be fixed, Beal said, Sherrill could fix it. He knew the nuances of every position, but then he had played seven of them with the Bear at Alabama.

Mostly, however, he ran the business of football, and the coaches coached. Historically, graduate assistants were little more than gophers with whistles around their necks. They felt totally separate and apart from the team and the rest of the coaches. Sherrill was different. He gave us respect. He made us feel that we, too, were an integral part of his staff. We probably weren't, but he made us believe we were.

And now, in the early spring of 1983, Beal, roughly the same age as a fifth year senior, found himself sitting across the desk from Jackie Sherrill. For some reason, the dark, deep-set eyes did not seem as intimidating as they once did.

You know we're going to have a 12th man kickoff team next fall, the coach said.

Yes, sir.

What do you think about it?

Beal didn't hesitate. I went to school here, he said. I played here. I know Texas A&M, I know its traditions, and I know its students. I believe it'll work.

There are a lot of doubters out there, Sherrill said. And skeptics.

I've heard what they have to say.

Do you still believe it will work?

It'll work.

Good. Sherrill stood up. As far as he was concerned, the meeting was over. Well, not quite. David, he said.

Yes, sir.

I want you to coach them.

David Beal was stunned. He knew the team would be rough around the edges. As a coach, he himself was a little rough around the edges. He just assumed that the coach chosen to work with the 12th man kickoff team would carry a wealth of experience out on the field. He assumed wrong. Yet, Beal knew that simultaneously he had just been given the greatest and most frightening challenge of his life.

How will I do that, coach, Beal asked and hoped Sherrill didn't hear the break in his voice.

You'll find a way. Sherrill shrugged. Curley's our special teams coach, he said. Curley will give you some pointers.

I appreciate the opportunity, Beal said as he stood to leave.

And David, there's one more thing, Sherrill said.

What's that, coach?

I don't want any kickoff returned for a touchdown. Sherrill paused, thought it over for a moment, then said, I don't even want the ball returned to the fifty.

His voice was low, barely audible, and filled with gravel.

Beal waited for him to grin.

Sherrill was out the door.

He had been dead serious.

Meeting adjourned.

It was the best day of their lives. During the summer of 1982, Sports Illustrated arrived in College Station to produce a six-page story on the creation of the 12th man kickoff team, and the magazine ran this picture of bright, energetic players who had made the last spring cut. For some, it would become the worst day of their lives. Not everyone featured in the photograph or in the article was selected for the first 12th man unit. For a brief moment, however, they had their day in the sun.

All of Aggieland became fanatical about the 12th man kickoff team, which, for the first time, connected the student body with the players on the field. When the 12th man team raced on the field, the crowd exploded with excitement and noise.

Chapter 8

From the beginning, David Beal had recognized the genius behind the idea of Sherrill's 12th man kickoff team. The students would feel a stronger connection with the football team. Ten of their own would be on the field. Their own flesh and blood were leaving their own flesh and blood on the turf of Kyle Field. As Sherrill said, scholarship football players live in their own dorm, they eat in their own dining hall, and, for the most part, they seldom cross paths with the Aggie students on campus or in the classroom. From their seats up in the stands, all students can see are names, helmets, and numbers. Nothing more. Just names, helmets, and numbers. Now when those students crowd into Kyle Field for home games, each of them will know, go to class with, live in the dorm with, go to the library with, date, or know someone who dates at least one member of the 12th man kickoff team. Those boys will put a face on our football team. They will bring the spirit of each and every one of those Aggie students down onto the football field with them.

All David Beal needed to do was find ten good men.

No. Make that more like fifteen or twenty good men.

Injuries were always a real possibility, especially on kickoff returns where knees and elbows worked hard before the whistle and even harder after the whistle had blown, where illegal hits, blocks, and cuts were as common as aspirin and band-aids, where injuries to those who happened to be a little too small, a little too slow, or a little too weak were not only a threat but a reality. Beal had to find ten who were all walking at the same time, who were capable of running at the same time, and he had to teach them the science of covering a kickoff. Lord knows, they didn't practice it very often in high school. No one did. In most high schools, covering kickoff was merely an afterthought. Send your fastest ten players out on the field, along with a kicker, and pray that your ten are faster, quicker, a little meaner, a lot tougher, and somewhat crazier than the other team's eleven. Somehow, for the most part, it usually worked out. Beal could teach them the right scheme, and his team would attack like a pack of mad dogs from every angle. They would learn just how much faster the college game was on their own. It would not take them long.

Beal walked toward Kyle Field, and he kept thinking about the ad that ran in the *Battalion*, the ad that casually mentioned *no prior experience required*. He laughed. If a kid had no prior experience, he was nothing more than a slow-footed goose in a shooting gallery. Then again, maybe they all were. Beal shoved his way into the offensive film room beneath Kyle Field. A lot more had crammed themselves into the room than either he or Curley Hallman had anticipated. The chairs were all filled. The rest were standing shoulder-to-shoulder, and a lot of them had spilled out in the hallway. Beal began passing around a yellow legal pad. He had numbered only sixty spaces on two pages, and, in a few minutes, he began hearing the pages being flipped and flipped again. It took awhile to collect two hundred and fifty names and phone numbers. The girls had already been turned away.

Beal looked across the grim, solemn faces of those foolhardy souls who had once played football and thought they could again. How long ago had it been? Most had not even considered that a few gallons of beer, probably more, had robbed them of their foot speed and waistline. Muscle had grown soft. The body had forgotten what it meant to hurt. To so many of them, that last Friday night high school football game seemed like last week or maybe the week before. Time had gotten away from them. Even a year away from practice would seem like an eternity, especially when a football field suddenly seemed longer than it used to be, and the forty-yard dash was no longer a dash. The mind was willing. The body was still telling lies. Sure I can go, it was saying. Nothing's really changed. Today's no different from yesterday.

There had been a time when the prospects could hit a brick wall and make it move, or at least rock back and forth. Here, the brick walls hit back and liked to hit back. But, on this particular afternoon, when the last chill of winter had dissolved into an early spring, none of it mattered. Sherrill said they could play. And no one doubted Jackie Sherrill for a minute. Beal laughed again. Meat on the hoof, he thought. Cannon fodder. They all looked so eager, their eyes wide, adrenalin bursting wildly through their veins. They had heard, as everyone did, that they would simply be asked to show up for a little while on Thursday and Friday afternoons. Go hard and fast. Cover a few kickoffs. Avoid a block or two. Make a tackle if the runner came your way. Spend the evening at the good old Dixie Chicken. And suit up on Saturday ready to play. Beal did not know whether to applaud or pity them. They all thought they had it figured out. They had no idea.

David Beal said, my idea was a simple one. Work with Curley Hallman. No one was better than Curley when it came to special teams. Hold the tryouts. Run everyone through a few sprints and agility drills. Check their quickness and speed. Let them do a little dummy work. See if we could determine who did or didn't have any natural athletic ability. At first, we were only trying to cut the squad from two hundred and fifty down to a reasonable forty or so, then let them put on the pads and throw them up against the likes of Ray Childress, Billy Cannon, Jr., Doug Williams, and Domingo Bryant. We wouldn't know a lot about them as football players until they hit somebody. Then it would all come down to this: who flinched, who could get knocked down, then get back up again, who could keep on going when his body felt like it was coming apart at the seams, who could play with pain, who had no sense of pain, and who would rather go home. You couldn't tell a thing about their faces. The tough ones sometimes didn't look it. Those who thought they had a mean streak played scared. A few of the skinny ones couldn't get both feet headed in the same direction at the same time. And a handful of the heavy ones were surprisingly quick.

Don't worry about the number of kids out there, Hallman told him. You won't have to cut that many of them. Mostly, they'll cut themselves. They'll know they can't make the grade long before you do.

But between now and that first kickoff against the University of California next fall, there were a lot of unknowns – two hundred and fifty of them to be exact. And the fear and uncertainty of the unknown would keep David Beal awake at night.

With so many crowded into the same room, some even stuffed into the small individual position rooms outside, Beal expected chaos, screaming and hollering, trash talking on one side of the room, bullshitting on the other.

But it was quiet.

God, it was quiet.

The silence was ethereal.

They were all ears, Beal said. They wanted to know what was going to happen next, when it was going to happen, and how soon they could make it happen. They leaned forward to hear every word I had to say.

Wow!

That's all I could think of.

Wow!

They were dead, solid serious. In a world that promised second chances but very seldom offered any, Jackie Sherrill was giving them an opportunity to come out and play college football long after they had all given up on the dream. It was almost too good to be true. For most of them, it was. My job was to whittle that room full of hopefuls down to a handful of genuine, honest-to-goodness football players. I hoped Curley had been right. I hoped that most of those who still thought they might actually be football players would do the hatchet job for me.

Next week, Beal began, we'll practice every afternoon at five o'clock. Will that conflict with any of your class schedules?

Twenty, maybe thirty, hands went up.

Beal took a deep breath. He was cautiously treading on unfamiliar territory. Football players never had class conflicts at five o'clock, or any other time for that matter. Their schedules were designed to accommodate football. Some said they could come at three o'clock, if that was all right. A few said they wouldn't have any trouble showing up on Wednesday, but they had labs on Tuesday and Thursday, so those days were out. These students did not and would never have a scholarship. They might not even be athletes, and football would never be part of their lives after college. Academics came first. Academics would ultimately make his first cuts for him. Some had the time it took to play, and some didn't. Life was full of choices. They had some big ones to make.

I thought we were just coming out a couple of times a week, someone said. Are you expecting us to be out there every day?

Beal smiled.

Next question.

Is that all we're gonna do?

What?

Practice kickoffs.

Beal smiled again.

Most of the prospects had walked into the meeting already dressed to work out. They were wearing shorts, new tennis shoes, worn-out tennis shoes, tennis shoes with no tread at all, sweat bands, head bands, worn-out T-shirts. They were ready to start running. Waiting until next week was a matter of inconvenience. What they were facing, Beal knew, took a lot of guts. Not courage. Guts. And there was a difference. I don't care if you are four-foot-one or six-foot-seven, Beal said. If you can run, and we evaluate you as a solid open-field tackler, if you are willing to give up your time and your body, you might be able to play. But it's not going to be easy. Don't get your hopes up. You'll get pounded. You'll run until you don't think you can run any farther, and then you'll run some more. You'll go home at night and hurt in places you forgot you had.

No one walked out.

It was a somber, grim-faced bunch of players who realized that every practice, every play, every hit might secure and keep them a place on the 12th man team – or eliminate them.

again. Dennis Burns cruised to a 4.6. And Ike Liles was right on their heels. James Barrett had a little speed, and David Beal began to feel better than he had since the day he sat in Sherrill's office. Things were happening now, he thought. Good things. All he needed were a few 4.7s, a 4.8 or two, and he might be able to put together a decent kickoff team, provided their thin, brittle, fragile-looking bodies didn't snap like matchsticks when some 270-pound linemen went in head first and removed their helmet, ribs, and a goodly portion of their sternum somewhere on the south side of midfield. It was all beginning to take shape.

Run.

They could hear Beal's voice in the background.

Run. Run. Run.

It kept a throbbing pace with their heartbeats.

Run you yellow-livered, dog-meated sumbitches.

That was Curley Hallman. He had sharpened and refined his vocabulary during years of coaching defensive backs. On a football field, he could communicate with the best of them. No one misunderstood what he told them. Being a dog-meated sumbitch to Curley Hallman was not a personal insult to one's heritage or lineage. In his eyes, they were all sumbitches. He had never seen a football player who wasn't.

Faster.

Get your head out from between your legs.

You can't quit now.

Get up, you little bastard. If you're gonna stay down on your hands and knees, you might as well crawl home.

The first cuts came quickly.

They were the easy ones.

Then came the second round.

Curley Hallman had been right.

Some of the prospects were fast. Some were slow. And some just walked away one afternoon and didn't come back.

Billy Pickard laughed a lot when he realized how many weren't coming back.

That was a good sign.

How many, Beal wondered, would be back? The last thing he told them before he left the room was, when you get on the field, give us everything you've got. It may not be enough, but it's what we want to see.

The door shut behind him.

Not a soul had moved.

As the *Battalion* reported, perhaps sixty percent of the prospects were Corps members, assuming no one else wore crew cuts these days. Some of the guys looked tough. We're talking downright mean, and it said so on a few of their T-shirts, which extolled the virility of some Corps unit. Then again, a few might think twice about this endeavor, so as not to get the hairdo mussed. The Aggie coaches say they are taking this business seriously, but I'm not sure about the players. With 36,000 people at A&M, they're bound to find someone.

The prospects came from all corners of Texas, from every dorm on campus, some wearing the khaki of the Corps, others the Wrangler jeans and boots of a self-confessed cowboy country kicker. They showed up in all shapes and sizes. For some, beer and cheeseburgers had taken a heavy, unmerciful toll. Their feet felt like lead. But, on a warm spring morning, they all possessed the same passion. They wanted to feel a football field beneath their feet one more time, to have one last chance to drive a shoulder or elbow into someone's midsection, to hear the crowd roar, to soak in sweat and liniment, to wear the Maroon and White, and breathe fire if necessary. It was becoming increasingly more difficult to wheeze and breathe fire at the same time.

Forty-yard dash times. That's what the coaches wanted to see. A 4.5 had promise. A 4.8 might work if the player had a little size on him. A five flat was out of the question. Can't make it down on a kickoff with a five flat or slower, Beal said. His stopwatch had absolutely no heart and little sympathy. A kid could cut it or he couldn't. The five flats began to pile up. For some, a five flat was as fast as they had ever run. In the Dalharts, San Sabas, and Sour Lakes of the world, it was sometimes fast enough.

But Tom Bumgardner blazed to a 4.5. Beal checked his stopwatch

Ike Liles had one thought as he looked around the innards of Kyle Field. It bore no resemblance to Stamford, and, if he happened to be one of the fortunate few to make the 12th man kickoff team, he certainly wouldn't be drinking tepid water out of a rusty faucet that drained through a PVC pipe. The coach told them all it wouldn't be easy. For Ike Liles, football had never been easy. The game was. But practices were as hard as the rock beneath his feet and no more palatable than the salt tablet he sucked on between drills. In fact, when Ike Liles drove away from West Texas, he had no intention of ever strapping on pads and walking out onto a football field again. Sure, he had been offered a chance to play for UTEP out in El Paso. But Liles was burned out. He had simply given the game everything he had, and the pain seared his soul long after the bruises healed. He wanted to get on with his life, so Liles married his high school sweetheart, Brenda, and, after a couple of years at Angelo State, set out for Texas A&M in pursuit of a degree in electrical engineering. Liles looked around and wondered exactly what he was doing in a room full of high school castoffs who had the audacity to possess some inner belief that they could play college football. Surely, they knew better. Surely, he knew better.

Liles, however, had a friend living above him in the married student apartment complex, and Randy Mitchell read in the school newspaper about the 12th man kickoff team tryouts. You ought to give it shot, he said.

It's been too long, Liles said.

You look like you can still run pretty good.

Got no reason to run anymore.

Go out, and I'll be your agent, Mitchell said.

You gonna work out with me?

Every step of the way.

Liles knew what it took to be a football player. Mitchell was a kicker, a cowboy, who felt a lot more at home roping cows than he did chasing a football. He pounded the free weights with Liles until his arm began to swell. He could barely lift it, and the pain was becoming unbearable. Ike Liles simply shook his head and ran toward Kyle Field alone. Randy Mitchell wouldn't be able to rope for another week.

And now Liles was sitting in the back of the film room, watching the players all jammed together in front of him. They were big sons of guns, he said. They all had broad shoulders, and none of them had any necks. They were the meanest looking guys I ever saw, he said. I had seen some pretty mean ones come through Stamford, but none looked that tough. A few of them could have made a rattlesnake squirm.

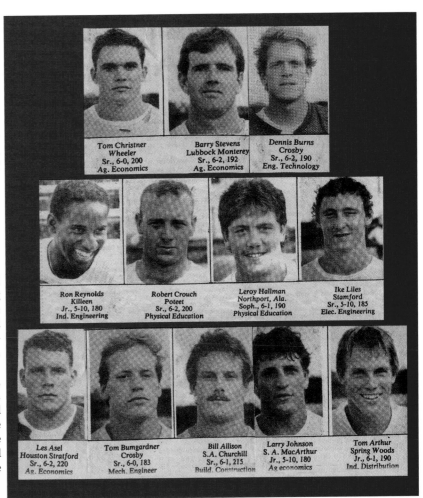

| Tom Christner Wheeler Sr., 6-0, 200 Ag. Economics | Barry Stevens Lubbock Monterey Sr., 6-2, 192 Ag. Economics | Dennis Burns Crosby Sr., 6-2, 190 Eng. Technology |

| Ron Reynolds Killeen Jr., 5-10, 180 Ind. Engineering | Robert Crouch Poteet Sr., 6-2, 200 Physical Education | Leroy Hallman Northport, Ala. Soph., 6-1, 190 Physical Education | Ike Liles Stamford Sr., 5-10, 185 Elec. Engineering |

| Les Asel Houston Stratford Sr., 6-2, 220 Ag. Economics | Tom Bumgardner Crosby Sr., 6-0, 183 Mech. Engineer | Bill Allison S.A. Churchill Sr., 6-1, 215 Build. Construction | Larry Johnson S. A. MacArthur Jr., 5-10, 180 Ag economics | Tom Arthur Spring Woods Jr., 6-1, 190 Ind. Distribution |

Throughout the country, newspapers were featuring stories and photographs of the 12th man team. Some ridiculed the unit, saying that its players had no place on the field. Others were captivated by an innovative idea and a team that represented the Spirit of Texas A&M.

Cadet Robert Crouch had been sitting down to dinner in Duncan dining hall when Jackie Sherrill came out of nowhere and announced, out of the blue, that he was forming a kickoff team to honor A&M's famed 12th man tradition. Crouch didn't hear Sherrill's exact words, but he interpreted them to mean that Coach was looking for a genuine bunch of hard-hitting, head-hunting Aggie cadets to form a kamikaze squad capable of running downfield and knocking somebody's kick returner clear into the middle of next week.

Crouch grinned. Hell, he thought. I can do that. I'd be a fool not to try out. After all, he had a lot to prove. Before walking away from Poteet, Crouch had been stopped in the hall by his old high school coach. I hear you're thinking about going down to A&M and walking on the football team, the coach said.

I've been thinking about it.

Don't bother.

Why not?

You'll never make it, the coach said. Don't get your hopes up and have some big bastard step on them. That's another league up there, and you just don't have the talent to play in it. High school is as good as you'll ever be.

When Jackie Sherrill made his surprise proclamation, Larry "Rock" Johnson had been sitting in Duncan Dining Hall as well. As the coach walked in, he said, a hush fell over the place. You could have heard a pen drop. Coach Sherrill commanded that much respect. You could tell that you were in the presence of someone who knew what he was doing. He had an aura of success about him.

Johnson had been a linebacker at McArthur High School in San Antonio and walked on to the football team at Texas A&M. He, too, had witnessed the changing of the guard, the sudden, unexpected move from Tom Wilson to Jackie Sherrill. It was, he said, the difference between night and day. No one ran scared when Wilson ambled out onto the field. Jackie Sherrill took no prisoners. I can count the number of times I talked to Coach Sherrill on one finger, he said, but if Coach had asked me to jump off a bridge, I wouldn't have asked why or which bridge. I would have jumped. He was hard. Lord, he was hard. After thirty minutes with him and his practice, hell would have been a relief. He was demanding. He could jump down our throats without ever taking his cleats off. But no matter what he put us through, we knew he loved us.

Rock Johnson warmed up before each practice by banging his head against the lockers. Once. Twice. As many times as it took. If he didn't shed blood, Johnson considered it an off day.

Dennis Mudd had been born to play football. He was sure of it. He had little patience for nonsense, and football settled disputes quickly and decisively. Football, he found, was the great equalizer. Football gave him a chance to fight back. He had loved Friday nights, and, after a game, he would usually head out to hunt rac-

Tom Bevans (8) and Tom Arthur (4) prove that members of the 12th man team could play big-time college football even though recruiters had overlooked them in high school. That first team helped create the mystique of wild and crazy bunch.

coons, especially if a cold front was coming in. Back in Yoakum, Texas, he was a Friday night star, and everyone knew his name and his number when he walked the streets on Saturday morning. Yoakum was a small town where everyone knew everybody else. If the football team won, the town was filled with tumult and shouting. If the team lost, it was a tough week. But there was always another Friday night beckoning on the horizon, and everyone was hungry for a win. Mudd hauled hay for a rancher on most Saturday afternoons, and generally he was able to pick up the replay of his high school game on radio. Football was king in South Texas, he said, and nothing was better than hearing your name called though the static by a hometown, play-by-play announcer.

Mudd's senior year had been marred by injuries. An ankle that should have broken. Torn cartilage in his chest that cracked and popped when he took a breath. Still, he refused to miss a game. Even when he was on crutches all week, Dennis Mudd was able to convince his coaches that he could still play. He wanted to play. And they needed him on the field. After the final game, a lasting hunger for football still dwelled within his heart. Two varsity seasons had provided only a combined seven wins, and he vowed that his football career would not end in Yoakum or defeat. He wanted more. He wanted one more chance.

Football, he thought, was life. Even as a sixth grader, Dennis Mudd was out in the barn behind the family farm, lifting weights that had been given to him by his brother-in-law. He didn't have a bench. He used a potato box. God had given him a little speed. He would build his own strength.

By the fall of 1981, Mudd had met with the A&M recruiting coordi-

nator. No scholarship was available, Dan LaGrasta told him, but you can always walk on the team. He promptly sent the Friday night star from Yoakum, Texas, to see Billy Pickard.

What are you doing here, Pickard had asked.

I'm here to play football.

Mudd, let me tell you something, Pickard said. You're not tall enough. You haven't gone to your first class yet. You don't know if you're fast enough. You don't have any idea what you're getting into.

Pickard glanced over Mudd's medical report from high school. Tonsils had rotted out. Most of a year lost to mononucleosis. A broken nose when he was ten. Surgery the summer before college so he could breath through his nose again. While recuperating, Mudd had leaned over to pick up a box, and the stitches popped. When his parents saw him spitting blood by the mouthful, they hadn't known whether to call the hospital or the funeral home.

Pickard frowned and shook his head. I'm not gonna let you play, he said. They cut on your nose for five hours, and if somebody hits you once in the face out here, we'll be picking up your ass in a pile of blood.

Dennis Mudd was stunned.

Tell you what, though, Pickard said. Go ahead and enroll in school.

Get the fall semester behind you, and if you are still interested, then come see me in the spring.

Those became the most miserable months of my life, Mudd said. Since I was in the third grade, I had told everyone I was going to play football for Texas A&M. When I drove out of Yoakum for College Station, the whole town believed I would be on the field wearing maroon and white. Now the whole town knew I wouldn't be playing. All they had to do was read the game story each week. My name wouldn't be in it. I hated school. I hated life. There was nothing fair about it.

Dennis Mudd was barely able to tolerate those long autumn months when others were playing football and he was standing in the stands, unscathed and unhappy. During the spring of 1982, as soon as he finished his first day of class, Mudd hurried back to Kyle Field and looked up Billy Pickard. He knocked on the door and walked in.

You said that I could come back after I had a semester under my belt, he said.

What kind of grades did you have, Pickard asked.

I had a 3.0265 grade point average in engineering, Mudd said.

Pickard nodded. Here's a key to a locker. Go see Sly about getting yourself some equipment.

Who's Sly?

Sylvester Calhoun. He and I work together. If I say you get a uniform, he finds you one. Now get yourself out of here.

Mudd turned to leave.

One more thing, Pickard said.

What's that?

If you bleed to death, don't blame me.

When Rock Johnson had been a walk-on freshman, he heard faint rumors about some oddball initiation ceremony, but had no idea what it was until the football seniors dropped him off one night twenty miles from school.

The temperature had plunged to twenty degrees.

It had been raining, and the clouds threatened more.

Ice had turned the grass to needles beneath his feet.

Rock Johnson was butt naked.

There were fifteen of us, Johnson said, and we had been told to steal a pig, grease it down, and drop it off inside a girl's dorm. We were all fairly modest and embarrassed. But after freezing all night, we didn't care who saw us, how many girls were in the dorm, or if the police were sitting there waiting on us. We were simply trying to find some place where it was warm. I would have sat down on a campfire, but the matches were wet.

The seniors, as usual, had picked the coldest night of the year, Rock said. They watered down the field outside of Cain Hall all day, and, when dark came, it was a solid sheet of ice. We stripped down, dove across the ice, slid from one end of the field to the other, warmed up with a little liquor until midnight, then leaped into the fishpond beside Rudder Tower, sat submerged with cold water up to our necks, and sang the school song. If we tried to stand up or sit down, somebody would tee off on us with a three-iron. Iron on cold hurts.

The Rock was blindfolded and left with the others out on a farm somewhere down a country road. They tracked down a pig, wandered around most of the night, searching for a familiar landmark or two, and finally trekked their way back into College Station. They crossed campus, doused the pig with a healthy dose of grease, and knocked on the door of a girl's dorm.

The door opened.

The Rock tossed the pig inside.

And left like a winged bat leaving the exit of Hades.

The girls were too busy running from, then after, the pig to notice how cold, how wet, or how naked he was.

The Rock glanced at the sky and saw the first hint of daylight creasing the clouds. He had football practice at six o'clock that morning, and, for the first time in a long time, he was too numb to feel the pain.

It took him three weeks, he said, to thaw out.

Tom Bumgardner knew he was a football player even if no one else did. For Crosby High School, he had been Mr. Everything. Bumgardner played free safety on defense, then moved onto offense as a halfback or wingback, and he even returned punts and kickoffs when it was necessary, and it was generally necessary. If someone was hurt, Bumgardner took his place. He was seldom ever off the field, and even when the final whistle ended his high school career, he was convinced that he should be hard at work on a college football field somewhere. But Bumgardner was cursed with the stigma of playing at a little 3-A school, and college coaches had a tendency to look past, over, and through any kid whose battle scars had a 1-, 2-, or 3-A attached to them. He was fast. He was tough. College coaches had merely patted him on the head and moved him along.

Tom Bumgardner had initially read in the *Battalion* that Jackie Sherrill had only opened the team up to Corps of Cadet members. That's bull, he said. Not good bull, but bullshit. Just because I'm not in the Corps doesn't mean I can't play football, he said. He was jealous. He was envious. Once again, he felt slighted.

Then came the second announcement.

Everybody had a chance.

Even those from a little class 3-A high school.

Tom Bumgardner squared his shoulders and headed to Kyle Field.

All he had ever wanted was a chance.

As *Sports Illustrated* would write: After walking on at Houston to yawns and then walking on at Stephen F. Austin to more yawns, Bumgardner decided to walk on at A&M as a 12th man candidate. Nobody yawned. Not this time anyway.

He was tired of always walking on.

Tom Bumgardner was ready to run – run hard, run wild, and run until everyone else was on their knees – and *Sports Illustrated* would later describe him as the shiniest diamond in this very rough-cut group.

Tom Arthur, like Bumgardner, had wound up at Stephen F. Austin after playing safety and outside linebacker at Spring Woods High School in Houston. There was one significant difference, however. Springs Woods played 5-A football, and Tom Arthur was on scholarship. His body may have been in Nacogdoches, but his heart, as always, was in College Station. He played one year for the Lumberjacks, then packed up and drove away before spring training of his sophomore year. Next stop: Texas A&M. It was 1982, the year Jackie Sherrill took over the football program, and Tom Arthur figured if he had the ability to play for Stephen F. Austin, he could surely play for Jackie Sherrill. He walked on and found himself slotted as the backup free safety to Wayne Asbury. Life for Tom Arthur was just about as good as it could get. The transfer rule trapped him, but he did not mind sitting out a year. His time would come. Tom Arthur was sure of it.

James Barrett, as much as anyone, exemplified the heart, the character, and the determination that made the 12th man unit a force to be reckoned with on any given Saturday.

could play a tough brand of football. He had been searching for some way to use him more, and the 12th man kickoff team just might be the solution.

Tom Arthur walked from one side of the field to the other, joining a bunch of nobodies in shoulder pads, who didn't have any more sense than to believe that the 12th man kickoff team had been created solely for their benefit. Arthur was no different from anyone else. It's me and nine others, he told himself. Me and nine others. That's who'll be the team. But what's gonna happen to all of those other poor bastards?

Shawn Slocum did not have a lot of concern. He was as a player, tough as nails and unafraid, a graduate of the same Bryan High School that had turned out such great Texas A&M players as Rod Bernstine, James Flowers, and Todd Howard. He had been invited to walk on at Texas A&M, then invited to become a member of the 12th man kickoff team. Shawn Slocum looked like a football player. He ran like a football player. He hit like a football player.

He had the 12th man kickoff team made without ever having to work out or try out. The coaches had all seen him before. They had known what Shawn Slocum was capable of doing for a long time. Now David Beal only had to find nine more starters. Tom Arthur might or might not be among them.

Shawn Slocum had a definite advantage. It helped to have a father who was defensive coordinator and assistant head coach for Texas A&M.

Then again, it might hurt to have a father who had grave concerns about a 12th man unit that had still not gone downfield in the face of an offensive firing squad gunning for them, who sometimes envisioned long kickoff returns in his nightmares, whether he was sleeping or not. R. C. Slocum's mind played the same game over and over, and he feared his defense would always be backed up against its own goal line, and those bunch of kids on the kickoff team would be to blame. They would try hard. No doubt about it. They would give a lot of effort. They were Aggies after all. But common sense said they should be up in the stands where they belonged.

He worked hard on the scout team under Coach Curley Hallman and learned the infinite number of ways he could be told just how worthless he was. Most of Hallman's words had four letters attached to them. Coach Hallman was hell on the field, Arthur said, but he squeezed the most out of you no matter how much screaming, yelling, and cursing it took. And Curley Hallman was the self-taught master of all three.

In time, Tom Arthur realized that walk-ons, good, bad, or indifferent, would have to swim the river of Hades in the dark, blindfolded and with a dead weight on their backs to ever garner much playing time. Scholarship players always received the first shot. The school had simply invested too much time, effort, and money in them. Whether, he liked it or not, there were seldom ever any other shots left.

In the spring of 1983, Tom Arthur waited for Sherrill after practice and told him, Coach, I'd like to be considered for the 12th man team.

You'll have to try out like everybody else.

I'll take my chances.

Then go for it, son.

Sherrill liked Arthur, thought he was a good athlete, and knew he

James Barrett had been a rock-solid linebacker for Rankin and helped lead the Red Devils to a state championship. But he had never lied to himself. He knew he was far too small to ever play in a conference where 220-pound linebackers were as fast as a lot of sprinters he had seen in high school. Small schools would no doubt give him a chance, but Barrett was and always would be an Aggie. It was part of his heritage. Besides, six years of football in junior high and high school were enough, so he decided to turn his energy to studying agricultural economics. Once he read about the 12th man kickoff team, however, Barrett felt his pulse quicken, and an old, familiar spirit of competition began to boil in his blood.

He talked it over with his mother.

You should give it a try, she said.

Barrett turned to his father, a survivor of Junction, a man who had borne the brunt of Bear Bryant's animosity and tenacity when he tore apart the Aggie football team and began to build it in his own image from the ground up.

It's going to be rough, Ray Barrett told his son. He knew. He, too, had played A&M football without a scholarship, a strong-willed and stubborn young man who had walked on and stayed on. Not even the Bear had been able to run him off.

I think I can take it, James Barrett said.

Ray Barrett sat in silence for a moment, then nodded. I think you can, too, he said.

His forty time was fast enough, a tick under 4.6. He could see the faint smile on Coach Beal's face, and that was always a good sign. He had a chance. He definitely had a chance to make his father proud of him. He had been proud of his father for so long.

James Barrett made the early cuts.

He put on the pads.

In practice, he went eyeball-to-eyeball with those 220-pound linebackers who were as fast as the sprinters he had seen in high school. But the sprinters didn't hit like the linebackers did. They descended on him like shrapnel shot from big guns, and Barrett went down, grimacing in pain, his ankle twisted badly beneath him.

It's over.

That was his first thought.

It's over.

It had not yet begun.

And it was over.

You'll be out at least a week, the trainer said.

A week might as well be forever.

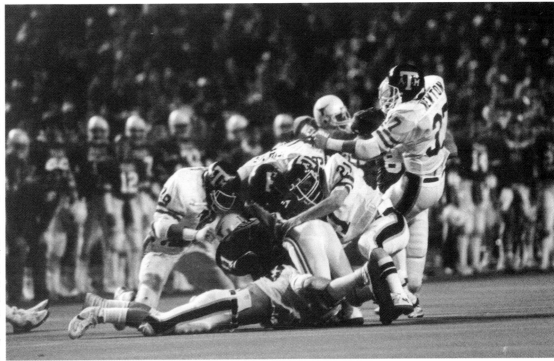

Even on the road, selected players from the 12th man team, helped generate the mad and swarming coverage that Sherrill wanted from his Aggie Team. It was always a collision waiting to happen.

even if he gave himself a head start. His old high school teammate, Tom Bumgardner, persuaded him make a run at the team, and, for some unknown and probably ungodly reason, something absolutely magical had happened during the past three years.

Beal clocked him with a 4.5 forty-yard dash time.

The stopwatch must be broken, Burns thought. He had never run that fast in his life. Then again, he was suddenly able to dunk a basketball, which he had never done before either, and he had added almost thirty pounds to his 6-3 frame.

Dennis Burns had not yet made the final cut, but suddenly he was silently beginning to wonder if, perhaps, he just might be able to play wide receiver for the Aggies. The afternoon in practice, when Ray Childress met him a step past the line of scrimmage and ran over him like gum on the bottom of his cleats, he knew better.

First, Burns had to figure out how to open his eyes.

Then, he looked up.

Ray Childress looked down. You okay, he asked.

Dennis Burns didn't know. He hadn't felt the impact, and it had been sudden and decisive. He still wasn't feeling a lot. He thought his toes moved. It might have been his eyelids. Dennis Burns would have smiled, but he didn't know where his mouth was.

For Dennis Burns, it was quite laughable. He had been a wide receiver at Crosby High School. That sounded fast on paper. It wasn't. He ran the forty-yard dash in five lingering seconds and had absolutely no vertical jump. If his cleats cleared the earth, he thought it was a good day. Burns played because he had great hands and the ability to catch everything thrown his way. But, alas, anybody who was crazy enough to play on a kickoff team only had to catch the ball carrier, and he wasn't sure he was fast enough to catch his own shadow

Tom Christner was a fifth-year senior, and his recollection of either football or winning had become a discarded memory. At little Class B Wheeler, a remote hamlet in the far reaches of the Texas Panhandle, Christner had seen his team lose only twice in three years. He had been an integral part of Wheeler's 31-game winning streak. He had played in the state championship game three times. But when Tom Christner hung up his cleats after the final game, he had no intention of ever wearing them again. A 175-pound offensive lineman didn't stand much of a chance at all at Texas A&M, and Christner was adamant about

Tom Arthur (3) and Jared Marks, a scholarship safety, had a reputation for blowing people up whether they were on the practice field running scout team against varsity or in a game.

wanting to wear an Aggie ring.

His father tried to encourage him. You might be able to play some football down there, he said.

I'm too small, Christner said, and a high school the size of Wheeler is too small for A&M to even want me. I doubt if A&M has ever even heard of Wheeler.

Didn't stop Jack Pardee, his father said. Pardee played six-man football, and he was a great player for the Bear at A&M.

It was another time, Christner said, and I'm no Jack Pardee.

At A&M, he was in the spring of his final year when he read about Sherrill forming an all-volunteer kickoff team. But it was limited to Corps members. If it was open to everybody, he bragged, I'd go out and make that team. A few weeks later, he read that anyone in the student body was eligible to try out for the 12th man squad.

You said you'd play, his friends told him. Now go prove it.

Tom Christner walked onto Kyle Field, looked around him and thought, I have no idea who I have to beat out. So he put his game face on, turned the ragged remnants of his game up a notch or two, and did his best to beat out everybody who dared to suit up and oppose him.

Barry Stevens was philosophical about it all. He and college football had made a gentleman's agreement when he left Lubbock Monterrey High School. It was a mutual decision. He no longer wanted to play, and college football did not particularly want him to play. His team had wallowed through a season of mediocrity, and now Stevens figured that, at Texas A&M, he was fortunate enough to be in the right place at the right time. I always believed life had a master plan for me, he said. So I kept my head down, worked hard, did what I thought was

right, applied for my commission as lieutenant, and, without really knowing why, marched out to Kyle Field to see what the 12th man kickoff team was all about. Every step of the way, Stevens kept telling himself to turn back. For once, Barry Stevens did not listen to his better judgment.

Coach Sherrill said he was looking for players who could run downfield and show a total lack of fear, he said. I knew how to run downfield, and I had never been afraid of anything in my life.

Then I walked onto the field and saw Jackie Sherrill.

He didn't smile.

He never smiled.

His eyes burned like smoldering coals, and I thought, God, please have mercy on my soul if I have to play under that man every day. I wasn't the quickest person out there. I wasn't the strongest. I was twenty-two years old, had not played football in five years, and here I was standing within plain sight of the Prince of Darkness.

But I would rather hit Billy Cannon, Jr., head on, at full speed, and without a helmet than tell Jackie Sherrill I couldn't do it.

David Beal stopped one of his charges after a demanding day and delicately tried to prepare him for the worst.

Son, he said, I'm sorry, but I just don't think you are quick enough or fast enough to make the team.

The hopeful wasn't shaken.

Don't worry, coach, he said, brimming with confidence. Just wait till you see me with my pads on.

Beal closed his eyes and walked away. Maybe if I don't remember his face, he thought, I won't feel so bad when I have to let him go.

As far as Keith Newton was concerned, Texas A&M was a good school for flag football. Nothing more serious, thank you. Absolutely nothing more lethal. He had been sitting in a shuttle bus, headed from class to home, when he stumbled across an article in the *Battalion* about the 12th man kickoff team. He was simply headed home, had a little time on his hands, and the thought of actually going over to Kyle Field, running a few wind sprints, and probably making a fool of himself never crossed his mind. If anything, Keith Newton knew his limitations. But three or four members of his intramural football team were fielding a few outdated dreams of fame and glory about playing on the kickoff team, so when they pulled on their cleanest, dirty T-shirts and showed up at Kyle Field to try out, Newton tagged along.

He watched David Beal test their speed, their agility, their quickness.

He was not particularly impressed.

I've got as good a chance out there as anyone else, he thought. So Newton peeled off his shirt, tightened the laces on his tennis shoes, found a place at the back of the line, and ran a forty-yard dash.

A 4.7, Beal said. Not bad.

Not great.

But not bad.

I can do better, Newton thought. Just give me a day or two. I can do a lot better.

From the stands, he had watched as a crew filmed the tryouts, and that, he hoped, just might give him the edge he needed to stand out in a crowd of two hundred or more players. Most of them were wearing T-shirts that were a faded, bleached, or a stained shade of white. He hurried back to his apartment and pulled on a bright red sweatshirt.

Every day, Keith Newton ran, some days harder than others, some days faster than others, but always he was on the field and running. Some worked out one day, then took a break. Some worked out another day, before class, after a lab, whenever they had a spare moment. Without fail, Keith Newton worked out every day, and, every day, he came to Kyle Field wearing the same sweatshirt.

Bright.

And red.

Day after day, no matter where he looked, no matter how hard he tried, Coach Beal could not miss seeing the bright red sweatshirt flashing up one side of the field and down the other. On film at night, he would sit in the dark, silent room and watch frame after frame of a bright red sweatshirt. It was here. It was there. It was everywhere.

Neither Beal nor Curley Hallman knew whether or not the slender Keith Newton could play football, hold up to the pounding, or hit with any hammer of authority.

But they knew who he was.

He was the kid with guts enough to wear an Oklahoma T-shirt.

Les Asel already had a busy schedule but believed that he had enough time left over to go out, run a little, endure some pounding in pads, tackle whoever had the ball, block whoever didn't, take a shower, and wander back home at night to study. Wouldn't be a problem, he thought. He was disciplined. He was a football player. He was a straight arrow, serving as a member of the A&M Air Force ROTC unit and student-body election commission.

He had been named the Outstanding Citizen and Outstanding Student at Stratford High School in Houston. And he came to the A&M spring game, carrying his economics 311 textbook, *Money and Banking – Economic Analysis of Banking,* under his arm.

He would play with the 12th man kickoff team, all right, but he wouldn't be on the field all the time. He had a test coming up. Between memorizing a couple of banking principles, he would dutifully place his book under the bench, go out on the field, and lay down a hit or two.

Banking.

Leroy Hallman (6) comes in hard and lays the leather to a kick returner. When Hallman hit, it was an eye-opening experience from a team that took no prisoners. He was the nephew of defensive backs and special teams coach, Curley Hallman.

Football.

It was all about addition and subtraction, and his job was to subtract the ball carrier from the ball.

What David Beal liked, however, was the fact that Asel was a big Aggie. He stood 6-2 and weighed in at 225 pounds. He could take a lick and deliver one. He was smart enough to understand the geometric angles of covering a kickoff and was never caught out of position. Someone might well make a long return someday, but it would not be anywhere within the vicinity of Les Asel. Get that close to him, and Asel would bust your tail and put you on your head.

Why did you come out for the team, Douglas Looney of *Sports Illustrated* asked him.

Coach Sherrill put out the call, Asel told him. Coach said he wanted us and needed us, and I'm answering the call.

That's not what college football is all about, Looney said.

It's what college football should be, Asel said.

Tom Bevans had done it all at Texas A&M. At least, he thought he had. Bevans had been a member of the Corps. He had worked on Bonfire. He had hauled logs out of the woodlands, stacked them tall like the Tower of Babel, and watched them burn. As a linebacker, who sometimes posed as a tight end at Spring Woods High School, he had walked on the Aggie football team and moved his way up to fourth-team safety. Not a big move, but a move all the same.

And now he was sitting alone in the bleachers, watching some friends from the Corps race up and down the fresh white lines of Kyle Field in pursuit of a place on the 12th man kickoff team.

You can do this, they had told him.

Don't need to.

Why not?

I'm already on the team.

It's the fourth team.

I'll get my shot.

Hell, his friends told him, you're a walk-on. Walk-ons wear burnt orange jerseys in practice.

What'll the kickoff team wear, Bevans wanted to know.

I hear it's red jerseys.

Why red?

It's better than burnt orange.

He couldn't argue with that.

At least come and watch us, his friends said.

So he had.

Day one, Bevans thought, they all looked a little foolish. The field was crowded. Everyone was running in different directions, and some were having trouble running at all. If that's the best Jackie Sherrill can find, he thought, then the Aggies may have some real problems next fall. Not a lot of quickness out there. Not a lot of size. As a fourth-team safety, Bevans certainly thought he had as much insight into the strengths and weaknesses of the football team as anybody else.

Day two, he asked the question that had been rattling around his mind all night. Exactly what are the coaches looking for when they choose the 12th man team?

Somebody fast, he was told.

Alan Smith (13 huddles with the 12th man unit, including Leroy Hallman (6), Tom Arthur (4), Tom Christner (3), and Tom Bevans (8), as they prepare for another battle downfield. The 12th man lived in fear of the dreaded touchback.

And big.

And mean doesn't hurt.

By day three, Tom Bevans believed he could qualify for at least two of the three. He knew he was big enough and probably mean enough. The coaches had already seen him in pads. They knew he packed a pretty healthy punch with those 207 pounds. He didn't mind throwing himself into the middle of a good fight, and he didn't bounce off of a lot of hits. They already realized his speed had never burned a hole in a pair of tennis shoes. Slow feet and a few pounds over two hundred would never earn him anything resembling a scholarship, and, although he hated to admit it, a fourth-team safety might never see the field on game day.

The 12th man team, he decided, could well be his ticket for a smattering of playing time. He had heard that Coach Sherrill was looking for a wild bunch resembling a suicide squad. Well, Bevans was a psychology major, so he could be as wild, as crazy, as suicidal as any of them. Of course, it was all a gamble. At least, that's what Tom Bevans kept telling himself. One bad kickoff return, and the team would probably wither up and die where it stood. But what the hell?

He walked down from the bleachers, vaulted over the fence, and began looking around for David Beal.

I'd like to tryout, he said.

Beal nodded.

Am I too late?

Beal shrugged. Not if you can play, he said.

I'd like to find out.

Beal looked around at the masses and the multitudes jogging across the field. It's a long shot, he said.

Everything about football is, Bevans said.

David Beal handed him a slip of paper numbered 252. His was the last number handed out in the spring of 1983.

David Bishop was living a lie. He was small at 5-11 and 150 pounds. He wore glasses. The *Bryan Eagle* wrote that he looked more like a walk-on for the glee club than a candidate for the football team. He ran the forty in 4.89 seconds, which, he conceded, was pretty slow, especially for a wide receiver. Footballs thrown his way by quarterback John Elkins bounced off his shoulder pads or sailed through his hands. But Bishop kept passing himself off as a genuine football player, and he showed no fear when it came time to shove his head in the meat grinder. I'm not out here to catch passes, he said. We're out here to do the dirty work.

The trouble was, David Bishop had never before played football. He wouldn't have been able to put on his uniform if Barry Stevens hadn't shown him where to place the pads. The helmet gave me a headache the first few days, he said, but then I started to get the hang of it.

No one but Bishop and a small circle of friends knew the truth, and they weren't passing any judgments or telling any tales. Don't admit you've never played before, he was told. They'll rip you up. It might prejudice the coaches. They're looking for a reason to cut players anyway.

They won't have to look hard to find a reason to cut me, Bishop said. Me being out here is the only reasy anybody needs.

He walked to the dressing room where the names had been posted for the first cut. If your name was scribbled on the list, don't bother to come back. That was the rule. It's over. You're out. David Bishop looked. He took a deep breath, not quite believing his eyes, and looked again. His name was nowhere to be found.

Tom Ray was a country boy, a farm boy, and farmers were a tough breed down around Floresville.

The dairy operation had been in his family for a hundred and eight years, and Ray had always lived in the home his grandparents had built a century or more ago. Dairy cattle, cotton fields, and tradition. That's what he knew best. Milk generally sold whether the cotton grew or not, and the Ray family was always at the mercy of the weather, which was always too hot and seldom too wet.

Tom Ray had been an all-district running back in high school, and he was a hot-shot, big-time sprinter, clocked as the thirteenth fastest 200-yard dash man in Texas. He could bench press 325 pounds and handle 600 pounds in the squat, but the speed and the muscle had not helped him find a scholarship in a Division 1 school,

At Texas A&M, he was merely a determined face in the maddening crowd, fighting for one of ten spots on the 12th man kickoff team. In the tryouts, he ran a 4.59 in the forty, fast enough to raise a few eyebrows, and Tom Ray had always been able to bring the lumber. He looked around after practice and recognized immediately that some of the players were definitely better than he was.

He hated to admit it, but he did. Tom Ray, however, had heard a few scattered rumors that David Beal might be carrying as many as twenty players when the season started, and nowhere on the field were there twenty players with more talent and ability than he had. He was sure of it.

Tom Ray went home at night and tried to soak the soreness from his bones. He did not remember hurting that much, that badly, or in that many places in high school.

Robert Crouch had been known to stretch the truth from time to time, but he never lied to himself. He knew he wasn't the best athlete on the field. His old high school coach had told him that. So Crouch worked to make up any deficit he might have by strapping on his running shoes and covering more miles more often than anyone else who happened to believe they were serious 12th man material.

Crouch was in a Marine Corps outfit, and he always crawled out of bed every morning at five o'clock, usually with just an hour or two of sleep under his belt, and hit the ground on the move. Historically, with the Corps, he would go a simple two miles. Now, he had begun to lengthen the distance to four miles.

Whatever it took, he told himself, I am going to be on that kickoff team next fall. If it takes ten miles a day, that's all right. He lowered his head, tried to shake the ache from his muscles, turned into the wind, and followed the flickering shadows around the track.

A girl he knew on campus roomed with Miss Texas, who had also been Miss Texas A&M, Sheri Ryman.

Crouch happened to mention one afternoon that he had become a dedicated runner, and he thought he saw Sheri Ryman's eyes widen with a flicker of interest.

Do you run at night, she asked.

Robert Crouch grinned.

I do now, he said.

So he would run the cinder ovals at five o'clock every morning for himself, then jog along at midnight alongside Miss Texas. It was a sacrifice, he knew.

But she said she felt a lot safer and a little more comfortable not having to run those late, dark hours alone.

A little extra roadwork, Crouch reasoned, never hurt anyone.

James Barrett (16) and Keith Newton (17) teamed up anchor a formidable first year for the 12th man team. Their exploits served to build a strong foundation for those teams that would follow on a field where they left their sweat and blood.

Chapter 9

Coaches Jackie Sherrill, David Beal, and Curley Hallman had drawn up their master plan in early spring. Let speed and athleticism make the easy cuts. Look in their eyes and determine who has a streak of fear lurking in their subconscious mind. Cut the number down to forty players before spring training. Let them put on the pads, stick them out there one-on-one, man-against-man, with scholarship players, then select the final ten players who would comprise the 12th man kickoff squad before summer began. A simple plan. Easy to execute. Shouldn't be a problem.

The final forty players, however, kept it from being so simple. No one quit. No one backed down. No one got hit hard enough to stay down. The final forty kept coming back for more. You dish it out was the attitude, and we can take it. Damaged and abused, physically and mentally, they tried to sleep at night with the harsh, brittle echo of Curley Hallman's cursing coursing through their minds. He's just trying to make us mad, they said. He just wants to run us off. We're not leaving. And no one did. Bruises turned different shades, from black to purple. Blood dried up. As far as they were concerned, the war had not yet begun.

As Robert Crouch said, I needed a jersey with a handle on it so someone could pull me up after every play. He pointed out, the coaches thought they could judge us by merely looking at us. They couldn't. They

still could not measure the heart or the spirit inside of us. They put our 40-yard dash times on paper, but that didn't work either. Sometimes, the slowest guys were out there making the toughest plays. We were mad men. Find the worthless peckerwood with the ball. That's what Coach Beal said. Then put him on the ground as rudely as possible. We did it. Every day we did it. Over and over we did it.

Other than that, we had no purpose in life.

The afternoon had grown long and weary. Tom Bumgardner was playing right cornerback on the scout team, and he saw the sweep headed in the other direction. He was completely out of the play and jogging across the field. No, he said. I was loafing. I never took it easy, my motor was always running, but, for whatever reason, I realized that I was fifteen yards away from the tackle, so I took the play off.

The pain came without warning.

It was a quick, numbing blast to the back of his head.

Sudden impact, and Bumgardner hit the ground before he knew he was falling. He lay there, dazed and confused.

Who hit me, he wondered.

Where did he come from?

I never saw him.

Curley Hallman had blindsided Bumgardner and taken him out

with one clean shoulder to the back of his neck. Curley Hallman had run across the field at full speed and drilled Bumgardner from behind. And now he was standing above the fallen player, telling him in a few well-chosen words, don't ever let me see you loafing out here again.

He never did.

Jackie Sherrill's scholarship players did not know what to think about a bunch of misfit volunteers from the student body who had come out to interfere with their practice, invade their turf, get in their way, cause more trouble than they were worth. Linebacker Greg Berry was an old-school Aggie, and he didn't like what he saw going on around him. As he said, when Jackie Sherrill arrived, we didn't know him from Adam, and he didn't know us.

We were convinced he was determined to weed out the players he didn't want, then go recruit nationally. We were afraid that if somebody didn't have a good spring, twisted a knee, or got hurt in any way, he'd lose his scholarship. Almost as soon as he hit town, Sherrill began canceling out any scholarships that had been offered by Tom Wilson, and that included one to my brother, Ray, who would have been the third Berry to play football for Texas A&M. One by one, I kept seeing my friends leave or be asked to leave the team. My recruiting class had thirty players, and it was ranked third in the nation. When I graduated, there were only seven of us left.

The Aggie scholarship players heard that the 12th man kickoff team project was nothing more than a patented Jackie Sherrill ploy to build a larger scout team. As Berry said, Coach wanted more butts on the field. Coach wanted more tackling dummies. Hurt somebody who didn't count. Keep the varsity as free from injury as possible. Berry said, by the time we wandered out of the locker room and began stretching, the 12th man team unit was already running wind sprints and doing their best to dislodge somebody's head in some of the damndest tackling drills I ever saw. Hit and get hit. That's all they ever did. Hit and get hit. They were all running around, not unlike chickens with their heads cut off, trying to be All-Americans in hand-me-down shoes and helmets.

So what did you do?

When they ran the scout team, we lined up and knocked the hell out of them. If they were crazy enough to get back up, we'd knock a little more hell out of them. We knocked out a lot of hell, but we never were able to knock those grins off their faces.

Greg Berry watched Jackie Sherrill on the field and said, Coach gave the appearance of being so arrogant that we believed he might be able to turn horse manure to gold. He kept twirling that whistle, looking to see who had it and who didn't, who could take it and who couldn't, who could play for him and who would be better off on the road to some other school. We watched the 12th man team and didn't particularly trust them. They would come at us like a herd of wild mustangs. They had nothing to lose. We did. If

they got hurt, Pickard would drag them off and forget them. If a varsity player was injured, we had a problem. If he was a starter, we had a serious problem. Jeff Payne was a linebacker and a strong religious individual. He didn't smoke, drink, or curse, and while we were working on the punt team in practice, a member of the 12th man scout team came down and rammed Jeff in the shoulder. It popped out of the socket, and Jeff was rolling on the ground in excruciating pain.

Sherrill was yelling, dammit, Payne, get up.

Jeff couldn't get up.

Sherrill walked over, grabbed him by the pads, and yelled, Payne, do you believe in God?

Yes, sir, I do, Jeff answered.

Sherrill dropped him. There, Coach said, you're healed. Now get your worthless self back out there.

Poor old Jeff. He was hurt. He was scared. He was afraid he would lose his scholarship. He crawled to his feet and went after the next punt regardless of how badly he hurt. He would rather die than get cut.

Jeff Payne had a certain amount of empathy for the 12th man team members even if no one else did. Early on, he had walked up to Tom Christner, as he did to others, held out his hand, and said, when I came here, I was a walk-on, too. I got lucky. I earned a scholarship. But I know what you're going through.

Varsity is pretty rough on us.

We try to be rough on everybody.

I sometimes feel like we're banging our heads against the wall, Christner said.

Jeff Payne grinned. I just wanted you to know I believe in you, he said. Keep your head in there, and you'll get the job done.

Tight end Mark Lewis realized that the 12th man was Coach Sherrill's team, and he tried to diplomatically ruffle as few feathers as possible. The idea sounds great to me, he said. Then his disdain for the unit crept into his words. Hopefully the other teams won't break anything on us, he said. And I'm afraid this 12th man team might affect some of

Coach Jackie Sherrill was building a new Texas A&M tradition around such 12th man playerss as Tom Arthur.

the scholarship players who work so hard at practice. Their only chance to play may be on kickoffs, and now they're having their jobs taken away from them. No animosity, perhaps. Just legitimate concern. Why the hell didn't Jackie just leave well enough alone? Lewis didn't say it, but he thought it.

Another scholarship player was asked, do you think these guys can cut it?

Sure, he replied, as long as the kickoff goes through the end zone.

Above it all was an underlying feeling of suspicion, resentment, and more than a little bitterness.

If you could play football at the collegiate level, prove it. Not just today. Not just tomorrow. But every day. It was not a one-game battle. It was a season-long war. Did you have what it took? Could you survive the grind? Could you bite the bullet, swallow the pain, and get back up when the cartilage was torn? That was what the scholarship athletes wanted to see. If you wanted respect, earn it. If you couldn't, go on back home and

Nothing felt better for an Aggie kickoff coverage team than to drill a ball carrier from the University of Texas. All games were important. It just felt better to drill a Longhorn.

leave football to players who had high-dollar scholarships that said they were football players. Walk-ons were a different class, generally second, if that high.

For the 12th man kickoff team, practice became a death march. Their baptism by fire began thirty minutes early. Long before any scholarship athlete wandered out of the tunnel, they were on the field, going nose-to-nose, in a winner-take-all series of tackling drills. Line up ten yards apart and charge. Helmet to helmet. Eyes spun. Heads ached. A whistle. A charge. Then get up, get in line, and do it again. Every day was an aspirin kind of day. Pain relievers before practice, during practice, and most certainly after practice. Beer was good. Whiskey was better. Neither would chase the pain away, but the aches became more bearable. Fractures. Broken bones. Pulled hamstrings. Charley horses. A hospital

was out of the question. Bartenders were easier to find than doctors, and Billy Pickard never complained about players taking their medicine from the Dixie Chicken.

So that's the way it was: thirty minutes of nose-to-nose tackling, two hours, maybe more, of running the scout team against the varsity, then along about six o'clock, while everyone else had drifted off to the locker room to clean their wounds after two hours of practice in the scalding, 120-degree heat of Kyle Field, members of the 12th man team lined up on the forty-yard line and spent another thirty minutes running belly flat and wide open down the field covering kickoffs. A kick. A block. Shed that block, dammit. A tackle. Breath gone. Sweat dripping. Joints throbbing. Do it again. And again.

Sprint, Beal yelled. You can't let up a minute. Sprint.

The players were nearing exhaustion.

The ball was in the air.

Go get the sumbitch, Hallman was screaming. No matter what, go get him.

Rock Johnson was leading the charge. He had bloodstains on his pants. It had been a good day. He reached down and got his hands on a loose football as it bounced away from the returner. Then Johnson muffed it. He hit the ground, and the ball rolled crazily and harmlessly away from his outstretched fingers.

Damn.

He knew the dog pile was coming before it hit him.

Damn.

That's the reason we call you Rock, Hallman screamed as Johnson dug his way out of the pile and limped back to line up for another kickoff. You thought it was because you were so damn tough. It's because of your hands. You got stone hands.

Rock Johnson wasn't laughing.

Neither was Hallman.

Coach Pettibone had always called him "Rock" because Johnson was almost too dangerous to have on the other side of the ball. He kept knocking out my wide receivers, the coach said. They would come out on a dead run, and Johnson would cold-cock them, hit them like a rock.

It wouldn't have done to call Johnson "Cold-Cock."

The name "Rock" worked much better.

Ike Liles lost his father, who had been a first sergeant and shot up pretty badly in Korea, then in Vietnam. His final wish was, bury me face down so the world can kiss my ass, Liles said, and his only advice to me was, Ike, don't ever let anybody call you a son of a bitch. Sooner or later, most everyone did. So I fought a lot. In fact, I fought every chance I got. In West Texas, it's what you did on a slow day. In high school, we'd get in a scuffle, and somebody would always jump in and break it up. So we didn't win many fights, and we didn't lose any. We just skinned up our knuckles and our faces a little.

Liles and the 12th man dressed separate and apart in the freshmen locker room. It was segregation at its best. Race had nothing to do with it. Being walk-ons, unwanted, and unappreciated second-class citizens did.

The scholarship athletes had their own private quarters. Sometimes, they weren't private enough.

After practice, Liles said, everybody would pull the tape and gauze from around their ankles, and it came off like a cast. We'd wad it up, throw it across the room, and try to nail somebody. A ball of tape sailed past me, hit the wall, and fell at Jeff Sciba's feet on the varsity side of the room. He casually picked it up and put it in his locker.

The next thing I knew, he was all over me like a wildcat with his balls in a trap. Jeff Sciba was a defensive tackle who weighed 260 pounds, Liles said, and if he wasn't mad, he was looking for a reason to get mad. We were nose to nose before I knew I was in trouble, and, by then, it was too late. He grabbed my hair, twisted my neck, lifted me off the floor, threw me down like he was trying to get snot off the end of his finger. Then he proceeded to thoroughly whip me in something roughly less than twenty-two seconds. I lost the fight about the time I knew I was in one. I still don't know why he came after me. I never asked, and he never said.

On the field, it was different. On the field, Ike Liles thought he had a fighting chance. James Flowers, the great defensive back, and I were in a tackling drill, Liles said. He thought I came in a little too hard, and I didn't think I'd come in hard enough. He thought we were running the drill at half speed. The 12th man boys never went half speed. We took our shots anytime we could get them. Fair. Square. No cheap shots. But if some hot-shot varsity athlete didn't keep his head on a swivel, we'd make it spin. James was a pretty boy. Didn't want to mess up his pretty face. Didn't like the way I was treating him. He threw a punch. I threw a punch.

We both stepped back so somebody could step in like a gentleman is supposed to do and break up the fight.

No one did.

Everybody just stood around, thinking they were about to see a damn good fight, and it might have been a good one, too. But we were just too tired to fight. I hit him in the helmet. He hit my helmet. We hadn't hurt anybody's helmet, but we sure did hurt our hands. The coach blew his whistle and let both of us save face, especially James' pretty face. If I had gotten another scar, no one would have known the difference.

Only now was Barry Stevens learning about the larger-than-life-size targets that scout team members wore squarely on their backs, their chests, their helmets. We were tackling dummies, he said. We were blocking dummies. We were probably dummies for being out there. We were always stum-

bling around in the line of fire, considered fair game by anyone wearing shoulder pads. Knock one of us out and the coaches would just go back up in the stands and find somebody else. We were expendable.

Barry Stevens had lined up at strong safety. He knew his responsibility. His job was to come up, give the quarterback a read on the option, and flare out to contain the pitch. Easy to remember. He could run it by the numbers. What they failed to tell me, he said, was that a 270-pound pulling guard was on his way around the line to clean my clock.

I read the quarterback.

I had the pitch man squarely in my sights.

I had him bottled up.

There was no place for him to go.

The guard hit me.

I never heard him. I never saw him.

The world turned a strange shade of green, then went black.

I was trying to catch my breath, and I could hear the coach from somewhere on the other side of never, never land yelling, do it again.

Hell, I was thinking, he's gonna run it again. Didn't kill me the first time. Gonna try it again. I'm a dead man walking.

I moved up on the quarterback.

Here came the guard.

The simple law of physics said I would lose.

I did.

And the coach was yelling, do it again.

Damn.

I wasn't young. I hadn't played competitive football in five years. I wasn't big. I wasn't strong. But I was smart enough to know he had my number, and he wasn't smart enough to realize his number was up. I moved up on the quarterback, just like my coach said I was supposed to do.

And here came the guard. This time, I knew he was coming. It took three times, but I finally had it figured out. I grabbed him by the jersey,

Tom Arthur (4) is on the move, ready to hit anyone who gets in his way. His mission was to make a tackle or blast the wedge so someone else could bring the kick returner down. The 12th man unit practiced an hour longer than varsity every day to become a deadly and finely tuned machine.

threw him aside, and drilled the quarterback with my helmet planted as hard as I could plant it in the hollow of his chest. He grunted as the air left his lungs, and he thought it might be for good. His legs buckled, and Sherrill was going wild. I thought Curley Hallman had some choice phrases, but Sherrill was inventing new ones as he came running up to me. I didn't know the man could run that fast. He was in my face, and his words had a fair amount of spittle attached to them. He was calling me every name but my right one.

You don't hit my quarterback, he screamed.

Never.

Leave my quarterback alone.

And that was my introduction to Kevin Murray. He was fast. He was smart. He had a strong arm. He could throw like a rocket. He was a great leader. And I had just put him flat on his back.

God, it felt good.

It was the scrimmage before the spring game, and Tom Bumgardner could see a glimmer of hope in his future. He might be working hard to make the 12th man kickoff team, but Jackie Sherrill had moved him to second-team cornerback. At last, someone had noticed. He had speed. He had moxie. He had what it took. Nothing could stop him now. Bumgardner's heart was pumping. His adrenaline was running on high octane. He tore through the blocker and slammed violently into the ball carrier. He did not arrive alone. Bumgardner felt someone jump on the pile, and his elbow was driven hard into the ground. A sharp pain ripped the nerve endings and shot out his fingertips.

He clenched his jaws and looked down. A turf burn, he thought. Thank God, it's just a turf burn.

By morning, his arm had swollen, and he suspected the worse. Before practice, he walked over to the field house and searched out Billy Pickard. Pickard absolutely hated us, he said. I was scared to death of him. Pain didn't bother him at all as long as we were the ones who were suffering.

I think the arm's broken, Bumgardner said.

You on that 12th man team?

I'm trying to be.

Probably lose your spot, Pickard told him. Serves you right.

I'm also running second-team cornerback, Bumgardner said.

Not anymore. Pickard grinned.

He sent Bumgardner to the infirmary, better known as the quack shack, and an X-ray confirmed the break. You'll have to have surgery to get the arm mended, a doctor told him. You have a real blockage in the blood supply that feeds your arm.

How long will I have to wear a cast, Bumgardner wanted to know.

The rest of the year.

Can I play football in a hard cast?

The doctor grinned. As long as you don't get caught, he said.

Curley Hallman was a hard case. No doubt about it. He hammered the defensive backs on his 12th man team without mercy. No matter how fast they ran, he wanted them down the field faster. No matter how hard they tried, it was never good enough. We're not out here to grade effort, he shouted. We want results.

Hallman verbally battered them. The excrement from a horse with diarrhea was about as nice a reference as he ever used. But he'd be damn if anybody else got in their faces. God have mercy on anyone who tried.

They were his charges.

They were his kids.

And, by damn, a few of them were pretty good.

If Curley Hallman abused them, it was tough love. It anyone else jumped down their throats, somebody was way out of line, and hell was a high price to pay.

In practice, it had been a train wreck. Jeff Nelson, one of A&M's elite receivers, cut sharply over the middle, hauled in a quick pass, and Tom Bumgardner leveled him. Nelson hit the ground hard. The ball rolled harmlessly away.

George Pugh, coaching the receivers, ran toward Bumgardner. You can't hit one of my scholarship receivers, he yelled.

That's what I'm here for.

Not down here, it's not, Pugh screamed. Who told you to go full speed?

We always go full speed.

I'm not losing one of my receivers over the likes of you, Pugh growled. If you get hurt, we can just drag your ass off. If he gets hurt, we got ourselves a problem.

I'm just doing what I'm supposed to do.

You ain't worth it, Pugh yelled again. You ain't worth nothin'.

By now, Curley Hallman, running hard across the field and out of breath, had reached the confrontation. His face was red. The veins were popping on the side of his head. He sure the hell is, Hallman screamed at Pugh.

You're man ain't worth a horse turd, Pugh said again.

He damn sure is.

And there they stood, neither blinking, neither flinching, a coach who had been a great player for Alabama spitting, sputtering, and verbally sparring with a coach who had been a great player for Texas A&M. Neither was giving an inch. Hell, they hadn't hit anybody who counted in a long time, but the thought was beginning to cross their minds.

They were on the same side.

They may as well have been a world apart.

You can't treat my player that way, Hallman said.

He can't hit my receiver that way, Pugh said.

Then, by gawd, don't send your damn receiver over the middle, Hallman said.

Have your man let up a little, Pugh said. We're not out here to kill each other. What does he think he is, a hot damn All-American?

You think Texas is gonna let up next fall, Hallman asked. Your man had better learn to take a hit and hold on to the ball.

If looks could kill, Hallman would have been a dead man.

Hallman stared with daggers up at Pugh.

Pugh stared with daggers down at Hallman.

For a moment, all was quiet. Tension had grown as lethal as the plague. Finally, Hallman put his cap on backward and stalked across the field. Pugh spit. Hallman was chewing nails. Pugh spit again.

Tom Bumgardner looked down at Nelson. Sorry, he whispered.

You didn't do anything wrong, Nelson said.

You ain't worth a horse turd, Pugh said under his breath, and Bumgardner had never felt more humiliated in his life.

Robert Crouch had been wide receiver and occasional quarterback in high school. Now he was a scout team linebacker. How did I get myself in that position, he wondered. Who did I upset? When Crouch woke up every morning, he knew that before the day ended, he would be squaring up against the great Billy Cannon, Jr., son of LSU's famed Heisman Trophy winner, a kid who was big and fast and had the heart and conscience of a serial killer. Cannon didn't like the 12th man team, Crouch said. No. Billy Cannon didn't like anybody. He was mean and proud of it. I decided the only reason he played football was

Alan Smith (13) hammers the ball downfield with Tom Arthur (4) and Leroy Hallman (6) gearing up for action, which was only a few yards away. Players on most teams throught kickoffs were a chore. For the 12th man, kickoffs gave them an opportunity to prove that, somewhere in the country, a college coach had made a tactical mistake by not recruiting them.

because he liked to inflict pain, primarily on me. He got to do it often.

Crouch being a linebacker didn't particularly mean that his job on the scout team was tackling anybody. No. That would have been too easy. It was his duty to serve as the surrogate running back, take a pitch, run as hard as he could, every time he could, and know for dead certain that Billy Cannon was moving up to cut him in half. We'd get the hell beat out of us, Crouch said, and then we'd hustle back, get in line, shake out the cobwebs, and wait for the privilege of being taken apart again. One big hit after the other. Full speed. No mercy. Faster, the coaches were yelling. Don't let down. Pick it up. And Cannon would hit me again. They wanted us to quit, he said. Hit us hard enough and often enough, and we'd throw in the white towel. *No mas. No mas.* That's what they thought. It didn't turn out that way.

In other drills, Crouch found himself with the daunting task of blocking Billy Cannon, who came across the line like a hired assassin on a thunderball, only faster. Cannon would one day become the number one draft choice of the Dallas Cowboys. There was no way I could take him on, man-to-man, Crouch said. So I began cutting him to take him down. No cheap shots. I stayed below his knees. But I kept on cutting his feet out from under him.

Crouch lay on the ground after one collision that left his chest sag-

ging somewhere down between his belt loops and kneecaps. Cannon reached down, picked him up by his shoulder pads, and shook him like a rag doll. Cut that crap out, he said.

I'm not trying to hurt you, Crouch told him. I'm just doing everything I can to make this football team.

You could ruin a knee, cutting me like that.

Crouch gritted his teeth. Listen, he said, I'll do whatever it takes to get some coach's attention out here, and if the only way I can block you is to cut you, then that's what I'm going on do. I'm not letting you or anybody keep me off this team.

Billy Cannon stared at him.

Silence.

He thought it over. I'll make a deal with you, Cannon said slowly. If you promise not to cut me anymore, on every fourth or fifth play, I'll let you block me.

Crouch nodded.

Cannon grinned and dropped Crouch to the ground with a thud. The rest of the time, he said, I'm gonna kick your ever-lovin' ass.

It wasn't much of a deal, Crouch knew, but it was better than he expected and as good as he was going to get.

One afternoon, Crouch looked up and saw Larry Edmondson, a

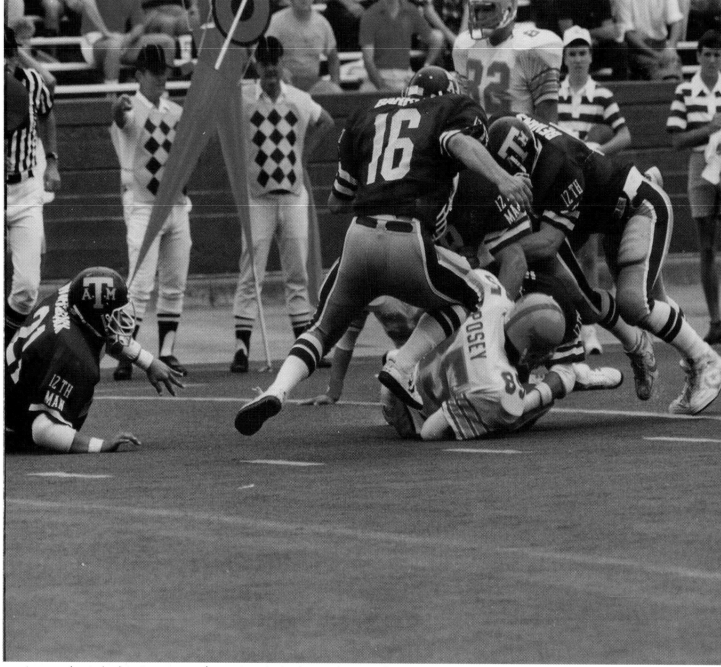

Mark Wurzbach (21) looks up as Brian Edwards (16) leaps into the fray. The 12th man well understood that the violent force of a team playing together was much more effective than a single man out to make a tackle alone.

graduate assistant, running across the field toward him. You're not a linebacker anymore, Edmondson told him. You've been moved.

Where?

To tight end.

Robert Crouch grinned. No more Billy Cannon, he thought. Never again would he have to face the meanest, toughest, hardest-hitting, most vicious man in the free world.

Crouch felt downright giddy.

He strutted across the field and headed to the far hash marks where the tight ends were huddled up. Coach George Pugh waved him over. What do you want me to do, Crouch asked.

In this drill, you gotta block the defensive end, Pugh told him. You think a worthless pile of dogmeat like you can do that?

Crouch nodded. Hell, he had been tangling with Billy Cannon. He

had already gone to hell and back. He was ready for anything.

You're gonna block him, Pugh said.

Robert Crouch looked across the line of scrimmage and came face to face with Ray Childress, who would one day be the number one draft choice of the Houston Oilers.

My God, Crouch thought, I've really made somebody mad around here. They want me dead or dying.

Before the afternoon came to a merciful conclusion, Robert Crouch was longing to line up against Billy Cannon again.

Ray Childress was different, he said. He'd knock us down, then smile about it. He would run right through you. He never tried to run around you. He didn't have to. I would have tried to cut him, but I just wasn't that strong. To cut down Ray Childress, I would have needed a double-bladed axe.

Larry "Rock" Johnson knew how to finish off a hard day without any concern at all for etiquette. He was a little undersized, the coaches knew, coming in at about 5-10 and a 185 pounds before practice began and about ten pounds less when the final whistle had blown. He ran a 4.7 forty on a good day, but Beal realized early on that, pound for pound, Rock Johnson was one of his five top players. When the players began their one-on-one drills, few 12th men prospects had any desire to line up against Johnson. He could take a good player and make him look bad. He could take a bad player and hurt him.

Since he had traded his burnt orange walk-on jersey for a chance to wear red, Johnson knew what to expect. I might not get there as fast as some of them, he said, but I got there harder than the rest of them. He left a few bruises and never worried about those of his own. When Johnson was on the scout team, Coach Jim Helms always knew that his running backs, at the end of the day, realized they had worked out in the twisted teeth of a rusty meat grinder. So he kept sending the likes of Johnny Hector, Ernest Jackson, Roger Vick, Keith Woodside, and Thomas Jackson against the Rock. Johnson made them pay a terrible price for every yard they gained. Indifference became respect. The harder Rock Johnson worked, the harder they had to work. When the Rock was running full bore, he had no kill switch.

You need a new drill, Johnson told Coach Hallman.

What do you suggest?

Put me on one goal line, Johnson said, and put the ball carrier a hundred yards away on the other. We both run as hard as we can and have ourselves a meeting head-on at the fifty.

He'll get to the fifty long before you do.

He'll wish he'd never crossed it.

At first, Hallman thought Rock Johnson was kidding. The eyes said otherwise. That's suicide, Hallman said as he walked away.

No, the Rock thought. It's Russian roulette, and I have the bullet.

So now Johnson was seated in a Huntsville pool hall. He was slamming full cans of beer against his head just to see how loud he could make them pop when the metal seams broke. One after another, he hammered the beer cans against his head. One was frozen. Johnson didn't know it. The beer can hit the side of his head like a chunk of cheap concrete, and the Rock felt his chair slip out from under him. He lay on the floor. He was bleeding like a stuck pig.

You gonna check on him, Tom Bevans asked Crouch.

Nope.

You think he's gonna be all right?

He's the Rock, ain't he?

Bevans nodded and lined up an eight ball for the side pocket.

Five minutes later, maybe it was less, Johnson opened an eye.

Where am I, he wanted to know.

Same place you been, Crouch said. You haven't moved.

How come it's so dark?

It's night.

Johnson crawled to his feet. He gingerly touched the side of his head. It's gonna hurt tomorrow, won't it, he asked.

Only when you put your helmet on.

Damn beer had a kick to it, Johnson said.

In March, the *Battalion* reported, Sherrill made a point of assuring "non-believers" that the kickoff team would not turn into a disaster. There's no question about that, he said. It will be successful.

Although it might seem there would be some animosity among the players as a result of the 12th man idea, Sherrill said he had not felt any need to talk to the team about the situation. Don't have to, Sherrill said. If these players go through and become a part of the team, they deserve a spot just like everyone else. But they'll have to earn a spot. They know that, but if one of the 12th man hopefuls performs well enough to earn a spot elsewhere on the team, then that position belongs to him.

They were all fighting for so few positions. The odds were stacked against them, and attrition had stolen all the bodies it would take. As David Beal said, some of them are small, but by watching their faces when they work, I'd be afraid if one of them hit me.

The 12th man team members slowly peeled off their red practice jerseys and pulled on Maroon and White uniforms for the annual spring varsity-alumni football game. It was real action. The score might not count for much, but the kickoff tackles would. A new jolt of fevered adrenaline hit their bodies and jump-started their hearts.

The *Battalion* reported, the team covered both kickoffs and punts, and only one return man made it past the 20-yard line. Still not everything went smoothly. We did have some problems, Coach David Beal said. I thought some of them weren't sprinting downfield fast enough. When they slowed down, too many people were bunched up in the middle. Beal did point out that the squad was hyped for the game, and that it helped their performance.

They were really excited about the game – their eyes were bugging out at the opening kickoff. The surprising thing to me, Beal said, is that most of the players knew how to tackle ahead of time. Their football knowledge really impressed me. After the first week, most of the players had the tackling form down. As far as motivating the players, Beal says he's had no problems. We've tried to go through some drills at half-speed, but these guys are so pumped up that they go full speed anyway. Beal said it's special to work with these guys because they're not recruited athletes. While they may be less talented, they work harder than the scholarship athletes because they know they've got to in order to play football. I expect them to work harder. Another advantage of working with the squad, Beal says, is that you only have to tell them how to do something one time. After that, Beal says, they'll do it right every time.

I think we did better than anyone anticipated we would, Keith Newton said.

We hit 'em where it hurts, Barry Stevens said.

Don't get too excited, Robert Crouch told them.

Why not?

We were playing old men.

Hell, Stevens said, there were some out there who's playing pro ball. A few others are looking for an NFL team, and they've got a damn good chance to find one.

They took it easy on us.

Newton shook his head. Aggies never take it easy, he said.

Tom Arthur (3) joins with the 12th man to spearhead a scout team tackle against varsity in practice. Jackie Sherrill always said that his 12th man team played so hard in practice, it made his varsity better. The 12th man never went half speed.

David Beal agonized over the decision facing him. He had forty players on his 12th man kickoff team: fifteen defensive backs, seventeen linebackers, four defensive ends, and four wide receivers. Most could play a little. A few could play a lot. For the most part, there wasn't an appreciable amount of difference between any of them.

He studied the names far into the night, writing down the plusses and minuses for each. One lacked speed, but he could hit. One had speed, but he would rather run down a ball carrier from behind than meet him helmet-to-helmet. They all had heart. They all had character. If some didn't play with a hangover, they couldn't play at all. Pain will do that to a man.

Jackie Sherrill had told him to wait until after spring training, then cut the list down to the top ten players he had. That's who we'll carry on the squad, he said.

I can't do that right now, Beal said.

Why not?

We can't afford to make a mistake.

It's your team, Sherrill said. Do what you think is best.

The forty had assembled in the meeting room, and Beal could see the hope, the anguish, the fear masking their faces. Emotions were so real he could reach out and touch them. They had all worked for this single moment in time. For some, the end would come with a word, not a collision.

This was it, they knew.

This was the day.

Only a few would be chosen.

It was so quiet, Beal could not even hear any of them breathing. Maybe they were afraid to breathe. Maybe it hurt to breathe. Gentlemen, he said, we've made our decision.

Shoulders stiffened. Jaws were clenched. The palms of their hands were coated with sweat. One mistake, they knew. One mistake in practice had meant the difference between making the team and losing out altogether. They searched their minds.

Which mistake had they made that cost them? Which day had they not run as hard as they could? Which practice would they love to have over again?

Gentlemen, Beal continued, we're bringing all forty of you back for the fall. The final cut won't be made until after two-a-days. Have a great summer, and do everything you can to get a little faster and a little stronger. I'm counting on you.

The players looked at each other. Tom Christner had left the field at the end of spring training bruised and bloodied. It didn't bother him. He had been bruised and bloodied before.

He fully believed that David Beal would make the final cuts before summer, and now Beal was saying, come back in the fall and we'll do it all again. Give the wounds time to heal and the blood time to dry, and we'll do it all again.

It felt like the forty of us were facing an execution, Christner said, and we had just been granted a reprieve.

That's all it was.

Nothing had really changed.

Their heads were still on the chopping block, but the axe wouldn't be sharpened again until August.

Shortly after Jackie Sherrill became head coach of the Aggies, he watched the Fightin' Aggie Band of Colonel Joe T. Haney and remarked to Billy Pickard, when our football can execute as well as the band, we'll win the Southwest Conference.

Chapter 10

Keith Newton limped home that summer. It was the first time he had allowed himself to limp since the spring scrimmage. He had run downfield, hadn't hit anybody, and nobody hit him, but suddenly Newton turned sharply one way, and his knee headed in a different direction. He heard the pop before he felt the pain, and the pain hit him like a stray rifle shot. He gritted his teeth and kept on playing. An injury might be a death knell, but, as long as Pickard did not find out about the bum knee, then the coaches wouldn't have a reason to cut him. Coaches were always looking for a reason, any reason. He'd be damned if he gave them one.

Newton would spend all summer jogging and finding his way to the gym as often as possible. The cartilage had been torn, but he was convinced that a few free weights and a lot of will power were as close to a faith healing as he would get. Leg curls. Leg lifts. Time after time. Rep after rep. Day after day. Surely they would help. Keith Newton did not even go see his hometown doctor. He made his own diagnosis. He would figure out his own cure. Newton did not want anyone to tell him his football career was over. If he ran hard enough and often enough, maybe, just maybe, the pain would go away.

Jeff Boutwell thought about joining the Corps of Cadets, but the Corps, he said, was way too intense. He thought he might play football instead. After all, he had been a 6-1, 200-pound linebacker for Cameron's state championship team and had turned down

an opportunity to play football for the Air Force Academy. Boutwell was convinced he could still play as well as anyone, and the 12th man just may have been created solely for his personal indulgence. I thought I could run through a stone wall if it didn't get out of the way, he said. He worked out for Beal, day after day, and every time the coach made his cuts, Jeff Boutwell was still on the list.

In practice, he learned what intensity was all about. The tackle drills opened my eyes, he said. They were jarring and sometimes paralyzing. I got hit even when nobody was shooting at me. I looked at the scholarship players I had watched on television and couldn't believe their speed and the physical violence they brought to the field. They didn't hit like the boys I played against in high school.

Boutwell's assignment, if he chose to accept it, and he didn't really have a choice, was to carry the ball for the scout team and take his chances in a running drill against Ray Childress. I hit the hole as the blocker rolled into Childress, Boutwell said. I found a little seam and broke into the open. Foot loose and fancy free. Felt pretty good. I stood a little higher and walked back to the end of the line. Out of the corner of my eye I could see Coach Register chewing out Ray Childress, and Childress was ready to explode.

Jackie Sherrill walked up. Same people, he said.

Jeff Boutwell abruptly turned around. Same people, he asked.

You run it last time?

Yes, sir.

Run it again, Sherrill said.

Childress was so upset, the blocker didn't stand a chance, Boutwell said. He hit me while picking up speed. I was lying on the ground and couldn't breathe. Childress jammed his hand against my chest and pushed himself up.

games with an honest-to-goodness all student, all-volunteer, non-scholarship 12th man kickoff team. The magazine dispatched Douglas Looney to College Station. The call went out for as many of the final forty as possible to return to school for a photo session, and James Barrett, enrolled in a college-credit course in Hawaii, caught the next plane home. Tom Bumgardner heard about *Sports Illustrated* being on campus that Saturday, but he had a hiking trip planned. He decided that a trek through the woods would be a better way to spend the morning than posing for a photographer. He ignored the call. It was be a decision he would always regret. The faces of so many would be showcased from coast to coast, the faces of those who did not make the final team.

The subhead on the article declared, since 1922, the Texas A&M student body – a.k.a. the 12th man – has stood ready to serve the Aggie football squad. This season, 15 die-hards will get a chance to "splatter people" on the kickoff team.

Looney wrote, the 12th man stands a good chance of being a lights-out failure. Send engineering students, who are a little slow, a little light, and a lot inexperienced, down the field against recruited college football behemoths, and … Well, the biggest and fastest, and strongest don't necessarily win everything, but they're not a bad bet to do so on every given Saturday against the 12th man. Almost all of the 12th man hopefuls played high school football, but none of them got any more than a smile from college recruiters. One of the 12th man candidates, freshman Rodney Pennywell, says firmly, failure is disgraceful. Aggies don't let Aggies fail.

Looney continued, during spring practice, Beal imparted to his charges the basics of tackling – keep your

Tom Arthur, primed to play free safety for the Aggies, was wearing No. 34 in practice. He is was working with with transfer quarterback John Elkins (17) and Darrell Smith (39).

Childress was screaming at Register.

Register was screaming at Childress.

A few expletives were tossed around like live grenades.

And all I wanted to do, Boutwell said, was catch another breath before I died. I knew football was a violent sport. Always had been. I didn't know it was a blood sport.

During the summer, the oddest of things happened. Up in New York, *Sports Illustrated* caught wind of Jackie Sherrill's ingenious, yet hare-brained scheme to go into battle during home

head up, put your helmet between the runner's numbers, lock your arms high around his chest – and stood back to watch. They didn't do any of those things, he recalled. They looked like two freight trains running into each other.

Very small freight trains, of course, as in narrow-gauge. But their enthusiasm goes to the heart of college football …

Quarterback John Mazur, a starter at USC two years ago before transferring to A&M, says, I hope it works.

Adds linebacker Jerry Bullitt, I'd like for them to be a little bit bigger and stronger, but ….

Defensive back Domingo Bryant sees some silver in the storm clouds, saying, They're running up and down the field busting people. They'll give me a chance to rest.

The starters don't mind the 12th man because they'll get plenty of action. The reserves, however, see the 12th man as cutting into their playing time on special teams. But with all the hoopla, no one wants to step forward and publicly ridicule the newcomers. Furthermore, because of (NCAA) travel restrictions, the 12th man team will appear only at home games.

The only real football player on the kickoff team, kicker Alan Smith, says of his 12th man colleagues, They impress me more than I thought they would. They're pretty bloodthirsty, but they're kind of green. Beal figures that Smith, who has an exceptionally strong leg, should kick the ball out of the end zone 90 percent of the time, and the coaches may feel relieved if he does.

Les Asel sees things differently, Looney wrote. We're hoping the Lord blesses us and gives us a 50-mph wind against our kicker every time, he says.

Even Sherrill admits, frankly, I have no idea what's going to happen the first time we kick the ball.

The 12th man members remain uncertain of their status with the regular players. They talk to us like we're their friends, says Asel. They slap us on the butt like everyone else. None of them know my name, but I know theirs. We don't really know what to think of them, and they don't know what to think of us. But if we ever screw up, we'll never be accepted.

Looney quoted Tom Bumgardner as saying, for a long time, we didn't even look at the football players because we didn't want to see if they were scoffing at us.

Robert Crouch got himself worked up, saw his eyes glaze over with maroon and white, and told Looney, we live on motivation and the sight of blood. Most of the blood was his own.

Said Asel, all of us have our dreams, one dream, and it's of us going down the field, making the hit, the ball coming loose, and all of us jumping on it. Then we will take the ball and get it bronzed.

Bill Allison, a junior from San Antonio, pointed out, everybody was talking about how Jackie Sherrill was making us the laughingstock of the nation. But we've got a lot of people who think they can do the job. We also know he's taking a big risk putting us out there. If I were him, I wouldn't do it. Allison was honest, if nothing else.

Yet, Sherrill simply grinned and told Looney, well, what if this 12th man team knocks the snot out of somebody, they fumble, and we get the ball on the one?

It made sense to him. He still believed his idea was a sound one.

And Lt. Colonel Don Johnson, assistant commandant of the Corps, agreed, telling Looney, I think they will have a commitment and a silent pact that nobody will score on them.

Colonel Joe T. Haney, director of the Corps band, said of Sherrill, he's smart enough to know what's he's doing. This may be the best kickoff team we've ever had.

His words would prove prophetic.

Jackie Sherrill was still fuming about his 5-6 record the year before. As he said, five-six isn't in my vocabulary. I'm a better coach than that. He did not bring his troops back in August and inflict them with the traditional two-a-days of practice.

Sherrill had three-a-days.

And he would have had more if the NCAA had let him.

The 12th man kickoff team began to resemble the grim aftermath of a MASH unit gone awry. James Barrett's ankle was still tender and

bothering him. Barrett never knew when or if it would turn under him again. Bill Allison went down with a bad knee. Shawn Slocum had a hairline fracture in his left leg. He was done for the season. And Rock Johnson was one beer can off the side of his head away from a concussion. He was sitting in the Dixie Chicken one night, and, for reasons known only to God and Miller time, some drunk had the audacity to pick a fight with him. The Rock felt a tap on his shoulder and looked up.

You're one of them 12th man guys, aren't you, the drunk said.

Johnson ignored him.

You'll are just a bunch of wusses, the drunk said.

Johnson did not respond to the insult. He did not look up again. He simply grabbed a glass of lukewarm beer on top of the bar and slammed it against the side of his head. He did not flinch or change expressions. The glass shattered. The beer spewed. The blood flowed. And the drunk eased his way softly back out into the parking lot. Some fights are won before they ever begin. The Rock looked up at the bartender and said, Don't worry. I'll pay for the glass. Just give me a couple of ice cubes, a towel, and another beer.

Keith Newton thought he had been able to rehab his knee. But in the middle of two-a-days, it popped again. This time, it wasn't so easy to stand back up. Cartilage had originally been ripped in the spring, and now it was really eroded, the doctors said. He was lying in the steam room, and the day had become more hot and humid than usual. We need to scope it, the doctors said.

Newton's shoulders sagged. Go ahead and cut on it, he said. I'm done. He closed his eyes. The room was dark. The dream was gone.

Tom Bumgardner was practicing with a hard cast. It was like a weapon, he said. And Bumgardner was growing a little more bitter with each day that passed. He had left spring training as the number two cornerback behind James Flowers on the depth chart. During the spring scrimmage game, he had brilliantly picked off an interception and was beginning to feel pretty confident about his chances to play. When he returned in August, Bumgardner discovered he had dropped a slot. Flowers was back, and nobody was taking his job away. Sherrill had gone out, which was his reputation and prerogative, and recruited the number one cornerback in the state. So, in practice, Bumgardner gnashed his teeth and began working even harder than he had before. What else was he to do? He had lost his spot, and the other kid hadn't even walked on the field yet. Nobody ever said the game was fair. Then again, Bumgardner thought, nobody had ever told him it was this crooked either.

During three-a-days, he dove to knock down a pass, crashed crookedly onto the ground, and felt his thumb bend sharply over the hard fiberglass cast. He heard a crack. The pain told him that the thumb was broken long before he saw the X-ray. It was a secret Bumgardner kept to himself. Neither Jackie Sherrill nor Curley Hallman ever knew about the broken thumb. Bumgardner certainly wasn't talking about it. He and pain had gotten acquainted several tackles ago.

Back in the spring, he had severely dislocated a shoulder. He glanced around to make sure no one was watching, popped the bad shoulder back in place, and he kept going, driving into Domingo Bryant day after day in Curley Hallman's eye-opener drill. The shoulder screamed with pain. Bumgardner screamed back. He and Bryant backed up until they were fifteen yards apart, and, when the whistle blew, charged forward like a pair of disgruntled rams on a mountain top, meeting head-on in the hole. Bryant wasn't that big, only about 180 pounds, but he was fast, and he was strong. He lived for contact. Bumgardner was dying a slow death. It felt like a sledgehammer pounding his shoulder. No. A sledgehammer didn't hit like Domingo Bryant. One afternoon, they collided, and Bumgardner's knees buckled. His arm was hanging loose from his shoulder. The sinew had unraveled from the bone.

You hurt, Hallman wanted to know.

No, sir.

I thought I saw you flinch.

Tom Bumgardner squared his shoulders, even his injured shoulder. His eyes were glazed, but he didn't blink. He couldn't blink. And he knew that Hallman would never see him flinch again.

For David Beal, the final decision hadn't gotten any easier. He had a core group that could run, had shown up every day without fail, had played when they hurt so badly they could barely walk, had done everything he had asked, endured every drill thrown their way. They had gone through the fires of damnation, taken the pain, and dished it out. They had gone full speed, balls to the wall, and given everything they had on every play. Beal looked in their eyes. They were maniacal.

He sat down with Jackie Sherrill and said point blank, I can't cut the team to ten or even twelve.

What's the problem?

I've got fifteen or eighteen kids out there who can really play. Take James Barrett, for example. Good kid. Hard worker. Tough as nails. I have him listed at number fifteen, and he may be as good as anybody I have in the top five. I don't want to lose him. Coach, it would be a shame to lose him.

Sherrill studied Beal's face.

He believed in hiring good coaches, then letting them coach. He gave them the freedom to make their own decisions. But they had to live with those decisions. David Beal knew that, and Beal had made his case. It was a reasonable one. Sherrill had placed his faith in Beal to find the players necessary to build him a great kickoff team. Average wouldn't be accepted. Mediocre was out of the question.

Can you cut it down to less than twenty, the head coach asked.

If I have to, I can.

We'll go with sixteen, Sherrill said.

No more discussion.

The forty had assembled as a group one last time. Robert Crouch had been one of the last to arrive. He had sat in his dorm room and stared at the wall all morning. He had been dreading this day for a long time. Within an hour, it could all be over. The work, the aches, the pains would have all been in vain. His stomach churned and was tied in knots. He walked out of his room to face the inevitable.

Crouch took a seat in the back of the room and waited.

No one was talking or laughing.

The room had a funeral feel to it.

Football careers would die today.

Coaches Sherrill and Beal walked into the room, their faces solemn. It was a day Beal had been worrying about since last spring. Twenty-three fine young men would go home heartbroken. They had given their

all, and it had not been enough. Beal held a sheet of paper, and Sherrill moved to the background.

If I call your name, Beal said, you have not made the team, and I ask that you excuse yourself and leave as quietly as possible. If you do hear your name, I want you to know how much I admire and appreciate the effort you have given us. It's a numbers game. It always has been. We have forty in the room this morning. Only sixteen will remain.

Silence.

There was nothing else to say.

Beal began reading the names.

One by one, players began quietly standing up and walking out of the room. As rough as they had been on the practice field, they were just as reverent when they left for the last time.

Heartbreak was etched in every face.

Nowhere was it etched deeper than on the face of David Beal.

Barry Stevens leaned forward in his seat. In his mind, he was counting off each name. All week he had heard gossip that the team would have no more than twelve members, but Sherrill must have changed his mind. The twentieth name was called, and then the twenty-first.

He held his breath and waited. He realized the names were being read off alphabetically. He wouldn't know anything until Beal reached "S," and "S" was coming up quickly, too quickly.

And then they were all gone.

Twenty-four of them had left the room.

Beal had come to "S," passed it on by, and still Barry Stevens, the old man of the group, was sitting on the edge of his chair. He wouldn't believe it until the names were posted. Errors did happen, he knew.

Sherrill nodded and glanced them over. He had his kickoff team. Without their pads, they looked awfully small, maybe even fragile. Win or lose, he was ready for battle. He hoped they were as well. Jackie Sherrill walked out of the room without a word.

Tom Ray stood outside in shock, a wave of nausea sweeping over him. He could not believe it. Neither could his friends. There must have been some mistake, he thought. Yeah, he said. He knew what it was. The mistake was thinking that Tom Ray could still play football, and it had been his mistake. Nobody but his. He had no one to blame but himself. Ray walked out of the shadows of Kyle Field without looking at anyone and hoping that no one was looking at him.

I immediately called my father and told him I was coming home, he said. I drove three hours to Floresville and spent the weekend on the farm, trying to decide whether or not I was even going back to school. I had been swept up in the 12th man hype. I had my picture in *Sports Illustrated*. Now I was nothing, just another face in the middle of thirty-six thousand faces on campus. I would never wear the twelve. I would never step foot on Kyle Field when it counted. I was devastated.

Ron Reynolds had been planning to attend college, then move on to a military career like the one his father, a retired Lieutenant Colonel, had experienced. Football had been left behind on the high school field in Killeen, but, he said, here was this guy Jackie Sherrill giving me a chance to play football for a potential powerhouse. It had taken a lot of swimming and weightlifting for me to get back in shape, but every hour was worth it. I just wanted to prove to myself I could still play. Beal was folding the sheet of paper, the head coach had left, and Ron Reynolds could not keep from grinning. It must be over, he thought. It must be official, and, damn, David Beal thought he could still play, too.

Keith Newton limped up to Beal, a curious look on his face. I didn't think I had a chance, he said.

Why not?

When the knee was scoped, I thought it was over.

Don't worry, you had already shown us what you can do.

It'll be awhile before I can play.

Beal grinned. He glanced from James Barrett's ankle, to Tom Bumgardner's cast, to Bill Allison's knee. That's why we took sixteen, he said. It's a rough game.

Beal stuck the sheet of paper in his pocket. On it were written the names of Bill Allison, Tom Arthur, Les Asel, James Barrett, Tom Bevans, Jeff Blair, Tom Bumgardner, Dennis Burns, Tom Christner, Robert Crouch, Leroy Hallman, Larry Johnson, Ike Liles, Keith Newton, Ron Reynolds, and, of course, Barry Stevens.

God help them all, Beal thought, as he walked out toward an unforgiving sun beating down on the fifty-yard line of Kyle Field.

A newspaper would describe the 12th man team has having seventeen hearts, thirty-four arms, as many legs, and one ambition: to earn a place on the Aggie football depth chart. He is short, tall, black, tanned, fair, blond, brunette, muscular, and dedicated, said the article. He is polite, personable, neat, and unassuming. Jackie Sherrill considers the members of his 12th man team as a real find, and he didn't even have to leave campus to find them.

When it came to football, Jeff Boutwell had always been the number one guy. In high school, he was lining up with the varsity squad by the time he was a freshman. On the day, David Beal made his final cuts down to seventeen players, *Sports Illustrated* hit the streets with its showcase, full-color article on the 12th man kickoff team.

Boutwell bought ten copies. He sat down at the counter of the MSC and began thumbing through the issue.

How come you bought so many, a waitress asked him.

It has a story on the 12th man team, Boutwell explained. My picture's in it.

Oh, the waitress said, her face brightening. Are you one of the 12th men guys?

I was yesterday.

What happened?

I've just been cut, Boutwell said.

The words were a crushing blow to his ego. They were a blow that hurt worse than a Ray Childress forearm to the chest.

Jeff Boutwell had been playing football for a long time. Never in his life had he ever been cut.

Robert Crouch immediately left the meeting, jumped into his car, and headed out toward Pflugerville, about two and a half hours away. He had a point to make. His old coach at Poteet had taken the job at Pflugerville, the same old coach who had told Crouch that he would never play football again, that high school was as good as he would ever be.

Crouch spun his automobile into the school parking lot, walked past the football office, and waited in the locker room.

His old coach stopped in his tracks when he saw Crouch standing there, leaning against the wall, his arms folded defiantly. Frankly, he had never expected to see Robert Crouch again.

Coach, I just came by to let you know I made it, Crouch said.

Made what?

The Texas A&M football team.

You wouldn't be bullshittin' me, would you, boy?

Just watch the newspapers, Crouch said.

The look on the coach's face, he thought, was better than a kickoff.

Jackie Sherrill, said members of the 12th man unit, was a football coach to be feared, admired, and respected.

After their long-awaited debut, members of the 12th man unit covered their first kickoff against the University of California. It was an on-side kick, recovered by Tom Bumgardner (9). A great call. A great play. Unfortunately, the ball only traveled six yards, and the Golden Bears wound up with the ball after all. They scored in two plays, leaving A&M stunned.

Chapter 11

The talk around campus and the nation turned to the University of California Golden Bears. How ironic? Jackie Sherrill and his coaching staff had whipped together the first and only all-volunteer, student-body, non-scholarship kickoff team in the nation, banking on the hope that a sixty-one year old tradition at Texas A&M would somehow make up for the fact that, outside of Sherrill and David Beal, no coach in his right mind or in Division I football wanted them on the field or in uniform. California, on the other hand, had ended the 1982 season by returning a kickoff for a touchdown, racing past the goal line after time had already ticked past zero, to defeat Stanford in a wild, frenzied, and bizarre explosion that would forever be known as "The Play."

Trailing 20-19, Cal's Kevin Moen glanced at the scoreboard clock and realized that the Golden Bears had a scant four seconds to make something happen. He fielded the squib kick on the hash mark of the forty-five yard-line, tried to scramble, had nowhere to go, and lateraled the football to Richard Rogers.

The mad rush had begun. Golden Bears running backs and linemen alike were weaving from sideline to sideline, moving in and out of traffic jams, running forward, then backward, heading one direction, then another, tossing the ball around like it was a live grenade, never slowing down, never catching their breath, always one pitch ahead of the next tackle, frantically dodging their way toward the goal line. Five laterals were what it ultimately took, including one blind, over-the-shoulder heave by Mariet Ford as his knees were scraping the ground,

or so Stanford claimed. Rogers touched the ball twice during The Play. So did Moen, who started it all, and he corralled the last pitch at the twenty-five, charging through and over the Stanford Cardinal band as it marched ceremoniously out onto the field, believing the game had ended in a maddening scrum somewhere around midfield.

If California had the magic to perform such a miracle and knock off Stanford in John Elway's final college game, just imagine what the Golden Bears would be able to do to a bunch of A&M misfits who, more likely than not, would be mistaken for mascots when they darted out on the field.

David Beal simply shrugged. If the Aggie band had been on the field, he said matter-of-factly, California would not have scored.

The seventeen members of the 12th man kickoff team had their lane assignments and knew their jobs. Their kamikaze scheme had been drawn up, memorized, digested, and practiced without fail for thirty minutes or more of every day. It was as familiar to them as the aches in their joints, the pain that jarred their psyche when their muscles and bones were twisted in directions that God had never meant for them to go.

Sixty-three left.

That was the kickoff coverage, an attacking, relentless assault, and each nuance of the rush downfield had been hammered into the deep, psychotic corners their brains. Forget the size. Forget the speed. Search and destroy. That was the attitude. That was the mission.

Alley guys would hold their lanes. Wedge busters would take out as many as possible as often as many as necessary. Ball guys had the afterburners. Their only aim in life was to find the man with the ball and knock something loose, if not the ball, at least the helmet. And the safety was the last line of defense. God protect them all if the safety was forced to make the play. Seven seconds. That was all the time they had. Seven seconds, and it was over. It had damn well better be over. Seven seconds, and some poor devil would be lying flat of his back. Six seconds would be better.

David Crisp reported in the *Battalion*, as kickoff nears, they have become much greater objects of public scrutiny than many of their teammates with far better athletic credentials. *Sports Illustrated* made them the subject of a six-page story. One of them, who figured his football career had ended two years ago, got a call from the *New York Times* one morning this week, then met with another reporter at lunch.

As Tom Bevans pointed out, my uncle lived in Philadelphia, and he called my mom one day and said, What the hell is going on down there? I'm reading about your son in the *New York Times*.

Texas A&M rarely made the pages of the *New York Times* and almost never when the story was a positive one. The *New York Times* preferred scandal. If only its reporters had seen the 12th man team after dark, on the streets, at the bars, and in the Dixie Chicken long before the statute of limitations ran out. The devil-may-care fights on a football field were commonplace. In the Chicken, they were the stuff of legends.

Before, after, and sometimes during practice, David Beal found himself fielding a never-ending allotment of questions by phone and in person from news people around the country, and most were asking him the same question: What happens if California runs a kickoff back for a touchdown?

Said Beal, we'll worry about that when or if it happens.

Les Asel, a victim of his own deepest fears, was convinced that California would be the ultimate test. They've probably been working on one play for us for months now, he said. They're gonna show us something we've never seen or thought about before.

They're brewing something up, Tom Arthur said. You can bet on that.

Paranoia? Probably.

Concern? Without a doubt.

Fear? Not on your life.

Some, especially those who resided within the leering press, still believed that the 12th man kickoff team was merely Jackie Sherrill's ultimate publicity stunt.

Or maybe a bad joke.

He'll ride it as long as he can, some wrote. Then he'll junk it.

Jackie's no fool.

He wants to win.

He can't afford to let a bunch of students cost him field position and games no matter how heart-warming the story may be.

The first time some team runs a kickoff back for a touchdown, the 12th man team may as well keep on running as well, off the field, past the bench, through the tunnel, out the stadium, across campus, and to a chemistry lab somewhere. These guys are probably pretty good in a chemistry lab. You don't want your football players taking chemistry, and you don't want your engineering majors playing football. That's not law. That's a pure and simple fact of life.

That was pretty much what the leering press wrote and what they whispered among themselves awaiting that first and fateful kickoff. The leering press, most of whom had never tackled anything tougher than a typewriter, had it all figured out.

Sherrill simply met their skepticism with humor. He told one group of A&M supporters, I'll probably be down on my knees with the yell leaders when the first 12th man kickoff comes. Then the smile faded from his face, and he turned serious. I would not want to be receiving the kickoff, he said, because those boys may not even hear the whistle. They'll start coming. And they'll keep coming. I've seen them. They can be an awful ugly bunch when they want to be.

No member of the 12th man would ever forget September 3, 1983. Game day had started slow, seemed to be lasting forever, and suddenly night was falling fast. This was it. This was what they had been fighting for. This was why their bodies had been tattooed with bruises that bore strange and curious shades of purple and green. This was why they had been vilified and glorified. This was the moment they feared would never come, and now it was staring them in the face. The trash talk, the boasting, the hype was all behind them. This, at long last, was showtime. It was time to put up or shut up.

The atmosphere in the 12th man locker room was electric. The players still didn't dress with the varsity, but none of them cared. Not

When Jackie Sherrill accepted the job at Texas A&M, he firmly believed he had the good fortune of walking into the best coaching job in the nation. He believed the Aggies had the potential of becoming a national powerhouse.

now, they didn't. Not tonight. The fact that there had been sixteen uniforms waiting for them was all that mattered. They would have slept in their uniforms if Billy Pickard had let them.

Barry Stevens wanted number six. After all, he was in squad six of the Corps.

David Beal handed him number twelve.

Stevens didn't want number twelve.

Trust me, Beal said, it's a good number.

What makes it so good?

I wore it.

It would be another twenty-five years before Barry Stevens awoke one morning and realized that he had worn the first number twelve of the 12th man kickoff team. It was indeed a good number, a number to be honored, and he had not even been aware of it.

As Beal told his troops, you can't be looking up into the stands for girls. I'll do that for you. Remember, a lot of people are here just to watch you play. We're here to have a good time and ricochet some people around. What we want you to do is go down and splatter people.

No one was worried. They knew how to splatter people. It was second nature by now. The give and the take. They had been splattered on the practice field for months.

Neil Landsman of the *Bryan Eagle* roamed Kyle Field to capture it all in print. It was the opening game of the season. The University of California had come to town. Jackie Sherrill was trying to resurrect a football program that kept falling on hard times. On the field, two of the nation's top potential powerhouses would line up for a genuine, old-fashioned, old-school slugfest. Landsman, however, knew what the sto-ryline was, and he understood why the stands were packed. The roar, the growl, rising up from the far side of Kyle Field was enough to make the hair stand up on the back of his neck. Not even Sherrill's first game on the A&M sideline had generated that much enthusiasm.

As Landsman noted in his column, TV cameras were everywhere, recording every movement of the 12th man kickoff corps. ABC, NBC, and CBS all had film crews in town. The non-scholarship volunteers had achieved historical significance.

You'd have thought Saturday night marked the first time actual students were playing in a college football game.

Earlier in the week, Tom Bumgardner had been interviewed, and the reporter asked him the usual question: what will happen if the 12th man messes up?

Only one person can mess it up, he said.

Who's that?

The only scholarship player lining up with us.

The kicker?

The one and only.

The story appeared in print, and Curley Hallman was immediately on the phone, dialing Tom Bumgardner's number. Jackie wants you to keep your mouth shut, he said.

What'd I say?

The wrong damn thing.

Next time, Bumgardner would know what to say.

Nothing.

He hid from the press and refused to answer his phone, afraid that some reporter might be on the other end of the line. If he talked now, it

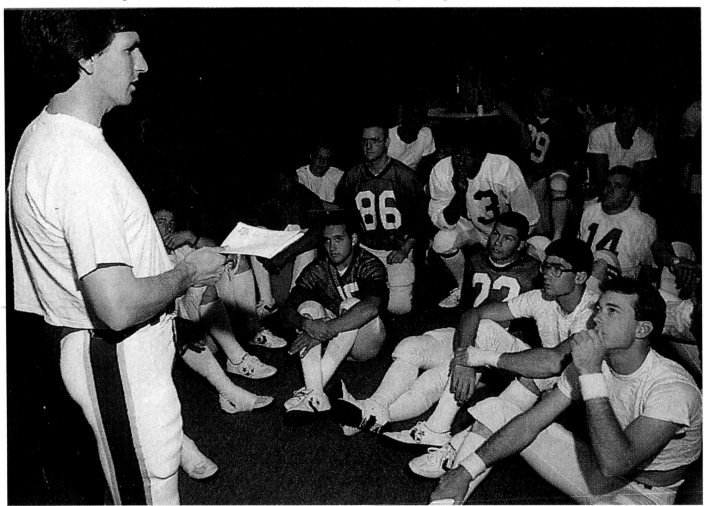

Young graduate assistant coach David Beal was given the challenge of coaching the first 12th man team. His only instructions from Jackie Sherrill were: Don't let anybody return a kickoff for a touchdown. Sherrill's words became his nightmare.

would be on the field.

Parents sat nervously in their seats. There won't be any amateurs down there, said Rock Johnson's father, J. R. It takes a lot of guts to stay on the practice field through two falls and two springs with little hope of getting out to play. It takes a lot of dedication to stick with something that long.

Rosemary Reynolds was searching for a glimpse of her son. She had always prayed that he would switch to a less dangerous sport, but there he was, Ron Reynolds, wearing maroon and white, and he didn't look out of place at all. I've tried to discourage him from playing football since he was in the sixth grade, she said. Obviously, I've not been very successful. In high school, they almost started giving me green stamps down at the emergency room because Ron was there so often with football injuries.

I hope Rock lays somebody out good, J. R. Johnson said.

I hope Ron doesn't get hurt, Rosemary Reynolds said.

That was the difference between a father and a mother.

Warm-ups were over, and Ron Reynolds was jogging back to the locker room. Rock Johnson was already inside, banging his head against the lockers. He wouldn't be ready to play until he saw the first sight of blood. His own would do fine.

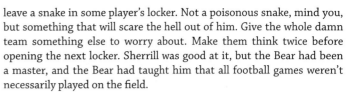

Jackie Sherrill met with the leering press. It was not one of his favorite chores, but he knew how to handle the writers, the reporters, the television faces in a box. A little sleight-of-hand never hurt much either.

If California returns the opening kickoff for a touchdown, he said, I'm going to have a lot of people throwing darts at me. They think I'm crazy anyway.

He laughed.

I've planted a record in my kicker's ear, Sherrill continued. It stays in there all night, and all he hears is, end zone, end zone, over and over and over. Kick it in the end zone.

Now the press was laughing, too.

That had been the set up.

For weeks, he and David Beal had watched the film, again and again, of California's kickoff return against Stanford.

Have we covered this, Sherrill wanted to know.

We've gone out and practiced against laterals, Beal replied. We've done it a lot.

Can we stop them?

We'll be okay, Beal said.

Sherrill sat in the dark and stared at the film. You notice anything about their kickoff return team, he asked.

It looks to me like the front line starts peeling back right before the ball is kicked, Beal told him. I've watched this film over and over, and I think we ought to be able to take advantage of that.
What are you thinking?

What if we surprise them?

Sherrill glanced over. He had a puzzled look sketched on his face.

What if we try an on-side kick, Beal said.

Sherrill nodded. He was always looking for an edge. He was always searching for some way get inside another coach's head and jerk his mind around for awhile. Confound him. Let him worry about something other than the game. Irritate the hell out of him. Make his skin crawl. Make him forget the X's and O's.

Maybe we should turn the heat up in the visitor's locker room, Sherrill once told his coaches. Or maybe we can turn the lights off in the dressing room at halftime, or paint it pink like they do up in Iowa, or

leave a snake in some player's locker. Not a poisonous snake, mind you, but something that will scare the hell out of him. Give the whole damn team something else to worry about. Make them think twice before opening the next locker. Sherrill was good at it, but the Bear had been a master, and the Bear had taught him that all football games weren't necessarily played on the field.

An edge.

That was all Sherrill wanted.

The fanfare surrounding the 12th man kickoff team had already crawled down inside California's head.

An on-side kick might be a dagger to the heart early.

Have you talked it over with Curley, Sherrill asked.

He and I have discussed the possibility.

What does Curley think?

Curley thinks it might work.

Sherrill grinned. Curley might be right, he said.

Jackie Sherrill knelt on the sideline and glanced at his clipboard. The thought did intrigue him, but he still had not made up his mind. Not for good, anyway.

California had won the toss.

The Aggies were kicking off.

The boys on the 12th man might as well get rid of their jitters. The nerves tangled in knots at the pit of their stomachs would leave as soon as they hit someone. They would get that chance, and they would get it early. Sherrill hoped they were up to the challenge. They had one shot and better not misfire.

He had brought them into the locker room in the early evening when no one was around but a bunch of walk-ons and their coach. Today, Sherrill told them, what you guys are doing is something special to you and to Texas A&M. Twenty years from now, nobody will remember who our quarterback is. But everyone will remember you and what you do here today.

We were confident. That's what Dennis Burns remembered. We were scared. But we were confident. It had been a nerve-wracking day.

As Burns turned to leave the locker room, Sherrill stopped him. Dennis, he said.

Yes, sir?

Don't let anybody get past you.

Burns nodded. He played safety. If anyone ran past him, they could all go home, preferably before the next kickoff and probably under assumed names.

The crowd was rising to its feet.

The tension was suffocating.

The razzle dazzle had come from California.

The mavericks were wearing maroon and white. They had a 12th man patch on their sleeves.

Richard Rogers, who captained California's special teams and who had lateraled the ball twice during the miracle return against Stanford, said, yeah, he had heard and read a lot about the 12th man squad, but he didn't think the Golden Bears would regard the Aggie unit differently from any other kickoff team.

What have you heard, a reporter asked him.

That they're coming down on kickoffs and try to kick the dog out of us, Rogers answered. It's great for the fans. But is it good for winning? I don't know if I would go that far. If you have to go up in the stands to find a football team, you might be in a little trouble.

On the Aggie sideline, Tom Arthur was growing more adamant by the moment. I just want our kicker to knock the ball down to about the ten-yard line, he said. I want to see what we can do. I think we'll do pretty well.

Alan Smith, however, had been listening to Sherrill. The man with the headset had the first, last, and ultimate word. The 12th man had begged him to sky the ball and leave it short, but he stayed with the Aggie company line. A kicker is going to try to put the ball through the uprights, he said. If the wind's with me, I'm sure I can do that. A lot of the scholarship athletes have been kidding me about how I'll have to make the tackle or how my health is in jeopardy. But these guys know what they're doing.

The starting unit of the 12th man team huddled around Alan Smith and David Beal. Eleven players stood among them. Only one had a scholarship. Their hearts were pounding wildly, threatening to hammer their way through the cavities of their chests. Sherrill walked over as nonchalantly as he could manage. They met his intimidating stare with silence. Dead silence. The world around them had lost its voice. Even the roar from the stands had been deadened and swallowed by the silence.

Let's on-side kick the ball, he said.

No rationale.

No explanation.

Just a simple, let's on-side kick the ball.

Which side, Smith asked.

Left.

Smith frowned and looked at Sherrill like he was crazy, wondering if the coach had somehow misplaced his sanity somewhere between the dressing room and the field.

The 12th man team looked at Sherrill like they knew he was crazy.

But no one debated the issue, at least not until the coach had walked away.

It's brilliant, Barry Stevens said.

He doesn't have any faith in us.

No, Stevens said, it's a stroke of genius.

He doesn't think we're good enough to tackle anybody.

No, Stevens said, Sherrill's gonna give us a chance to recover an on-side kick and make a play before California ever touches the ball.

Someone glanced over at Dennis Burns and said, hell, you're fast enough to catch the damn thing in the air, and we've got six if you do, and California ain't got nothing.

Burns felt the fire in his belly, and it was growing hotter by the moment. He would be on the left side, near the hash mark, and his job was to keep an on-side kick from bouncing out of bounds. He might catch the kick. He might not. But he knew one thing for certain. It sure as hell wouldn't be going out of bounds.

The game film had been right.

California was peeling back in full retreat before Alan Smith's foot touched the ball. The squib kick tumbled end over end and crazily to the left, bouncing one way, then another. It ricocheted off the leg of Leroy Hallman as he charged downfield, and Tom Bumgardner had a clear shot at the football as it danced drunkenly toward the sideline of a vacant field. Just he and the turf and the pigskin. Nothing else. The ball seemed to lay on the ground forever.

No one else was even near Bumgardner, and the world was spinning around him slow motion. He kept grasping and clutching for the ball, unable to tell the difference between the sound of his heartbeats and footsteps.

Bumgardner leaped on the football and rolled over, holding if tightly against his chest.

The crowd went wild. The Aggies on the sideline went wild.

Sherrill grinned broadly, which was as close to going wild as he

would ever be.

David Beal thrust a fist in the air. He couldn't believe his eyes.

California was stunned.

Then Sherrill began to count, and his grin was replaced with a scowl.

Six yards.

Damn.

The ball had only gone six yards.

How did the strongest damn kicker in America come up with the weakest damn kick he ever saw?

The Aggies had the ball.

Didn't matter.

California had a first down.

The referees could count, too.

Six yards. The ball hadn't gone the required distance.

R. C. Slocum turned away in disgusts, or maybe it was despair. His worst fear had been realized. Put the damn 12th man kickoff team on the field, and his defense would be facing a short field every time. The disgust passed in an instant. What was past was past. What he did for the rest of the game was the only thing that mattered.

As John Wagner wrote in the *Battalion*, the only scholarship player on the 12th man kickoff team messed up its debut. Alan Smith failed to kick the ball the required ten yards.

Damn, Hallman thought. Tom Bumgardner had been right.

No one felt worse than David Beal. The fabled and fateful on-side kick had been his idea, and Sherrill had gone along with him. Shrewd? Perhaps. A calculated risk? No doubt. But the kick had failed. Now Sherrill would face the blame, and he would accept it without passing the buck to anyone.

But worse, California had taken over at the Aggie 46-yard line. The Bears scored two plays later. Sherrill had listened to him, and A&M was losing. Beal felt nauseous. He glanced toward Sherrill, but Coach was already moving on. The last play was over. Good or bad, he could not do a damn thing about it.

The next play was all that concerned him now. Sherrill would never mention the on-side kick to Beal, simply telling sports writers after the game, it may have been over-coaching on my part. Maybe we should have just let the 12th man go after them.

The Aggies were in a hole quickly and early as California steamrolled to a 17-0 lead at halftime. A&M stormed back with a third quarter field goal. The 12th man took the field one more time, and the world for them all was about to change.

The kick was in the air and coming up short of the goal line.

Ike Liles found a gear he didn't know he had. I had never seen him run that fast, Beal said. He was running faster than when we timed him in the forty.

Tom Bumgardner lay just off his shoulder, picking up speed, and both players were looking for somebody to hit.

Anybody.

It did not make them any difference.

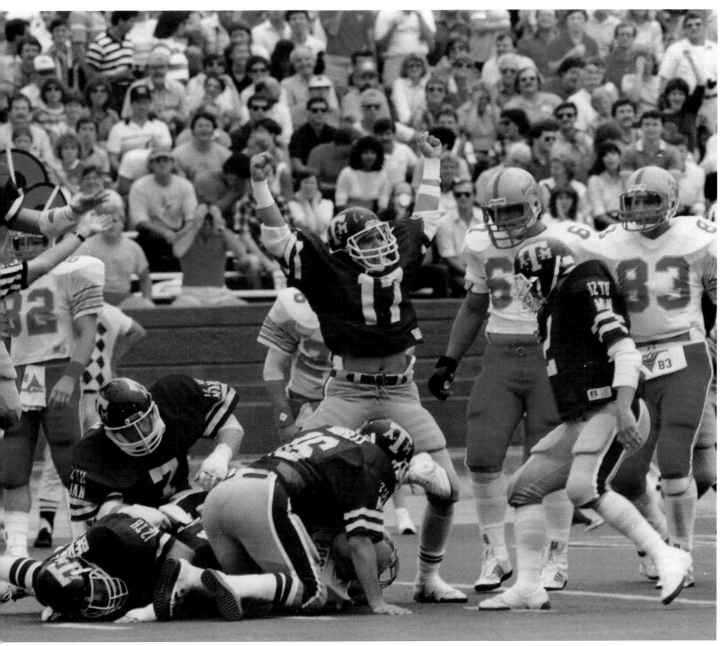

Sean Page (17) waves his arms in triumph and Danny Balcar (2) looks on as David Coolidge (7), and John Burnett *6) help bring a sudden halt to the kickoff.

I was more fired up than nervous, Ike Liles said. I was a ball guy, pumped full of adrenaline. I thought I was fast, but Bumgardner had moved a step ahead of me. He was really cooking. The blocker came up, and Bumgardner took him out like he had been hit with a ball peen hammer. There wasn't anything left for me to do but make the tackle. The runner juked, and I hit him before he jived. I had a clean shot at him. I wanted to make one of those clean-your-clock kind of plays. But it was just a regular tackle. He didn't feel any pain. The crowd didn't see anybody get blasted. I just grabbed his legs, held on, and help came from every direction.

It was, however, the shot heard around the college football world.

As Neil Landsman wrote, the 12th man lived up to its build-up and more. It was magical. Ten student volunteers made a routine tackle, and Kyle Field exploded. Until then, the game was Dullsville. Leading 17-3 in the third quarter, the University of California was seriously dominating Texas A&M.

But regardless, when the scrawny band of walk-ons scampered

on the field, Aggie fans started screaming. They rocked the East Kyle grandstands. The 12th man tackled Dwight Garner at the 17. Nothing sensational. But the crowd acted like the student volunteers had saved College Station from foreign invaders. And members of the special unit were jumping all over each other. After a mere tackle, they were throwing high-fives and hopping like guys on pogo sticks.

The fever was contagious. The fans went bonkers, and so did the Aggie players, who, in the first half, had looked spiritless, like zombies. After just one attempt, California never returned another kickoff. Twice Cal fielded kicks in the end zone and settled for touchbacks. To the 12th man, it was a sign of respect. Forget a five-lateral return that finished with a dash through the Corps. No, the visitors didn't want to tangle with Texas A&M's rowdy volunteer force.

The 12th man changed the game. The first half was a yawner; the second half was a thriller ... Rallying desperately, the Aggies scored 17 points to tie California, which appeared on the verge of collapse. Afterwards, Cal Coach Joe Kapp admitted the crowd's roar rattled the Golden

Tom Bumgardner with his defensive backfield coach Curley Hallman, who had the reputation of being demanding and hard-nosed. It was, his believed, to squeeze every ounce of talent he could from the 12th man team members.

Bears.

Homer Jacobs would years later write in the *12th Man Magazine*, The Spirit of Aggieland and the swashbuckling of Sherrill had come together in a tackle by Liles at the Cal 17-yard line. Like the Junction Boys before it and Red, White and Blue Out after it, this was one of those defining, spine-tingling Aggie moments.

The roar from the stands had reached decibel levels that surpassed even the normal, frenzied crowd noise rocking Kyle Field. It was a wall of sound, a deafening assault on every ear drum in the place, spilling across campus and even shaking the foundation of the Dixie Chicken. An amazed Joe Kapp said of the students and the fans,, they don't have a 12th man. They've got at least thirteen with all that noise.

Ike Liles appreciated the undying faith that Jackie Sherrill had in his kickoff unit. He had read where some were saying that Sherrill would scrap the idea in a pulse beat if the Aggies fell behind. Well, the Aggies had fallen behind, and Sherrill kept running his volunteer team back on the field time and again.

He even gave the 12th man team credit for jerking the Aggies out of their doldrums and dragging them back into the game again. Sherrill said, offensively, we had just moved the ball in the third quarter, and we kicked off and made a big hit. The tackle Ike made affected the whole atmosphere.

Unfortunately, it wasn't enough.

With the scored tied at 17-17, California kicked a field goal with 1:20 left on the clock, but Kapp unexpectedly broke the golden rule of football by taking the three points off the board after A&M had been guilty of roughing-the-kicker. The penalty gave the Golden Bears a first

and goal at the two-yard line. Kapp wanted a touchdown. Three points, he knew, could wilt in a hurry. His quarterback, however, fumbled the snap, and the Aggies recovered.

Momentum had worn maroon and white the whole second half, and Sherrill knew A&M had just dodged a bullet. He wasn't about to play for a tie, not at home, never at home and especially not in the season opener.

He had a minute left. He took a chance. Get the ball to the eight-yard line, he reasoned, and Mazur would have room to operate the passing game. He didn't need a lot of yards. Just a few, eight to be exact. So

Sherrill called for a sweep, a gutsy play if it worked and probably second-guessed for the rest of the season if it didn't

It didn't.

Jimmie Hawkins cut wide, hesitated, was caught and spun down by Ron Rivera for a safety. And California left A&M in dismay at the wrong end of 19-17 score.

Sometimes you gamble and roll the dice, Sherrill said. It just didn't come up. Cal didn't win the game. We lost it. But the team never quit. It's young, and it's going to get better. Count on it.

The Aggie alumni shook their heads. It all sounded so familiar. Blame the youth. Blame the inexperience. Blame the on-side kick. Blame the pitch play in the end zone. None of it really mattered. They were just as troubled by the three bad punt snaps, the two missed field goals, and those ten penalties.

Thank God for the 12th man kickoff team. It had been the lone glimmer of hope in a night that began and ended on a bitter note.

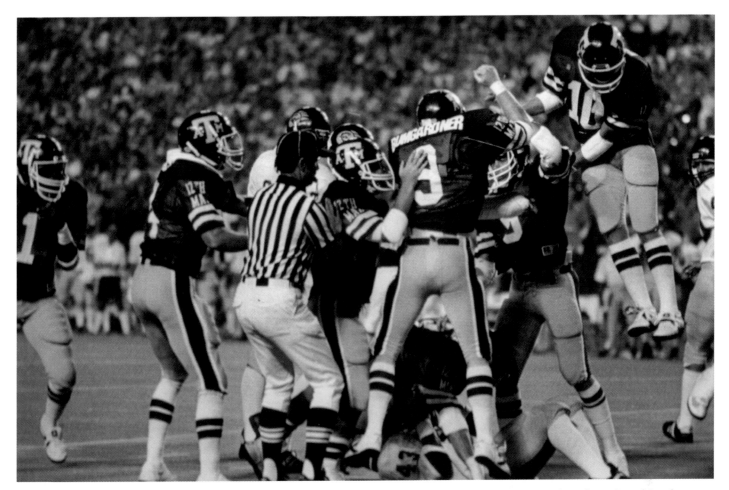

Ike Liles, buried beneath the pile, made the first tackle for the 12th man team against the University of California. Tom Bumgardner (9) and Larry Johnson (5) lead the swarm to the ball with Dennis Burns (10) coming over the top and Ashley Eddington (1) closing fast. The tackle proved for all of the critics that the 12th man would not be a flash in the pan.

Chapter 12

Jackie Sherrill was enamored with the potential of his 1983 Aggies, but he also feared the deadly mistakes that could haunt and demoralize a bunch of players so young and inexperienced. The mistakes had a tendency to come at the oddest and the worst of times. He had a left-handed quarterback, John Mazur, who looked a lot like the Snake, Kenny Stabler, when he threw the ball. Sherrill knew. He had played with Stabler. Mazur was a thoroughbred when he passed, but a plodding plow horse when he tried to run. Sherrill held his breath and hoped for the best. Let Mazur stand tall in the pocket, and nobody was better. When he was forced to dodge the rush, however, he was a lame duck in a shooting gallery. Sherrill did have a couple of freshmen studs at quarterback, Kevin Murray and Craig Stump, but he was not ready to throw the babes to the wolves. Not yet anyway. The season was only one game old.

Sherrill had been prompted by graduation to replace his entire starting backfield, but the Aggies did have three strong fullbacks, Ira Valentine, Jimmie Hawkins, and George Smith, and, in time, the running back corps just might be the strongest facet of the A&M attack. Mazur could turn in either direction and hand the ball off to the power of Anthony Toney or the speed of Keith Woodside and Rod Bernstine. Shea Walker had great hands and absolutely no fear at split end. Jimmie

Williams and Don Jones both possessed speed to burn at flanker. Matt Darwin anchored the offensive line, nicknamed "The Pack" by Jackie Sherrill. Ken Reeves was the best pulling guard in the Southwest Conference, Tommy Robison at right tackle was considered an early round NFL draft choice, Rich Siler was a bruiser at tight end, and Greg Porter at left guard was the backbone of the offense.

The defense was in the All-American hands of Ray Childress and Billy Cannon, Jr. Both were beasts, Childress the giant and Cannon, who could run faster and hit harder than anybody on the team. Childress had great inner strength, and Cannon had demons driving him to the top. His father had won the Heisman Trophy for LSU, then later went to prison on a counterfeiting charge. Cannon played angry. In practice. In games. He was looking for someone to kill or at least leave broken and in pain.

Sherrill loved to study players and move them around, usually against their will, finding positions where they could succeed. He was a chess master on the football field, and he certainly knew the difference between the kings, the rooks, and the pawns. He already had his pawns in place. He had the 12th man kickoff team. Now he had switched the tall, lanky, hard-hitting Domingo Bryant from strong safety to free safety, shifted Billy Cannon from safety to linebacker, and was still try-

THE WHITE HOUSE

WASHINGTON

September 23, 1983

Dear Coach Sherrill:

The efforts of the Twelfth Man unit of your football team have been brought to my attention.

The spirit of the football fans at Texas A&M is legendary, and I know it has been a great factor in the team's success over the years. The Twelfth Man unit is an excellent way to capture that spirit and show your opponents what loyalty to the home team really means.

My best wishes to you and all the students of Texas A&M, and especially to the hardy volunteers of your Twelfth Man unit.

Sincerely,

Ronald Reagan

Mr. Jackie Sherrill
Athletic Director and
    Head Football Coach
Texas A&M University
College Station, Texas   77843

Each member of the 12th man kickoff team received a letter from President Ronald Reagan, extolling his admiration for the all-volunteer unit.

Jackie Sherrill could live with one bad snap on a punt. Mistakes happen. But three of them? In one game? It was ludicrous. And it was a bad situation not easily corrected. The art of deep snapping was practiced by many but perfected by only a few. Good deep snappers did not grow on trees, at least not any on the outskirts of College Station.

On Monday night after the loss to California, Sherrill gathered his players around him and asked, have any of you ever had any experience as a deep snapper?

Silence.

No response.

Eyes found it easier to look at the ground than at the coach. He was calm. His voice was steady. He was mad as hell.

Does anybody know a deep snapper, Sherrill asked.

I do, said Shea Walker. My brother. He did it all the time in high school, and he was pretty dadgummed good?

Where is he now?

In school.

Where?

Here at A&M. Shea Walker shrugged. He's probably back in his dorm right now.

Get him out here. Tomorrow's soon enough.

The next afternoon, Shawn Walker ambled out onto the football field. He was lanky, almost fragile, and couldn't have weighed more than 175 pounds with a bowling ball dangling from his belt.

My God, thought Sherrill, he's just a skinny little kid that some defensive lineman will eat alive. The rules said a team couldn't run over a deep snapper, but if Walker went downfield in coverage, he was dead meat.

Sherrill was running out of options. He was desperate.

You play any college football, Sherrill asked.

No, sir.

Right out of high school?

I'm afraid I'm a junior, Coach, Shawn Walker said. I haven't done any deep snapping for two or three years.

Sherrill shrugged. Let's see what you've got, he said.

Nothing ventured.

Nothing gained.

The ball shot back to the punter like an arrow, straight and true.

ing to figure out what to do with a raw but talented quarterback from down the road in Hempstead. Johnny Holland was a little too large to line up under center, not quite fast enough to roam free in the defensive secondary, and maybe not strong enough to handle the duress of a defensive end. But, Lord, how Johnny Holland could hit. Jackie Sherrill had never recruited a quarterback who was tough enough and powerful enough to hit that hard.

New players. Young players. Raw talent. A little hope. A lot of worry. The pieces were there. But would they all fit together, and would

The punter didn't even have to move his hands. Shawn Walker was dead on target.

Sherrill turned to Curley Hallman. He's it, Sherrill said. Work him and I don't care if he never goes down on a punt. See what you can do to keep him from getting killed.

Jackie Sherrill asked Tom Bumgardner to speak to the Quarterback Club after the Cal game. He always had a football player show up at the meeting with a member of the coaching staff to deliver an updated version of the state of the team and, with the buzz on campus circling around the exploits of his glorified kickoff unit, he might as well send a member of the 12th man team.

The bitterness of defeat was still stinging as Bumgardner stood up, walked to the podium and said, we were just glad we were able to get the crowd going, and I thought the crowd noise did as much as anything to get the defense back in the game. The defense played great from then on. Ike's tackle certainly changed the momentum, and we all felt lucky that we were able to make a contribution.

Short talk.

Heartfelt.

Applause.

And Bumgardner sat down.

R. C. Slocum stood up and, in that folksy, Southern drawl of his, told the Quarterback Club, we had a good and solid game plan prepared. We practiced hard. We worked hard. We played hard. Those kids on the 12th man team really had nothing to do with it.

Bumgardner felt the air suddenly go out of his chest. Maybe the air had been sucked out of the room. I knew Coach Slocum never acted as though he liked us, he said. I just didn't know he would dismiss us and our efforts as easily as he did.

President Ronald Reagan in the White House shows off his own individual 12th man kickoff team jersey.

Ike Liles, as expected, received the 12th man Most Valuable Player award for the California game. On a maroon velvet backing, they had placed his name.

Ike Lyles.

Damn, he thought. This is probably the only of these I'll ever win, and they misspelled my name.

How could they?

I was the only Liles in Stamford.

He went down, had another "Liles" plate made, paid for it himself, and stuck it over the typographical mistake. The finished product looked homemade, he said, but it was correct.

On September 23, President Ronald Reagan sent Jackie Sherrill a letter on White House stationery that said, the efforts of the Twelfth Man unit of your football team have been brought to my attention.

The spirit of the football fans at Texas A&M is legendary, and I know it has been a great factor in the team's success over the years. The Twelfth Man unit is an excellent way to capture that spirit and show your opponents what loyalty to the home team really means.

My best wishes to you and all the students of Texas A&M, and especially to the hardy volunteers of your Twelfth man unit.

Each member of the 12th man team received the letter, along with an autographed photograph of President Reagan, smiling proudly and holding his own 12th man jersey.

Keith Newton walked onto the field without a limp. The brace around his knee helped a lot. It had been four weeks after his surgery, and the helmet felt good on his head. He had never expected to wear one again.

I'm ready, he told Beal.

You sure?

Doctor says I can play.

You probably need to sit out a few games, Beal said. We'll work you

The 1983 season had a bad beginning, and it was growing worse every Saturday. Sure, the Aggies beat up on Arkansas State, 38-0, but they were ambushed by Oklahoma State, 34-15, and demoralized on the High Plains of Lubbock when the only sign of any offense came on the strength of a Texas Tech field goal. The Aggies fell 3-0. The defense had been a wall of concrete with only a few hairline cracks, but as Neil Landsman wrote in the *Bryan Eagle*, every time the defense gave the ball to the offense, A&M imitated a chorus line ... one, two, three, kick. He also wrote, is there any Geritol in the house? Know any unemployed Sumo wrestlers? How about 250-pounders with mean streaks who are free Saturday night? The anemic Aggie offense needs help. Yards are rare, much less first downs. Forget about points. A street gang would have been gentler than Tech on quarterback John Mazur. They jumped him when he left the huddle.

In reality, the season had been a long shot in spite of Sherrill's undying optimism. He believed that his offensive line compared favorably to any group he had at Pittsburgh. But "The Pack," as he called them, had packed up, packed it in, and vanished. And now Greg Porter, for reasons known only to Greg Porter, had quit the team. Rumors floating around College Station said he had grown frustrated and was suffering from a pinched nerve. The game had ceased being fun for him. Rumors had been known to stray from the truth. Ken Reeves was suffering from a pulled groin muscle, and tackle Nate Steadman was hampered with shoulder problems. Freshmen were being forced into the Aggie lineup, and, unfortunately, they were playing like raw freshmen. On occasion, starting center Matt Darwin had been moved to guard. There was no end and little hope in sight.

If a record of 5-6, as Sherrill had said, was not in his vocabulary, then 1-3 was akin to a foreign language. He told his team, practice is going to get tougher, so damn tough you won't recognize it. You can't sit around on Sunday and feel sorry for yourself, he said, so on Sunday afternoon, the day after being thoroughly embarrassed by Oklahoma State, Tom Christner received a frantic phone call. Get down to the field, he was told. If you're not already there, you're already damn late.

What's going on?

Coach Sherrill's got his stinger out. He didn't like what happened yesterday.

Nobody did.

We've got practice.

Nobody practices on Sunday.

Coach Sherrill does.

He hauled the Aggies out to the practice field and put them through a full scrimmage. It's not punishment, Sherrill said. But there's something missing, and I've got to find out what it is. The Sunday practice was long. It was hot. It was a two-car collision, and, for hours, the cars kept colliding over and over. Coaches were screaming and cursing with every breath. The plays were live. Full speed. No quarter. No prison-

James Barrett (16) bolts downfield with an open seam ahead of him.

back in, but it may take awhile.

I understand.

His eyes said he was lying.

He did not understand.

Keith Newton had been ready to play by the time the surgeon rolled him off the operating table.

He stood on the sideline and watched the California game.

Ike Liles made the tackle.

It could have been him.

That was it. The watching was over. By the second game, Keith Newton was on the field and starting again. Where he knew he belonged to be. He didn't feel the brace, and it had not slowed him down. A hit or two, and he forgot he was wearing one.

ers. No surrender. Blood was optional.

Billy Pickard was screaming at Sherrill, you're gonna kill 'em, Coach. Heat exhaustion. They've had enough. You better let up a little. Sherrill did not let up at all. The trainers were running hard, keeping the players on their feet and water down their throats. Jackie Sherrill wanted more. He was demanding more. The hits were violent. The atmosphere was violent. Other than the day being Sunday, the 12th man team didn't see any difference.

Game after game, Alan Smith, the barefooted sidewinder, kept driving the ball into the end zone. But still the collisions came. There might not be a runback, but those on the 12th man team took their pound of flesh from every man they could find wearing the wrong color of jersey. The 12th man only knew how to play the game one way, breathing fire and brimstone with malice aforethought. They were invincible, they thought, wandering somewhere on the borderline between insufferable and immortal.

If Smith's kick landed anywhere near the goal line, somebody was going to get hurt. The runner. The blockers. The wedge. They loaded up, eyes peeled, ears laid back, elbows pumping, and kept firing. The 12th man took out everybody standing, and pain no longer bothered them. Their bodies hurt every day anyway. Knock them down, but don't turn your back. Never turn your back. They don't stay down. They like to hit back. They have a gene missing, the one that marks the difference between a saint and a psycho.

Against Oklahoma State, Tom Bevans had been the proverbial hammer. It was his job to throw himself against the center point of the wedge like a bowling ball, take out as many Cowboys as possible, and leave the lanes split wide open for the ball guys.

Go fast.

A tempest in a storm.

Make it thunder.

Send the lightning down in ragged bolts.

Make sudden stops.

Bevans slammed into the wedge, and the wedge didn't budge. He outweighed me by a hundred pounds, maybe more, Bevans said, and he was steamrolling toward me. All I could see were his eyes, and he was not scared of me. We were so close I could smell the onions on his breath. Day-old onions. He had a beard. I didn't even have a whisker. He was a man and casting a broad shadow, most of it muscle. I saw him coming, and I heard him leaving.

Bevans' chest bore the distinct tracks of cleat marks.

He tasted blood, and this time it didn't taste so good.

The ground spun crazily beneath him. His head was on a windmill, and the storm was blowing hard, and the lightning was flashing crazily inside his brain. Bevans crawled to his feet and frantically tried to decide which sideline was dressed in maroon and white. He could no longer tell the difference.

What the hell are you doing, Robert Crouch asked him.

I don't know, Bevans answered. Are we fixing to kick off?

We just did.

Bevans shuddered. I hope like hell that's the last one today, he said.

Tom Arthur wasn't quite sure what he had done wrong.

But one thing was for certain.

He hadn't done it right.

Dammit, Mike, the coach yelled.

I'm sorry, coach, Arthur said. But Mike was my brother. He played here a few years ago.

The coach threw up his hands in disgust. He was close now, screaming, and Tom Arthur could feel the spray of spittle peppering his face. I don't give a damn if you're Tom Arthur, Mike Arthur, or Shit Arthur, the coach yelled, you're not doing it right.

Thank God, it wasn't Coach Sherrill, Arthur thought. He could look at you, and you'd crumble like a clay pigeon in a hailstorm. He could put you away, and he didn't have to say a word. One look from Sherrill, and you'd start digging your grave.

When the season began, the only team to take the 12th man seriously was the Texas Aggies. A&M's opponents had little regard for the kickoff team. Line 'em up. Knock 'em down. We'll run past 'em. That was the belief anyway. As David Beal told his troops, other teams want to prove you wrong, want to prove you're a mistake. And when you're backed in the corner, you have to fight or get whipped.

He knew they might get knocked around, but they would never be beaten. He had watched them day after day in practice. They would run

Dean Berry (45) follows the flight of the football, ready to hit somebody, anybody, who is not wearing maroon and white. His sterling play allowed him to become the only member of the 12th man team to ever play a position, linebacker, during a game.

unafraid into the ragged teeth of a big thicket chainsaw, and none of them ever wanted to rotate out or go to the back of the line. They simply stood up, brushed the dirt off their faces, and began looking for another chainsaw. They didn't mind living with a cramp, an ache, or a break just as long as the coaches realized they had the ability and the tenacity to deliver the same kind of pain to anyone who dared run back a kickoff toward them. Beal did. Sherrill did. Hallman did. Pettibone did. Register did. The others tried to beat them into submission. It didn't work.

The Aggie varsity worried that the 12th man team would make a wrong turn, a bad decision, or break down at any minute. Long returns. Touchdowns. The very thought of student volunteers in helmets and cleats kept everyone but Jackie Sherrill and David Beal afflicted with the restless sweats at night.

At first, Dennis Burns said, I could hear the opposing teams razz us all the way down the field. They called us every name they could think of, and most had to do with our being overmatched, out of place, cowards, scared, a joke, and, more often than not, compared to various and sundry parts of the female anatomy. The only way we could shut them up was shut the return down. Mentally, we drew a line in the dirt at the twenty, and we dared anybody to cross it. Few did.

The reputation of the 12th man unit was growing. As James Barrett told the *New York Times*, some people say they'll try to run right over us, but that would be a mistake. We're going to be hitting.

Leave a tattoo.

That was the thought.

Leave a tattoo that looked an awful lot like the number 12.

Tom Christner was surprised. After those few first games, he said, we could look downfield at the kickoff return team and see that they were more nervous than we were. They looked scared. They had scholarships. Some had dreams of playing in the NFL. They knew we were out there to barrel our way downfield, make the big hit, hurt them as badly as we could hurt them, and take them out for good, one at a time or the whole damn bunch. It didn't matter. Nobody played dirty. It's just that they cared about their bodies, and we didn't. We were flying higher than a kite and playing like we had just escaped from an asylum. We were coming after them like mad dogs in search of a bone with meat on it, and they had nowhere to go. They had to live with the consequences. We didn't. We just wanted to rock and roll.

As Aggie linebacker Greg Berry said, we didn't trust them at first. But after a few games, we began to realize that they were the most dedicated kickoff team in the nation. Certainly, nobody worked harder. And those teams coming into College Station were having to kick, scratch, and claw as hard as they could just to make it past the 20-yard line. These guys might have been a little small and a little slow. But they were for real.

Teams were learning not to take the 12th man unit for granted any more. No longer was the unit merely an afterthought. Teams began to game plan for the Aggie kickoff team.

Tom Arthur was chosen to make the trip to Lubbock. The Red Raiders had been studying game film. They played the scheme back again and again, looking for flaws, searching for a weakness, trying to determine just how they could slow down a pack of wild and howling dogs.

They changed their kickoff return tactics and threw the wedge away. Spread the field. Don't bunch up. Keep them looking left, and hit them from the right. Blindside the little bastards. Cold cock them from behind if necessary. Don't stick anybody up in their faces. Don't line up with big, slow-moving targets. Make the 12th man go out and search for somebody to hit, then come after them from angles they had never seen before. Let Jackie chew on that for awhile.

The Red Raiders crosschecked Tom Arthur on the kickoff. He did

not see, hear, or suspect anyone was coming until his world caved in and suddenly turned upside down. It was, he said, the hardest I had ever been hit.

The impact snapped the strings on his shoulder pads, and the pads ended up dangling haphazardly over his helmet. Arthur opened one eye, then the other. He was crumpled in a place he had never been before. He was lying in the middle of the Texas Tech cheerleaders.

He winked.

The 12th man team was being honored for its gallantry in action. No one disputed that. But most of the unit secretly harbored a belief that, one day, they would be sent on the field as a position player. They had seen the enemy up close, felt its wrath, and the only thing the enemy possessed that they didn't was a scholarship.

Ike Liles ran strong safety on the scout team and thought he just might have a chance to find his way onto the field even when A&M wasn't lining up for a kickoff. Maybe not with the first team or even the second, but play nevertheless. He said, I busted my head against the wall every day and was never scared of anyone. I was the only one on the field who didn't think I was a little guy.

The Aggies, however, were four deep at strong safety, and Liles kept being methodically moved down, never up, the depth chart. He was hell on the kickoff team. He was forgotten otherwise. The defensive coaches didn't bother to give him a look, not a real look anyway. After awhile, he stopped going to meetings with the other defensive backs. He simply went out and took out his anger and frustration on any poor sonuvagun running back a kickoff.

As he said, we got a lot more respect from the players than we did the assistant coaches. They buttonholed us on the 12th man team, locked us in a box, and threw the key away. Now if we could have just persuaded Alan Smith to quit bombing those balls into the end zone. Sixty yards is a long way to run for nothing. Sure, I'd hit somebody, but there wasn't a lot of satisfaction in it if he wasn't carrying the ball. I would have stomped on Alan Smith's bare kicking foot if I had gotten the chance.

Dennis Burns was running at wide receiver on the scout team, lining up to face Wayne Asbury, who grinned and said softly, you ain't gettin' past me, boy

Burns gritted his teeth.

No way.

Burns tensed his muscles.

Don't bother comin' my way, Asbury said. It's the wrong way. I'll take you out. That's what I'm supposed to do. Take you down and take you out. Maybe for the count.

Burns flexed his fingers.

You ain't gettin' past me, boy.

Burns cut right.

Asbury cut sharply left.

Asbury got there before Burns did.

Catching the ball was no problem. Neither was holding it. But Burns could not get himself free. There was daylight out there somewhere, but he wasn't having any luck finding it. Wayne Asbury had crawled inside his skin. Burns went left. Then he darted right. He spun one way and then back the other. He hit Asbury with his helmet, his knees, his elbow, his shoulder, any weapon at his disposal. He hit the defensive back

Dean Berry (1) and John Burnett (6) come swarming in a hurry to support a Danny Balcar (2) tackle.

head on, grabbed his jersey, and tried to toss him on the ground. Burns sprinted. He stutter-stepped. He tried to stop and go, fade, then fly He juked and faked, but only rarely did Burns see what the field was like on the other side of the whirling dervish squared up in front of him, a defensive back that clung to him closer than body odor.

Asbury kept his promise.

When I went down, Burns said, I went down hard. Maybe not for the count, but then I always stopped counting before I got to ten.

Roy Kokemoor was, without doubt, the oldest graduate assistant at Texas A&M. He had been a former head coach in high school, but he wanted to break into the college game, and he was willing to start at the bottom. So he walked away from a good-paying job and

was now earning two hundred dollars a month for the privilege of working under Jackie Sherrill. He had been assigned to join Curley Hallman in the defensive secondary. It was a curious combination. Hallman was incendiary. Kokemoor had a temper, all right, but he also had a gentle side. Hallman beat them down. Kokemoor did what he could to build them back up. Hallman would drive them through a brick wall. Kokemoor would open the door for them. Both men burned with a passion for football.

In practice during a sweltering afternoon when the temperatures had broken well past the top side of a hundred degrees, Kokemoor glanced across the field and saw Tom Bumgardner tangling with a wide receiver.

Football was combat.

It was all about winning and losing.

And only one could win.

Whip the next worthless low life before he whips you.

That's what it was all about, and fighting, whenever the occasion

Kokemoor was almost in tears.

He was sucking hot wind to catch a breath.

He looked up at Bumgardner and wheezed. I love the intensity, boys, he said. His voice was barely audible. But can one of you boys stop fighting long enough to bring me a cup of water. Cold. Hot. Just make sure it's wet.

Dennis Burns saw Jackie Sherrill coming down from his watching post high atop the tower, and he felt his muscles tense. Nothing good ever happened when Sherrill came down from the tower. Sherrill walked into the middle of a heated hamburger drill, and Burns could tell by the scowl on Sherrill's face that he was not a happy man, which meant nobody on the field was happy. In the drill, an offensive lineman squared off against a defensive lineman while a running back lowered his head and charged through a hole no more than five feet wide. It was close quarters and violent.

Coach Sherrill expected the players to give him their best at all times, Burns said. When they didn't, he would get in there amongst them. He blocked. He tackled. He took the ball and came at you as hard as he could, and Coach Sherrill could flat lay a hit on you. He didn't have the speed to run around you. But he could run through you, and, Lord help you, if you didn't lower a shoulder and knock him to the ground. He did not like the weak or the slackards.

The backs kept bursting loose and running free, which was fine for the offense, but it galled Sherrill, who preached defense in a voice filled with a heavy dose of fire and brimstone. He jumped between the linemen, grabbed a defensive end's jersey, and shouted, can't any of you worthless reprobates tackle the ball carrier?

Johnny Holland didn't hesitate. He grabbed a spot in the drill, shed the block as easily as a matador sheds the bull, and spiked the running back between the eyes with a massive forearm. The ball carrier stiffened and went down like a wild pig with a rifle slug in his forehead.

Holland grinned. That's my flipper, he said.

Sherrill nodded. Johnny Holland was indeed being wasted at quarterback. Rock Johnson dug in and waited for Ray Childress to hit him like a jackhammer. Not many people could rock the Rock. Childress could. He was just a big old teddy bear, Johnson said. He was quiet. He had nothing to say. But when he hit you, there was hell to pay, and I paid every day of my life.

He had a certain gleam in his eyes. He loved to kick my face in.

No. That's not quite right.

Ray Childress loved to kick everybody's face in.

Change the shape of their grin.

Childress didn't have to beat his chest or stomp around like Godzilla or do any trash talking. His play said everything you wanted to know about him. He was at A&M, going to classes like everybody else, but he had one mission and one focus in life: He was determined to play professional football. Ray Childress did not take any nonsense off anybody.

Coach Jackie Sherrill burned with intensity on the sidelines.

arose, was never out of the ordinary.

Kokemoor understood how tempers could flare, then flame out of control, but he preferred that his players bring blood during games when it counted. He began running across the field.

Bumgardner remembered, we had this wide receiver who fought with everyone who tried to defend him, especially if the defensive back happened to be on the 12th man. Scare tactics is what it was. Down and dirty scare tactics. I've got a scholarship. That was his attitude. Don't touch me, boy. You ain't got nothing.

Well, maybe not, but I had his tail in a double-barreled wringer. I stood him up at the line of scrimmage.

He grabbed my facemask.

I grabbed his helmet.

It came off, and I flung it angrily to the side. The helmet struck Coach Kokemoor as he ran toward us, hit him dead on, nailed him in the family jewels.

He went down to his knees.

I heard him grunt.

I saw his eyes roll back with pain.

And I'm thinking, this is not a good way to impress the coach. I may have been worthless before. I'm dead now.

Speed. Now you see him, now you don't speed. Football was always about speed. It couldn't be taught. It couldn't be coached. It was a God-given gift, and those who had it never understood why. Offense. Defense. Speed was what mattered, maybe all that mattered, which was the primary reason why Sherrill continued to be so intrigued with the potential of Tom Bumgardner

During practice, Sherrill brought in several of A&M's former high-profile football players to work with his team. Many had found careers in the NFL, and one was running back Curtis Dickey, who could cover a lot of ground in a hurry. Catch him now, or you couldn't catch him at all.

Bumgardner was on the scout team, playing defensive back, when Jimmie Hawkins grabbed a short pass, spun once, broke free, and headed with a quick burst toward the far sideline.

Bumgardner was coming hard, and he had the angle.

Hawkins was flying.

Dickey, wearing dress slacks and leather-soled shoes, was running down the sidelines, step for step with the running back.

Bumgardner had narrowed the gap.

Hawkins was looking for another gear.

And as he ran, Dickey was yelling, don't let that white boy catch you, Hawk. Don't let that white boy catch you.

Bumgardner was only a step or two away now.

Hawkins had thrown his head back.

His legs were a blur.

You can't let that white boy catch you, Dickey kept yelling. He was still yelling when the white boy did.

Bumgardner drove Hawkins to the ground, and they both rolled into a disjointed pile of twisted arms and legs at Dickey's feet. Dickey looked down at them for a moment, then walked away, shaking his head in disbelief and disgust. White boys don't run like that, he told Sherrill. You got yourself a fast white boy.

Rock Johnson rattled a lot of ball carriers. When he drove his helmet into their chest, they went down quick and hurt for a week. But he hardly ever ran any of them down. As he said, I couldn't catch a cold on a cold, wet night.

Billy Cannon, Jr., tried to help him with his speed.

He ran with Johnson every day.

But as the Rock said, I would be sprinting, and he would be jogging. I had fire. But Billy Cannon was smoke.

Day after day, they ran, and finally Cannon threw up his arms in despair. I'm sorry, he said.

About what?

You're not gonna get any faster.

Sure, I'm getting faster.

Cannon looked at him hard. Rock, he said, you know that story about the turtle and the hare?

Yeah.

It's a lie.

Tom Bevans, after two years in khakis, made the decision to leave the Corps. It was all about choices, he knew, and, for the moment, studies and football, sometimes in that order, took precedence over everything else.

There was a definite conflict between classes and practice. As soon as a professor spoke his last word, Bev-

ans would run madly toward Kyle Field. If practice had already started, he said, I was a condemned man. Anybody who arrived late was a condemned man. We had to run the bleachers carrying twenty-five-pound cinder blocks under each arm. We called them Aggie blocks. We ran until our arms gave out, then we kept on running. There was a heavy price to pay if you dropped one. We found out we could tolerate things we didn't know possible.

Classes ran late far too many times, and I did a lot of running with cinder blocks. My arms ached. My head hurt all the time. My helmet had originally been laid to rest somewhere in the 1950s. It didn't protect much, but it was old school, and I loved wearing it.

I kept a jar of aspirin beside my bed, and I took a handful before practice and another handful when I got back to my room at night. Bayer and Deep Heat. I wouldn't have survived without them.

Barry Stevens earned his commission as second lieutenant in the Corps. In the afternoons, he put on his Class A uniform with the officer's bars on the shoulder and strode smartly across campus on his way toward Kyle Field.

Corps members saluted him as he walked past.

He was someone important, an officer and gentlemen.

A short walk later, he entered the dark chambers of a locker room, traded his freshly starched uniform for one that had been handed down one too many generations ago, and ran toward the practice field like a lamb being led to slaughter.

Tom Arthur brought speed and athleticism to the first 12th man team.

It's celebration time for Jeff Boutwell (11), David Coolidge (7), Mark Wurzbach (21), Rick Tankersley (20), and Ronnie Glenn (9). When a team only a had a few plays a game, it looked forward to excelling every time downfield.

Chapter 13

Jackie Sherrill had seen enough. Jackie Sherrill had endured enough. Games, more often than not, were won at the quarterback position, and John Mazur had not lived up to expectations. He had great size and a great arm. He worked hard, had a good grasp of the offense, and was an unselfish young man, but, under his leadership, the Aggies simply weren't driving the ball down the field. The defensive corps, to no one's surprise, had become the strength and the anchor of the team, but, unless the defense pitched a shutout, A&M was in trouble. At Southern Cal, John Mazur had lost his starting job to a freshman. It was about to happen again. Something was definitely missing from the Aggie attack, so Sherrill made the move he had been hesitant to make.

Like a riverboat gambler running short of chips, the coach decided to go for double or nothing. He turned to a freshman quarterback. Kevin Murray was considered the future, and his future might as well begin now. In reality, Sherrill had little choice. He made the move and was determined to live with the consequences.

Mistakes. They were bound to happen.

But Sherrill was looking far down the road, and he believed that Murray had the arm, the quickness, the speed, the command to take them the distance, no matter how far the road stretched out in front

of them. Sherrill had glimpsed a dim light at the end of a long, dreadful tunnel when Kevin Murray took control toward the end of the debacle with Oklahoma State. The freshman completed four straight passes, including a 38-yard touchdown to Jeff Nelson.

He looked like he belonged, and, for Sherrill, there was no reason to wait any longer.

As Sally Wilson in the *Dallas Morning News* reported, Coach Jackie Sherrill compares Murray's arm to the rifle attached to Dan Marino's chest. (Murray's nickname is Magnum.) He scrambles and reacts so adroitly that he has been given control of 70 percent of plays from the line of scrimmage. Murray, with 4.5 speed, is a threat outside the pocket as well as in it.

Murray, Wilson wrote, had read an article about the pressure being piled on top of a freshman quarterback starting for the first time for a team whose record had sunk to a dismal 1-3. He was green, she reported, and the offense was a pale shade of yellow. In the past eleven quarters, the offense had scored no points. Murray put down the sports section and laughed. Who is this guy, Murray said to himself. He doesn't know me. What gives him the right? This is my opportunity. I love proving critics wrong.

The Aggies promptly went out and shocked Houston, 30-7. No. They defeated Houston. They shocked the Aggie alumni. It was, however, an ignominious beginning. The Cougars scored first, then Murray struck back with the quickness of an irritated rattlesnake, leading A&M to thirty points in thirty minutes. The schooling of Kevin Murray had only begun. The Aggies tied Baylor, 3-3, when Thomas Everett, the Bear defensive back, blocked an Alan Smith field goal attempt in the last quarter. It was a game the Aggies knew they should have won, the kind of high-profile game they needed to win if A&M ever hoped to dig itself out of a hole growing deeper by the week. More than anyone Sherrill understood that it would be a long, hard climb out of the ditch.

That was the last straw. Robert Crouch was mad as hell, and he wasn't going to take it anymore. All afternoon long, the Baylor wide receiver had been searching him out on the kickoff and coming up alongside like a bolt of blindside thunder.

Now the play was over.

The tackle had been made.

The whistle had blown.

And the Bear wide receiver flashed out of nowhere one more time and scissored Crouch's legs out from under him. He went down as if he had been shot. In war, Crouch decided, anybody who didn't shoot back carried a white flag. As the wide receiver rose to his feet, Crouch drove an elbow into his ear hole. The helmet shuddered. The receiver's head snapped back.

No one saw.

No second whistle.

At least, Crouch was hoping that no one saw.

He jogged innocently toward the bench, and his eyes met the unmistakable glare of Jackie Sherrill. He turned and headed toward the end of the bench. I'll just pretend I don't see him, Crouch told himself, and maybe he'll forget.

John Roper eased up alongside of him. Coach Sherrill wants to see you, he said.

Crouch stared ahead, not wanting to meet the judge, jury, and executioner all on the same play. He say what he wants, Crouch asked.

He wants a piece of you, Roper told him.

I was afraid of that.

He saw the elbow.

Crouch didn't know whether to run or walk, so he did a little of both. Sherrill was waiting for him. Sherrill was probably timing him.

Crouch wished he had run faster.

I saw you hit the kid, Sherrill said.

He had it coming.

It could have cost us if the referee had seen it.

Yes, sir.

Sherrill's voice had the cutting edge of a rusty butcher knife. I don't want to lose a game because some lamebrain 12th man kid can't hold his damn temper.

No, sir.

You gonna do it again?

No, sir.

By the way, Sherrill said when Crouch turned to escape the coach's wrath, you're right. The little bastard did deserve it. That was a helluva good hit.

Kevin Murray and Texas A&M kept rolling, sputtering from time to time, but managing to defeat Rice, 29-10 and earning Sherrill his first road victory at Texas A&M. He wasn't particularly proud of the way the game unfolded, saying, sometimes we played well, and sometimes we didn't.

Murray may have been the difference. Kevin's a money guy, tight end Rich Siler said. He likes to go for the big plays. He's a gambler. He likes to take chances.

A cloud of unexpected controversy began to darken the career of Kevin Murray. He had been signed as an eleventh-round draft choice to play baseball for Milwaukee, received a bonus of $35,000, spent ten weeks of his life in the Brewers Rookie League, played a mere thirty-one games in the ball club's Instructional League, and decided he had could hit wide receivers better than a curve ball.

Murray left baseball for Texas A&M, and the Brewers sued. They obtained an injunction to keep him out of football, trying to enforce a provision in his contract that prohibited Murray from participating in any outside activities that could cause an injury. Milwaukee hinted at, but never produced any evidence, that Murray had been given a few illegal inducements to trade sports and head to College Station. Milwaukee knew what made headlines. And when the leering press was involved, hard facts be damned.

A judge ruled that the quarterback could play for the Aggies until the case was settled in court, but the threatened legal battle and the great unknown that lay ahead in a courtroom played games with Murray's mind all fall. By November, the ordeal was over. The suit against Kevin Murray, Coach Jackie Sherrill, and Texas A&M was "dismissed without prejudice," a high-dollar legal term that simply meant the case had been dropped.

At SMU, the game came down to a foot, probably less, that could have been measured either way. The Mustangs led 10-7. The game had slipped into the fourth quarter. Time had become critical, but the Aggies were on the move, driving the ball to the Mustang one-yard line and facing second down. On the previous play, A&M thought Jimmie Hawkins had scored. SMU was praying he came up short. His dive over the top was marked down inside the one-yard line. Home field advantage had reared its ugly head. As Sherrill said, it was either a poor call or an inadvertent whistle. His momentum never stopped. Hawkins had been hit in the air, knocked back, then spun his way into the end zone. A second dive hit a stone wall, and Sherrill was facing fourth-down. A 10-10 tie was only a field goal away, but Sherrill wanted a win. If it had been a yard, he said, we would have kicked a field goal. But it was less than six inches, so we went for it.

Said SMU defensive tackle Mitch Willis, the Aggies were so close to the goal line you could place half a burnt cigarette between the nose of the ball and the end zone. It was that close. It might as well have been a mile of bad road. Kevin Murray's sneak went nowhere.

The half a burnt cigarette had not moved.

As John Lopez wrote in the *Battalion*, the better than 60,000 Aggie fans cheered, the SMU players signaled no touchdown, and the A&M players signaled touchdown. The only person in Kyle Field who didn't seem to know if Murray scored was Bob Jones, the referee.

As the players walked angrily off the field, Tom Christner fell in behind Ray Childress. He could tell that Childress was seething inside. They passed the door, and Childress suddenly rammed his fist through a small window, sealed with chicken wire.

The glass shattered.

The chicken wire broke. Childress was beyond pain.

Sherrill felt empty inside. We gained a lot of respect, he said. On that particular day, he would have traded respect for a win.

Dennis Mudd, the walk-on, was frustrated. He had liked Tom Wilson and was shocked when he heard the news that Jackie Sherrill was taking command of Aggie football. Why do they need to hire a Yankee from Pittsburgh, he wondered. No one understood him. No one wanted to understand him. He would walk right past you, twirling his whistle, and act as though he didn't see you. I was way down at the bottom rung of the ladder, and Sherrill didn't even know I was in school or care I was on the football team.

Dennis Mudd simply shook his head with disgust when those reports about the 12th man kickoff team started making their way across campus. Sherrill can't even coach a real football team, Mudd thought. Why is he doing some fool stunt like this?

Mudd found out.

All season, he said, he had been a meat-squad running back against the varsity. But now Mudd had become the ignominious meat-squad running back against the 12th man unit, chosen to run back kickoffs in practice. Why not? Somebody had to do it, and he was as disposable as an old pair of socks. The 12th man had been hammered around on the scout team all day, and they were more than willing to stay an extra thirty minutes for the privilege of taking out their anger, frustration, and revenge on him.

It got old the first day, Mudd said. The kickoffs were live. They came at full speed, time after time, and they came racing downfield like scud missiles. They weren't wimps. They were psychos. Mudd felt as though they might be his next of kin, and if they hit him any harder or any more often, somebody might well be looking for his next of kin. He loved defense, strong safety to be exact. Because of Mudd's quickness and agility, however, the A&M coaches decided he was better suited to be a running back. Sure, he had carried the ball in high school, but Mudd had been a natural on defense, recording 120 tackles while playing on one leg during his senior year.

He stared across the field at the 12th man squad. Maybe, that's where he belonged, Mudd thought to himself. Maybe he should throw in with them. They hit like he hit. They knew how to crack heads. His was a prime example. Mudd had once ridiculed Jackie Sherrill's idea for the 12th man. Suddenly, it was beginning to make sense. Suddenly, the all-volunteer team didn't seem nearly as outlandish as it once did. He wondered if Sherrill was still looking for any volunteers.

Arkansas and its poor, old, forty-thousand-dollar-a-year, Coach Lou Holtz, came hog calling all their way into town. Arkansas was a perennial powerhouse, but Holtz was crying the blues, and no one could cry as well as he did. His team had the flu bug, he said. As many as forty players were under the weather. He was shedding tears for the leering press and saying that he hoped beyond hope he would have enough players left to suit up and play on Saturday. He feared that the game just might have to be played in the emergency room.

Maybe he had been right. On the field, the Razorbacks appeared to be befuddled and bewildered. Kevin Murray sliced and diced Arkansas with four touchdown passes, but perhaps the turning point came when the 12th man kickoff team shook up Kyle Field by forcing a Razorback to cough up a fumble in the fourth quarter. They crucified the ball carrier, Sherrill said, and it was without doubt the biggest play of the game. The

Battalion reported that the 12th man play, which the Kyle Field crowd liked better than Bevo burgers, was a supreme final blow against an Arkansas team that hadn't given up so many points to the Aggies in thirty-three years. Before the play, the Razorbacks were merely behind. After it, they were beaten. The play was pure hard-eyed football, but those shoulder pads cracked together with the sweet sound of vengeance. It was as final as gunning down your enemy, counting your coup over his body, then doing the California Quake on his grave.

It was also Sherrill's answer to critics who had belittled the expensive coach, the struggling Aggies, and their gimmicky exploitation of 12th Man tradition. The 12th man team, which struck me when I first heard of it as the dumbest idea since sleeper-beepers, has in fact been one of the brightest spots on an Aggie ball club that happened to be walking in tall cotton.

Arkansas had been ranked nationally in the Top Ten, and the Razorbacks had their backs to the wall. It was time to make something happen. Alan Smith hit a kick high into a clear sky, and the 12th man came charging downfield like a maroon and white version of the Light Brigade.

Before the game, Wally Hall, a sports reporter for the *Arkansas Gazette*, had written: The 12th Man. What a joke.

The joke was running on all cylinders and gaining ground.

Keith Newton, brace and all, and Tom Bumgardner slammed into the ball carrier. We stuck him pretty good, Newton said.

The ball popped loose.

And Tom Arthur leaped on it.

A year's worth of dreams all came to pass within a split second. Wally Hall be damned.

Wally Hall could take his joke and shove it.

As the team raced triumphantly to the sidelines, Curley Hallman walked out to meet them and asked, who caused the fumble?

A couple of us hit him, Bumgardner replied nonchalantly. I know I was one of them. He shrugged.

Curley Hallman shook his head. I don't think so, he said.

Newton was wobbling off the field, shaking his head, trying to get both eyes focused at the same time and looking in the same direction. The hit hadn't ~~crossed his eyes~~, but it surely did rearrange the pupils. He started to answer, then thought it might be better to just find some place and sit down. The bench wasn't soft, but it was handy. He slumped down, holding his head with his hands. He closed his eyes. When I open them, he told himself, it will all be better. It wasn't.

The Arkansas game ball was given to Leroy Hallman.

At practice the next afternoon, Sherrill stood up and told his players, we took a good look at the game film last night. The film doesn't lie. I'm giving the Arkansas game award to Keith Newton. He had a lot of help, but he was there first.

Sherrill made points with the 12th man team by righting a wrong. As Dennis Mudd said, Leroy was Curley Hallman's nephew and had been given preferential treatment from the day he set foot on campus. We all knew Leroy hadn't caused the fumble, but when the announcement was made that he had, it was viewed as more internal self-promotion, and that rubbed a lot of people the wrong way. When Coach Sherrill stepped up to make the change, he grew in our eyes as someone who was fair and committed to doing the right thing.

Two years later, Bumgardner was seated at his brother's home watching a taped replay of the game. He studied the hit time and again, frame-by-frame, and a big grin crossed his face. There was Newton. There was Arthur. There he was as the Arkansas returner snapped his head back. No sign of Leroy Hallman. He may have been twisted up somewhere in the dog pile, but he didn't have any Arkansas red on his helmet. Any doubt lingering in Bumgardner's mind had all been erased. He, Newton, and Arthur had indeed done the damage the day the Razorbacks fell. He quickly left the room and immediately called Tom Arthur long distance.

We've been vindicated, was all he said.

Lynn Ashby, a featured columnist for the *Houston Post,* remembered the game this way. The kickoff and the group of Christmas help, known collectively as the 12th man, runs down the field, he wrote. A strong wind, a strong leg, and a good kick put the ball beyond the end zone.

This is a beautiful fall afternoon, perfect for a college football game. The bands are playing, the students are yelling, the alumni are drinking. Down on the field, the Arkansas Razorbacks look pretty sharp. They have beaten the Aggies like a drum for years, winning 10 of the last 12 games. Indeed, Arkansas Coach Lou Holtz has never lost at College

Station. A&M kicks a field goal, and the 12th man runs back on the field. The kickoff sails into the Brazos ...

Sectional football games have the glory and the despair of war, and when a Texas team takes the field against a foreign state, it is an army with banners. Nowhere is this more evident than here at Kyle Field, where it is now halftime. The Arkansas band takes one look at the Aggie band and refuses to leave the stands. One cannot blame them. The Aggie band fills up the field.

The Texas A&M army resumes its battle, which, thus far, has been going poorly. Once again, A&M kicks off. Apparently they would rather have the wind on this gusty day than the ball. The 12th man comes out and nails the receiver on the 15. The game grinds on as the Aggies score, then score again. Then again. The 12th man is spending more time on the field than the starting lineup. The Aggies are pounding Arkansas, 24-9 ... The Hogs score once and go for two points. By the end of the third quarter, it is 24-17.

With 7:58 left in the game, the 12th man staggers out onto the field. They are not used to such labor. The ball sails down the field where it is taken by a Razorback named James Shibest, from Houston. He is hit by the A&M Class of '84. The poor fellow goes down, the ball goes up, and the Aggies have it. The 12th man gets a standing ovation and, later, one of the game balls.

No one is laughing at the 12th man anymore.

When the 12th man team came downfield, a tackle sometimes looked more like a catch-as-catch-can wrestling match.

worse than usual. The brace felt heavier than normal. He was dragging around the field.

Take it easy.

That was the attitude.

Loosen up.

Stretch a little.

Jog a little.

Get your body ready for tomorrow.

That's the way it had always been on Friday before a Saturday game.

Hey, Newton, Sherrill yelled, walking toward him.

Yes, sir.

What's your trouble?

Nothing, Coach.

Well, dammit, if you're not going to run, you can just keep your worthless pile of dogmeat here, and we'll take somebody else.

Keith Newton turned and started running. Faster. Ever faster. He forgot about the knee and the brace. Half-speed became full-speed, and he kept reaching frantically for the accelerator. It was already mashed as far down as he could mash it.

To Tom Christner, Jackie Sherrill looked mad. He acted mad. His face was a grim, agitated slab of granite. Start running, he told his players. Start running, he told the 12th man team.

And they ran.

Keep running, Sherrill yelled. Harder.

He ran us down the field, Christner said. He ran us out of the stadium. He ran us down to the pool where the swimming and diving team worked out. Then he yelled, now get rid of your shoulder pads, jump in, and cool off.

Texas A&M was staring face to face with a possible, though implausible, bowl bid. A win over TCU, and the Aggies just might slip unexpectedly into the Independence Bowl. It was still regarded as a Leftover Bowl, but the Aggies were growing weary of staying at home during the holidays. They were ready to go anywhere. Bad bowl, maybe. But a damn good party.

Dennis Mudd displays the unbridled and enthusiasm and emotion that came to typify the spirit of the 12th man kickoff team. When the unit was on the field, they went on hard every play. They were playing for themselves and the student body both.

Sherrill had always told his 12th man unit, somewhere on a Saturday afternoon or a Saturday night, some kickoff team somewhere in the nation is going to run downfield and force a fumble that decides the outcome of a ball game. Somebody will do it. This week. Next week. Every week. It may as well be you.

Against Arkansas, Sherrill and the 12th man kickoff team had made believers out of each other. Now, he was telling the *Bryan Eagle*, I wish we could go back and start over. We probably could be 8-1 or 7-2. But you can't go backwards.

A&M had lost three games by a total of seven points. One less penalty. One less fumble. One less mistake. One less bad decision. One more break. The season could have been so much different.

It was as close to an off day as the 12th man unit received, the Friday before a Saturday game when players worked out in sweats and allowed their deep bruises to climb to the surface of the skin and change to a pale shade of purple. Sherrill always selected a couple players from his 12th man unit to travel out of town, and Keith Newton had nailed down one spot. He wasn't about to lose it. His bad knee was hurting

The game suddenly turned sour. Just before halftime, word filtered down that Virginia Tech would get the Independence Bowl bid to play Air Force regardless of the Aggie performance against TCU. Emotions had been running high. They were crushed.

And finally the game turned bitter. Texas A&M slipped away from Amon Carter Stadium with a 20-10 victory that disgusted both teams. The game moved slowly, was an uninspired, penalty-marred, mistake-filled drudge. According to the *Houston Post*, it, more or less, resembled a twenty-car pileup on artificial turf.

Both Sherrill and TCU Coach Jim Wacker walked angrily off the field criticizing the officials. If the officiating doesn't get any better, Sherrill said, still steaming from the bad call in A&M's 10-7 loss at SMU, then the conference ought to wipe the slate clean and start over. David Crisp wrote in the *Bryan Eagle*, Wacker said the officials appeared to be intimidated, a charge as serious as accusing John Wayne of having been a sissy.

It was, all in all, a most unpleasant affair.

Down the road, the 12th man team could see them coming, those bastards from Texas. And it would be their day to shine. They were sure of it. Joe Kammlah wrote in the *Bryan Eagle,* ten men will streak down Kyle Field, their bodies targeted for a Texas Longhorn ball carrier. For a good many, it will be their first and last shot to play in THE GAME. The 12th man team is giving up less yardage per kickoff than the varsity team that does that chore on the road games. The 12th man team, on returns, has given up an average of 13.6 yards. The road team has given up an average of 18.8 yards.

The 12th man had become a precision unit, finely tuned and running like clockwork.

On Saturday, THE GAME would be more like a clockwork orange.

Burnt orange.

The 12th man had one mission. Keep those bastards from Austin as far away from their end zone as possible and give them a new meaning of pain, one that would stay with them for a long time.

The 12th man had one problem, however. Those bastards from Austin were ranked number two in the nation, were undefeated, and, with a victory, just might have a chance to play in the Cotton Bowl for the mythical national championship.

Jackie Sherrill, as much as anyone, understood that the rivalry game with Texas transcended all boundaries. It wasn't life or death. It was worse. It is the game you live with 365 days, he said. And the Bryan Eagle reported on the rivalry, calling it city slickers versus sod busters, aggie jokes, A&M's Bonfire, male yell leaders, Corps of Cadets, time-worn fight songs unlike any other in the world, the 12th Man, and all the other dusty traditions that still prevail. For Texas, the biggest tradition is winning.

Sherrill read the story and thought it should burn with Bonfire.

Those bastards from Austin had better win while they could.

He was about to change all of that.

The shadows hovered like a great flannel shroud around the stack of logs. The masses had flocked to the Bonfire site, old and young, students and alumni, farmers and engineers, stock raisers and stockbrokers. The football seniors huddled together on the edge of a platform stage jutting out from the face of the stack.

Dennis Burns was standing around by himself, hands in his pockets, staying out of the way, looking down at the multitudes who were making their way toward the logs. For years, he had been down there in the middle of the Aggie faithful. Never in his wildest imagination had Dennis Burns ever let himself think that he would be standing up on stage come Bonfire night.

Curley Hallman ambled up and told him, be sure to thank Coach Sherrill for giving you the opportunity to play.

Burns frowned. He was used to Hallman being in his face, but usually the coach was screaming at him. Tonight, there was a calm amusement in his eyes.

What are you talking about, Burns asked.

You're about to go out there and make a talk, Hallman said.

Why me?

Why not?

You could have given me some advance warning, Burns said. His nerves were running on straight adrenaline now and threatening to derail at any minute. It felt as though it was being pumped directly to his veins. What'll I say, he wanted to know.

I already told you.

So, when the time came, Dennis Burns stepped forward, awkwardly took the microphone, looked down at the hordes in maroon and white, and, he remembered, I thanked Coach Sherrill for giving us the opportunity to play on the 12th man team. I thanked the rest of the coaches for putting up with us. I thanked the varsity players for allowing us to be a part of their team. I thanked the student body for their support. And I said something about beating the hell out of t.u.

It was, he said, the longest and most frightening twenty-eight seconds of his life. By comparison, kickoffs and the punishment that came with them were a slow walk in the park.

Dennis Mudd had drawn the ill-fated black bean and was too excited to realize it. He was among those freshmen and walk-ons selected to battle Cisco Junior College in a JV game. As far as he was concerned, the game offered legitimate playing time, and, at a robust two hundred pounds, Mudd was assigned the fullback duties.

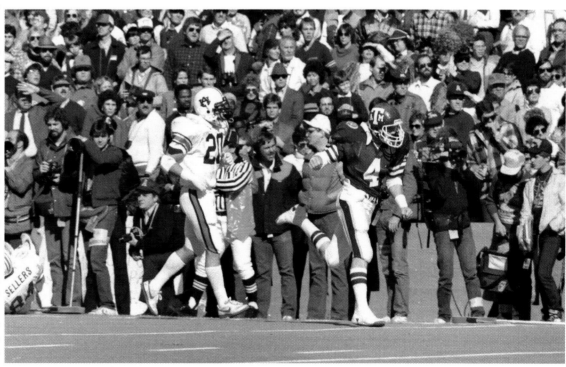

Dennis Mudd (4) beats his SMU blocker and races madly down the sidelines in search of the ball.

On the fourth play of the game, he was the lead blocker on a sweep left. He hit the linebacker, and, in an instant, separated his shoulder and fractured his collarbone. Mudd rose to his feet in agony but refused to leave the game even though the pain bordered on being unbearable. When he finally took his shoulder pads off, he heard head trainer Karl Kapchinski spit out the four words he dreaded most: *out for the season.* He might be out, but Mudd faithfully suited up for every game and stood on the sidelines, watching the 12th man become a team of rock stars while he was wallowing in his own misery.

The pain began to subside a little. The throbbing did not go away, but it wasn't pounding so hard anymore. Mudd decided he could play. Bite the bullet. If I ignore the pain, he told himself, then it's not there. Before the Texas game, Pickard saw him walk into the locker room one afternoon before practice. What the hell are you doing here, he wanted to know.

The shoulder's doing fine, Mudd said. I think I'm ready to play again.

The hell with that. Pickard spit. Don't bother to put your pads on, he said. I've spent the whole damn semester putting you back together. I'm not about to start picking you up in pieces again.

Texas had the swagger, all right. And Sherrill told the leering press, you can only play a certain number of games each year on emotions. The rest of the time, you have to line up and play on ability. The stadium will be crowded. I hope the play on the field will be crowded, too. When his players went back to the locker room after warm-ups, they found that Sherrill had new uniforms waiting for them. The Aggies, for the first time all year, would be wearing solid maroon.

The wind was gusting to thirty-five miles an hour, and A&M took advantage of the gale to jump out to a quick 13-0 lead. Texas might be undefeated and hanging on to the dream of a national championship, but the burnt orange had not yet been able to carve out a first down, and the Aggies were lining up with hostility in their eyes and fire simmering in their guts. Beating Texas would at least ease a measure of the heartbreak that all of those close losses had inflicted on them.

A&M kicked off once more, and Alan Smith dumped the ball to the goal line.

Between the thud of the kick and the thud of the ball carrier's head slamming into the turf, the game dramatically turned.

So quick.

So sudden.

So unexpectedly.

Tom Bumgardner recalled, I saw the football bounce awkwardly on the six-yard line. The kick returner picked it up, and I dove for him. We were all closing in like a herd of raging bulls, and two of us got there at the same time. At least, I thought we both got there at the same time.

Somebody hit him early.

Bumgardner hit him late.

He saw the dreaded yellow flag falling to the turf about the same time he heard the whistle.

Fifteen yards.

Instead of being penned up on the nine-yard line, Texas was on the twenty-four. The dominoes had started to fall, and the crash was deafening. During the drive, Domingo Bryant hit the Texas quarterback out of bounds, and the Longhorns were in business just on the shy side of midfield. A long pass, a race to the end zone, and Texas was right back in the game. The Aggies had stumbled, and they never recovered.

Momentum had shifted in a single heartbeat, and those bastards from Austin thundered to a 45-13 win. Sherrill blamed the late hit by the 12th man for the defeat. It broke our backs, he said.

Tom Bumgardner was mortified.

He had been playing hard.

And it cost him.

Hell, he thought, it cost the whole team.

That night, Bumgardner did not sleep much, if at all. That night, Jackie Sherrill watched the game film, a frustrated man sitting alone in a dark room with the reflection of the screen ricocheting off a grim face.

The next day, he dispatched David Beal to find Tom Bumgardner.

Coach was wrong, Beal said. He sent me over to apologize to you. You had a great hit, and it wasn't late. You didn't make a mistake. The yellow flag did.

The referees had exacted their measure of revenge.

They had defied all tradition, rationale, and common sense when it came to discussing the X's and O's of big-time college football. And, according to a headline in the *Austin American-Statesman*, the 12th man silenced taunts with talent and extra effort. Brad Buchholz, wrote in the newspaper, every time they line up for a kickoff, the players hear someone cackle from across the field. Invariably, some 210-pound linebacker tells the players to hold onto their helmets to keep their heads from popping off. Someone always tells an Aggie joke. Even now, someone always has a taunting word for Texas A&M's 12th man kickoff team.

I'll never forget Houston, said sophomore Leroy Hallman, a regular member of the all-volunteer 12th man team and a star high school player from Tuscaloosa, Alabama, who had moved to third-team free safety. When we went out on the line, all of those guys just looked at us and laughed All of them laughed. They just stared at us and made jokes. A lot of people still think we're a joke. Every week, there's somebody popping off about us in the papers before we play a new team. I remember SMU said they were gonna scatter banana peels on the field and then watch up slip and fall. I tell you, though, they had their chance to run one back against us. But they set the ball down in the end zone instead. There must have been something that changed their mind.

The 12th man has compiled a better record against kick returns than last year's bigger varsity squad. A much better record. In five home appearances, the 12th man has limited the opponents to only 74 total yards – and an average return of 12.3 yards. A&M's varsity unit – a scholarship group that executed kickoffs in road games, has allowed an average of 19.3 yards per return.

They have exceeded all expectations, said David Beal, the former Aggie quarterback who coaches the 12th man team. When we were working in the spring, you could see they had talent. Still you didn't know. But all the repetitions they've had, working over and over in practice, has really made a difference.

Week after week, the 12th man is upstaged by Aggie placekicker Alan Smith, who kicks the ball halfway to Hearne most of the time ... But even when we see the ball going into the end zone, said Hallman, we're still looking for someone to hit. I try to get my licks in. If someone's in the way, I hit him.

Still others adopt a more wistful attitude. It would be nice if Smith would just miss one once in a while, said senior Tom Christner, from the Panhandle town of Wheeler. You know, just when he got to the ball, if he'd just slip just a little bit.

Ironically, most Aggies agree that the 12th man unit makes its greatest contribution by merely showing up. It's kind of a spiritual thing, said Tom Arthur. It gets everyone in the stadium motivated – from the people in the stands to the players.

They're great at making things happen, said linebacker Darrell Smith, a sophomore scholarship player from Pasadena. When those guys go out on the field, the crowd gets about eighty percent louder for about ten minutes. It carries over for a long time. Believe it or not, I think the crowd gets just as loud every single time it happens. I've got a lot of respect for every single one of those guys. They always go out full speed, willing to break their necks for us. It takes a lot of courage to do what they do. I don't know if I'd have enough courage to do it myself.

Finally, there is Christner, a quiet, soft-spoken agricultural economics major who spent three years watching Texas A&M from the stands before trying out for the 12th man this year. Now, the former class B football player from the Texas Panhandle finds himself playing in front of 60,000 fans on a Saturday afternoon. I never dreamed something like this could ever happen. When I left high school, I never thought I'd ever wear pads again, said Christner. I really look at this as an honor, an honor to be on the very first 12th man team. I think it will be a special thing to tell my grandchildren someday.

For the original sixteen members of the 12th man kickoff team, the season was over, it sometimes seemed, before it had really ever be-gan. The unit had been maligned and ridiculed. But their performance was exemplary. Throughout the nation, those who knew little or anything about Texas A&M, the university, had become quite familiar with the 12th man team, the walk-ons who slugged it out with elite scholarship football players in practice and in the games, the little guys who had stood toe-to-toe with the big guys, rolled up their sleeves, and knocked the big guys on their collective asses.

The 12th man represented the student body of Texas A&M, to be sure. But they also represented every fan in every corner of the country who yearned to achieve something that the world kept telling them was impossible to accomplish. They symbolized every hope that had not materialized, every dream that had shattered. They faced fear and refused to back down. They faced adversity and never quit. Pain did not take a day off even when they did. As Barry Stevens said, our bodies hurt every day. Mistakes? Sure, there had been a few. But when it was all said and done, the 12th man kickoff team led the nation in allowing the fewest number of yards per return.

As Jackie Sherrill said of them, the kids on the 12th man team were a little hungry about making things happen. They got knocked down, but they wouldn't stay down. Robert Crouch said, Coach believed that we played like he did, with more heart than talent, with more desire than ability, with more guts than sense. We probably played better than we should have played because Coach Sherrill trusted us, and, to a man, we didn't want to let him down.

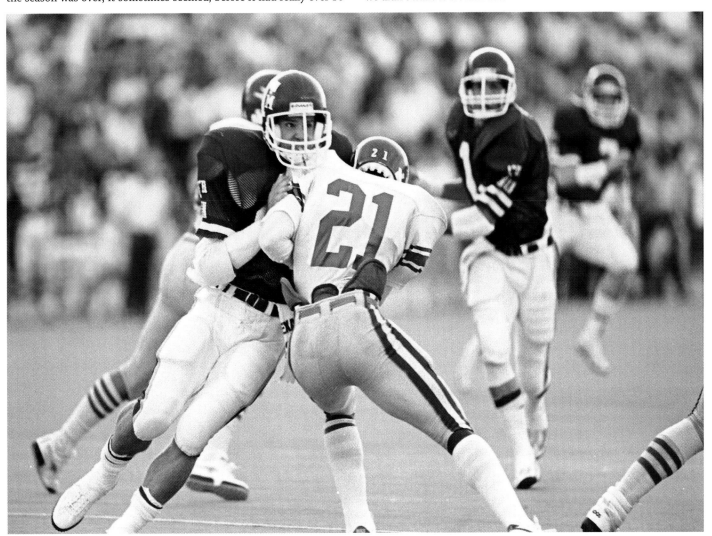

Dean Berry (1) and his frenzied pack of 12th man team mad dogs come barreling through the wedge. On every kickoff, the thought was basic and simple: You can stop one of us, perhaps. Good luck. But there's no way you can stop us all.

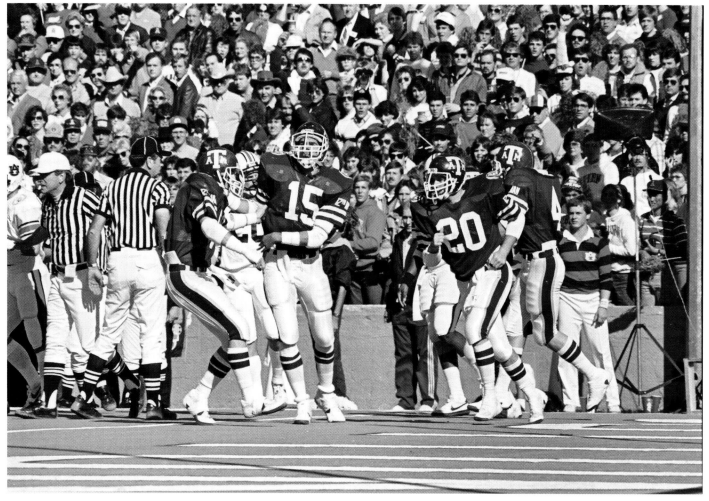

Tony Pollacia (15), Rick Tankersley (20), and Dennis Mudd (4) congratulate each other after another tackle. Even though the 12th man kept receiving a new infusion of blood with a new set of players each other, the tradition held strong.

Chapter 14

Roy Kokemoor had been as close to the 12th man kickoff team as anyone. As a graduate assistant, he had worked with defensive backs coach Curley Hallman during the 1983 season, and Kokemoor kept sending the 12th man scout team into battle against the best and the brightest that Texas A&M's varsity squad had to offer, propping them up when they could barely walk after a knee-jerk, blindside hit, wiping the blood from their faces, clearing the glaze from their eyes, and kicking them back into the skirmish to fight tanks with pitchforks one more time. Can't quit, he kept telling them. Got to keep going. Pain's all in your mind, he said. Won't hurt long. Won't hurt forever. But sometimes, Roy Kokemoor lied to them. He always believed that the members of the 12th man unit were a lot better than anybody gave them credit for being. The leering press loved them. But not even the leering pressed believed in them. Sports writers kept waiting for Jackie Sherrill's iconoclastic idea to blow up in the Aggie faces. The 12th man squad wasn't a novelty, Kokemoor said. It wasn't a stunt. It was a time bomb when the ball was teed up.

David Beal had been in charge of the inaugural team in 1983, but now Beal was moving on to concentrate on his own graduate studies. Jackie Sherrill had a team without a coach. He glanced over a list of possible names, made a quick decision, believed he had the right man already in place, and walked over to the cubicle where Roy Kokemoor was once again trying to digest the nuances of the Aggie playbook. Sherrill,

who never wasted words, got right to the point. They're all yours, said.

Who are all mine?

The 12th man kickoff team.

Kokemoor took a deep breath. What do you want me to do, Coach, he asked.

Sherrill frowned. Didn't you hear me, he asked. I said they're yours. You'll be their coach. Not me. He turned and walked away. The decision on what to do with the 12th man team no longer troubled him. One problem. One problem solved. Sherrill had other things on his mind at the moment.

In reality, he had become the controversial centerpiece in a tale of two cities. In College Station, Sherrill was expected to be the magician who would forever change the fortunes of Texas A&M football. Yet, in the minds of many Aggies, his first two seasons had been abysmal and unacceptable. With Sherrill at the throttle, A&M had stumbled to a 5-6 record in 1982, then shown only minimal improvement the next year, flirting briefly with a bowl bid before stumbling home with a 5-5-1 mark badly scarred with a bitter loss to Texas. Many of the school's most devoted alumni were no longer merely wondering if Sherrill had been worth a million dollars. They were beginning to worry if he had even been worth their trouble.

Back in Pittsburgh, however, there was weeping and wailing and the gnashing of teeth. No bitterness. Just lamentations. As Bob Smizik of the *Post-Gazette* wrote, when Sherrill left, the Pitt football program took a hit from which it is still staggering. Early in the third week of January in 1982, a simmering feud in Pitt's athletic department, one laced with intrigue and backstabbing, came to a full boil when the highly successful Jackie Sherrill, feeling disrespected, bolted for a big-money deal at Texas A&M. No one realized it at the time – people thought the program was bigger than the coach – but Sherrill's departure was the beginning of a slide that has become a full-blown avalanche. Pitt was poised for another national championship run. Almost nothing could stop them except the departure of Sherrill. He demanded and received discipline. His players liked him, respected him, and even feared him a bit. He didn't say much, but when he talked, people responded in a positive manner. He had an uncanny eye for talent – in players and assistant coaches both.

Before Sherrill's sudden departure from Pittsburgh, he told *Press* columnist Pat Livingston, I get the feeling there are people at Pitt who don't want me around here any more. He was beginning to have the same thoughts at Texas A&M. The Aggies certainly weren't pleased with a two-year run of 10-11-1.

Neither was Jackie Sherrill. He firmly believed that his football team had been the victim of his own celebrity status. Texas A&M had been beaten by Boston College in his inaugural game, and Sherrill sensed an immediate letdown among his players. As he told the *New York Times*, because of the focus on my coming here, the players felt they would be an instant success. When they weren't against Boston College, they felt they weren't any good because the coach must be. It affected their perception of the whole season.

At the moment, Sherrill preferred to talk about how he had brought order to the program, how he had boosted the graduation rate among the players and was helping them mature as young adults. As the *Times* reported, he is confident that he is building the type of season first envisioned for him.

But where, the Aggie faithful wondered, were the results?

Pressure on Sherrill began to mount. There were rumors of disharmony among members of his high-powered coaching staff, as well as a streak of discord rising up within the players, growing dissension that had been triggered when Tom Wilson was fired and kept festering with every on-the-field disappointment. Al Carter of the *Houston Chronicle* would write, for the most part, Sherrill has remained serene and self-assured. He retains an air of invincibility and a conviction that even the losses are part of a larger plan that is, in fact, working. Associates say a weaker man might have panicked by now, but Sherrill hasn't. He had his program to build.

As he stalked out of Roy Kokemoor's office, he could not be bothered with either the concerns of his graduate assistant coach or the 12th man kickoff team. He had faith in them both.

Roy Kokemoor immediately saw the irony of it all. The 12th man team was made up entirely of walk-on football players, he said. And now they had a walk-on coach. They were all volunteers, and so was I. I wondered if they would have any faith in a coach who was earning a mere two hundred dollars a month.

He glanced briefly over the roster lying on his desktop. He did have a nucleus of some strong players returning: Tom Arthur. James Barrett, Tom Bevans, Jeff Blair, and Ron Reynolds. Keith Newton should be at full speed. He had a season of playing with a knee brace under his belt.

Hopefully, Bill Allison had finally recovered from a bad leg. And, from all reports, the hairline fracture had healed in Shawn Slocum's leg. Good as new. That's what the doctors said. And only the Good Lord knew exactly how much he was counting on Slocum. That boy can play, Kokemoor told himself. If the 12th man unit had anyone who resembled a full-fledged, genuine, high-powered, helmet-in-your-ear-hole hitting machine, it was Shawn Slocum. He had talent. He was a natural leader on the football field. Shawn Slocum could indeed make a difference.

Kokemoor was thrilled with the assignment. But, he said, he was also scared to death. He kept wondering, what if I'm the coach who gives up the first big runback for a touchdown? What if I'm the coach responsible for the demise of the 12th man team? Some believed that the kickoff unit, for the most part, had been hauled to Kyle Field from a rusty scrap heap in a second-hand junkyard, and, in an instant, the team and the whole idea could be just as easily scrapped and thrown away for good. David Beal had been constantly tormented by the same thoughts.

Kokemoor walked out of his office and headed toward the field. Those were the kinds of worries he would have to exorcise from his mind. If players feared the worse, he decided, then they would play in the shadow of their own fear, and the worst that could possibly happen would probably happen. No. His players would never run onto the field afraid that some hot-shot kickoff return artist might take the ball the distance. Instead, he would simply focus their attention on one single facet of the game. Keep the ball inside the 20-yard line. The twenty was a great wall. Don't let anybody through it or past it.

He kept remembering the old Vince Lombardi story. A slow-footed quarterback had thrown an interception, and the speedy defensive back was running wide open for the goal line. The quarterback, in spite of his lead feet, caught him and brought him down as time expired. How was he able to do that, Lombardi had been asked. Simple, the coach replied. The defensive back was running for a touchdown. My quarterback was running for his life. That was the 12th man, Kokemoor knew. Every time they stepped on the field, they were indeed running for their lives. The hammer was cocked to bring them down. But keep the ball inside the twenty, and the life span of the team just might last forever.

For Shawn Slocum, it was a new beginning. When the spring of 1984 rolled around, he had his mind set on two goals. He was dead sure that he would be covering kickoffs as a member of the 12th man team. That was a given. He was also determined to move up the depth chart as linebacker. He may have been a little smaller than most, but no one could deliver the impact of Shawn Slocum. All he needed was a break or two.

Some members of the 12th man unit were upset, even bitter, that Slocum, the son of a coach, had been given a varsity helmet to wear in practice. They wore helmets that had been dented and scarred while they were probably still in junior high. They deserved better. Slocum was the only member of the team who was given better. It did help, they knew, to have friends in high places.

The varsity helmet did not do him a lot of good. In practice, Slocum went to his knees with a concussion. It's a severe bruising of the brain, the doctor carefully explained to him. You need to take some time and let it heal. It's vitally important for the brain to be completely healed before you try to get back on the field. More than likely, it will happen again.

Slocum listened. He wasn't concerned. He was a football player, and bumping heads together was what football players predictably did on a normal day. He would be careful. He would lead with his shoulder, not his head. But when the going got tough, Shawn Slocum did everything he could do to impress a coach other than his father. And if he had to hammer some ball carrier with his helmet, then he stuck his head into

R. C. Slocum, the Aggie assistant head coach and defensive coordinator, adjusts his game plan with Jackie Sherrill. The two teamed up during the 1980s to form one of the most formidable coaching tandems in the nation.

Dennis Mudd took a deep breath. I'm afraid I can't try out until the fall, he said. My shoulder won't be ready until then.

Roy Kokemoor nodded. We'll see how it looks in the fall, he said.

More than anyone else, Mark Wurzbach wanted to play football at any university where R. C. Slocum was serving as the defensive coordinator, and that happened to be across the street at Texas A&M. He had heard Slocum speak at his Bryan High School football banquet and thought that the Aggies just might be able to use another 6-1, 195-pound strong safety who had decent speed and could get from point A to point B in an awfully big hurry if there was a collision waiting for him on either side of Point B. He waited for a scholarship, and, when one wasn't offered, Wurzbach considered playing for some junior college, then transferring to A&M. But why waste two years? Now was as good a time as any to become an Aggie.

Mark Wurzbach walked onto the football team during the autumn of 1983, was handed his burnt orange jersey, and, after a day or two, realized that he was trapped deep in the mire of a numbers game, and there was very little chance for him to escape. Ninety scholarship athletes roamed the field. Walk-ons were running everywhere he looked, and the only walk-ons receiving much attention or any playing time were on the 12th man team. It did not take Wurzbach long to figure out that his future, if he had one in football, meant prying his way onto a specialized kickoff unit that swaggered across campus like cult heroes, had open invitations to every party in town, and knew every girl they wanted to know and a few they didn't.

He tried out for the 12th man team in the spring of 1984, and, he said, I ran the forty in 4.85, which was barely fast enough to make the first cut. My speed could put a stopwatch to sleep. I thought, well, I may not be the fastest or the smartest guy out but by the time I get through this tryout, the coach will know I'm the hardest working guy he has. If we practice an hour, I'll give him an hour and a half. If we practice all day, I'll be here all night. They can't run me off. I'm too slow to run off.

As a blistering sun beat down on Kyle Field, tempers began to flare. Wurzbach tore into scholarship athlete Ken Ford, and the simple block-and-tackle drill, the most basic of all drills, he said, suddenly caught fire, became a backwater skirmish, and, almost without warning, raged into a small-scale war.

Curley Hallman raced up and shoved his way between them.

Ford was snarling like a back-alley dog.

And Wurzbach didn't care if Hallman kicked him off the team. He wasn't leaving without taking another pot shot at Ford. If nothing else, he wanted to knock the prestige out of his scholarship.

Hallman shoved Ford out of the way. He would deal with him later.

the pile at full speed and let his body follow. Impact. That was football. It was all about impact.

The second concussion was as bad as the first.

During the latter days of the fall of 1983, the future had all seemed so simple for Dennis Mudd. He began working to rehabilitate his shoulder after breaking a collarbone in a JV game. Weeks earlier, he had been able to bench press more than three hundred pounds. Suddenly, virtually overnight, it was all he could do to raise a broomstick over his head.

David Beal had promised him a chance to tryout for the 12th man team, but Beal was gone. Mudd felt that his last chance to play college football had taken a wrong turn and left him trailing far behind.

What did Roy Kokemoor know about Dennis Mudd, either good or bad in the spring of '84? His shoulder was still in bad shape, and now it was a struggle for him to push more than a hundred pounds above his head. Mudd saw stark reality staring him squarely in the face, and he didn't like what he saw. Football players who couldn't lift more than a hundred pounds weren't football players. They were pretenders. No. They were jokes. He wondered if he was washed up before he ever fired another shot in anger on the turf of Kyle Field.

Kokemoor gave him a glimmer of hope. You've been with us awhile, the coach said. You've worked hard. I've seen you. Sure, I'll be glad to give you a shot.

Then again, maybe he wouldn't deal with him at all.

Hallman grabbed Wurzbach by the shoulder pads.

Wurzbach gritted his teeth. Hallman was one volcano lava rock short of an explosion, hot enough chew a bar of iron and spit nails. His eyes were aflame.

Fights were part of the game. But varsity players were the cream of the crop and should damn well be respected as the cream of the crop. Walk-ons were simply the cream that had curdled. For walk-ons, hurting a varsity player was as risky as sitting on a powder keg and smoking a two-bit cigar.

Great, Hallman told him through clenched teeth.

Wurzbach snapped his head around.

What?

He had expected to feel the blast.

The blast had not yet rocked him.

That's the kind of intensity I like, Hallman said. That's the kind of fight we need out here to make our players better.

He turned and walked away.

No cursing.

No screaming.

No threats.

Wurzbach grinned. Well, he thought, I may have a chance out here after all.

On the football field, Bobby Middleton viewed himself, with a certain amount of humility and insanity, as an assassin. His motor never quit running, the only speed he knew was break-neck, and if he was afraid of anything, Middleton hadn't quite figured out what it was yet. It had never bothered him to get hurt or to hurt somebody else. Pain was the great equalizer, he thought. It bridged the gap between those who could or would and those who didn't even bother to try. Bobby Middleton was a linebacker, a damn good linebacker, too, and he had a year of varsity football under his belt at the University of Missouri. He would have no doubt stayed, but his family moved to Texas, and Middleton, being the good son, came along to help out on the family's polled Hereford ranch during the summer months. Texas A&M had been a likely choice since Middleton was an animal science major. He sat out of school and worked the cattle for a year, then asked his old Missouri coach to call A&M recruiting coordinator Dan LaGrasta and suggest that he meet with Middleton to explore the possibility of playing football for the Aggies. Good kid, the Missouri coach would say. Good, hard-nosed player. Bobby's got a lot, and he gives you all of it. He doesn't leave anything on the field.

How big a kid is he?

Six-one and 228 pounds. Not an ounce of fat on him.

Could he play for you in Missouri?

Already has.

Yes, LaGrasta said when he and Bobby Middleton sat down at a McDonald's in College Station, there might well indeed be a scholarship available for him.

Yes, A&M did hold back a few scholarships for big-time athletes who might be transferring from other schools. No, he could not offer one until Coach Sherrill had a chance to see Middleton in practice. No, neither game film nor another's coach's recommendation was enough. Certainly, he thought it was a good idea for Middleton to meet with R. C. Slocum since Middleton was a linebacker and Coach Slocum was the man in charge of the Aggie defense.

Middleton and Coach Slocum sat down with only a desk between them. Face to face. A boy looking for a promise. A man who made no promise but offered the hope of one. Then again, boys hear what they want to hear and believe what they want to believe. Go ahead and enroll in school, the coach said. Walk-on for us, and let's see how you do in two-a-days. Then we'll talk about some scholarship money.

Middleton watched Slocum walk out of the room. He knew that something was wrong, but he couldn't quite figure it out.

Then the truth hit him.

He could not recall R. C. Slocum once looking him in the eyes.

John Burnett had a burning passion to play football for Texas A&M. Even in the fifth grade he would tell those who asked, and those who didn't, that he would one day be an All-American line-backer for the Aggies. His dream was to play on a championship team that defeated the burnt orange of Texas. The trouble was, John Burnett suited up in high school at Rockwall, better known as the "Angry Orange." Not burnt, but orange all the same. Not a good sign.

He was recruited by Baylor and Texas Tech, even had an offer to play for the Air Force Academy, but John Burnett was waiting on a scholarship from Texas A&M. After all, Jerry Pettibone had come around a few times when his recruiting trips carried him into the Dallas area.

But no scholarship ever arrived. Burnett was disappointed, but he turned his back on the Air Force, ignored Tech and Baylor, and went where his heart led him, which meant he traveled the long road down Highway 6 to A&M. During the fall of 1983, Burnett watched the Aggies play from his seat in the stands. One single thought kept tumbling over and over in his mind: how can you give up on a dream?

When the spring of 1984 rolled around, John Burnett had made up his mind. He walked on the Aggie football team, riding his bike every day from Crocker Hall to Kyle Field. On the first day, he walked up to his locker, turned to Sly Calhoun, and asked, why doesn't my locker have a nameplate above it? I see that the other lockers do.

Calhoun shrugged. Not for sure you'll be here long enough to get your name over a locker, he said.

Sly, Burnett said, I'm here to stay.

Calhoun grinned. I've heard that before, he said.

John Burnett looked around him. Bare walls. Locks that wouldn't lock. Dim lights. He suspected that forgotten cells in some third world archipelago had the same feel and ambiance. Here I am, he thought, a refugee from the "Angry Orange," wearing a walk-on's burnt orange jersey, a linebacker wearing cheap, low-top Converse shoes that didn't have cleats. My jock strap had a hole in it. My socks were at least ten years old. And my locker didn't even have my name over it.

How, Burnett wondered, am I ever going to be an All-American linebacker in a situation like this?

He told Roy Kokemoor, look, coach, I want to play. I'll do whatever you want me to do. But I've got to play.

Kokemoor sent him out onto the practice field as a 6-3, 205-pound offensive lineman whose sole mission in life was to block a bonafide All-American, Ray Childress.

Childress could have destroyed me, he said.

Childress treated him worse.

Kokemoor liked Burnett's spunk. Thought he saw the mentality of a double-fisted jackhammer in his attitude. As the practices tuned into confrontations in cleats, provided a player wore cleats, he suggested that Burnett try out for the 12th man kickoff team.

I'm not a kickoff kind of guy, Burnett answered. And he said under his breath, Doesn't anyone around here understand? I'm destined to be an All-American linebacker. If I can just find a way to stay on the field, I'll make an impression. The only way he would ever be noticed, Burnett decided, was to buck up and knock Childress off his feet. Day after day, he tried. He had the desire. Childress had the strength. He was tough. Childress, on the field, was disruptive. He thought that bones merely

Ronnie Glenn (9) is out front as the charge of the light brigade heads downfield.

termined was the size of the numbers on the scoreboard. Odessa Permian did not simply defeat teams in those days, Odessa Permian sent them back home with their pride and uniforms stained with dirt and disgrace.

I was playing Pop Warner football, Chad Adair said, and we had a big, burly, Odessa Permian linebacker named Bucky Taylor helping us learn the game. No X's. No O's. Just fundamentals. His job was to get the kids motivated. When he looked at you, it was either get tough or go home. I was in my one-handed stance during practice, and I'm staring at my teammate. We're both spitting and grunting, and the ball hasn't even been snapped. I think I'm tough, and he thinks he's tough.

Bucky Taylor is standing right on top of me. He's screaming, kill him! Kill him! I'm flinching, but I'm not moving. He grabs my pads, picks me off the ground, and throws me across the line of scrimmage as hard as he can. The other kid and I collide, and we both fall flat on the ground. From that moment on, I never feared the pain of impact again.

When I arrived at Texas A&M, I heard rumors that the 12th man team was a suicide squad.

Didn't seem that way to me.

In West Texas, we just called it football.

gave him a chance to break something. It was a year of painful memories, Burnett said.

Burnett made the sacrifice. Didn't mind. Knew it was part of the game. He was wondering how many other All-American linebackers had suffered the same gut-wrenching disappointment that ripped out his heart and stomped the sucker flat.

Chad Adair could play linebacker at 185 pounds in Friendswood High School. Texas A&M was not that impressed with 185-pound linebackers and did not recruit him, not as a scholarship player anyway. The 12th man team, on the other hand, was a viable option, one where speed and self-discipline were critical traits. Hard work didn't hurt any either. Adair knew he was strong enough. He could bench press 350 pounds, and he was aggressive. Maybe it was natural. Maybe it was learned, even inherited. However, it was birthed in the dust-driven sandlots of Odessa football.

Adair had grown up, sitting on a cinder block fence, watching the feared and dreaded Odessa Permian football team as it marched with fame and fury across the West Texas prairie.

As Adair said, that instinct to hit and take somebody apart came from the notorious Odessa Permian Mo-Jo. Football wasn't a sport in that part of a world. It was a religion, a ritual, and on Friday nights, Adair went to witness the great sacrifice. When teams walked onto the field and saw Permian, dressed in black, not unlike an executioner, watching for them, waiting for them, they knew already they were a beaten bunch, and they hadn't even touched a football yet. The only thing left to be de-

Dean Berry walked onto the campus of a football program that had not wanted him. But then, no other team wanted him either. He had waited throughout his senior season for the letters and the scholarship offers to make their way to Abilene Cooper. If any had been sent, they were lost along the way. Berry dutifully went to class day after day at A&M, studying to become a petroleum engineer, but his heart wasn't in it. His grades were on the borderline between bad and good, depending on how you looked at them.

He had pledged Phi Kappa Alpha fraternity, but it left a bigger void than it filled in his own empty universe. Beer. Parties. Girls. Wasted nights and empty mornings. Classes were places to sleep, and grades be damned. He had left all sense of ambition lying beside the highway on the outskirts of Cisco. Or maybe it was Eastland.

By the spring of 1984, Dean Berry knew he needed a serious change in his life. He was on a dead end street, traveling at high speeds and looking for a detour that didn't exist. He was wound tight, his nerves on edge, and he was searching for a new roadway to take him some place he had never been before. Dean Berry found his way to Kyle Field.

Berry's brother, Greg, had helped anchor a good Aggie defense even during hard times, serving as the team's defensive captain his senior year.

By now, however, Greg was gone, and Dean Berry had grown to 6-1 and 190 pounds. He was on the ragged edge of a fragile cusp. A few pounds too light. A step too slow. Berry had never been that fast, but, he

said, I had a little athletic ability. I was aggressive. I played hard. I could hit as hard as anybody and harder than most. The coaches knew I was a Berry, and they knew I had the DNA to play football. He began jogging a little to get back in shape.

He was treated better than most walk-ons, and he was the first to admit it. A&M's coaching staff still remembered Dean as the skinny little kid who showed up on game day and hung around with his big brother.

Don't know if the kid can play, they said, but he comes from a damn good family.

Can he hit like Greg?

Damn few do.

As much as anyone, Berry understood the importance of walk-ons to a football team. He said, if a coach didn't have walk-ons out running the scout team, getting themselves beat up and butchered on a daily basis, then he had to send out second and third teamers to face his varsity and bear the brunt of their onslaught.

A coach could end up with half of his football team crippled or injured.

Scholarship athletes did not want to run that kind of risk. It didn't matter to walk-ons. We were there because we wanted to be even though we knew we were always within one hit of being dragged off, tagged, and discarded. I suited up each day, knowing it might be my last, wondering how much damage I could do before they hauled me away.

Dennis Mudd had always been quite content to hibernate away in his hometown of Yoakum, but now he had rented a U-Haul trailer, loaded up his weights, and was on his way to North Carolina, assigned to work in an engineering co-op program sponsored by the Weyerhaeuser Company.

Make a little money, fifty dollars a month. Get some on-the-job experience by helping engineers with their portable tree de-barking operation while earning a few credits toward his degree. It seemed as good a way as any to spend the spring of 1984.

As Mudd walked into the North Carolina woodlands, his boss said, I guess you were wondering why we hired you for this job.

Mudd nodded.

Well, his boss continued, we saw on your resume that you played football, so we figured you'd be strong enough to move the heavy equipment around for us. Mudd shrugged. He didn't mind the hard work, but he was glad he hadn't told them about his busted shoulder, the one with the compressed fracture.

He lived in a remote trailer park outside of Plymouth. By March, Mudd was bench pressing 225 pounds, and he kept hauling Weyerhaeuser's heavy equipment around the Carolina highlands. Tough duty. As good as a weight room.

During those long, hot summer months after he returned home, Mudd wrestled unruly cattle around the auction ring in Cuero. By the time fall finally rolled around, he was ready to find out just what it took physically and mentally to batter his way on the 12th man kickoff team.

Only a year earlier, he had been the poor devil running kickoffs back in practice against the special forces unit. He knew how they hit. He knew they liked to take their shots, load up, lock, and fire again. This year, some other poor devil would be taking those kickoffs back, and

Dennis Mudd (4) paid his dues as a walk-on before emerging as a leader on the 12th man unit. He brought to the 12th man unit the same flair and devotion to football that he had displayed at Yoakum High School. To the right is Corey Linscombe.

Dennis Mudd at last had a chance to hit back. He had previously been at the bottom of a pile. Now he aiming to instigate, then disrupt the pile. If he were lucky, the streaks of blood staining his jersey would belong to somebody else.

Roy Kokemoor found out that Mudd had gone to high school in Yoakum, and he asked, do you know J.C. Hermes?

I was a linebacker, Mudd replied. Coach Hermes was my defensive coordinator.

J. C. and I were friends down in Brenham, Kokemoor said. Been friends a long time. If you played under Hermes, you can probably play.

Dennis Mudd breathed a sigh of relief. Maybe at long last, he thought, his luck was finally changing, but only if he could just keep that crooked little fracture in his shoulder from tearing apart again. The doctor said it wouldn't. But what did he know? The doctor had never been hit in a fit of anger by Johnny Holland.

Chad Adair had never considered himself to be a speed merchant, although he had worked hard enough to lower his forty time from 4.75 down closer to 4.6. He was on the field running wind sprints, striding step for step with John Roper.

The faster Adair ran, the faster Roper would go.

Step for step.

Almost shoulder to shoulder.

Chad Adair should have been satisfied.

He wasn't.

John Roper was running backward.

Spencer Baum looked around the practice field and began to wonder why he had actually gone to the trouble of trying out for the 12th man team. He was far outside his own personal comfort zone. Baum had come from a small ranch south of Mineral Wells, and he had grown up raising cows and calves, always aware that long hours, a hard life, and a struggling bank account were about all ranching ever promised anyone. It was the only life he knew or understood.

In high school, Baum, at 6-3 and 195 pounds, had played outside linebacker and offensive linemen in a program where positions were usually handed out according to size rather than ability. He sifted through a few junior college offers but chose instead to attend Texas A&M and begin his pursuit of a medical career. At the moment, he had no idea whether he wanted to be a physician, a dentist, or a veterinarian. He just wanted the word "doctor" written in front of his name. As far as he was concerned, Spencer Baum had raised his last calf.

Baum jogged unsteadily across Kyle Field, staggered by the number of dreamers who all foolishly believed they just might have the fortitude and the talent to play for the 12th man team. I didn't know the number of kids who showed up that morning, he said, but it was a damn big number. Spencer Baum was motivated by one overriding factor. I had watched college football all of my life, he said. I wanted to see how I measured up, or if I measured up at all.

He had always been shy and unassuming.

He was awed by the Aggie tradition and the thought of actually playing football on a field where the maddening crowds were so loud he wouldn't be able to hear himself think. He had been to the games during his freshman year. He knew how deafening it could get. His singular hope was to someday reach the sidelines and, on a Saturday that few would ever remember, do his part, no matter how small, in helping the Aggies hammer out a victory. Make a block. Make a tackle. Get in somebody's way. For Spencer Baum and the 12th man team, dreams were indeed small.

He wondered if they were real or merely imagined. Baum trotted over to watch as the deep snapper worked out with the punter, and linebacker Todd Howard snarled at him, hey, you damned idiot walk-on 12th

Jeff Boutwell (11) is on the prowl, even after a disgusted and disappointed ball carrier tosses the ball to the referee.

It's all over but the shouting for Dennis Mudd (4), Ronnie Glenn (9), Rick Tankersley (20), Bobby Middleton (18), Danny Balcar (2), and Tony Pollacia (15). They have struck again, and SMU is learning the heavy price a returner has to pay.

man, get the hell out of here.

I stood there like a deer in the headlights, Baum said. I thought for a minute that Howard was joking. I started to smile, then looked at his eyes. He was dead serious. As far as he was concerned, I was just out there taking up space. Probably his space.

Spencer realized he was not fully prepared for Texas A&M's brand of college football where speed was the holiest of all talents a player could have. If he were tough, fine. Jackie Sherrill could coach tough. If he were fast, great. No one could coach fast. I was in good shape, Baum said. I had been working hard in the weight room. In practice, we beat up on each other like a pack of angry dogs all going after the same bone. But, unfortunately, I had white man's disease. My forty time was only 4.8. There were some players out there on varsity who could low-crawl the forty yards faster.

You need to get your time down, Roy Kokemoor told him. I know you can hit. I've watched you. You've got the head for the game, and you've got the desire. I just need you to be able to run a little faster.

How much faster?

Kokemoor smiled. When you get there, he said, you'll know.

Two-a-days had ended.

Bobby Middleton had made his mark. He was sure of it. His weight had increased to 238 pounds, and still there was no place for any fat to hide. He was, without a doubt, as strong as any linebacker on the team, probably stronger, bench pressing 400

pounds and establishing a new Aggie squat record with 525 pounds.

He was, as Roy Kokemoor said, as solid as a wrecking ball.

Middleton had a knack for the football. He had the size, the strength, and for a 238 pounder, he could run fast enough. Middleton couldn't chase a rabbit down, perhaps, but the rabbit might run themselves to death trying to get past him.

Day after day, he said, Coach Slocum didn't even act like I was on the Aggie football team. As far as he was concerned, I was just another walk-on, and walk-ons had a purpose but no promises. I stopped him after practice one afternoon and said, coach, you wanted to wait until after two-a-days before we talked about finding me a scholarship.

You're in school, aren't you?

Yes, sir.

You're out here playing football aren't, you, the coach said.

Yes, sir. But who's paying for it?

Be patient, Slocum said. It'll all work out.

Slocum ambled away. He still hadn't looked Bobby Middleton in the eyes. His gaze had been focused on the scholarship athletes across the field. Middleton realized it would never work out.

No matter how hard he worked, he remained a player without a position, a man without a team. He would never be given any playing time. He would never earn a letter. He would never set foot on Kyle Field. He would merely be a watcher from the sidelines. Game day would be nothing more than a day to recuperate from the aches and pains of practice. He felt a violent rage rush through his brain.

He wanted to hit somebody.

He wanted to hit somebody hard.

Roy Kokemoor gave him a chance.

They stood in the shadow of the bleachers, Bobby Middleton and Roy Kokemoor. One was ready to explode. His shoulders were trembling.

TEXAS A&M

FOOTBALL OFFICE · COLLEGE STATION, TEXAS 77843 · 713-845-1241

July 23, 1984

Tom Arthur
10010 Knaboak #37
Houston, TX 77080

Dear Unemployed, Beach Bums and Work Pretenders:

So you want to work forty hours a week for a living. Join the crowd and make sure you realize going to school, football, and weights are not all bad. Some day you will think back and remember your college days and friends as one of the best times of your life.

The summer is going good. All the coaches are in the office working, breaking down films of next year's opponents, working on scouting reports, and recruiting lists. Coach Roper is working out and dieting, he even ran two 220s last week and lost 15 pounds. It was the first running he had done since 1965. Coach Slocum now owns Coach Davis. I think Coach Davis should give up golf. I saw Curley backpeddling down Highway 60. He didn't intercept any cars. I heard Coach Ruel and Coach Summers telling high school coaches how to hold good. I'm doing good except the IRS and Louisiana Downs are about to break me.

Seriously, have a great summer and be in shape on your return because the early season games are won by the team in the best condition.

Sincerely,

Paul Register

Paul Register
Assistant Football Coach

P.S. Coach Helm's hair is red again.

During the summer, A&M coaches sent out letters to players to make sure they came to two-a-days in the proper condition and right frame of mind.

He kept opening and closing his huge fist.

Son, Kokemoor said quietly as he folded his arms, have you heard about the 12th man team?

They go down on kickoffs, don't they?

They're pretty good at it.

I came here to be a linebacker.

I can give you a chance to get on the field.

From what I hear, you have to be pretty fast to make the team, Middleton said.

What's your forty time?

Probably a 4.75 on a good day. Middleton shrugged. From what I'm told, he said, that's not fast enough.

It is for somebody as strong as you are, Kokemoor told him.

Middleton paused a moment, then asked, what would you want me to do with the 12th man?

I want you to break though the wedge.

When do we practice these kickoffs?

We come out thirty minutes early and stay thirty minutes after the rest of the players leave.

In this heat?

It's always this hot.

Will it get me a scholarship?

I'm afraid not.

What do I get for it?

Roy Kokemoor smiled. You get to be famous, he said.

He watched Bobby Middleton walk away. In a game where the man who gets there first and hits the hardest wins, being mad was good. Middleton had a short fuse. He might hurt somebody. Kokemoor's smile broadened. He might round them all up, find the man with the ball, then nail his backside to the ground until he whimpered. Then hit him until he quite whimpering. Roy Kokemoor needed as many Bobby Middletons on the team as he could get.

No university, large or small, wanted a pretty decent quarterback, and only the little colleges were trying to attract pretty decent punters to the far distant corners of Texas, out where little towns had as many traffic lights as Dairy Queens and only one of each.

Ronnie Glenn packed away any hopes of playing big-time college football and decided to walk on the Texas A&M baseball team. After all, Coach Mark Johnson had told him, son, if you can run, hit, and throw fairly good, I'll keep you. So Glenn went out and ran, hit, and threw fairly good in the fall workouts. Coach Johnson kept pitchers to throw batting practice and catchers to work in the bullpen. The trouble was, Ronnie Glenn was neither.

He felt a much greater kinship with the 12th man kickoff team, and he had only watched them from the stands high above Kyle Field. In the spring of 1984, he signed up, ran a 4.65 in the forty, and was fast enough to still be hanging around when the squad was cut down to forty. I knew that a lot of guys were back from the original team, he said. But I decided to keep coming back until somebody told me I wasn't welcome anymore.

Lots of bodies out there, he knew.

Lots of faces.

Lots of bodies and faces running around with no name.

Foolish mistake, he thought.

Ronnie Glenn wrapped a wide piece of white tape across the front of his helmet and used a magic marker to write his name in big, bold letters. Whether the coaches liked him or not, they would at least know who he was.

In punt coverage drills, Glenn lined up, shot the gap, and blocked the kick.

It made Curley Hallman mad.

Then Glenn rammed his head into the scholarship punter.

And Hallman was furious.

The punter crumpled in a heap.

Now Hallman was screaming.

He didn't like me, Glenn said. He didn't like me beating his blocker. He didn't like me for running into his punter. He didn't like me for putting his punter's on the ground. But he knew me. I made sure he knew me. I worked out with the defensive backs, and every time Curley Hallman turned around, he had me and my piece of white tape staring him in the face. He cussed me. Lord, he cussed me. But he called me by my name when he did.

Glenn, after weeks of enduring the wrath of Curley Hallman, gradually came to realize that the defensive coach wasn't angry at him. He was upset with his scholarship players. Hallman kept raving and ranting, pointing his finger at Ronnie Glenn, and yelling, look at him. He's a walk-on. Ain't nothing but a damn walk-on. He didn't get your scholarship. Glenn wasn't given anybody's scholarship. And he's busting your tail on every play.

During the first year of the 12th man, injuries dramatically cut down the size of the original seventeen players. In some games, David Beal had understood what Dana X. Bible must have felt when he went looking for E. King Gill. Beal would anxiously look down the bench, and about the only members of the 12th man unit he had were on the field. If he needed a sub, he was flat out of luck.

In 1984, Jackie Sherrill and Roy Kokemoor made the decision to keep a few more. Besides, Sherrill kind of liked the way the 12th man bunch, wild as it was, ran the scout team. Full out and full bore. None of them ever slowed down or slacked off. If they got a clean shot, they took it. If the shot wasn't clean, they took it anyway. Sherrill grinned to himself. In time, he thought, these boys just might be able to whip his varsity players into a damn good football team.

Of the final forty players invited back in the spring of 1984, only twenty-six of them returned in the fall for two-a-days. I'm going to keep twenty, Kokemoor said.

Ronnie Glenn looked around.

He liked the odds.

I knew I was better than six of them, he said. I just didn't know which six.

For Kokemoor, like Beal before him, the first two hundred or more cuts were not really that difficult, at least not from a football perspective. Speed, athleticism, and agility all took a heavy toll, and it weeded kids out in a hurry. Some of them were cut out to play a higher level of football. They had the mental toughness for it. Some would never be any better than they were during their junior year in high school. When it came time to knock heads, others fell by the wayside. Class work and long hours were an obstacle that many could not overcome. Pain, for some, was too much to bear. Injuries whittled away a few who might have been able to play. Breaks. Torn muscles. Popped hamstrings. Shoulders dangling. Concussions.

And Kokemoor was worried because Shawn Slocum had gone down with his third concussion. He was smart, the coach said. He was intense. Nothing could stop him when he strapped on his pads. But his head and his brain kept getting rocked and bruised. A man can only take so much, and then it becomes hazardous to his health.

Shawn should have hung up his cleats. But as soon as the cobwebs dissolved in his mind, as soon as the glaze melted from his eyes, as soon as he could remember his name and figure out if I was holding up one or three fingers, he was pulling that helmet strap a little tighter and looking

for someone else to bury. God, I hoped we wouldn't be burying him.

Those last half dozen cuts were the hardest to make.

One player was as good as the next.

Same speed.

Same intensity.

Same attitude.

Kokemoor would lead his charges out two at a time, and, at the 50-yard line, he placed one on the east hash mark and the other on the west. They glared at each other. They flexed their muscles. They pawed the ground. Their eyes caught fire and smoldered.

They charged.

Twenty yards apart, and they were coming as hard as they could run. They couldn't deviate from the midfield stripe, Kokemoor said, and they couldn't slow down. When they rammed into each other, it was like a couple of trains trying to beat each other to the same bridge. I could almost sense that the field shook at the point of impact.

I watched to see who flinched.

I kept the ones who didn't.

And if neither flinched, I'd splash some water in their faces, line them up, and send them crashing into somebody else.

Some would have died before they flinched.

Jackie Sherrill brought his varsity players out early one afternoon to watch.

Some shuddered.

Others turned their eyes away from the spectacle.

A few stared, completely mesmerized.

One walked away and he was heard mumbling, my God!

Roy Kokemoor would say, when I suck down my last breath, I will still remember those guys. They had principles, even when they were going wild.

They had character. They had desire. They had discipline. They believed they could make a difference. I was convinced that if the whole kickoff team was headed in the same direction with the same goal in mind, not a damn thing on earth could stop them.

Every one wanted to make the tackle. Sure. That was only natural. But it was more important for each of them to make damn sure he knocked somebody down so a teammate could make the tackle.

When the ball carrier hit the turf, they all took credit for it.

The hardest thing I ever had to do was walk up to a kid, look him in the face, and say, I'm sorry, son. It just hasn't worked out.

He was hurting.

I was hurting just as bad.

Then I would go home and agonize over my decisions. I never lost faith in the ones I kept. I always feared I had missed on a player who needed a second chance and never received one. The thought haunted me then. It still does.

During the summer, Coach Paul Register had written to each of the Aggie football players, including those who labored on the 12th man kickoff team. Tom Arthur opened his letter and read:

Dear Unemployed, Beach Bums, and Work Pretenders:

So you want to work forty hours a week for a living. Join the crowd and make sure you realize going to school, football, and weights are not all bad.

Some day you will think back and remember your college days and friends as one of the best times of your life. The summer is going good. All the coaches are in the office working, breaking down films of next year's opponents, working on scouting reports and recruiting lists. Coach Roper is working out and dieting; he even ran two 220s last week and lost 15 pounds.

It was the first running he had done since 1965. Coach Slocum now owns Coach Davis. I think Coach Davis should give up golf. I saw Curley back-peddling down Highway 60. He didn't intercept any cars. I heard Coach Ruel and Coach Summers telling high school coaches how to hold good.

I'm doing good, except the IRS and Louisiana Downs are about to break me.

Seriously, have a great summer and be in shape on your return because

Much to their disdain, members of the 12th man team trot off the field after a kickoff sails into the end zone. No chance for a runback. No chance for a tackle for Tom Christner (3), Tom Bumgardner (9), Tom Arthur (4), and Ike Liles (7).

the early season games are won by the team in the best condition.
   P.S. Coach Helm's hair is red again.

Texas A&M eased its way precariously into the 1984 season running hot and cold, usually out of gear and sometimes out of gas – coughing, clutching, and clattering every mile of the way.

The Aggies were frustrating to watch and frustrating to coach. They opened with a win over UTEP, but a Miner's field goal with 1:39 left in the game bounced off the left upright and saved A&M from the disgrace of a humiliating tie. A&M placed its football fortunes in the mystical, magical hands of Kevin Murray, but Craig Stump had to come off the bench and throw a pair of fourth-quarter touchdowns or the Aggies might not have survived a scare from Iowa State. Two wins. Neither of them impressive.

A shock wave of nausea and desperation swept across Kyle Field when Murray dove for a first down deep in Arkansas State territory during the final, frantic moments of the third quarter. It was as though an entire stadium heard the sickening crack of the quarterback's ankle break when he tumbled onto the turf.

The Aggies came back to win, but only by a scant two points. Murray missed the last-minute heroics. He was being rolled into the emergency room. Texas A&M stood 3-0, but nobody was feeling very comfortable about the season. The wins, some feared, had all been an illusion. The losses would be for real.

Texas Tech battered its way to a 30-12 victory. They made the big plays, Sherrill said with a shrug. We didn't. Houston came away with a 9-7 win when Alan Smith's 57-yard field goal attempt came up short with little more than three minutes left in the third quarter. And, a week later, with almost four inches of rain relentlessly pounding Kyle Field, Baylor's Bears slipped and slid their way past A&M, 20-16.

Seasoned veterans in the leering press were having a difficult time trying to recall if football had ever been played in worse conditions. Sherrill had gambled in the game, taking a soggy page from Dana X. Bible's old playbook. He quick kicked, but Anthony Toney's punt was blocked, setting up Baylor only eight yards away from a touchdown.

The Aggies did freewheel their way past Rice, but who didn't? Texas A&M had SMU bottled up, throttled down, and virtually hammered into submission. Leading, 20-7, and driving deep for a touchdown in the third quarter, however, the Aggies found a way to self-destruct. Same old story. Same old ending. Craig Stump was hit, and he coughed up the football. SMU unceremoniously stole the momentum, and A&M was never able to right a sinking ship.

The Mustangs marched to three quick touchdowns, and the Aggies came stumbling home with a 28-20 loss that threatened to crack their fragile psyche wide open. If anything bad could happen, it did, and it did on a regular basis.

A&M was cursed, and the curse was hanging over Kyle Field like a brooding flock of vultures. Dead. Dying. It didn't matter. The vultures could smell the meat, and the meat was rancid and spoiled.

Not all of the 12th man action took place on the field. Taking a break solely for medicinal purposes are (left to right) walk-on fullback John Miggins, Warren Barhorst, Kirk Pierce, Brian Edwards, Garry Sorrell, David Fry, and Sean Page.

Chapter 15

In the beginning, Keith Newton was convinced that teams never got around to putting in any game plan designed to stifle or suffocate the downfield shenanigans of the 12th man kickoff team. Their thinking was simple, though flawed. We're bigger and faster and stronger than those sumbitches are, so we'll grind them into the dirt and let them chew on our dust.

Can't stand up to us.

Can't beat us one-on-one.

Can't catch us.

There's no reason to give those boys a second thought. By mid-season, however, teams were beginning to worry. The 12th man unit began seeing stunts and crossing patterns, and there was a new scheme facing them virtually every week. This was football. The 12th Man could make adjustments on the fly or be run off the field.

At SMU, Keith Newton never saw Russell Carter coming.

His eyes were downfield.

His head was on a swivel, maybe, but it was certainly swiveling in the wrong direction.

Carter came out of nowhere, Newton said, and what in the world was an All-American safety, destined to play professional football, doing on the kickoff return team? He should be behind the bench taking care of his knees, not out in the path of a suicide squad trying to take him apart. Common sense said, Russell, get off the field.

I didn't see him enter the first ear hole, Newton said. But I certainly knew when he exited the second one.

Newton never expected his head to stop aching. It had been aching since the early days of August.

He did expect the fog to clear from his eyes. He just didn't know if it would be today or next week. As he said, I felt better now. I knew Carter was out there, and I knew where he was. He was no longer an unknown.

He was no longer lying in ambush. The first time, he had me in his sights. On the next kickoff, I put the crosshairs between his eyes.

Somebody else could make the tackle. Russell Carter was mine, and I could take a lick if it gave me a chance to deliver one. I couldn't hit as hard as Carter. But he certainly had no idea I would be searching him out either. Nobody sought out Russell Carter.

Blindside was good.

Mark Wurzbach's feet hurt. The shoes Billy Pickard had given him were too small, too tight, too short, and he felt like they cut off the flow of blood to his toes when he laced them up. His toes were numb. It hurt to run. Hell, it hurt to walk. And he had to run everywhere he went.

Pickard didn't seem to care. As long as anyone could remember, he had been an ornery old maverick who was fired up when he awoke every morning and still fired up when he went to bed at night. He lived and died Aggie football and believed that only the toughest of the tough was ever good enough to play. He was crusty and grizzled, and he had been in the hellhole called Junction, working shoulder to shoulder with Bear Bryant, when Elwood Kettler collapsed, writhing on the ground and groaning with pain. That damn girl, the Bear had said. Get him off the field and out of my sight. As the quarterback's limp body was placed on a stretcher, the coach told Pickard, if he's not well enough to practice this afternoon, just send his butt on back to College Station.

Pickard had been worriedly standing in the emergency room when

Ronnie Glenn (9), Rick Tankersley (20), and Mark Wurzbach (21) help whip the Kyle Field crowd into a frenzy.

Kettler was X-rayed.

Boy's hurt pretty bad, the doctor said grimly. We need to keep him here tonight.

Pickard shook his head. Doc, you just don't understand, he said. Coach don't believe in players getting hurt. He grabbed the quarterback around the waist and said, you're just gonna have to straighten up and fly right, Elwood. Coach is waiting for us back at camp.

Pickard still did not believe in players getting hurt or staying hurt. He was pretty good at popping dislocated fingers, shoulders, and toes back in place. A scream now and then never bothered him, as long as it wasn't his scream. If you can't take the pain, he always believed, you shouldn't be on the field. If you didn't leave a little blood behind, you weren't playing the game right anyway.

Pickard, so many of the 12th man unit believed, had absolutely no interest in providing the best equipment for those who, he reasoned, should have never left the stands. He never threw anything away, and he had piles of threadbare uniforms, and worn-out pads lying around. No need to buy the 12th man a lot of new equipment, he said. They don't know the difference and would probably ruin it anyway.

The pads may have been junk, Pickard said, but we always had new shoes for the boys. Don't know if they fit or not, but they were new. And I made sure they had the best helmets I could give them. I knew their collisions were just a violent as anybody else's. A lot of them thought they had bad helmets. Worthless helmets Memories dim. Maybe they just got hit on the head too many times.

At the end of practice, Wurzbach brought him the shoes that hurt his feet so badly. These don't fit, he said.

Let me tell you a little secret, Pickard said.

What's that?

There's a helluva lot more shoes around here that don't fit than do. Pickard grinned.

Maybe it'd be better if I had a scholarship.

Be better for you.

Better shoes?

I've seen you run, boy. Shoes won't help you a lick.

When Bobby Middleton left for practice, he was upset. By the time he pulled on his uniform, he was mad. When he reached the field, he was furious. He took his wrath out on anyone who stood in his way. Even at night, when the aches and pains of the day were deadened by various grades of whiskey, both good and bad, Middleton's anger was always seething deep inside him.

He could play the game as well as anyone. He knew. He traded blows with the best of the best every day of his life, and nobody had gotten the best of him yet. Why weren't the coaches able to see that? He had played at Missouri. He could damn sure play for a team so bad it was losing more games than it won.

I was called crazy, he said. I was known as the bowling ball. I played every day in practice like I was one tackle short of being a starter. Varsity hated it. They hated to line up against me. And I was only trying to prove a point. I was looking for a chance to light somebody up. I never let up. Knock me down. Stomp on my face. I didn't care. If I could get back to my feet, I'd knock you to hell and back on the next play.

Even when Jackie Sherrill walked down the field, Bobby Middleton would run directly toward him as hard as he could, head down, arms pumping, knees driving like pistons, picking up speed with every step, swerving at the very last moment, coming so close to the Coach that their shoulders brushed against each other. He never said a word to me, Middleton said.

He never acknowledged me. I was giving him and Texas A&M everything I had every day in practice and every Saturday on kickoff coverage, and Coach Sherrill didn't even know I was alive and kicking.

Bars.

They helped ease the frustration.

Girls.

They helped him forget the mental anguish.

He could deal with the physical pain just fine.

Middleton's room in Cain Hall, C-119, was the party place, better known by 12th man and varsity players alike as the "Bobby Mania Deli." When someone was throwing a party either on or off campus, my room was where the pre-party party began, he said. The word would go out, and by the time I finished a beer, the room was packed. Football, if only for a few hours, took a holiday, and Bobby Middleton felt in perfect harmony with the world around him. No anger. No frustration. No bitterness. There might be a fight or two. But, by morning, no one remembered who had fought or why.

Matt Gurley, a scholarship athlete who had been moved to fullback, and Middleton were walking onto the practice field together. Jackie Sherrill was striding ten feet in front of them. He never looked behind him. But suddenly Sherrill stopped on the white lines and let the players pass. His eyes never shifted toward them.

Middleton, Sherrill said quietly and somberly, if I hear you've been in trouble one more time, you'll never step on Kyle Field again.

Middleton kept walking.

So did Sherrill.

Gurley was looking for some place to hide. If Middleton had been in trouble, he knew he wasn't far behind. They had been convinced that Coach had no idea of the sin and bootleg corruption going on in the Bobby Mania Deli.

How'd he know, Middleton asked.

He's got a sixth sense, Gurley replied.

Middleton was grinning. Best day I've had since I've been out here, he said.

Gurley looked at him as though he were crazy.

Sherrill knows who the hell I am, Middleton said. He grinned. The Coach actually called him by name. He didn't know whether or not any coach knew his name, and here was Jackie Sherrill, the head man himself, the commander and chief, actually speaking the word *Middleton* out loud and on the field. The threat be damned.

For weeks now, Dennis Mudd, probably against his will, had been changing his mind about Jackie Sherrill. Coach may have been a Yankee from Pittsburgh, but he grew up in Mississippi and played for Alabama.

His work on Bonfire had not merely been a one-year publicity stunt, and neither had his 12th man kickoff team. Sherrill was a man of his word, a man you could trust, Mudd said. He looked you in the eye. He told you what was going to happen, whether you liked it or not, and he made it happen. He followed through with everything he said. He never lied to us. He said we would cover kickoffs, and we did. No matter how good the opponent was, no matter how great the kick return man might be, he had Kokemoor line us up, and he sent us downfield. Sherrill was a handshake kind of guy. His word was his bond. I felt like he was becoming one of us.

Then again, Jackie Sherrill may have always been one of us.

Jimmy Hawkins was returning punts in prac-

tice, and Kokemoor pulled out ten members of his 12th man unit, in no particular order, and told them to set a wall on the run back. Pick out a player, he said, any player, and take him to the ground.

We set the wall to the left, Mudd said, and we all took out our man. For whatever reason, Hawkins darted right. He had no intention of following a bunch of walk-ons. He had a scholarship. He was a budding star. He was afraid we might get him killed.

Curley Hallman was screaming at him. The red shirts had you a wall where you could have walked in for a touchdown, he said.

Why do you even have a bunch of red shirts out here in the first place, Hawkins asked.

Hallman stepped back, stared at him for a moment, then barked, if you don't shut up, I'll tell these red shirts not to knock anybody down, and somebody's coming in hard to take your head off. And if he doesn't, I will personally take his damn head off.

The practice had not gone well, and Jackie Sherrill was a dark shade of livid.

He lined his varsity offense up against the 12th man scout team and announced, no more drills. No more jogging around with your lazy, good-for-nothing attitudes. No more taking it easy or taking a play off. We're going live. And may the best team win.

Ronnie Glenn (9) looks down at an ill-fated Houston ball carrier who was surrounded by the number twelve and has suddenly reached the end of the line.

Preparing for an all-our 12th man assault are Ronnie Glenn (9), Ashley Eddington (22), Mark Wurzbach (21), Bobby Middleton (18), Jeff Boutwell (11), and Dean Berry (1). They were headed downfield with their pistols cocked.

team, caught McLemore's eye, and nodded. In a graveled, somber voice that even the Bear would be proud to own, Sherrill announced, gentlemen, today I am quitting. I am no longer the Texas A&M coach.

A funereal silence fell around the team.

All sound escaped the room.

Jaws were clenched, eyes were widening in disbelief.

Gentlemen, Sherrill continued, I am turning the team over to Ivy McLemore, who obviously knows more about coaching than I do.

He tossed his cap, his whistle, and his clipboard toward the sportswriter, who was afraid to move or even breathe.

Ivy, the Coach said, his voice still devoid of any emotion, they're all yours now. Get 'em ready for Texas.

Jackie Sherrill walked out the door.

The cold, seething eyes of ninety-five players turned to stare at Ivy McLemore. He had no idea what to do, so he did nothing. McLemore, with darting eyes, was too busy searching for a way out. If he could find it, he was gone. Ivy McLemore left the coaching profession before he ever picked up the whistle.

Jackie Sherrill was on the practice field, waiting for his teams when the ninety-five players wandered from out of the darkness and ran, puzzled and perplexed, back into the sunlight. They looked over their shoulders, and Ivy McLemore was nowhere in sight.

He was on his way back to Houston to write about that one brief and frightening moment when he had been anointed as head football coach at Texas A&M. He never mentioned anything about Sherrill re-

signing again.

For Jackie Sherrill, the season had been a disappointment. A&M had fewer wins than he expected, and even the wins were too close for comfort. Something was missing. Other than the 12th man on kickoffs, his team had not been able to work the Aggie faithful into a wild, unmitigated frenzy. The crowd remained far too quiet, considering the fact that they were students and alumni of Texas A&M, had a reputation for being as rowdy as they were loyal, and could always be counted on to cram their way into the stands at Kyle Field on any Saturday night or afternoon.

The Aggie faithful had done absolutely nothing to inspire his football team. They sat on their hands. They yawned. They gossiped among themselves, and most were spreading rumors that Jackie Sherrill had been a bust. They were waiting for him to pull off the greatest magic act of all, turning A&M into a winner, and for the most part, they had lost the faith. Churches were many. Revivals were often. Prayers were hardly ever answered in College Station.

Jackie turned to Bobby Middleton. The boy was a headache. He might even be a head case. But Bobby Middleton was a player. He was a little rough around the edges. He was always one hit away from taking on the whole football team. You big ones line up, and you little ones bunch up, because I'm gonna whip every damn one of you before I leave here today. That was Middleton's philosophy when it came to football. Others had fire in their belly. Bobby Middleton burned. In practice and in games, Sherrill noticed, he was always jumping up and down like some kind of maniac.

Sherrill made it a point to stop him as he left the practice field. Middleton, he said.

Yes, sir.

I need you to get the crowd fired up.

What do you want me to do?

Sherrill shrugged. You'll figure out something, he said.

I guess I can act like a nut.

Sherrill grinned. You always act like a nut, he said.

Middleton asked the trainer to cut up a large towel into a smaller one. He took a magic marker and scrawled "12th Man" in big letters. He came running out of the tunnel on Saturday afternoon, waving that towel violently in the air.

The crowd saw him, and a deep-throated growl began to sweep across Kyle Field. The noise grew loud, then louder.

Bobby Middleton jumped up and down like the maniac he was.

And he kept waving that towel.

The other team looked at me and the rest of the 12th man like we were crazy, he said. They didn't know we were about to run down and shove that towel down one of their throats. Well, not really. I didn't want to lose the towel. They had no idea what we were about to do.

But the crowd knew.

And the harder, the more rowdy and rambunctious Middleton waved his towel, the louder the roar of the crowd became. The noise was reaching a crescendo it had not approached in a long time.

The crowd knew what was about to happen.

And they couldn't wait.

So that's what it takes to get A&M out of its seats, Sherrill told himself. A towel and a head case waving it.

He grinned. At the moment, he had a lot more head cases than he did towels.

In the restless, agonizing days leading to the TCU game, it all came together. Out of the blue and quite unexpectedly. Whatever had been missing was suddenly and firmly in place. The players may have feared Sherrill. But either on or off the field, they were terrified of Ray Childress, an animal, a hulk who had been nicknamed "Manchild" in high school. Doug Williams, the Aggie starting right tackle said of him, Ray was one of those quiet guys who usually just went about his business, and it

took a lot to flip his switch. But once that switch got turned on, you better get the hell out of the way.

For most practices, Sherrill would get his players fired up by having them circle around and watch Childress and Williams go one-on-one like two battering rams, beating each other to a pulp, maybe, but never into submission. That's the way football is played, the Coach would say.

Ray Childress was tired of losing, and he kept reading in the newspapers that Jim Wacker's Horned Frogs were coming to College Station and tread recklessly all over the Aggies on their way to a Southwest Conference championship. After all, TCU, as Jim Wacker kept yelling in that raspy voice of his, was in the midst of an "unbelievable" season, and A&M was merely a pothole to step across as they traveled toward the Cotton Bowl.

The Frogs, of course, did have the much heralded, hard-running Kenneth Davis, known as the Temple Tornado. Davis was even being mentioned as a possible Heisman Trophy candidate. Posters of him were everywhere, and they were life-size. TCU was ranked nationally in the Top Twenty, and the Aggies? Well, the Aggies were just rank. As far as the leering press was concerned, it was a clash of two programs headed in opposite directions. Wacker's Horned Frogs were on their way to the top while Sherrill's Aggies were again in an ill-fated free fall toward the bottom. Apparently, so many of the Aggie faithful felt the same way. The crowd that afternoon was abysmal.

Only a handful more than 38,000 slipped with disdain and embar-

Wave the Towel!

Burnt Orange Lettering? Yes, fans, that was the coloring on the first batch of 12th Man towels received this season by The Student Aggie Club. Of course, we sent them back.

Have your money ready before the next home game to purchase a **Maroon**-lettered 12th Man towel from our student club members. There will be a booth in the field next to Cain Hall and one in the MSC for all fans who failed to get a towel last year.

12th Man towels show your just like your membership in The Aggie Club. Students get a special opportunity to join The Aggie Club — only $12 for a 12th Man. It's a real bargain.

Proceeds of the towel sale serve to offset a portion of the cost of trips for club members to out-of-town football games and at the end of each year, the student club donates money to worthwhile projects at the university.

Last year's proceeds went to the A.P. Beutel Health Center and to the endowment of spring sports.

The 12th man towel became so popular that the Student Aggie Club began selling them for $12 each, and the money raised was donated to benefit worthwhile campus projects.

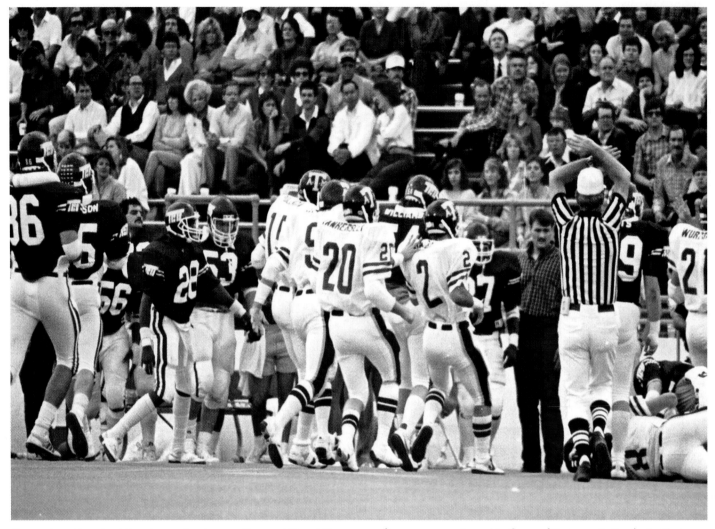

Even when they had the chance to play on the road, the 12th man unit was an unstoppable force with Tony Pollacia (15), Ronnie Glenn (9), Rick Tankersley (20), Danny Balcar (2), and Mark Wurzbach (21) always in the center of the storm.

rassment into Kyle Field. Empty seats. Empty hopes. Empty promises. Two more games, and the Aggie faithful would not be forced to endure any more losses or suffer any additional humiliation. They had grown tired of mediocrity. They had no idea what was going on inside the Texas A&M locker room.

On game day, Dennis Mudd remembered, Coach Slocum had us foaming at the mouth. He kept saying, TCU has stepped on your field. Your field. And they're out there right now, thinking they can beat you. That's what they believe. They're gonna whip you from one end of Kyle Field to the other if you're not ready to play today.

Then suddenly Ray Childress stood up.

The silence was shattering.

His broad shoulders cast a broad shadow.

Doug Williams said, he must have had a hard rock to sleep on instead of a pillow the night before, because, let me tell you, he really had a problem that day.

Childress did not rant. He did not rave. He screamed. He looked out at his team, a bunch of underachievers who had not lived up to their billing or Aggie expectations, and he growled, I have not lost to TCU since I have been at A&M, and we are not going to lose this game today.

He angrily slammed his left fist against the podium, and it cracked.

The podium, not the hand. It wouldn't have mattered. On that particular day, with blood running like jet fuel through his veins, Ray Childress would not be denied.

No one doubted him.

No one would dare face him in the locker room if the Aggies lost.

A win.

Nothing but a win.

Moral victories didn't count.

It was unreal, Sherrill recalled. Ray was determined that he was not going to let a losing season happen if he had to make every tackle and every touchdown himself. The team could damn well follow him or quit. By the time the team hit the field, the players were as fired up as Childress. In those few moments, Dennis Mudd said, I heard Ray Childress say more words than I had heard him say during the last three years.

Childress had demanded a change in the football fortunes of Texas A&M, and many would feel that his brief, fiery pre-game speech may have been the most poignant and heartfelt in the annals of A&M football history.

As Childress said, I was playing mad at that point, but that's pretty much how I played anyway. When the center snapped the ball, I'd just go after it. It, whatever it was, didn't stand a chance.

TCU was cocky, probably even overconfident.

The whistle blew. Pads and helmets were slammed violently together, and the sounds of impact ricocheted across the field like gunfire in a small border war. Overconfidence, the frogs learned, was a terrible thing. The Aggies ganged up, wrung it out of them, and stomped it beneath their cleats.

A&M rose up to protect its home field with a bitter 35-21 upset, and Childress finished the game with fourteen tackles, ten of them unassisted. He forced a fumble, knocked down a pass, and sent one TCU quarterback to the showers early and in pain. He was a dominant force, and Wacker summed it up by saying, we just couldn't block Childress. He was a big reason they played tougher than we did.

Mudd would remember, a guy tried to cut Ray's knees, and he didn't like it a bit. He picked the guy up by his face mask, twisted him around, and threw him back on the ground. No referees ever blew a whistle. They just stood there and marveled at carnage Ray Childress had been able to unleash on the Frogs.

Roy Kokemoor did not have time to savor the win for very long. The crowd had not yet cleared the parking lot when he got the word.

Have you heard, a trainer asked him.

About what?

Shawn Slocum.

What about him?

He suffered a concussion.

Kokemoor winced in shock and disbelief.

How many does that make?

Four.

Shawn Slocum was a warrior. He needed Shawn Slocum. The 12th man needed him.

Kokemoor looked up at the trainer and said, Shawn's not coming back, is he?

Not if he's smart.

A battle with those bastards in Austin was looming in the distance, and the 12th man team members was chomping at the bit. It was the last road game of the season, NCAA travel restrictions had been lifted, and Jackie Sherrill told them, we're taking you with us.

A year ago, Texas had missed winning the national championship by a mere four points in the Cotton Bowl. The Longhorns fell to Georgia 10-7 on a muffed punt that set up a Bulldog touchdown deep in the fourth quarter. Texas hadn't forgotten, Texas was blasting its way toward another Southwest Conference title, and Texas had not yet exorcised the demons that donned burnt orange the moment the fumble hit the ground.

Only Texas A&M stood in the way.

Texas laughed.

The Longhorns were quite familiar with the strife that was threatening to unravel, then tear down Aggie Football. A&M was a rival. Sure. A win over A&M could atone for a lot of sins that had occurred in the Cotton Bowl. But a win over A&M no longer had the sting that it once did. A&M had lost its stinger.

Then came the kickoff, nothing special or out of the ordinary, high, end over end, a floater if nothing else, settling down to rest just shy of the goal line. Texas would have the ball, and A&M would be battling feverishly for its life in the dark, foreboding innards of Austin's Memorial Stadium.

It was the kind of kickoff that members of the 12th man were always dreaming about.

Said Keith Newton, I was racing downfield as hard as I could go, and I didn't have any lane responsibility. My job was to simply find the ball, go to it, and create as much chaos as possible when I got there.

Some Longhorn blocker suddenly came out of the blue and steamrolled me. I never saw him. I hit the ground and immediately rolled to my knees, trying to dodge the onslaught of freeway traffic bearing down on me in orange and white. The ball carrier was coming right over the top of me. The blocker had knocked me into his path.

I reached up and grabbed his legs. There was no heavy impact, no pile-drive tackle that blasted him back toward the goal line, just a twisted mass of arms and legs, and he went down inside the twenty. If I had rolled right instead of left, I would have missed him altogether. But that was a different day for us. On that day, everything was going our way.

Indeed it did. All year, Jackie Sherrill had known he had the pieces. On a mild autumn evening, before a stunned crowd of 81,309 fans, playing before a national television audience, the pieces all finally began falling together. It was about time, he thought.

Craig Stump kept passing to Jeff Nelson and Jimmy Teal, Anthony Tony unleashed a brutal ground assault, and the Aggies had battled to a 20-0 advantage by halftime. Domingo Bryant blocked a field goal attempt, Scott Polk picked up the loose ball and returned it to the Texas seven-yard line, and Eric Franklin kicked a pair of field goals as A&M silenced the orange faithful and shocked the Longhorns, 37-12.

Texas A&M had beaten Texas for the first time in three years. No. Forget that thought. Jackie Sherrill had finally beaten Texas, and the wise old heads within the Aggie faithful nodded among themselves and thought it was about time. As Dennis Mudd said, the TCU upset had been our signature victory. The win over Texas proved it wasn't a fluke.

As the lights were dimming in Memorial Stadium, Tom Bevans stole away for a few minutes and walked out across the Texas campus. It was empty. Somewhere down on Sixth Street in Austin, a little beer was flowing, but those who had come to celebrate were trying to wash away the disappointment that ached like ulcers in their bellies.

He looked up. The tower always blazed in burnt-orange lights after a Texas victory. The tower was dark. Bevans laughed out loud. It was, he said, the best night of his life.

Three busses rolled through the darkness and back into the College Station in the late hours. One hauled the offense. One was loaded down with the defense. And the bus trailing along behind carried the 12th man kickoff team, along with University President Frank Vandiver, the deans, and the dignitaries of Texas A&M. Vandiver had been right. He told anyone willing to listen: Jackie Sherrill had indeed been the single, most fortuitous hire of his administration.

Bevans glanced out the window and had trouble believing his eyes. University Drive had been shut down. The campus was too crowded. The yell leaders were standing on the roof of the Dixie Chicken. Thousands of students were jamming the streets.

It was Thanksgiving, and no one had gone home. If they had left the campus for a turkey dinner somewhere, they had found their way back before the busses came rolling triumphantly into town.

Tom Bevans soaked it all in. He had never seen a sight quite like it before. It was a bittersweet moment. Bevans was finished, he knew. It was over. The long ride home had marked the end of the last football day he would ever experience on the field. The bruises would heal. Someday they would.

The pain would fade. Even the adrenalin coursing wildly through his veins would lose its steam. But if there had to be a last day, Tom Bevans decided, this was the way to spend it.

Ready for the kick with their adrenaline pumping hard are Ronnie Glenn (9), Larry Johnson (5), David Coolidge (7), Bobby Middleton (18), and John Burnett (6). The fuse was burning, and when the kick came, the 12th man exploded downfield.

Chapter 16

The face and the future of Texas Aggie football had been caught up in the restless winds of change.

Jackie Sherrill knew he had the weapons, and by 1985, his triggerman, Kevin Murray, was back. The bionic ankle should be as good as if it had never snapped. Now Sherrill was bringing in an offensive coordinator who had the imagination necessary to unleash the kind of air and ground assault that would carry A&M to heights its football program had not experienced for a long time.

He hired Lynn Amedee from Vanderbilt to install a balanced and sophisticated attack designed to take advantage of Murray's rocket arm and quick feet. Murray recalled, Jackie showed us films of the Commodores tearing up Alabama in Tuscaloosa.

Then we watched Vanderbilt tearing up Florida down in the swamps of Gainesville. I was thinking: Damn, we're going to be running this offense? Now, that was exciting.

Joe Avezzano had fled a head coaching job in Oregon, bringing A&M offensive linemen a demanding and uncompromising new work ethic: work to get it right, and then work some more. Linebacker coach Bob Davie was on board to help solidify a stalwart R. C. Slocum defense. Bob Boyd was taking on the tight ends. His most vital role, perhaps, would be persuading Rod Bernstine that his future lay in catching the ball, not carrying it. Sure he was a good running back. The world was full of good running backs. He could be a great tight end.

The rebuilding had been long, arduous, and painful. But at last, Sherrill had outstanding athletes from three superior recruiting classes. The chemistry within the coaching staff was harmonious. Stubborn players had finally quit fighting his ideas and were beginning to accept his

philosophy. Those clinging defiantly and desperately to Tom Wilson's way of football had all gone, and Sherrill was convinced that the Aggies were ready to go to war against any enemy as the team he had always envisioned them to be.

Despite the fact that the 12th man kickoff team had become a well-oiled, well-run, fine-tuned machine, some of the coaches still held their collective breath when the unit clamored on the field like a maverick herd of raging runaway bulls. Roy Kokemoor needed only ten good, stout-hearted men to start, and he usually had most of those coming back with a little slobber-knocking game experience under their belts. That wasn't enough, he knew, Kokemoor was still in the market for ten more good, solid prospects who could be thrown to the wolves and toughened up to play for the next few years. Jackie Sherrill was out recruiting on a national level.

Kokemoor and Curley Hallman were recruiting just as hard, but their territory hardly ever extended past the outer limits of Texas A&M. They would look over the odd assortment of candidates who showed up each spring and kept wondering where the real athletes were lurking on campus. Most of the new breed came to try out in tennis shoes, but it was disconcerting to see entirely too many of them wandering haphazardly into Kyle Field wearing hiking books and metal baseball spikes.

Kokemoor turned his attention to a handful of walk-ons who possessed a little speed and some natural athletic ability. He had already seen them in action. They had a chance to help the 12th man. Hallman, like Sherrill, was obsessed with speed. Can't play without speed, he said. Can't even suit up without speed. In the spring of 1985, Hallman made his way over to take a look at the track team. He was scouting a sprinter from Cuero, where football was as passionate as a Friday Night revival. The track star had a reputation for being pretty fast. Didn't know if he could play football, but he was pretty fast. Son, Hallman said, if you put a little meat on your bones, you might have a shot to be a safety. The sprinter had no interest in being a safety.

Sean Page did.

He was a football player at heart, but, being wise beyond his years, Sean Page realized that he had already taken his last snap, and it had been on a high school field in San Antonio. His senior year at Churchill had been mediocre at best, and football had left a bitter taste. At Texas A&M, he said, I was floundering at track. A speed burner in high school was always chasing somebody else's tail lights in college. I thought I was fast, then I saw what speed was really like. I was running in slow motion. They were a blur.

However, if Curley Hallman needed someone who could put on shoulder pads and run a little, then I thought I just might be the man he was trying to find. He said he wanted kids who could play on the 12th man kickoff team. Fast. Tough. Take the pain. Wouldn't quit. Said he wouldn't be making the final decision. Said a coach named Roy Kokemoor was the man in charge. He'll get you in shape, see if you can hit a lick or take a punch, and let you find out what it's like to get run over by an eighteen-wheeler headed in both directions at the same time. Before Hallman was out of sight, I had turned in my track uniform and was on my across campus to find this man called Kokemoor.

With a ball carrier lying in his wake, Rick Tankersley (20) receives congratulations from his 12th man brothers.

As Sean Page recalled, there had to be a hundred ways to reach College Station. Some came along the banks of the Brazos River, others by a Lear Jet into Easterwood Airport. For those who arrived from Houston, Waco, and on farther west, it was a route of choice, the same for those who ventured from Dallas and beyond, even from the cursed, dirt robber-lands of Oklahoma.

I had taken Farm to Market Road 50, the way my dad had taught me. FM 50 was no shortcut. The tabletop flat route was an unlit two lane with no shoulders, interrupted with stop signs for dirt roads that periodically spilled traffic usually accompanied by farm implements directly into a driver's path. Fields of crops crowded the roadway in reluctant defiance.

Outside of drought or winter, the fields along FM 50 came alive with color and swayed with winds created by passing trucks. During the growing season, gold and blue daredevil crop dusters cruised just above the ground. They seemed to bank out of the clouds and come from nowhere, cutting bold swaths down above the crop rows and protecting the fruit of a farmer's labor.

While I was still a pup, my father, a product of the Fightin' Texas Aggie Class of '49, packed me up each year and religiously drove FM 50 towards Texas A&M in search of those crop dusters. I was the ever-vigilant lookout. And every fall, the farm to market route would be littered with white, snowflake ruminants of one crop just picked and bailed. Cotton. I once wondered aloud what snow was doing on the road at that time of year. My father just shook his had and said, son what you see was left behind by Coach Stallings. One day you might understand. As we approached College Station, my father would proclaim that only out in the fields of Nowhere, Texas, could one see Kyle Field this far from campus. Only out here, where it all began, could one see so far so clearly.

FM 50 seemed to go on forever. I had to be at Kyle Field an hour before the game or I would not be among the hundreds of other pups allowed to congregate behind the end zone near the bleachers and beneath the old scoreboard, fighting for the chance to snag one of Tony Franklin's booming practice kicks as they routinely sailed into the "peanut gallery" during the pre-game. A successful grab provided the opportunity to throw the prematurely worn-down, over-inflated kicker's ball back onto the field of play. Surely, a coach somewhere was watching to see which kid possessed the next Ed Hargett arm.

Kyle Field became a beacon of dreams, and I would proudly tell my father that one day I would play on Kyle Field. One day I too would run out the tunnel onto the hallowed turf where boyhood idols and legends roamed. But the dice were loaded. My father, painfully aware of the future harsh realities that would be presented by my small stature, only shook his head sadly, but wisely, and simply said he hoped for it but didn't think it would happen.

Dennis Mudd (4) and Mark Wurzbach (21) exchange excited high-fives after spearheading another critical tackle.

course, there were the rodeos. Eight seconds on the back of a bull didn't seem long until you were chewing dirt and dung at the end of a six-second ride. In fact, Motley said, I was the best six-second cowboy in West Texas. At Western Texas College, he took rodeo for physical education credits and crawled on two bulls every Wednesday.

Pain?

There was a little.

Glory?

A few of the girls thought so.

At 6-2 and 195 pounds, Butch Motley was probably a little too large to rodeo and keep riding those bulls, but the junior college did not have a football team, and he had already turned down an offer from UTEP.

The recruiter had told him, we don't have any more scholarships, but we'd like you to walk on. I can get you a job to help pay your tuition, room, and board. It's as good as a scholarship. Maybe even more money.

What is it that you want me to do, Motley wanted to know.

The recruiter shrugged. We'll have you out on campus turning water off and on somewhere, he said.

It wasn't much of a job.

But then, Butch Motley didn't think much of UTEP as a football school.

He rode one last bull just to prove to himself that he would never be afraid of fear. He wanted to leave the arena on his own terms. He stayed aboard for the full eight seconds, figured he couldn't do any better, and turned his back on the agony and ecstasy of rodeo, packed up, and drove east toward College Station. Texas A&M had a pretty decent engineering school. At least those were the rumors around Novice, and with any luck at all, there wouldn't be any bucking bulls or rodeo chutes to distract him or tear his arm apart again. The cast had finally been cut off, and the healing was coming along just fine as Motley, on a cold, blustery January day in 1984, drove away from the high plains and into a new, unpredictable life on the edge of the Aggie campus.

He rented a room in a trailer house, but the heater didn't work. The water froze, and the temperatures kept plunging toward zero. Ice peppered the ground outside. Butch Motley had all of Texas A&M he wanted, and he hadn't gone to class yet. He threw his clothes together and climbed into his car, ready to head west toward home again. Hell, he thought, a smart man would have never left. He turned the key in the ignition. The engine sputtered but wouldn't run. It didn't even threaten to run. Butch Motley was stranded. He was an Aggie whether he wanted to be or not.

When Motley walked across campus, he was always wearing a big straw hat and cheap red plastic sunglasses. He looked for all the world like a cosmic cowboy and in no way resembled a football player. By the spring of 1985, however, he decided that a role on the 12th man kickoff team might be as close to riding rodeo bulls as he could find, and he did miss the bulls. Motley wandered down from the stands in Kyle Field to try out.

I wasn't the fastest guy around, he said, and I knew speed was more

L arry "Butch" Motley thought he was as tough as they come, and he may have been right. He had grown up in Novice, in far West Texas, affectionately known as the Broomwood Capital of the World. He worked most summers under an unforgiving sun, picking broomwood and mistletoe, blasting juniper cedar from the prairie sand, dodging mesquite thorns, fighting wasps, and sometimes dueling rattlesnakes that had climbed under the cool of a rock ledge. Then, of

important to the coaches than breathing. I barely kept making the cuts but knew on the last day that Kokemoor's final decision would be based on whoever ran the fastest forty times. I could hit like a jackhammer, but the coaches were worried that I might not get downfield fast enough to hit anybody like a jackhammer. I didn't want to run the forty. If I ran the forty, I was dead. The stopwatch was a killer. I prayed for rain.

The gods must have listened.

The sky opened up, and the pouring rain sizzled when it touched the hot ground at Motley's feet.

Kokemoor ushered his charges inside. Couldn't run the forty, he decided. Too stormy outside. Not enough room inside. Kokemoor had only one option left. He let those final prospects square up and run into each other. He would keep the ones who stayed on their feet, and he kept his eyes on Butch Motley. The boy had some size on him and could hit pretty well, he thought. He had no idea that Motley cut his teeth on six-man football, out where they scrimmaged the wind. Sometimes they scored, and sometimes they didn't.

C orey Linscombe often felt as though he had spent enough time in Purgatory. Back in Judson High School, on the outskirts of San Antonio, he had been an all-district outside linebacker and punter, a 190-pounder who dared to believe that Texas A&M just might give him an opportunity to earn an engineering degree, as well as a spot on the Aggie football team. Time would prove that both assumptions were correct.

High School had begun so well for him and ended so badly. As the top team in a weaker district, Judson had won thirty consecutive football games. Then came the sudden transition to a more competitive league, and Judson fell on hard times. Linscombe found himself enduring two mediocre seasons, and during his senior year, he suffered separated ribs. He could play with the pain all right. He just couldn't lift weights. And he knew he would have to be a lot stronger before casting his lot with Division 1 football.

Corey Linscombe spent the winter of 1983-84 in the A&M weight room. Hour after hour, day after day, he battled the weights, testing his fortitude, fighting through the aching muscles. He had a singular goal in sight.

He walked on the Aggie football team.

His condemnation to Purgatory had begun.

On the scout team, as an outside linebacker, Linscombe sometimes dropped in pass coverage and found himself dueling with a speedy array of wide receivers. Lord, even the tight end was fast. And sometimes he rushed the passer, going one-on-one with 300-pound offensive linemen. Lord, they were big.

One pushed him into the quarterback.

Craig Stump went down.

Jackie Sherrill went berserk.

A quarterback, he kept screaming, was off limits.

That is, a quarterback was off limits until the day Corey Linscombe was handed the football and told to line up under center. I had always been pretty athletic, he said. I had a little speed, but was never faster than a 4.7 in the forty. And I could the throw the ball fairly well. Of course, I had never played quarterback before.

After he had been hammered a couple of times by linebackers bigger, stronger, and faster than he was, Corey Linscombe understood why varsity quarterbacks had the coach's protective shield around them.

At the end of spring practice, he had moved up the depth chart and was listed as the third-team outside linebacker for the Texas A&M football team.

Not bad, he thought.

Not bad all.

When the new freshmen arrived in the fall, Linscombe discovered that he had dropped off the bottom of the depth chart, kicked aside, and probably for good.

Long year.

Tough times.

By the spring of 1985, he was talking seriously to Roy Kokemoor about a position on the 12th man kickoff team.

D uring Christmas of 1984, Rick Tankersley sat down with his family for dinner and casually mentioned to his uncle that he might give the 12th man team a shot when he returned to Texas A&M. The volunteer kickoff unit had become something of a national

Rick Tankersley glances around while awaiting for the offense to score again in front of a packed Kyle Field. In the background are John Burnett (6), Chad Adair (12), Tony Pollacia (15), and Aggie punter Todd Tschantz.

Tony Pollacia (15) leaves a TCU player lying in the dust. Short run. Sudden stop. Only one man left standing.

phenomenon. His roommate had decided to try out, and Tankersley thought he just might have the right stuff to play. Doesn't take a whole lot of skill or talent, he told everyone. It's more like being in the middle of a demolition derby with pads on.

His uncle laughed. The whole family laughed. The thought of Rick Tankersley from little old Canyon, Texas, playing Division 1 football for a big-time university like Texas A&M was just about as absurd as anything they had heard lately. At the moment, playing for the 12th man had only been an idle and maybe a passing thought. Now Rick Tankersley was afflicted with a burning desire that he had not felt before. Tell him he couldn't do something, and he would move heaven and earth to get it done.

Roy Kokemoor said he would take twenty players, and he had fifteen back from the year before. Rick Tankersley rolled up his sleeves. The odds were slim, he thought. Hell, he liked the odds. He said, I was standing in the middle of the line, watching every one around me. Some were bigger and stronger. Some were scared to death. When they dove into that hamburger drill, I heard them grunt and saw them wince. They closed their eyes and crumpled to their knees. Dead weight, he knew. They were dead on the hoof and didn't know it yet. I suddenly realized that, oh, yeah, we're playing real football out here, and it's a vicious sport. Some hadn't put on pads since junior high, and they had forgotten the suffering that comes from trying to beat a train to the next crossing. A couple of guys just turned, walked off, and never came back. I was a hitter, always had been, and it didn't take long to tell who the hitters

were. My chances were improving every time we got in each other's face. Knock somebody out and cut down the odds. That's all I thought about. But still my knees were unsteady. The whole weeding out process was an absolute nightmare. Some were excited to be included in the final forty when the list was nailed to the door. Not me. The final twenty was the only number that counted.

Tankersley worked all summer, running hard and lifting weights, he said, like a mad man. He returned to school with an additional twenty pounds of muscle packed on his 5-11 frame, and two-a-days began to leave bruises on top of bruises that were taking an abnormally long time to heal. On the morning before the Alabama game, the prospects were herded together for their last hurrah. Kokemoor lined them up, face mask-to-face mask, and members of the scholarship team circled around them, not quite sure what these animals were trying to do. As Tankersley said, they had seen a lot of collisions in their time but never train wrecks like this.

He sought out red-headed Cory Allen, a former walk-on tight end who had played offensive tackle at 180 pounds for Industrial High School in Vanderbilt, Texas. Cory was a hard hitter, Tankersley said. I wanted to go one-on-one with him because I knew he would do his part. If I made an impression, it had to be against the toughest sonuvagun on the field, and not even the scholarship players had any burning desire to mess with Cory Allen. We slammed into each other, knowing that we were probably both fighting for the same spot, maybe even the last spot, and the shock, the violence of the sudden impact turned our bodies to rubber. I felt my knees go. I saw Cory falling to the ground. God, no, I thought. What kind of carnage is this? Neither one of us will be the last man standing.

That's it, Kokemoor said. I've seen all I need to see.

That single hit, Tankersley said, probably put both of us on the team. Kokemoor called him aside and said, Tank, you're one of the last guys I'm looking at. If I put you on the 12th man team, you'll work hard, you'll get beat up on the scout team every day, and you probably won't play at all this year. All I'm asking you to do is work hard enough to get ready for next year. So I don't want you coming up every day after practice or during a game and begging to play.

Tankersley remembered, I woke up the next morning completely depleted, sick as a dog, physically exhausted. I didn't go to school and called Kokemoor, telling him, you won't believe this, coach, but I gave everything I have, and now I can't get out of bed. If you let me miss today's practice and catch up on my sleep, I won't miss another day.

A long, agonizing pause. Then Kokemoor said with a brittle voice, Tank, I sure hope I didn't make a mistake.

Danny Balcar was up early, always early. He walked across the drill field each morning when the day was still pitch black, knowing the 12th man team had to be on the training table by six-thirty if they wanted their ankles taped before practice. Varsity came staggering in at eight o'clock, but if a walk-on happened to be late, he would be thrown off the table to make room for a player who counted, one who had size, speed, talent, and, most of all, a scholarship.

Balcar would practice, shower, and go directly to his first class. As the afternoon wore on, he had a tendency to cut his last class short, leave early, miss any study session that might be scheduled, and head to the 12th man workouts. He had to choose between education and football, and for a nineteen-year-old, it wasn't a difficult decision to make.

Danny Balcar was fast. He had blazing speed. He never doubted that he would make the team. Anybody who flirted with a 4.4 forty was regarded as a godsend. If he could hit at all, he had a place nailed down. Balcar, however, worried more about the walk-on who stood 5-8 and weighed 200 pounds. He looked like Barney Rubble and wasn't fast enough to stop a stopwatch, Balcar said, but he was always there. His nose was always broken, his face was bloodied, he limped back to the locker room each day after practice, and when it was all said and done, he would be left behind. All he had was not nearly enough. God gave some people heart, and others he blessed with speed. Balcar was gambling that when he found himself going downfield on his first kickoff, he would have a little of both.

Tony Pollacia considered himself a triple walk-on at Texas A&M. Grades in high school had never been particularly important to him. Tests were merely a chore that helped him kill time before football practice at Round Rock, so neither his grades nor his SAT score had been high enough for him to be accepted at A&M. During the summer months, he enrolled in four classes on campus, and on his first test in psychology, he earned a good, solid 52. For the first time, reality struck Pollacia. I'm gonna fail, he thought. No doubt about it. A&M is going to send me home, and I can't go home with a 52.

The sun beat down on him. Sweat covered his face. He was chewing on fear, and he did not like the taste. Pollacia said, I sat on a bench in front of the Sul Ross statue in a state of anxiety and depression, and in the shadow of old Sul Ross, I had an epiphany. I can do better than this, he thought. I don't have to let these classes whip me. I can find enough time for everything else. I might as well take a little time to study. He finished the summer with a 3.0 average.

In the fall, he walked on the campus at Texas A&M as a full-fledged freshman.

In high school, Pollacia had run the 400-meter relay and the mile relay, and he was invited to work out with the A&M track team. Might make it. Might not. Never know if you don't run. That was the only promise he had.

Tony Pollacia walked on the Texas A&M track team.

He endured the indoor track season, running the 600 meters, then moved on to the 400 meters outdoors. Pollacia also hooked up with the two-mile relay team, and after earning a letter in track, he fully expected to receive a scholarship.

None came.

He talked to the coach, and this was the bottom line: there were no scholarships available to a runner who never seemed able to break into first, second, or third place, regardless of the event. Pollacia hung up his track shoes for the final time and headed for the door.

He read in the *Battalion* about tryouts for the 12th man kickoff team, and he thought, I'm big enough, I'm fast enough, and, Lord knows, I've been playing football as long as we've both been around. I know how it's done and what it takes to get it done. What's the worst thing that can happen? They can kick me off the team, but they can't kick me out of school.

Tony Pollacia walked on the 12th man team.

He had been walking on forever, it seemed.

Now it was time to run.

Ed Silverman had matured late. In high school, he had been moved to tight end, to wingback, to an outside linebacker position, playing at 180 pounds and never able to run any faster than five flat in the forty. He was always looking for a permanent spot on the team, never quite finding one, running at night against that harsh West Texas wind and through the Amarillo sandscapes in an effort to increase his speed. By the time he had finished growing, by the time he was able to run a decent 4.7, Silverman had wasted a high school career and was fully established at Texas A&M with an eye set on Veterinarian School. He joined the Corps, he said, because his life needed discipline and structure. Just maybe, he thought, the 12th man team would give him the chance to finally find out if he could play football. High school was nothing more than a faint blur and a bad memory.

Freshmen in the Corps were always subjected to crap-outs by upper classmen, especially those with rank, and Ed Silverman was no exception. Pass a cadet officer, he said, and I would immediately be on the ground, doing pushups and sit-ups until my muscles ached and refused to cooperate anymore. Then I would do ten to twenty more. Such was life in the Corps. When he decided to try-out for the 12th man, Silverman went on a crash course to get in shape.

Every day, he would knock on a sophomore's door in the Corps dorm and explain that he had broken a rule and come by for his crap-out. I didn't have the self-discipline I needed to keep doing those pushups and sit-ups on my own, he said, so I let the upperclassmen in the Corps yell and scream at me, and I kept doing pushups until I was in good enough shape to play football again.

Kokemoor took him aside and said, if you want to know how to hit well enough to make this team, watch Kip Corrington. He's a technical perfectionist. And keep an eye on Jared Marks. He blows people up. Kokemoor was right. Ed Silverman had a knack for knocking people down. But when he stepped on the field against Jared Marks, he knew what it felt like to be blown up.

Silverman wanted more reps in spring practice. He wanted the coaches to notice him. He sidled up to Ronnie Glenn and asked, can I take your place in line?

Not a chance, Glenn snapped. I'm not about to lose my chance to nail somebody's hide to the wall. Ask somebody else.

If I saw any hesitation in any walk-on in front of me, I'd jump in front of him, Silverman said. Most didn't mind. Most weren't eager to test he last remnants of their manhood against Kip Corrington or Jared Marks. It was asking for disaster. I didn't particularly want to face them either, but I felt like I had a gun at my head. Time was running out, and every hit, either good or bad, counted. I would rather bleed now than be rejected later.

David Coolidge. Russ Birdwell. Paul Luedtke. They had all followed the same pitiless, punishing, and precarious route. Neither of them wanted to leave football behind when those Friday night lights went dark. Each wanted one last chance. Each defied the odds, but it did not take long for them to understand the power, the politics, and the broken promises of college football.

Once a walk-on, always a walk-on.

Coaches had a habit of looking through you and past you but seldom at you. Chances of ever moving into the starting lineup were negligible. Chances of playing at all weren't much better. As Coolidge said, I came to practice every day like I was coming to play a conference game. The varsity players had their game of the week. I had my game of the day. Starters went half speed and would just as soon walk through the plays. On the scout team, we went full bore, knowing full well that every tackle, every play might be our last. I would rather hit somebody and walk away limping than stand on the sidelines and watch.

Paul Luedtke was known as *The Commander*. He was a take-charge kind of guy, who came out of Pflugerville as a defensive lineman, barely weighing 185 pounds if he was dripping wet with his jock, socks, and cleats on. He had been the largest player on his high school team, and by stuffing himself with the culinary overload in Cain Hall, Luedtke became a 200-pound outside linebacker. I was miserable when I went back to my dorm room, he said. I kept complaining to my roommates about the stomach aches and indigestion that resulted from gorging myself with too much steak, shrimp, and baked potatoes. One plate. Then two. Maybe more. None of them expressed any sympathy.

Russ Birdwell had been invited to walk-on as a 6-2, 205-pound wide receiver, and he spent his freshman year competing alongside members of the 12th man kickoff unit on the scout team. They weren't like the rest

For the 12th man team, every kickoff was showtime, especially in the Cotton Bowl. Ready for battle are John Burnett (6), Rick Tankersley (20), Brian Edwards (16), and Ed Silverman (19). .

of us, he said. They were a wild bunch, partly mad and mostly crazy. The walk-ons were working to learn a position. The 12th man players were head hunting. If I had been smart, I would have gone ahead and been a part of them. But it took another year for me to make up my mind. I kept gambling that I was good enough to move up the depth chart. In reality, though, I knew that everyday when I came to practice, likely as not, I would find my locker cleaned out and my equipment gone. No explanations. No one to say they were sorry. No one to thank me for the time and the sweat and the blood I invested on Kyle Field. Billy Pickard, some believed, had two loves in his life. One was Aggie football. The other was cleaning out a walk-on's locker.

It did not take David Coolidge or Paul Luedtke that long to make a decision. With the 12th man unit, Coolidge said, we thought me might have a chance to get on the field. They were good. They were solid. They would either run through a barbed wire fence or take the fence apart barb by barb. It didn't matter. No matter how good each of the players were, however, I knew I had a better chance to beat out one of them than I did trying to wrestle playing time away from the likes of Domingo Bryant, James Flowers, and Chet Brooks. A 12th man was always vulnerable. A scholarship was chiseled in stone.

Luedtke liked his chances. Even against varsity, he said, on most days I could give them a pretty good run for their money. But they didn't always come from the same place the same way, and they had a nasty habit of hitting me when I wasn't expecting it, and I was always expecting to get hit. I never realized how hard the ground could be and what kind of damage it could do to the back of your head. I didn't see much of a future in being a live tackling dummy who never got to play. With the 12th man team, I had the opportunity to actually knock down somebody wearing a jersey other than maroon and white. The 12th man was my chance and my only chance to feel that I was a genuine Texas A&M football player. The 12th man had a role to play. The walk-on may as well have been the unknown soldier.

Although Birdwell was working out for Roy Kokemoor, he kept his eyes Jackie Sherrill. He was the most intimidating man I ever saw, Birdwell said. He had the look of a man who could have whipped Goliath without the slingshot. I had complete confidence in Coach Sherrill and the program he was trying to build, but I had no idea of what he was looking for in the members of his 12th man team. Speed. Sure. Strength. Definitely. But Coach Sherrill was always looking inside his players. He wanted to know what made them tick. We knew what made him tick. Intensity. Maybe that was it. Maybe intensity was what mattered most to him.

Russ Birdwell should not have worried.

Jackie Sherrill wasn't paying any attention to the try-outs. Even when he walked past, even when he stopped to look over the drills from time to time, he had other, more pressing matters on his mind. As far as the 12th man unit was concerned, Jackie Sherrill only had one simple rule, and it was carved in granite. Don't let any of the jackasses from hell run one back on you. The rest of the decisions lay upon the shoulders of Roy Kokemoor.

Dan Pollard had a choice to make. He had joined the Corps of Cadets just as his father had done more than two decades earlier. He was Old Army all the way. Pollard knew it would be tough and probably unforgiving. But then, if his father had survived the demands and rigors of military training at A&M, he was determined to make the grade as well. A chip off the old block made the decision to get his block knocked off.

During the spring of 1985, Pollard joined his old high school teammate, Sean Page, on the 12th man try-out practice field. If all they want

is speed, he thought, then I can bring them a little speed. After all, Pollard had been a track man back at Churchill in San Antonio, running the 100-yard dash, the quarter-mile relay, the sprint relay, and the mile relay. For good measure, he even threw himself into the long jump. Maybe Dan Pollard might have a legitimate chance. Maybe he hadn't hung up his cleats for the last time after all. In track, however, no 300-pounder had ever been standing there at the tape to level him at the end of a 100-yard dash. Track could wind a man. Football was combat.

The Corps and the 12th man team, however, were consuming Pollard's every waking moment. His day began early when he was still sleepy and ended late when he was wracked with pain. In between, of course, he had his exams, and studying was a little more difficult than it had been before. The A&M experience began to overwhelm, then suffocate him. In the Corps, Pollard was a member of the Bloody Cross outfit, and each day, members of Company K-1 ran as many laps as possible around the quadrangle during a twenty-minute period. In fact, the Bloody Cross was running all of the time. The unit took pride in being able to endure as much or more than any other outfit. If nothing else, Dan Pollard's physical condition was as good as it had ever been. On the football practice field, the running really began in earnest, and it was punctuated by the kind of punishment that could only be handed out by someone a foot taller, a hundred pounds heavier, and usually almost as fast as he was. He knew it would be hard, but not that hard.

The Corps was Pollard's master. The pursuit of a spot on the 12th man team became his sole and undying ambition. He knew it would be difficult, but he was determined to do both. Cuts came. Pollard remained. The competitors were all whittled away. Pollard was still hanging on. Then came the final and fateful day.

The coach called out eighteen players. Pollard's name had not been among them. He and the few still grouped together on the sidelines squared their shoulders, took deep breaths, hardened their muscles, gritted their teeth, and lined up against each other on opposite hash marks. The day of reckoning was upon them. They all knew that a big headache was waiting somewhere near midfield. Kokemoor only wanted to see who flinched, who blinked, who turned away, who backed down just before the critical moment of impact. Pollard says, I wasn't the biggest, and I wasn't even the fastest. For whatever reason, I was one of the last two guys chosen.

On the practice field with the 12th man was a hard and humbling experience. Then Pollard would join his Bloody Cross outfit to make those short, quick sprints around the quadrangle when his lungs were threatening to burst. His legs were always burning. Running had become a way of life.

Of course, Dan Pollard was no longer able to march with his Corps unit from the quadrangle to Kyle Field on game day, passing the spirited crowd that lined the street. He was already warming up on the field. It was a sacrifice he chose to make.

But he wore a 12th man patch stitched on his sleeve.

And one day he would be wearing his senior boots.

It was, Pollard decided, a formidable combination.

Tom Ray was resentful, even though his raw feelings were buried deep inside him. He did not particularly care what those wild-eyed band of tail kickers and head removers were doing in the 12th man unit. He should have been on the original team. He damn sure earned a spot, but Tom Ray had been cut. Just before the first game, he had been told in no uncertain terms that his presence was no longer needed on Kyle Field. That was his interpretation anyway, so he had remained a student, rooted for the Aggies the next two years because that's what Aggies did, but no longer did Tom Ray harbor any foolish

Out to inflict a little pain and a lot of damage are Jeff Boutwell (11) and Chad Adair (12), along with the rest of a thundering herd that had number twelve stitched proudly on their jerseys. There were good days and bad. No one remembered the bad.

notions about playing football.

Don't give up, James Barrett kept telling him.

I'm through with it.

You ought to give the 12th man one more try.

They've seen me, Tom Ray said. They know what I can do. It wasn't enough.

It's different now.

Tom Ray shook his head. He had lost his interest in football, he said But it was a lie, and he knew it. Ray kept faithfully working out, lifting weights day after day, and, somewhere in the backside of his mind, he wondered if the fire still burned hot enough for him to give the 12th man another try, another chance, another risk of failure. James Barrett had faith in him, and Tom Ray certainly did not want to let Barrett down. So, he reasoned, what were another few wind sprints, agility drills, and physical – no, violent – contact? All the coach could say to him was *no thanks*. Ray had heard it before, and it might not hurt so badly the second time.

His family motto down on the ranch had always been: We get it right the second time, or we do it again.

Tom Ray made the decision to do it again.

Doug Middleton knew his chances ran somewhere between slim and non-existent. There weren't a lot of opportunities for high school cello players to find their niche in college football, especially when the cello players had never strapped on pads or a uniform before. But Middleton had heard Ray Childress speak at Bonfire in 1984, and he said, Ray was so fired up, he fired me up. He didn't say a lot, but he was speaking volumes to me, and I would have run down and signed up for the 12th man that night if anyone had been around to take my name. I wanted to be a part of a game and a team that Childress was so passionate about.

Middleton, at 6-2 and 210 pounds, was certainly big enough to impress a coach, but he had no idea who the 12th man coach was. He wandered around the athletic offices until he stumbled into a small cubicle occupied by Roy Kokemoor.

Mister Kokemoor, he said, I'm interested in being on the 12th man kickoff squad. What do I have to do to better my chances for making the team? You tell me what to do, and it's done.

Well, we won't have our tryouts for another forty-five days, the coach said. You don't have time to get any stronger. So I'd suggest you start running wind sprints as hard as you can and long distances as often you can. Where did you play in high school?

I didn't.

No football?

I played the cello.

Roy Kokemoor immediately wrote Doug Middleton off and forgot him long before Middleton reached the far end of the hallway.

When Middleton tried out, he said, I was nervous. I was anxious. I was a little overwhelmed. My feet had never touched a real football field before, and I had no idea what to expect. Bert Hill, the strength and conditioning coach, walked out the door and bellowed, oh, yeah, it's a great day to be alive this morning. I'm looking good, and I'm feeling good. He flexed the massive muscles clinging to his body.

I was standing at the five-yard line on the south side of the field, Middleton said, and Dana Batiste followed Hill out the door, wearing gray shorts and a white T-shirt. He stopped, looked at us, and his big grin turned into a belly laugh.

Why is he laughing, I asked.

You have no idea what's in store for you, Kokemoor said. He does. You're the dummies that Dana and his friends are going to block, tackle, demoralize, and demolish over the next few weeks.

It won't be so bad once I get my pads on, Middleton thought.

He had no idea how to put them on.

Middleton's thigh pads did not fit quite right, so he and tightly wound a roll of tape several times around the pads, his uniform, his thighs. Doesn't look too good, he thought, but it should keep the pads in place. He jogged out onto the field, and Sean Page grabbed him by the shoulders. Boy, we're in college now, Page said, not high school. You don't want to look like you did in high school. Get that damn tape off as quick as you can get it off.

Then how do I keep the pads from falling off, Middleton asked.

Page sighed. It was going to be a long spring, he decided.

It would get longer. Before practice, Page said, the 12th man had it own personal and private session where we did basic fifth-grade tackling drills. Nothing fancy. Nothing unique. We just went jaw-to-jaw and kept rattling somebody's cage while we were still listening to the rattle of our own. For thirty minutes, we did hitting drills from all angles, straight ahead, from a foot away, from hash mark to hash mark, from sideline to sideline, from what seemed like Hearne and Highway 6 to Kyle Field. We were out there butting heads – Roy Kokemoor didn't mind sending the smaller guys like me against the bigger guys – and the scholarship players were laughing at us. They couldn't help themselves. We could have felt intimidated, and sometimes we did.

Were we doing it wrong, I wondered. Hell, that's the way we did it in high school. Schemes may change, but techniques didn't. We kept butting heads. They kept laughing.

Then the coaches threw us onto the scout team for a few more hitting drills since we were warmed up and frothing at the mouth. That meant we dug in, held our ground, and let the varsity players take turns pounding us. Hit us high. Hit us low. Hit us often. Don't back down. Get back up. Here they come again. We were cheap commodities. If we broke down or got hurt, nobody cared. There were a lot more human tackling dummies where we came from.

For us, it was just a privilege to be out there. We wore our bruises like purple hearts.

On more than one occasion, Danny Balcar and I found ourselves in the corner of the end zone, trapped in the middle of Sherrill's inside drill, and the goal, I finally figured out, was to knock us into an eight-foot chain link privacy fence that encircled the practice field. We left a lot of skin on that fence, but at least we were on the right side of the fence. We could have been on the outside looking in.

When Balcar pulled off his jersey, he had the imprint of the metal fence squares carved into his back. I thought that was pretty funny until I woke up the next morning and saw the size of my own bruises.

Eagerly awaiting another Aggie score, which sends them back out on the field again, are Rick Tankersley (20), Dean Berry (1), and Dennis Mudd (4). No one cheered the offense like the 12th man unit. Another touchdown. Another tackle.

Chad Adair (12) and Mark Wurzbach (21) are running wild and free in search of a collision. Before the play is over, they will be in the middle of one, the more violent the better. The bigger they were, the harder they fell. The small went down quicker.

Finally we had to run back and cover wide receivers on their "go" routes, Page said. Over and over. Down the field running wide open. Again and again. A step behind. Never a step ahead. Anytime we got the chance, we knocked those smiles off their faces. It didn't happen often, but, Lord, it felt good when we had a hard, clear shot that snapped their heads back. Nobody promised us that we could come back tomorrow or even stay the rest of the day. For those of us trying to worm our way onto the 12th man team, pain was the only guarantee.

The scholarship players did not have a mean streak, just a competitive one. They wanted the coaches to notice them, Page said, and we were getting in the way. We were always in the way. After awhile, we began to realize that getting in the way wasn't all bad.

Billy Pickard gave Balcar and me shoulder pads designed for wide receivers because we were so much smaller. I wondered why Mark Wurzbach, Ronnie Glenn, and David Coolidge were laughing at us, and by the time practice had ended, I knew.

I was the first one in the locker room trying to trade those wimpy little pads for some real ones. It was a matter of survival. I needed all of the protection I could get. Didn't care how big the shoulder pads were as long as they were big enough to absorb enough of those damnable shocks to keep me alive.

In August, before the fall campaign began in earnest, the scholarship athletes were working diligently to get ready for the first game of the season. Members of the 12th man team, Page said, were simply getting ready to face the final cuts. We worked harder. We ran harder. We hit harder. August was hot. The sun was unbearable. Practices wore us down to a nub. We ran on the field but could barely walk home. I think it was easier on Kokemoor if someone called it quits. He hated to cut someone. He watched over us like we were his cursed little children.

All my friends were going to the Student Union and buying their game tickets. I went along with them, stood in line, and dutifully bought my tickets, too. I had no idea if I would be watching the games from the stands or the sidelines.

A week and a half before Texas A&M departed for Alabama, Roy Kokemoor took a dirty dozen from the final forty and ran them out on the field. This is the core of my 12th man unit, he said. From this group, I'll select my starters. I have an idea who the next eight or nine will be, but I haven't quite yet made up my mind.

Sean Page looked around him.

He was not on the field.

Another full week of practice, and only a handful of spots remained open. Kokemoor took Sean Page aside and said, son, I'm looking for some speed guys who can cover the whole field. Keep everything in front of them. Not let anyone past them. I can go ahead and put you on the team, but you won't play a down the whole season.

I understand, Page said.

Do you still want to be on the team?

More than you'll ever know.

Sean Page was one of the last chosen in 1985. He thought back and remembered the day Jackie Sherrill walked into the room after the registration forms had been signed. Gentlemen, the Coach had said, do you want to be a part of this? It's lots of work. And you won't play a down. Good luck.

Hell, Page thought, Sherrill was a straight shooter if nothing else. Page might not play, but he would strap on his cleats on most Saturdays in the fall, and he felt as though he was among the ones most blessed.

Ed Silverman had trouble making practices. He was committed to a number of science labs during the late afternoon, and there were some weeks he barely made it to practice at all. He knew that the final workouts before those last critical cuts would take place on Thursday afternoon. He had the memo folded up in his pocket. He had it memorized. It was the one day he could not afford to miss. It was judgment day.

On Wednesday, he finished up his lab for statistics 301 and hurried down to the field. As usual, he was running late.

Where in God's name were you, Rick Tankersley asked. There was a frantic sense of urgency in his voice.

In lab.

Dude, Tankersley said, you missed it.

Missed what?

Kokemoor made the final cuts today.

I thought it was Thursday.

Sherrill changed his mind.

Kokemoor had no doubt been under enormous pressure to create the final roster. Ed Silverman had always known he was probably on the bubble, and the bubble burst. It felt, he said, as though he had been kicked in the gut. All that time. All that effort. All of those hopes. Gone. I would have gladly missed a statistics computer lab to play football. I was never angry or upset at Kokemoor. The coach did what he had to do.

I decided to walk-on, keep my face and my name in front of the coaches, and get ready for next year.

A few weeks later, Ed Silverman came down with mononucleosis and missed the rest of the semester.

By now, John Burnett had decided that maybe, just maybe, he actually was a kickoff kind of guy. The dream of becoming an All-American linebacker had been left in the dust by the terrible devastation that Ray Childress had inflicted on him. Burnett made the long-suffering discovery that he just couldn't stop a heavy truck on a downhill grade with its brakes burning out, and Childress was always coming downhill and at a furious rate of speed and power.

His equipment hadn't changed. It was still as old, as worthless as the year before, but Burnett was on his way to becoming a card-carrying member of the 12th man kickoff unit, which meant he had achieved a certain kind of status and recognition on campus. Not an All-American, perhaps, but somebody special all the same.

Burnett walked into the locker room, found Sly Calhoun, and said, I'm still here.

Sly nodded. So you are, he said. He handed out a new jock strap, a new pair of socks, and, by the end of practice, John Burnett had his name nailed firmly above his locker. He was no longer living in obscurity.

Billy Pickard had quit snickering at Doug Middleton and started laughing out loud, laughing to his face. Karl Kapchinski was issuing equipment, and Pickard asked Middleton, hey, boy, are you one of them 12th man red shirts?

Yes, sir.

First year you ever played?

Yes, sir.

You a senior?

Yes, sir.

Pickard laughed again, harder this time. I can't believe it, he said. I see here where you're majoring in psychology, and you're not smart enough to know better than to play as a senior and get your brains beat out.

Kapchinski laughed along with him.

Middleton would go home at night, he said, with bruises the size of softballs, and he didn't even remember getting hit. R. C. Slocum was my position coach, and he acted like he was disgusted with every move we made. It seemed as though we were a waste of his time, and, frankly, I can't say as I blamed him. He was obsessed with making his defense better. But then, that's what he had been hired to do. And, more than anyone, he had the uncanny ability to build the best, the strongest, the most aggressive defense in the nation. He had a wrecking crew before anyone knew what it was.

During two-a-days, Doug Middleton had gone head-to-head with Butch Motley, lost his balance, twisted a knee, and banged up his ankle. In a game that demanded speed, it was tough to compete when he could barely walk. There were times when he began to wonder if he would ever walk without a limp again.

The pads came off. Doug Middleton wasn't able to practice for a week. Then it was two weeks. He had a stress fracture and became one of Hill's Raiders. Bert Hill put us through hell in an effort to get us back on the field, Middleton said. He did not want any slackards around. He had no use for slackards. He had no use for me. I thought about quitting, but then decided, no, I'll see this through to the bitter end, which meant that neither Billy Pickard nor Bert Hill nor Karl Kapchinski were singularly or collectively tough enough to run me off.

The final cut came down to Doug Middleton and Mike Blachiki. One had played football. One hadn't.

Blachiki was Roy Kokemoor's final selection.

I decided to hang around and play as a walk-on, Middleton said. They could show me the door, but there weren't enough of them to drag me through it.

Blachiki suddenly and unexpectedly turned in his uniform. Didn't have time for both schooling and football, he said. Had to make a deci-

Bobby Middleton (18) left an indelible mark, usually bruises, on the teams he faced. Few had the power to hit as hard as Middleton.

Mark Wurzbach (21) blasts off the line in a dead sprint.

sion. Football lost out.

Middleton ran as quickly to Kokemoor's office. Let me take that spot, he said.

Kokemoor smiled and shrugged. I guess I should have picked the one who wanted it so badly in the first place, he said.

Jackie Sherrill was always working on a new angle, trying to figure out how he could make his team a little better, a little faster, a little more lethal in the fourth quarter. He recruited a track star and brought him out to practice. Was he just as fast in shoulder pads? Could he take a lick? Had he ever been knocked down before? Had he ever been hit by anything harder than the tape at the finish line?

Chet Brooks was sitting in the stands watching as David Coolidge lined up as a scout team defensive back. Come on, *Cool Breeze*, Brooks yelled. Let's do it today, boy.

The track star ran a skinny post.

He's a burner, Brooks yelled.

Coolidge crucified him. Just a couple of walk-ons out for a casual afternoon collision. Coolidge had nothing to lose. The track star could see the end of his sprint career flashing through his subconscious.

Damn track's got a wall on it, Brooks said. He was laughing now.

Only Sherrill and the trainers were watching.

The track star crumpled to the ground like wrinkled cellophane from a day-old pack of cigarettes.

Ten-yard dash, Brooks was saying to anyone who happened to be listening. Short dash. Ain't who crosses the finish line that counts. It's who gets up.

The track star lay flat on his back.

Flamed out, Brooks said. Threw a tennis shoe.

The helmet rolled to one side.

Chet Brooks was on his feet, walking out of the stands. He shrugged and looked in the direction of Sherrill. Hey, Coach, he said, somebody call the track coach. This one's through running for the day.

He liked a good hit whether he delivered it or not.

All Chad Adair had asked for was a simple, no-holds-barred chance. Now he had one. He trotted in on the scout team and was told, you're out here for one reason. Don't let anybody get to the quarterback. I don't care what you do. Keep those sumbitches off the quarterback. Block 'em. Cut 'em. Hold 'em. Separate their heads from their feet. Rip their balls off. But keep those sumbitches off the quarterback.

Adair looked across the line of scrimmage.

He had to block John Roper.

Then Aaron Wallace.

Then he was supposed to square up and do it all over again.

Roper would have a good head of steam. Always did.

Wallace hit scout team linemen like speed bumps worn down by too many tire tracks. Most of the tracks belonged to him.

If I can make something happen, Adair told himself, it'll leave a good impression on the coaches, and – who knows? – I might even get some extra playing time.

In my head, I had it all worked out, he said. I knew Roper was coming. I had him dead in my sights. I didn't have to knock him down. I simply had to slow him down a couple of times. A second was all we needed. Maybe two seconds if I was lucky. Just give the quarterback time to deliver the football.

No problem.

I was a pretty damn good blocker in high school. I thought I could slow down any moving object, no matter how big, no matter how strong, for a second. Maybe two.

Roper charged.

He went through me like butter, Adair said.

Dan Pollard began his career at Texas A&M as a bonafide engineering student, but he admitted that he didn't quite know exactly what an engineer did. It's just that he was aware the university had a damn good engineering school, and engineers generally didn't have a lot of problems finding a good job. He diligently went to class but gradually saw his grade point average drop into a steep decline. It seemed as though the more ground he made up on the football field, the more he lost in the classroom.

At eight o'clock in the morning, he would be listening to a lecture that had something to do with engineering and chemistry. His bruises ached. His aches ached. Pollard made his first three classes. He made only three more the rest of the semester.

He was a football player, he told himself.

Not an engineer.

Yet, in the midst of it all, Pollard realized that he was part of a special unit that had more notoriety on campus than it did on the practice field. His arms were black and blue, unless, of course, the bruise turned purple and green. He had a stinger in his shoulder, and the nerve endings in his arm, down to the tips of his fingers, felt as though they were on fire.

Billy Pickard gave him a spider pad to place under his shoulder pad. Don't need it, Pollard said through clenched teeth. I'll tough it out. He feared Pickard. Pickard had too much power within the inner circle of A&M football. Pickard, he said, had the ability to make life unbearable for us. Pickard could cut you, and Coach Sherrill would never find out. One day you would be on the team. The next day, you were gone.

The boy got hurt, was all Pickard ever said or ever had to say. The 12th man realized that he kept a scurrilous and guarded account of the number of injuries a player endured, and no one ever knew just how many injuries it took to be one too many.

Pollard's shoulder was hammered again.

The fire in his arm blazed hotter.

This time, he accepted the spider pad.

Pickard be damned.

Pollard had better equipment in high school. As a member of the 12th man team, he was given a helmet with foam inside, he said. It was similar to the splintered old helmet he had worn in Middle School. Varsity had new helmets with a liquid-filled cushion protecting the head.

From time to time, however, Sylvester Calhoun took pity on us, Pollard said. He would sneak us better pads and shoes, helmets and uniforms any time he could. If we happened to walk through an empty locker room and find a better piece of equipment lying around, we borrowed it. We borrowed it for a long time. If no one found out, we borrowed it for the rest of the season. Some of the scholarship players felt sorry for us. They would tell Pickard they had lost or ruined their pads and shoes, get new ones, and then come over to our side of the locker room and donate them to us.

We weren't as talented as they were.

We would never be as good as they were.

But we were Aggies, and Aggies took care of their own.

A quiet and undeniable optimism about the football team was beginning to work its way across campus as Jackie Sherrill unleashed one of the most physical and highly competitive spring trainings that the Aggie faithful could remember. It had the same kind of edge and intensity that Bear Bryant brought to Texas A&M, they said. Sherrill didn't need Junction to whip his team into shape. The hot afternoons hovering above Kyle Field would do just fine. Bring the whip. Sharpen the spurs. Cinch the saddle up tight. Sherrill was throwing his minions into the raw side of hell.

The Aggies had pulled themselves off the mat to upset TCU, then drum Texas soundly to finish strong in 1984, and with those two victories, A&M began to glimpse the million-dollar promise that Jackie Sherrill had made in the midst of a three-ring circus that surrounded his hiring three years earlier. The future wasn't even now. The Aggies would be dominated by sophomores and juniors. That meant 1985 would be good and '86 just might be even better.

Kevin Murray was back with his rocket arm. Craig Stump had a critical year of experience under center. Anthony Toney, Roger Vick, and Keith Woodside could run either inside or wide. Flanker Jeff Nelson and split-end Shea Walker could go get the ball with the best of them. The offensive line was anchored by Doug Williams, Louis Cheek, Randy Dausin, and Matt Wilson, with Jerry Fontenot and a giant of a man, 6-7, 378-pound Marshal Land, ready to wear down any defense that might have the grave misfortune of confronting them. The wall of defense was on the broad shoulders of linemen Rod Saddler, Guy Broom, and Sammy O'Brient, as well as linebackers John Roper, Steve Bullitt, Todd Howard, Larry Kelm, Dana Batiste, and Johnny Holland, who, as Sherrill had known all along, found it infinitely more satisfying to drill a quarterback

than be one. Ballhawks roamed the secondary: Domingo Bryant, Jimmie Hawkins, Terrance "Chet" Brooks, James Flowers, and Old Faithful, Kip Corrington.

R. C. Slocum's defense was, as always, solid as a stone wall. No weathering and no cracks. His defense could put fear in the hearts and souls of mankind. Whether A&M ultimately won or lost, however, was tucked away in the offensive genius of Lynn Amedee, and he liked it that way. Amedee had introduced a multiple offense he called the run-and-shoot. It's balanced, he said. If we pass for three hundred yards, we ought to be able to run for three hundred yards. Jackie Sherrill preferred to call it a "controlled" offense. The I-formation was gone and placed in cold storage. Out of the way. Forgotten.

As Amedee explained, we'll use the short pass instead of a run, and our passing will be based on our receivers making the adjustments necessary to take advantage of whatever scheme we're facing. They have to read the defense just like the quarterback does. Line up with us, and you won't know where we're going. Blitz us, and we'll burn you deep.

He seemed quite sure of himself.

Jackie Sherrill, John Burnett said, never lost sight of the big picture. We should be the big dog, the Coach kept saying. The head, not the tail. He had to turn the entire Aggie football culture around. For so long, the team had played as though it was content to have a decent season and occasionally win a big game. Sherrill wanted to win all of the time. He knew he had to change the Aggie mind set.

During those first three years, Jackie Sherrill, constantly in the wake of withering criticism, had clung firmly to his basic philosophy. Build from the bottom up. Don't ever panic. Take care of your own business, and don't worry about what you can't control. Do your best, and hang the rest. Too often, the Aggie faithful were talking among themselves about the possibility of hanging him.

During 1984, the wolves had definitely been howling. Gallows humor prevailed among the assistant coaches, and some staffers had been seen plotting escape routes on napkins in the dining hall. But after the disastrous collapse in Arkansas, the team came together and began to click on more cylinders than it had in the past. The 6-5 record wasn't exactly the promised land, but it did signal hope that the program had finally turned the corner. His 1984 team could have easily folded, Sherrill said, but it never gave up. A group of young men sat up, rid themselves of mediocrity, and molded themselves together as a team. The strident chords of discord among them were laid to rest.

The leering press had mixed reviews.

Al Carter, a constant critic in the *Houston Chronicle*, wrote, the Aggies have changed head coaches nine times in the past thirty-seven years. That just about averages out to a new head coach every four years. Sherrill is entering his fourth season in 1985. Either history or the Aggies will have to change. It's the irresistible force against the immovable object with the career of Jackie Wayne Sherrill caught in the middle.

Carter picked the Aggies to finish seventh in the Southwest Conference. Carter loved to badger a loser.

Lynn McKinney, in *Texas Sports World*, wrote, the 1985 season is critical for Sherrill. As losses mount, even his million-dollar contract becomes less a factor. Aggie former students don't like a losing season even if the team beats Texas. They want the Cotton Bowl. If Jackie Wayne Sherrill can't take them to Dallas, they'll find a coach who can.

Athlon's Southwest Football was the first to recognize that a new day had dawned upon the sacred confines of Kyle Field. The publication turned its back on conventional wisdom and predicted that Texas A&M was at last ready to take a run at the conference championship. It said, this is the year Jackie Sherrill's building program lights up the sky.

At A&M, it was win or else.

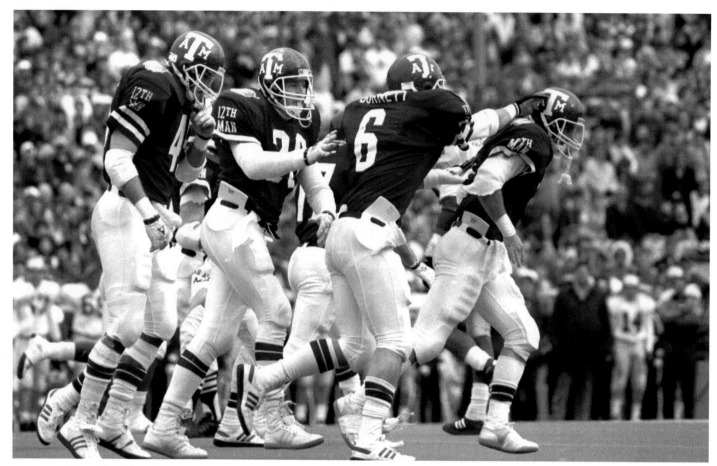

Racing off the field in triumph are Dean Berry (45), Garry Sorrell (26), John Burnett (6), and Harold Huggins. Berry traded in his No. 1 during his senior year to wear No. 45 since he had been added to the varsity roster as a linebacker.

Chapter 17

Jackie Sherrill had always been the master motivator. He loved the thought of crawling down inside the hidden corners of somebody's head, worrying, then confusing, the hell out of an opposing coach while, at the same time, figuring out a way to teach his own team about leadership and unity and the will to win no matter how imposing the odds might be. In August, he sent out letters to 12th man team members and scholarship players alike, saying, I hope your summer has gone extremely well and that you have been preparing yourself mentally and physically for a great year.

That was what Sherrill expected.

A great year.

In his mind, anything resembling a good year would be an absolute failure, one weighted down with mockery and mediocrity.

Most of the Aggie faithful were merely hoping against hope that the Aggies would receive an invitation to some bowl, any bowl, even a Leftover Bowl game.

For Jackie Sherrill, it was Cotton or bust.

Sherrill called his team together and gave them a page filled with black dots that could be removed and placed on the hour-hand numbers of their wristwatches. Any time you check the time, he said, you can look down and see those dots. Those dots represent Texas A&M, your team members, and our goals for the season. The dots will be used exclusively by coaches, by the team, by friends, and by family members. We're all in this together.

Before one critical game, he brought a box filled with car keys to the locker room. He handed a different key to each player. Take it, he told them, and put it in your shoe, shove it down your socks, or tape it somewhere inside your uniform or on your pads. Don't lose it. Keep it with you every minute of the game. Because sometime during the fourth quarter, when you are battered and bruised and bone-tired, you know you can reach down, take that key out, and start your engine one more time.

Sherrill had his Aggies revved and ready to roll.

One question mark continued to hang like a dark, morbid shadow above the A&M coaching staff. Who would do the kicking? The heir apparent to the booming leg of Alan Smith was Eric Franklin, the kid brother of Aggie barefoot legend Tony Franklin. Eric had a unsettling tendency to misfire far too often on his field goal attempts, and, even worse, his kickoffs resembled shots fired from a pop gun. Sherrill had grown accustomed to Smith driving the ball deep into the end zone. Eric Franklin, on the other hand, seldom hammered the ball past the ten-yard line. Short field position was deadly field position.

Enter Scott Slater, the great unknown. He had been a free safety at

Fort Worth's Richland High School, but he walked onto the Aggie football team as a kicker in 1984. Spent the season in anonymity. Wore an orange jersey. Kicked the ball day after day. Kicked it high. Kicked it far. Nobody noticed. He had the stigma of being labeled as a dreaded walk-on, which carried with it the kiss of death. He may as well have been exiled on a desert isle. Slater wasn't large. He wasn't imposing. But, he said, I had the God-given ability to kick the ball out of sight.

Jackie Sherrill did not have a scholarship for him. But then, neither did any other Division 1 program. The Aggie coaches told him, however, come on down and let's see what you can do. No promise, no guarantees, which was the usual line. But we will take a good look at you. For a year, nobody had looked his way at all.

Scott Slater, during the fall of 1985, was one of a half dozen walk-on kickers who had gathered on Kyle Field. Determined. Nervous. Drained. Wondering if it had all been a scam. Most had been kicking the way walk-ons historically kicked. Pop flies. Low liners. Wobbles. Spirals. And a few that occasionally turned over. Not a ball had been kicked hard enough to leave any scratches.

Sherrill told them all, I need someone who can kick the ball out of the back of the end zone.

He was holding two footballs.

From sixty yards, Slater stepped up and drilled the first one through the uprights. High. Far. Made it look easy. Room to spare. Then he drilled the second football through the uprights.

Give me another football, Sherrill said quietly. When a trainer did, he handed it to Scott Slater and said, do it again, son, and you have yourself a job.

Slater ripped the third football through the uprights.

Three days later, promptly at seven o'clock on a Saturday evening, Scott Slater found himself standing on the forty-yard line, getting ready to kick off to Alabama.

Freeze frame.

Slater was quietly telling himself as the noise of the crowd faded from his mind: So this is what it's all about. Set your goals. Take advantage of whatever talent you might have. Be willing to put in a lot of hard work. Forget the disappointments. Hope for a little luck. God was indeed taking care of me.

He charged forward, and the ball was in the air.

Nobody was bringing it back.

For Jackie Sherrill, going to Alabama was going home. He had played and bled for the Bear on Legion Field. He had been involved in two national championships with the Crimson Tide. He would be facing off against an old teammate, Ray Perkins, who had been chosen to replace the Bear. Both men still grieved, knowing that Bear Bryant had died a mere twenty-eight days after retiring from Alabama. No teams to coach. No games to play. No life worth living.

I'll have some emotions when I walk on the field, Sherrill said. I've got some teeth buried at Legion Field, some blood on Legion Field, some sweat and some tears. But that's not going to make a difference in the game. If Jackie Sherrill and Ray Perkins lined up and played, there would be maybe twenty people in the stands. It's going to be Alabama against Texas A&M.

Ronnie Glenn had been having a difficult time controlling his nerves. Texas A&M was on its way to Birmingham, and he was back in College Station. Out-of-town games, all but the last one of the season, were off limits for members of the 12th man. It was, he decided, time for a little road trip. He and his best friend, scholarship wide receiver Greg Dillon, loaded up his mother's van in Houston and pulled out in the pitch black hours of an early Friday morning, not long past two o'clock.

They were traveling up from the South, winding through unfamiliar territory until they ran into something that looked a lot like Legion Field. Mark Wurzbach, David Coolidge, and Bobby Middleton were not about to be left behind. They followed I-45 north to Dallas, then connected with I-20, driving hard and furious through the heart of the Deep South. As the country song said on the radio, they were moving on.

Roy Kokemoor heard they were on their way to Alabama, and he passed the word to Jackie Sherrill. Well, Coach said with a grin, if the boys arrive on their own at their own expense, we'll have some equipment waiting on them. Kokemoor allowed his 12th man interlopers to sneak through the gate during pre-game warm-ups and dress out for the game. They stood on the sidelines, wearing redshirt freshman jerseys, and Glenn spent his evening on Legion Field as Lafayette Turner. No one knew the difference.

They didn't play. They didn't go down on kickoffs. But they were immersed in the deafening chorus of boos that arose when A&M returned to the field, and they began to understand the vagaries and the glories of Alabama football.

The ghost of the Bear won, and the Tide rolled to a 23-10 victory. The crowd noise was unbelievable, Sherrill said. It led directly to four critical illegal procedure penalties against the Aggies, and penalties were the difference in the game. As Ronnie Glenn recalled, the noise was so loud I could feel the ground vibrating. Craig Stump started the game for A&M and had a good first quarter, completing five of six passes. But down on the sidelines, it was Kevin Murray giving his team encouragement, walking to each offensive player, shaking his hand, and saying, the rope's getting tight. We've got to pull together. Don't give up. Finally he was back under center, connecting on 13 of 20 passes for 158 yards, and A&M was on the cusp of making a glorious comeback. But Alabama's running back, Craig Turner, bolted thirty-two yards for a touchdown with 1:07 left to ice the win. For Jackie Sherrill, for Kevin Murray, for the A&M team, it was a long, quiet, and miserable flight home.

Sherrill was convinced that the noise level in Legion Field had done as much to defeat the Aggies as the Alabama team itself. He needed the crowd to rock Kyle Field. As he said, our fans yell when we have the ball. They want to see something happen. But the noise deadens dramatically when the defense runs out. From one end of Legion Field to the other, it was wild, raucous, and boisterous all night.

He had an idea. A year earlier, he watched Bobby Middleton whip the crowd into a frenzy with a single, ragged-edged homemade towel. Maybe he needed a stadium filled with towels. Jackie Sherrill did his best to follow protocol and not step on any traditions at Texas A&M. He sought out the Aggie head yell leader, the self-imposed guardian of Kyle Field, and said, son, I need to ask your permission to implement a little idea I have about getting the crowd fired up on game day.

What's that, sir?

I want to print up some white towels for my 12th man team to bring out here and wave around their heads during the games.

Can't, sir, the head yell leader said.

Why not?

This is sacred ground, the yell leader said with authority. Nothing artificial can ever touch this field, sir.

I think it'll be a good way to whip the fans into a frenzy, Sherrill said. It's time they started rocking the stadium.

I'm sorry, sir. Towels aren't allowed.

Sherrill nodded and walked away. What did he mean that nothing artificial could ever touch the field, the Coach wondered. It may be tradition, and he respected tradition more than most. Sherrill glanced down. The whole damn field was artificial turf. He turned toward the athletic office and went to look for Robert Crouch.

Crouch had been a member of the original 12th man kickoff team, but, in 1985, he was working in the offices of recruiting coordinator Tim Cassidy and trying to nail down enough credits to finally earn his degree. Crouch was writing letters for coaches, keeping up with potential Aggie recruits, calling players at night, and making sure they knew that Jackie Sherrill and Texas A&M were definitely interested in them and their abilities on the football field. He looked up as Sherrill stormed into his office.

As usual, the Coach got right to the point. Crouch, he said, get me a towel. Don't want a big one. Little one will do fine. Make sure it's white, and print the "12th Man" in big, maroon letters in the middle. I'd like to see a sample.

When?

Now.

On his way home, Crouch dropped by the printing company that sponsored his softball team and asked the man in charge if he would mind printing up a sample towel for Sherrill's approval.

You gonna pay for it?

Not the sample, Crouch said.

The printer had no interest in wasting a perfectly good golf towel on one of Robert Crouch's lame-brained ideas, and Crouch had as many as anyone and more than most. The printer doubted seriously if Jackie Sherrill knew anything about the towel anyway. He picked up one that had already been bought and thrown away, placing the "12th Man" in bold, maroon letters on one side. On the other was a logo for the Brazos County Golf Tournament.

Will this do, he asked.

Crouch nodded that it would.

He had the towel ready for Sherrill early the next morning. The Coach came in, studied it for a moment, and said, make the towel a little smaller and print me up a couple of thousand of them.

When do you need them, Coach?

Now.

It was as much time as Sherrill ever gave anyone.

Before the next game, the Aggie hostesses began selectively handing out the 12th man towels at the gate. Sixty thousand of the Aggie faithful. Two thousand towels. No one knew exactly what the odd little towels were for, but they were free, and everybody who could jerk one away from an Aggie hostess wanted it.

In the tunnel, each of the 12th man tightly held a towel.

What'll we do with it?

Beats me.

The only one who knew was Bobby Middleton. He had waved one before. Watch Middleton. He'll get it right.

The towels weren't anything special, Chad Adair said. They looked pretty much like ragged old hand towels with the "12 Man" printed on the side. I figured they would be pretty good to use when we dried our hands, but it wasn't raining.

I guess we ought to start waving them when we run out on the field, someone volunteered. For whatever reason, Coach thinks it'll get the crowd into the game.

Danny Balcar shook his head. He didn't know whether to laugh or cry. I thought, without a doubt, that this was probably the stupidest thing anybody around here had ever done, he said, and they had done some pretty stupid things with the 12th man. But, like a good soldier with an order he didn't understand, Balcar began half-heartedly waving the ragged old towel above his head and hoping that no one would be paying any attention to him when he came charging out of the tunnel. Crazy, he thought. Foolish. Maybe we're supposed to use them to wipe the blood from our faces.

Adair remembered, we ran out of the tunnel in a straight line, then fragmented in as many different directions as we could go. We were waving the towels, cracking them like a whip. Some of the guys were jumping up and down and yelling like mad men. A few were in a dead run alongside the stands, whipping the towels back and forth wildly above their heads.

The crowd watched for a moment in curious silence.

Then the crowd exploded.

The noise was rising in a great swell above Kyle Field. It sounded something like a thunderstorm when a jet was flying low and burning the treetops. Adair looked up, and damned if there weren't another thousand or so towels bobbing up and down amidst the procession of fans streaming into Kyle Field.

Tony Pollacia squinted and glanced up into the stands, searching

Place this dot on the Center of your Watch Crystal

Webster says, "The dot is used as a multiplication sign." Use this reminder to multiply our strengths as we "TOGETHER" build a "CHAMPIONSHIP CHAIN."

Share these with family and friends →

AT TEXAS A&M
"THE BEST...
IS YET TO BE!"

Our Attitude is Multiplying and "TOGETHER" we are building a "CHAMPIONSHIP CHAIN."

Dear Friends of Texas A&M,

Once again, our football team wants you to join it in our commitment goals for 1987. These watch dots are for the exclusive use of our players and coaches to share with family, friends and staunch supporters of our program.

We concluded our "Character to Continue" and the Cotton Bowl with a challenge theme "TOGETHER" we are building a "CHAMPIONSHIP CHAIN." Our team worked hard during spring training on continuing to build on our strong foundation. Our players have dedicated themselves to working together to build a championship chain. They feel that the "BEST IS YET TO BE."

Their commitments contain ideals and principles that our young men can use throughout their lives. Thank you for your continuing support and for being on our team. "TOGETHER" we are building a "CHAMPIONSHIP CHAIN."

Jackie Sherrill
Head Football Coach

DESIRE ★ DISCIPLINE ★ DEDICATION ★ DETERMINATION

Jackie Sherrill was a master motivator. He always found some unique way to fire his team up, even having them, their friends, and family place dots on the hour hands of their watches. Check the time. Remember the team.

for his mother and father. They both had been given towels by an Aggie hostess, and he wondered if they were waving the towels as wildly as members of the 12th man. Game day was dreary, bleak, and threatening to rain. His father had folded up the towel and stuck it inside his cap to keep his head dry in case the storms came.

As Jackie Sherrill recalled, the hotel and motel owners in College Station did not speak to me for the rest of the year. The fans hit town, spent the night, and when they left for the game, they took the hotel and motel towels with them. Waved the hell out of those towels. Never got around to carrying them back. On campus, the official 12th man towels kept selling out as quickly as we could get them printed.

Texas A&M bounced back from its ill-fated journey to Alabama with a 31-17 win over Northeast Louisiana, then thundered past Tulsa, 45-10, with a stunning 702 yards of total offense. Lynn Amedee had promised balance, and the Aggies rushed for 346 yards and passed for 356 yards. Kevin Murray had 309 of the passing yardage, along with four touchdowns, on only twelve completions. It was the second best offensive game in the history of the Southwest Conference. As Sherrill said, now we would be able to put a lot of pressure on teams.

The gods of good fortune had finally found their way to the Aggie side of the field, no matter where A&M happened to be playing. In the lost wasteland of Lubbock, Texas Tech fell, 28-27, when Red Raider players and coaches frantically tried to call a time out before the final extra point or points that could have tied or won the game. Tech had no timeouts left. A delay of game. A five-yard penalty. Pressure up the middle. An incomplete pass. A bizarre game. A bizarre finish. It was, according to Texas Tech linebacker Tim Singley, another heartbreaking loss for the Red Raiders, left stranded in a confused state of shock, disbelief, and despair. Losses were part of the game. But how they lost was unthinkable.

John Lopez wrote in the *Bryan Eagle*, wild, emotional, down-to-the-wire games are nothing new to Red Raider fans who are perhaps the most hostile hosts in the Southwest Conference. But for the teams that can get out of Lubbock alive, history has proven that an emotional win at Jones Stadium can go a long way in putting together a good season.

As Chet Brooks said, this game really helped us prove to ourselves and to others that we're the kind of team that will come up with a way to beat you.

So the Aggies were 3-1. Good, maybe, better than expected, perhaps, but still a long way from Cotton.

For the first and only time in its history, the Texas A&M kickoff team was going into battle with ten walk-on players, a walk-on kicker, and Roy Kokemoor, the graduate assistant who referred to himself as a walk-on coach. Scott Slater felt a close kinship with the unit. He was one of them.

Jackie Sherrill began telling him, in no uncertain terms, kick the devil out of the ball, Scott, the farther the better.

The 12th man kept demanding, kick it high, and kick it a yard or so short of the goal line. Give us a chance to go down and clean somebody's clock. Touchbacks were the bane of their existence.

Scott Slater grinned. Give somebody a little hope, it said, and scary things can happen. He possessed the uncanny ability to lift the football skyward, angle it left, and drop it down somewhere between the left hash mark and the sideline about a yard or so shy of the end zone. The team called it sixty-three left, and by the time the football fell gently into the cradled arms of some kick returner, he was surrounded by

the sound of reckless and thundering feet. The hammer was about to drop, and he didn't know which of the ten hammers would nail him first. Mostly, they all got there about the same time.

Coach David Hardy had been a former A&M kicker, and Slater said, he took me from being a kid who could kick the ball a long way to one who actually knew where the ball was going. He taught me technique, foot placement, hip placement, and a proper follow through. He taught me accuracy.

Ronnie Glenn realized that one serious drawback was facing members of the 12th man kickoff team. On Friday nights before a game, the scholarship athletes all went to a movie. The 12th man members were left to their own devices, and very few of those devices were completely honorable.

On the night before playing Northeast Louisiana, assorted players from the 12th man had gathered, as usual, and were holding court at a club on the outskirts of College Station, drinking far too many Jello shots, straight melon liqueur downed from a shot glass. Pass the melon. Pass the glass. Pass on or pass out. The liqueur looked a little like lemonade, Glenn said. It had all the finesse of a ball peen hammer. The first shot had a pretty good taste. Light. Cold. Nothing more than a good fruit juice. And wasn't fruit juice healthy? The 12th man members kept wondering among themselves if the liqueur at the bottom of the bottle was just as good as the nectar at the top, and there was only one way to find out.

The next day, Glenn said, I felt horrible. I woke up and crawled out of bed, but it was entirely against my will. The floor was a long way down. Hell, I couldn't reach it without standing up. I thought, well, I'll run downfield a time or two and do my job, then I'll find a nice, quiet place at the end of the bench, make sure that neither Kokemoor nor Sherrill get a close-up look at my eyes, and wait for the dull ache to find some backdoor exit from my head. But we kept kicking off. Over and over, we kept kicking off. I was afraid the scoring would never end.

We always played hard. Some probably even played better than they were capable of playing. A few of us were playing with a hangover. My head pounded with each step I took. My body ached every time I hit the wedge. Damn. He saw me coming. Why didn't he get out of the way? It has a hard lesson I learned that day, the kind of lesson that's not soon forgotten.

I kept running downfield, praying, God, please don't let one of them sober-headed jackasses come up and gut punch me. Lord, I couldn't stand the thought of lying face down before sixty thousand fans and leaving melon liqueur stains all over the turf of Kyle Field.

Maroon and yellow had never been a good mix.

For David Coolidge, life amidst the frenzy and furor of Kyle Field was good and getting better with every kickoff. On the first one against Northeast Louisiana, he had outside containment and saw the running back cut suddenly right. He cut left. And, as Coolidge said, the ball carrier came right at me. Didn't even try to miss me. Just speed and power. He had one aim, and that was to run over me like I was road kill stretched out in the middle of a two-lane blacktop. I guess he thought it was nothing more than a big-time scholarship player knocking down some cross-eyed geek from the student body. I don't know what he was thinking when he picked himself up off the ground.

A promising beginning, Coolidge thought.

The promise was shattered.

Mike Tolleson (32) walked on the Aggie football team and fought it out in practice for two years before joining the 12th man team. Coach R. C. Slocum, holding Tolleson's baby, always had a soft spot in his heart for Tolleson's courage.

Before the third game in 1985, David Coolidge broke three bones in his left hand. He told the coaches, I was running through a door when somebody suddenly slammed it. The door broke my hand before I knew what was happening.

He was lying. God, he was lying, trying to keep a straight face and coating each of his well-chosen words with a desperate plea for mercy. He had practiced them every step of the way to the locker room, and he hoped that no one saw the nervous flicker in his eyes.

David Coolidge had been playing Nerf basketball in his apartment and rammed his hand into the back of the couch when he drove past the coffee table for a dunk. Dumb move, he thought. He hoped the coaches never found out the truth, and he watched Rick Tankersley take his place on the starting team. Coolidge, in desperation, had his hard cast removed, and he wrapped an Ace bandage around a metal splint to keep the broken bones in place. To hell with the broken hand. He had lost his job and wanted it back. Coolidge covered kicks in practice, and, if anyone asked him about the injury, he would simply nod and say, the hand's fine. Doesn't hurt at all. Good as new.

There he was, lying again.

On the scout team, Coolidge made a valiant, though futile, effort to maneuver his way around Jerry Fontenot, big and wide and powerful. The hand jammed hard against Fontenot's shoulder pads, and he felt the pain shoot violently up his arm. His fingers went numb. The hand began to swell. It hadn't hurt that badly when he broke it.

Karl Kapchinski did not particularly care one way or the other if Coolidge had an injury. Bad hand. Bruised hand. Broken hand. It didn't matter to him. Coolidge was a 12th man. Coolidge was a nuisance. Billy Pickard was cursing him with a vocabulary of words he made up as he went along. In Pickard's eyes, David Coolidge realized, he was just one more worthless problem to deal with, and Pickard didn't have the time or the patience to deal with walk-on trash. His only hope was that David Coolidge, in a fit of late-blooming wisdom, would have the decency and good sense to call it a day and quit.

An X-ray at the Quack Shack told Coolidge what he already feared.

Too bad, the doctor said. It's the same three bones. If they had healed, and maybe they did, you broke them again. David Coolidge felt like cursing and tried to remember the odd assortment of names that Pickard had called him. Coolidge used them all and he used them well. It didn't make him feel any better.

John Burnett, the 12th man scout team, and the rest of the Aggie linebackers were in the midst of heated drills on a hot afternoon when Jackie Sherrill climbed down from his tower and hurriedly walked toward them. The drill had gone awry. John Roper had messed up again, and when Roper messed up, hell was only a step away.

No. No. No, Sherrill was yelling.

Burnett said, the Coach pulled out Roper, showed him the proper way to run the drill, gave him a new technique to work on, slapped him on the back, and walked away.

Linebacker Coach Bob Davie watched him go, then brought his crew up into a tight circle around him. Jackie Sherrill is the head coach, he said flatly. He deserves our respect, our loyalty, our dedication, and our attention. When he is around, you do the drill exactly the way he wants it done. But, by gawd, when he leaves, we'll do it my way.

Mike Tolleson had long dreamed of following in his father's footsteps at Texas A&M. Back in the early 1960s, David Tolleson had played for Hank Foldberg, who took the philosophy of three yards and a cloud of dust to a whole new level. With luck, A&M managed three yards every three downs and usually choked on its own dust, winning six games in three years. At 5-8 and 225 pounds, Mike Tolleson knew he was too short, too slow, and too weak to play big-time college football, but he walked on at A&M anyway. Maybe with a little luck, he thought, he might catch lightning in a bottle. He recalled, we had 122 walk-ons during the spring of 1983. By the time we played our first game against California, only fourteen were left. By the time the season ended, only eight walk-ons were still around. Mike Tolleson was one of them.

He had guts. He had staying power. He had played for Celina High School, and Celina had a reputation for practicing harder and going for longer hours than any other team in North Texas. The workouts had been physically demanding. If nothing else, Tolleson had endurance and stamina, and A&M had not yet recruited anyone rough or ornery enough to run him off. If they think A&M is hard, he thought, they should have tried to survive Celina.

During his first drill, as a former running back, Tolleson carried the ball into a combat zone patrolled by Billy Cannon, Jr. The collision was shattering. Cannon thought I'd get out of his way. I didn't. He was meaner than a horned toad with his stinger up, Tolleson said, and he was looking to annihilate someone. He did.

Tolleson struggled to regain his footing. The ground felt like sponge, or maybe it was quicksand. The fence surrounding the practice field was spinning around him. Pain jolted his head and his stomach. He jerked involuntarily once, then twice, and threw up.

A coach walked over, looked down, frowned, and said, as honestly as he could, son, this might not be your sport.

Tolleson wiped the vomit from his face, brushed it haphazardly off his uniform, stood up, tried to regain his balance, and got back in line, waiting his turn, waiting to carry the ball again. So this was big-time college football, he told himself. Hell, it wasn't a bad as he thought it would be.

Tolleson knew he ran the ball a second time that day. He didn't remember it. The day was a blur, and his mind kept moving in and out of a dense fog. He would have never found the locker room if someone hadn't pointed out the way.

His position coach, R. C. Slocum, ultimately took Mike Tolleson under his wing. Maybe it was because Tolleson was a survivor, a good kid who tried so hard and always gave more than the Good Lord had given him. Slocum often thought, if Tolleson had grown another six or seven inches and cut his forty time by three hundredth of a second, he would have had college coaches camped all over his door step. But, alas, he was condemned by his own size and foot speed, so he labored in anonymity on the Texas A&M scout team. When Tolleson didn't make the travel squad, however, Slocum slipped him sideline passes. Tolleson drove to almost every game, no matter where it might be played, for a chance to be as close to the action as the white stripe of the sideline.

That's all Tolleson ever did.

Watch.

Walk-ons practiced. Walk-ons bore the punishment handed out by varsity players a head taller, a hundred pounds heavier, two steps faster, trying to prove they should be a starter or remain a starter. Walk-ons even suited up for home games. They had numbers, and their names were printed in the program.

But walk-ons didn't play.

Pure and simple.

On game days, the field was off limits to them.

Mike Tolleson was a player. Simple fact. No one would dispute it. But time was running out for him. He had run the practice field for so long it felt old and worn under his feet. By 1985, he had made a critical decision in his football life. He wanted to feel the turf of Kyle Field at least once when it counted. He went to see Roy Kokemoor.

Getting beat up on a regular basis by Johnny Holland and Larry

Kelm was bad enough, but now Coach Register was running Rick Tankersley into the line against Guy Broom. He hit me once, Tankersley said, and coach was mad. He was always mad. Even when he was feeling on top of the world, he was mad.

Hit him again.

Tankersley was rocked. Guy Broom didn't go out of his way to be mean, he said, but he did live just on the far side of being crazy. The boy wasn't quite right. Put a helmet on him, and he was a killer.

Hit him again, Register yelled

This time, Tankersley said, Guy Broom threw me into the stands.

Register had been screaming and cursing, but finally he took a deep breath and stepped back. He seemed quite pleased with what he had seen. I think we've hit these boys enough, he said.

The only disappointed player on the field, Rick Tankersley said, was Guy Broom.

Before one game, Jackie Sherrill strode into the dressing room and said, I've just seen Guy Broom's mother out there, and she told me that if we don't win today, she's coming in here and whipping me pretty good I'm asking you to do your best today, gentlemen, because, to tell you the truth, I'm more scared of her than I am Guy Broom.

Jackie Sherrill was a man obsessed. Only perfection would satisfy him. He ordered for the kickoff drill to be run at full speed. No, faster than full speed. And hit the man as hard as you can, he said. No, harder than you can. Somebody's head was in dire straits. It could be yours, Danny Balcar said, or somebody else's. At the moment, Coach Sherrill didn't care.

Where's my 12th man unit, the Coach yelled.

The team came running.

Line up, Sherrill said, and take somebody out.

Live?

Just like you do it in a game.

Full speed?

If you have any left.

He walked over to the varsity return team and snapped, see that group over there? They're a bunch of damn walk-ons. You have scholarships. If you can't return the ball against a bunch of damn walk-ons that nobody else wanted, you might as well pack it in and go home.

Varsity was enraged.

The 12th man was fired up.

Sherrill stood back to watch the fireworks.

God, how he loved the fireworks.

Jimmy Shelby cradled the football, took a cautious step up field, didn't know whether to zig or zag, did neither, and Cory Allen cut him down like an old oak tree.

Shelby was Sherrill's ace, number one, starting kick returner, one of the nation's top recruits. A speed merchant with afterburners. The Aggies were expecting great things from Jimmy Shelby.

Shelby lay on the ground.

Both eyes burned with pain.

He tried to roll over. He couldn't.

Shelby had both of his shoulders separated.

It was the last time Coach Sherrill let us go live against the varsity return team all year, Balcar said.

So much for fireworks.

Another day. Another collision. One day was no different from the next. The drills never changed. Neither did the punishment. Cory Allen swaggered to the front of line. He was a tough as they came, a fanatic on the field, a hitting machine, who could take a moving object head on and move it backward a step or two. Didn't matter who it was or what it was. Ask Jimmy Shelby. It had been a week since he could use both of his arms without pain. Players always knew what kind of helmet Cory Allen was wearing. He would leave the helmet's logo tattooed on their chest.

He glanced up and saw Butch Motley facing him ten feet away. Well, he thought, this ought to be a good one. Motley was always ready for a little contact. He didn't think the drill was any good unless somebody blacked out on his feet. Allen grinned, heard the whistle, tightened his gut, and charged forward. Hell on wheels. Flying low. Flying hard. Flying out of control. Something had to give. Something snapped.

A pain shot through Allen's shoulder.

Worse than a knife blade.

Cory Allen was on his knees, then face down on the field. He kept trying to get his legs back under him, but his legs refused to cooperate. He tried frantically to move his shoulder and couldn't. He wasn't paralyzed. He just wouldn't move. His face was twisted in agony that had never before been introduced to Cory Allen.

Damn.

Allen didn't feel pain regardless of how badly it hurt.

Never did.

Never would.

He shook his head to clear the fog, failed miserably, and stumbled back onto his feet.

You all right, Motley asked.

Allen didn't answer. He tried. Words had fled his brain. Instead, he walked to the back of the line, trying to stretch his arm, waiting to work his way toward the front again, waiting for someone else to batter, hoping to God it wasn't Butch Motley again.

He saw the face.

It had no features.

He looked at the number on the jersey.

It had no shape.

Cory Allen charged.

The effort was there. But he cringed just before the collision, and Cory Allen had never hesitated before. He staggered. The pain turned to nausea and was dumped as sour as bile into the pit of his stomach. His arm felt as though it had been torn off his shoulder.

The first time, Allen thought he could walk off the injury.

The second time, he knew something was wrong, dreadfully wrong, something that grit and gumption alone would not be able to cure.

The doctor would tell him, son, that's one of the worst shoulder injuries I have ever seen, and he had seen a lot of shoulders banged up.

Cory Allen was on the operating table for a long time.

Butch Motley never apologized for the hit. It wasn't dirty. It wasn't a cheap shot. I knew if I hadn't gone full speed against Cory, he said, I would have had my head handed to me in a sling. Cory Allen would have taken an apology as pity, and I wasn't about to let him think I was disrespecting him with pity. He was too much of a man for that.

Cory Allen did have one request. He looked up at Butch Motley and said, you can bring me a beer after they get through cutting on me.

I will.

Don't lie to me.

I'll be there.

Motley was standing in the hallway when the nurses rolled a groggy, half-conscious Cory Allen back into his hospital room.

Under his arm, Motley carried a brown paper bag.

In the bag was a beer.

Cory Allen grinned. It was the last thing he remembered before taking a long swig of lukewarm beer and throwing up on the bed.

The nurses were appalled.

Butch Motley was nowhere to be found.

Ironically, for most of the season, Cory Allen and Jimmy Shelby ran the bleachers of Kyle Field together. They kept their legs in shape. At the moment, their shoulders were worthless.

They talked.

And laughed.

Jimmy Shelby was afraid Cory Allen might hit him again.

The wide receivers had work to do, and those who had more speed than sense on the 12th man were lining up as defensive backs on the scout team. Sean Page said, there was one receiver who always came after me hard in practice. He was lining up on the hash mark. He gave me a look of utter disdain and ran a curl route, sprinting forward fourteen yards in an effort to convince me that he was going deep, waiting for me to turn my back, then curling back toward the line of scrimmage. He would be clear. I would be tied up in knots, my head going one way while my feet went another. The play worked if he sold it well enough. He didn't try to sell it at all. Didn't need to. Wasn't worried about me. I was a walk-on.

The pass came in high.

I had a cocky wide receiver in front me, some bastard who thought I was a notch lower than the road kill stuck to the soles of his shoes. His back was exposed.

I grinned. I had my shot. I hit him as hard as I could.

He went down and came up swinging. He was 6-3, weighed over two hundred pounds, and had obviously been in a few fights before. Before he had a chance to cold cock me, Tony Pollacia jumped on his back, and every wide receiver and defensive back on the field leaped into a melee that was probably one swing away from becoming a genuine, old-fashioned, down-home blood-letting. I sneaked a glance over to the sideline. Our offensive coordinator, Lynn Amedee, had sat back to enjoy a good backyard brawl, and Roy Kokemoor was wearing a smile as big as Dallas.

Pollacia would say, we took care of our own. When it was them against us, whoever them might be, you could count on all of us being there together and at the same time.

On that day, Page said, I felt like I became an official member of the 12th man. I would remain one for the rest of my life.

Life itself is a lot like that. When you get your shot, you better take it. It may never come your way again. No fear. No hesitation. No experience required.

Practice had finally ground to a halt, and Mike Tolleson gathered with the team around Jackie Sherrill, kneeling on one knee as he began his usual end-of-the-day talk. Sherrill suddenly stopped in mid-sentence, and those intimidating eyes of his focused on a walk-on who had wearily sat down on top of his helmet.

Coach Sherrill stood up and walked through the players, parting them like Moses going through the Red Seas, making his way to the kid's side, Tolleson said. He looked down. You could almost feel the heat rising up within him.

Get off that damn helmet, Sherrill snapped. It's worth more than you are.

From that moment on, the walk-ons knew where we stood, Tolleson said. In Celina, I had been somebody. I had state championships to prove it. Now I was a nobody. Just like that. From one year to another, I became a nobody. Overnight, a nobody. At least on the practice field I

It took a team with players like Ronnie Glenn (9) and David Coolidge (7) clearing the way for the bone-crushing tackle.

was a nobody.

Coach Sherrill always told us that Highway 6 ran both ways. It brought you into College Station. It could take you right back out of town. We called it the midnight train. When we came in and found another locker empty, we'd simply say, well, it looks like the midnight train came through again last night.

Doug Middleton watched from the sidelines. He had beaten the odds and earned a spot on the 12th man. During two-a-days, there had been brief moments when he thought he might have been able to actually work himself into the starting unit. Everyone always did. A good hit or two was all it took for a young man to become delusional. Maybe he could one day start for the 12th man. Maybe not. Hunt a few heads along the way. Lose his a few times. Now Middleton would never know. The ankle had been hurting too badly for too long

In reality, Middleton understood that he had a uniform simply because Mike Blachiki had decided to trade football for the classroom. Now he was surprised to see Blachiki back on the field, gesturing frantically, and talking to Roy Kokemoor. Blachiki was probably the better player, Middleton knew, and Blachiki didn't have a bad ankle.

Middleton had a uniform today. Old. Tattered. Threadbare. Didn't fit. But it was his. The uniform might be gone tomorrow. Middleton held his breath. He wanted to start. There was no doubt about it. But it was more important for him just to remain on the 12th man team.

Blachiki wanted his old spot back.

Middleton was injured.
He had never played football before
He couldn't play now.

If anyone was expendable, he knew, it was Doug Middleton. R. C. Slocum even ridiculed his stance as a linebacker. The defensive coordinator kept telling him, son, you look like you're sitting on a toilet seat. You can't do any damage sitting on a toilet seat.

Middleton felt as vulnerable as he had ever felt. His fate was being decided, and it was in someone else's hands.

He saw Kokemoor shrug and tell Blachiki, you're a good kid and a pretty good football player. But I'm afraid I don't have any spots left.

What about my old one?

We have it filled by a kid who's got the grit to stick it out.

I hear he's injured.

Maybe, but he hasn't quit.

Linebacker Larry Kelm was standing beside Middleton. He turned and said, it looks like the kid wants to jump on the bandwagon. Kelm laughed. Hell, he said, the bandwagon's already gone, Middleton, and you're still riding on top.

Tony Pollacia (15) and his towel-waving antics became legendary. When Texas A&M won its first Cotton Bowl under Coach Jackie Sherrill, the Dallas Morning News chose to run this photograph, in color, on the front page of its Sunday paper.

Chapter 18

By 1985, Jackie Sherrill, as John Lopez wrote in the *Bryan Eagle*, had done some soul searching and decided to get back to doing what he does best. He is one of the best in the game when it came to coordinating plans of attack. He walks the sidelines, making most of the decisions. But he's leaving the play calling to Lynn Amedee, who has proven to be an expert at dissecting defenses. And Sherrill is letting R. C. Slocum have a free hand with the defense. Instead of talking about next year, the Aggies have begun talking about next week.

After trailing early, 9-0, A&M came thundering back to score nineteen straight points in a convincing 43-16 win over Houston. Tom Ray's job was to find a crease in the defense, fly past the wedge, and go to the ball. He was running downfield against the Cougars, had the ball carrier in his sights, and, boom, he went down. Didn't know he was in trouble until the hit rolled him up from behind.

Good, he thought. I've been clipped. A penalty. Fifteen yards. As good as a tackle.

Tom Ray looked around for the flag.

None had been thrown.

He threw up his arms in protest and looked angrily down at the culprit who had drilled him from behind and brutally taken his feet out

from under him.

Good hit.

Hard hit.

Illegal hit.

He was staring into the face of Sean Page.

Rick Tankersley had been given his chance, and he wasn't about to waste or lose it. David Coolidge was over on the sideline, nursing a broken hand, and Tankersley was facing Houston with a chance to prove that he really did belong on the field at Texas A&M. He had the game of his life. After an Eric Franklin field goal, he came down like a wild stallion that had broken free of his reins, drove the ball carrier down on the three-yard-line, and on the next play, linebacker Dana Batiste busted through to bury Houston quarterback Gerald Landry for a safety. Those two points are mine, Tankersley thought. He gladly gave them to Batiste. The only place they counted was on the scoreboard.

Twice more on kickoffs, Tankersley took on 250-pound linebackers, and twice more he left them lying in his wake as he found the ball and made the tackles. From that day forward, no one considered ever moving him out of the starting lineup. He felt both sympathy and empathy for David Coolidge. He really did. Coolidge was a friend. But if Coolidge came back, he would have to find another hole to fill. There were nine of them. Tankersley was not giving his up.

Out on a farm on the edge of Claude, Texas, Tankersley's father had settled down on a tractor, plowing a field, listening to the radio. He had once been a big-time Texas athlete himself, the holder of the state record in the mile relay. But a spinal cord injury kept him from getting around as well as he once did.

He tuned into the Aggie game on a portable radio, and he heard his son's name called. Once. Twice. Three times. He smiled, and the field didn't seem as large as it had before lunch. The tractor was running a little more smoothly, and his back wasn't hurting nearly as badly as it did before breakfast.

An article in the *Houston Post* would say, the University of Houston kickoff returner was on one knee in the security of his end zone when Texas A&M's Bobby Middleton pin-balled off a couple of blockers and flew toward him. The play was over – a routine touchback. But across the width of the Kyle Field turf, Middleton's teammates kept coming. They have a dedication and lack of concern for personal well-being seen more frequently in Beirut.

The statistics show that the 12th man is more than a curiosity. It's working. No kickoff has been returned for a touchdown against the squad. On ten kicks this year, opponents have averaged 14.7 yards a return. On the road, where Aggie scholarship players man the kickoff team, opponents have averaged 26.4 yards a return.

According to Sherrill, some 12th man players have reached the verge of receiving scholarships. He doesn't anticipate any would accept a scholarship, however, because it would disqualify them from being a member of the 12th man.

To be a guy who wants to cover kickoffs, the Coach said, you've got to be crazy. You've got to have a lot of cold blood to you.

Tony Pollacia could barely move. His back was killing him. Too many helmets to the kidney, he figured. During the Houston game, his knee was hyper-extended.

Now his knee didn't want to move. Pain bolted through him whenever it did. It hurt to sleep, and it hurt to stay awake. But unless the bone was showing through the skin, Pollacia said, I was on the field.

The limp was bad enough, but what bothered him worse was fear. During the second game of the year, he had been moved to the first team, and as he said, that spot was mine. I'd be damned if anybody else took it.

If I could limp, I could walk. If I could walk, I could run. If I could run, somebody was in trouble. Mostly it was me.

With the Houston win solidified on the scoreboard, Jackie Sherrill was looking down the road, telling the leering press, our game next week at Baylor could be for all the marbles on down the road. The marbles rolled off the table and broke. Once again, Grant Teaff's Baylor Bears lay in wait and ambushed A&M, 20-15. A drained Jackie Sherrill could merely throw up his hands and say, Baylor played very well. They hung in there when they fell behind, and they came back to win the game. We did not execute when it was third down and twenty-five, and Baylor did.

A lost Aggie fumble at the Baylor three spelled the difference. So had a roughing the kicker penalty when the Bears had been forced to punt from their own thirteen-yard-line with two minutes left. Sherrill had been holding cotton. Now he looked at his hands, and they were empty. He had expected to ride away from Waco with his Aggies leading the Southwest Conference. Now Baylor was in the driver's seat. First, A&M would have to take care of its own business against TCU and hope for a miracle.

Rice was no problem, and the Aggies left Houston with a 43-28 win. The big test would be powerhouse SMU, and ESPN television cameras were being hauled into Kyle Field. It may not have

been a game for the ages, but it helped fortify the foundation that Jackie Sherrill was so intent on building.

On the first kickoff against SMU, Dennis Mudd knew what he had to do. He was the ball guy, and it was his job to make sure the return scheme was disrupted regardless of the mayhem it took. If he did his job, an alley guy would be right there for an easy tackle. Mudd would bust the wedge, bust it wide open, and leave the ball carrier standing naked before the world. No blockers. No protection. Dead meat. Give some alley guy a clean shot at him.

The wedge was there.

The ball carrier tried to outrun his blockers. He cut to the edge, and Mudd went airborne. I hit him in the ear hole, he said, and knocked him backward eight yards, he said. The returner was off balance but still on his feet when Ronnie Glenn drilled him.

Ronnie made the tackle.

I did the damage.

Rick Tankersley had a bead on Reggie Dupard, who, in some circles, had begun to challenge Auburn's Bo Jackson in the Heisman Trophy race. In the back of his mind, Tankersley was remembering the last advice Roy Kokemoor had given the 12th man team. Keep your lanes, he said. Keep them tight, don't let anybody get a seam, and know you have Tankersley back there containing the whole field. Just go wild. Go flat out. Do what you're supposed to do, and if Tankersley does his job, nobody scores. If Tankersley fails, then it's a touchdown. Nobody felt the pressure like Tankersley.

For us that night, he said, the stakes had never been higher.

Slater kicked off. Reggie Dupard had the ball. And, Lord, he was fast. He beat the 12th man to the corner and was on the edge in an instant, a blur of blue and Red. All he needed was a step. Nobody on the 12th man could catch him. Maybe nobody wearing maroon and white could catch him. Dupard turned toward the goal about the time Rick Tankersley reached out and slammed him across the chest with his arm. No time to square up. No time for a tackle. No way to hit his legs. Dive, and he would have had an arm load of dead air. Desperation had many weapons, and Tankersley used the only one at his disposal. He simply swung his arm. The blow stunned them both. Dupard went down, and Tankersley's arm went black.

Tankersley said, I was so excited, I ran home after the game to watch the replay on ESPN. Television showed the tackle in slow motion. I hit him all right. I had the black arm to prove it. I slowed him down and spun him around. Ronnie Glenn knocked him to the ground.

It was a good night for Ronnie Glenn.

Spencer Baum was an alley guy, and he said, Scott Slater flipped a pooch kick high down to the 20-yard line and toward the hash mark.

The running back was nowhere around.

A tight end camped under the kick.

He thought about fair catching the ball.

He didn't.

The football touched his fingers.

Spencer Baum cut him down.

It was the only solo tackle I ever made, Baum said, but it came on the student body side of the field, and I could hear them all yelling my name. I swaggered across campus with a smile on my face for the rest of the year.

The feeling was electric.

A&M had squeezed out a heart-pounding win over SMU, 19-17, but Eric Franklin kept the Aggie faithful on edge and on the edge of their seats all night. He misfired on a 45-yard field goal in the third period, then saw an extra point attempt sail wide after the second Aggie touchdown. For Franklin, however, the game would be one of redemption. With 1.46 remaining, he calmly trotted onto the field and drilled a 48-yarder, not straight, perhaps, but true.

Dennis Mudd said, the stadium was filled with a dead silence when Eric lined up for the kick. The ball was in the air, and we were holding our breath. It cleared the goal post by a quarter of an inch, maybe less. Rod Bernstine and I were hugging each other when I heard someone yell, hey, we have to go out and cover.

Roy Kokemoor gathered his kickoff unit around and told them, if we beat SMU, we have a chance to go to a pretty good bowl game. They don't have much time left. But they have time to score. The kickoff's big, and the game is all on your shoulders now. Don't mess it up. The 12th man carried his final thought with them as they marched onto the field for the final kickoff. One kick. A handful of seconds run off the clock. A tackle. And the bowl game express was in high gear. As Mudd ran on the field, he was looking for his towel. Damn, he thought. It's gone. I must have lost it in the celebration.

Against all odds, SMU had one last chance, and the Ponies would cast their fate on the outcome of a desperate gamble. Head Coach Bobby Collins knew that a bunch of student-body volunteers were coming down to cover the kickoff. He decided to see if a little sleight-of-hand magic might confuse them, lure them out of their positions, and leave their scheme in disarray. Fake right. Go left.

In the middle of all the excitement and adrenalin rush, Collins wanted to see if the inexperience of the 12th man would show its ugly face. Those kids just might fall for it. He called for something new, something the 12th man might not have ever seen before. He called for a throw back on the kickoff. His reasoning was sound. He had watched the film and knew all about sixty-three left. With the 12th man converging like keystone cops to the left side of the field, his kick returner would juke right, then suddenly stop and fire the ball in a backward lateral across the field. If the play worked, there wouldn't be an Aggie within fifteen yards of the ball carrier. And, hell, it just might work.

The daring throw back surprised everyone at Kyle Field except the 12th man. We knew Coach Collins had done it before, Ronnie Glenn said. We knew it had gone for a touchdown. We had seen it on film. We were ready for it.

Reggie Dupard was doomed from the moment he caught the ball. The Mustangs had set their wedge farther back than usual, creating a protective shield in front of the ball carrier, but that didn't matter. Bobby Middleton single-handedly caved in the wedge, and Dupard was swarmed as soon as he turned and tried to throw a long, off-balance lateral. Roy Kokemoor remembered, Middleton disrupted the play, and Dupard was never able to get the pass off. If he had, I don't know what would have happened. Ashley Eddington was the only player we had covering the other side of the field. Ashley was fast, but was he fast enough?

SMU had a speedster waiting on the far side of the field. He was wide open. The ball never reached him. Mudd ripped off his helmet to raise it like a gladiator who had just survived the last charge of the lions, and that's when he saw it. His 12th man towel had been rolled up and stuffed inside his helmet. The towel would be going to a bowl game with him after all.

Jackie Sherrill wasn't surprised with Eric Franklin's winning field goal. I didn't send Eric into the game to miss, he said. We were able to turn that train wreck around and get it back on track.

It could not have come at a better nor more fortuitous time, not with a national ESPN television audience looking in and representatives from the Bluebonnet, Holiday, Cotton, Independence, and Sun Bowls

taking copious notes. They may have come to watch the famed Pony Express, but they left with a pretty good feeling about A&M. According to the Associated Press, the win was the biggest in Sherrill's A&M coaching career. It was the first time Sherrill's troops had defeated a ranked opponent. It was only the second time they had come from behind in the fourth quarter to do it. Until then, Denne H. Freeman wrote, about all the campus coffee shops had to talk about was Sherrill's brilliant innovation to have a 12th man kickoff team composed of members from the student body.

Cotton was growing again.

The stakes were indeed getting higher. Seven bowl representatives stuffed their way into Kyle Field to watch the Aggies defeat Arkansas, 10-6, in a defensive nightmare that helped remove the sting of a 28-0 insult in Fayetteville the year before. By now the Fiesta and Liberty Bowls had joined the pack. A&M not only stifled the storied Arkansas wishbone attack, A&M broke the bone and left it lying in splinters. ESPN's cameras were back, monitoring those 58,000 fans who kept chanting, we want cotton, throughout the entire fourth quarter. Sherrill could not agree with them more. He already had his mind focused on TCU. We took each game and started building blocks, he said. Now we were down to the end of the season, and there were just a couple of blocks left. The biggest thing about this team was its character. He told the leering press, it has been an uphill struggle. I'd be lying to you if I said it wasn't very hard. But of all the teams I've ever had, this is the best young team I've ever been around.

It all boiled down to one single, fateful Saturday afternoon, and for the first time in forever, the Aggie faithful were actually rooting for those bastards in Austin. A&M needed Texas to defeat Baylor if it had any outside chance at all of capturing the fabled Southwest Conference championship that had eluded them for the past eighteen years. Of course, Texas A&M, as Sherrill liked to say, had to first take care of business with TCU. Then the Aggies could let the coming war on Thanksgiving Day settle the feud once and for all. Sherrill was locked and loaded.

ESPN arrived in Fort Worth before the Aggies did. ESPN was a struggling young television network in 1985, trying to get a firm foothold in the cable marketplace, and it was letting the drama unfolding around Texas A&M's unpredictable football fortunes build its ratings. For ESPN, the saga of Jackie Sherrill and the Aggies had all the makings of a good, old-fashioned, down-home, backstreet soap opera. The clash with TCU wasn't merely a game. At least, that's what the leering press said. It was a massacre. The Aggies won, 53-6, but the most deafening roar erupted with 4:44 to play in the second quarter as A&M eased ahead 22-0. Word reached Amon Carter Stadium that Texas had knocked off Baylor, 17-10, leaving the door ajar for the Aggies to rumble into the Cotton Bowl. Only Texas stood in the way, and Sherrill said, I don't know the last time it came down to Texas-Texas A&M in the last game of the year. I do know we seat 72,000, and there will no doubt be 85,000 showing up.

In reality, the last time A&M and those bastards from Austin squared off to battle for the outright conference title was November 25, 1943, three days before Jackie Sherrill was born.

Paul McKay wrote in his *Bryan Eagle* column, the manly 12th man kickoff and KAMIKAZE SQUAD made the trip to Fort Worth, and squad stats will show that the 12th man boosted the body count considerably. The 12th man's sole function is to kill a ball carrier inside the 20.

Their most memorable moment against TCU, however, occurred with the Aggies leading 46-0 early in the fourth quarter. A&M had just scored. The 12th man was huddled on the sidelines. Just another kickoff in a day filled with kickoffs. Almost a yawner. Kick it deep. Knock some-

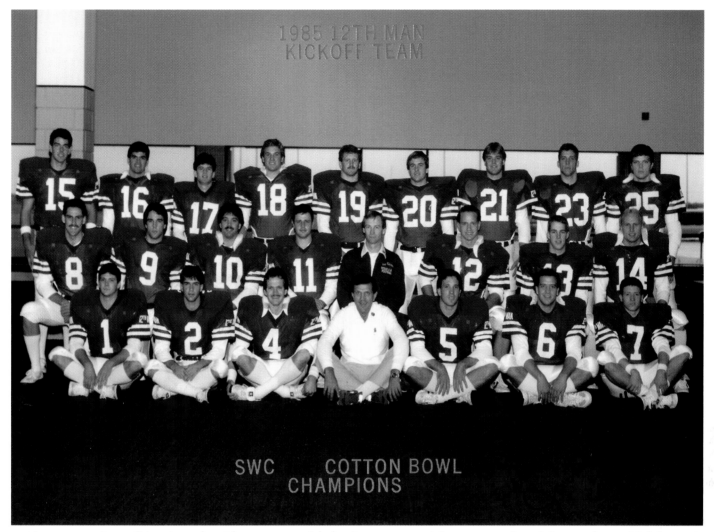

1985 12TH MAN
KICKOFF TEAM

SWC   COTTON BOWL
CHAMPIONS

12th man members of the Championship Team were (sitting) Dean Berry (1), Danny Balcar (2), Dennis Mudd (4), Coach Jackie Sherrill, Spencer Baum (5), John Burnett (6), David Coolidge (7). Second row (kneeling): Doug Middleton (8), Ronnie Glenn (9), Corey Linscombe (10), Jeff Boutwell (11), Coach Roy Kokemoor, Chad Adair (12), Dan Pollard (13), Paul Luedtke (14). Third row (standing): Tony Pollacia (15), Tom Ray (16), Sean Page (17), Cory Allen (19), Rick Tankersley (20), Mark Wurzbach (21), Chris Probst (23), and Larry "Butch" Motley (25).

body down. And get ready to go home.

Then all hell broke loose.

Dennis Mudd swore he heard a coach tell Scott Slater, pooch kick right. Maybe not. He said, I saw Sherrill talking to Slater, and, sometimes when he was excited, Slater didn't hear a word the Coach was saying. He just wanted to get out there, kick the ball, and see if he could drive it into the next county. Danny Balcar remembered Sherrill tapping his clipboard and telling the 12th man team, you've been getting beat up all day out there, so here's your chance to take your shot. Coach turned to Slater and said, kick it short and lob it.

Slater kicked it short.

And he lobbed it.

Mudd said, by the time Scott dropped his hand, I was already running wide open. Curley Hallman had worked with us in practice all year long. The timing was precise, and it was perfect. We reached the ball and passed it a split second before Slater kicked it. We were always offside but always too close for a referee to blow his whistle.

Mudd knew where the ball was going. The TCU kick return team turned around and began retreating downfield, he said, and Slater hit the ball like a lob wedge into the wind and sky high. It bounced somewhere just inside the 30-yard line. Dean Berry and I were running hell-bent-for-leather toward the ball. I was outside and got there first. Just as I cradled the ball in my arms, Berry hit me, and he hit me pretty good.

Didn't mean to. He was diving for the ball, too. And the loose football rolled out of bounds.

The leering press couldn't believe.

TCU Coach Jim Wacker couldn't believe it.

Suddenly, Jackie Sherrill couldn't believe it either.

He was aghast.

Texas A&M was ahead by forty-six points, and the Aggies had just tried, of all things, an on-side kick. It looked like Jackie Sherrill was pouring salt on old wounds, the sports reporters would be writing. And Sherrill was on the phone to the press box. Coach Bobby Roper grimaced as he handed the headset to Roy Kokemoor.

What the hell is going on, Sherrill was shouting.

I don't know, Kokemoor told him.

Did you call that on-side kick?

No, sir, I didn't.

Sherrill angrily threw his clipboard to the turf. He turned around and grabbed Slater by the shoulder pads as his kicker trotted off the field. What the hell was that about, he asked.

Sorry, Coach, Slater said. I screwed up the kick. I looked up too quick and hit it off the side of my foot.

Scott Slater didn't blink. That was his story, and he was sticking to it. He sticks to it still. It was, he said, the only time he ever made the pages of *Sports Illustrated*. It was a rather humiliating moment to be on the pages of *Sports Illustrated*. Kick the Aggies, he said. That was always the case. But, hell, this time it was kick the Aggies kicker.

Sherrill explained it this way. Slater was supposed to kick the ball high and drop it down between the 10- and 20-yard lines. We didn't want to get the ball back to their deep people. He just missed the ball.

The 12th man team waited for Sherrill to wink.

He never did.

Jim Wacker simply shook his head, threw up his hands, and said, it sure was certainly a strange call leading, 46-0. An unbelievable call, he thought, quietly removing the heart of a Horned Frog team that had lost its glitz and glamour and wasn't so unbelievable anymore.

Here came the television cameras back down Highway 6. They weren't about to miss the finale. Not even storybooks had these kinds of endings. As Ronnie Glenn said, Texas A&M had become the choirboys for ESPN. Some had even begun to refer to it as the "ESA&M" network. On New Year's Day in 1984, Dennis Mudd had sat in a domino parlor in Hallettsville, Texas, watching the Cotton Bowl on a battered old television set in the corner and thinking, that's where we're going someday. Someday might be closer than he had imagined at the time.

All week, Texas A&M students were going as crazy as the 12th man team they adored. They camped out all night for the privilege of buying football tickets, or at least for the privilege of placing their names in a lottery that would ultimately choose the blessed few eligible to buy tickets. Cain Hall, generally open to visitors until the night before games, had become Fort Aggie. Security was that tight. Jackie Sherrill shut it down in the early hours of Tuesday morning. He even outlawed sports

reporters from *The Daily Texan*, the student newspaper at The University of Texas, from attending Aggie practices. The days were growing colder, and Bonfire was taking shape.

Mark McDonald wrote in the *Dallas Morning News*, students are cutting down trees by hand, stripping the timber to logs, and dragging them to be picked up by heavy equipment donated by A&M boosters. The so-called "push" is on as students labor round the clock to stack raw lumber into something resembling a towering multi-layer wedding cake. As Bonfire burns, many will stay for hours, roasting marshmallows and themselves to see how long the center pole supporting the massive collection of wood will last before the flames take it down. Tradition says that the longer the center pole stands, the better the team's chances the next day.

Texas A&M was hoping it would stand strong and tall for a long time on the night before Thanksgiving, the night before Coach Fred Akers brought Bevo and his illustrious band of braggadocios Longhorns to town. It was not the best of times for those bastards from Austin. Two years after Akers had played for the national championship, many of those wearing burnt orange wanted him fired, tarred and feathered if possible, and run out of town. What have you done for me lately, Fred? A win over A&M could salve a lot of scars and heal a lot of wounds, provided they weren't already terminal.

For the first time since 1943, Texas A&M and Texas would be playing for something more than pride. As Jackie Sherrill said, this state has always been very much swayed in its economics, its politics, and socially by graduates of either A&M or Texas. That's what makes this more than a football game.

A journey to the Cotton Bowl was at stake, and those bastards from Austin had made that journey nine times since the Aggies earned their last trip. As one reporter wrote, unless the bookies are dead wrong or Kevin Murray breaks his ankle again, the Texas Aggies, a dry hole for eighteen years, would rumble past the state's official college football team – on Jackie Wayne Sherrill's birthday, no less – and gush all the

Looking a lot more professional and a lot less fierce off the field are, left to right, Dennis Mudd, Tony Pollacia, Dean Berry, Rick Tankersley, and Danny Balcar. They had gathered for the Cotton Bowl's pre-game dinner, honoring players from both Texas A&M and Auburn. Suddenly, all of those painful, punishing moments on the practice field had been forgotten.

way to Dallas. All Texas Coach Fred Akers said was, I expect it to be a hectic, noisy, high-energy football game.

Billy Pickard, with the most important game of the past two decades facing him, was beginning to have some empathy if not pity for the way he had treated the 12th man team. It was all Coach Sherrill, he said. There were no committees, no suggestions, no anything. It was solely his idea. I told him he was crazy and that there was no way it would work. He said, well, we'll do it.

I said, yes, sir, we'll do it.

Billy Pickard was a company man.

He had survived a lot of athletic directors and football coaches. Regimes came and went at Texas A&M. Billy Pickard stayed. In time, his name would be symbolic with Texas A&M athletics. He was the bedrock.

He and Jackie Sherrill had a special relationship. I could talk to him the way others couldn't and get away with it, Pickard said. He knew I been with the Bear. He knew I had been with Gene Stallings and the Bear at Junction. All of us, Gene, Jackie, and me, had been connected to the Bear. We knew what it took to win. But sometimes, Jackie had some harebrained ideas. The 12th man kickoff team was one of them.

I didn't think it would work. I didn't think it would last. But once we did it, those boys were a magnificent bunch. They probably thought we were hard on them. They thought we pushed them to the limit and sometimes beyond. But we just wanted to toughen them up. That's the way we did it in the old days. That's the way some of us still believed we should do it. Knock them down every day. Knock them down as often as you can. Then play with those who don't stay down. If these boys thought we were hard, they should have signed up to play with the Bear.

At first, I had no reason to believe in the 12th man team, Pickard said, but after a few years, after they proved themselves, it looked like Jackie had been right. Those boys busted their tails out in a game, and we busted their tails on the practice field. They took a lot, and they kept coming back for more. I wouldn't have bet a plugged nickel for their success. I would have lost the nickel. They made a believer out of me. But none of them ever saw me go soft on them. They may have been good today. I tried to make them better for tomorrow. Jackie thought the 12th man pushed his varsity. They couldn't have done it if we hadn't pushed them, and we pushed them beyond all limits. We didn't have practice for the faint of heart. If they wanted somebody to baby them, they should have stayed home with mama.

Sports pages said they were crazy. Pickard knew they were crazy. Sherrill may have been tripping on the edge of insanity himself. Chad Adair remembered the Coach tying a longhorn steer to a goal post during each day of practice. We couldn't run downfield without seeing that steer, he said. He was always out there and always in our way. Before the game, Coach Sherrill handed each of us a square that had been carved from a steer's horn. It had A&M on one side and our name and number on the other, and the Coach said it came from that old steer we had seen in practice. It didn't, but he said it did, and we were believing everything he was saying. Coach said that's what he did to longhorns. He wasn't just out there singing about sawing off horns. He was cutting them up and handing them out to us. He didn't have any respect for that longhorn. He didn't expect us to have any mercy on the steers either, especially the ones wearing burnt orange. We were ready to kill any longhorn that got in our way by the time the first kickoff was in the air.

At Bonfire before the Texas game, Corey Linscombe, one of two seniors on the team, spoke briefly, then Dennis Mudd grabbed the microphone, ambled to the front of the stage and looked out over the growing sea of maroon and white as it faded into the darkness far beyond the flickering glow of the flares. Ags, he said, I want you to dig real deep into

your pockets tonight, and I want each of you to pull out a nickel and send it in care of Texas University, Austin, Texas, to the attention of the Fred Akers unemployment fund.

Dennis Mudd had not been attending church as regularly as he knew he should have. I was spending so much time with my studies and football that I kind of put the Good Lord on the back burner, he said. I didn't have any time for him. Now, I was hoping he had some time for me.

Mudd knew he had to get out of his dorm room as soon as possible. Too many people calling. Too many people wanting tickets to the game. Too many people asking if they could bunk down on his couch or his floor for the weekend. The phone was ringing constantly and off the wall, so he spent a night at his sister's place to escape the chaos.

He was headed toward her home in College Station after Bonfire when he drove past a Catholic Church. He turned the car abruptly into a parking lot and went inside, walking all the way down to the front of the sanctuary. The lights were on. The church was empty. Dennis Mudd sat down on a pew. Lord, he said, I really don't know why I'm here. But I thought it might be the right thing to do. We're playing Texas come Thursday, and I just wanted to make sure you were up there and looking out for us.

Before the Texas game, Paul Maguire with ESPN was interviewing members of the 12th man unit, and he asked Tony Pollacia, what made you decide to go out for the kickoff team?

Only one reason, Pollacia said.

What's that?

It's a great way to meet girls.

Maguire grinned. He didn't doubt it for a moment. On the air, he would say of the 12th man, these guys are stranger than fiction. They're wacko. I played on special teams myself, so I know what it's like. You have to be a little bit nuts to do it.

Tom Ray ran out of the tunnel and gazed up into the stands of Kyle Field. The night was chilled and growing colder by the minute. It seemed as though everyone from end zone to end zone was waving a 12th man towel, he said. Lint was flying and floating down onto the field, and, for a moment, I thought it was snowing. We could have sold a million towels if we'd had them.

Jerry Cox, a former student, understood the impact that Sherrill's idea for a 12th man kickoff team had made both on the school and the program. He said that the 12th man team was the key, critical, ingredient that linked the football team with the Texas A&M student body. That link ignited a new energy, spirit, and feeling that forever changed Kyle Field, he said. It was a brilliant strategy, That number twelve on the jerseys meant something special to those who crowded into the stadium. A great tradition was no longer just a tradition passed down from generation to generation. Sherrill had made it real.

Johnny Holland would say, I remember coming out of the locker room and feeling the stadium shaking. The 12th man towels were everywhere. I think the 12th man tradition really hit home that night, and I understood what it really meant. I think the fans that year – and every year – at Texas A&M played a big part in our football team. But that year, they were really outstanding.

Jackie Sherrill glanced up into the stands, completely surrounded by sound. At Bonfire, he had asked Aggies to make Kyle Field, on Thanksgiving, the loudest night in the history of the stadium. The volume had

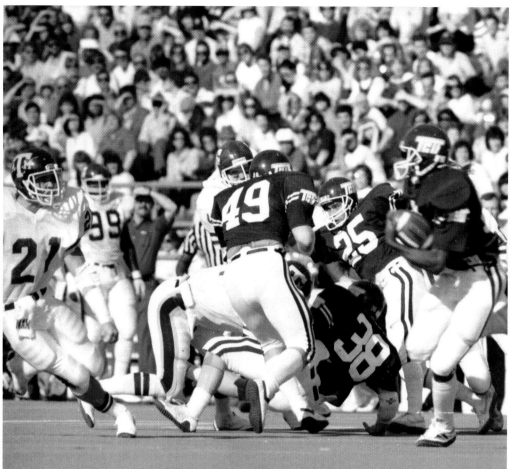

As the TCU ball carrier tries to bounce outside, he comes into the range of Mark Wurz-bach (21). One is varsity. One isn't. The scholarship player doesn't have a chance.

Freshmen members of the A&M Corps of Cadets picked up the Aggie yell leaders and marched off for a nearby pond and a traditional dunking ceremony. Two students unfurled a bed sheet and paraded it around the field. The sign read: Give Jackie A Raise. In the flush of victory, A&M fans would agree that the investment in their million-dollar coach had been well spent.

Lynn Ashby, a columnist for the *Houston Post* and an avowed apologist for The University of Texas, provided his own biased account of the game: The Aggies win the coin toss and elect to kick off. Onto the field runs the 12th man – amateurs recruited by A&M to tackle whoever catches the ball. The 12th man only goes out on the field when A&M is kicking off. Take a good look at them. This the only time they'll be on the field tonight. After a long defensive struggle, the Aggies luck out and score. Onto the field runs the 12th man. Towels spin in the stands like so many terry cloth propellers. The rest of the first half is uneventful. Second half begins. The Aggies, by supreme luck, score again. The 12th man takes to the field. I think they've got more playing time than anyone, remarks a Canadian. I rip up his visa. Busy lads, those 12th men," says the Canadian.

Odd, said I. They seem to be out on the field again.

That's because it's 21-0.

reached deafening heights, and the steady roar was growing wilder, more intense, more raucous, more out of control with every passing moment. He could barely hear his own thoughts. Sherrill grinned. Let that damn Texas quarterback try to audible now. He doubted if anyone could even hear the snap count.

Movement seems to be going in the wrong direction. A&M runs up and down the field at will. For the first time in history, the 12th man is being substituted due to fatigue. I think they've run out of towels, says a Canadian. You can never find a border patrolman when you need one.

The game eventually ends with the worse trouncing an A&M football team has ever inflicted on a UT team. Oh, well, says a Canadian brightly as we are leaving the stadium. There's always next year.

Yeah, I agree. That's what worries me.

The game wasn't close. Akers had been right. It was hectic and noisy and filled with high-energy. But it wasn't close. A&M defeated Texas for the second straight year, and the score, 42-10, was merely incidental.

Dallas Morning News columnist David Casstevens captured the mood of Kyle Field when he wrote, as the clock ticked, ticked, ticked down the seemingly endless fourth quarter, sold-out Kyle Field began a celebration that would go on and on into the wintry night. Kids. Students. Parents. The old school ties. They stood, crouched, hands on knee, barking yells. Arm in arm, they swayed drunkenly, deliriously, to and fro. They kissed. They hugged. A few, you guess, cried. They savored every delicious moment. It wasn't quite the same magnitude of say, V-E Day, or the night Lindbergh landed in that field in France.

But don't tell the Aggies and their long-suffering fans that A&M's 42-10 rout wasn't a moment of historic proportions. When the clock finally expired at 10:44 p.m. and this one was officially over – it had been over, for all practical purposes, since late in the third quarter – goodness what a scene. From high above, Kyle Field looked like a giant anthill stirred to life. Fans spilled onto the field.

It was a sad touch of irony. Throughout the season, Cory Allen had been running the bleachers, staying in shape, trying to rehab a bum shoulder, wondering if he would ever go downfield on a kickoff, praying that all of his hard work had not gone for naught. The doctors had cleared him to play before the previous game, but the game against TCU was on the road, and Allen had been left behind. Now he had strapped on his armor of maroon and white and was gazing out upon an enemy in burnt orange.

In a single and violent collision in practice, Butch Motley had separated Allen's shoulder. Sent him to surgery. Ruined a good year for him.

Now, however, with Texas on the field, Motley was injured and unable to play.

Roy Kokemoor hurriedly sent Cory Allen onto Kyle Field to take Motley's place.

Allen said, as slow as I was, I went down on a kickoff, slipped through a seam when a 12th man wedge buster did a pole job on some

Longhorn blocker, cleared my path for me, and I came face to face with an unprotected ball carrier.

Just me and him.

That's all.

Me and him.

The way I had always dreamed it would be.

My eyes locked onto his, and he could see a train wreck coming. He knew he had the speed to run past me. But he made the mistake of hesitating. Even a slow guy like me could catch you if you hesitated. I hit him, he went down, and I was jumping up and down beside him like a little kid.

For Cory Allen, it had been a short season.

I was, he said, a one game, one hit wonder.

Chad Adair believed that the college game was played at a much more serious and business-like level than he had ever experienced in high school. He was no longer a stud, he said, and football was not nearly as glamorous as it had once been. On this particular night, however, with the far end of the field ablaze with the color of burnt orange, the glamour had returned. He met Mister Eric Metcalf face to face, and neither player was interested in pleasantries or small talk.

Metcalf was the son of a former professional football player Terry Metcalf, and he was, 12th man members said, the scariest kickoff returner of them all, a scatback, a waterbug, who darted and dashed, an illusion in cleats who could turn sharply on a dime and cut out a nickel in change. I got to him, Adair said, but I didn't blow him up. He was going every which way at once. His head was headed east. His feet decided to go west, and I was able to spin him around, then pull him down before he ever got himself turned north and south.

The next time, it was Rick Tankersley bearing down relentlessly on Eric Metcalf, who had broken into the open field. Roy Kokemoor had told him, watch Metcalf's hips. Wherever his hips are pointed, that's the direction he's gong. Follow his hips. If you watch his head or his shoulders, you're dust.

I was praying and praying hard, Tankersley said, and God must have heard me. I grabbed a leg before his hips could change directions and jerked it out from under him. I never saw his face. I was afraid to look at his face. When I stood up, I still had his left leg in my arms, and I was driving it back over his head. It was Thanksgiving, and I had his legs apart like a wishbone on a turkey platter. I didn't need to make a wish. Mine had already been granted. I was pumped. The adrenaline was flowing, and I couldn't control my emotions. Didn't even try.

It was everything Corey Linscombe expected it to be. Nerves. Adrenaline. Fear. He had outside containment, and Eric Metcalf dashed to the outside. Eric Metcalf was coming his way. I thought I had him boxed in, Linscombe said, but Metcalf could run through a keyhole.

There he was. Then he wasn't. A flash. A flicker. And Metcalf was gone. That was the fear. One minute you'd see him, Linscombe said. The next minute you were asking yourself, where'd he go?

Eric Metcalf was a freshman.

The keyhole was closing fast.

He stepped out of bounds.

Metcalf was wise beyond his years, Linscombe thought. His own psyche would live to fight another day.

Dennis Mudd had deep worries and deeper fears about Eric Metcalf, who had run the forty in a blazing 4.2. If he beat you a step, he was gone. He was fast. He was elusive. What's the best way to keep him stacked up, Mudd asked Kokemoor.

The 12th man coach shrugged. Just run down as hard as you can, he said, and Metcalf will probably run into you. If you miss him, don't worry about it. Just stay ready. He'll be coming back around your way before you know it.

Mudd was as anxious as a pig in a packing plant. He said, a Texas blocker hit me pretty good, and it made me mad. This guy was big, and he blocked me straight up, so I grabbed his helmet from behind, twisted his head and tried to throw him down. I lost my balance, and he shoved me to the ground, then fell on top of me. There wasn't anything athletic or graceful about either one of us. It wasn't even a decent fight. I was kind of ashamed to be a part of it.

The yellow flag hit the ground at his feet.

Mudd was petrified. He had just been called for a personal foul, given up fifteen yards after the tackle, and now he was afraid to go back to the sidelines.

Jackie Sherrill was waiting, and Sherrill did not like stupid penalties, and all penalties, he said, were stupid.

A second yellow flag hit the ground.

It was, Mudd said, the most beautiful flag he had ever seen.

Off setting penalties, the referee said. We'll kick it again.

Mudd saw Metcalf gather in the football at the 14-yard line and immediately cut sharply to the right. He stopped and spun to the left. Metcalf could see daylight. But then, he could see daylight through the hole of a needle.

The daylight turned dark.

The 12th man had him hemmed in, trapped, and the 12th man was coming hard.

Metcalf, willing to take the easy way out and live to fight another day, stepped out of bounds.

He had gained fourteen yards, Mudd said. He had run eighty yards, but he only gained fourteen.

Mudd ran off the field.

He saw Sherrill walking toward him. Oh, Lord, Mudd thought, he's still mad about the personal foul. He's gonna kill me. I may never see the field again. Biggest game of my life, and I've had a personal foul.

Great recovery, Sherrill said to all and to no one in particular.

He slapped Dennis Mudd on the back of his helmet.

I felt like I had been given a second life, Mudd said.

Tony Pollacia had burst down the middle. I was like a bowling ball, he said, trying to knock down as many pins as I could. I raced toward the wedge. It broke down and faded away.

There was no one but Pollacia and Metcalf and the football.

Miss him, and he's away, a magician on the loose, a streak in burnt orange, a road runner searching for a faster gear and usually finding it.

He juked, Pollacia said, and I stumbled to my knees. He darted past me, and I reached out an arm. Instinct. Desperation. I don't know. By the grace of God, I grabbled an ankle and tripped him up. I'm down, and he's down on the 14-yard line, and he's not going anywhere. The streak had been struck.

As Pollacia bounded off the field, Butch Motley asked, did you nail him good?

Plastered him.

Pollacia was laughing. When they all watched the film, he knew, it would be Motley's turn to laugh.

He had always dreamed about making a play at home against Texas and hearing his name called out by the announcer on the P.A. System. Now it had happened.

He wondered if anyone was listening.

Ronnie Glenn had new life as well. On the kickoff, the football sailed into the end zone off Scott Slater's toe for a touchback, but the

12th man had flashed past the tee a tick too early. Close. But not close enough. Hallman was fuming.

Offside.

Step off five yards.

Kick it again.

This time, the ball fluttered to the goal line, and two people on the field were excited by the moment.

Eric Metcalf wanted to run the ball.

Ronnie Glenn wanted him to run.

Glenn sliced past the wedge and slammed into the ball carrier. Metcalf bounced backward, changed directions, and Mark Wurzbach hit him square in the chest and drove him into the ground. Until Rick Tankersley dragged him away, Wurzbach kept punching and gouging and trying to rip the football out of Metcalf's arms.

It looked like a street fight, Tankersley said. Metcalf wanted a penalty. Wurzbach wanted the ball. Metcalf was ready to go home. Wurzbach wanted him to know he could take his quick-darting, flash-and-dash somewhere else. It wasn't going anywhere on Kyle Field. We scored a lot that night. We kicked off a lot. Metcalf got hit a lot. Getting out of bed the next morning wasn't going to be easy for him.

Dean Berry remembered, there was nothing more mystical than going to war with Texas at Kyle Field. It was cold and gray at game time, with fog hovering above the stadium. The cannon fired, and smoke hung heavy across the field. It was a surreal sight on a surreal kind of night. We won and knew we were headed for the Cotton Bowl. A kid came running out on the field, asking me for my pads or my chinstrap. I wasn't a star, but he didn't care. I was wearing an Aggie uniform. In a wave of excitement, I gave him the pads that I wore to keep the artificial turf from tearing the skin off my arms and elbows. The next day, I realized what I had done and knew that the Cotton Bowl would be played on artificial turf as well. I asked Billy Pickard if I could have some new elbow pads.

Don't have any, he said.

What do you mean, I asked. This is Texas A&M. Surely you have some more elbow pads lying around somewhere.

Are you one of those 12th man guys?

I am.

Then we're out, Pickard said as he walked away.

Dean Berry had to find his way down to a sporting goods store and buy his own.

During the week, Jackie Sherrill had brought in a bale of cotton and dumped it in the A&M locker room, a bold reminder of how important the Texas game would be. When we walked back in after the game, Doug Middleton recalled, there was cotton everywhere. Players were ripping the bale apart and throwing cotton at each other. We had it in our faces, in our hair, and a few of the players were down on the carpet rolling in cotton. It had been piled a foot deep on the floor.

Middleton picked up a handful, put it in his pockets, and took the cotton home with him.

A year earlier, Rick Tankersley had been seated for Christmas dinner in his West Texas home and mentioned that he might try to walk-on the 12th man kickoff team down at Texas A&M. Everyone had laughed at him. That's ridiculous, they said. Why, that's downright absurd.

He sat down for Christmas dinner in 1985, and no one was laugh-

ing anymore. Rick Tankersley was on his way to the Cotton Bowl.

Jackie Sherrill realized that his team would be scattering far and wide for the holidays. It was a time to go home for awhile, and a lot of his players hadn't seen home for a long time. Sherrill gave them a date, December 25, and a time to be in Dallas. Have yourself a good time, he said. Enjoy the holidays. Don't get into trouble. And everybody get to Dallas the best way you can. No bus. No plane. No car caravan. Just find your way to Dallas. It was, after such a long, dry spell, a good place to be on New Year's Day.

Dennis Mudd left his home in Yoakum, headed down the road to Schulenburg, and picked up Danny Balcar for the journey north. Here we were, Balcar said, two boys on top of the world and on our way to the Cotton Bowl in an old beat-up pickup truck. We must have looked like the Beverly Hillbillies going to Hollywood. Mudd had never driven to Dallas before, and I had never seen Dallas. All I knew was that if we drove north up Interstate 35 far enough we would eventually run into it. It's a big town, Mudd said. But when you come from Schulenburg, they're all big.

Auburn with the great Heisman-Trophy winning Bo Jackson was on its way to the Cotton Bowl as well, and bookmakers in Las Vegas had established the Tigers as seven-point favorites to whip the upstart Aggies. Jackie Sherrill wasn't concerned with either the odds or the point spread. Let the gamblers lose their money. All he wanted to be was a single point better than Auburn.

Sherrill's mind was trying to wrap itself around five critical issues facing his team. Would his outside people be able to successfully shut down Auburn's running lanes? Did A&M's linemen have the ability to handle Auburn's offensive bulk up front? Could the offensive line of the Aggies successfully punch holes in the vaunted Auburn defense? Did Auburn have the firepower in the secondary to stop Kevin Murray? And how would the 12th man unit fare against the likes of Bo Jackson and Brent Fullwood, if, perchance, Jackson, with his raw power and speed, was sent out to return kickoffs?

As Sherrill quietly told the leering press, in every game, you figure that your players are going to win some of their match ups, lose some, and play even in others. The key to the game is for your players to play better than anticipated.

Just how good is Murray, a reporter asked.

Before he got hurt, Sherrill said, Murray probably was in the same category with Joe Namath. He has that special arm. Our tight end poured water down the back of Kevin's shirt the other day, and, in retaliation, Murray knocked him down with a pass during Friday's practice.

Behind closed doors, Jackie Sherrill meant business. The NCAA was cracking down on athletes who received tickets to a big game, then turned around and sold them for a handsome profit. It smacked of serious violations, the NCAA said. Some hot-shot, high-dollar booster could be using the scheme to pay ungodly sums to college football players. Buy a ticket for a thousand dollars. Buy a bunch of them. Easy come. Easy go. Sherrill shuddered.

Tony Pollacia remembered, Coach lined us all up and down the hallway. He was sitting at the far end behind a table. The Cotton Bowl tickets were stacked in envelopes before him, and each of us would be receiving four tickets to give to our families.

Coach Sherrill made each one of us walk up, stand before him, and

Along with Coach Jackie Sherrill, the Aggie football team wase led onto the storied Cotton Bowl turf by Sean Page (17), Tony Pollacia (15), Jeff Boutwell (11), Rick Tankersley (20), Bobby Middleton (18), and Mark Wurzbach (21).

look him dead square in the eyes. Who are the tickets for, he asked.

Family, I answered.

You have any intention of selling them?

No, sir.

God help you if you do, son.

Yes, sir.

Coach Sherrill stared at us like he was a psychic reader, and he could tell if we were lying to him. He didn't need a polygraph machine. He could look at us and know.

I didn't lie to him. I would have never sold the tickets. They meant too much to my family.

But when I walked away, I still felt guilty.

In another time, when Jackie Sherrill was playing linebacker for Alabama, Pat Dye had been working for the Crimson Tide as an assistant coach. Pat put many a knot on my head, Sherrill said. He taught me to be tough. It's ironic that I started the season coaching against one of my teammates, Ray Perkins of Alabama, and now I'm going against one of my former coaches. This game will be like an older brother playing a younger brother. There will be some special feelings on the field.

Perkins had told him, Bo Jackson is the best running back in the world, college or pro. And Johnny Majors, Sherrill's old mentor at Pittsburgh, said, Bo is the most dynamic all-around back I've seen. He's the most explosive since Tony Dorsett, and he weighs forty more pounds. Bo was a definite concern. We'll try to slow him down, Sherrill said. Nobody stops him. Bo Jackson, was, as Auburn Coach Pat Dye said, a genetic wonder. He had rushed for 1,786 yards and scored seventeen touchdowns in his mad, unbridled gallop toward the Heisman Trophy.

A reporter asked Sherrill, what's gonna happen if Auburn decides to run Bo Jackson on kickoffs against your 12th man team?

Sherrill shrugged and said, those guys can stop a train. What makes you think they can't stop Bo Jackson?

Members of the 12th man team, along with the scholarship athletes, were bedded down in the elegant and luxurious Hyatt Regency Hotel. They were playing Aggie football. They were in Dallas. They were on their way to the Cotton Bowl. If they had been treated any better, they couldn't have stood it and the law wouldn't have allowed it. They ate steaks and stuffed every suitcase they had with free and expensive Cotton Bowl-sponsored gifts.

However, while Sherrill's staff in the Hyatt was monitoring the varsity squad twenty-four hours a day, 12th man team members were left to come and go as they pleased. No curfews. Nobody looking over their shoulders. All they did was let common sense be their guide, and common sense failed to make the trip to Dallas. But, Sherrill had said, if I hear of you getting into any kind of trouble, I'll send you back home to you mama and daddy. No questions asked. As Dennis Mudd said, we took turns looking out for each other. If somebody needed to get back to the room before daylight and didn't know his right from his left, we didn't simply put him in a cab and ship him back to the hotel by himself. Too risky. Somebody rode with him. No one was ever left alone. We took turns riding a lot of cabs in Dallas.

For Corey Linscombe, it marked the end of a perfect year. He had been married during December of 1984, and wives were allowed to travel with the team to Dallas.

He and Denise had their own room in the Hyatt, and she had been given permission to go everywhere he went to celebrate the Cotton Bowl festivities.

On the field of the Cotton Bowl, long before the game began, Sean Page (in the shadows) captures the special day with a photo of (left to right) David Coolidge, Mike Tolleson, and Mark Wurzbach.

Denise was on a pedestal.

He would be on a football field.

Singularly and together, they were treated like royalty.

It was, Linscombe figured, exactly the way a first anniversary was supposed to be.

R. C. Slocum was in a bad mood. Our guys looked like they had too much turkey over the holidays, he said. It was his mission to give them a little conditioning and see if he could get them back in shape during the next five days. That's what he told the leering press anyway. In reality, he and Sherrill were working the Aggies until their tongues were dragging the field, then they kept running the team until the players started tripping over their own tongues. The practices were not for the weak of heart. Sherrill had waited a long time for the Cotton Bowl. He had no intention of taking it lightly. The Aggies had not come to merely play. The Aggies had stormed Fair Park in Dallas to win. Moral victories might as well leave town. Moral victories were for the losers.

In the middle of the third practice, Sherrill blew his whistle and gathered his team around him. His eyes were a little more deep-set than normal, perhaps a little darker and a lot more intimidating. Dennis Mudd said, all afternoon he had been watching us drop too many passes and miss too many tackles. We were dragging. Nobody was sharp. Sherrill heated up his practices. Even if it happened to be December, even if the days were cold, his workouts became as heated as a war zone. We practiced two hours. He blew his whistle. I thought we were going back to hotel. For Sherrill, the clock had started over. We would be out there another two hours. We could get practice right. We could play with intensity. Or we could practice without stopping until New Year's Day. He was building us up, Mudd said. Nobody complained. We were all scared to complain. Sherrill was sharpening the knife. He wasn't leaving anything to chance.

Before the pre-game meal on game day, Sherrill walked into the dining room and whistled loudly. His team had been called to order. A deathly silence hung over the tables. Nobody dared breathe. I know you've been bottled up and are tired of taking out your frustrations on each other, Sherrill told his troops. I know you're straining at the bit and ready to go. Just be patient a little while longer. In a couple of hours, I'll turn you loose on them.

Before the game, CBS announcer Brent Musburger gave each of the 12th man members a five-second interview. He asked one question: why did you try out for the team? The answers were varied. Because my mama wanted me to, said one. It gives me a better chance to meet girls, said another. I missed football, said a third. Chad Adair went before the camera, took a stance not unlike the Incredible Hulk and said, the Terminator movie has just come out. And I'm the terminator.

The first half was a battle, and Auburn was battle-tested. Texas A&M was treading on new ground. And here came Bo. Sean Page recalled, I was on the sidelines watching Bo run a toss sweep around the end. Our starting defensive back was big, and he had the angle. Bo suddenly put it in another gear and came around the corner, blowing past our cornerback and up the sidelines past us. I saw a 230-pound freight train in blue and orange headed toward us and then, in a split second, right past us. I had never seen anything before or since quite like Bo Jackson on a dead run.

The Aggies trailed 13-12 with time running out in the first half. Eric Franklin had missed two field goals, and Sherrill was fuming. A&M moved to the Auburn 19-yard line, facing fourth down, and Sherrill did not hesitate. He grabbed the shoulder pads of walk-on kicker Scott Slater, shoved him toward the field, and said, kick it.

Me?

Kick it.

Slater said, here is the scene. I'm a freshman. I'm a walk-on. I've never kicked a field goal in college before. I'm in the Cotton Bowl. I'm kicking for the lead. And I am scared to death. My knees are wobbly. I'm having trouble running straight. I can't catch my breath. I just want somebody, anybody, to put an arm around my shoulders and tell me that everything is going to be all right.

Shea Walker, the holder, looked back as Slater lined up the kick.

Slater, he yelled.

Yeah?

Don't screw it up.

The kick was right down the middle. A&M grabbed a 15-13 lead.

Early in the fourth quarter, Auburn ratcheted its offense another notch and drove eighty-eight yards to the Aggie six with A&M holding on to a precarious 21-16 lead. It was Bo Jackson time. He gained four yards on first down, found no hole or seam at all on second down, and watched Sammy O'Brient shut the door to the goal line on third down. The game had come down to fourth and inches. For Sherrill, it was fourth and life. As Mike Forman wrote in the *Victoria Advocate*, the frustrated Tigers called a timeout and decided to go with their Heisman Trophy winner again on fourth down. But with a partisan Aggie crowd of 73,137 roaring and waving their white towels in unison, Jackson never even came close to crossing the goal line. Junior linebacker Larry Kelm got penetration to slow the Auburn running back, and freshman linebacker Basil Jackson completed the tackle, which resulted in nothing but a one-yard loss for America's premier running back.

I knew we had to dig deep inside, Johnny Holland said through clenched teeth. It was do or die.

Bo Jackson was mad. I could have scored if I had gone around the end, he said. But I don't call the plays. The coach calls the plays. With six minutes left, Auburn again faced fourth and two, and again Jackson was handed the ball. This time he did race wide. Wayne Asbury met him at the corner and drilled him for another one-yard loss. Oh, well. Same situation. No difference. Mickey Herskowitz wrote in the *Houston Post*, the Aggies simply surrounded Jackson. He had a great individual effort, but so did Custer at Little Big Horn. The Aggies had too many weapons. As Bo told the leering press, they just wanted it badder than we did.

Herskowitz concluded, in a fitting end, time ran out with the Aggies kicking off after their last touchdown, and their 12th man unit, their non-scholarship players, their students, on the field. The timing could not have been deliberate, but it made an interesting statement at the end of an impressive game.

As Dennis Mudd walked off the field, all he could see in his mind was a small boy sitting beside the driveway of his home in Yoakum, Texas, looking down a long and narrow road that wound its way toward a glow of bright lights, barely visible in the haze and shadows that hovered over the farm fields of an early Friday night. That's where I'll be someday, the boy had told his dog, down where the lights are bright, and they're playing football. And that's where he was, beneath the bright lights, standing on sacred ground that had been scarred with cleat marks, his cleat marks.

The small boy had never thought that the long and narrow road would one day wind its way to Dallas. He knelt and looked around him. It was as he had always known it would be. And he wondered if those beyond the Cotton Bowl stadium had been able to know who was winning by the size of the roar of the crowd. Back in Yoakum, in the front yard, he had always known. He smiled quietly. He was in Dallas, and the small boy deep inside had made the trip with him.

John Burnett was stunned. He read the list, taped to the door, the one that held the names of those Aggie football players receiving Cotton Bowl rings. His name wasn't on the list. He scanned it again. The names of a lot of the 12th man team members had been left off. Burnett tracked down David Coolidge.

That's not right, Burnett said.

Maybe you ought to talk to Coach Sherrill on our behalf, Coolidge replied. Maybe it was just a mistake.

I'm not going alone.

I'll go with you.

Burnett and Coolidge sat down in front of Jackie Sherrill's desk. Both were walk-ons. Both had sacrificed blood, sweat, and mostly blood for the 12th man team. Both had worked hard for the past two years. Neither had ever had the courage to talk face to face with Coach Sherrill before. Their nerves were raw and on edge.

What's the problem, Sherrill asked.

The names of a lot of the 12th man team members have been left off the list to receive Cotton Bowl rings, Burnett said.

Is your name on the list, Sherrill asked.

No, sir.

It definitely should be, he said. Sherrill glanced away, deep in thought. Finally he drawled, we have a coach's meeting at four-thirty

today. We'll go over our roster name by name. Those who deserve a ring will certainly receive a ring. And, boys, if either of you disagree with our decisions, any of them, you can come see us and give us your reasons why we're wrong.

That was more than either Burnett or Coolidge could have ever hoped to achieve.

The changes were made.

A new list was taped to the door. Burnett grinned. The starters, and those key members who contributed mightily to the 12th man kickoff team in practice and on the field, would have their Cotton Bowl rings. The long hours, the hard work, the aches and pains, they hardships they endured had not been in vain.

For Jackie Sherrill, the season had been win or else. He felt a sense of relief and vindication when the final seconds counted down on the Cotton Bowl scoreboard. He had won. He had won his way. He had won in style. Now, what would the leering press and Aggie faithful want from him, he wondered. Another pound of flesh? And how many times would he have to win to keep the wolves from howling outside his door, or did the leering press simply make its living by howling on the safe side of somebody's door? In Texas, his door was always open. The leering press wrote from afar. The leering press was afraid to go in.

Pete Herndon wrote in the *Battalion*, even after Texas A&M had upset Texas, 47-12, in Austin last year, the Aggie fans still kept one foot in the water, preparing to jump off Coach Jackie Sherrill's ship if A&M didn't produce in 1985. Several times last season, especially after losses to Tech and Baylor, some Aggie faithful considered standing Sherrill in front of the cannon cadets fire after an A&M score. Why not, one A&M student said. We aren't scoring any points. If we don't do something, that old howitzer is just going to get rusty again. But during the course of a 9-2 season, a SWC championship, and a Cotton Bowl match-up with Auburn, Sherrill has gone from being in front of a cannon to being canonized – at least in the minds of Aggie fans.

Al Carter reported in the *Houston Chronicle*, the Texas Aggies were the best at the finish. By far, the best. Baylor peaked a month too soon. Texas peaked a week too soon. Arkansas never really peaked. But the Aggies saved their best for the last, mowing down SMU, Arkansas, TCU, and Texas all in the month of November. It strains the mind to think this is basically the same team that opened the '84 season trying its best to lose to the likes of Texas-El Paso and Arkansas State.

Yet, in his darkest hour as a college football coach, Jackie Sherrill wrung out his staff, laid down the law to his team, and it worked. The infamous Aggie death march never materialized. But Sherrill didn't do it alone. Offensive Coordinator Lynn Amedee created artwork out of a unit who's past playbook looked like alphabet soup.

Up in Dallas, Randy Galloway, in the *Morning News*, was predicting that Sherrill could actually be dangerous to the health and job security of every other coach employed in the Southwest Conference. He wrote, while other coaches were drumming him regularly on the field during those first three seasons, there was always a hidden fear factor for SWC schools.

What if a football monster suddenly came to life on Highway 6? What if Mr. Slick could defy Aggie history, grab this sleeping giant by the feet, pull it out of bed, and slap some fight into Ol' Sarge? Sherrill can give hope to the nation's most loyal alums, give hope to the nation's most spirited student body, and give Reveille a bite and a bark. There would be no place to run or hide for the rest of the conference.

At least Galloway understood more than anyone else that a monster was indeed on the loose.

Dean Berry (1), Corey Linscombe (10), Danny Balcar (2), Bobby Middleton (18), and Rick Tankersley (20) form a formidable defensive wall against kickoffs.

the football field. That was his lot in life. Hard to make an impression, he thought. Easy to get overlooked. Just as easy to get lost. He was a little short by football standards. He was a little too heavy for his height by football standards, weighing in at 225 pounds. But Roy Kokemoor could not believe his stopwatch. The boy's speed was pretty good by football standards. Damn if Warren Barhorst, built like a cypress stump in a river bottom, wasn't running a 4.5 forty. Kokemoor raised his eyebrows and had him run again. Same time, give or take a tick or two.

He called Barhorst into his office. You have a little speed, son, he said, and that means I have a spot for you. Kokemoor paused a moment, then asked, have you been at A&M your whole college career?

No, sir.

Where else did you go to school?

Stephen F. Austin.

Play any football?

Yes, sir.

Roy Kokemoor winced. The news hurt him worse than it did Barhorst. Well, you have the makings of a real good 12th man player, the coach said, but I'm afraid you'll have to sit out a year. Transfer rule, you know. You'll practice every day. You'll work hard. You'll learn a lot. But unlike the other walk-ons, you won't be able to suit up for games. Your situation has a lot of drawbacks, but I think the 12th man is worth it.

So did Warren Barhorst.

He bought two tickets to every game that fall. He stood in the stands and watched those who had punished him every day at practice. I couldn't even tell anyone that I was on the team, he said. They would have thought I was lying. Game after game, I was in the stands, and my teammates were all headed downfield on kickoffs. They were basking in the glory of it all. I was anonymous. They had the uniforms. I just had the bruises, and it began to eat my guts out. I was frustrated. I knew I was good enough to play, and, yet, I couldn't get on the field. The transfer rule was a killer.

In practice, Coach Sherrill gathered us around him and began to talk about a pyramid. Doesn't matter where you think you are, he said. Might be on top, in the middle, or at the bottom. Just remember, a pyramid is not a pyramid without all of you. It's worthless if any of the blocks are missing. It seemed as if he were talking about me. I may have been in the stands, but I was still part of that pyramid. I was part of that team.

The pounding at the end of the day left him staring down the barrel of a rifle that held one last bullet, and the bullet bore his name. He often felt as though he were holding a pair of deuces against a full house in a game of cut-throat poker, and the knife never left his throat.

If it weren't for the pain, Barhorst sometimes thought, he would have no feelings at all. He saw the bruises. He could taste the blood. It soured on his stomach. At the end of one hot, grueling practice, he stopped Dennis Mudd, who was working with the 12th man as a graduate assistant, and told him, I'm a walk-on. I'm a junior. I only have one more year to play. I don't get to suit up or even stand on the sidelines. The games go on without me. They have me beaten down to the point I have to force myself to get back up. I don't even want to get out of bed in the morning. Is all of this really worth it?

to go against someone who was afraid to hit back, Silverman said. There was no pain involved when it came to hitting someone as soft as a pillow, but you couldn't impress the coaches that way. No doubt, Scott and I were willing to take a hit. We'd stand in line, glance over to see who we would be lining up against us, then trade places until we knew we would be meeting each other head-on. Scott and I kept pounding each other.

The more we hurt each other, the better we liked it.

The pillow bodies didn't last long.

They packed up their bruises and were sent home.

On the day before the first home game against North Texas State, Kokemoor called Ed Silverman aside. I have something for you, he said. It was a jersey.

Number nineteen.

Tough guys don't cry, Silverman told himself.

Warren Barhorst loved the game of football, but Friday nights in high school, he knew, never lasted forever and seldom until next week. He had been a hot-shot running back at Jersey Village in Houston and thought he might have a chance to play for the Lumberjacks of Stephen F. Austin. After two years, Barhorst limped away from the field for the last time with a bad hip and a separated shoulder. There were better things to do in college, he knew, such as study a little, attend a few classes, and prepare for the rest of his life, which had absolutely nothing to do with football. He followed the footprints of a brother and sister, letting them lead him to Texas A&M. Warren Barhorst would have been perfectly happy as a student-body Aggie if that damn advertisement in the *Battalion* had not jerked his attention toward tryouts for the 12th man kickoff team.

He was destined to be one amongst the three hundred out roaming

Mudd, just coming off the 1985 championship season as the 12th man captain, stared at him and didn't hesitate. Warren, he said, I know it's hard. I know it has to be discouraging. I know it doesn't seem fair. But one day you just may make a play that will change your life forever.

Kirk Pierce had labored far too long on the outskirts of anonymity. He had been Canton's number one athlete in high school, and he missed the glory of it all. For a time, he had lined up as a running back for Stephen F. Austin, but, down deep, he wanted to be an Aggie. No. He wanted to be an Aggie football player, which was difficult for a small-town boy who worked hard just to measure up to 5-9 and 175 pounds.

Pierce was able to run the forty in the high 4.4s, and Roy Kokemoor told him, you might have a real chance of playing for us if you can put on a little weight and add a little muscle without slowing yourself down.

For Kirk Pierce, it would be uphill all the way.

Vince Palasota, in reality, had probably even been too small to play cornerback for the Mexia Blackcats, but somewhere down beneath that 5-8, 138-pound frame beat the heart of a man who thought he was as big, or at least as tough, as anybody who ever strapped on a helmet and a pair of shoulder pads.

These were his credentials: undersized, started for a team that never made the playoffs, determined to prove everyone wrong, cursed with a never-say-die attitude. At A&M, he was jumping at every chance he had and rapidly running out of chances. Palasota walked on the Aggie baseball team and was cut. He walked on the Aggie swim team, even though his high school had never fielded a swim team. You have a lot of raw talent, he was told, but you'll have to train and train hard for the next three years before you even have an opportunity to make the team. The coach's words cut him as well.

For Vince Palasota, football became the only sport left. Of course, there was basketball, but basketball coaches weren't beating the bushes for a 5-8 point guard. As a walk-on for football, he had been told that he would be tested on his speed and his size.

He ran a 4.5 forty.

That was fast enough.

Better weigh at least 150 pounds, or they won't even look at you, he was told.

He didn't have enough time to stack on another fifteen pounds, he figured, so Vince Palasota, with weight belts taped around his waist and ankles, confidently stepped onto the scales, and watched them measure him out at a good, solid 157 pounds. His grin had a swagger.

I held my breath, he said, afraid that I would be busted at any moment.

No one checked him.

No one obviously thought the little man from Mexia, Texas, was worth the trouble.

Palasota was undaunted. He headed straight for Jackie Sherrill's office. His hard stare met the coach's dark, deep-set, intimidating eyes head on. Palasota didn't blink. In Mexia, hard knocks were a way of life. He lived with them. He had beaten

most of them. They had left their scars on his body, but not his psyche. I want to play football, he said. I know I'm fast enough, and if you give me a chance, I'll prove to you I'm mean enough.

Sherrill shuffled through the stack of forms on the desk. Son, he said, it says here you only weigh 157 pounds.

I run a 4.5 forty.

You'll get rolled on every play.

I want a chance to put on the pads against those guys.

It's not the same as playing in Mexia, Texas. Sherrill shrugged. But I won't discourage anyone from walking on, he said. There comes a time in life when people need to know if they have what it takes to succeed – in life, as well as football. Can't tell them. Can't convince them. They have to find it out on their own. Besides, kids came out to walk on all the time, Sherrill knew. Big kids. Small kids. Fat kids. Slow kids. Kids with a dream. Kids on a dare. On rare occasions, someone who could actually help the team. But mostly, the kids didn't last. The little ones never did. I don't run them off, he said. After they've been hit a few times, the smart ones know they can't play without me ever saying a word.

Vince Palasota lasted.

For two years, he was a walk-on wide receiver, running kickoffs back every day against the 12th man unit. Coach Sherrill had been right, he said. I ran hard. I ran as fast as any of them. I was as mean as any of them. I got rolled on most every play.

Butch Motley (25) plays to the crowd. Around him are Alec Cuellar (22), Mark Wurzbach (21), and Dennis Kotara (27).

Brian Carpenter had entered a brave new world. In high school at Bridgeport, he played golf, tennis, basketball, baseball, and ran track. Somewhere along the way, he never got around to playing football, which made it even more ludicrous when Carpenter decided to walk onto Kyle Field and try his hand at knocking down ball carriers who were foolish enough to think they could find a break in the seams of the 12th man unit. Brian Carpenter, after all, was no stranger to the Kyle Field turf. He was out there every game day, playing a trombone and marching with the Aggie band

Colonel Joe T. Haney, legendary bandmaster, told him, if you have a chance to play football at Texas A&M, then you should go play. If you get hurt or don't make the team for some reason, you can always come back to the band. I'll have a trombone waiting for you.

The track coach tried to persuade him to ignore the perils of football and walk on as a quarter miler. In high school, Carpenter had run a 48.1 in the 440, but his knees were beginning to wear out on him. He had a little speed. He had a lot of heart. At Bridgeport, nobody ever passed him on the last corner. No matter what it took, he dug down deep and refused to be beaten. But now the kick was gone. At A&M, though, he found himself chasing the will-o-the-wisp wind sprints of Olympic sprinters. He had never known that a man's legs could carry him that fast. It was a new day, and his knees hurt worse with every lap around the long oval.

Football was the last viable athletic option available to him, if someone could just help Brian Carpenter figure out where his pads went and how to put them on. He ran a 4.51 in the forty, which made him one of the three fastest players at the tryouts. Of course, no one could outrun Danny Balcar. He was, Carpenter said, the fastest white guy on the planet. But then, Carpenter knew he was a lot faster than Bobby Middleton. Of course, he couldn't hit like Middleton. No one did. Middleton played like a Mafia hit man. One helmet. One bullet. It was all the same.

Brian Carpenter sat down with the registration form he needed to fill out. Where did you play high school football, it asked. What position did you play? What honors did you receive? All district? All State? Carpenter had nothing to write down but his name and his phone number. He doubted seriously if either Sherrill or Kokemoor cared much about his expertise in the marching band. Kokemoor glanced the form over, sighed softly, and sent Carpenter out to play wide receiver.

Kevin Murray hit him with a pass. I thought it had been shot from a cannon, Carpenter said. I had never seen or felt anything quite like it in my life.

A few passes bounced off his helmet.

Some ricocheted off his hands.

He even managed to hang on to a couple.

Kokemoor moved him to running back.

What'll I do, Carpenter asked.

See those big boys over there?

Yes, sir.

Take the ball, put it under your arm, hold on tight, run as hard as you can, and see if you can get past them.

What happens if I get past them?

Don't worry, son, Kokemoor said, patting the back of Carpenter's helmet. We'll worry about that when it happens.

Carpenter grabbed a football, held on tight, and slammed into Rod Sadler. It was an eye-opener, he said. It was like running into a slab of concrete. It might be some time, he decided, before he had to worry about running to daylight. He simply ran to the dark.

I had never been in a high-speed collision before, Carpenter said. There were four of us in line, and we took turns carrying the ball. Andy McDonald and I also took turns wiping the blood off each other. Twenty-five years later, he would still have a few fingers that he couldn't straighten out.

Garry Sorrell had cleaned out his locker for the last time at Calallen High School in Corpus Christi and never gave college more than a passing thought. His friends were all in school somewhere and mostly broke. Garry Sorrell was earning ten dollars an hour as an electrical worker at an oil refinery, and he said, I was making more money than I had time to spend. I was on top of the world.

He was helping assemble a start-up unit one night, and the electrical engineer on the project was puzzled and perplexed as he valiantly tried to spark some life into a stack of equipment gone dead. The unit wasn't cooperating, the engines were silent, the whole job had been ground down to a standstill, and the refinery was losing money with every passing second. Sorrell watched for awhile, looking over the engineer's shoulder, then sat down beside him and began totally re-engineering the blueprint. I believe if you make those changes, he said, it's got a good chance to work.

The engineer did.

The unit roared to a start.

He looked up at Garry Sorrell and asked, what are you making on this job?

Ten dollars an hour, Sorrell said proudly.

Well, the engineer replied, I'm making a hundred thousand dollars a year, and you're better at this than I am. Every day you're not in college is a day you're wasting.

Sorrell shrugged. If he did become an electrical engineer, he decided, he might as well go to Texas A&M. Ten whole dollars an hour had made him feel like a rich man. A hundred thousand dollars a year bordered on being preposterous. But if he could earn it, Garry Sorrell was hell bent on finding some way to spend it.

He was twenty-two years old. He was a college freshman. He had not put on his cleats or hit anyone legally in almost five years, and Garry Sorrell walked onto the Texas A&M football team. In high school, he weighed 195 pounds, ran a 4.4 forty, and had been on the sprint and mile relay teams. Suddenly he found himself in the midst of a sudden and unexpected growth spurt.

His shoe size had gone from ten and a half to twelve, and his weight was loading up the scales at 225 pounds. He wasn't a sleek, well-oiled, stripped-down, streamlined running back anymore. The Aggies moved him to outside linebacker.

Roy Kokemoor and Burnis Simon, a graduate assistant, looked over those who were suiting up for the first time. New faces. New names. New hopes. Old expectations. Somewhere in the crowd might be at least one or two who could play for the 12th man. They were always looking. They were always recruiting. Buried in all of that mud, and, Lord, there was a lot of mud, he might run across a diamond.

On the first day of practice, Garry Sorrell pulled on that damnable orange shirt that walk-ons were cursed to wear and ran out looking for somebody to hit. Hell, he liked to hit. He had always been a hitter. He had just as soon play football if everybody had forgotten to bring the ball. Just line up and start hitting whoever was closest or ran the slowest. He might not be the last man standing, but Sorrell knew he would damn well be among them.

On the first drill, he charged, and someone with an unknown name and unfamiliar number came his way.

The ground rocked.

Heads rolled.

The crack sounded like a pistol shot.

Garry Sorrell broke three screws in his helmet.

He face was awash with blood.

Holy Mother of God, Burnis Simon yelled as he came running up. I'm gonna name you First Blood. Hell, get that orange shirt off. You're on the 12th man team now.

What's that, Sorrell wanted to know. He had no idea what the 12th man team was all about. Never heard of it before. Been buried deep in an oil refinery. Maybe too deep.

It means you'll be wearing a red jersey from now on.

The next day, when Sorrell walked into the dressing room, he found a red jersey hanging in his locker.

One hit had changed it all.

He never knew whom he hit. He only knew the player without a name didn't come back.

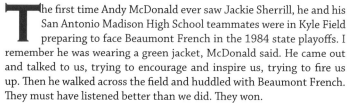

The first time Andy McDonald ever saw Jackie Sherrill, he and his San Antonio Madison High School teammates were in Kyle Field preparing to face Beaumont French in the 1984 state playoffs. I remember he was wearing a green jacket, McDonald said. He came out and talked to us, trying to encourage and inspire us, trying to fire us up. Then he walked across the field and huddled with Beaumont French. They must have listened better than we did. They won.

As a freshman at Texas A&M, McDonald was walking across campus when a friend told him, I'm trying out for the 12th man team. Want to come along?

I thought, well, I would like to see the inside of the stadium at ground level again, McDonald recalled, so I said, why not?

It was a whim, nothing else.

We went through the tryouts like marines at Quantico. I figured out in a hurry that size and speed might be important, but the real secret was convincing your mind that you could do it, that you could take the pain without buckling, that you could hit somebody regardless of how big he was, that you could run somebody down no matter how fast he was. We practiced day after day, and, after awhile, it became a real grind.

I could run downfield and take out a wedge in my sleep.

Pain was as natural and as normal as breathing.

Our only mission in life was simple: point yourself down hill, pick up speed, find a gear you didn't know you had, and don't leave anybody standing in your path.

Charles "Bubba" Hillje didn't mind the hard work.

He was used to it. Even while at Texas A&M, he and hard work remained personal acquaintances. During Christmas break, he would go back home to Cotulla in the far, remote reaches of Southwest Texas and trap raccoons, bobcats, and coyotes. He served as a guide for out-of-towners in search of the elusive whitetail deer. During the hot summer months, Hillje cleared land with a bulldozer, dug postholes, built fences, strung barbed wire, worked on the callused end of a root plow, and burned off brush while the heat lying heavily on his shoulders would sometimes rise to 110 degrees in the shade, if, perchance, Cotulla had possessed a decent shade.

He was paying for his college tuition, and just off campus, he, like so many others, went down twice a week to sell plasma for a little money to buy beer.

In high school, Hillje played linebacker, tight end, and offensive lineman for a team that barely had enough players to scrimmage. He punted. He kicked off. On a ball club known as the doormat of a great district, he managed 137 tackles in nine games to earn first-team, All-Southwest Texas honors during his junior year. Four games into his senior season, however, Hillje tore ligaments in his ankle. The plethora

When the 12th man team met a ball carrier head-on, he was buried under a defensive avalanche, led here by Bobby Middleton (18), Dennis Mudd (4), Ronnie Glenn (9), Corey Linscombe (10, Tony Pollacia (15), and Rick Tankersley (20).

of phone calls from football recruiters suddenly dried up. The postman did not bring any more heart-warming, personal notes from coaches. Only Army bothered to recruit him, and when Hillje showed up to look around West Point, the military simply assumed that he would become a cadet. No welcoming committee was beating the drums to announce his arrival. No coach was on hand to shake his hand. He came and left without Army really ever knowing he was there. Instead, Bubba Hillje accepted an ROTC scholarship to A&M. In the back of his mind, however, he was still thinking about football.

Hillje sent Tim Cassidy some game film, and Cassidy told him, why not walk on? Hillje thought about it for a few days, and then decided, I may not be good enough to start, but maybe I'm good enough to go downfield on special teams.

He had no idea how special the team would be.

Garry Sorrell walked up to him during practice and asked, do you like that orange jersey you're wearing?

I'd do anything to get rid of it.

Come on over to the 12th man, Sorrell said, and we'll get you a red jersey.

Might as well, Bubba Hillje thought. It's a damn sight closer to maroon than the one I'm wearing.

In the spring game, Bobby Bostic was a warhorse running wild.

He was covering a kickoff.

His father was on the sidelines.

Bostic said, I made the tackle and caused a fumble. It was the play of the night. My father was so excited about watching the game that his video camera was hanging down loose, taping close-ups of the turf at Kyle Field.

I knew I made the tackle.

He knew I made the tackle.

In his mind, with his own eyes, my father captured a memory that would last him forever. His video camera didn't catch it at all.

For David Fronk, all 6-3 and 245 pounds of him, this might be the year. Two had already been wasted. Oklahoma State had recruited him as a punter when he played high school football for Trinity Valley in Fort Worth. The prep school was small, had little exposure to the outside forces of big-time college football, and only the Cowboys, then Tim Cassidy at Texas A&M, seemed to be impressed at Fronk's ability to average 44.7 yards a punt. Didn't make any difference who the competition might be. Big Schools. Little schools. That was a long way to consistently punt a football. There had been All-Americans would couldn't punt that far. As usual, the Aggies had run out of scholarships, but Jackie Sherrill did take notice of the freshman's booming punts in practice.

The 1986 12th man team was comprised of, front row, Dean Berry (1), Danny Balcar (2), David Joiner (4), Spencer Baum (5), John Burnett (6), David Coolidge (7), Doug Middleton (8), Ronnie Glenn (9), and graduate assistant coach Dennis Mudd. Second row: Corey Linscombe (10), Jeff Boutwell (11), Chad Adair (12), Sean Page (17), Bobby Middleton (18), Cory Allen (19), Rick Tankersley (20), and Mark Wurzbach (21).

Who's that, he asked Curley Hallman.

The kid from Fort Worth.

We need to keep him.

Fronk had been told that the Aggies seldom if ever kept a second punter on the squad, but Sherrill walked up out of the blue and told him, Fort Worth, you earned yourself a spot.

No scholarship.

Just a spot.

Better than nothing.

But not much.

For two years, David Frank never left the bench. A walk-on punter, he found out, simply hung around on the periphery in case an emergency ever happened to arise. None had. He kept hanging around until he grew tired of hanging around.

Even from the beginning, Fronk tried to make his presence known during scout team practice. After all, he didn't punt all of the time, and he did have the ability to run a 4.65 in the forty, which was pretty fast for a man carrying 245 pounds, some of it muscle. Coaches found him a slot at tight end.

During my first year, I was a mere 18-year-old kid, Frank said, and I was looking across the line of scrimmage at the cold, uncompromising eyes of Johnny Holland. His motor was always running, and, suddenly, my 245 pounds didn't feel so big anymore. I knew why potholes hardly ever stopped a long-distance hauler. He had a gear I had only heard about.

Fronk, according to the playbook that afternoon, was listed as the third receiver on the play. His assignment was to run a 10-yard slant to the far side of the field. Basically, it was to keep a straight face, lie to the linebacker, make him think you were going somewhere you had no intention of going, and then get the hell out of the way so a real football player could catch the ball.

Fronk made his cut.

He took one more step.

Johnny Holland slammed a forearm to his head.

Fronk bent backward like a cheap ten-penny nail.

The hit was so devastating that Fronk figured it would take two, maybe three days, to clear the cobwebs and ease the throbbing in his temples. He tried to open his eyes. They were already open.

When he pulled himself back off the ground, he looked at Holland and asked, why did you do that? I wasn't even the primary receiver on the play. Hell, I wasn't even the secondary receiver on the play.

Holland grinned. I just wanted to let you know I'm here, rookie, he said. Welcome to college football.

By the time Fronk reached his junior year, he had made the decision to cast his lot with the 12th man team. He doubted if anyone really wanted to see him punt anymore. No one had thus far. Those days of kicking a football were far behind him. In fact, in all reality, they had probably never left Fort Worth. The 12th man, he said, offered him a chance – no matter how small – to finally step across the white line and see if he could survive a disaster or cause one. Besides, I could swing a wrecking ball as well as anybody out there, Fronk said, and even if I wasn't the fastest, I could make up for it with hustle and grit.

Fronk decided he had nothing to lose. All I had to do, he said, was go out and blow somebody up. Not a difficult job. You put your mind to it. Then you put your body to it. You looked across the line of scrimmage, found your target, and convinced yourself that you were a meaner sonuvagun than he was. Then you proved it. The man in my sights had two choices. He could run toward me or away from me. On 12th man kickoff coverage, neither option lasted very long. .

It was like shooting a dove on the fly, only a little more brutal. Catch him. Knock him down. Stomp on him. Don't get caught. It wasn't gut instinct. We practiced it. All the time, we practiced it, especially the part about stomping and not getting caught.

For the rest of the year, no coach asked David Fronk to punt a football. Just as well. His leg was much too sore to punt.

During the spring season, before the bruises had grown too large and too purple, before Jackie Sherrill had lost his temper one too many times, while the Aggie spirit and enthusiasm were reaching an unprecedented level of confidence, the players on the Southwest Conference Championship team were awarded their Cotton Bowl rings and honored with a banquet at the Duncan dining hall.

Doug Middleton was standing in the corner with his parents, and Jackie Sherrill walked straight toward them.

I wasn't a star, Middleton said.

I was a walk-on.

I was on the 12th man.

On the football field, I was a nobody

Jackie Sherrill had never sat in my living room and recruited me to play football for Texas A&M.

I'm not for sure I ever heard him speak my name, not even in anger.

He looked at my mother and my father, and he said, I deeply thank you for allowing your son to play football for us.

He was somber.

He was sincere.

It was a gesture Coach Sherrill did not have to make.

But he did.

And, all season long, Middleton said, I had never gone downfield on a single kickoff.

Jeff Boutwell was beginning to feel like the daring young man on the flying trapeze, working without a net or anyone to catch him when he fell. In 1983, even after his picture appeared in a *Sports Illustrated* article about the original 12th man kickoff team, he had been unceremoniously cut from the team. A name left off the list. Good enough to make the top twenty, perhaps, but not the top seventeen.

A year later, he tried out again and had the same expectations but was certainly expecting different consequences. Boutwell was convinced that he could earn his stripes simply because he was a year older and a year wiser, even though he still wasn't a step faster. Boutwell carried 215 pounds, but he ran a 4.78 forty and settled into the life of an alley guy, a player who stayed in his lane, covered a specific area of the field, and blasted blockers out of the way while the ball guys flew like devils from the backdoor of hell on their search and destroy missions.

During the early days in practice, he was always figuring out a way to be first in line, to try and make a strong impression on the coach, any coach, and, God forbid, carry the football. Offense was all glory, Boutwell thought. Offense was where he ran at full speed, searching for a new power supply when the old one ran out, and was lit up by the likes of Johnny Holland, Todd Howard, Domingo Bryant, and Kip Corrington. They would double you up pretty good, he said, rattle your brains a little, and I would go home in the afternoon, bruised from head to toe with impressions of the jersey mesh tattooed on my back and chest.

Boutwell made the decision to move himself, without ever asking for a coach's permission, to a defensive position on the scout team. Offensive linemen might be big and strong, he surmised, but they spent more time grabbing, clutching, and holding than they did putting somebody on the ground. Of course, in his ill-fated logic, he failed to take into account the tight end.

He came out to block me, Boutwell said, and I hit him. Head-to-head, I hit him, and the world suddenly spun once, flipped twice, and went dark. I tried to open my eyes, and everything I saw had a silver lining. What I was looking at wasn't supposed to have a silver lining.

You all right, somebody asked.

I guess.

The words sounded so muffled, so far away, it was like being inside

starter, and neither aches, pains, concussions, nor a separated shoulder would keep him off the field.. He had four long years of catching up to do.

B obby Bostic never thought he had a chance. He came from a little wayward town in Louisiana, down on the gulf, cut off from the main world by the Atchafalaya Swamp, and he played defensive back and wide receiver for a little 1-A Catholic high school in Morgan City, the heart of Cajun Country. His heart had always been loyal to LSU's Tigers, and he figured it always would be. His father, on the other hand, was an Aggie, and Bostic finally heard enough hard-core, dining room, maroon and white sermons to leave his beloved Tigers behind and transfer across state lines to Texas A&M.

He knew all about the 12th man kickoff team. His brother had tried out for the unit, made the first cut, but didn't survive the rest the spring training.

Bostic was a quiet, unassuming, soft-spoken young man determined to prove that, on the football field, he had a lethal side as well. The cuts kept coming up. The team kept being whittled down. His name remained on the list.

Much to his surprise, Bobby Bostic was introduced by Coach Jackie Sherrill to speak about the exploits of the 12th man at an Aggie club meeting in Lafayette, Louisiana.

a tunnel, Boutwell said. The headache that night was excruciating. It was my first experience with a concussion. I choked down a mouth full of aspirins and the next day, I was back on the field.

It was a year in the eye of a storm. It was a long year. It was a year filled with delusions and disappointment. Each day brought its risks. Saturdays offered no rewards. Jeff Boutwell stood on the sideline and watched. His day was coming, he knew. It must be coming. At the moment, it was nowhere in sight.

By 1985, his diligence paid off. Boutwell had worked his way onto the first team. All the aches, all the pain, he finally decided, had been a worthwhile investment. During the week before the first game, he ran downfield during practice, found himself caught and entangled in a crossfire between two blockers, was wearing pads that didn't fit, felt as though his left arm and collar bone had abruptly parted company, and went down with a separated shoulder.

On game day, Mark Wurzbach moved into his position. Wurzbach was my backup, Boutwell said, and Wurzbach was a helluva player.

He went in. He never came out.

Again, Jeff Boutwell stood on the sideline and watched. Even when his shoulder had been screwed tightly back in place, he mostly stood and watched. He did find his way onto the field a time or two, but, more often than not, he was merely the twelfth man on an eleven-man kickoff team.

During the fall, Boutwell worked on Bonfire and crawled up the logs to sit on top of the outhouse, the crown jewel of the stack.

He looked out over the campus.

He contemplated his fate.

No one had worked harder.

No one had played less.

Where was justice, he wondered.

When 1986 came around, he knew. Jeff Boutwell would become a

During the summer, he attended Coach's Night being held at Lafayette, just up the road and past the Atchafalaya bayou from Morgan City. The quiet and unassuming Bobby Bostic walked in and found a seat at the back of the room. He had driven north to hear whatever words of wisdom Coach Sherrill decided to spread among the Aggie faithful. As soon as the meeting ended, he planned to ease quietly back out of the room and head home again. No one would ever know his name or realize he was there.

Sherrill wouldn't let him. At the podium, the Coach paused, looked out over the crowd, and called Bobby Bostic up front, introducing him, along with Jerry Fontenot, to those who were congregating like a group of underground solders behind enemy lines. LSU had no use for Aggies in their midst. LSU had no use for anyone not wearing purple and gold. Sherrill draped an arm around Bostic's shoulders and said loudly, this is one of my 12th men. He represents the A&M student body on every kickoff. He represents the alumni. He represents you.

Sherrill ended his talk with his usual question and answer session.

There we were, Bobby Bostic said. I was standing alongside Jerry Fontenot. He was a starter. He was All-Conference. He was an All-American. He was as good as anybody playing for Texas A&M and would spend years in the NFL with the Bears and the Saints.

But I was on the 12th man kickoff team.

Most of the questions that night were for me.

The mystique had not tarnished.

Texas Aggies '86

TCU Game   November 22, 1986 $2.00

Brian Edwards, left, and Mark Wurzbach were featured on a 1986 game day program, an honor historically reserved for members of the Aggie varsity team. By this time, the special unit was looked on a rock stars on the Texas A&M campus.

Chapter 20

Jackie Sherrill never wavered in his support of the 12th man kickoff team, not even when opposing coaches, his own coaching staff, and an overabundant number of doubters among the leering press thought he had sacrificed the inner sanctity of college football in order to take a blind, uneducated, and ridiculous stab at preserving an ages-old tradition. The 12th man unit had proven once again that those who preach something can't be done are usually run over by people doing it. By 1986, members of the all-volunteer team had become the darlings of college football. Not unexpectedly, teams began coming out of the woodwork in an effort to implement their own personal versions of Sherrill's folly.

The University of Alberta boldly instituted a 13th man team since football on the Canadian side of the border was played with twelve men anyway. In the Big Eight, Kansas State called the Texas A&M athletic department, trying to find out what steps the Wildcats needed to take in order to produce their own twelve-man kickoff team. Coach Stan Parrish gave the idea a legitimate chance, and he had almost two hundred students trying out. He selected eight. After a kickoff or two, he let them all go back up in the stands where he and they both felt a little more comfortable. The boys might get hurt, he said. They might give up a long return, he said. Lord help us, but they were a nuisance, he said. As Jackie Sherrill always believed, only at A&M, with its historic tradition of E.

King Gill alive in everyone's mind, could a 12th man kickoff team be successful. The unit was four years old by now and no longer an X-factor in his game plans. He knew what the team could do. The opposition knew what the team could do. Nobody had stopped them yet. Their coverage still had not been penetrated or broken. It was solid. Granite solid.

After the spring semester, Roy Kokemoor departed for a head coaching job at A&M Consolidated High School, and the fate and the fortune of the 12th man kickoff team were handed to another graduate assistant, Burnis Simon, who first walked onto the A&M campus in 1980 as a player without a position. Every Sunday, he found a note in his locker that said fullback or wide receiver or linebacker or safety or cornerback. Before the season ended, Simon had occupied every position available on special teams, with the exception of the kicker. He had been recruited by Tom Wilson. His versatility had made a lasting impression on Jackie Sherrill, a man who, more than anyone else, understood the fortitude and courage it took to line up at a different position every week or every year or every time he turned around. Sherrill

Texas A&M football, under Jackie Sherrill was a slam-bang, no-holds-barred war, especially down in the trenches where games were won or lost on the intensity and tenacity of the players.

played seven of them for the Bear. Burnis Simon had been a player after his own heart.

Simon began to believe that Sherrill had been able to tap into his routine as a player and a person. He knew my schedule, Simon said. He knew if I was attending class or not. He sat down and talked with me if he saw a sudden change in my demeanor. He had us out working on Bonfire. He made sure we knew, understood, and stood by the traditions of Texas A&M. He made sure I came back to school to earn my degree. He taught us there was life after football, and he preached the values of self-discipline and the importance of family. At Texas A&M, the football team was our family. Coach Sherrill was even able to take a group of guys unfit to play on any college football team in America, stitch a number twelve on the arm of their jerseys, and persuade them to run downfield at full speed and in a straight line, then knock out anyone who happened to get in front of them. That was the 12th man team. Now they were mine. Those guys had never allowed a touchdown, and I prayed that the first one wouldn't come on my watch.

I called them crazy.

They thought it was a compliment.

I called them uncontrolled and reckless.

They thought I was bragging.

We went into the season with the roughest, toughest bunch of kids Coach Kokemoor and I had been able to scrape up, and sometimes I thought we had been scraping the bottom of the barrel. We threw them against the best kick returners in the country, and the kick returners didn't have a chance. They had to fight to get back to the 20-yard line. Only on rare occasions did they get there. In practice, I threw them in to run the scout teams, and, from whistle to whistle, they made the whole team better. As Coach Sherrill said, put scholarship player on scholarship player, and they tended to slack off and go half speed. Put one of the 12th man members out there, and the scholarship player couldn't afford to go half speed. If one slacked off, he'd get his bell rung. Lord, the 12th man liked to ring those bells.

Dennis Mudd knew that his days on the football field were numbered. He thought they had ended. Jackie Sherrill had other ideas. Just before the summer of 1986 drew to a close, he summoned Mudd and told him, I want you out there helping Burnis with the 12th man team. Burnis will be in the press box with Curley during games. I want you on the sideline keeping order. You've been one of the 12th man. You know what I expect.

Sherrill didn't ask Mudd to become a graduate assistant.

He told Mudd that he had become a graduate assistant.

And Mudd had never told Jackie Sherrill "no" in his life.

Billy Pickard had his coaching gear waiting on him when Mudd reached the locker room. Now he would see what life was like on the other side of the bench.

Bobby Middleton was the craziest one of all. His helmet never fit, Simon said. It slipped down on his nose with every hit, and sometimes I couldn't recognize him for the blood on his face. I just knew it was Middleton because he had blood on his face. In one practice, I took him out of a drill.

You can't do that, he said.

Why not?

I gotta play.

Your nose is broken.

It won't stay broke long.

Burnis Simon shook his head. I need a right tackle in there now, he said. You can't play right tackle. You're not big enough.

Yes, I can.

They'll kill you.

I'll take that chance.

Burnis Simon shrugged and walked away. So that's the way it was going to be. The size of their hearts outweighed their common sense, which all seemed to disappear the moment they pulled on their helmets and laced up their cleats. Simon braced himself for the ride and knew it would be a wild one. Roller coasters had an easier track.

Andy McDonald no longer paid much attention to the name his parents had given him. Everyone called him Ears. He sent the name "Andy" packing. Ears stayed.

He also made the mistake of telling Burnis Simon that he had played on the offensive line in high school. So every day, without fail, Ears McDonald found himself squared up against the likes of Richmond Webb or Leon Cole, and he had only one idea running through his mind. Hit first. Hit hard. Hit quick. Hit often. Hit them before their motor started running.

Take it easy, Ears, Richmond Webb said loudly. Why you be coming so hard?

Have to.

This is practice, man.

Not for me.

Richmond Webb shook his head and walked back to the line of scrimmage. Still, you don't have to be coming so hard, he said.

McDonald's sister made him a T-shirt, and he wore it every day just to make sure that no one ever forgot. On it, she had written: "Ears Be Coming Hard."

Roy Kokemoor had always told Spencer Baum to keep his head in the game. He didn't mention that he might get his head knocked off, or at least disassembled. Pick up the pieces and go on. Hell, leave the pieces where they lay. I'm coming back out here tomorrow anyway, he said.

Melvin Collins was running back kickoffs in practice, and as Baum said, Collins looked like Conan the Barbarian. He was nothing but speed and muscle.

I saw the collision coming.

Two cars on a dead-end street. No place to turn. No detours. No reason to stop.

Our heads snapped back, Baum said.

Mine went farther back than his. I dropped like an anvil. And Kyle Field became a blur. My eyes dilated. It was though I was having an out-of-body experience. I looked down on myself. I wasn't moving. Everybody was staring at me. Nobody was moving.

He spent the night in the quack shack, and Spencer Baum, the brain, could not, for the life of him, remember his class schedule. He knew he had classes somewhere on campus, but he had no idea what they were or where they were located. Something far back on the ragged edge of his subconscious told him that he had a test coming up. But was it pathology? Or physiology?

I drew a complete blank, Baum said. No form. Full of darkness. I couldn't remember anything.

It would take a week before he did.

Baum did make sure he found his way to Kyle Field every morning and every afternoon. There was a lot of pressure, he said. Members of the 12th man team were throwaways. We could be replaced. If we weren't there, nobody missed us.

David Coolidge knew the rules. He knew how to break them.

Let's go half speed, the coaches said.

There was no such thing as half speed.

You can't hit low, the coaches said.

Hell, if that's what it took to nail somebody's bare hide to a bare wall, Coolidge told himself, hit the bastard low. Between the lines, he was not thinking about friendships. He was trying to work his way back into the starting lineup, and he had learned well the gospel, according to Jackie Sherrill, who had stern sermons and few beatitudes.

Football was not a contact sport.

Football was a collision sport.

Keep working, he told himself. Keep getting better. Even when on the ground, keep swinging. The injury was behind him. He was playing football again, and he was playing for Texas A&M.

David Coolidge moved closer to the line of scrimmage, his eyes never leaving the running back. It was his job to make the tackle or turn the ball carrier inside.

He closed the gap.

Randy Wylie, a pulling guard on the sweep, hit him like a rock.

His eyes spun like a pinball machine run amuck.

He hurt all over.

Coolidge climbed back to his feet, squared himself, and here came the running back again.

He closed the gap.

He knew Wylie would be there.

He knew Wylie would cut him into a pile of pulpwood chips before the drill had ended that day. Coolidge didn't wait to get drilled again this time. He charged the ball carrier. If Wylie hit him, Wylie would have to catch him.

Wham!

Wylie caught him. The guard reached down to pick him up. You 12th guys are insane, he said. We keep beating up on you, and you let us keep beating up on you.

Coolidge grinned.

Keep coming, he said to himself. Keep coming, and if you get there a step late, I'll make your running back hurt as badly as I do.

It didn't happen often.

Lord, it felt good when it did.

As Sean Page told him, well, *Cool Breeze*, that's what it's like to be a full-fledged member of Jackie's own personal Side Show.

It was the year Sean Page had been waiting for, his year to break into the 12th man team's starting lineup. His rookie season, at times, had been a nightmare. His defensive backs coach, Curley Hallman, had a few favorites on the 12th man, as well as on varsity, Page said. Mostly, he thought the rest of us were in his way. He was exceptionally hard on the second and third teamers. If he ran us off, and he had no qualms about running us off, Hallman certainly wouldn't be losing any sleep over it.

Hallman could be brutal, Page said, but we were scared to death of Jackie Sherrill. Some kept referring to him as Darth Vader, but never to his face.

When we messed up, those dark, deep-seated eyes of his would cut through us like a welding torch.

When I saw him coming my way, I turned and headed to the far end of the bench.

If Sherrill talked to you, only two things could happen, and both were bad.

He'd chew you out.

Or he'd cut you.

During the summer, Sean Page contracted hepatitis and mononucleosis, which led to an enlarged spleen. The doctor wouldn't clear him to

Butch Motley (25) and the 12th man receive their final instructions before taking the field.

play. Sherrill had no intention of letting him play. If a player was injured or couldn't get back on the field, Page said, Billy Pickard and Karl Kapchinski took great delight in cleaning out his locker. No sympathy. No court of appeal. If you broke a bone or maybe separated a shoulder, you were allowed back one time. Do it again, and you were out the door so fast you never heard it close. On the 12th man team, we hid our injuries. We hid our limps. We even hid our broken bones. But, I wondered, how in the world do you hide hepatitis and mononucleosis?

Every day, he checked his locker.

Every day, he saw his uniform still hanging there.

He wondered if Pickard and Kapchinski were merely playing games with him. Sean Page was physically unable to practice, so why bother with him? Why don't we wait until he's ready to come back, then throw his uniform away? Might as well throw it away. Too old. Too worn. Too ragged. Nobody else would want it.

On the 12th man unit, Page said, you always suffered from a bad case of paranoia, if nothing else.

Butch Motley was drowning in tests, he had already missed a couple of practices, and he hadn't been able to sleep since the morning he woke up and realized that he was drowning in tests. He was a month behind in his studies and losing ground every day. He was tired. He wasn't thinking straight. He was in a foul mood, and his fuse was short and already burning. When I showed up that day, he said, I smelled bad, looked bad, felt bad, and had a worse temper.

On a punt drill against scholarship players, Motley smashed through the line and collided with Chet Brooks, a good guy and great player. Everyone on the 12th man team respected Brooks. Motley respected Brooks. Nobody cared if he was always trash talking. To Chet Brooks, trash talking was merely a form of personal conversation.

As I turned around to go line up for the next snap, Motley said, Chet pushed me. His mood was as foul as mine. I spun around and gave him a good shove. There we were, a couple of roosters fighting. That was all. Chet reached out and grabbed my facemask. I grabbed his, and we proceeded to try and twist each other's head off. The players broke it up and separated us real quick. I always said that I won the skirmish

because Chet had to go in and have his fingers taped up. But I knew I was in trouble.

Coach Sherrill had a hard and fast rule against fighting with his starters. Coach Sherrill, however, never said a word to me. He turned the whole shooting match over to his scholarship players and let them hand out the punishment. I kept hitting the line but always found the big end of a sledgehammer waiting for me. I thought the punt drill would never end, and I knew damn sure the pounding would never end. They all took turns knocking me down. Line up. Knock me down again. I had more ups and downs than an elevator. In the past, somebody had always been there to help me to my feet. On that afternoon, I got up the best way I knew how, which was slow, painful, and somewhat erratic. One leg was working, but the other was lagging behind.

Spencer Baum was playing outside linebacker, he said, when John Burnett came up to him with a bright idea. Simple. But bright.

He gave us all a piece of white tape.

We stuck it across the front of our football helmets.

And we used magic markers to write our names in bold letters across the tape.

Burnett was tired of the coaches and scholarship players always saying hey, you 12th man guy, come on.

Now they knew we had names.

They may not call us by our names, but, by damn, they knew what they were.

Sean Page told Billy Pickard he needed a new helmet. His old one had one too many dead foam cells on the inside. Couldn't trust it anymore.

Pickard tossed him a helmet. Take this one, he said without smiling. It's brand new.

Page looked it over. Had a few scratches. Had the number eight written on the side. Page had seen it before. This helmet's not new, he said. It belonged to Jeff Nelson.

Don't worry about it, Pickard said. He was a wide receiver. Didn't get hit much. Didn't use his head much. The helmet's as good as new.

Page immediately went to find Sly Calhoun. Hey, he said. I need a new helmet.

Can't help you.

Why not?

You got a little head, Calhoun said. We didn't buy many helmets for little heads. Only had one left.

I'll take it.

Can't. Gave it to the fish scholarship kicker.

He's just a kicker, for God's sake. He's a freshman. He's not gonna ever see the field. Why does he need a new helmet?

Calhoun shrugged and grinned. Scholarship, he said. The boy's got one. Get yourself one of them, and somebody around here will probably buy you a new helmet.

Steam built up inside the members of the 12th man unit. The constant beating wore down their bodies and flattened their psyche to the thickness of a stale tortilla. They knew they couldn't cure what ailed them, but they found a way to mask the pain and lessen the stress that gnawed at their gut. The prescription tasted a lot like beer, and liquor seemed to have a healing power all of its own.

The house at 807 Holleman – loosely occupied by Garry Sorrell, David Fry, and John Gregg – became famous in a notorious sort of way. As Bubba Hillje said, for the next three years, it became the official unofficial frat house for the 12th man team. Parties started big and had a habit of growing a lot larger before daylight. In the back of the house, there was always a homemade craps table, fashioned from plywood with a piece of green velvet glued on top. With a little luck and a lot of friends, two kegs of beer could be miraculously transformed to twelve and one time to seventeen. A never-ending line of people spilled outside the door, waiting to get in, and the line was often strung around the block.

Garry Sorrell explained, we'd all put a few dollars in the pot to see how many kegs we could buy, but by eleven o'clock, the kegs were usually empty. We passed the hat, and complete strangers, as well as our varsity players, dropped in a ten or twenty dollar bill. Then somebody would head out to Graham's Central Station for another beer run. In the back, people crowded around the craps table, stacking those coins, folding that green, and rolling those dice. The House always won. We took their money to pay bills, and by the time we heard the school busses running outside, everybody began staggering out the door, trying to remember where they lived. Sometimes we stacked them like cord wood and let them sleep on our floor.

It took gall and guts to run the house on Holleman Street. It bordered on the law enforcement offices of a DPS trooper, constable, and Brazos County Sheriff's deputy. They kept an eye on us, Hillje said, and they wandered on in from time to time. Didn't need an invitation. Didn't need to RSVP. The door was always unlocked and usually open. However, nobody with a badge ever tried to shut the house down as long as the activities, illegal or otherwise, were kept under the roof and out of the street.

We didn't have time to get any sleep, Sorrell said. Didn't need any sleep. We weren't planning on going to class anyway. We just considered that the numbers on the dice rolling around the craps table as part of a statistics course and opened another beer.

The 12th man unit had its own initiation and indoctrination for rookies wedging their way onto the kickoff team.

It was called *wahooing* beer.

As Bubba Hillje pointed out, the convenience stores in College Station weren't allowed to sell beer after two o'clock in the morning. We lined the rookies up and, from time to time, drove them all over town. They slid into their best disguises, kept their faces well covered, waited until ten minutes after two, walked into a store carrying a handful of money, picked up a case of beer, and swaggered up to the counter.

How much for this, the rookie asked.

Man, I can't sell you no beer at this hour, the clerk would say.

The rookie would slap the money on the counter, usually a few cents more than the price of a case, yell, WAHOO, and run like hell to a waiting getaway car, usually a F350 Ford pickup truck belonging to Garry Sorrell. Its bed was rusted out so badly you could see the pavement racing along beneath the cracks, and it was held together by a few strands of rust that passed for baling or barbed wire.

Sorrell called it his RT for ranch truck. He had found it virtually abandoned and shoved back beneath the underbrush alongside the road. A farmer sold it cheap. Thought it was worthless. Probably was. Wouldn't run until Sorrell tinkered on the engine and hammered it back together. Didn't run fast. Might not run far. Made a damn good getaway truck.

As the first days of autumn fell on College Station, the sororities all began to break out their formal fall mixers, where a host of genteel and lovely young ladies of old money and good breeding invited the finest of A&M's young gentlemen for an evening of weak cocktails and strong conversation around the country club swimming pool.

The 12th man team was the hottest group on campus. No mixer would be complete without a chance to mingle and mix with the fine young All-American looking men who raced down Kyle Field like Hollywood's finest on Saturday afternoons. The fine young men not only possessed helmets and numbers, they had clean-shaven faces as well, and most, if given the chance, could even speak in complete sentences.

We came wandering into the country club as loose as lost geese with a case or two of cheap beer already under our belts, Andy McDonald said. The club was located on the right side of the tracks, and we all came from the wrong side.

Nobody was mad.

Not even upset.

The fight was rigged.

Just a couple of good old boys showing off for the ladies.

Somehow it all got out of hand. There was a sudden splash, and a cascade of water sprayed over the patio, drenching a few high-dollar coiffeurs. No one confessed. No one pointed any fingers. No one was bragging. And absolutely no one, sober or otherwise, remembered how the golf cart ended up in the swimming pool.

It was the last sorority mixer invitation the 12th man received that fall. No one was upset. A country club was never quite as good as the house on Holleman Street.

The next day at practice, the red shirts with red eyes were all wondering if word of their somewhat dubious behavior had reached the all-knowing office of Jackie Sherrill. When he looked at them, they knew that he knew, and they waited for the wrath of God to fall like brimstone on their shoulders.

Sherrill walked up and, in a soft voice, said, don't worry about the golf cart, boys. I've got your back on this one.

I guess he paid for it out of his own pocket, McDonald surmised. He never said, and we never asked.

It was Friday night, and the varsity had gone to the movies. Members of the 12th man were left to roam the streets. They weren't looking for trouble, but they did manage to stumble across it from time to time. Ronnie Glenn was sneaking back into Cain Hall, and he had no idea how many hours it was before dawn. He knew it couldn't be many.

I saw a cop at the front door, he said, so I slipped through the bushes and around to the window outside my room. I knocked on the window, hoping my roommate, Shea Walker, would hear me. No answer. No response. I started to tap on the window pane again but saw the shadow materialize and realized that someone was standing behind me. I turned around and looked into the dark face of a coach.

The coach was scowling. He grabbed Glenn by the neck. What the hell is going on, he asked.

Ronnie Glenn straightened his shoulders and said with a certain air of dignity, sir, I was returning from the library, studying for a test, and, when I walked up, I thought I saw something shiny lying on the ground. I saw the reflection in the moonlight. I came back here to see what it was, and that's when you walked up.

Do you really expect me to believe a lie like that, the coach asked.

Honest to God, Glenn said, that's what happened.

Glenn looked down.

The coach looked over his shoulder.

Damn, if there wasn't a dime lying at his feet, looking up through the dirt, shining in the moonlight.

Glenn knew his was guilty.

The coach knew he was guilty.

Neither one of them could explain the dime.

Across the length and breadth of the Southwest Conference, Jackie Sherrill was a marked man. He was wearing the latest version of a Cotton Bowl ring, and those who had ridiculed him were beginning to fear that he would have a stake in their hearts for a long time. The football monster– so aptly described by the typewriter of Randy Galloway – was loose and on the verge of running wild. As R. C. Slocum had said, the key thing for us was being able to get the right players here. Those first couple of years were crucial for us. We needed credibility to sell Texas A&M, and Jackie Sherrill gave us that. He gave us something to hang our hat on.

In 1985, Texas A&M dominated the conference. A year later, Sherrill had even loftier expectations. Before the season began, his Aggies were ranked in the top ten nationally, and some were spreading the word that A&M just might be the team to beat for the National Championship. Pressure was growing heavier with the printing of each new press release, but the kind of pressure that suffocated so many great coaches was the elixer that fueled Sherrill's massive ambition to be the best. He invested every waking hour in his drive to the top.

He also possessed a brain that was no stranger to spilling out the oddest and most controversial of ideas. At least, that's what the leering press kept writing. Sherrill was searching for ways to place Texas A&M football on the national landscape, and he had realized, from day one, that no one would ever take the Aggies seriously if their non-conference schedule were comprised solely of such teams as North Texas, Northeast Louisiana, and UTEP. Sherrill had a burning ambition to take on the big boys. Sherrill wanted to throw the gauntlet down to teams looked upon as national powerhouses. In spite of those, who once again thought he had lost all vestiges of sanity, who warned him against the idea, Sherrill had visions of heading to Baton Rouge on a Saturday night. Death Valley was what LSU called it. Death Valley was a name no one dared to dispute, especially those who had the misfortune to dueling the Cajuns in the parking lot after dark.

During 1983, Sherrill had flown to Baton Rouge to watch LSU battle Florida State, and his old mentor, television analyst Frank Broyles, asked him what he was doing so far away from College Station.

I'm talking to the LSU athletic director, Sherrill replied. I'm trying to get the series between LSU and A&M back like it used to be.

Broyles looked at him and said, you're crazy, Jackie. You'd have to be crazy to play them at Tiger Stadium.

The last time Sherrill ventured into Baton Rouge was 1965 when he was a linebacker for Bear Bryant, and the game was scheduled for the daylight hours. Coach Bryant had flat, and wisely, refused to play LSU at night, he said. There was a different atmosphere between day and night at Tiger Stadium. An LSU game in Baton Rouge was a happening. People came out of the rice fields and sugar cane fields to be a part of it.

Lynn Amedee, an old Tiger himself, knew first-hand about the angry, ribald, carnival-like emotions festering around LSU home games. The fans were rabid, and, more likely than not, the fans could make a difference in the game, he said. They got those tailgate parties started sometime on Wednesday, and the sound was deafening. To have a chance, you had to take the fans out of the game early. If you weren't ready to play, you could be embarrassed and run out of town. The Aggies just had to remember one thing, however. They weren't playing the people in the stands, just the people on the field with them.

Burnis Simon sat down with Jackie Sherrill and said, I know we have travel restrictions, Coach, but I also believe that we have some boys on the 12th man team who deserve a chance to play against LSU.

Who do you want to take?

Middleton, Coolidge, Page, Berry, Wurzbach, Glenn, Sorrell, and Boutwell would do you a good job, Simon replied. Mix them in on your varsity kickoff team, and I'll guarantee they won't let you down.

You want the whole damn bunch.

Burnis Simon grinned.

They're your responsibility.

I'll accept that.

If they lose the game for us, it's your job.

Burnis Simon grinned. Then my job's safe, he said.

Sherrill's face was grim, but Simon noticed there was the faint glimpse of a smile tucked away in the corner of his eyes. Or maybe it was just a reflection of the sunlight coming through the window.

We didn't take the bus, David Coolidge said. We flew to the LSU game. I had always worn number seven, and I told my sister, who drove to Baton Rouge, to be sure and watch out for number seven on the field. Pickard handed me a jersey with number eight on it.

What's this, I asked him.

You're number eight, aren't you, he said.

I've always been seven. Coolidge was mad now. He knew Pickard had never bothered to learn his name. He did think Pickard would bring along the right jersey.

You're number eight now, Pickard said before turning away.

My sister looked for number seven all night, Coolidge said. My friends back home watching on television looked for number seven. There was no number seven on the field that day. It was though neither number seven or I even existed.

Number eight did just fine. No one noticed.

Jeff Boutwell looked out the bus window as it eased slowly toward the stadium. There were tailgaters everywhere he looked, all grilling any creature that hadn't been able to crawl fast enough across a lake or a parking lot. The smell of smoke, he said, and the burnt aroma of barbecue splashed with beer were overpowering. Tables were filled with crawdads, and the Cajuns were pulling the little critters out of boiling, salty water and sucking their heads.

They were cussing us, Dean Berry remembered. The fans were ruthless. We could either play LSU in the stadium or fight them in the parking lot. It didn't matter to them. They were all drinking from a bottle of Jack Daniel or stronger, and when one little old lady who could have been my grandmother stepped out of the crowd, smiled sweetly at our bus as we passed by, and flagrantly shot us the bird. I knew it was going to be a long day.

Garry Sorrell remembered, it didn't matter whether those LSU fans were five years old or ninety-five years old, they were treating us like we were a bunch of mass murderers. When we climbed off the bus, we had to walk through a police gauntlet for protection. They were throwing whatever they had in their hands, beer cans, whiskey bottles, rocks, wads of tinfoil, toilet paper.

Don't feel bad, a policeman said.

Why not, Sorrell asked.

Bubba Hillje (13) had a career with the 12th man team that was intertwined with triumphs, disappointments, and raw emotions. He played hard for both Jackie Sherrill and R. C. Slocum, and during his senior year, he would make his last bittersweet stand on the Rio Grande in El Paso's Sun Bowl.

It's not personal, he said. They treat every team this way.

And then there was Mike. A tiger mascot. A real, live, genuine tiger mascot. Mad when he woke up that morning.

They positioned him next to the door of the visitor's dressing room, Boutwell said. Coach Sherrill was talking to us, going over the game plan for the final time, and we could hear Mike roaring. They were out there, poking him with a long stick, slapping the side of his cage, trying to rile him up to make sure he was good and mad and growling as hard as he could by the time we ran out of the dressing room. He was so close to the door, we could smell his breath, and it was a little unsettling to see him leaping across the cage at us. We were pumped up. Mike was pumped up. His teeth were flashing like daggers, and we had to fight our way past the tiger just to get to the field.

Everybody in the stands hated us, Boutwell said, so the 12th man raced up and down the sidelines, waving our towels. It was our way to thumbing our noses at 79,000 people who just may have been a little crazier and a lot more liquored up than we were. We were separated from the LSU fans by a chain link fence, and the first couple of rows were so close they could reach out and touch our shoulder pads. They offered us a good cussing, and they were pretty good at it. Then they offered us all a beer. No good will. Just a chance to get us drunk. Didn't think we could play well drunk. They'd never been to the house on Holleman Street.

Jeff Boutwell had never seen Johnny Holland so intense. Holland had graduated from Hempstead High School, and so had LSU's great running back, Harvey Williams. Holland had done his best to recruit Williams to A&M, and the Aggies thought they had a better than average chance of landing the number one running back in the state. But at the last minute, Harvey Williams unceremoniously turned his back on A&M and signed with the Tigers. Williams always claimed he hadn't made up his mind until signing day when he walked down the hall to pen his signature on a letter of intent. He said he heard some fellow students singing "The Aggie War Hymn," and, at that moment, he decided to cast his fate with the Tigers.

Johnny Holland had not forgiven him.

Holland was focused, Boutwell said. He had the look of an assassin in his eyes. Every time Harvey Williams touched the ball, Holland was all over him like ugly on an ape. As Larry Bowen of the *Bryan Eagle* wrote, Holland knocked Williams silly with a hard hit that sent the freshman stumbling to the sidelines. Williams would finish the game with a scant fifty-six yards and a hip pointer, both compliments of Johnny Holland.

On A&M's second kickoff, Ronnie Glenn busted into a blocker at the 10-yard line, blasting through like a dynamite cap and leaving Williams alone and unprotected. The wedge was in shambles. Williams was like quicksilver, always one shift, one slant, a single step from going the distance as quick as the snap of a bullwhip. He looked right. He looked left. All he saw were Aggies. Nothing but Aggies. He went down at the fifteen, buried and fighting for air instead of yards. Glenn stood up and grinned. Score one for the good guys, he thought.

In the fourth quarter, Glenn finally had a chance to personally introduce himself to Harvey Williams. The kick was high and deep, and Glenn broke free again. He wasn't nearly as strong as those massive blockers who made up the wedge, but he was faster and a step quicker. Williams caught the ball near the goal line, and when he broke, Glenn hammered him with the force of a tire tool swung in anger. The illustrious Harvey Williams felt as though he were juggling hand grenades with the pins coming loose. He had not planned on being caught, much less nailed, by a volunteer walk-on, which was as surprising as a bolt of lightning from a blue sky.

Williams hit the ground first.

Thud.

A heavy thud.

He also got up first.

Ronnie Glenn wasn't sure he could get up at all. As he limped groggily toward the sidelines, Wurzbach asked, are you okay?

I think it's a stinger.

Get some ice. Wurzbach grinned. If it's not broke, you can play, he said. Hell, you can still play if it's not broke bad.

The game started so well for the Aggies. It turned ugly after halftime. Before the largest crowd in LSU history, before a national television audience, A&M turned the ball over five times in a hot, sweltering September evening and lost 35-17. It's very simple, Kevin Murray told the leering press. The Aggie quarterback just didn't play well. He didn't get the big plays when we needed them. Kevin Murray had looked in the mirror, then spelled out the blame where it belonged. He was too much of a man to do otherwise.

During two-a-days, Dean Berry had moved his way up to third-team linebacker. I had been having some good practices and turning a few heads, he said. Even Berry was surprised when R. C. Slocum walked up to him before the LSU game and said, get ready, son, I've decided to play you're a little. I'm counting on you.

Berry's emotions, within a single breath, reached an all-time high. His work on the scout team had not been a lost cause after all.

During the game, he stood beside the bench.

And he waited.

He made sure he was close enough to Slocum so the defensive co-ordinator would not have to go looking for him. He was ready whenever Slocum needed him.

And he waited.

The game dragged on.

The seconds ticked down.

At the final whistle, Dean Berry, other than racing down on kick-offs, had not reached the field. He had never been more disappointed or down and out in his life. His weekend became a lost weekend.

The bitterness didn't last long. Berry's father had always told him, son, they are going to play their best players. It was not what Berry had wanted to hear, but he knew it was the truth. A week later, he hoped there had been a cornerstone of truth behind his father's words because R. C. Slocum sent him into the game to play linebacker against North Texas State. It was his moment in the sun. No tackles, perhaps, but Dean Berry could look around and see himself standing shoulder to shoulder with the varsity. He was one of them. God does answer prayers after all, he thought.

Harold Huggins had waited a long time for North Texas. After playing fullback for Churchill High School in San Antonio, he had spent a couple of years at UTSA, then decided to move on to Texas A&M. He had a couple of friends on the 12th man team, Dan Pollard and Sean Page, but he had no intention of ever putting on his cleats again. He had cleaned his conscience of football. There had been good times in high school, but the good times had all faded in a hurry. Huggins was in class most of the time, he had a job managing one of the city swimming pools, and football, he knew, was damn near a full-time commitment. Page told him, I made the team, and you and Pollard both were a hell of a lot better than I was in high school. The power of persuasion finally convinced Huggins to tryout. Didn't mind practice. Didn't mind the violence. Didn't mind the collisions. The cuts, however, were brutal. He saw grown men walk away with tears of disappointment in their eyes. He kept hanging on. Didn't know why. Didn't care why. He kept taping himself back together and hanging on. The names of the final selections were taped to the door, and Harold Huggins had earned a spot on the 12th man unit.

North Texas would be his first test in battle. Harold Huggins would be going downfield on his first kickoff. He couldn't wait.
I knew Texas A&M would score a lot of points that day, he said. I knew that a bunch of touchdowns translated into a lot of kickoffs. Even a rookie stood a pretty good chance of tasting a little sweat and blood that day. It would be his time to shine.

But practice got in the way.

Jackie Sherrill had not been pleased with the sloppy performance of his Aggies down in the heart of Cajun country. He did not like losses. He did not like mistakes. He could not correct the loss, but with God as his witness, he could eliminate the mistakes. Practices during the next

week were harder than usual.

Harold Huggins didn't care. He liked the drive, the pressure, the competition. He raced downfield, searching, he said, for some unsuspecting soul to terminate at the point of contact. Whether he happened to be carrying the ball or not was inconsequential. Huggins always said, if I have to run that far, then I'm gonna hit something in cleats.

He planted his foot.

His ankle rolled.

The hit came moments later.

The pain arrived late.

Against North Texas, Harold Huggins was on the field all right, but he was slumped over crutches with a pin in a broken foot.

His assumption had been correct. Texas A&M did score a lot of points that day, forty-eight to be exact, and the 12th man team went down on a lot of kickoffs. For the offense, everything clicked whether Murray or Craig Stump was under center. The game did not wash away the bitter taste left over from the LSU loss, but it helped. Huggins believed one of those tackles on kickoff coverage would have been his, but he would never know for sure. A pair of crutches could flat cut down on a man's foot speed.

Only Rick Tankersley did not bask in the thrill of victory. He tore a hamstring, and, he said, it felt as though somebody had taken a muscle and ripped it out with his bare hands. It would be, he knew, a long and forgettable season. No practice. No games. No hits. No tackles. No glory, If he didn't go the beer joints with Shawn Slocum, he would see no action at all, which was why Tankersley wound up at the wrong place at the wrong time, looking for the wrong man to fight. Slocum wasn't afraid of anybody, he said. A series of concussions had cut short his football career, but he still had the mentality of a linebacker, especially when he emptied a bottle or two. Never saw a tackle he couldn't make. Never saw a fight he couldn't win. When Shawn Slocum walked through the door, he already had his fists clenched, and his eyes were darting wildly around, seeing if they could find for the biggest guy in the room. I thought he might be off his rocker. I knew I was off mine for just being there.

He and Tankersley were at the Roxie, standing impatiently in line to order their beers.

I don't think there's anybody in here I can't whip, Slocum said.

Not tonight.

Bunch of little drunks in here, Slocum said. That's all I see. A bunch of little damn drunks.

That's what was worrying Rick Tankersley. When there was just as bunch of little drunks, it always wound up with him and Shawn Slocum taking on the whole lot of them.

Takes ten or more to make it a fair fight, Slocum said. He looked around to see which ten might be drunk enough to go to war. There were three, maybe. Eight if he had time to wait a spell. But, hell, the night was still young. I bet the bouncer could put up a damn good fight, Slocum said. Hell, the bouncer gets paid to fight.

Look, Shawn, Tankersley said, I'm here to find a girl. That's the only reason I came. So if you start a fight, I'm calling the cops on you.

Girls are easy to find, Slocum told him. A dime a dozen. Cheaper on the weekends. A good fight is a once-in-a-lifetime experience.

Hell, Shawn, Tankersley said, for you, it's a once-in-a night experience. He felt a twinge in his hamstring. The tear hadn't healed, and sometimes he felt as though it might never heal. He looked around for the girls. Only a few had made it to Roxie's. It wasn't a good night to troll. Hell, he thought, if it weren't for the damn hamstring, a good fight might be a damn good way to spend the evening after all. Down and out at Roxie's. Hell, it sounded like a country song.

A triumphant Coach Jackie Sherrill rises to the top of the Southwest Conference with another title and trip to the Cotton Bowl.

Chapter 21

Brian Carpenter found a note taped to the door of his dorm room. It was short and cryptic and to the point. Coach Sherrill wants to see you, the note said. Be at his office at one o'clock.

Carpenter sighed. It was not a good omen, he thought. I did something wrong. Coach finally found out I never played football in high school. He knows I was in the Aggie band. He doesn't think I have a place on the 12th man team. He doesn't believe I have the right stuff. He's gonna cut me.

Carpenter walked into Jackie Sherrill's office promptly at one o'clock. His jaws were clinched. He was afraid to blink.

Come on in, Brian, Sherrill said.

Well, that's a good sign, Carpenter thought. Coach at least knows my name.

His chest wasn't as tight as it had been.

Son, I'm moving you into Cain Hall, Sherrill said.

Now Carpenter was beginning to feel a whole lot better. Coach was taking him out of his dorm and giving him a room where the real football players lived. Maybe I've done something right after all, he decided.

Sherrill said without fanfare, I'm rooming you with John Roper.

The smile faded on Carpenter's face. Roper was a great player, he knew, but he had come from the rough side of Houston, the wrong side

of town, where gunshots and stabbings were commonplace. John Roper had a reputation for being as mean as a snake and possibly as vicious as a grizzly, only slightly bigger, a little faster, and a lot stronger.

Jackie Sherrill leaned across his desk. Son, he said, let me explain your job as a member of the 12th man team. Every day, I want you to pry John Roper out of bed every day and make sure he gets to his one o'clock class on time. If he doesn't attend class, he is not going to be eligible to play, and we need him. I've already explained all of this to John, so if he doesn't want to get up, don't try to fight him or antagonize him. Just come get me. He won't fight me. He won't fight me but once.

Thus began the strange, symbiotic, odd-couple friendship between a football player who would one day sign a professional contract with the Chicago Bears, and a football player who didn't have the slightest idesa of how to put on his pads.

They roomed together.

They ate lunch together.

Carpenter walked Roper to his one-clock class to make sure he was never late.

In practice, when Carpenter ran the ball, John Roper tried to knock him back into the middle of last week and usually succeeded. When we collided, Carpenter said, I never won.

Roper reached down and picked him off the ground. Sorry, Roper said, but I had a little too much gin last night. I'm hungover and my head hurts. Brian, dammit, if you just don't run that hard, then I won't hit you that hard.

Carpenter nodded. He heard Bob Davie yell, run it again.

Don't run so hard, John Roper said under his breath.

Carpenter came as hard as he could.

Now his head was hurting. No. It was dangling by a thread. No. The thread had already broken. He felt like he had a hangover, and Carpenter couldn't remember a drop of gin ever touching his innards.

The game with independent Southern Miss was, as always, an absolute nightmare. The Aggies dominated defensively, sacking the Golden Eagle quarterback seven times, holding USM to ninety-nine yards of total offense, and only allowing USM to penetrate A&M territory twice during the game.

Unfortunately, if Scott Slater had not kicked three field goals, the Aggies would not have escaped with a 16-7 victory. Those who had boldly predicted that A&M might be rolling downhill toward a national cham-

Lord, where was everybody?

Miss the tackle, and the 12th man would forever live in infamy, especially in a game where the Aggies were desperately fighting to put any points on the board. A runback for a touchdown was unforgivable. A runback by Southern Mississippi would condemn them all to purgatory. He could almost hear the cell door slamming shut.

Coolidge sliced his way past the blockers, jarred the ball carrier, spun him around, knocked him off balance, and gave him a solid introduction to Kyle Field turf. One step and he would have been gone. He hadn't had time to take the step.

It was a good day after all.

For Coolidge, it was as good as it got.

Purgatory would have to wait.

The 12th man unit wasn't coming today.

When we scored midway through the second quarter, Dennis Mudd was so pumped that he started head-butting us on the sideline.

One problem.

We were wearing helmets.

Mudd was a coach. He wasn't. He bled right along with us.

On Sunday, while everyone was having ice placed on their bumps and bruises, while they sat in the whirlpool and let the hot water soak away the pain, the 12th man player of the game was announced.

The award goes to David College.

That's what he said.

Not Coolidge.

College.

He glanced at the players, and everyone was snickering, trying hard to keep from laughing out loud. So that's the recognition I get for pulling on old number seven and going out to bleed, he told himself.

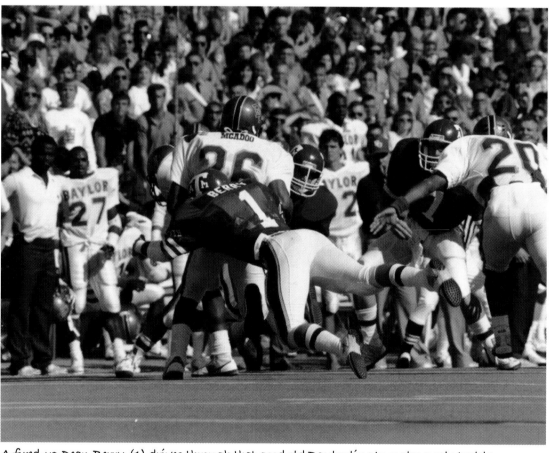

A fired-up Dean Berry (1) drives through that good old Baylor line to make a solo tackle.

Russ Birdwell had seen the train go rolling down the tracks early in the evening, long before the party turned soggy with warm beer, never stale, but warm and plentiful. It was Friday night, varsity was watching a downtown movie, and members of the 12th man were slowly drinking themselves down to their first kickoff against

Texas Tech. The lowly Red Raiders. The hated Red Raiders. Damn the Red Raiders. Hand me another beer. No. Hand me two. Birdwell stood outside on the porch and watched the lonesome old train as it slowly disappeared into the distance.

He turned to a friend, who had driven down from Lubbock, and said, you know, I'd like to ride that train someday.

Buy yourself a ticket.

I'd rather jump on when it comes rolling past again.

You're crazy.

So I've been told.

Where does it go?

pionship had quietly tossed their hopes aside and thrown themselves off the bandwagon.

For David Coolidge, it was both a moment to remember and a memory to forget. He crashed down on a kickoff against the Golden Eagles and saw the ball carrier with darting eyes cut toward the middle. Two blockers were out front and leading the way.

He had the angle.

The ball carrier had daylight.

To the other side of town, Birdwell said.

Nobody's stopping you.

Nobody indeed.

By two-thirty, neither Birdwell nor his friend thought he was particularly crazy.

They heard the train before they saw it. Both began slipping and sliding as they hurried alongside the track, and when the train slowed down, they jumped on a flat car and felt the hot wind sting their faces.

Damn fine feeling, Birdwell said.

Riding the rails,

Free as birds.

Headed for God knows where, or at least to the other side of town. That's where trains went. Over there somewhere. They always stopped on the other side of town.

When we reached the other side of town, Birdwell said, the train didn't even slow down. It passed the city limit sign on a dead run and was picking up speed.

We gotta jump, he said.

Can't, his friend told him.

Why not?

This sumbitch is going forty miles an hour, maybe faster.

The ground was flying along beneath them.

Rocks.

Grass.

Weeds.

Big Rocks.

Higher weeds.

A blur in the night.

By the time the train jerked its way into the outskirts of Reagan, it began slowing down because of some work on the bridge. We didn't have a choice, Birdwell said. Get off now or we might wind up in Waco, and I didn't even know if the damn train would stop in Waco.

We jumped, hit the ground, and started rolling. The ground felt like a John Roper elbow in the face. We were in the middle of nowhere. The night was pitch black. We heard wild dogs howling. At least, they sounded wild to us. I know damn sure they were mad. Highway 6 was on our right. I figured we were probably fifty miles from College Station.

Our breath still smelled like a brewery.

Russ Birdwell and his friend walked into town and found an all-night service station. The attendant looked up and saw them, wearing shorts and sweat shirts and covered with grease, dirt, and grime. Their faces were black. Their hair was lacquered with suet. They looked like oil slicks in tennis shoes.

Sir, we'd like to use the phone, Birdwell said.

The attendant studied him.

The boy was damn polite for an oil slick in tennis shoes.

He reached into the cooler, gave each of them a Gatorade, then made the call himself. He called the Reagan police department. He thought we had escaped from the prison in Huntsville, Birdwell said. The police had a good laugh when I told them our story. The attendant had a good laugh. I knew we must have broken a few laws. The police figured we had suffered enough. I could see the first steaks of daylight rising above the trees, and it dawned on me that I had a football game at one o'clock. Reality sobered me up in a hurry. I didn't think Coach Sherrill would delay the game if I were running a little late.

Russ Birdwell and his friend stood alongside the highway, waiting for any signs of early morning traffic. The headlights were few and far between. Birdwell wasn't sure it was even safe to ride with someone foolish enough to pick up a pair of oil slicks in tennis shoes. They hitchhiked their way back to College Station and arrived on campus at high noon.

There was no time to shower, Birdwell said. I washed the grease and dirt off my face and hands, left it on the rest of me, suited up, and slipped in with the team that was already on the field warming up. I hoped no one noticed. If they did, no one cared.

I sat exhausted on the bench. No sleep. Long train ride. Longer

walk back. The aftermath of a good beer party was pounding my head.

I wanted to play against Tech.

My ego wanted me to play.

I prayed for the chance to play.

And I hoped to God that Coach Simon wouldn't send me in.

The Aggies cruised past Texas Tech, 45-8, with Red Raider quarterback Billy Joe Tolliver, from whistle to whistle, running for his life. Defensive end Rod Saddler said, with people flying at you from every angle, I think you would tend to get a little rattled.

What's the defensive scheme you use, a sports writer asked.

Oh, said Sadler, we just jump in there and fly around a lot.

The University of Houston didn't offer much resistance, and A&M hammered its way to a 19-7 win that was not nearly as close as the score indicated. Scott Slater kicked four field goals, which gave him eleven for the year, not bad for a walk-on. Murray's eighteen completions enabled him to break Edd Hargett's school career record of 408. By halftime, the Cougars had managed only one first down and one yard of total offense. It didn't get much better the second half. The game gave Jackie Sherrill a sense of personal satisfaction. It marked Texas A&M's first win in six games at the Astrodome and its first win over the Cougars in Houston since 1952.

John Burnett had burst past the wedge and was running down a clear lane when the clip came. It was brutal, he said. Felt like I had been trying to outrun a cyclone with a good tail wind, and it caught me from behind. My head snapped back. My legs buckled. I fell on my wrist and broke it. All I could see was the ball carrier speeding past me and headed for midfield. We were, as usual, one of the nation's leaders in the fewest number of yards allowed by a kickoff team, and I couldn't force myself to look back over my shoulders. It wasn't the pain. I knew he was riding high with one of the longest returns I had ever seen, and he had broken it past me. I was the culprit. I was on the ground, and he wasn't.

Two flags went down.

One flag would have been fine, Burnett said. Thank God for two.

Both referees had seen the clip, and the ball was coming back.

John Burnett had no idea when he would be back. It didn't take nearly as long as he had feared. He wore a cast, wrapped in foam, for the rest of the season. Before every game, the referees checked carefully to make sure the cast wouldn't be viewed or used as a dangerous or lethal weapon. Burnett grinned. He would take any weapon he could get.

Burnett kept playing.

The wrist refused to heal.

The bones had gone dead.

It would take surgery and a screw to finally put the wrist back together again.

When Baylor came to town, it was a family feud. Across the field, clad in green and gold stood Ray Berry. Full of emotions. Most of them mixed. He had wanted to go to Texas A&M. His father and older brother had played football at Texas A&M, and he had a younger brother, Dean, firmly entrenched on the 12th man team. Ray Berry had even been recruited to play for the Aggies, but the scholarship offer came from Tom Wilson. When Jackie Sherrill hit town, all previous offers had been quickly suspended, then shredded.

Sherrill had no interest in knowing the names or the players who appealed to Tom Wilson. He would go out and find his own. But time and again, Sherrill would say, I made a grave mistake by letting Ray Berry go. The Aggies had a great linebacker corps, to be sure, but Ray Berry

Dean Berry (1) prepares to square off against his brother, Ray, an All-Conference linebacker for Baylor. Understanding the importance of families and family rivalries, Coach Jackie Sherrill named Dean one of the Aggie team captains for the game.

was All-Conference and destined to play for the Minnesota Vikings and Seattle Seahawks. Sherrill named Dean Berry as one of his captains for the Baylor game, and the two bothers met face-to-face at midfield. For Sherrill, it was an admirable gesture.

Sean Page was sitting in the back of the dressing room, pressed against the wall, when Jackie Sherrill walked into the room. Texas A&M was in the midst of a roller-coaster winning streak after the humiliation in Baton Rouge, and he knew that Baylor, if no one else, had the talent to derail the Aggie Express. After all, Page had played with the Bears' quarterback in high school. He knew Cody Carlson had the God-given ability to pick a good team apart and surgically slice up a bad one. He feared Cody Carlson, but not nearly as much as he feared Jackie Sherrill.

As David Coolidge remembered, Baylor was a good team and always on the verge of being great. However, it seemed that Coach Sherrill held a festering grudge against Baylor Coach Grant Teaff for ridiculing and criticizing his idea to form the 12th man team. Coach was slow to forgive. He never forgot.

Butch Motley remembered, Sherrill was never a rah-rah, get excited, come in yelling and screaming, fire 'em up kind of coach. He could get you ready to play, but he had a different approach. Coach Sherrill simply gave you the facts, made sure you had a grasp of the game plan, pump you up mentally, and let you fire up your own emotions.

None of them had ever seen the Jackie Sherrill who came storming into the dressing room that afternoon. He told his team about reading a book written by Grant Teaff. In it, Teaff casually mentioned that the Baylor alumni had told him, as long as you win the sixth game of the season, you'll always have a job coaching the Bears. Well, Baylor's clash with Texas A&M usually managed to be the sixth game of the year.

Motley said, Coach Sherrill suddenly held up a wristwatch for everybody to see. It was an official Baylor Cotton Bowl watch from some years past, he said, and someone had mailed it to him. Sherrill yelled, this is not a damn Timex. It's a Rolex. And I don't think any more of the Baylor Bears that I do this watch.

Jackie Sherrill wheeled around and threw the watch as hard as he could against a rolling blackboard, which had been conveniently placed behind him.

The Rolex exploded.

Glass shattered, Vince Palasota said. Tiny diamonds scattered and bounced across the floor. A ruby rolled under a chair. The watch fell in hundreds of fragments.

Motley remembered, the room grew deathly quiet. Then suddenly it erupted. We all started whooping and hollering and jumping up and down. We burst out of the room and raced out of control onto the field.

It was the most fired up I had ever seen a Texas A&M team.

Coolidge said, we were running on raw emotion, and by the time we could see the scoreboard with clearer heads and a sharper focus, we were behind 17-0.

Mickey Herskowitz re-lived the game in the *Houston Post*: The experts in the press box nodded knowingly, he wrote. This was a day when the Texas Aggies had lost their carbonation completely. They were so flat, a danger existed that the nation's 11th-ranked team might get plastered by a scary margin. But if ever a team was qualified to dig out of a ditch, it had to be those blessed farmers from the Brazos Bottoms. Trailing for more than fifty-six minutes, Texas A&M staged a comeback that sent the historians flipping through the calendars and their coach all but flipping his lid.

At halftime, Sean Page said, R. C. Slocum made some of his patented adjustments in the nickel and dime packages, and Coolidge recalled, Slocum was upset because his defense had not played up to its potential. In a calm, monotone emotionless voice, he told us: There comes a point in life, gentlemen, when you realize that there are people always depending on you. The dry cleaners is depending on you bringing in your clothes. The mechanic is depending on you bringing in your car. The barber is depending on you for a hair cut. This afternoon, gentlemen, I am depending on you. Your family is depending on you. Your friends are depending on you. Aggies everywhere are depending on you. You can't afford to make any more mistakes. You can't afford to let us down.

No one, no one, could coach a defense like R. C. Slocum.

Period.

It was a new Aggie team that somberly took the field for the final thirty minutes of play. Baylor had led by ten twice, by six twice, and by three on three occasions. The Bears had never trailed. Even with Baylor out front 30-24, Kevin Murray said, I felt like we were finally in command. Johnny Holland glanced at the scoreboard, grinned, and predicted, boys, this one is ours, 31-30. Johnny Holland was a prophet. Ken Sury wrote in the *Battalion*, on the final touchdown, Murray was at his best, hitting two key third-down strikes to tight end Rod Bernstine to keep the drive alive. His last toss of the afternoon was a bobbled catch in the end zone by wide receiver Tony Thompson that sent the majority of the 74,739 spectators into a frenzy. A beleaguered Grant Teaff told sports writers after the game, spell the win Murray. He escaped our pressure and did the job. On third down, he was just incredible. In those situations, he got the ball there by an eyelash. It was like he was throwing rocks through a slat.

Chet Brooks stood up and said, we see this Aggie team as a machine. We'll get you from California to New York. No one had any idea what he was talking about, but the leering press thought it made a damn good quote.

The 31-30 win, years later, would be voted as the greatest game of the decade. Those who witnessed it would not disagree.

For Butch Motley, it was indeed a day to remember. The nobody bull rider from Nowhere, Texas, walked away with two tackles on kickoffs, and the second one turned a little bizarre.

Slater kicked toward the scoreboard end of the field, Motley said, and the ball hooked left, which was my side of the field. Ronnie Glenn took out a three-man wedge with a hell of a hit. I was following right behind Glenn and took a clear shot at the ball carrier. He crumpled back on his heels, fumbled, and I frantically tried to crawl over him to grab the football before it rolled out of bounds. I just wasn't quick enough. The sidelines snatched it away from me.

I was pumped.

The team was pumped.

And in the television booth, Lynn Swann ignored me altogether and gave Glenn credit for the tackle. Well, he didn't actually call Ronnie Glenn by name. He was on the air, screaming that our punter and backup quarterback Craig Stump had made the tackle.

Stump and Ronnie Glenn wore the same number nine. Swann didn't have a clue.

Glenn was slow to rise to his feet. He looked like the leaning tower of Pisa, Motley said, and didn't know which way to lean. The day for Glenn became definitely darker than it had been. He took off his helmet and looked at it. It was bent, and it was scarred with swatches of green and gold paint, Baylor green and gold paint. He grinned as he started to fall. Motley caught him before he hit the ground.

You all right, Dennis Mudd asked when Glenn reached the sidelines. He had seen players with the staggers before.

Have we scored again? That was all Glenn wanted to know.

Not yet.

I'll be ready when we do, Glenn said.

The kickoff was a boomer, end-over-end and landing five yards deep in the end zone. I was supposed to blow up the wedge, David Fronk said, cause a wreck and create a little holy havoc. Didn't take a lot of skill. Took a lot of guts. That was second nature. I thought the Baylor kick returner was going to take a knee, but then he stood up. I never slowed down. Find a blocker and take him out. Open a crease for the ball guys. That's all I was thinking. I saw the blocker, and I hit him just as he turned his back to me. I was in the air, and he was slowly turning around. I saw his back and nothing else. There were no brakes in mid-air. Flags were going up while he was going down.

In the midst of what sounded like 80,000 screaming fans, I could hear one voice.

An unmistakable voice.

The grim reaper must have a voice like that.

Dammit, Fronk.

The voice belonged to Coach Sherrill, and I knew I was in trouble.

He was standing on the 50-yard line.

I ran off the field at the twenty.

Where is he, Sherrill was screaming as he stalked down the sideline. Where the hell is he?

Who?

Fronk.

About that time, he saw me.

Fronk, come here. Dammit, son, Sherrill said, I don't care if that son of thistle-eatin' jackass is looking straight at you with his butt, you can't hit him.

It won't happen again.

You're damn right, it won't happen again.

You gonna bench me?

Hell, no, Sherrill barked, but, by damn, it won't happen again.

After the game, Butch Motley ran into his old 12th man coach, Roy Kokemoor, now roaming the sidelines as the head man for A&M Consolidated High School football. He said, I have some players who always watch out for your number twenty-five on kickoffs.

Why me, Motley wondered.

They say your either knock the hell out of someone, Kokemoor said, or somebody knocks the hell out of you. Makes good theater.

Two of A&M's great traditions at Texas A&M were the Corps of Cadets and the 12th man team, represented by David Fry.

Chapter 22

The Aggies had won five in a row. Rice made it six as A&M marched away on the favorable side of a 45-10 score. I had a nightmare about Rice beating us, Chet Brooks had said. I woke up in a cold sweat with owls flying around my head. There would be no upset, no more owls than usual, and the ones who did make their way into Rice Stadium weren't flying very high.

Kevin Murray fired a 26-yard touchdown pass to flanker Rod Harris, the fortieth of his career, re-writing the Southwest Conference record book and breaking the tie he shared with A&M's Edd Hargett and SMU's Chuck Hixon.

It had become a dam with too many leaks. The 12th man kickoff team was no different from the little Dutch boy with too few fingers. There were simply more holes breaking loose on kickoffs than the 12th man could plug. It was sandlot football, a Chinese fire drill, and the famed 12th man precision had begun to fall apart like a cheap suitcase.

Butch Motley said, one of the first rules for covering kicks was that you never, never, ever let one of the front-line blockers get a piece of you, block you, or slow you down. We were supposed to pooch kick, but Slater rifled one of his patented line drives, and the returner took the ball on a dead run. One of our wedge busters lost his balance and fell, taking down another one of his own men. The dominoes were beginning

to fall. Danny Balcar, maybe the fastest guy on the whole team, outran the coverage. A huge hole suddenly flared open on the right side.

The 12th man was in the middle of a perfect storm.

The ball carrier blasted through the hole with Ronnie Glenn and Motley trying desperately to cut the angle. Thank goodness, Glenn caught him around the fifty-yard line, Motley said. If the ball carrier was waiting on me to catch him, he would have still been running. It was the longest kickoff return ever against the 12th man, and I had the misfortune of being the first one coming off the field.

Jackie Sherrill came running up, spitting out words that you couldn't use in either mixed company or in church. I tried to tell myself that he was yelling at the whole kickoff team, but he was looking squarely at me. I simply stood there and waited for him to run out of gas. Whatever I told him, I knew, would be the wrong answer.

When Coach Sherrill paused to catch his breath, I cut a beeline for the end of the bench and hid out until we scored again. Coach was too mad to recognize my face or remember my number. Numbers didn't matter. He gave all of us new names that game.

The next week, Kevin Murray took the Aggie road show to SMU, and A&M beat the clock one more time. Larry Bowen of the *Bryan Eagle* wrote, used to be, the Aggies never lost – they just ran out of time.

Lately, even the clock has been no threat. It was the second time in three weeks that the tenth-ranked Aggies stared a loss in the face and rallied to win. This time it was 39-35. After SMU scored to take the lead with 2:53 left in the game, Murray moved A&M fifty-one pressure-packed yards in four plays, capped by the winning pass to Keith Woodside.

I always have confidence in Murray, Chet Brooks said. When he's lined up behind center, you can score in a hurry. He can put it in the end zone in a New York second. Said Sherrill, this team probably reaches down and gets a little more extra than any football team I've ever been on or coached.

Two members of the 12th man kickoff team, Ronnie Glenn and Dean Berry, had traveled to Dallas. For Berry, it became a quick trip to the twilight zone. On the opening kickoff, while his parents were running late and listening to the game on the radio, he ran smack into a black abyss from which he could not escape. He may have been hit head-on. He may have been hit from the side. He may have been hit with a hammer. Dean Berry had no recollection at all of the impact.

He said, I was sprawled on my back, looking up at the face of God through the opening high above Texas Stadium.

A trainer knelt on the ground beside him, waving smelling salts under his nose. Wake up, the trainer kept saying.

Berry opened his eyes. How long have I been lying here, he asked.

Three minutes at least.

Get me off the field.

They took my helmet off, Berry said, and, for the next five days, I lived in a far different world. My brain must have hit the back of my skull like a freeway collision. For the rest of the game, I sat on the bench, looking up at the scoreboard, asking anyone who happened to be nearby, who's winning? What's the score?

After awhile, no one would sit beside him.

On the long bus ride back to College Station, with dazed eyes and a dull throb beating out a strange rhythm in the back of his head, Berry kept asking, who won?

We did, Glenn said.

What's the score?

Doesn't matter.

Did I look bad out there?

No answer.

Tell me, Berry said. Did I look bad?

After the fifth time Berry asked the same question, Glenn turned to him and said, you looked like a dumb ass. Now shut up, and go back to sleep.

Ronnie Glenn stood up and changed seats.

Back home, his friends told him, too bad, Berry. You missed one helluva game.

The final score against TCU did not relieve, soothe, or alleviate the simmering feud between Jackie Sherrill and Jim Wacker. The Aggies ushered the Frogs out of town with an embarrassing 74-10 massacre even though the final accumulation of points was put on the scoreboard by Aggies who had seldom ever dirtied their uniforms in a game. Earlier in a week, Sherrill had agreed with most coaches and sports pundits when he told

the leering press that TCU had the best talent in the league. Before the season began, he even predicted that the Frogs should be the surprise team in the SWC.

Well, the Frogs promptly dropped to 1-6 in conference play, had eleven starters injured, and Wacker was upset, believing that Sherrill had criticized the coaching job he had done. Great talent. Bad coach. That, to him, was the between-the-lines inference. Wacker struck back, and the words he had for Jackie Sherrill in his pre-game press conference were not particularly kind or forgiving ones. Most just figured the TCU coach was still fuming about A&M's controversial on-side kick the year before. But Kevin Murray told the cadre of sports writers, Wacker always has some negative things to say to the press. I didn't expect him to say anything nice. It's just his nature. He likes to downgrade people. It comes back in your face. It did today.

How many points could the first team have scored if Sherrill had left you in for the full sixty minutes, Murray was asked.

No telling, Murray said. Maybe ninety.

Why not a hundred?

I don't dislike TCU that much, he said.

It was, however, a record-setting day in Aggieland: 708 yards of total offense, 38 first downs, and 74 points. Rod Bernstine passed Jeff Nelson as A&M's career reception leader with 98 catches, not bad for an old running back who fought the move to tight end. Shea Walker moved into second place with 94 catches. And Scott Slater tied Alan Smith for the A&M single season record of 18 field goals.

John Burnett had made the sacrifice. He dutifully worked on the scout team as a linebacker, always hoping he would play the position in a game, knowing he would probably never be good enough to start but believing he had the raw talent to line up and stick somebody

David Fry (14) waves the famous 12th man towel as he, Sean Page (17), John Burnett (6), and Danny Balcar (2) head off the field after another successful day of kickoff coverage.

at the line of scrimmage. He wanted as many chances as he could get. Burnett would have been satisfied with one.

Bob Davie turned to him as the scoreboard kept lighting up like a pinball machine. Get ready, John, he said. You're going in.

Davie's words hit him like an electric shock.

He grabbed his helmet.

TCU fumbled.

The Aggies recovered.

Bob Davie turned to him again. Forget it, he said.

There was enough disappointment to go around. The Aggies exploded to a fifty seven-point lead late in the fourth quarter, and Curley Hallman walked down the sidelines toward Sean Page and David Coolidge.

He looked at one, then the other.

Which one of you plays left cornerback, he asked.

We didn't know what to think, Page said. It came out of the blue, and the thought of a walk-on, a member of the 12th man team going onto the field to play a position, was the ultimate dream come true.

I looked at Coolidge. He looked at me.

We both raised our hands, Coolidge said. That irritated Hallman. He knew one of us was lying. He just couldn't remember which one worked out at left cornerback.

Then we pointed at each other.

That really made him mad.

To hell with it, Hallman said, throwing up his arms, the next time TCU gets the ball, you're both going in. Get loose.

The Aggies began a methodical six-minute drive. Six minutes of hell. A few yards. A few first downs. Time kept slowly ticking away.

Page and Coolidge nervously watched the clock on the scoreboard. Score quick, or punt, they were thinking. We were fired up, Coolidge said.

I was warming up like a professional gymnast, and Page was squeezing a football so tightly I'm expecting to hear the damn thing pop. We were actually going to play cornerback for Texas A&M, and the rest of the 12th man team was as excited as we were.

We'll play cover three, Hallman said calmly. Stay a little deeper than usual. Stay nine yards off the ball. We know they're gonna throw. You've worked hard. Here's your shot. Keep the ball in front you, and you have a chance to make a play. Don't let anybody get behind you deep.

What happens if they complete one deep, Page asked.

It's not gonna happen.

What if it does?

Just keep running, Hallman said.

At the thirty-five yard line, the drive stalled. Sherrill called for a punt. Page and Coolidge strapped on their helmets. A punt. A few more seconds off the clock, and they would be on the field. Two minutes were left in the game.

Craig Stump punted.

TCU nailed him.

A penalty flag hit the turf.

Roughing the kicker was the call.

First down, A&M.

The dream faded as quickly as it had begun.

Sean Page and David Coolidge removed their helmets and watched the offense run off the final 120 seconds of the game. I felt like we had just won the lottery, Coolidge said, only to find out at the last minute that we were one number off. Somewhere, E. King Gill must have been looking down on us. We were the 12th man. Our destiny, like his, was on the sidelines, ready when the team needed us, not, I guess, when we were ahead 74-10.

David Coolidge (7), Danny Balcar (2), Chad Adair (12), and Dean Berry (1) huddle before going downfield on another one of the 12th man team's kamikaze missions.

On the scout team, Ed Silverman was wearing the red number twenty-four jersey of Arkansas All-American safety, Steve Atwater.

He's extremely aggressive on run support, graduate assistant Jim Hughes kept telling Silverman. You've got to go out there and believe you're Steve Atwater. We want you to play just like he does.

How's that?

See those running backs over there?

Yeah.

Take them on one at a time.

I can do that.

And knock brickload from hell out of them.

One at a time.

It's better that way.

So that's what I did, Silverman said. I spent the week knocking bricks from hell out of whoever carried the ball. By Friday, I didn't answer unless somebody called me Atwater. The number twenty-four looked good on me. It felt good on me. I thought I was as good as Atwater until I saw him play.

Jackie Sherrill didn't call him Atwater.

Just Silverman.

And he gave him Sherrill gave him the award as Scout Team Player of the Week.

The trap was awaiting the Aggies in the most abominable places of all to play football, War Memorial Stadium in Little Rock, Arkansas. Larry Bowen wrote in the

Bryan Eagle, this time, the patented A&M comeback came up short. How short? Thirteen yards, a couple of inches, and four points. When Kevin Murray's final desperation pass for Roger Vick fell incomplete, Arkansas escaped with a 14-10 upset.

In the *Houston Post,* Mickey Herskowitz wrote, the Aggies have had their hearts and their hopes broken before in the Ozarks. If they go on to reach the Cotton Bowl, however, this one may not rank in the top five. Still, they learned a costly lesson. Dreams do not always beat the clock. Sometimes, the train runs over Little Nell.

Spencer Baum wasn't exactly afraid of Jackie Sherrill.

He just never wanted to be standing too close to him.

The volcano could explode at any minute, and those standing the nearest would be the ones covered with ashes, usually the verbal kind, salted with a few colorful expletives that dictionaries had yet to define. The closest I ever got to Coach Sherrill, Spencer Baum said, was the day we took the team photograph.

I wore number five. Jackie Sherrill walked up and stood between numbers four and five.

None of us smiled.

Network television personalities were swarming over the Texas A&M campus, wondering, along with the Aggie faithful, whether or not Jackie Sherrill had enough miracles left to beat the long odds and lead his team back to the Cotton Bowl. An ambush the color of burnt orange was lying in wait. Texas stood in the way. The Aggies would need both barrels blazing when they barreled into Austin.

Brian Carpenter watched Lynn Swann of ABC Sports amble out to the practice field to interview Sherrill. The wide receiver had once sparked the famed Pittsburgh Steelers Super Bowl run during the 1970s, and Swann still looked as though he hadn't lost a step. Fit. Trim. He even walked with the graze of a gazelle. Probably still ran that way, too, Carpenter thought.

Defensive back Chet Brooks glanced over at Swann and said, you better be glad I wasn't in your face. Brooks laughed. You'd still be trying to catch your first pass.

Chet Brooks could do a lot of things better than a lot of people.

None of them could beat him when it came to trash talking. His common sense, however, was seldom on the same page with his words.

A few minutes later, Jackie Sherrill walked up and threw a pair of cleats at Lynn Swann's feet. These ought to fit, he said.

Sherrill nodded at Brooks, and yelled, get up here on the line. You think you're a damn hall of famer. See if you can defend one.

Carpenter remembered, Kevin Murray dropped back, Swann darted downfield, and Chet was all over him. Swann made one quick and sudden move, then another, finally spun back, and had Chet's legs twisted under him like a pair of broken pretzels. Murray dropped the pass in his hands, and Lynn Swann was gone.

As Swann jogged back up field, he paused beside Chet Brooks and said, son, you have a little work to do before you play at the next level.

Chet was still trying to untangle his feet, Carpenter said. For once, he had nothing to say.

It was a tale of two teams that, virtually overnight, had swapped places in the Southwest Conference. Well, they hadn't actually swapped places. A&M had bumped Texas rather rudely off of its glorified pedestal and taken the top spot for its own. For once, the Aggies were looking down on the 'Horns, and Texas was not enjoying the view from the bottom. A&M was a step away from the summit. Texas was on a downhill slide. As always, Jackie Sherrill said, the road to the Cotton Bowl traveled through Austin, and the highway had long been stained by the spillage of bad blood. The Aggies were in the driver's seat, and those bastards from Austin had just fallen to Baylor, 18-13. With a 5-5 record, the Longhorns no longer needed a road map to Dallas, but Fred Akers desperately needed a win just for the outside hope of keeping his job. Sherrill knew that Memorial Stadium had historically been a tough place to play. Yet, he said, the crowd noise really doesn't affect you unless the guy on the other side is putting a knot on your head.

Most of the noise was being generated by Longhorn safety John Hagy, who was quoted in the *Austin American-Statesman* as saying, the Aggies are arrogant and stupid people. I hate them. I hate their coach. I hate their team. I hate their town. The Aggies told me in high school I wasn't good enough to play for them, not that I've lost any sleep over it. But where I went to school, at San Antonio Marshall High, everyone goes to A&M. When they come back, they're stupid.

Something happens to them over there. The Aggies are all unclassy – their coach, their quarterback, their people, their community. As far as I'm concerned, they're all a bunch of cockroaches. When A&M recruited me, I told Coach Sherrill that I bleed orange, and he said – you know how serious he is – *son, I assure you, you bleed red.*

In reality, Texas A&M was in a no-lose situation. A win, said Ed Silverman, sent the Aggies to the Cotton Bowl. A loss re-directed us to Miami and the Orange Bowl. In fact, when we ran out onto the field, the Texas fans were throwing oranges at us. Even Hagy had said the Longhorns had one goal in mind, and that was to come out, whip us, and send Arkansas to the Cotton Bowl. Most of us had never seen the beach in Miami, but we all wanted another conference championship. Going to Dallas on New Year's Day would be just fine. Besides, this was Texas, and I wanted to beat Texas even if it meant I never saw a beach in Miami.

Kirk Pierce was standing calmly behind the bench when the orange hit him.

He looked around.

The Texas fans were laughing.

He did what any self-respecting 12th man headhunter was supposed to do. He casually reached down, picked up the orange, and threw it back.

Harder this time.

He smiled, glanced around, and saw Jackie Sherrill staring at him. The glare cut to the bone.

In the training room, thirty minutes before kickoff, a trainer had been wrapping ankles when Danny Balcar asked him, do you know how to make a plaster of Paris cast?

Sure.

When you wrap my wrist, Balcar said, put a plaster of Paris cast under the tape.

How much?

Oh, from my elbow to my wrist will do fine, Balcar told him.

The trainer sighed. If you get caught, he said, I didn't do it.

By the time I get caught, Balcar replied, it won't matter. He ran out of the training room, trying hard to remember John Hagy's number.

Butch Motley (25), with Danny Balcar (2), Bobby Middleton (18), and Chad Adair (12), raises a hand in triumph. The day was good. But, as far as the 12th man was concerned, any day on the field covering kickoffs was good and getting better.

tion you scream into the night, "Is there no God?"

And Jackie Sherrill answers, "Yo."

Don't you hate him, too, for what he did to Fred Akers down in Austin? The poor little fellow got fired because Sherrill stripped him naked and burned his clothes. He took the whole State of Texas away from The University of Texas. The Football Capital of Texas is now College Station. Remember what they told you about that strange school with all those strange customs and rituals? And everyone connected with the place had this fierce pride, except they had nothing to be proud of except academics and a band that hasn't taken a wrong step in at least a hundred years? That was the Aggies. Never lost a halftime or a slide-rule contest. Hardly ever won a football game. But you were warned that if the right man ever arrived to coach the team, if someone could come in and channel all of that hocus-pocus, pride, and alumni money in one single direction, there would be a monster roaring down Highway 6 and no one would be safe. Don't you just hate it that Jackie Sherrill has built that monster, and, at the moment, it appears nothing can stop it?

It was the week before Christmas, and Kirk Pierce was a scout team fullback, trying to replicate Ohio State's plays against the famed Wrecking Crew. He was blast blocking Adam Bob, and the tailback cut through the crease and scored. He said, I heard those dreaded words from R. C. Slocum. He was cussing and yelling and telling us all to line up and run it again.

Burnis Simon helped Pierce to his feet and said, Rock, you better strap it on and blow him up good this time.

Pierce nodded, but he knew something had gone dreadfully wrong with his shoulder. Probably a stinger, he thought. It wasn't the first. A stinger was simply one of those hazards confronting a member of the 12th man team every day of his life. The numbness wouldn't last long.

Never did.

He blasted Adam Bob again.

The tailback cut through the hole and scored.

We were fired up, Pierce said. Slocum turned his profanity up a notch or two. He was upset. Adam Bob was catching hell.

My arm was dangling loosely from my shoulder.

No pain.

No feeling.

Nothing.

We ran the same play again, but I wasn't able to go quite as hard.

The tailback was tackled. Slocum wasn't nearly as upset as he had been. I walked back to the huddle, getting slaps on the helmet for doing a good job, but no high fives because I couldn't lift my arm.

No one on the field knew Pierce was injured.

Simon had asked him, you get your shoulder messed up?

Pierce only shrugged. He said, I wasn't about to let anyone know I was hurt because I figured I'd be kicked off the traveling squad for the Cotton Bowl. No ice. No pain medications. No injections. Just a little beer. That was all I thought I needed. Can't cure it. Numb it. Pain was the closest ally Kirk pierce had.

When the alarm woke me up the next morning for practice, he said, I reached to hit the snooze button, and my arm dropped to the floor, completely unresponsive. I kept telling it to move, and my arm wasn't listening to a damn thing I told it.

Kirk Pierce did what any self-respecting member of the 12th man would have done. He packed several bottles of Advil, took them religiously by the handfuls for the next few days, and went to Dallas. Dig deep, he told himself. Go hard in practice. My shoulder can't be hurt any worse than it already is. So let the Wrecking Crew bring it on. I may not play against Ohio State, but I'll do what I can to make damn sure the Aggie defense is ready to play.

In the fifty-first Cotton Bowl, Texas A&M would be facing the storied Buckeyes from Ohio State, and all week Coach Earle Bruce was preparing his team to face the illustrious 12th man. Sure he had a game plan to confuse Kevin Murray, he hoped, but Bruce told the leering press that he was employing a 12th man team on his offensive and defensive scout teams in order to better simulate the Aggies' famed unit. He wasn't leaving anything to chance.

Back during two-a-days, Garry Sorrell had been pinned down, and David Fry teamed up with Warren Barhorst to shave "A&M" in the hairs of his chest. Big joke. Big laugh. It could only happen to Garry Sorrel. He couldn't wait for the hair to grow back, but word quickly spread around campus that Sorrell had a chest unlike any other player around. He quickly discovered that girls really liked the hand-shaven version of "A&M."

Not so bad after all, he thought.

He kept it.

Before the Cotton Bowl game, a woman reporter from the *Dallas Morning News* asked him for an interview. She had brought a photographer with her.

Sure, he said.

Let me see your chest, she said.

What?

She grinned. We've heard all about it, she said.

Garry Sorrell shrugged. I thought about asking her to return the favor, he said.

Kevin Murray, on the first day of 1987, found himself back in the Cotton Bowl record books, but this time his name was on the wrong side of the ledger. He threw five second-half interceptions, saw two returned for touchdowns, and the flu-ridden Texas Aggies fell to Ohio State, 28-12. All-American Chris Spielman stole two of the passes, and Murray would say, he was sneaking around, and normally they use a safety for that. That's why I had such a hard time. It wasn't so much what he did, it was what we did. It was ugly. Spielman simply shrugged and said, I don't think it was one of Kevin Murray's better days.

Murray referred to Spielman as a spy.

Spielman grinned. I certainly didn't have sunglasses and an overcoat on, he said.

During a crucial moment in the game, it appeared that Keith Woodside had reached the end zone with a pass for the two-point conversion. Officials ruled he was out of bounds. After the game, Sherrill was questioned about the controversial decision

I remember what the Bear said when I played at Alabama, and Joe Namath tried to sneak over the goal line in the Orange Bowl against Texas, Sherrill answered with a slight shrug. The officials said he was short. Namath came back to the sideline and said, coach, we scored. All Bear said was, if we had scored, son, the official would have raised his hands. That's how I feel about this on

They were just a bunch of big old country boys from Ohio, Ronnie Glenn said. We had to hit them as hard as we could to bring them down. Sean Page remembered, I was excited to play the famous Buckeyes and wanted a chance to get after the big slow factory worker kids from up north. They were big. I'm not for sure they were slow. Wide receiver Chris Carter was a man among boys in college. We couldn't stop him. On two occasions, I thought we had interceptions, but Carter went up and made the big play. Over and over, he made the big play. He caught only four passes for sixty-one yards. It seemed like he had a dozen catches.

For Butch Motley, it was a single and infuriating moment in hell. A&M had just scored the 12th man believed the Aggies had time to come all the way back, and the thought in the huddle was: Hit him hard, cause a fumble, and get the ball back in Kevin's hands. When Murray was firing darts, no lead was out of reach. Rick Tankersley made the tackle and Motley was driving hard. Hit him hard. Cause a fumble. The words were rattling around his head when Motley dove desperately into the Ohio State ball carrier. He came in high, flying low. Late hit. Obvious even to the Aggie faithful, who were more than a little prejudiced, and especially to Sherrill, who was seldom in a forgiving mood. Motley had let his emotions get the best of him, and, he knew, if a man didn't use his head, he might as well have two assholes.

Early whistle.

The play was over.

Late flag.

Motley knew he was as guilty as sin. An aggressive mistake, perhaps, but a stupid mistake just the same. He lay face down on the field and thought, oh, my Lord, now the whole Aggie nation will know my name, and they won't like it. If I had found a hole, even a crevice, in the ground, he said, I would have crawled inside and stayed there.

Instead, he jogged toward the sidelines, head down, heart aching.

Jackie Sherrill met him. He wasn't yelling, Motley said. He wasn't screaming. He was as calm as I had ever seen him. Why did you do it, son, was all he said. I looked at him. I didn't know what to say. R. C. Slocum came running up and said, it's a holding penalty on them, Coach. Sherrill walked right past me. He had already forgotten me. I felt like the weight of the world had been lifted from my shoulders.

When the members of the 12th man unit ran off the field after the game, they were swarmed with kids wearing miniature maroon and white jerseys, all begging for someone to sign their programs. Said Motley, it was easier to sign our autographs than explain to them why they probably didn't really want them.

Jackie Sherrill had no idea at the time, but Kevin Murray had played his last game in a Texas A&M uniform. As Sean Page said of him, Murray was a quiet, introspective guy on the field, and his execution was exemplary. He was a strong leader and a great player. He deserved a better ending to his career, but that was what being a quarterback was all about. Glory when it's going good. Blame when it doesn't. He and that rifle arm of his took us to two straight Cotton Bowls, and, in the annals of Texas A&M history, that had never happened before.

It was a contrast of thoughts on the sidelines. If Rick Tankersley (20) and the 12th man played, it was because the Aggie offense was succeeding. If Todd Tschantz (4) went out to punt the ball, it meant that the Aggie offense had stalled out.

Chapter 23

David Fry never saw a fight he didn't like. He never saw a fight he thought he could lose. Football to him was nothing more than an organized fight. Sure, there might be twenty-two on the field, but only two of them counted. David Fry and the man he was seeking out to leave crumpled up in a pile of unrequited devastation.

Fry had played linebacker and fullback for Anderson High School in Austin, and he considered attending The University of Texas, but, he said, I walked around campus, saw two chicks kissing, and decided I could find a better place to go to school. Since he had aspirations to become a veterinarian, David Fry wound up at Texas A&M. He said, I had already given football everything I had, and at 5-9 and 190 pounds, I knew I was too small to play big-time football and too proud to play anywhere smaller.

The 12th man kickoff team, however, was another story. Girls had little interest in those run-of-the-mill boys running around campus, he said. I was just part of the crowd, and it was a pretty damn big crowd. Girls would stand in line to date a member of the 12th man. Girls always had a smile for a member of the 12th man. I became a member of the 12th man team as soon as I could get out there and find somebody to whip in practice.

He hadn't played much the year before.

It didn't matter.

He dated a lot.

They told me the games would be hard and practices harder, he said. I guess they knew what they were talking about. In high school, I rode bulls for the rodeo team. I had been riding bulls since I was a little kid, and not even going up against A&M's varsity on the scout team was as tough as riding bulls. In football, I knew I probably wouldn't die. I wasn't so sure when I climbed on top of a mad bull. When the chute gate opened, I could only hear one person screaming. My momma. When I ran out onto Kyle Field, there were seventy thousand people screaming. But no one was up there pointing at me and saying, that boy's got a chance to die today.

Before the Texas game in 1986, David Fry read where John Hagy had the gall to tell a sportswriter that the Aggies were nothing but a bunch of cockroaches, and Hagy's cockeyed statements rubbed him the wrong way. Fry hadn't played in the game, but he kept those words locked away on the inside door of his mind. Saw them every time he closed his eyes.

On January 31, the night before he turned twenty-one, Fry drove to Austin with a fake ID and wound up at a bar on Sixth Street. For all practical purposes, he had merely gone home to celebrate his comof age. He had decided to use his fake ID one final time before becoming legitimate. David Fry did things like that. In the bar, he stumbled across John Hagy.

A word or two passed between them.

A curse word or two passed between them.

Finally Fry said, why don't you step outside, and we'll settle this little argument.

Fine, Hagy said.

Fry walked out onto the sidewalk. The glow of neon pierced the darkness.

He waited.

Hagy didn't come.

David Fry went back inside the bar to get him.

Fry hit him once, and Hagy went down.

One-on-one.

Mano-a-mano.

One would walk out that night under his own power, Fry knew, and Hagy, in spite of his brazen words, wasn't nearly as tough as a good, honest bull ride.

We were on the floor, Fry said, and I'm trying to rearrange portions of his face. I suddenly looked around and realized that I was surrounded by eight legs that looked a whole lot like a bunch of tree trunks.

Four Texas linemen had encircled us, and one was wearing Roper boots. His foot came up and caught me in the head, and I'm thinking: this is not going to be a good way to turn twenty-one. I think two of the big sonuvaguns would have probably been enough, but all four jumped on top of me.

When David Fry staggered out of the bar, he had a broken nose, a fractured mandible, and was trying hard to keep a loose tooth from departing his mouth.

He was a bull rider, owned a black belt in karate, and had been undefeated in thirty-two karate tournaments.

David Fry had just walked away – no, limped away –from the only fight he ever lost.

The next morning, his mother was appalled when she walked into the room and saw his face.

What happened, she wanted to know.

Got in a fight.

Oh my Dear Lord, she said. When you're home, we live with the devil.

She had placed a box with a new cowboy hat on the table.

Happy birthday, David.

She yanked up the box and angrily left the room.

I never did get the birthday present, he said.

Kevin Murray had grown weary of the unrelenting turmoil that kept circling his tenure at Texas A&M like a pack of turkey vultures on the prowl. On the football field, his exploits, his rifle arm, his leadership qualities, his ability to win against all odds had become legendary. With Murray in charge, the Aggies had stormed their way to back-to-back Southwest Conference championships and two straight Cotton Bowls. However, he had not been able to escape the whispers of NCAA improprieties and violations that had dogged him since the Milwaukee Brewers, in a frantic effort to retain his services on the baseball field, passed rumors that Kevin Murray may well have landed at Texas A&M solely because, in so many words, the Aggies had more financial enticements for him than professional baseball did.

The Brewers could never back up their charges with proof, only fourth-hand whispers and third-hand, hearsay innuendos. The NCAA

Brian Kotara (27) sees a dream come true at the Cotton Bowl.

could never back up baseball's charges with any hard evidence, but, much like old bird dogs looking for a new bone or an old bird, college football's investigators kept chasing down cold trails hoping they would stumble across a hot one.

For the past two years, Murray had been linked to a Dallas businessman whose only transgression was hiring the quarterback as a summer intern. The leering press did its best to indict the business man in print, keeping his name in front-page headlines, and camping on his front yard with their television cameras all hours of the day and night. He's paying Kevin Murray way too much money for a summer intern, newspapers and television reporters claimed. He has given Murray a new sports car to drive. The leering press was running amuck in its attempt to discredit Texas A&M coaches, a quarterback, and a Dallas businessman, all of whom spoke to the NCAA but left reporters dangling in the dark. However, the leering press never bothered to check and discover that, through the years, the businessman had hired more than two-dozen Aggies as summer interns. He had worked his way through Texas A&M and realized how difficult it was for students to pay for their education.

So, yes, he had probably paid Kevin Murray more than the job was worth. Then again, he paid all of the other Aggie summer interns the same exact salary that Murray earned. They were students, worrying more about their GPA than passing rating. A young lady who worked in the accounting department earned more, but she didn't play quarterback. The leering press had absolutely no interest in her.

The Dallas businessman gave the NCAA investigators the tax and pay records of all his student interns. He showed them photocopies of the checks Murray's mother had given him to lease the sports car. The leering press more or less ignored the fact that Murray still had most of his $35,000 baseball bonus, which made him fairly solvent and able to pay for almost anything he wanted during the 1980s. He wanted a sports car, and the checks came in like clockwork. The NCAA closed its books and walked away, clearing Jackie Sherrill and the Dallas businessman of all allegations that had smeared their good names. The leering press, however, kept right on digging, even though they were never able to locate any fire. When it came to Kevin Murray, they didn't even find the smoke.

The Southwest Conference was in turmoil. The NCAA came down hard on SMU as recruiting violations led to the death penalty, and investigators were hovering around schools in the Southwest Conference like beady-eyed rodents searching for road kill, picking at the bones, digging through the scraps, searching for any shred of evidence that might indict and convict someone else.

As Jackie Sherrill said, in a disappointing move that threatened to cripple the power, the prestige, and the credibility of the conference, coaches began pointing fingers at each other, throwing out their own rumors and gossip, often trying to pass it off as truth. If they had any luck discrediting another coach or another university, they thought it might enhance their own recruiting efforts. It didn't take long before everyone had been smeared. The coaches hadn't helped themselves. They had wrecked the conference.

Sherrill hired a media consultant to educate the team on answering questions, loaded or otherwise, from the leering press. He told his team, if an NCAA investigator talks to you, tell him what you know, if you know anything, and tell him the truth. If you don't know the answer, just go ahead and tell him that you don't know.

Be forthright.

Be honest.

Don't beat around the bush.

Don't hide from anyone.

Don't hide anything you know from anyone.

The investigator sat down across the table from John Burnett, opened his briefcase, and removed a tablet. He sharpened his pencil and said, name, please.

John Burnett.

Were you ever recruited to play for Texas A&M.

Yes, sir.

Did you come for a visit?

Yes, sir.

Who was the recruiter?

Coach Jerry Pettibone.

The investigator leaned across the table and said in a soft, soothing voice, now I'm going to ask you a few questions that are a little more sensitive. Remember, when you answer them, you will doing a great service for the integrity of your university. Do you understand?

Yes, sir.

Now, have you ever received a gift from a former student at Texas A&M?

Tommy Bolcerek (25) has the ball carrier wrapped up as Garry Sorrell (26), Rene Casas (9), and Trent Childress (17) converge on Baylor. When they all arrived at the same time, there was no exit or escape. The run had come to sudden end.

Yes, sir.

The investigator sat up straight in his chair. He had hit a nerve. His eye quivered. There was more urgency in his voice. Would you mind telling me what it was, he asked.

It was a car, Burnett answered.

Now the investigator was trying hard to conceal a smile. His eyes were like those of a rattlesnake mesmerizing its prey. He began scribbling frantically in his notebook. What kind of car, he asked.

A Camaro Z28.

A bold, brazen look crossed the investigator's face. No time to waste. He went for the kill.

What former student was it, he asked.

Duke Burnett, class of 1966, Burnett said. My father bought me the car for Christmas.

The investigator sighed wearily, snapped his notebook shut, and left the room without another word.

Kevin Murray decided he had accomplished all he could at Texas A&M, and maybe he had a career awaiting him in the NFL. He had the arm, but no one knew if his bad ankle would hold up. With all of the hits he was sure to take, another year of college football certainly wouldn't help him and could easily ruin any chances he might ever have to play in a professional league. So, as a junior, Kevin Murray declared for the NFL draft, leaving Texas A&M and Jackie Sherrill with a lot of unknown, untested, but highly recruited talent at quarterback. For the Aggie faithful, two Cotton Bowls weren't enough. They were lobbying for three, and Sherrill was wondering if Craig Stump, Lance Pavlas, or Bucky Richardson could successfully drive the train to Dallas.

John Klein wrote in the *Houston Post*, the priority in the spring was clear. Craig Stump, Murray's backup and a starter in 1984 when Murray was injured, stepped into the starter's role. Stump, a gritty competitor but lacking in the natural skills that made Murray so dangerous, is an efficient operator of the Aggies' complex offense. Lance Pavlas, the whiz-kid freshman redshirt, suffered a severe elbow bruise and lost a lot of valuable time.

No one, not even Klein, was bothering to write about Bucky Richardson, tough, hard-nosed, a quarterback with a running back's mentality, still motoring along far below the radar. Richardson had been a wishbone quarterback who had managed to escape the recruiting clutches of LSU, and Sherrill had decided to keep a redshirt on him for the year. He had faith in Stump, with the multi-talented Pavlas waiting in the wings. No reason for Richardson to lose a year of eligibility for a few meaningless plays during the season.

Graduate assistants came and went at Texas A&M, and Burnis Simon, like Roy Kokemoor and David Beal before him, had moved on for a better paying job. It was getting harder and harder to live on two hundred dollars a month. The 12th man team was turned over to Chris Massey, who had been coaching at Cy-Fair High School in Houston before Paul Register persuaded him to take a huge pay cut and make the trek to A&M a year earlier. Massey had been twenty-seven years old and single. He had a chance to include college football coaching experience on his resume, so he decided to invest the time toward earning his master's degree. In 1986, he had worked with R. C. Slocum on the defensive side of the ball, and now Sherrill was asking him – no, telling him – that it would be his fate in life to make sure a bunch of student walk-ons kept the nation's top kick returners out of the end zone.

Massey watched three hundred show up for tryouts, saw the stars dancing in their eyes, knew that a few of the chosen ones would have the good fortune of being laid out cold as a wedge every day. He began, he said, trying to find out who would go down on kickoffs and strike somebody without being shy about it. Almost any of them could run in a straight line with varying forty times, but Massey was searching for players who had a move or two, who could dip and dodge the first onslaught of blockers, who would not back down when a bulldozer with a football was trying to out maneuver, outsmart, and outrun them. For the 12th man, it was always an altercation in cleats.

Massey, with the help of another graduate assistant, Jim Hughes, began working to narrow the walk-ons down to a manageable number. As always, those who had been an integral part of the 12th man unit the year before were back on the field, trying out again. Couldn't rest on their laurels. Couldn't take it easy. The Cotton Bowl ring didn't mean a thing. They were battling to make sure their places weren't stolen or snatched out from under them by a bunch of new guys who had never borne the bloody brunt of a Dana Batiste blast in practice. As Massey said, they had left blood on Kyle Field before. Last year hadn't been enough.

We had twenty slots open, he said, but, in reality, as many as thirteen or maybe fourteen places would be filled by players who had already spent time on the 12th man team. Most of them had never been starters, but they had a little experience, primarily on the scout team, knew what to expect and what was expected of them. As many as three hundred other kids – most of them wading knee-deep in manure – were fighting for those last six or seven spots we had available.

Massey, in his mind, already had one of them filled. He had coached Blake Dwoskin at Cy-Fair, knew he would play with the devil-may-care spirit that flowed through the veins of the 12th man, and wanted him out front in that critical first line of defense on kickoffs.

As a high school senior, Dwoskin, playing free safety, had led the state of Texas in interceptions. He had enrolled to play at Sam Houston State but found himself a wife and spent the next year and a half working in the construction business, framing houses, while she attended school. Dwoskin, however, knew he was an Aggie at heart, and he would always be an Aggie. He was already attending classes at A&M when Chris Massey called.

I'm married now, Dwoskin told his old coach. I'm not for sure I have a lot of free time to devote for football.

I don't want to hear that, Massey said.

Besides, I'm too little to play college football.

I know what kind of football player you are.

That was high school.

Makes no difference, Massey told him. I don't care how big the ball carrier is or how fast he is. He doesn't have more than two legs, and I think you can knock them out from under him.

Well, Dwoskin admitted, I've done it before.

I'll see you on the field.

What are my chances?

There are no guarantees, Massey told him, but if I hadn't believed you could make the team and help us, I wouldn't have called.

Blake Dwoskin sighed and shook his head. I haven't played in almost three years, he said.

The game hasn't changed, Massey replied.

It may have passed me by.

I've seen you run, Massey said. Nothing passes you by.

Now, Chris Massey thought, if he could just track down a half dozen more Blake Dwoskins, his job might be a little more secure. The phone rang. He answered and heard the unmistakable voice of Jackie Sherrill at

The Texas Aggie football team, sprinkled with members of the 12th man team, Doug Lawson (21), Bubba Hillje (13), Brian Carpenter (5), and Rene Casas (9) respectfully follow the time-honored tradition of Farmer's Fight.

the other end of the line.

I want you to pick forty players for the 12th man team, he said. What?

I want forty players on the 12th man team. Not twenty. Forty.

But Coach, Massey said, it's difficult enough to find much playing time for twenty kids. Forty will be impossible.

Sherrill snapped, that's what I want, Chris. Find me forty. You may have to look a little harder but they're out there. And Chris?

Yes, sir.

I don't want forty lukewarm bodies on the field. I want forty who can play for the 12th man team.

Why so many, Coach?

Well, Sherrill said, the tension easing from his voice, there's a big difference between the usual walk-ons and members of the 12th man team. The 12th man plays to a higher standard, to a different level, especially in practice. Walk-ons don't hit as hard as my 12th man players do. Hell, on the scout team, I have scholarship players who don't hit as hard my 12th man players do. I want as many of them on the practice field as possible. They'll make the team work a helluva lot harder. They'll make the team a helluva lot better.

Forty, it'll be, Massey said.

Sherrill hung up the phone.

Chris Massey knew there were no points to argue. He said, the members of the 12th man team were just regular Joes, but when they put on those red jerseys in practice, when they put on those A&M uniforms for a game, something extraordinary happened to them. Overnight, without anyone ever understanding why or how, they became better than they were supposed to be. They knew how to die standing up. It happened every year.

The 12th man kickoff team had been launched in a flurry of scorn, ridicule, and national headlines and, by 1987, had settled into a position of respect, admiration, and national prominence. No longer, as Sherrill pointed out, was the unit being looked on as a fluff and puff publicity stunt. Phyllis Miller reported in *The Twelfth Man Magazine*, the statistics, which cannot be shaded or twisted, speak for themselves. In their four years of existence, the team has held kickoff returns by the opposition to an average of 15.2 yards. No one has ever scored a touchdown against them. In fact, no team has managed to run the ball past its own 39-yard line. The squad has also established a reputation for their fanatical, wide-open pursuit of ball carriers. The 12th man team is a curious mixture from Butch Motley, a cowboy type, to the cool, sophisticated Spencer Baum. Motley is classified as a headhunter, and Baum is the bomber. Sherrill says, the crazy and tough image that surrounds the squad is not an image. They are crazy and tough. They are dedicated, and they are determined. They have literally transformed the stadium. They have meshed the student body and the athletes together, and the student body is now part of what is happening on the field. The crowd is now louder and more involved and a real factor in every game.

According to Jeff Boutwell, the most frequent question asked of him had been, do you play on the 12th man team or the real team?

Boutwell, without hesitation, always responded the same way. We are the real team, he said.

Brian Edwards had no intention of giving up football. High school, he decided, was just one short step away from college ball, and he had started at various times as quarterback, strong safety, and tight end at Sugarland, a large 5-A school with a great football program. It had always been his ambition to play Division 1 football for the University of Texas. Edwards had been an ardent fan of the burnt orange for as long as he could remember, but somewhere along the way, he took a wrong turn, lost the sight of Austin in his rearview mirror, and walked on at Blinn Junior College – one of two hundred players trying out for thirty-two scholarships. During the last scrimmage before the last cut, Brian Edwards hit the fullback, got his hand caught and twisted between the two helmets, and broke a finger.

Blinn needed players right now, Edwards said, and I wasn't any good to them. I could practice. I just couldn't play. He stayed around anyway, and by the fall of his sophomore year, Edwards had worked his way into the starting lineup at safety. Once again, he began to wonder if maybe, just maybe, there might be an outside chance of his pulling on a burnt orange jersey someday and playing football for the Longhorns. His weight had gone from 185 to 215, he hadn't lost any speed, and he had no intentions of losing a dream.

Blinn was a suitcase college. Most of its students were commuters, and on the weekend, the campus woke up empty. Blinn even played its football games on Thursday nights just so there would be enough students around to form the semblance of a crowd in the stands. On a free Saturday night, he traveled to College Station to watch Texas A&M play Arkansas, knowing that the Aggies had a conference championship well within reach. I was sitting in the student section, Edwards said, but I was still a Longhorn at heart. The Wrecking Crew was beating the hell out of Arkansas physically, but late in the game, the Razorbacks were driving. It was fourth and one. The crowd was going crazy. I was going crazy, and I didn't even like Texas A&M. Arkansas pitched the ball, and here came Kip Corrington blazing into the Arkansas backfield to drop the ball carrier for a two-yard loss. That was the game, and I was up there high-fiving everyone I saw. I came back to College Station for the Texas game. It was cold, and I was wearing an A&M jacket. The Aggies won and headed for the Cotton Bowl. I decided to go to the Cotton Bowl myself, just so I could watch them. Somehow, I became an Aggie before I ever admitted it out loud to myself.

During the spring of 1986, Brian Edwards met with R. C. Slocum. Football, as always, was on his mind. We don't have any scholarships left, the defensive coordinator said, but we'd certainly like for you to walk on.

Tell me when, Edwards said.

Burnis Simon, who had been coaching the 12th man team at the time, watched for awhile, thought Edwards showed a lot of potential, ambled up to him and said, why don't you come over here and work out with the 12th man.

If it'll get me on the field, all right.

Simon smiled. See all of those walk-ons out there wearing orange jerseys, he said.

I'm wearing one myself.

They're never gonna play, Simon said. I don't care how hard they work, they're never gonna play. Simon's smile grew broader. The guys with red jerseys, they have a chance to play every Saturday, always at home and sometimes on the road. We see the field more often than some scholarship players. When they were in high school, that was as good as they ever got. We're getting better ever week. Count on it.

Edwards said, I dreamed all of my life of wearing an orange Jersey. But the next day when I came to practice, I found a red jersey hanging in my locker. Looked a lot better than orange. Felt a lot better than orange. Didn't show blood nearly as bad.

In retrospect, R. C. Slocum said, Jackie Sherrill's idea for the 12th man kickoff team was a stroke of genius. I wasn't so sure at the time because I knew how important it was for those kids to be effective on the field. Well, they were effective. They gave us everything Sherrill had hoped for, and they tied together the basic 12th man tradition that lived at the very heart and soul of Aggieland. He took the 12th man concept off the printed page and put it on the field where it counted. It meant a lot to the kids. It meant a lot to the student body. Those former high school players from other universities who came to our games at Kyle Field watched and wished they had a chance to play like the 12th man did. I think they were a little jealous.

Slocum pointed out, the concept had created such positive press across the state and the nation that we began using the 12th man team as a recruiting mechanism to bring in walk-ons who all saw themselves as potential members of the kickoff unit. It was important for us to have a strong walk-on program with as many good high school athletes as we could find. You can't effectively practice day after day by just using scholarship players. We needed some solid, hard-nosed players to run the scout team. Even though we had no scholarships for them, we never failed to offer those high school athletes the chance to come to Texas A&M and walk-on.

Will I ever get a chance to play, they asked.

Maybe, we said.

How much of a chance?

We would simply smile and say, well, you could come on down and be part of the 12th man team, Slocum said.

For high school athletes, those were magical words.

Slocum pointed out, what we got for our walk-on program and ultimately for our 12th man team were good, rough-edged, hard-hitting high school football players. They had a little talent, but they would never be down-to-down guys at the college level. Yet, they were absolutely tough as nails on kickoffs. We had good times on Sunday watching their efforts on the game film. They took pride in what they did. We saw some wild and reckless collisions. They were taking on blockers twice their size and knocking them down, diving over the top of piles, fighting and scratching and playing as though there was no tomorrow. They were their own harshest critics. If one made a mistake, the coaches didn't have to say a word. The 12th man, as a group, would take the guilty party aside and make those corrections for us.

We were tough on them.

We were hard on them.

We pushed them to the outer limits of their ability and made them as good as they could possibly be. They may have hated us as coaches, but, ultimately, I believe they respected us. I know that we respected them as a kickoff team and admired the tireless, thankless, day-to-day whipping they took on the practice field,

For years, a lot of teams had simply gone through the motions on kickoffs, Slocum said. The fire was missing. They were content to merely bring the ball out as far up field as they could so the real game could begin. Most didn't practice kickoffs a lot in practice. A few didn't practice kickoffs at all.

Opponents would come in, look around Kyle Field, see the 12th man team jumping up and down, waving those towels, and, the next thing they knew, those crazy bunch of maniacs were flying downfield ready to shoot first without ever bothering to ask any questions. The ball carriers were not nearly as lacksadaisical as they had been. They became concerned and sometimes a little hesitant. There were health issues at stake. Tackles weren't enough. Inflicting a little pain on the way to the ground was the preferred method of punishment. If all the kick return team did was simply go through the motions, Slocum said, then they were treading on dangerous and treacherous ground.

Kirk Pierce wasn't sure, but he thought his world had ended. He knew he was small. He knew he was fast. He knew that his time on the football field depended on his ability to be as strong or stronger than those who were roughly the size of a cement truck and as mean as a bulldog on a gunpowder diet. Pierce seldom budged the scales beyond 185 even after a pair of steaks at Cain Hall. But he could bench press as much as 400 pounds. He didn't merely step up and defy the odds. Kirk Pierce obliterated them.

Then, just before the Cotton Bowl, came the stinger, the shoulder separation. It was bad. Pierce had always known it was bad, but he never had the shoulder X-rayed. He kept the trainers in the dark. But his right arm refused to cooperate with the rest of his body. The strength had slipped away, he could only bench press 134 pounds, and even that was a struggle.

It was a sober awakening.

Kirk Pierce had been invincible, he thought.

Bullet proof.

He did not want to quit. He did not want to give it up. He did not want to waste the dream.

Kirk Pierce became a weight-lifting machine.

Every spare minute, he was in the weight room.

He awoke and went to sleep at night with the loud, metallic sounds of free weights being tossed around in the back of his mind. He was addicted. Add another pound. No. Put another five pounds on the bar. Maybe ten. Hour after hour. Day after day. My Lord, they said, how can the little guy get so much weight above his head. It's a miracle. No. It's ridiculous.

By the spring of 1987, Kirk Pierce beat the odds and became a card-carrying member of the Texas A&M Top 10 Club, which was both unanticipated and unexpected from a walk-on who was too short and too small to ever play football at the collegiate level. He registered 440 pounds in the bench press, 395 pounds on the incline press, 450 pounds in the squat, 1,250 pounds in the leg press, and his power clean topped out at 250 pounds. When the amount of weight was all added together, he stood there among the mountain of men and muscle, who carried scholarships and formed the foundation for the Aggie football team. Little Kirk Pierce ranked number seven.

Bert Hill, our strength and conditioning coach, made me pee in a bottle every week to make sure I wasn't taking steroids, Pierce said. It damn near killed him to give a Top 10 T-Shirt to a 12th man member. He still thought I must be a fraud, and he had watched me lift.

John Gregg knew he was wasting his time. In Austin's Anderson High School, he had been a receiver, defensive back, and kick returner, a little speedster who weighed 160 pounds soaking wet. On a good day, he could stretch to 5-9, but only if the tape measure shrunk. And, as far as he was concerned, every day was a good day. He was blessed with quick feet and could slip through the eye of a needle if the wind didn't stop him first. John Gregg roomed with David Fry, and Fry had the uncanny ability to convince a man, who knew better, that he could drink too much, fight too much, catch a good-looking woman or two, and there weren't any bad-looking women, and he could play for the 12th man team.

Fry talked.

Gregg listened.

He had nothing better to do that afternoon, so he found an old pair of shorts, laced up his tennis shoes, and headed to Kyle Field. He said, when Coach Massey finally posted the names of those who had survived the last cuts of 1987, damned if my name wasn't on the list.

So maybe John Gregg wasn't tall.

So maybe he wasn't big.

So maybe he wasn't as fast as he thought he was.

Chris Massey saw the kind of raw toughness he liked in John Gregg. He was ready to burn some powder.

In practice, Bucky Richardson fired a pass, and Gregg's finger went numb. No feeling at all. Then it began to throb, keeping time with the beat of his pulse.

Got a problem, Massey asked him.

Jammed it. That's all, Gregg said.

The doctors looked at the X-rays and decided otherwise. I'm afraid you broke it, said one of the physicians at the quack shack. But don't worry. We'll fix it up for you.

Not today, Gregg said.

You can't go around with a broken finger, the doctor said.

Sure I can. I'll get it fixed when the season's over.

That's not a very smart thing to do, the doctor said.

I'm with the 12th man team, Gregg said. If we were smart, none of us would be there.

Brian Kotara had seen both sides of the coin, and one had been as worthless as the other. He had come drifting into College Station from the little Texas Panhandle town of Pampa, a 5-10, 170-pound tailback and safety. He had already seen the handwriting on the wall and knew that it had a lot more to do with an engineering degree than football. His mind realized that big-time football was no longer an issue, but his heart could not overlook the chances that the 12th man kickoff team afforded students like Brian Kotara, students who still had more grit and gumption than good sense.

In 1986, working in the spring for Roy Kokemoor, he ran fast enough without the pads and hit hard enough when he finally strapped them on, which, by all accounts, was a good combination to have for someone who specialized in either sneak attacks or full frontal smackdowns. For Kotara, however, he said it was a bizarre feeling. I hadn't been in pads for more than a year, and I seldom ever had any reason to hit anyone weighing over two hundred pounds. Until spring training got underway, we were just running around in shorts and tennis shoes, showing how fast we were. The pads separated the men from the boys. Being fast only meant we reached the point of contact a lot quicker. No use slowing down. We knew we were going to get busted on every play, so there wasn't any use in delaying the impact or the pain. We no longer counted the number of times we were knocked down. We lost count. We didn't even count the number of times we crawled back up on our feet again. It didn't matter. If we couldn't stand, we couldn't run. If we couldn't run, we couldn't play.

Because Scott Slater came to Texas A&M as a walk-on kicker, he always considered himself a part of the 12th man team.

Kotara came into spring training as a fourth-team alley guy. He worked his way up to a position on the second team and believed that, with a little luck, he might well be within striking distance of a starting job. He had earned his promotions. He had the scars to prove it.

Fate dealt him a miserable hand.

Fate left him a card short.

Roy Kokemoor departed Texas A&M, and if he had left any notes or personal observations lying around, they had all been trashed. When those battling to make the final cut for the 12th man returned for two-a-days as summer spilled into August, they discovered a new graduate assistant, Burnis Simon, in charge of the kickoff team.

He was new to them.

They were certainly new to him.

He remembered a few faces, a handful of names, and little else.

Burnis Simon had only been able to track down Kokemoor's early depth chart, the one he wrote before practices became a full-scale conflict. He could not locate the coach's last one.

Brian Kotara found that he had been dropped unceremoniously back down to the fourth team. He was devastated. It was tough to handle, he said. There was no time left to climb back up the chart again. Coach Simon had his list. He stuck to his list. I was on the bottom of his list and didn't make the team. He tried to talk me into walking on, but I had grown to fully understand the precarious landscape of Texas A&M football. Walk-on players were treated as a sub-human form, and the 12th man team was only a notch above.

By 1987, Brian Kotara had a clean and unblemished slate. Chris Massey was in charge of running the 12th man show now, and he had absolutely no idea who Kotara was. Massey just knew that the kid from Pampa was a player. Sean Page, after three years, had the starting safety position nailed down, and Kotara was promptly plugged into the team

behind him. That's great, Kotara thought. Page will be graduating, and, if I show Massey I'm as crazy as the rest of these guys, the job will be mine and all mine next year.

He had a goal.

He had a plan.

Nothing could stop him.

Kotara also practiced as a ball guy, running on all cylinders, out front and on the loose, headed straight for the scout team kick returner. He planted his foot when the ball carrier broke wide, felt a pop, and realized his knee had twisted at an unnatural angle as he made the tackle. I knew something major had happened, he said, and it wasn't good.

A torn ACL in his knee had knocked Brian Kotara down and out for the season. He made a valiant effort at rehabilitating the knee, but time was running out for him. He wondered if he would ever be given the chance to come back and battle again for a spot in the starting line-up. Nobody was more easily forgotten than the injured. When a coach looked around for you, Kotara said, he was looking for someone to play. After awhile, he no longer bothered to look.

Kotara made the 12th man team. Nobody had given up on him. He made it with a limp. Thank God, Sherrill had wanted forty of them.

David Fry had never been what he called a skilled football player, not even in high school. My coach called me Omar, the rock chunker, he said. I had to chunk the damn football. I certainly couldn't catch it. I had brick hands. I couldn't catch a cold standing naked in the middle of Alaska.

David Coolidge (7) has the ball carrier firmly in his sights as the rest of the wild bunch close in hard and fast.

David Fry was more like a chunk of concrete on the move, only a little more solid and a lot tougher to block. When he drove his shoulder into your chest, you hoped you'd be able to catch your next breath before he nailed you again.

Fry was athletic. He had broad shoulders and a barrel chest. Football, he believed, had been invented with twenty-two man pileups in mind. He loved to start them or end them. It didn't really matter as long as he had an elbow in somebody's ribs. As Brian Carpenter said, on the playing field, David Fry was as mean as a desert rattlesnake. It's just that he could strike a lot quicker.

I thought I had a good chance to make the 12th man team, Fry said. I ran a 4.52 in the forty. I had been lifting weights for as long as I could remember and couldn't wait for somebody to throw us into the hitting drills. The game was on then. Just me and whichever crazy peckerwood wanted to go up against me. Didn't look for them. They found me. Didn't take long to weed the weak ones out.

Nobody weeded out Cory Allen.

He was the only guy I was ever afraid to fight, Fry said. I saw Cory get upset at a party one night, and he ripped a stop sign out of the ground, concrete slab and all. He shouldn't have done it. We should have told him not to do it. Nobody had the guts to stop him. I said, Mister Allen you just go ahead while I hold your beer for you.

David Joiner knew that the map had a lot of roads intertwined on its surface, and he sometimes felt as though he had taken them all, never quite knowing where the next highway would take him and wondering if the traveling would ever slow down or stop.

As a wide receiver in high school, Joiner had received a few calls and letters from Texas A&M, but nothing serious. The Aggies were little more than an idle curiosity on the football landscape. Nice of A&M to write. But who really expected David Joiner to play so far from home. His father was a career military man, stationed with the Pentagon in Washington, D.C., and the state of Texas was a two-day drive away even if the car was running hot, the highway patrol had cleared the freeways, and he didn't bother to sleep. Hell, College Station might be a day's drive after he crossed the state line in Texarkana.

As a result, David Joiner began his excursion into the world of college football at Shepherd College on the banks of the Potomac River in West Virginia. It was a four-year NAIA teacher's college, and Joiner knew he would be able to find both the degree and experience he needed at Shepherd to become a football coach, which was all he had ever wanted to do.

As a receiver in practice, the nose of the football tore the pinkie off of his right hand, and Joiner found it difficult, if not downright impossible, to either throw or catch the ball. The coach stuck him in the defensive backfield, but he said, I was too scared to be a defensive back. All I had ever done was catch the ball and run away from people. I didn't want to be hit, and I never really tore into anyone until I played for the 12th man.

When his family moved to Texas, David Joiner transferred his football allegiance to Stephen F. Austin, then traveled the road southwest to College Station as a junior. The transfer rule forced him to sit out a year, but Joiner dutifully walked on and, as the fifth receiver for the Aggie football team, believed he might actually have a chance to play in 1987.

Alas, Jackie Sherrill went out and recruited the great feet and soft hands of Rod Harris, and Joiner became an afterthought. The 12th man would be his only redemption.

Don't worry, he had been told by coaches. Even though you're having to sit out a year, we'll still let you travel with the team.

The day before the Aggies departed for Baton Rouge and a bayou brawl with LSU, however, Joiner heard a knock on his door. A coach was standing there. We've had to give your seat to someone else, he said. I'm afraid there won't be room for you.

Joiner worked hard.

He practiced hard.

There was never any room for him.

I remained an orange shirt, Joiner said, the lowliest of the low, just a shade below the scum of the earth. In practice one day, Coach Register called all of the orange shirts together and said, I want you to pretend like you have the ball. Run as hard as you can and see if you can get past the line of scrimmage.

I looked up, and there was Rod Sadler grinning at me. I hit the line at full speed, and I was pretty fast. Sadler almost killed me, and I knew what being hit was all about it. It was an eye-opening experience. No, it was an eye-shutting experience. I liked it better when I caught the ball and ran away from people. I wouldn't be doing that anymore.

The practice was almost as hot as R. C. Slocum's temper. His linebackers thought it was a walk-through. Maybe. Maybe half speed was fast enough. But Slocum had those competitive fires rampaging through his belly, and he didn't like the idea of his defense giving up a touchdown no matter where they might be playing – the practice field or the Cotton Bowl.

John Gregg was split out as a receiver. He was the hot end. He knew what play he was running. He knew what the ending would be. The ending was never good.

He would cut across the middle.

The linebackers would converge.

And one of them would do his best to tear John Gregg in half.

It happened every day.

It happened again and again and again every day.

This time, Gregg snared the pass a step quicker than anyone was expecting, and he was gone. The linebackers slowed down without giving chase, and John Gregg was running free and easy, his feet barely touching the ground. At least that's what it felt like to him. Not a thing in the world quite like it. Enjoy it now, he thought. It's not gonna last.

Slocum was upset, Gregg said. He made damn sure his defense was just as upset. On the next snap, I went down twenty yards, cut abruptly to the middle, and saw Dana Batiste coming my way.

He was the freight train, and I felt like a bug on the track in front of him. Now matter how fast I moved, it wouldn't be fast enough.

Dana eased up.

He wanted to learn his defensive assignment, but he had no interest in removing the top half of my body from the lower half.

My eyes were on him, not the ball.

I missed the pass.

Slocum didn't care what I did or didn't do. But he lit into Batiste with all he was worth. Slocum left no doubts. Batiste had a job to do, and he'd damn well better do it, or the coaches could find someone else who might possess the killer instinct that Batiste was sorely missing. No heart. No guts. No tenacity. No position. Hell, Slocum said, he had

a whole room full of linebackers looking for a place to play, and they weren't scared of hitting a worthless walk-on. A worthless walk-on was as good a name as any coach had called me for while.

When Gregg lined up again, he knew there would be hell to pay, and he had already paid hell enough that day. Hell kept him in debt for most of the year.

There were days, Gregg said, when we practiced in a slaughterhouse. This was one of them.

When the team wasn't living up to Jackie Sherrill's expectations, Blake Dwoskin said, he ran us through shotgun alley.

It wasn't offense against defense.

It wasn't scholarship players against walk-ons.

Sherrill lined us up, and he left a single running lane only five yards wide. There was a running back with a blocker out front, and both were facing a defensive lineman or a linebacker.

The drill was simple.

Block the defensive player, or the running back was in trouble.

Coach Sherrill's primary aim wasn't complicated, Dwoskin said.

He wanted to destroy the man with the ball.

He looked at me, and I knew what was coming.

I was the man with the ball.

It was too good a day to waste, Kirk Pierce thought. Spring was only a week or so away, the sun lay warm on his shoulders, and he was driving with David Fry through College Station in his new 1987 Conquest Turbo.

They drove past a Taco Bell.

See that slogan that says run for the border, Fry said. Let's do it.

You want a taco?

Hell, no, I want to run for the border.

Which way is Mexico?

South, unless they've moved it.

Before the sun rose again, Pierce and Fry had wheeled into Laredo. Mexico was only a few steps away. They walked across the river, past customs, and sat down on the curb, paying a young boy to keep bringing them bottles of beer, cold, warm, tepid, stale, cheap, or otherwise.

It didn't matter. Long before they were able to quench their thirst, they ran out of money.

Needed an ATM machine, but that was back at a bank in Laredo. Couldn't afford a taxi. The driver took their camera. More money only meant more beer. Thank God for the ATM.

By the time Pierce and Fry returned to College Station, they were sunburned, had gone far too many hours without sleep, and were suffering from severe hangovers, eyes glazed, heads throbbing, shoulders sagging, muscles aching.

They staggered into the weight room.

Gary Coster, a tight end, ran up to Kirk Pierce and asked, where have you been?

Mexico.

We've got the weight lifting competition this afternoon.

Doesn't' mean a damn thing to me. I'm a walk-on.

The hell it doesn't, Costner said. I've put up money that says you're gonna win the bench press.

Let me tell you a little secret, Pierce said.

What's that?

You've just lost your money.

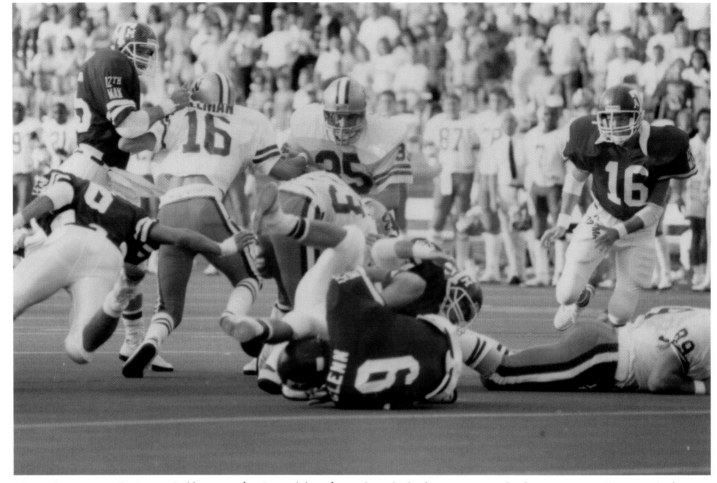

The 12th man wreaks havoc, led by Ronnie Glenn (9), Brian Edwards (16), Dean Berry (45). Garry Sorrell was at the bottom of the pile. He had tackled a blocker and the ball carrier both, and the TV announcers kept calling him the crazy one.

Chapter 24

Warren Barhorst would always be a big believer in fate. In March, with spring practice looming just around the corner, he decided that he and his sweetheart had waited long enough, and they began planning a wedding. He was a senior. College football had always seemed to be just one snap beyond his grasp, if not his reach. He had transferred from Stephen F. Austin and sat out a year, wearing the dreaded orange shirt and going to practice every day as a walk-on. He threw himself into the middle of a brawl each time someone stuck a football under his arm, and he was always wondering who would step up to hammer him senseless next. After awhile, the faces and numbers all looked the same. Only the size and speed were different. It wasn't long before the size and speed all began to look the same as well. Too many sacrifices, he thought. Too few rewards. Hell, there hadn't been any rewards.

Warren Barhorst wasn't one to walk away from adversity. Never had been. Never would be. But maybe, he thought, it was time to finally leave football for good.

All of the long hours, the unforgiving, demanding work, weren't worth the payoff of going out and maybe covering a single kickoff during the course of an unforgiving, demanding season that offered him absolutely no assurances of playing time. Of course, Dennis Mudd, a year earlier, had told him he might one day make one play that would ultimately change his life. More likely than not, one play would be forgotten before the sun cracked through the next morning.

Barhorst was a realist, and there was, after all, a real life waiting on the far side of the goal post.

Barhorst sat down with his prospective father-in-law, Ray Highsmith. I want to marry your daughter, he said, and here's my plan. I'll keep going to school, but I'll get a job so I can support her.

His thoughts, stumbling over each other in his mind, were: it's time I grew up, became an adult, and put away football along with the rest of my childish things. Better things to do with the rest of my life. I might as well get on with it. Simple decision to make, and he had made it.

Highsmith looked at him with the wisdom of a man who understood the turmoil raging within the heart of the young man and said, Warren, there's only one way I'll allow you to marry my daughter.

What's that, sir?

You don't quit football.

Tommy Bolcerek was certain of one thing. He had lost the last football game he would ever lose. As a linebacker and tight end for Brenham high school, he had suffered through a 2-8 record on a team that probably wasn't good enough to finish 2-8. He would be happy if he never heard another referee's whistle or walked back to the huddle trying to breathe while keeping the grass and dirt from staining his teeth.

Bolcerek was 5-10, weighed a solid 205 pounds, and was running the forty-yard dash, trying desperately to earn his way onto the Texas A&M baseball team. He looked up and saw a graduate assistant for football motioning him aside.

Have you ever heard of the 12th man kickoff team, the GA asked.

Sure. Who hasn't?

We're looking for players, and I think you just might have a shot to make it.

Frankly, Bolcerek told him, I still don't have a very good taste of football in my mouth.

We're not asking you to eat the damn thing, the GA said. We're wondering if you want to play football.

Bolcerek shrugged. Let's see how it goes with baseball, he said.

It didn't go well.

He pulled a hamstring in the alumni game, foolishly trying to show off and steal second base simply because his older brother was catching. The injury was devastating to him. Bolcerek lost out on any outside opportunity he might have had of landing a spot on the team. Could he hit? Maybe. Could he run? Not a chance.

He decided he might as well spend his time lifting a few weights and jogging a little, once the hamstring quit hurting, then wander on over to Kyle Field in the spring to see exactly what the 12th man tryouts were all about.

His forty time was usually around 4.8. Not fast enough, he had been told. If you can't break 4.8, then you might as well forget football and especially the 12th man. Jackie Sherrill liked speed. A 12th man had to fly downfield faster than the kick returner could make it back up field. Simple formula. The game really wasn't a complicated sport. Whoever got to where he was going the quickest won. It didn't say so in the rule book. But it was so.

Tommy Bolcerek began running the Kyle Field bleachers throughout the winter. He fought the cold rains and ice that hung like sheets upon the stands. Some days were hot and sweltering. Others were caked with mud. Sleet struck his face as though they had been shot randomly from scatterguns. The winds never let up or went away. Tommy Bolcerek kept running. Early and late, he kept running. Before a test and sometimes during a test, he kept running.

By the time Chris Massey let him run against the stopwatch, Bolcerek said, God and hard work had knocked five-tenths of a second off my time. A 4.75 looked pretty good, and it was good enough for Billy Pickard to throw him a red shirt.

David Fry looked down at the practice equipment he had been given. He had expected better. It was old. It was worn. The jersey was threadbare. The shoes didn't fit. The helmet wouldn't have offered much protection in a good rainstorm, he said The air bags in the helmets had all blown out five years before they were issued to the 12th man, and I wasn't for sure whether either the jersey or the jock strap had ever been washed. As a unit, the 12th man smelled to high heaven. After awhile, no one noticed.

Garry Sorrell had gone to Billy Pickard and said, honestly enough, we need new cleats. These are worn down to a nub.

You're walk-ons, Pickard said. You don't need a damn thing.

Sly Calhoun had overheard. He didn't say much, was always hanging around, and overheard everything. The next day, everyone had new cleats in their lockers. Sly was sly, and he felt deeply about the success and the health of the 12th man. He dutifully took care of them as long as he could keep Pickard from finding out about it.

Sorrell always wore a T-shirt that said: Jack Shit.

Fry bought one that said: I Know Jack Shit.

He often thought that he played football on the same field with Jack Shit. There sure were a lot of them around.

Fry missed practice one afternoon, and the head coach called him in to his office. Why, was all Sherrill wanted to know.

My girl friend's car broke down, Fry replied. I fixed it.

What's gonna happen if the car breaks down during a game?

At the moment, Fry said, I was tired, I was hurting, and I was lathered up with a craw full of sand. I had been hit one too many times to give a damn anymore. I didn't care if Sherrill kept me or kicked me off.

Coach Bob Davie answered for him. Don't worry, Davie said. Fry's a good man. He won't miss another practice.

You sure?

We need him. On the scout team, he's a damn good linebacker.

Doesn't mind getting hit?

Lives for it.

Can he help make the team better?

Fry likes to go home with somebody's ass in his hip pocket.

Sherrill nodded. Sherrill kept him.

The day would come when Jackie Sherrill had second thoughts.

It was just a drill in practice.

No, said David Fry, it was a hitting drill. They drilled, and the 12th man drilled them. If they thought they were too good to get hit, then they should have stayed home.

Fry slipped off of a block, tackled Bucky Richardson, and drove his helmet into the quarterback's gut.

Richardson's eyes flipped back in his head. He lay on the ground, doubled up, writhing in pain, trying to take a deep breath, wondering why all of the air had departed his lungs.

Coach Sherrill was mad, Fry said. His coaches were mad. The whole lot of them had a burr under their saddle. Coach Sherrill looked at me and said, get this worthless rattlebug off the field.

As Fry walked off the field, he was grinning. Well, he told himself, at least Coach Sherrill knows my name: Worthless Rattlebug.

Had been called better. Had been called worse.

For David Coolidge, it all ended much quicker than it began. He was a senior. He had become an anchor for the 12th man team. He had two Cotton Bowl rings, and he was working hard to prepare for a season where, with any luck, he might have the chance to play an actual position in a game.

That was the dream.

That would be the ultimate moment.

After all, Coolidge and Sean Page had come within two minutes and one roughing-the-kicker penalty of taking the field as defensive backs in the 1986 TCU game.

This would be his year.

No doubt about it.

But, once again, an injury hammered him in practice just before the first game with LSU. He tore a knee ligament, and Coolidge would spend the rest of the season in rehab, wondering if he would ever walk again, much less run, on a knee that didn't ache nearly as badly as his heart did. The season was passing him by.

The game was passing him by. He longed for one more practice. He longed to take one more hit. He longed to have his bell rung one last time. He thought long and deep, then finally told himself, hell, Coolidge, you must be as crazy as they say you are.

David Fry was majoring in football. No doubt about it. He had spent his life planning to become a veterinarian and realized that it would take the best of grades for him to be accepted in A&M's Vet School. God had given him a good brain. Some said he was as smart as anyone they had ever seen, and Fry's grades for three years were on the plus side of 3.5.

Then came his senior year.

Then came the 12th man.

I knew I'd be starting, Fry said, so I gave myself a week off from classroom work. Worked hard on the field. Practiced hard on the scout team. Took it easy when the sun went down. Thought I needed a break. I didn't need to go to class. I had the books. I'd just go down and study at the Dixie Chicken like everybody else.

The first week went so well for Fry, he said, I quit the second week as well.

I had a test coming.

Hadn't gone to class.

Didn't take any books to the Chicken.

Didn't know what the test would be about.

So I skipped the test.

Besides, science was boring as hell.

Statistics was even less interesting.

By now, I decided, I'm so far behind there's no reason for me to go to class at all until next semester. Maybe I didn't need to be a vet anyway. Maybe I'd just become a football coach. Hell, I knew all about football. It was simply a game where people kept stomping on each other, and, sooner or later, somebody scored. Not much to it.

David Fry would end the semester with a 0.0 grade point average.

He waited for the hammer to fall.

It didn't.

That wasn't so painful, he figured.

He worked no more or no less in the classroom and wound up the next semester with a 0.0 grade point average, too.

When it was all said and done, and he had made his last tackle for the 12th man, David Fry buckled down, went back to the classroom, studied hard enough to remedy his past transgressions, and worked his way into Vet School. For David Fry, football had always been more difficult than grades, and football was a snap.

The run for Cotton began again, and the Aggies were wondering if there was life after Kevin Murray, Johnny Holland, Roger Vick, and Rod Bernstine. The Aggies would miss them all. Jackie Sherrill even believed that A&M might have had a good shot at the national championship if Murray had stayed in school. Couldn't worry about what might have been but wasn't. Yesterdays had a nasty habit of always leaving. Sherrill and his coaching staff began trying to figure out how they could upset the time-worn form charts by becoming the first team to win three consecutive conference titles since those bastards from Austin had capped a six-year title streak in 1973. No other team had ever won more than two straight outright league championships.

Can we do it again, Sherrill wondered. That's the question everyone was asking. I don't know, he said. There's no question that it's tougher to repeat today than it ever has been mainly because of the limit on scholarships. When Texas was winning in those years, there was no limit. You could have forty-five or fifty kids in a recruiting class, and that makes an awful big difference. Coach Bryant used to say that for every sophomore you start, you're gonna lose a football game. At A&M this year, we're starting freshmen and expecting those freshmen to win games for us. Yet, if some of the young players come in and take somebody's job, that simply means we're a better team. Sherrill shrugged. He looked at the team's tough early schedule and said, I have no idea how good we'll be or how much we'll struggle. We'll just line up and find out.

Arkansas had climbed to the top of the pre-season polls with the Aggies named as a solid choice to finish no better than second. But Arkansas will feel the pressure, Sherrill said. We felt it last year, and it's not the best thing in the world.

The year before, as a transfer-walk-on, David Joiner witnessed a close-up and personal view of the dynamics between Jackie Sherrill and his coaching staff. They were all strong-willed men, self-assured, brimming with confidence, and fortressed within their own opinions. They all respected Coach Sherrill. When he spoke during practice, they knelt on one knee and took their caps off. It had all the reverence of a prayer meeting. Unlike the 12th man, none of them were afraid of Sherrill. He would not have hired a coach with a weak backbone.

Lynn Amedee was working an offensive drill, Joiner said.

Jackie Sherrill was watching.

Kevin Murray had been throwing swing passes to Roger Vick and Keith Woodside.

Jackie Sherrill suddenly stepped in and abruptly told Amedee. I want you to change the receiver's steps when he's running his route. He's doing it all wrong.

Amedee's face clouded with anger. Jackie, he barked, you hired me to run your damn offense. Now let me run the damn offense or fire me. If you're gonna run it, you sure as hell don't need me.

The 12th man team shows up for the Cotton Bowl extravaganza. Among the group are Harold Huggins, Ed Silverman, Sean Page, Russ Birdwell, Kirk Pierce, Danny Balcar, Warren Barhorst, Chad Adair, John Burnett, Garry Sorrell, David Fry, Brian Edwards, and Dean Berry.

From that moment on, Joiner said, Lynn Amedee ran the offense. Of course, he apologized the next day. After all, Sherrill was head coach. His opinions and his authority should never be questioned. Amedee said he was sorry for losing his temper.

You coach the offense, Sherrill said. You call the plays.

Thanks.

They'd better win games.

That was Jackie Sherrill, Warren Barhorst said. He didn't coach to have a job or keep his job. He didn't coach to keep the alumni or his players happy. He didn't coach for the honors he received. Jackie Sherrill coached to win.

John Gregg had seen the look in David Fry's eyes before. The practices had been brutal. Fry had grown tired of being a tackling dummy. He couldn't take his frustration out on Jackie Sherrill. Hell, in spite of all he endured, David Fry loved Jackie Sherrill.

But, damn, he wanted to take it out on somebody.

If you were looking for a fight and Fry went through the door first, Gregg said, you were out of luck. By the time you walked into the room, the fight was over.

Gregg and Fry were headed for the Dixie Chicken when they saw some drunk pick up a rock and throw it through the window. The glass shattered and ricocheted all over the parking lot.

Fry grabbed him. Why the hell did you do that, he asked.

Because I damn well felt like it, the drunk said.

The drunk looked down and spit in David Fry's face.

The next time he spit, he was spitting teeth.

Harold Huggins (24), Brian Edwards (16) Dean Berry (45), and Danny Balcar (2) celebrate and congratulate Garry Sorrell (26) after his tackle against the University of Washington.

Members of the 12th man team were convinced that their infamous party at the house on Holleman Street just might well be the social event of the year. Black ties not required. Shoes optional. Sororities, at least those who could show up under assumed names, had indicated they would be flocking to the shindig. The scholarship players, provided Jackie Sherrill did not have their curfew screwed too tight around them, already had the party penciled in on their social calendars.

We've got to fix the place up a little, David Fry said.

What do you have in mind, John Gregg asked him.

Pot plants. Fry grinned. Girls like pot plants.

Well, make up your mind, Garry Sorrell said. You can either buy pot plants or beer. We don't have the money for both.

You got your truck, Fry asked.

Yeah.

Still running?

Was yesterday.

Then let's take it for a little drive.

Fry, Sorrell, Gregg, and Butch Motley spent most of the night, driving up one street and down the next. It was dark. The self-respectable of College Station were sleeping. If a house happened to have a potted plant or a hanging basket out front, the boys simply backed up the pickup truck, climbed a few fences if necessary, and took it.

When Texas A&M put down new turf at Kyle Field, the maintenance crew had rolled up the old carpet and stuck it out of sight. The 12th man boys found the old, worn-out turf, took a roll from the 50-yard line and used it to carpet the patio.

From a dentist office, Gregg said, we hauled away a couple of trees that had been planted in wooden barrels as big as our ego. As Sorrell said, we had more plants than Moody Gardens.

The 12th man knew that beautiful plants were a big draw, especially when coeds were headed their way. Made them seem a little more civilized and helped soften their outlaw image. Girls loved outlaws as long as they knew the boys only bent the law and hardly ever broke it.

A year earlier, Sorrell, Fry, Gregg, and Brian Carpenter had driven around and collected baskets of plants and flowers for another get together long before any of them ever decided to bunker down in the house on Holleman Street. They knew they were tempting fate. They were good about tempting fate.

After they had made their last haul, a police car turned the corner and drove in behind them.

What are you boys doing, the officer asked.

We're decorating for a party, Sorrell had said.

Where'd you get the plants?

We borrowed them, Fry said.

I'm afraid you're gonna have to take them back.

How about tomorrow?

Tonight.

We're not really stealing.

I'd hate to explain that to the judge.

The policeman started to walk away, then slowly turned around and said, boys, I hope you've learned your lesson. This is your one freebie at Texas A&M.

We returned them all, Fry said. Every house we had visited had a plant or a hanging basket in the yard by the time the sun came up. We just couldn't remember which plant came from which house. I doubt if anybody ever noticed.

After a successful career on the 12th man team, Dennis Mudd, right, was chosen by Jackie Sherrill to serve as a graduate assistant coach, keeping the unit prepared and, more importantly, in check on the sideline.

Now, Sorrell was worried.

He doubted if the statue of limitations was up on their first haul, and now they were guilty again of the same damn crime.

Either fortunately or maybe unfortunately, it got a little easier the second time.

Crime always does.

His conscience never bothered him. The thought of a cold cell did.

Sorrell kept looking up and down the street as the first hint of dawn sneaked through the darkness. No police car was in sight. The first freebie was already on the books. They might not be so fortunate the second time.

As the Aggie football players waited to take the field against LSU, walk-on Alec Cuellar remembered Jackie Sherrill walking into the dressing room, staring down at the team with those intimidating eyes of his, and saying, gentlemen, the first game of the year may be the most important game of the year. The road to the Cotton Bowl starts here. What happened last year may as well never happened.

Sherrill removed his Cotton Bowl watch and held it at arm's length above his head.

LSU doesn't care what we did last year, he said. You shouldn't care what we did last year. The only year that counts is this year.

Sherrill paused dramatically, then yelled, to hell with last year.

He threw the Cotton Bowl watch against the wall and smashed it.

Jackie Sherrill was hard on watches.

The motivational tactic had not worked against Baylor.

It didn't have a prayer against LSU. The watch had been ticking toward disaster when it broke.

The Tigers came roaring into College Station, and as Lloyd Brumfield wrote in the Battalion, once again the Aggies started the season embarrassingly unprepared. As a result, they suffered a 17-3 defeat at the hands of a Louisiana State team that appeared to be a tad overrated. We got the same dreary story of penalties, mistakes, and offensive confusion that adds up to a dismal loss. The Aggies started the 1987 campaign using a stuffy, conservative offense that the Tigers devoured. It was run on first down, run on second down, pass on third, and punt on fourth. The Aggies didn't even complete a pass until six minutes into the second quarter. Actually, they completed one earlier, but it went to the wrong team. Craig Stump started, and Lance Pavlas entered the game in the fourth quarter.

Neither had been particularly effective. Both looked great on paper. The games would not be played on paper, and Sherrill was staring in the face a growing dilemma. He realized that, whether he liked it or not, he would spend the rest of the season with a quarterback controversy on his hands.

Jackie Sherrill did not blame the play calling of Lynn Amedee. Couldn't afford to.

Lynn Amedee didn't have Kevin Murray anymore.

Brian Carpenter remembered, when the game began, Kyle Field was so loud we had difficulty talking to each other when we warmed up in the end zone. Garry Sorrell looked over at me and yelled, if heaven is half as good as this, then we've all made it.

Before the game, LSU running back Harvey Williams, who almost became an Aggie, criticized A&M and its traditions, telling Sports Illustrated, I don't get off on all that military and uniforms and yell leaders. And that dog – Reveille – that dog is so sorry. I can't stand that dog.

Neither was Williams particularly impressed with the vaunted 12th man kickoff team. They were dogs, too. Lord, how he hated Aggie dogs. Those boys are slow, he said. Small. Walk-ons. He never gave walk-ons the time of day. They could eat his dust and spit mud. He was obviously far too great a running back to worry himself about any kind of trouble that a bunch of walk-ons could cause him. He said, I figure I ought to break a touchdown on them. That was a conservative estimate.

For Brian Carpenter, it was his first time downfield.

It marked the first time he had ever hit someone other than an Aggie in practice.

He was looking for the ball.

He found it. Then found the man who held it.

He slammed into the kick returner and looked him in the face.

Didn't recognize him.

Didn't know the number.

Didn't mean a thing.

Brian Carpenter, who never played football in high school, had just taken both ends of the illustrious Harvey Williams and buried them in the turf of Kyle Field.

Harvey Williams had been wrong. Dead wrong. He did not break a touchdown on the 12th man.

Sam Martin almost did.

The Aggies were trailing, 10-3, when Sean Page ran onto the field as the 12th man safety for the second-half kickoff. He had seen a lot of action. He had made very few plays. Tackles were generally made far downfield in front of him. If the ball carrier ever broke through the crease and reached the safety, the 12th man was facing dire circumstances. Only one man was left to make the play. The odds had suddenly become about as low as they could get. It was a game like any other game, Page thought. Be ready. Keep your eyes open. Keep your head on a swivel. Wait for somebody to make a tackle. Jump up and down. Wave your towel. Take your seat on the bench again.

Sam Martin grabbed the ball on the kickoff.

Sam Martin broke it. By the time he reached his own 45-yard line, Page said, it was just him and me, face-to-face. That's all. A fleet-footed athlete. And a walk-on. He saw daylight. I saw the tragic ending to a wonderful fairy tale. I thought, Oh, my God, here he comes, and I'm going down in history. I'm destined to be the one who ends it all. He's gonna score, and the 12th man is going into the trash heap. It's over. If he gets past me, it's over. As a kickoff team, we had become too predictable. Scott Slater almost always kicked the ball to the left side of the field, and LSU had been watching too many game films. They knew where the ball was going as well as we did, and LSU set up the wedge toward the other side, the empty side of the field. And here he came in a dead sprint. Wide open, through the seam, past the wedge, running wild, his eyes flashing, his legs churning. Sam Martin

had found the soft spot.

A walk-on volunteer and fifty-five yards separated Martin from paydirt. Page said. I saw Scott Slater out of the corner of my eye. He was coming hard, and Martin caught sight of him in his peripheral vision. He veered sharply toward the sidelines. He had never broken stride when I hit him. He was past mid-field, and I hit him. He was bigger and faster. I was more desperate. He was a step away from a touchdown. I was a step away from oblivion.

We went down in a heap. I held on until I heard the whistle, and even then, I was afraid to let go. I wanted to celebrate, but we were behind by a touchdown, and the 12th man just given up its longest return. As I ran off the field, I could hear Coach Sherrill screaming. He was as mad as a wet hornet. I kept running until I reached the far end of the bench. It may have been a meaningless non-conference game to the rest of the world, but it was the most meaningful tackle I had ever made. It meant the 12th man would take the field again.

When Monday's team session with the coaches ended, Slocum met with Dean Berry, who had fought his way up the ladder and was running second-team linebacker behind the armored tank they called Dana Batiste. Slocum didn't beat around the bush. You're now running first-team linebacker, he said, his voice filled with conviction.

What about Dana?

You want the job?

Yes, sir.

Then don't worry about Dana.

My emotions exploded and hit the ceiling this time, Berry said. He knew that the coaches had been extremely upset with the loss to LSU, and there had been rumors that Sherrill was ready to make some wholesale changes. The team had embarrassed him. It would not happen again. Dean Berry finally had the chance he had always wanted and

Bubba Hillje (13) and Trent Childress (17) have one goal in mind, and that is to stop the ball carrier inside the 20-yard line. Get there fast, and do a little damage along the way. They have done their job.

The 12th man unit had no problem playing hurt. Kirk Pierce exhibits a severe turf burn on his arm. Bite the bullet, play with pain, and keep going. It was their basic motto.

David Joiner had grabbed a pass near the sideline, and Kip Corrington, a tall, thin, raw-edged time bomb, slammed him hard against the chain links of a fence surrounding the practice field. It was nothing new. He had been thrown into the cyclone fence so often that, after practice, he and Sean Page would count to see who had the most bruises. They looked a lot like tattoos before they turned purple.

I knew the knee was hurt, Joiner said. I expected the worse. I figured I had a torn ACL. I had two options. I could have the doctor check it, or I could forget about the pain and keep playing. It was my senior year, and I had no intention of losing my spot on the 12th man.

He ignored the knee.

He figured it wouldn't kill him.

If I ran hard enough, he said, it didn't hurt so bad.

It would be another seven years before David Joiner finally underwent surgery to repair the knee.

It was the one drill everybody dreaded. It had nothing to do with one player trying to hammer another into submission. It was a time when players had to dig down deep and battle the inner turmoil churning within their guts. It took place in the open end of the horseshoe, Blake Dwoskin said.

We'd run in place as hard as we could.

We'd hit the turf.

We'd pop up.

We'd run in place.

Time and again, it never changed.

Run.

Hit the turf.

Pop up.

Run again.

Our legs were turning to rubber. We couldn't breathe. The heat was beating down on us without any relief. Our muscles cramped. Some were throwing up. Somebody was always throwing up.

We hoped Coach Sherrill would let us quit, Dwoskin said.

But he didn't. He wouldn't.

Coach Sherrill was doing the drill with us, and if he wasn't running out gas, then we'd better not be running out of gas either.

Against the University of Washington, the A&M defensive pressure was relentless as the Aggies ran away with a 29-12 victory.

By the time the game ended, Huskie quarterback Chris Chandler was no longer the nation's leading candidate to win the Heisman Trophy. He had been battered, blitzed, and bruised.

He was sacked four times, he fumbled twice, and Chandler was only able to complete 11 passes for a meager 120 yards. Dean Berry may have been wearing a big cast on his hand, but Sherrill had not lied to him.

If Texas A&M kicked or received, even on punts, Dean Berry was in the game. The pieces may have been small, but he had been able to put a few of the broken ones back together – enough to ease, if not alleviate, his years of disappointment.

Carrying around a battered and broken hand, Berry had been dropped to third-team inside linebacker and pretty much forgotten. When my hand heals, what are my chances for playing, Berry asked Slocum.

Well, son, the coach said, you're a real good athlete but not as good as the two in front of you.

The season would pass. Dean Berry never got a snap at linebacker.

never believed possible. Neither Sherrill nor Slocum would regret their decision, he told himself.

It would be a Monday for unbridled excitement.

It would be a Monday when the dream slipped away for good.

In practice, Berry fell awkwardly during a drill, caught his hand in the bars of some offensive lineman's facemask, and knew the hand was broken the moment it happened. He heard the snap. He felt the wave of nausea before he felt the pain. I didn't bother to tell anyone until practice was over, he said. I kept hitting, and I kept hurting. I was running first team linebacker. A simple little break wasn't going to stop me.

The doctor studied the X-rays and said, in simple terms, that the hand had suffered a splintered fracture.

For Dean Berry, the fracture meant he wasn't a linebacker anymore. You had to use your hands to play inside linebacker, and my hand was virtually useless. The cast did not interfere with his ability to tackle, so Berry had not lost his spot on the 12th man. But his hopes of ever playing linebacker for Texas A&M on game day were shattered. He lay awake that night and stared at the ceiling, the room as dark and empty as he felt. It had all come apart, and he knew he would never be able to put the pieces back together again.

Jackie Sherrill, however, had other ideas. At a team meeting, he called out, where's Berry?

Dean Berry froze. I was afraid I was in trouble, he said.

Where's Berry?

Berry slowly stood to his feet. Here, I am, Coach, he said.

Sherrill looked at the cast weighing down his hand and asked, can you play with that thing?

I can hit all right. I use my head and shoulders for that anyway. Berry shrugged nonchalantly. I'm a senior coach. Pain is no longer part of the equation.

Sherrill nodded. We're gonna find you a place to play, he said.

Berry grinned. I knew I must have done something right, he said.

Vince Palasota (1), Garry Sorrell (26), beside the referee, Trent Childress (17), Tommy Bolcerek (25), and Kirk Pierce (10) knew no fear and had no doubts in their ability to draw a line in the dirt and keep the opposition on the other side.

Chapter 25

Sherrill was becoming concerned about his 12th man team. The quick Steve Jones of Washington, the nation's fourth leading kick returner, bombed A&M right out of the chutes for thirty-eight yards. Scott Slater was given orders to squib kick the ball, but he nailed a hard line drive. The 12th man had trouble locating the ball, and it reached

Jones much quicker than anyone anticipated. Slater had made one mistake. He didn't make a second, flying recklessly across the field and knocking Jones out of bounds at the 44-yard line.

As Larry Bowen of the *Bryan Eagle* wrote, the 12th man usually runs down the field like a group of convicts who just escaped. They were a bit more reserved on the first trip downfield against Washington. All of us were a little timid at first, said Dean Berry.

We weren't going down like we have in the past because we were afraid of letting that guy get by us. We were just trying to get him down instead of going full speed like we usually do.

The statistics spoke loudly. In 1983, the 12th man had allowed an average return of 13.1 yards. It was 16.6 in 1984, 14.2 yards in 1985, and 18.1 in 1986, but, during the chaotic days of 1987, the average return began to edge higher than it had ever been before. Nobody was pleased. The 12th man team was bewildered. Sherrill's temper was not yet boiling, but it was growing closer by the game.

Said Chris Massey, I guess we were going against the law of averages. Sooner or later, now matter who you put out there, the law of averages said somebody was probably going to break one. The odds of a return being broken were becoming greater every time we went out there and covered a kickoff.

Jackie Sherrill didn't give a damn about the law of averages.

He did not believe in them.

Neither did the 12th man. After Jones broke free for thirty-eight yards, the kickoff team settled down, laced their cleats tighter with fire and fear, bowed their necks, and held the Huskies to only a scant forty-three yards on the next three returns.

Jackie Sherrill made the change he dreaded to make. Under the signal calling of Craig Stump and Lance Pavlas, his high-powered offense had fizzled, moving as though a cylinder or maybe a sparkplug was missing. It limped along, looking like a world beater one minute and the end of the world the next.

Sherrill took a deep breath, hoped he wasn't making a mistake, and removed the sacred redshirt from Bucky Richardson.

He turned the offense over to a true freshman, who, Sherrill said, felt a lot more comfortable running the football than he did throwing it. The Aggies hammered their way past an old nemesis, Southern Mississippi, 27-14, as Richardson and Darren Lewis both rushed for more than a hundred yards.

Sometimes, a man's wishes weren't worth the trouble. In high school and on the practice field, David Joiner said, I had always played on grass. Nothing but grass. Deep down, I had always wanted to know how it would feel to play on turf.

Now he knew.

He didn't like it.

David Joiner had carpet burns stacked on top of his carpet burns.

And the heat was sweltering, unbearable. With an unmerciful sun

Lubbock, as always, was a deadly and disappointing place to be in October. The Aggies lost to Texas Tech, 27-21, as two last-ditch passes went for interceptions. Ronnie Glenn, along with Dean Berry, was on the traveling team, and he said, the cowbells were ringing so loudly our heads hurt. We had to keep our helmets on because the Red Raider fans began throwing bottles at us as soon as we ran out of the tunnel.

As Sherrill had said, it was good to be the champion. It was damn hard to defend the title. Against Houston, the defense came through one more time, shutting down Andre Ware, one of the nation's most potent and prolific quarterbacks. The Wrecking Crew blitzed and blitzed, then blitzed some more. Sherrill had joked earlier in the week about dropping all eleven players back in pass coverage, especially after Texas Tech had burned the A&M blitz and toasted the secondary. Instead, the Aggies peeled their eyes back and went after Ware as if he had a bulls-eye painted on his jersey.

Ware's intimidating assault on the Houston record books came to an abrupt halt. He was dropped for sacks seven times and held to no more than a 120 yards, well below his season passing average. He looked mortal for a change. The Aggie offense misfired and backfired

Danny Balcar (2) and Doug Middleton (8) lead the cheers as the offense moves steadily downfield. To the right are Chris Probst and David Coolidge. The quicker the score, the quicker the 12th man returned to the field. It was all about kickoffs.

beating down on Kyle Field before the game, a team trainer had taken a thermometer out and placed it at midfield.

What's it say, Joiner asked.

Near as I can tell, it's 147 degrees, the trainer said, but it may be off a degree or two.

If it were, Joiner thought, it was a degree or two to the hot side.

and came out firing blanks. As Tammy Hedgpeth wrote in the *Battalion*, the switching of the quarterbacks was like a merry-go-round. Not one of them took a leadership role. Sherrill was hoping to find a quarterback who had the cunning and the tenacity to come in and take charge. He was still looking. A young team. An inexperienced team. It was like saying we have bad luck, Hedgpeth wrote. It's just an excuse. The Aggies won, 22-17, but the nails were already bitten back and the fingers bloody by the time the game finally came to a merciful end with two straight sacks of Ware. Houston was dancing inside the A&M 25-yard line when the music stopped.

Even the 12th man, Jackie Sherrill's rock of Gibraltar, was beginning to reveal a few unexpected cracks. Brian Edwards made two game-saving tackles of kickoff returns as James Dixon burst like a missile up the middle. Containment had been shoved rudely aside, and that was an unpardonable sin. Hedgpeth wrote, if you can't rely on the 12th man kickoff team, then who can you rely on? Once as impenetrable as the Great Wall of China, the 12th man team had fallen back on its heels, lost confidence in itself, was more afraid of giving up a touchdown than making a tackle. Coach Massey was sweating bullets. He pointed out, there are only three people on the unit with any experience – Dean Berry, Ronnie Glenn, and Danny Balcar – so we're putting a lot of new faces in the game. The 12th man still had Sherrill depending heavily on them and the student body cheering wildly for them, but the team had lost its swagger.

Reporting on yell practice before the Houston game, Anthony Wilson of the *Battalion* wrote, the 12th man members must have gotten caught up in the emotion and heat of the moment because they said some incredibly foolish things. They talked about how they were going to mash, maul, mangle, and generally be all-around tough guys once they took the field. They were going out and kick a little butt and beat the ever-livin' daylights out of Cougar High's smurf-sized returners. Undoubtedly, Houston's James Dixon, who is tenth in the nation in kickoff returns with a 28.7 average, must have been shaking in his red smurf-shoes. All the 5-foot-10, 185-pound Dixon did was return five kicks for 171 yards and a 34.2 average. In the fourth quarter, Dixon broke a return for 53 yards, the second longest ever against the 12th man, before being dragged to the turf on a touchdown-saving tackle by kicker Scott Slater. If Slater had not stopped Dixon from scoring, his touchdown probably would have won the game for Houston. Another startling statistic about the 12th man is that Slater is tied for second place on the squad in tackles. The leading 12th man tacklers, Brian Edwards and Garry Sorrell, have only three tackles, and Slater is just one behind them.

R. C. Slocum read the column and nodded. It was as he had always suspected and feared. As Wilson so eloquently pointed out, the 12th man had consistently let opponents start drives with excellent field position. The A&M coaching staff, he wrote, should give serious consideration to benching the 12th man the rest of the season. The Aggies have three remaining home games. Two of those are against conference foes Arkansas and Texas. If A&M loses either of those games, their Cotton Bowl hopes will turn into toilet bowl reality. The bottom line is that it would be a real pity to lose a championship due to special team play.

Slocum wondered if Sherrill had read the column, too.

If Sherrill had, he never mentioned it.

For the 12th man team member, the towel was his symbol of courage, honor, and duty on field. It represented his love and devotion for his team and his school. When waved overhead, the towel did a pretty good job of raising the noise of Kyle Field another decibel.

team meeting.

Alec Cuellar was clutching his strip of balsa. He was always on edge and on the edge of his chair when Jackie Sherrill walked into the dressing room.

Sherrill, he said, looked out across the room and said, I want you to understand exactly why I gave you a piece of balsa wood. By itself, it's not very strong. It's brittle.

Sherrill picked up a piece and, with a quick snap of his fingers, broke it.

Then he reached down and grabbed several strips of balsa wood that had been glued together.

Sherrill banged it against the wall.

He hit it with a hammer.

The balsa wood held strong and solid.

An individual standing alone is pretty weak, Sherrill said, but when everyone sticks together, and we all work together as a team, nothing can break us. You can become very good.

It was his style, Cuellar said. When Coach Sherrill drove a point home, he knew how to illustrate it so that we would never forget.

E ach member of the Texas Aggie football team found piece of balsa wood, about three inches wide and ten inches long, in his locker. On it was stapled a note that read: Bring this to the next

B aylor had historically put the fear of God in Texas A&M. When the Aggies and the Bears tangled, the scoreboard would be lit with a giant fireworks display. The Aggies did their part. With

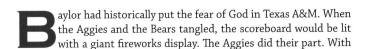

Bucky Richardson at the helm, they blasted the scoreboard with an impressive thirty-four points. Baylor's game plan went woefully awry. The Bears only managed eight first downs, fifty-two yards rushing, and ten points. Jackie Sherrill once again had his sights aimed at the Cotton Bowl. Officials from the Peach, Bluebonnet, Independence, and Holiday Bowl attended the game, but they all filed into the Bear's locker room. Baylor had hung "Think Cotton" signs all over the stadium, but as darkness descended on Waco, the banners were quietly taken down.

Rice wasn't able to stop the Aggies nearly as often as penalties did, and A&M managed to flee Houston with a 34-21 win. It could have been a dogfight, Sherrill said, but the Aggie faithful outnumbered the Rice fans, the Aggie defense ratcheted its game up a notch when its back was pressed against the wall, and Bucky Richardson joined Keith Woodside in gaining more than a hundred yards on the ground. Owl coach, Jerry Berndt said simply, I think we lost the game because in the third quarter we couldn't put any points on the board.

That would usually do it every time.

Louisiana Tech proved to be less trouble, falling, 32-3, even though it sometimes seemed that A&M had been sleep walking for four quarters and having a difficult time taking the game seriously. A non-conference encounter. Small school. A frantic, last-minute replacement for the Mustangs of SMU, whose football program had suddenly been derailed by the NCAA. SMU's games had been cancelled and its schedule ripped up and thrown away for a year. The death knell had sounded in Dallas.

The killer instinct may have been missing from A&M's scholarship players, but not from the 12th man. Garry Sorrell said, we covered eight kickoffs that day, and the only thing better than going down on eight kickoffs was going downfield on nine. On every one of them, however, somebody cut my knees with an illegal block. I kept looking around for a flag. None ever hit the ground. Well, I thought, if the referees don't have a real interest in throwing any flags, I might as well get myself up and fight somebody. If they won't stop those illegal cuts, I'll do it myself. That was our mentality. If we can't outscore you, we'll at least outkick and outfight you.

For Kirk Pierce, it was a day of reckoning. He needed every one of those eight kickoffs. For two years, he had played behind Dean Berry, and with forty seconds left in the game – and with A&M kicking off for the last time – Kirk Pierce finally made his way onto the field.

He was fast.

He was a ball guy.

The ball was in the air.

And he was looking for a reason to prove why his teammates called him Rock.

In practice, the scholarship players had a grudging, then a growing admiration for the tenacity of those wearing a number twelve patch on their game-day jerseys.

As David Joiner remembered, they would clue us in when they knew the drills had suddenly reached a boiling point.

Wide receiver Tony Jones looked at him and said, the man's got his stinger out.

What's new?

It's on. We're coming after you.

David Joiner sighed and kept an eye out for Rod Sadler. Sadler was a menace. He hardly ever talked to me, Joiner said, and when he did, he was usually standing over me, looking down while I was spitting out dirt and grass stems, and saying, are you all right, punk?

No. But I sure as hell didn't tell him.

Aaron Wallace was a physical freak that God had blessed with abilities other football players only coveted. He was big. He was strong. He was fast. He never worked out, David Fronk said. He never lifted weights. He smoked two packs of cigarettes a day, sometimes more if he had them. He was strong enough to turn a pothole inside out with one yank. God invented Aaron Wallace for the sole purpose of playing football.

As a tight end on the scout team, Fronk was told, hook the linebacker and keep him off the quarterback on the option play.

Wallace had been told, you better not let that walk-on son of a ditch digger hook you on the play.

The ball was snapped.

Wallace charged.

Fronk took a quick step to the left, shaded Wallace to the outside, and hooked him, sealing off the linebacker while the quarterback dashed for daylight.

Aaron Wallace wasn't just upset, Fronk said. He was mad enough to bite the head off a hammer. He wanted to kill me. He had loafed on the play. I had gone as hard as I could. Wallace looked at me with those angry eyes of his and said, it's just a drill, man. It's just a drill.

The scout team lined up again.

Fronk waited for the staccato of the quarterback's cadence.

But before Coach Bob Davie even said set, before the ball was snapped, while the quarterback was still standing over the center surveying the defense, Fronk said, Wallace suddenly tore madly across the line of scrimmage and cold-cocked me.

You win one. I win one, Aaron Wallace muttered. Now it's your turn. See if you can stop me.

Nobody stopped Aaron Wallace when he turned his motor on and shifted to another gear, a gear the rest of them didn't have.

I knew without a doubt, Fronk said, that it was going to be a longer than usual afternoon.

On Fridays, while the varsity was walking through plays during its final dress rehearsal before game day, the 12th man was shoved aside, and told, as pleasantly as possible, to stay the hell out of the way. They were exiled to the far end zone.

For awhile, they passed the time playing flag football.

Then it turned into full-speed, high-impact tackle football.

In shorts.

Without pads.

Finally Jackie Sherrill told them, you boys keep that up and you're asking for trouble. It's a damn good way to get hurt. It's a damn good way to ruin your careers.

That surprised them.

At the moment, they hadn't realized they had a career in football.

Contact, maybe.

Collisions, perhaps.

But damn little of what any of them would call a career.

So Brian Edwards came up with the idea of walking football.

Don't run.

Walk.

It was half-speed, half-ass, low-impact football, and it was easy for the 12th man to understand why Edwards had invented the game.

Nobody could walk faster than Brian Edwards.

Jackie Sherrill came to practice mulling over an idea on an innovative tactic the Aggies could implement to confuse the Razorbacks. He loved to confuse other coaches and other teams. Again,

Celebrating three consecutive Southwest Conference championships are Ronnie Glenn (seated), kneeling (left to right) Chad Adiar and Sean Page, Standing (left to right) Dean Berry, Warren Barhorst, John Burnett, and Harold Huggins. In the back are Danny Balcar and David Fry. It was the time of their lives, a great time to be a Texas A&M football player.

Sherrill was looking for an edge, and he thought he had found one. His thoughts centered on All-American safety Kip Corrington.

This is what we'll do, Sherrill said. We'll change Kip's number, hide him in the defensive backfield, and Arkansas will have trouble finding him. They won't know where he is, so they can't run away from him.

Won't work, Dana Batiste told him.

Why not?

Kip's the only white player you got back there, Batiste said. I don't care what his number is. Arkansas can find him.

A showdown with Arkansas was dawning on the horizon, and the *Bryan Eagle* reported, R. C. Slocum signaled a defensive call from the sideline, and his Texas A&M defense huddled. *Forty-four mess*, safety Chet Brooks said, and the players smiled. Good call, they thought. Too bad it wasn't the play Slocum called. Or recognized. Or devised.

Slocum was looking for repetitions, not innovations. Slocum was running his players through a series of drills to assure himself they understood the signals. He admitted later to being a little intense. In two days, the Aggies were to play Arkansas in a game that could eliminate them from Cotton Bowl contention. They also would be playing their first wishbone team. He wanted perfection.

Slocum squinted at his defense as the scout team quarterback's sharp signals stabbed the November air. Ball snapped, the best defense in the conference went into motion. Safeties Brooks and Kip Corrington blitzed up the middle, nose guard Sammy O'Brient dropped back into safety, and the defensive tackles ran out to the corners.

Slocum's brow wrinkled. What is this, he asked. Run it again, he said. The players tried but were laughing too hard. Don't worry about it, coach, Brooks said. We have it under control.

So they did. The Aggies were first in the league in pass defense and second in rush defense. They had allowed opponents only 3.7 yards per play. Nobody in the SWC was better. Sherrill said he wanted his players to be loose and aggressive. Offenses are too regimented to have a personality, he said. Defenses are off-the-cuff, quick-tempered, the bad little boys at the party. Loud, profane, funny, attacking. They chew on offenses. They get a team down and then tell them how they did it.

We don't see it as talking trash, Brooks said.

And if an opposing player disagreed?

I just tell him to look at the scoreboard, Brooks said.

Nobody liked the arrogant Aggie defense.

The arrogant Aggie defense didn't give a damn.

Arkansas had been the pre-season favorite among the leering press that earned its livelihood covering Southwest Conference football. Most

After being bruised and battered in practice all week, the 12 man team – Vince Palasota (1), Greg Nehib (2), Bubba Hillje (13), Garry Sorrell (26), and Tommy Bolcerek (25) were ready to deal out a little punishment of their own on game day. For them, it was payback time.

Garry Sorrell remembered, when the game started, it must have been 120 degrees on the field. The heat was insufferable, but before halftime, a cold front came roaring through out of the north. It was a wet cold, and the day became so dark it looked a lot like night. TCU turned on the lights, and we changed into long-sleeved shirts.

Ronnie Glenn hated TCU's home field. The turf was old and starting to unravel, he said, and the Frogs were using a carefully devised kickoff scheme with their up-front players crisscrossing the field to pick us off one at a time like snipers. I had to get past the front line of blockers before anyone reached me, and I was afraid that the zippers holding the artificial turf together would trip me up and slow me down. Coach Sherrill called for one of his famous squib kicks. I cut past the line of blockers, and, as the returner picked up the ball, I dove. The hit drove the TCU ball carrier backward. He went one way. The ball bounced in another direction, and A&M's William Thomas fell on it.

Maybe that will silence the critics, Glenn thought.

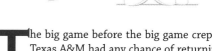

of the sports writers predicted an offensive bombardment when the Aggies and Razorbacks hooked up in a war as lethal as a nuclear blast. Whoever scored last would probably score the most. That's what the newspapers reported, so it must be true.

The Hogs never had a chance.

The vaunted but one-dimensional Arkansas wishbone attack gained only forty-five yards during the first forty-four minutes of the game, and A&M proudly marched away with a 14-0 win. Said Chet Brooks, the goose egg on the scoreboard speaks for itself. Craig Stump, withering away on the sidelines, came off the bench to engineer a 78-yard, sixteen-play touchdown drive that erased any dying prayer the Razorbacks had for a date in Dallas on New Year's Day.

There were a lot of players who really hung in there, Sherrill said, and Craig was one of them. We started off the year not really performing well, and I kept saying that it wasn't the quarterback's fault, at least not all of it. Craig never let it get him down. He was ready to respond and come in when we needed him most. As Doug Hall wrote in the *Battalion*, fumble, stumble, and fall. So went Arkansas' Cotton Bowl hopes.

In Fort Worth's Amon Carter Stadium, Darren Lewis unleashed a formidable bolt of thunder and lightning, racing for 194 yards on just sixteen carries as A&M battered a worrisome but troubled TCU team, 42-24. With the Frogs leading in the fourth quarter and the Aggies facing a stiff wind, Lewis fumbled a pitchout from Stump but picked up the ball on the bounce and raced eighty yards. TCU Coach Jim Wacker, who was never at a loss for words, found himself at a loss for words. Finally he was able to mutter, we had this one, but the ball bounced funny in this crazy game. Maybe I should have been a basketball coach. Sherrill only raised his eyes skyward and said, when that happened, I knew that somebody besides an Aggie was on our side.

The big game before the big game crept inexorably into sight. If Texas A&M had any chance of returning to the Cotton Bowl for the third consecutive year, the Aggies had to overcome the same formidable task it had encountered since football was invented. It must beat Texas again. It seemed as though nobody in the State of Texas had slept for days. On Sunday, the Aggies didn't rest. They practiced. Bonfire was growing log by log. Jackie Sherrill participated in A&M's famed elephant walk, even striding briskly through the water and mud in his suit, tie, and high-dollar leather shoes. Many were disappointed he hadn't walked on the water. It would have been a better sign. In Austin, the Longhorn faithful were holding a candlelight pep rally on the south side of the campus mall. Texas was trying to rekindle the old-fashioned, time-honored, occultic Texas hex, burning red candles in an effort to break its losing streak against the Aggies. They should have been orange. Red didn't do a thing for them.

When Sherrill and Texas Coach David McWilliams met in Houston for the annual Aggie-Longhorn Day at the Touchdown Club, toastmaster Cactus Pryor said, the stakes are high. It's not life or death, but playing for the Cotton Bowl with the loser going to the Bluebonnet Bowl is like playing for "life" or a lifetime in Wichita Falls.

At the infamous house on Holleman Street, David Fry could not resist the overpowering urge, or perhaps its was temptation, to shoot something, anything.

He pulled out a 9mm pistol and fired fifteen times in and around and into John Gregg's helpless barbecue pit. I would have hit it every time if the damn thing hadn't kept moving, Fry said.

Gregg heard a knock at the door.

He opened it, and a squad of policemen walked in. What's going on here, one of them asked. We heard shots.

Nothing's happening, Gregg said.

Nobody's shooting anything around here, Fry said. He looked out of one eye and then the other.

The policeman looked down and began to count. He found at least ten bullet holes in the floor, no doubt made by the 9mm pistol David Fry was still clutching in his hand.

The case went to trial, and John Gregg walked into the courtroom to testify. He still wasn't sure if he was testifying on behalf of David Fry or the barbecue pit. He did not know whether shooting a barbecue pit was a felony or a misdemeanor. He sure hadn't pressed charges. Something about seeing Fry holding the 9mm, however, had unnerved the policeman.

David Fry did not see any reason to waste good beer money on an attorney, so he made the decision to represent himself in court.

The judge looked down at him, frowned, adjusted his glasses, and said, Mister Fry, it says here that you were shooting at a barbecue pit.

That is a mistake, your honor.

What's the mistake?

Sir, David Fry said with as much dignity as he could muster, I was shooting at a snake, and the barbecue pit simply got in the way.

Did you kill the snake?

Damn fast snake, sir.

We had a big game coming up, Gregg said. I guess the judge liked to watch us play. Knew we needed every good or ordinary player we could get. He laughed and had mercy on us all.

All year, Jackie Sherrill kept bugging Chris Massey.

How are the boys doing, he would ask.

All right, I guess.

Any of them getting into any trouble?

Why do you ask?

They sometimes practice like they have a hangover, Sherrill said.

They play better that way.

Jackie Sherrill thought it over for a minute, then nodded his head. They probably do, he said.

Jackie Sherrill was enforcing a strict curfew for the game. But, as Bubba Hillje said, curfews never bothered the 12th man. Nobody kept a watch over us. They didn't care when we came or when we went. If we got hurt, drunk, or jailed, the program wasn't in any danger of losing a scholarship. We came and went as we pleased. We all wandered out sometime after midnight to work on Bonfire. The game was growing closer. The stack was growing ever higher.

Brian Carpenter remembered, the night was cold and dripping with rain, and the ground had become a river of mud. The rain kept falling, the temperature was dropping, and we spent most of the night carrying logs. Along about four o'clock in the morning, we sat down on the curb and shoved a case of beer between us. We were tired and thirsty and chilled to the bone, but we didn't have a care in the world.

Suddenly Jackie Sherrill walked up beside them. He looked down. He saw a few glassy eyes and the case of beer.

What are you boys doing, he asked.

Getting in the spirit, Kirk Pierce told him, munching on pork skins, dipping them in a bottle of Tabasco sauce he had borrowed from Cain Hall. It wasn't stolen. He would take the bottle back. It would be empty when he did.

Carpenter looked up. You want a beer, he asked.

No.

Want some pork skins, Pierce asked.

Sherrill grinned. I'm riding the crane up to the top stack, he said.

Any of you want to come with me?

Can't do it, David Fronk told him. We're not allowed up there. We're not seniors.

Neither am I, Sherrill said.

No, Fronk thought, gods don't have to be seniors.

You boys be careful, Sherrill said as he walked toward the stack. He still had a couple of hours to wire logs together before sunup. At Bonfire, he was able to keep his sanity.

If you played for Coach Sherrill, Garry Sorrell said, and he knew you were giving him everything you had on the field, then he took care of you. On the field, he was full of intensity and all business. He was larger than life. Away from the field, he came real close to being a genuine, caring human being.

Michael Guerra, a Red Pot, remembered, we were in the middle of "push," and the weather was horrible. A typical November cold front was hammering us, and the site was soaked with rain. You had to be crazy or a frog to get out in it, and we only had a dozen or so working on Bonfire that night. They could only manage to put one log at a time on the stack. Duncan Field was virtually deserted.

It was shortly before two in the morning, and I saw Jackie Sherrill come sloshing through the mud. He ruined a lot of shoes in the mud around Bonfire.

Guerra grabbed a freshman by the arm and told him, hit every dorm you can and tell every outfit on campus that Jackie Sherrill is on the field.

The word spread and spread quickly.

Within thirty minutes, Guerra said, we had almost four hundred out in the mud and quagmire, working amidst the smell of burning diesel and oak wood smoldering in the parameter fires, hauling and crawling over those logs.

Jackie Sherrill could draw a crowd in a hurry.

He wasn't looking for one.

Longhorn kick returner and running back Eric Metcalf still remained as the most lethal break-away threat facing the Aggies and, particularly, the 12th man. Chet Brooks said, I just finished watching him on film for about an hour, and I'm still dazed from all the moves he has. Sherrill told his team, you can think you have the game pretty well under control, and all of a sudden on one play, he'll go eighty or ninety yards. You can't get down on yourself because Metcalf is going to make great plays. Count on it. And it's dangerous to try and overcompensate because you may leave a big hole behind you. No matter what you think might be happening, you have to take care of your assignments and stay in your lanes at all cost.

Eric Metcalf had the unbelievable ability to put the fear of God in the hearts of Aggies everywhere, especially those hearts beating in the A&M coaching staff.

Even the 12th man team knew that Metcalf was not just another run-of-the-mill college game-day kick returner.

He was a game breaker, as fast as a West Texas prairie fire in a windstorm, and they lined up with a wary and cautious fear coursing through their veins.

To David Fry, however, Metcalf was just another number with a football under his arm.

Rodeo bulls had tried to kill him. Metcalf, he said, wasn't as big as a bull. His first step might not even be as quick as a top-notch national finals rodeo bull out of the chute. Metcalf was a flyer, not a stomper.

David Fry drilled Metcalf, hammered him back on his heels, then tossed him to the ground. He stood above the Texas running back and lifted both arms above his head like a roper who had just tied the legs of his rodeo calf. Fry looked down at Metcalf, and yelled, yippee-ki-yay, you little runt-headed turd jumper. How's your jumper now?

For the first time in four years, the game was a slugfest and a barnburner in the best of the Texas A&M-Texas tradition. It was a rivalry that lived up to its name. The Aggie offense managed to work some fourth-quarter voodoo magic and conjure up ten points with Bucky Richardson coming off the bench to lead the last drive and Keith Woodside breaking three tackles and bolting twenty-four yards for the final touchdown. A&M escaped with a 20-13 win.

I had never been nervous before a game, Brian Edwards said. You line up. You hit somebody. The butterflies are gone. That's the way it had always been. But now a title, a championship ring, and a trip to Dallas all hung in the balance. In the locker room, my nerves and emotions were on such a roller coaster ride that I was afraid I might throw up at any moment.

It could have been a magical night. Late in the game, we scored, the cannon fired, smoke was blowing across the field, and I could see the faint outline of eighty thousand fans, their faces blurred by the haze. They were going absolutely berserk. That single moment would be locked in my memory bank forever.

It lasted only a moment.

Then I grabbed my helmet to get ready for the kickoff.

The magic turned sour.

We had shut down Eric Metcalf on kickoff returns, Ronnie Glenn said. But after we went ahead late in the game, 20-13, Curley Hallman, our special team's coach, turned around and yelled, I want the varsity kickoff team on the field. The 12th man was already heading to their positions, and his words jerked us back to the sidelines.

It had not been the greatest of years. But it had been a great night. Yet, for the first time in five years, the first time since Sherrill conceived the idea, the 12th man, as a unit, would not be going downfield on a home-game kickoff. Only Ronnie Glenn and Dean Berry, who had been moved to the regular unit for away games, ran onto the field. It didn't feel right. Hell, Glenn thought, it wasn't right.

The 12th man unit stood on the sidelines in dismay. They waved their towels. Their eyes were still focused on a championship. Their blood still ran maroon.

They only had one question for Hallman: Why?

It was my call, Hallman said. I did what I felt like I needed to do. Metcalf was too dangerous for me to risk it. If he returned the ball for a touchdown, we were in trouble.

Maybe Curley Hallman had made the right decision. Maybe not. But A&M was going back to the Cotton Bowl, he thought, and nothing else mattered.

Coach Jackie Sherrill gave the Texas Aggie football team the attitude, the character, the raw talent it needed to dominate the Southwest Conference, winning three straight titles for the first time in A&M history.

Jackie Sherrill leads the Aggies with Vince Palasota (1) and Dennis Descant (8) on the field. Players came, and players graduated, but Coach never lost faith in the 12th man team. He believed in them, and they never let him down.

Chapter 26

In Dallas, on New Year's Day, the Aggies would be facing the traditions and the golden-domed helmets of Notre Dame. That was special. For the second time in three years, A&M would confront the daunting and formidable talents of a Heisman Trophy winner, the hard-running, high-flying Tim Brown. He would take the field as the most feared and frightening kickoff returner in the nation.

The 12th man had its work cut out.

Larry Bowen wrote in the *Bryan Eagle*, one of the most intriguing match ups will pit A&M's 12th man kickoff coverage team against a player voted the nation's best, a sure-fire, first-round pick in the National Football League draft. It looks like a mismatch. But it doesn't sound like a mismatch.

We've gone against a lot of good guys, said Ronnie Glenn. Tim Brown is another good return man. He has a little asterisk by his name because he's a Heisman Trophy winner, but that's not going to make him run any faster in the game.

If Brown ran any faster, it would be criminal, Bowen wrote. He used his 4.38 speed in the 40-yard dash to earn first-team All-America honors as a return specialist. If Brown gets his hands on the football, it will be up to the 12th man to get their hands on Brown.

There was a lot of pressure on us, Dean Berry said, because a lot of people had lost confidence in us. We had to try that much harder if we ever hoped to earn back the respect we had before.

It had not been a good beginning to the season, Glenn admitted, but we finally buckled down and started doing our job, going down and hitting people instead of running around and waiting for them to hit us. Like the old days. We re-fueled our attitude a little, then a lot.

During the last four games of the season, the 12th man had allowed an average kickoff return of only about ten yards.

It was an incredible statistic.

But was it good enough?

For a critical kickoff, Hallman had pulled the team against Texas.

Would the unit have a chance at redemption?

The 12th man, after the Texas game, wasn't even sure it would be allowed to take the field in the Cotton Bowl. The 12th man wasn't sure if the team would receive an invitation to Dallas.

Jackie Sherrill had been upset a time or two. But Jackie Sherrill was constantly in pursuit of perfection. He stayed upset a lot. For him, playing the 12th man team against Tim Brown had never been in doubt. The 12th man was tradition.

And Jackie Sherrill was not about to buck or back down from tradition he revered so mightily.

The 12th man team became a wall of determination and dedication that few kickoff returners were ever able to penetrate. During their glory days, no one ever returned a kickoff for a touchdown. For Jackie Sherrill, that was the unpardonable sin.

The 12th man was his idea.

Whether the team played or not would be his decision.

And his mind was already made up.

John Burnett remembered, we saw Coach Sherrill walking our way after practice, and we didn't know what his verdict might be. Take us. Leave us. Bench us. Play us. We all held our breath.

He paused just long enough to look us in the eyes and say calmly, game's on.

It was a challenge.

The adrenaline rush was so great it almost clogged our veins.

That was all he ever said, but, in two words, we knew he still believed in us.

Dana Batiste said the scholarship players had never lost faith in the 12th man. We all fought together and bled together, he said. On the scout team, they fought us. The coaches would keep trying to calm them down, telling them, boys, this is just practice. We're afraid somebody's gonna get hurt. Let's slow it down a little.

Can't, Kirk Pierce said.

Why not?

If I knock somebody to the far side of hell and he don't get up too fast, it's my ticket to the Cotton Bowl.

On game day, Batiste said, the 12th man fought with us. They never let up and didn't know what it meant to quit. They made us better during the week. Even when we just wanted to take it easy and walk or trot through practice, they went full speed. We had to go at full speed. Slack off, and some wacko on the 12th man rocked your boat. The 12th man

hit as hard in practice as any other team hit you on Saturday. They stuck with us, and we stuck with them.

John Lopez, a former Aggie student, wrote in the *San Antonio Light,* Notre Dame's Tim Brown won the Heisman Trophy. A&M's Harold Huggins almost won all district honors as a Churchill High School senior four years ago.

Brown runs a 4.31 in the forty. Huggins runs a 4.6, give or take a tenth, mostly give.

Brown has All-American moves. Huggins has All-American looks and not much else. Brown is lightning. Huggins is a heavy fog. Brown has everything. Huggins doesn't even have a scholarship.

So let's try to put the potential head-to-head match-up in the proper perspective. We have Brown, the Heisman Trophy-winning phenom returning kicks against the likes of Huggins, the typical Aggie 12th man team member. We have this tough kid from San Antonio and others like him trying to stop the best football player in America.

I like our chances, said Huggins. Tackling the Heisman winner just makes it sweeter.

If Huggins sounds crazy, well, he is. That's a prerequisite for the 12th man. They're not normal guys, said Jackie Sherrill.

The team has never given up a return for a touchdown and has forced three fumbles. Brown had three kickoff returns of at least ninety yards, and when it came to facing him, Huggins said, we've gone up against some pretty good return men in the past, and we survived. We'll just run down the field, crazy as hell, and try to create a little havoc or a big train wreck like we always do.

Call Sherrill crazy, too, Lopez wrote, but he says the 12th man team will indeed play against Brown, and Sherrill says he will instruct the A&M kicker to send the ball deep to Brown. We'll play the 12th man against anybody, Sherrill says. These guys love the challenge. They're like no other players you know. They'll be out for practice thirty minutes before everybody else. They work out with the scout team. Then they stay and cover kickoffs for thirty minutes after practice. And they actually enjoy it.

Tim Brown, who had gone to high school in Dallas, said, you always hear about the 12th man. But I would say the challenge lies with me and my teammates. They're the ones who have to block eleven crazy guys trying to tear my head off. From what I've seen, those guys may not be on scholarship, but they're pretty talented. I'm sure they could go to other places in the country and play.

Jackie Sherrill headed toward Dallas, the driving force and guiding light behind A&M's success at ending an eighteen-year drought at the Cotton Bowl. He said, that lock has been broken. The Aggies are flying where they should be flying. They should not have been caged all this time because A&M has deserved a winner.

Across town, Notre Dame Coach Lou Holtz was telling the leering press, I've been to the Orange, Fiesta, Sugar, Gator, Bluebonnet, Peach, Liberty, Tangerine, and Rose Bowls, but I've never been to the Cotton Bowl. When I was in Fayetteville, everyone in the conference was eligible for the Cotton Bowl except Arkansas. At least that's the way I felt. We never could get down here. Now, nobody in the Southwest Conference is allowed to come but Texas A&M.

Sherrill looked at the game film Notre Dame had sent him, then called Lou Holtz and asked, why didn't you send me the real film? All we got was the slow film.

I have news for you, Holtz said. That is the speeded up film. The boys just look slow because they're wearing black shoes.

Speed.

It was a killer.

The game would all come down to speed.

Who had it and who didn't.

And Tim Brown was the fastest of them all. He's like a draft when he goes by you, the Michigan State Coach had said.

Brown said of his runbacks, sometimes I break tackles. Sometimes I run by people. I find it hard to explain. I really don't know what's going on, except I'm trying not to get hit. I watch people trying to tackle me, and it's a pitiful thing to see.

Harold Huggins remembered, Coach Sherrill had confidence in us. I often had my doubts. He didn't. He had this crazy idea that we could stop Tim Brown, and we believed him because we believed in him. Besides, he told the newspapers, the 12th man is gonna kick their butts. He had that look in his eyes. I knew we'd better get it done, or he would kill us. No "ifs" or "buts." We were dead.

Sean Page pointed out, the coaches had decided to put the real players on one floor of the Hyatt while the 12th man team was relegated to a lower floor. It was easier for the coaches to enforce curfew and keep the varsity from running footloose and fancy free in Dallas. The guard posted at our doors was a graduate assistant only a couple of years older than we were. We had a better deal and a better time than the scholarship players.

They were afraid of Jackie.

We seniors on the 12th man had nothing to lose. Not a scholarship. Not even our reputation. We were regarded as a bunch of kamikaze loons already.

We also had a couple of engineers on the team, and we learned how to rig the fire escape doors to allow lovely young ladies access to our floor. It wasn't any trouble at all to sneak them past locked doors and through a dark stairwell. However, I learned that it was a lot more difficult for a slightly inebriated college coed to climb eleven flights of stairs than it was for a twenty-one year old male working feverishly to get her in the room before anyone, especially a coach, saw them.

It was a real challenge to convince a young lady to climb those stairs more than once, but I do recall carrying one up on more than a few of the nights we were in Dallas. It seemed like the gentleman thing to do.

During Cotton Bowl week, we were driven to Lawry's Steak House, Blake Dwoskin said. Very few of us had ever been to a place that nice. We felt like royalty.

We could order any steak on the menu we wanted.

We could have it cooked any way we wanted.

I think Coach Sherrill liked it better when we ordered it raw.

It was after midnight, and Ronnie Glenn heard a knock at his door. Who is it, he wanted to know.

We've brought your snacks, came the reply.

Who sent them?

Jackie.

Glenn opened the door.

The team managers handed him a brown paper bag.

There was beer in the bag.

Coach Massey had caught a lot of heat because our play had been so erratic throughout the year, Brian Kotara said. Before the Cotton Bowl, practices were tough and physical. Then they became violent. Sudden impact on the field felt more like head-on-collisions on a Dallas freeway. Some of us wondered if A&M would have anybody still standing when the kickoff came.

Downfield, the fiery Curley Hallman held up his hand and, with the number of fingers he was waving in the air, signaled the play he wanted his scout team defensive backs to run.

Kotara squinted. Hallman was standing at midfield, Kotara had moved into a cornerback slot on goal-line defense, and for the life of him, he could not see Hallman's fingers.

Did he raise one, two, or a half dozen? I didn't know what I was supposed to do on the next play, Kotara said. None of us did. We looked at Coach Massey.

Don't worry about the number of fingers Curley is waving, Massey said. All he wants you to do is one thing.

What's that?

Put somebody's head in the dirt.

Darren Lewis hit the line.

Brian Kotara hit Lewis.

And somebody head was in the dirt.

It wasn't Darren Lewis.

Chris Massey had it all figured out. Metcalf had been a shake-and-bake waterbug on the field. Not even Metcalf knew when his legs would suddenly change directions and head another way. Tim Brown was fast. Lord, he was fast. But he ran straight up and usually in a straight line. Metcalf was elusive. Brown simply cracked through hole and was gone. You see him. You hear him. He's a vapor.

Hem Brown up, Massey told the 12th man. Don't create a seam, or he'll find it. Keep him in a phone booth with the door locked, and he can't run away from you.

Stay in your lanes.

Stay tight.

Don't try to free lance and make the big play.

And everything else will take care of itself.

CBS television mentioned to Jackie Sherrill before the game that the network wanted to interview some member of the 12th man team. Anybody would do.

See John Burnett, Sherrill said.

A microphone was stuck in Burnett's face, and all CBS wanted was a quick sound bite.

What's it like being on the 12th man, came the fluff question.

It's always been my dream to play for Texas A&M, Burnett said, as sophisticated as possible, and in my final game I want to get a lick on the Heisman Trophy winner.

So this was Texas A&M. It had lost an All-American, Kevin Murray. Jackie Sherrill had juggled three signal callers all year, always trying to find the hot hand, watching them flirt with both success and disaster, knowing that almost every game would ultimately be won or lost with a different quarterback under center. The Aggies weren't supposed to win the Southwest Conference, and they obviously didn't stand a chance against the green and gold mystique of Notre Dame. By the opening kickoff, every prayer and rosary bead in every Catholic home in America would be shaking.

Notre Dame, said Jackie Sherrill, immediately found itself in the middle of a street fight. There's no question about the image of Notre Dame, he said, but our players have grown a little tired of reading about how good they were.

R. C. Slocum said, Notre Dame scored quickly, and Lou Holtz was moving Tim Brown all over the field. It was a new scheme, one we had not seen on film, one we had not practiced against. I pulled our team together at halftime and drew up a brand new defensive formation that our kids had never seen or run before. They learned on the fly, and it did not faze them. Now it was Notre Dame's turn to make an adjustment. They didn't, or couldn't, and we slammed the door shut on them.

The *Dallas Times Herald* wrote, The Aggies – five-point underdogs – blocked and tackled with such firm conviction that their runners averaged five yards a crack on first down, and their defense forced four turnovers, allowing just 86 yards in the second half. A&M did not have a fumble, interception, or penalty until the last five minutes of the third quarter, when the issue was already decided. Strangely, the same Texas A&M team that spent September and October looking for a good quarterback suddenly found two. Freshman starter, Bucky Richardson, voted most valuable player on offense, ran the option for 96 yards. His two touchdowns blended nicely with the 5-for-7 passing of his backup, red-

shirt freshman Lance Pavlas.

The final score was 35-10.

The final score was incidental.

The showdown, the most intriguing battle of all, as the leering press wrote, would take place between Tim Brown and the 12th man kickoff team. Both had heart. One had speed. One against eleven, and no one gave the eleven much of a chance. It would be the ultimate duel in college football.

Tim Brown had returned the first kick to the 30-yard line, and Danny Balcar said, fifty percent of me was scared to death while the other fifty percent of me wanted to hit somebody. So I hit somebody who was bigger than everyone else on the field. My head snapped back, and, for a moment, I went blind. I could hear just fine. I could hear the crowd going wild, but I couldn't see. I didn't know why they were going wild. Suddenly my vision popped back into place, but I couldn't hear. I suddenly went deaf. I saw Lou Holtz. I saw his lips moving. I could not hear a word he said.

Are you okay, someone asked.

I didn't answer, Balcar said. I couldn't read lips.

Brown had broken containment and was flashing up the middle of the field. If I don't cut him off, he's gone, John Burnett thought. I was on his blindside, and I doubt if he ever saw me until we hit the ground.

My teammates dragged me to my feet.

I pulled off my helmet, and it was scarred with gold paint from Tim Brown's helmet. Notre Dame gold. Heisman Trophy gold.

Burnett ran off the field and found Sly Calhoun. He held out his helmet. It has a splash of gold on it, he said.

Sly grinned. Don't worry, son, he said. I'll have it in the bag for you as soon as the game's over. It'll be waiting for you when you get yourself back to school.

For the rest of the afternoon, Tim Brown was unable to find a crack, a crease, or a seam, and he felt as though he had been penned in the back corner of a corral that had been built without a gate. There was simply nowhere to go.

A&M squibbed a kick, Ronnie Glenn elbowed his way past the wedge, and he became the only 12th man to ever record at least one tackle in all three Cotton Bowls.

All year, the 12th man had been criticized, ridiculed, and maligned, even benched by Curley Hallman in the crucial game against Texas. However, on a cold New Year's Day in Dallas, the 12th man unit, against odds that had spit disgrace and venom in their troubled faces, rose up not unlike the Light Brigade and made the single play that forever defined their existence.

Chet Brooks was pacing the edge of the field on crutches. He had broken a foot against Texas, and throughout the afternoon, he kept dragging himself along the sideline, always seeking out Tim Brown, wherever Tim Brown lined up. He was in Brown's face, in his ear, crawling into his mind and raising the sport of trash talking to a level it had seldom reached before. Brooks turned to Brian Edwards and said, if you tackle that son of a jackass, take that smart-aleck towel of his away from him.

As Russ Birdwell (25) keeps the Spirit of the 12th Man alive and well, Warren Barhorst (11) awaits his turn. It has been a hard two years, but when his time finally arrives, Barhorst will be ready to meet the challenge. An explosive meeting with Tim Brown of Notre Dame awaits him, a moment that will forever provide the 12th man team with legendary status.

Warren Barhorst had stood on the sidelines all afternoon, watching as, one by one, the 12th man team members lost their towels on the field. It was as though Notre Dame had one mission in mind, and that was to infuriate, intimidate, and embarrass the kickoff team. When a member of the 12th man unit was blocked to the ground, some Notre Dame player grabbed his towel and raced off the field, waving it like a hunter's trophy high above his head.

Behind him, Barhorst could hear Brooks yelling wildly, in case anyone was listening, and it was difficult to hide from a voice that loud and excruciating, take the towel away from that son of a jackass. I played against Tim Brown in high school, and, if you take his towel, it'll drive him absolutely insane.

Barhorst wrapped his own towel tighter on his belt. He had not played. He might not play at all. The Aggies were scoring at will, but, he said, as much as Coach Sherrill loved us, he hated us. There was always a deep-seated fear lurking in the back of his brain that we might make a serious mistake and put his football team back on its heels and in trouble. Not even Coach Sherrill knew how much it meant for us to be a member of the 12th man team. We would have worn practice jerseys to games to cover kickoffs.

The Aggies lined up for another kickoff. There had been plenty of them, and the fourth-quarter clock was ticking down toward victory. Massey turned to Warren Barhorst. Go in for Fry, he said.

Barhorst would never forget the moment. The 12th man was thundering downfield, and, he said, I glanced over and knew immediately that we had a big problem. The person next to me was no longer in his lane. He was nowhere to be seen. Some blocker must have picked him off and left a hole wide enough for Brown to drive a truck through.

Brown saw the gap and was coming with his throttle wide-open, ready to end a day of A&M domination and Notre Dame frustration with one mighty run. Just another couple of steps. That's all it would take. He reached down to find his get-up-and-go gear.

Brian Edwards burst through the wedge. He had a bead on Tim Brown and was ready to pull the trigger, but a blocker spun him around and knocked him off balance. Edwards took a frantic swipe at Brown and missed as the Notre Dame legend barreled past, headed for glory.

God gives you instincts, Warren Barhorst said.

Practice sharpens them.

In a game, it happens.

Brown was a stride away from going for six.

Barhorst dove and grabbed Brown around the hips. It was a classic tackle. The gazelle with a Heisman Trophy hung ceremoniously around his neck plummeted to the ground. He had already been reading his name in the record books. Barhorst ripped the page out, and Brown immediately vanished beneath a pile of assorted players who had the number twelve stitched on their jerseys. Brian Edwards found himself in a cocoon of bodies, and he was frantically searching for Tim Brown's towel. Somebody wearing green and gold grabbed his helmet and tried to twist his head off. Down beneath it all, with elbows and fists flying around his head like the teeth of a lumberjack's chainsaw, Warren Barhorst dug methodically for Tim Brown's towel. He knew it had to be stuffed somewhere in the Heisman Trophy winner's belt.

When Barhorst finally fought his way out from under the pile and pulled himself to his feet, he had the towel with gold Notre Dame lettering clutched in his hand.

He did not wave the towel triumphantly.

It was the defining moment for the 12th man unit. In the 1988 Cotton Bowl, Warren Barhorst (11) stole the monogram towel belonging to Notre Dame's Heisman Trophy winning Tim Brown. Brown immediately and unexpectedly chased down Barhorst and hammered him to ground with a violent forearm. It triggered one of the great fights ever on Cotton Bowl turf.

He did not rub it in Tim Brown's face.

Barhorst began casually jogging toward the bench.

Chet Brooks had his souvenir.

In the television booth, announcer Brent Musburger, in a typical Musburger moment, was yelling into his microphone, Jackie Sherrill told us he was going to use the 12th man on his kickoff coverage team, but Sherrill has sent in a ringer. Tim Brown has just been tackled by one of A&M's starting defensive backs, William Thomas. Sherrill snuck one in on Notre Dame.

Think about it, Garry Sorrel said.

Warren Barhorst was 5-9.

William Thomas was 6-4.

Barhorst weighed 225 pounds. He looked like a block of wood.

Thomas weighed 175 pounds. He looked like a ten-penny nail.

Barhorst was white.

Thomas was black.

Warren Barhorst has just made the play that every one will remember for a lifetime and beyond, and Brent Musburger couldn't even get his name right.

Barhorst never saw an irritated and frustrated Tim Brown running at full speed toward him. It was anger on the hoof, the miserable and shameful end to a miserable day. Brown swung, and his powerful forearm caught the back of Barhorst's head like the dull, blunt edge of a tomahawk.

Barhorst went to his knees. I fumbled the towel, he said.

Brown grabbed his towel, wheeled around, and must have felt like the last man trying to escape the Alamo. The 12th man team was on him in a swarm. Varsity players from both benches were boiling out onto the field like a nest of mad hornets.

Sean Page remembered, I was running off the field, laughing, when Brown sped past me, making a line straight for Barhorst. The next thing I knew, half of Notre Dame's bench, along with two green elves, one a mascot and the other a head coach, joined the war. I looked for someone my size, but Holtz and the elf were already gone or taken, so I turned my attention to the nearest Notre Dame uniform in sight, which placed me face-to-face with the Irish's All-American center. It wasn't pretty. He kicked me around pretty good before he realized he was in a fight. I don't think he ever realized he was in a fight. He ripped my helmet off, and to this day, I firmly believe my worthless chinstrap prevented induced premature cranial separation from my cervical spine.

The fight ended as quickly as it began, and the *Dallas Times Herald* reported, it was the most celebrated Cotton Bowl tackle since Alabama's Tommy Lewis came off the bench to stop Rice's Dicky Maegle in 1954.

Barhorst said, after the play, Notre Dame was done. Its players no longer had any fire. Coach Sherrill was on the sideline yelling that Brown should be thrown out of the game. The referees did not listen. They walked off a 15-yard penalty against Notre Dame, but they weren't about to tarnish a Heisman Trophy winner by kicking him off the field. It didn't matter. The last time anyone saw Tim Brown, he was walking up the ramp and out of the Cotton Bowl stadium. He was through. He had a pro career awaiting him. He did not want to chance running back another kickoff. The 12th man, he feared, just might ruin that pro career. The *New York Times* reported, Tim Brown ended his college career on the sideline as Holtz tried to keep him from the angry Aggies' 12th man.

Brown simply explained, I wanted my towel back. It had my initials on it. It had my number on it. I didn't know I'd be called for a penalty just for trying to get my towel back.

He looked around for sympathy.

He found none.

I didn't celebrate, Barhorst said. Frankly, I was scared. I had started a fight on national television and feared that I had disgraced a university I dearly loved. It was my last game and probably my last play, and now I figured I was in trouble.

Warren Barhorst would not live in infamy.

In a split second, in a game already won, in a desperate attempt to find a souvenir for a scholarship player who had always defended the honor and the courage of the 12th man unit, he became the living symbol of the kickoff coverage team.

Even those who did not know a lot about Texas A&M knew the name of Warren Barhorst.

A year earlier, when Barhorst was contemplating the idea of leaving the 12th man to devote full time in pursuit of his education, Dennis Mudd had told him, one of these days, Warren, you may make a play that will change your life forever.

So he did.

In the locker room, the national press, including television cameras, microphones, and tape recorders, gathered around Warren Barhorst, like a swarm of leering locusts, almost as close as Tim Brown had been, close enough to feel the heat and smell the sweat. Everyone wanted to ask another question. Everyone wanted to hear another answer.

The little guy had gone up against the big guy.

The afterthought had dueled the legend.

The legend lost.

Long live the little guy.

Damn it was a good story, and the leering press, if nothing else, knew a good story when it unfolded before them.

Across the room, Bucky Richardson, the top gun who had engineered the upset victory, the freshman who had lost his redshirt and been voted the game's most valuable offensive player, sat virtually by himself. He had the stats. He never had Tim Brown's towel.

Time, fate, and circumstance.

The three connections to destiny always followed in the shadow of Jackie Sherrill's broad shoulders.

Richardson didn't mind. He basked in the glory alone.

He didn't need a crowd.

John Burnett walked out of the dressing room and into the late afternoon of a perfect Cotton Bowl day. Too hot. Too cold. Too windy. Too wet. None of it would have made any difference to him. It was a perfect Cotton Bowl day.

He saw an older gentleman approach him.

A stranger.

A stranger wearing maroon and white.

He was a mountain of a man, and his eyes were moist with tears.

He took Burnett's hand and shook it firmly. Thank you, son, he said. You have no idea what this means to us old Aggies.

Burnett said, all the crap from coaches I had taken on the practice field, all the pain I had endured, all the frustrations and disappointments I had experienced were suddenly worth it. I was just a kid with a dream. For the old Aggies, however, this game represented what life was all about. Until that moment I had never really understood, but I saw his tears, and now I would never forget. I had not become an All American player. Maybe this was better.

A few days later, Warren Barhorst's mother finally caught up with him by phone. Her son was skiing on the slopes of Colorado. David Letterman called, she said.

What does he want?

He wants you to be on his show.

Why me?

For a little while, you had Tim Brown's towel.

Warren Barhorst had suddenly become the folk hero of everyone who had ever rolled up a pair of shirt sleeves, defied the circumstances, and hoped to accomplish more than was realistically possible. Not all of them had won. Most had lost. But to them, Warren Barhorst had proven that, once in a great while, when the moon and planets happen to be aligned at just the right angles in a daytime sky, good things really did come to those who valiantly fought on and refused to quit.

Barhorst called David Letterman.

It was too late.

Yesterday's hero had become this morning's afterthought.

Back in the classroom, the marketing professor walked in and announced, well, we had a pretty good win up in Dallas.

The students whooped it up.

We also have a celebrity in our midst, the professor said. Mister Burnett, will you please stand up.

John Burnett stood.

I heard Mister Burnett being interviewed on television, the professor said. He said he wanted to get a lick on the Heisman Trophy winner. Mister Burnett, I just didn't know you swung that way.

Laughter.

A red face.

So much for fame.

It was the final day of practice, a beautiful fall day, Doug Lawson said. The sun was shining. The sky was a deep blue. There wasn't a cloud overhead, and a faint chill had broken a typical Texas hot streak. He remembered, you could hear the grass crunching beneath your shoes when you walked.

Nothing could be better, he thought.

Nothing at all.

Dammit, Lawson! He could hear Jackie Sherrill's voice booming in the background. Don't walk off this field. We run off this field.

The grass crunched a little more crisply when he ran.

Dean Berry's dream had come full circle. His father and brother Greg had served as football captains at Texas A&M. His brother Ray had been named captain at Baylor. For so long, Dean Berry had no hopes of ever playing football at the collegiate level. In high school, he had been ignored, neglected, and cast aside by recruiters. His greatest fear was not being able to carry on the family tradition.

His senior year at A&M was a godsend.

He was named captain of the 12th man team.

The family circle remained unbroken.

Dennis Descant (8) fires up the 12th man unit as Trent Childress (17), Brian Edwards (16), Garry Sorrell, Dan Leyendecker, and Tommor Bolcerek look on. If Jackie Sherrill wasn't motivating them, they were on the sidelines motivating themselves.

Chapter 27

It would be a season of discontent, turmoil, and regret. When it began, the Aggie faithful had climbed to the top of the world, filled their recent past with bags of cotton, and could envision absolutely no reason why a national championship should not be the next logical step for Jackie Sherrill and Texas A&M. After all, the Aggies were no longer fighting for recognition throughout the sports world. The Aggies had been chosen to make the journey to Giants Stadium in the Meadowlands of New Jersey and battle the Cornhuskers of Nebraska in the 1988 Kickoff Classic. When Jackie Sherrill headed north, he packed his 12th man team on the plane with him. They were no longer novelties or postscripts in America's press.

The *Newark Star Ledger* reported, Garry Sorrell has major college size for a defensive back at 6-2, 210, but absolutely no speed. Vince Palasota has an abundance of speed, but at approximately 5-7 and 160 pounds, no size. Brian Edwards is neither big nor fast enough to be a big time college football player. Except, all three are. There probably isn't another big-time program we could play for in the country, said Sorrell. There are nineteen other players like Sorrell, Palasota, and Edwards on this year's Texas A&M roster, the article said, all just a touch too short, a few pounds too light, a step or two too slow to be considered by big-time

college programs following productive high school careers. None were offered scholarship. All walked on at Texas A&M. And now they're all major college football players with six of them making the trip East with A&M. They are very much a part of what is probably the most unique unit in college football. None of the 12th man players have any false hopes about playing, other than on kickoff coverage. In fact, since the unit was formed, only one, linebacker Dean Berry, has managed to get game time at a position. We're just happy to have a chance to play, said Palasota. That is our reward.

When word filtered down to Palasota that he had been selected to travel with the team north, he was elated. His years of hard work had finally paid off. The skinny kid from Mexia, Texas, had arrived. He seriously doubted if anyone else from Mexia had ever gone farther north than the Red River and certainly not to New Jersey, which may not have been a foreign country but certainly seemed like one.

The week before the game, Palasota tore the ligaments in his knee while playing a game of pickup basketball on campus. He began walking on an unsteady leg. Pain shot through the knee like hot needles, but he kept a stoic face and let his helmet hide any reflections of the way he really felt. Seeing a doctor was obviously out of the question, Palasota said. If I missed one practice, one drill, one hit, I might never get my job back. So I taped the knee and boarded the plane.

He was aware of the constant, throbbing pain. No one else on the team was. It seemed as though every nerve ending in his knee had been ripped apart and left to fester. Vince Palasota grimaced, then grinned. He had played with pain before.

Jackie Sherrill told a New Jersey sports writer, when I selected players for the 12th man team, I was looking for guys who were crazy, guys who had no regard for their bodies, guys who wanted to hit you. When we play an opponent, they're very aware of our 12th man. They better be, or they're going to get slapped upside the head.

Texas A&M and Nebraska, the nation's second-ranked team, slugged it out for four quarters, and the *New York Times* reported, The Texas Aggies were not going to take this game sitting down. They never do. The Twelfth Man by the thousands stood throughout the evening. The "Aggie War Hymn" carried through the humid air. Their cannon exploded far more often than the fans who had come from Nebraska had hoped. Everything about the Aggies – their cadets, their tradition – suggests a mission. And the Nebraska Cornhuskers made the unpleasant discovery that a team on a mission can create a difficult evening. The A&M defense was aggressive, punishing.

But when the sound of the final whistle ricocheted through the confines of Giants Stadium, Nebraska's children of the corn had escaped with a 23-14 win. Jackie Sherrill's annual and frustrating dilemma of losing the first game of the year had struck him again.

On his return to College Station, Garry Sorrell was furious. The Newark newspaper had written, for all the world to see, that he had absolutely no speed, and Sorrell considered himself to be as fast, if not faster, than anyone on the 12th man team. That was his strength. He had a little pop all right, but Garry Sorrell, more than anything else, was a flyer.

He reached up and ripped his name off his locker.

He plastered down a wide strip of white tape.

And on it, Garry Sorrel wrote: "Absolutely None."

The season proceeded to grow worse. For several years, ugly rumors and closed-door accusations had probed and prodded the teams in the Southwest Conference. One, SMU, had suffered the death penalty. NCAA investigators continued to regard fiction as fact, just as long as someone would point a crooked finger, and Jackie Sherrill watched as coaches throughout the SWC kept falling all over each other in a conscientious effort to hide from their own improprieties, if any existed, by indicting someone else. No. By going ahead and indicting everyone else. Not a lot of proof, perhaps. But hearsay was raining across the conference as thick as an autumn thunderstorm. The leering press was working under the basic premise that everyone was guilty. We'll sort out the sordid details later, its editors said. And big-city newspapers, as well as the talking heads on television news, began weaving their own personal ideas and ideologies of truth with the threads of contradictions.

Texas A&M, especially now that Jackie Sherrill had cast aside and buried the losing image that plagued the Aggie faithful for so long, had become the SWC's most vibrant lightning rod for controversy. The NCAA, it often seemed, had an unspoken and unwritten vendetta. The NCAA had never forgiven the dastardly horde in College Station for its failure to implicate either the school or Kevin Murray for any wrongdoing. Forget reality. The NCAA wanted a sacrificial lamb. And the *Dallas Morning News*, ready to fan any flame that cast dispersions on the Aggies, was reporting that a few good old boys in the Aggie network were throwing a sizable amount of money around. A past-tense running back named George Smith suddenly came out of the blue to tell reporters that he had been paid hush money for not exposing any irregularities or transgressions that might have taken place within the football program. No facts. Only allegations.

Sherrill shook his head in disgust.

A day later, at a press conference, George Smith completely recanted his story, admitting he had received a small personal loan and been paid for some yard work, but nothing else. He said he had made up the story because he planned to write a book, and he believed that the pay-off angle would make it more interesting. In my best interest, Smith said, I included things in the book that were not and are not true. He denied that either Sherrill or assistant coach George Pugh had paid for his round-trip plane flights home to Georgia and said he had only been given a couple of hundred dollars, maybe as much as four hundred, for performing minimal work at Sherrill's home. He had sold out Texas A&M in the hope of selling a few more books.

David Eller, chairman of the Texas A&M Board of Regents would tell the media that the board backed Sherrill a hundred and ten percent and that it expected no further accusations to surface against Sherrill. It didn't matter. The deed had been done, and the vultures in the NCAA and leering press both descended on College Station. It was a definite rush to judgment. No. It was a stampede. Even new A&M President William Mobley announced that an investigation would continue despite the board's support of Sherrill. For Mobley and the board, a power struggle had been unleashed. Jackie Sherrill and the Texas A&M football team found themselves caught in the middle.

Linebacker Dana Batiste was as mad and as upset as anyone had ever seen him. George Smith just wanted to make a quick dollar, he said. Somewhere along the line he was told that it's all right to tell lies, if you have to, in order to take a shortcut to a pile of money. Smith wanted a big pile even if it hurt a man and a university that had been good to him and good to all of us.

Before the contentious month of September ended, the NCAA ruled against Texas A&M, placing the football team on probation, preventing the Aggies from making a run at its fourth straight Southwest Conference title and forbidding them to participate in any bowl game at the end of the season.

For Jackie Sherrill, the Aggie faithful, and the football team, it was a conviction without a trial. It felt as though the NCAA had decreed: we'll sentence them now and see if we can find any supporting evidence later. There may well indeed have been some rule violations, but none that could be tracked directly to Sherrill. It was impossible to keep a tight rain on overzealous alumni running amuck no matter how hard a coach tried. Any coach. Any school. Any conference.

As Layne Talbot (4) prepares for another kickoff, Dennis Descant (8), Bubba Hillje (13), Andy McDonald (24), Doug Lawson (21), Rene Casas (9), and Garry Sorrell (26) are ready to lead the 12th man on another bombing run. The moment before kickoff was when the adrenaline began to flow. When the hit came, adrenaline would be rushing like high octane fuel.

The 12th man kickoff team had its own demons to exorcise. A year earlier, the unit had worked hard, practiced hard, played hard, and, as always, partied hard, but the results for 1987 had been fraught with erratic, unreliable, and inconsistent play. Cray Pixley wrote in the *Battalion*, throughout the early years of the 12th man, the team compiled an impressive list of stats and had a better return coverage than the varsity team. Then, in 1987, the team hit a patch of bad luck and fell below par. Houston's James Dixon returned a kickoff fifty-nine yards, breaking through the yardage that the 12th man had jealously guarded for four years. In that one run, the reputation and prestige of the 12th man received a serious blow and seemed headed for a tumble from the pedestal of honor.

Jackie Sherrill remained staunch and unwavering in his support of the unit, no matter how troubled or unpredictable the team's kickoff coverage had been. He told Pixley, the 12th man will be here for as long as I'm here.

Prophetic, if nothing else.

Pixley wrote, the guys have no need or intention to shove aside the sad truth. They know about last year. Several of them played through last season's foibles and failures, but in the tradition of optimists and winners, that was then – this is now. The 12th man athletes know they have ground to make up and are dying for a chance to show that they are new and improved. This year, the 12th man team has a goal – just ask them.

We want to be the best kickoff team in the Southwest Conference,

Bubba Hillje says.

Garry Sorrell pointed out, we needed something to focus on instead of just running down the field and trying to hit someone. We knew we only had a certain number of plays to shine, and the kickoff was our specialty. We had to do it well.

Sherrill had never doubted them, their intensity, or their dedication, not even when Curley Hallman, at his own volition, kept them off the field for a single kickoff against Texas. Said Sherrill, we have some determined and confident young men out there.

They had been solid for most of the 1987 season. They had been tight. They had been brazenly selfish with the number of yards they allowed on returns. In several key games, the opposition had only managed to dig out an average of twelve yards or less. On rare and unfortunate occasions, a ball carrier broke loose and tore up large chunks of Kyle Field turf, gaining too much critical yardage and winding up too far downfield, making it hard on the defense and frustrating for R. C. Slocum. On those days, the stats ballooned out of sight. One kickoff might destroy them all.

Chris Massey had departed, and Graduate Assistant Jim Hughes, who played middle linebacker at McNeese State, was given the formidable responsibility of returning the 12th man to the status of its original glory. He said, these guys are playing for pride, and the time they sacrifice for the 12th man unit cuts significantly into their school, their jobs, and other activities. They work as hard as scholarship players, and their enthusiasm makes them a vital and a special part of the Aggie football team. Being a part of the 12th man is a big commitment.

The exorcism had begun.

Doug Lawson tightened up his tennis shoes and mentally checked out those who had gathered at Kyle Field to begin a no-holds-barred, catch-as-catch-can, winner-take-all competition for those last few empty slots on the 12th man team. These must be guys just like me, Lawson told himself. Pretty good athletes. None of them great athletes. They had learned the game, but it didn't come naturally to them. Every one of them, however, was dreaming about the prospect of playing college football at the highest level in the land.

Lawson had long realized that, sometimes, the best athletes weren't on the field. For whatever reason, they didn't have the discipline it took to succeed, and those who wanted it more, those willing to fight for a spot, often shoved the gifted athlete aside.

He had seen it more than once.

He brought a little fight to the field with him.

Doug Lawson had reached a height of 6-2 in the sixth grade, but he said, I couldn't see very well, I wore contacts, I had absolutely no co-ordination, and I was about the size of a No. 2 pencil. As a freshman, he barely weighed over 150 pounds, but in the small Tahoka 2-A school in far West Texas, Lawson was one of the largest players on the squad and immediately rushed to varsity. Our coach was old school, he said. No matter how hot it was in practice, and West Texas had its share of scorchers, we diligently took our salt pills and were never given a water break. Practices were so hard, demanding, and unforgiving that the whole senior class quit and walked off the field. The coach thought he could toughen us up, but as the day wore on, my mouth was like cotton. I couldn't even spit. I could barely breathe. Guys were dropping all around me. Couldn't run. Couldn't walk. No longer able to crawl. By the end of practice, I was the only player still on his feet. So I became a starter. We were the coach's first class to ever have a losing season. He thought it would get better. We won only three games in four years.

At Tahoka, Lawson found himself in a box. He became the strongest, the fastest, and the quickest player on the team, but he remained locked into the center position on offense. On the defensive side of the ball, Lawson lined up as a nose guard against the running game and outside linebacker when a pretty good passing quarterback rolled into town. He was fast. No one could block him. I never tried to get any faster, he said. Didn't see any point in it. We just lined up and slugged it out.

During the summer, Lawson worked as a farm hand, driving a tractor from sun-up until sundown, then he began lifting weights and running sprints up and down his dry, dusty, home-town football field. He labored on the wind-swept and sun-seared plains of Tahoka, referred to by some as God's country. Maybe. It would take God to love a country like that, he said.

Doug Lawson wanted to play college football. Ranger Junior College gave him a chance. Ranger offered a scholarship and financial aid. In reality, Lawson said, we had a real good running back at Tahoka, and he was my best friend. I think the Ranger coaches recruited me so they could get him. I was their insurance.

Jam box music throbbed down the dorm hallways all night long. Lawson went to sleep with the staccato sounds of dominoes being slapped against a worn table top. Hard drinking and loud laughter were accepted as the norm. Studies were optional. Lawson said, Ranger was stacked with Proposition 48 All-Americans who were there for one reason. Get their grades up and go play for a major college program. For the first time, I saw real athletes, and realized I probably didn't measure up.

He found the athletes even larger and a lot faster when he reached Texas A&M.

Tahoka and Ranger had been rough. A prison camp chain gang would have been an easier life. So Doug Lawson had no qualms about playing for the 12th man team. How much harder could it be?

Rene Casas had to be quick. He lived on the edge of the world in the South Texas town of Freer, where a boy grew up hunting deer and dodging rattlesnakes. Get quick or die. At 185 pounds, he played inside linebacker for a school that was fortunate to have as many as two dozen players on its football team. He was determined to go to Texas A&M and earn his way, regardless of the cost, onto the notorious and often infamous 12th man unit. A younger brother, Adan, would receive a scholarship to play for TCU, but Rene Casas realized that a star-crossed Aggie kickoff coverage team offered him the only hope he might ever have to step on a collegiate football field.

Casas met with Tim Cassidy.

He still weighed 185 pounds.

He ran a 4.5 forty.

Pretty quick, Casas thought.

Pretty fast.

There are five thousand guys in Texas who weigh 185 pounds and can run a 4.5, Cassidy told him, honesty being one of his strong points. For Texas A&M football, we're looking for 4.3 guys.

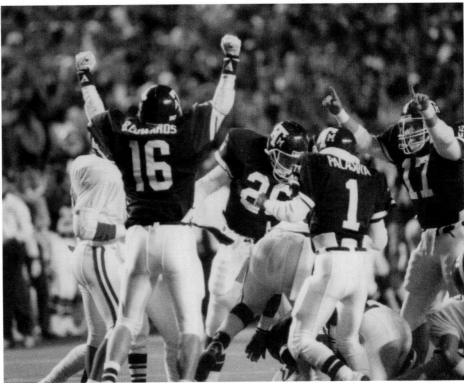

Brian Edwards (16), Garry Sorrell (26), Vince Palasota (1), and Trent Childress (17) have a reason to celebrate. They brought the lumber, and nailed a ball carrier in place inside the 20-yard line. Big hits. Big pileup. They lived to fight again.

The dream began to fade like smoke in a South Texas windstorm. All I had was heart and desire, Casas said, but would heart and desire be enough?

He didn't think so.

Rene Casas, as a freshman, was overwhelmed. Freer had a population of 1,200. The student body alone at A&M was at least 40,000. On a good Friday night, Freer football drew three hundred fans, maybe a few more. The Aggies played before 72,000. Freer was fighting to simply be better than another 2-A school. A&M was fighting for the Cotton Bowl. Warren Barhorst tried to talk Casas into going ahead and reaching for his dream. Give the 12th man a shot, Barhorst said. You have nothing to lose.

I'm not that good.

Are you fast?

Yeah. I think so.

Are you scared, scared to get hit?

Hell, no, which was the kind of answer anyone would expect from an eighteen-year-old, who believed that fear was akin to one of the seven deadly sins. But there will be hundreds trying out, Casas said. They're probably all bigger and faster and stronger than I am.

No, said Barhorst. They're all just as nervous as you are.

What makes you say that?

I was one of them.

Casas nodded. It had been easy to give up on a dream. Fortunately, the dream had no intentions of giving up on him. He began lifting weights and running. His forty time kept edging downward, never to 4.3, perhaps, but a great deal faster than it had been in high school.

He religiously read through the *Battalion* day after day, looking for some mention of a date when the try-outs would be held. When the article finally did appear, however, it was small, and he overlooked it. He missed the try-outs as well. I wanted to cry, Rene Casas said.

He had been nervous.

Now he was mad.

By the time he was a junior, Rene Casas was committed to the 12th man. Four years had once seemed such a long time to him, but now his four years were quickly running out. Like the rattlesnakes he had once dodged in Freer, it was time to strike.

Trent Childress was certainly big enough to be a fullback, maybe even big enough for a linebacker. He was 6-0, weighed 215 pounds, had played for a major high school football program at Sugarland, just outside of Houston, and listened intently while Jim Wacker offered him a scholarship to TCU.

I'm sorry, coach, Childress said. I appreciate your interest, but I'm afraid I'll have to turn the scholarship down.

Why, son?

I'm going to Texas A&M.

Jim Wacker raised an eyebrow. Did the Aggies offer you a scholarship, too, he asked.

No, sir, Trent Childress answered as politely as he could. I'm going to play for the 12th man.

You're crazy, son.

I understand that's a requirement.

A&M promise you anything?

I haven't spoken to anyone at A&M.

I want you, Wacker said. A&M obviously doesn't.

Let me ask you one thing, Childress said.

What's that?

Does TCU have a 12th man team?

Jim Wacker left without bothering to answer.

Childress walked onto Kyle Field for the first time as a freshman in 1988. The coaches carried forty players into spring training, Childress said. They cut it to thirty. One decided to concentrate on his studies. Nine went down with injuries. By the time we all came back for two-a-days in August, the 12th man team only had eighteen players. Coach Sherrill wanted twenty. He knew the high risk of injury. He needed at last twenty lambs to throw into the slaughterhouse he called practice every day. The coaches had to convince two walk-ons to join the 12th man unit. Those who had been cut stayed cut.

The first day of practice in full pads had not gone so well. The drills were sloppy, Childress said. Some of the players were a little tentative. Others were rusty. A few on the varsity just didn't have their hearts in it. A summer out of pads had softened them all.

I need a running back, Sherrill yelled.

I'll go, said Brian Edwards.

Jackie Sherrill looked around at the names taped on the helmets and barked, Childress, get in there.

He knew what Brian Edwards could do.

Let's see how some fresh blood works out.

The freshman fullback took the ball, looked up, and suddenly realized he was staring across the line of scrimmage at Adam Bob, Basil Jackson, Dana Batiste, and Aaron Wallace.

Name your poison.

Adam Bob beat the trap and bolted through the line, Childress said. He hit me harder than I had ever been hit before. I'm dead, I thought. I hit the ground. I lay there, trying to breathe and wondering why my lungs had folded up and dried out. I told myself, well, it'll never get any worse than that, and you survived. I had always feared the unknown, and now the experience wasn't unknown anymore. I knew I could take anything they had, as often as they could bring it, and get back up again.

Adam Bob's hit became a liberating experience.

Dan Leyendecker had every intention of walking on Texas A&M's football team as a freshman. As a junior middle linebacker for Laredo United High School, however, he had been chop blocked, tried to make a tackle while he was still on the ground, and had a ball carrier's knee drive sharply into his left shoulder. He knew the injury was lingering long after it should have healed.

At Laredo, he had even moved to tight end, but the shoulder couldn't hold up to the constant pounding, and he wound up as a Power I running back, tough enough, just not quite fast enough.

He wasn't particularly concerned when he took his physical examination at A&M. After all, his shoulder hadn't bothered him for more than a year. Time and rest could heal a lot of wounds and erase a lot of scars, he decided.

Leyendecker had no trouble passing his exams in the classroom.

He flunked the physical.

The doctor explained, you still have a rather wide gap between the socket of your shoulder and the bone. I'm afraid you'll dislocate the shoulder, or it will fall out of place every time you hit somebody.

What's the chance of me ever playing again?

Surgery could put it back together for you.

How long will I be out?

A year. Maybe more.

Dan Leyendecker still had four years of school lying out there in front of him.

No problem.

He had plenty of time to recover. He was a patient young man. He chose the knife and settled down to life with the Corps of Cadets.

During his junior year, Leyendecker and a high school teammate, Alec Cuellar, probably stayed up too late one night, maybe even tested a bottle or two of liberating spirits, and decided to walk on the football team. Maybe the shoulder would hold up, Leyendecker thought. Maybe it wouldn't. There was definitely only one way to find out.

He and Cuellar took a lot of hits. They cracked a few skulls and had their own battered from time to time. Hard days. Short nights. Quick hits. Dull pain. Aspirin by the handful. Unfortunately, if they hadn't played against varsity, they would not have played at all. A lot of risks. Damn little recompense. When the most important thing in life was taking a clean shot at a scholarship player, Leyendecker said, you knew that life had lost a lot of its meaning.

Bubba Hillje sat Leyendecker down after practice one day and said, look, you're a pretty fair football player. I've watched you, and I've gone up against you a few times. You've got some potential. I'll guarantee you one thing: you have a much better shot at playing time if you go out for the 12th man.

Leyendecker nodded his head, looked up Jim Hughes, and the coach told him, you have a little size, and we need some size on our wedge busters. But we expect even a big boy like you to run the forty in at least 4.6.

Leyendecker ran.

He bowed his head, leaned with the wind, and made a mad dash toward the tape.

The stopwatch was his only competitor.

✳ The Bus Trip From Hell: Itinerary ✳

Departure:
Time: 12:00 p.m. (noon)   13 January 1990
Please arrive at least 45min. early. Bus will leave on time!

Place: Bus terminal 1500 Westloop North by Northwest Mall loop 610 to Northwest Freeway (Highway 290) Houston, Texas

Other: Beer will be provided, along with traveling crapper and complementary party bags (barf bags). Will need EXCESS funds for New Orleans and body tags to identify unconscious individuals. For information call Dennis Descant (713) 466-3736

Destination: French Quarter New Orleans, Louisiana (Baarbon St.) Arriving approx: 6:45pm Departure will be 3:00am. from drop off point. Late comers will have an extended vacation in New Orleans.

Arrival: The ravaged remains of all participants will be shipped back to point of origin at approx 10:00 am. It is recommended that all survivors have alternate means of transportation at this time.

Not even the 12th man team ever left town without an itinerary. But a trip to New Orleans for Garry Sorrell's bachelor had the potential of being a journey to the heart of never-never land.

Jim Hughes nodded. A 4.58, he said.

Leyendecker grinned. I loved running on that artificial turf, he said. It made me feel like I was a whole lot faster than I really was.

He left class on the day when the final list of names for the 12th man team were to be posted and walked briskly toward Kyle field.

My balls were in my throat, he said, and my stomach was tied in knots.

The list was taped to the door.

He was almost afraid to look.

Leyendecker quickly, nervously glanced over the names and saw his staring back at him. Hillje had been right. He did have a chance for some playing time now. His balls were still in his throat, and his stomach was still tied in knots, but Leyendecker ran all the way back to the Corps dorm. In short spurts, he said, I may have done better than 4.58.

Alec Cuellar did not have a choice. He was the next in a long line of Aggies. He had been going to games at Kyle Field since he was in the third grade. He was in high school when he saw A&M put the clamps on Bo Jackson in the Cotton Bowl. He told himself, I want to be one of those guys. When his father handed him a ticket to college, there was no question that the trip would end in College Station.

Alec Cuellar marched into the office of Tim Cassidy and said, I want to walk-on and play football at Texas A&M.

Cassidy did not like to discourage anybody.

He would never tell any kid that he didn't have a chance.

They would find out soon enough and on their own.

How tall are you, Cassidy asked.

Five-ten.

Cassidy wrote it down. What do you weigh, he asked.

Cuellar squared his shoulder and said, a hundred and fifty pounds.

Step on the scales for me.

Cuellar did.

The scales registered a hundred and thirty, and Cassidy frowned. I thought you told me you weighed a hundred fifty, he said.

I thought I did.

Cassidy stifled a laugh. We have a uniform for you, he said. I hope you're big enough to wear it.

I'll bet you one thing, coach.

What's that?

There's no one down there big enough to stop me.

Tommy Bolcerek had either been a really good or an awfully bad influence on Derek Naiser, depending on how he looked at it.

The two had squared off against each other in high school.

The two had fought on the field.

Now, Bolcerek was telling him, maybe it's about time we have a chance to fight together.

Maybe.

Derek Naiser wasn't so sure.

He had been a slow-footed quarterback for Columbus High School, and, most important of all, Naiser realized beyond a shadow of doubt that he was a slow-footed quarterback. He had absolutely no illusions or hopes about ever achieving stardom on a college football field. He had already turned down a few offers from small colleges, had come to Texas A&M because his father was an Aggie, and had absolutely no interest in walking on the football team. Crazy idea the first time he heard it. Was getting crazier by the minute.

But this is different, Bolcerek said.

What makes it so different?

I'm on the 12th man, Bolcerek said, and you're as tough as anybody else we have on the team. You can play.

Maybe Bolcerek was right, Naiser thought. Maybe he was tough enough to play. Maybe after taking all of those hits as a quarterback, he would have a chance to go in there and inflict a little pain on somebody else. He had a lot of inflicting to do. I had the fire and the intensity it took, Naiser said, and I certainly wasn't scared to hit anyone.

That was before he met John Roper.

Roper came low and met me running full bore, Naiser said. Wider. Bigger. Faster. Stronger. Full blast. He rammed his helmet into my head, and I could feel my helmet as it rattled. Hoped to hell it wasn't my head. I saw a black hole and did my damnedest to keep from falling in.

His mind was strung together with cobwebs.

He stood up in a fog.

It could have been a daze. No. It was foggier than a daze, gray and thick. More like a flannel funeral shroud.

The day grew dark much earlier than I thought it should, Naiser said. I saw a lot of numbers on a lot of jerseys and wondered if I should be adding them up or just forget them.

He forgot them.

For a moment, he forgot everything.

Don't worry, Bolcerek said. Roper just has a bigger helmet than you do. That's all.

Derek Naiser cursed Tommy Bolcerek that day. Maybe not out loud. But he cursed him all the same.

Dennis Descant, at 6-2 and 220 pounds, knew he was probably not the best candidate to play special teams. He had thundering hooves, and, on a football field, he usually reached the point of impact, but he was hardly ever out front, leading the charge.

In his Jersey Village High School locker room, however, he ran across a poster of Jackie Sherrill standing with his 12th man team around a statue of E. King Gill. One of Descant's coaches, who happened to be a Texas A&M graduate, walked up and said, those guys are freaking nuts. Every time you see them play, they're headed downfield on a search and destroy mission.

That's pretty neat, Descant said.

It was more than neat.

He wanted to be one of them.

What does it take to become a member of the 12th man, Descant asked his coach.

They're always looking for speed.

How about somebody as big as I am?

Depends on how fast you can run.

You've seen me run. You think I have a chance?

There's only one reason why you wouldn't.

What's that?

You'll never make it if all you do is sit around and think about it.

He was right, Descant said. I might be too slow. I might get cut early or late. I might never make the team at all. But I knew I wouldn't be able to live with myself if I didn't give it a shot.

Dennis Descant lasted one cut.

Then he was gone.

He shrugged. Well, he thought, I'm already out here. I have a locker. I even have a uniform. I might as well hang around and keep playing. Nobody runs walk-ons off. They usually crawl off on their own.

His practices began to turn a few heads, and, by 1988, Dennis Descant had landed a spot on the 12th man team. Just maybe, he thought, a poster with his picture alongside Jackie Sherrill might someday hang somewhere in the Jersey Village High School locker room. And some coach might point him out and say, there's one of the freaking nuts. Every time he plays, he's out on a search and destroy mission.

Dreams came in all shapes and sizes.

Garry Sorrell (26), Brian Edwards (16), and the 12th man team clown around with walk-ons on picture day. The Dave twins are numbers eleven and twelve. Bubba Hillje is at the bottom of the pile, where he usually showed up in games with a ball carrier on the ground. The players have a break. They are not yet worn down by the grind and constant pounding of practice.

Chapter 28

For the members of the 12th man kickoff team, it was quickly becoming a curious and distorted season that none of them quite understood. The loss to Nebraska has been disheartening. The rumors of scandals and hush money and rules violations ranged far beyond their personal knowledge and comprehension. They only knew, from what they read, that the NCAA had invaded campuses all across the Southwest Conference like a swarm of locusts searching for a program to devour. The spectre, then the reality, of probation had been devastating for them. At the moment, all they had left was a chance to play football, and their first game would be a long time coming. They were itching for a good fight. It might not cleanse them of the frustrations they felt, but a brain-jarring hit or two certainly wouldn't hurt.

The home opener had been scheduled with Alabama, but there were threats of Hurricane Gilbert rumbling up from the Gulf of Mexico. Big storm. Heavy rains. Bad winds. Crimson Tide Head Coach Bill Curry decided not to gamble with the weather. He chose to stay home, keep his team out of the air and off the field, and respectfully requested for Texas A&M to postpone the game until, perhaps, the end of the season. Sher-

rill obliged.

Alabama became the laughingstock of the country when game day dawned bright, clear, and sunny at College Station, staying that way for the rest of September. Hurricane Gilbert did not get close enough to A&M for the Aggies to even smell rain, must less face the danger of drowning in it. The storm roared ashore down in Mexico, and, as near as anyone could figure, didn't disturb a single football game that day.

The circumstances surrounding the Alabama game, however, symbolized the season. Everything that could possibly go wrong, it seemed, had settled down like a nuclear cloud around Texas A&M. Old rumors, new rumors, manufactured rumors from the leering press kept hounding Sherrill during every moment he was awake. The NCAA brought in more sharp-tipped shovels, hoping to uncover a little dirt and finding none of it at the feet of Jackie Sherrill.

The *Bryan Eagle* reported that the year provided Sherrill enough lowlights to qualify for a coal-mining permit. The NCAA ruined Jackie's autumn, the article said, and he believes that the NCAA brought down the probation sword on the Aggies solely because of him. They thought

Jackie had too much power, Sherrill said. They think I control the whole school. They went after us for no reason.

They kept going after A&M.

They still hadn't found a reason.

Loose talk.

No hard facts.

Sherrill straightened his shoulders, stood tall, and told the leering press, I am responsible for the program. I am responsible for seeing that things run properly. In college football today, it's very difficult to sit there and say nothing has happened or ever will happen. Our responsibility is to do everything we can do to avoid it.

Rogue alumni everywhere, despite their good intentions, could make an error in judgment, break a rule they didn't know existed, spend a spare dollar or two they should have kept in their pockets, and cast a bad light on a program without any coach of any school ever knowing or finding out what they had done. It was the nature of the beast. Nothing was more dangerous than passionate, fanatical alumni.

The NCAA, Sherrill said, had based its rulings on incorrect and un-

would take a deep tank dive before the year had run it course, and Sherrill was saying, we want to win out and set the tone for next year. We're serious about winning the rest of the games we play.

The leering press sneered. Sports writers were too busy placing the Aggies in an empty grave to hear him.

The 12th man had been battered but not into submission. All they could do to hide from the rumors circling the campus was practice, practice, then stay after practice for a little more practice. They had pounded on each other until the bruises had welts, and the welts had cuts, and the cuts had scabbed over.

Jackie Sherrill was as frustrated, maybe more so, than the rest of them. Brian Carpenter remembered, the linemen had not performed up to his expectations during one drill, and Coach ran into the midst of them. His face was red. The veins were popping on his head.

No helmet.

No pads.

Just a red face.

And bulging veins.

Sherrill bowed his back and screamed, hit me. Hit me.

No one moved.

Hit me, he yelled, louder this time. Hit me.

A lineman plowed into him.

Sherrill didn't budge.

If you can't hit harder than that, he said, you sure as hell can't play for me.

No one dared touch Jackie Sherrill.

But, Carpenter said, they did unload the lumber on each other for the rest of the afternoon.

SMU ball carrier fair catches a pooch kick while Trent Childress (17) is being held as he attacks from the front. Bubba Hillje is ready to lower the boom before forcing himself to pull up to avoid a penalty. Dennis Descant (25) is coming fast. No daylight. No place to go. Same old story.

substantiated accusations, and he pointed out in a stern voice that, in time, he and Texas A&M would both be vindicated. He knew in his heart, however, that the NCAA was marching him in front of their legal firing squad and would forever keep him locked in their sights.

The calendar turned, the season moved into October, and, other than the six who traveled to New Jersey, the 12th man as a unit had not yet taken the field. LSU had risen up to tear down the Aggies, 27-0, and the Cowboys of Oklahoma State destroyed a proud A&M team that had been run off the track and derailed by the NCAA, 52-15. The Aggies were 0-3, had not suited up for a home game yet, and desperately needed a win. The Aggies were listless, down on their luck, and needed a spark.

Sherrill kept pressing his players and assistant coaches hard, doing what he could, emptying whatever bag of tricks he had, to keep them from giving up or letting down because of probation hanging like a noose over their heads. The so-called experts were predicting that A&M

Rene Casas was fast. He had made the travel team to the Kickoff Classic in New Jersey, but he found himself running as a ball guy on the second team. Find the ball. Find a crease. Shoot the crease. Find the ball carrier. Keep the seconds to a minimum. Keep the hit to the maximum. He's caught the kickoff once. Make sure he won't be so eager to catch the ball a second time and certainly not a third.

In practice, Casas watched the first-team ball guy head downfield, make a sharp cut, and without warning, go down even though he had been running wide open and alone. No one was near him. No one had hit him. Suddenly he was on the ground.

Strains.

Sprains.

Splints.

It happened all the time.

He blew out both knees, Casas said.

Such were the breaks of the game.

He had surgery.

He never came back.

It was tragic for him, Casas said. It was fortuitous for me. I had not earned the starting spot. I had inherited it. I damn well wasn't going to give it up without a hell of a fight, and no one was willing to fight that hard to take it away from me. From that point on, I was guaranteed to have at least one play a game, either the opening kickoff or the second half kickoff. That might be all. Just one. It was up to me to make the most of it.

The drill had dragged on, and Dan Leyendecker was lining up at fullback. Two scholarship offensive linemen were out front, shoulder-to-shoulder, blocking for him. Two scholarship defensive linemen had been given the singular purpose of separating the ball from his arms, the helmet from his head, or his head from his shoulders. It didn't matter to them which came first.

His job was to shoot the gap, provided, of course, there was a gap.

A faster player might have gotten there in time.

A hole suddenly opened up, but only for an instant, maybe less time.

Bam!

Hole closed.

He was flat on his back.

Sherrill decided to let Leyendecker keep running the ball until he was ready to drop.

Dan Leyendecker was a 12th man.

He didn't drop.

He was busted time and again, but he didn't drop. Pain never bothered him when it turned numb.

Leyendecker shot the gap and found a step, maybe two, of running room before the defense slammed the door and rattled his bones. The defensive linemen went down in a heap on top of him. The offensive linemen fell backwards on top of him.

Leyendecker lay at the bottom of the pile.

I'll never forget how flat I felt as I lay there, he said. Couldn't breathe. Couldn't get up. Couldn't even move. So I started calculating. There were at least twelve hundred pounds lying on top of me. I ran the forty in 4.58 seconds. So exactly what had been the ratio of impact?

It was sometimes a detriment to have your bell rung while studying engineering at Texas A&M.

Vince Palasota (1) is on the road with scholarship players William Thomas (11), Cornelius Patterson (14), and Shane Garrett (80). Coach Jackie Sherrill chose a few of the 12th man members to make out-of-town games.

the ground face first. He felt as though a wrecking ball had exploded into his sternum.

Cuellar rose slowly but triumphantly to his feet.

Jackie Sherrill grabbed his face mask and jerked Cuellar's head around. Why in hell did you do that, he yelled.

I was told to rush the passer.

Rush him, yes. Hit him, not on your life. Sherrill paused a moment, then said, Cuellar, I can replace you. I can't replace Pavlas.

Enough said.

Quarterbacks were definitely on the far side of the *don't hit me zone* in practice. Don't touch or even breathe your bad breath on a quarterback. Lance Pavlas was definitely off limits.

Pavlas dropped back, eased to the left, his eyes searching downfield for a receiver, knowing he had all the time in the world, aware that no one in his right mind dared lay a hand or, God forbid, ram a shoulder into a quarterback in practice.

He looked left.

Then right.

Didn't bother to look behind him.

Alec Cuellar cut him in half.

Pavlas grunted as a burst of air exploded from his lungs, and he hit

Doug Lawson was getting ready to run wind sprints. He grinned and eased up alongside a handful of defensive linemen. Big Boys. Heavy boys. Thick thighs. Built like logging stumps.

I'll blast one out, Lawson told himself. I'll show those big, old boys what real speed is all about.

They all hit the finish line, and Lawson, head down, was running as hard as he could.

He was still a step behind.

That's when I finally understood, he said. There's only so much a man can do to get any faster.

Real speed is a gift that God hands down.

And sometimes he packs it in a body that weighs damn near three hundred pounds.

Texas Tech was on the way, and the long, interminable wait for the 12th man was almost over. They could finally line up against unfamiliar faces with unfamiliar names and make their presence known with a gentle shoulder to the rib cage, a misplaced elbow to the bridge of a nose, or an accidental helmet to the chest. Someone among them had read a rule book. It said that the object of the game was to win. The book may have said "how." The 12th man did not read that far. They would figure out "the how" on their own.

For Bubba Hillje, it was a game that couldn't come soon enough. He said, I had gone through so many disappointments that I was ready to quit. I died a little bit when Alabama was a no-show. It was a real letdown. But now I could see the end drawing near. The wait was almost over. I had old shoes, but it was a new season.

Like a majority of the 12th man squad, Hillje was taking the field for the first time. Only three members of the thirty-three unit had any experience in live game situations – Brian Edwards, Kirk Pierce, and Garry Sorrell.

We had seven guys who had never gone down and covered a kick-off, Edwards said. Now they were going to be playing in a game in front of 70,000 people, and it was going to be difficult to make sure they concentrated on their positions. They all had the ability. They could hit and swarm to the ball. They were as dangerous a group as we had ever had. But the distractions of suiting up and playing big-time college football could be suffocating. I knew. I had been in their shoes.

A year earlier, the 12th man team had faced three of the top five kickoff returners in the nation and ended the season by allowing an average of 23.1 yards a return – good for most teams, a bitter, infuriating disappointment for the 12th man. Now came 1988, and Kirk Pierce said, we had virtually a whole new team on the field, and those of us who had not played very much were ready to get out there and get after somebody. We were like lightning waiting for a storm. Probation may have snuffed out the fire in some of the players. It kindled the fire for me. As far as I was concerned, Texas Tech was a bowl game. I didn't like those sheep-herdin' sod busters anyway.

On kickoffs, the 12th man team would be facing the mighty mites of Texas Tech, Tyrone Thurman and Wayne Walker. Each had scored on runs of seventy yards or longer in Tech's 27-21 victory over A&M a year earlier, Thurman on a punt return and Walker with a pass. It would not be easy to stop them. They were will-o-the-wisp receivers, Kirk Pierce said, quick-footed darters with afterburners blazing in their tailpipes. They could go a long way. They had to get past us first.

For the Aggies, it was good to be home.

Texas Tech would have preferred being elsewhere, anywhere less crowded and confusing. The Red Raiders limped away from an inhospitable Kyle Field and headed back to the high plains with a 30-13 defeat hanging over their heads.

Bubba Hillje would never forget his confrontation with Texas Tech. He wanted to win, obviously, but the score was of little consequence to him. After so long, after two years, Bubba Hillje was a starter for the 12th man.

He said, I remember thinking that there wasn't a drug or narcotic anywhere in the world that could have given me the rush I felt running out onto the field, waving my towel, and looking across that sea of white towels in the stands.

I don't remember feeling the first collision, but the adrenaline rush was crazy.

The crowd noise was overwhelming. But, as soon as the ball was kicked, the world grew quiet around me.

The silence was eerie. I felt as though we were playing in a vacuum, and the earth began rotating in slow motion.

Dan Leyendecker could barely feel the turf beneath his feet as he raced downfield, watching Layne Talbot's kick sail toward the left corner of the end zone. Everyone had an assignment, he said, and we didn't want to let Jackie Sherrill down. We didn't want to let our buddies down. We didn't want to let the student body down.

Three of us – Trent Childress, Tommy Bolcerek, and me – called ourselves the Backside Bellies for obvious reasons. We had a little gut hanging over our belts. We weren't built for speed. We were built for collisions. On the first kickoff, we swung toward the ball carrier, and he must have thought he was running through a minefield.

He was quick all right.

A will-of-the-wisp.

A darter.

He had no place to dart.

He tried to thread a needle, but the eye of the needle closed.

We hit him.

I didn't know how far he had run.

I just knew he wasn't going to run any farther.

Hell, I thought, none of us on the 12th man might be any good, but together we could cause some pain and cause it in a hurry. I had always been told, the bigger they are, the harder they fall. Well, I liked the little guys. They didn't fall as hard. They fell a lot quicker.

We had our bounty.

For the rest of the game, the Backside Bellies just tried to stick together, break down the wedge, and blow somebody up. More than a few heads would roll between whistles.

At Mexia High School, Vince Palasota had been voted "Most Likely to Succeed," "Most Handsome," "Most Intelligent," and "Most Conceited" by his classmates. He was cocky. He had a chip on his shoulder. He was, some said, the biggest little man they had ever seen.

Palasota was driven. He hated the fact that days had only twenty-four hours in them because he usually had twenty-five or more hours worth of work to do between sunrise and sunrise.

Football knocked the conceit out of him. On occasion, after running back a kickoff or two against the 12th man team in practice, the features of his finely chiseled face began to turn the color purple. Palasota would look in the mirror and realize he might not qualify for 'Most Handsome' anymore.

Palasota could wash away the blood, the bruises would heal, and the swelling never lasted much longer than a week.

He turned his life over to the team trainers.

They gave him bottles of aspirin. The pain would leave in time, they said. He did his best to mask the aches until it did.

Alec Cuellar had a simple but demanding life. He wore the uniform of the Corps of Cadets to class. He wore a burnt orange jersey as a walk-on, then a red jersey as a 12th man, in practice. He lived and breathed the traditions of Texas A&M.

The Corps, after the constant and grueling hazing Cuellar had endured during his freshman year, was a little less hectic, but school and academics were becoming increasingly more difficult. From two-o'clock in the afternoon until seven at night each evening, football abused his body, beat down his state of mind, and not even he could figure out why or how Alec Cuellar kept gritting his teeth and pulling himself back up every time he was knocked to the ground.

He had been a walk-on.

A nobody.

He had become a member of the 12th man.

A nobody with a certain amount of class.

He caught passes that no one, other than a 12th man, wanted to catch. He was a running back when no one, other than a 12th man, wanted to carry the ball. He stuck his head into a defensive buzz saw when no one, other than a 12th man, wanted to have a clash in cleats.

There were some on the field and even on campus who simply said Alec Cuellar was one of those football scrubs.

He only grinned. He didn't mind what they said about him. He had two championship rings and two Cotton Bowl rings.

It was more than he had been promised.

Alec Cuellar had paid for every one of the rings with the same blood that had always given him life. Nothing had changed. Not really. The 12th man was life.

Brian Carpenter had enrolled at Texas A&M for one reason. He wanted to be a doctor. He just didn't know what kind of doctor.

He caught his foot on the artificial turf in practice and felt the ankle pop out of place. Its only chance to heal was rest, the trainers said. Days off. Maybe even weeks off. Brian Carpenter did not have either days or weeks to give the injury. He kept on running with the scout team. He kept on going downfield. The pain nagged him on every play. It was never too great to stop him. It did keep him awake at night.

Finally, Billy Pickard told Carpenter, maybe, you ought to just go into town and see a podiatrist.

What's a podiatrist?

He's one of those doctors who works on feet. Sore feet mostly. Maybe he can help you.

A podiatrist made Brian Carpenter a special brace to wear on his ankle, one that would take the brunt of the pounding and alleviate some, if not all, of the pain.

It was a miracle, Carpenter said. I had never heard of a podiatrist.

In time, Brian Carpenter became one.

Pain, at times, did have its benefits.

For Texas A&M football, it had been a rough start, but with the win over Texas Tech, the Aggies regained some of their swagger. They shoved the controversy and the disappointment of probation aside, tried to block the harassment of the NCAA from their minds, and concentrated on becoming the team that Jackie Sherrill believed them to be.

They squared their shoulders, laced their pads on a little tighter, re-ignited the fire in their bellies, and stormed to consecutive victories over Houston, Baylor, Rice, and Louisiana Tech. A&M was on a roll and picking up speed.

Bubba Hillje (13), Vince Palasota (1), Rene Casas (9), and Kirk Pierce (10) fully understand the pressure that is clouding the future of the 12th man kickoff team. It's a new day under a new coach, and no one really knows what to expect.

Trent Childress (17), Kicker Layne Talbot (4), and Vince Palasota (1) are on the move, waiting to cause a train wreck. Talbot believed he could tackle with the best of them.

David Fronk had inherited number 7.

Trent Childress wore number 17.

At a distance, it was easy to confuse the two.

During a kickoff against Houston, a yellow flag hit the ground.

What happened, Jackie Sherrill asked the referee.

Late hit.

Who did it?

Number 17.

As Childress jogged off the field, Sherrill grabbed him and yelled, dammit, Childress, you just cost me fifteen yards.

Wasn't me, Coach.

The hell it wasn't.

The next day, after spending a night in the film room, Sherrill looked up Childress on the practice field. I'm sorry, he said.

Childress frowned. About what, he asked.

The penalty wasn't on you after all.

Sherrill never mentioned it to Fronk. It was too late anyway. The play was over, and none of them would ever have a chance to play it again. A lot of guilt was passed over and forgotten between the setting and the rising of the sun. Sherrill stood tall when he was right and even taller when he made a mistake.

Against Baylor, Dan Leyendecker had raced downfield four times and been clipped four times.

Whistles.

But no flags.

The Bear blocker wasn't trying to merely cut me, which would have been bad enough, Leyendecker said, he was doing everything he could to steal my 12th man towel. Ever since the Cotton Bowl, when Tim Brown lost his, every team we played came after us with the deadly intent of ripping off one of our towels.

That was like stealing the Holy Grail.

He nailed me, Leyendecker said. We both hit the ground. We came up swinging and kicking. When he left the field, he sure as hell didn't have the towel. I'm not for sure he had all of his teeth.

The Aggies scored with less than a minute to play. The Bears came after the 12th man unit one last time with revenge on their minds.

Trent Childress said, the Baylor blocker was lying in wait for Leyendecker and hit him from behind. Could have broken a leg or torn up a knee. When Dan went down, the Bear player began kicking him hard in the back, then on the side of his head. I don't guess he was worried about a penalty. Game over. Baylor had lost. Kick him out. He didn't care. Dan was curled up, trying to protect himself, and the guy kept kicking him.

Childress and Tommy Bolcerek bowled into him. One came in high. One came in low. Both came in hard.

It was no longer football.

The game no longer counted.

He stood 6-6 and must have weighed 300 pounds, Childress said.

We hit him for all we were worth and didn't make much of a dent. He turned around, and I could see in his eyes that he wanted to beat the hell out of one of us, maybe both of us, and he didn't care who he clobbered first.

He started to swing.

The punch never came.

The Baylor player never had a chance, Childress said. John Roper jerked me away, and Aaron Wallace jerked Bolcerek back out of the fight. They were mad as hell. Roper went to work on the Bear who had kicked Leyendecker, and Wallace was ready to take on the whole Baylor team, either singularly or collectively. They might as well bring the bench with them. They would sure as hell need it.

Not much of a fight, really.

The Bears didn't get our towels, Childress said. But they certainly unfurled a white flag. Didn't mind playing Roper when it was a game. Didn't want anything to do with him when it was a fight.

Roper and Wallace took turns beating the dog out of us in practice, Bolcerek said. But nobody else, especially no one on another team, had better try. The scholarship players came to the defense of the 12th man. It was a glorious day. We felt like we had come to the party with an invitation to stay.

The battle with Louisiana Tech provided the 12th man team with the kind of game it always wanted. Fifty-six points. Eight kickoffs. A lot of time on the field.

The last kickoff came with forty seconds left on the clock.

Kirk Pierce had played behind Dean Berry for two years, and now, on a regular basis, he had a chance to personally seek out a ball carrier and see what kind of damage he could inflict.

Pierce blew up the wedge, then realized that the kick returner had swung back to the open field. Nothing but daylight. Six points might not mean much on the scoreboard. Six points would drive a knife in the heart of the 12th man.

Pierce took flight.

I had been a cornerback in high school, he said. I had the angle, and I knew what it was like to make an open-field tackle.

He was running for a touchdown.

I was running for survival.

He had elite speed.

I had desperate speed.

At midfield, Pierce slammed headlong into the ball carrier and drove him five yards into the bench.

The ball carrier was ready to fight.

Pierce was ready to fight back.

Neither had enough energy left to raise their fists.

Derek Naiser said, I was racing after the ball carrier with my blazing 4.7 speed and realized immediately that Rock Pierce was the only hope we had. I probably could have caught him, but we would have been at least fifty yards past the end zone when I did.

On Monday, Pierce was stuck in a study lab and arrived late for practice. As he ran onto the field, a trainer pointed over his shoulder and told him, Sherrill wants to see you.

Oh, hell, he thought, Coach is upset because I'm late. He's under a lot of pressure, and I may have just blown his fuse.

Pierce tracked down Sherrill on the far side of the practice field, every nerve taut and raw. I was scared, he said.

Rock, Sherrill said, that was a helluva effort you made the other day. You saved us. You got up when you could have stayed on the ground, and you never hesitated. You ran him down and saved us. That, son, is what this game is all about.

Forty seconds left.

A thirty-nine point lead.

And Jackie Sherrill was still looking for someone to do more than he may have been capable of doing. It wasn't just a game he was talking about, Pierce said. It was life. Coach definitely understood how the game of life should be played.

Andy McDonald had suffered a stinger in his shoulder.

Nothing unusual about that.

He walked away from virtually every practice with his shoulder aching from a stinger. When you get a 40-yard running start and hit somebody at full blast, you have a tendency to knock your shoulder around a little, he said. Stingers were so common that none of us worried much about them.

That night in Cain Hall, McDonald reached across the dining table, as usual, to steal a French fry, and his arm suddenly flopped on the plate. He could not raise it. He could not move it. He had no control over it. No pain. Total inertia.

Andy McDonald was helpless.

The training staff immediately sent him to the team physician who conducted an EMG on the shoulder. The prognosis wasn't good.

You have nerve damage, the doctor said.

Can I still play?

You may have permanent nerve damage if you keep getting the shoulder knocked around, the doctor said. About all you can do is rest it. Time will heal the nerves. But don't keep using the shoulder for a battering ram. It's too risky.

Andy McDonald nodded. He would take some time off. He would give the shoulder a few months to heal.

But there was always next year. Next year, McDonald would play.

The doctor be damned.

Danny Balcar (2) and Butch Motley (5) come down hard on a ball carrier as Bobby Middleton (18) races off the field. They only had a few plays a game. They made the most of every chance they had.

With two-a-days behind them, the 12th man unit relaxes on picture day with Dennis Descant's mother. Making up the team are, on the ground, Garry Sorrell (26). First row, left to right: Doug Lawson (21), Trent Childress (17), Brent Clements (3), Dennis Descant (25), Bubba Hillje (13), Craig McPike (11), Andy McDonald (12), and Darin Dave (12). Back row, left to right: Brian Carpenter (5), Dave Thelan (16), Rene Casas (9), Lyn McDonald (11), Steve Sarkissian (15), Jerry Elliott (7), John Bulovas (2), Todd Atkins (14), Torrin McCoy (8), and Robert Segura (23).

The *Chicago Tribune* published an article showcasing the phenomenal exploits of safety Kip Corrington.

Beside the story was a big, full-color photograph of a blond All-American football player wearing number ten.

Kip Corrington wore number ten.

So did Kirk Pierce.

The photo was one of Kirk Pierce. It even had his *number twelve* printed on the sleeve of the jersey.

Kip Corrington was an All-American, it said.

A 12th man did not receive such an honor.

Kip Corrington was a straight-A student, it said.

Kirk Pierce's grades did not quite measure up.

Kip Corrington was looking at a career in the NFL, it said.

Kirk Pierce would be watching the NFL on television.

Pierce was walking across campus when a co-ed ran up to him, holding a copy of the *Tribune*. My grandfather lives in Chicago, she said, and he sent me a copy of this article.

Pierce smiled.

She smiled back.

I recognized you from the picture, the coed said. My grandfather says you're the guy I ought to marry.

Kirk Pierce looked her over.

If she never learned the truth, he thought, it just might be a match made in Chicago.

Texas A&M stumbled against Arkansas, losing a heart-breaker, 28-24, in a game that sent the Razorbacks to the Cotton Bowl.

Arkansas would have been in Dallas even if the Aggies had gone undefeated in conference. Probation was the albatross, and, for A&M, it was stifling, if not downright suffocating.

Ahead lay Texas.

Ahead lay the best rivalry game in the conference.

The leering press did not care.

The leering press wanted Jackie Sherrill fired.

Even the campus newspaper was urging Sherrill to resign, and Dana Batiste kept referring to the *Battalion* as Judas, the betrayer.

A victory would give the Aggies a 6-1 record in conference play. A win would not cure the wounds or make them go away. A win, however, just might ease the stress and misery that dogged their every footstep. The Aggie defense, mad at George Smith, mad at the NCAA, mad at being shut out from a bowl game, and mad at the world in general, marched defiantly into Memorial Stadium, clubbed those bastards for Austin senseless, and rode back home on the crest of an 18-0 victory. Jackie Sherrill knew how to beat Texas.

Rene Casas and Derek Naiser came thundering downfield and blasted Eric Metcalf before he was able to get his motor running during a first-half kickoff.

As Naiser said, the 12th man blew a hole in the center of the wedge, and no one touched me. Metcalf started to juke right. Then he started to juke left. He tried to juke one too many times. We caught him in the middle of his jukes.

We were hyped up, Casas said.

Metcalf had fear in his eyes.

The 12th man, he figured out, had come to personally punish him.

Metcalf knew that he was a step away – maybe even a night and a bowl game away – from playing on Sunday with a big bonus and a larger contract from some team in the NFL, or he might be a step away from losing his career forever.

The crazies could kill him.

He had no doubt.

He saw it in their eyes.

They had probably been trying for years.

Sooner or later, one of them would get it right.

As a sophomore and junior, the thought had never crossed Metcalf's mind. He simply threw caution to the wind.

As a senior, the wind had thrown caution back.

Throughout the game, Derek Naiser said, he heard two phrases erupting from the Texas side of the field.

Catch it, Eric.

And, oh, my Lord.

Not again.

It was early, Casas said. The game still hung in the balance, but I could sense that Metcalf was a little reluctant to head up field with the same wild, reckless abandon he had possessed in the past. Throughout the game, the defense had taken a lot out of him.

We were simply trying to get out of the game with a win.

He was just trying to get out of the game in one piece.

Metcalf ducked to soften the blow, if, perhaps, there was any chance in hell it could be softened.

He fumbled.

Dan Leyendecker said, I had gotten behind the blockers and saw the ball pop out of Metcalf's arms. I thought for a moment I was going to catch it in mid-air with nothing between me and the end zone but twenty yards of open field. The 12th man had never scored before. This was our chance.

The ball bounced crazily off a Texas helmet and fell harmlessly to the ground.

Casas looked up and realized that the A&M coaches were frantically pointing to the ground. He looked around and saw the ball bouncing free. He and Naiser dove. They were a fraction of a second too late.

In a mad scramble that looked more like an old-fashioned rugby scrum, Texas recovered.

The Longhorns had the ball. There wasn't a damn thing they could do with it. In an illustrious, All-American career, the elusive Eric Metcalf had never beaten Texas A&M.

The Aggies had been deprived of a bowl game, but Jackie Sherrill, in spite of the accusations, allegations, and falsehoods trailing after him, allowed A&M to shoot for one final star. He began referring to the postponed Alabama game as the Hurricane Bowl.

The leering press thought it was pretty clever. His team, however, was more concerned with their coach than Alabama. After the Texas win, the fire boiling inside them was snuffed out, and they saw the future lying in a bank of dark clouds.

The Crimson Tide won, 30-10, but at A&M, the game was almost an incidental afterthought. Played. Lost. Forgotten. Quickly.

Seldom had Vince Palasota ever experienced the unexpected sensation of fear. Usually when a kickoff return team came onto the field to face us, he said, their starters were on the bench taking a breather. Most of the blockers up front were generally a motley collection of second

and third teamers. They were big, all right. They were fast. But we could handle them.

He lined up at safety.

The hits, the tackles, the clips, the cuts, the abuse, the action almost always took place far up field in front of him. Palasota had the last chance to stop a ball carrier if he broke containment. Palasota had gone for games without ever venturing close enough to the opposition to smell the sweat on their jerseys.

Alabama was different.

Alabama was launching a crusade against the 12th man.

Alabama trotted its All-Americans on the field.

Derrick Thomas curled a sneer, pointed at Palasota. I'm coming after you, he said.

He bolted up field in a flash, and nobody touched him, Palasota said. No reason to. He wasn't blocking. He wasn't protecting the ball carrier. We ignored him. His singular purpose in life was to take me out. Alabama's game plan had been for Bobby Humphrey to blast his way past our wedge busters, outrun the contain men, and by the time he broke into the open, Thomas would have me flat on the ground and out of his way.

Derrick Thomas came with long, powerful strides, and he caught Palasota viciously across the head with a forearm the size of a small tree, probably hardwood.

He could have paralyzed me, Palasota said. Or worse, he could have killed me.

Why? That's all I wanted to know.

Derrick Thomas glanced back over his shoulder to find Humphrey and lead him unscathed to the promise land. He should be past the twenty and almost to the forty by now. Thomas had cleared the way for him. Nothing but smooth sailing ahead.

His eyes kept darting around, looking for Humphrey.

Bobby Humphrey was nowhere in sight.

Bobby Humphrey was somewhere under a pile just outside the 20-yard line. When he blasted his way past a wedge buster, a headhunter, blasted him.

Good plan.

Great tactic.

Didn't work.

The 12th man team, even with seven rookies when the season started, had bounced back into national prominence, covering forty kickoffs and holding the opposition to an average of 14.7 yards a return.

No team in the nation was better.

Jackie Sherrill did not have to leave Texas A&M. No one, he said, forced him out. The board of regents worked diligently to keep him in command of Aggie football. The NCAA, after its long, arduous, two-month investigation ended, reported that Sherrill had not broken any NCAA rules, saying that the Aggie football program would not be given any further sanctions. In its own internal probe, Texas A&M's vice president for finance and administration, Robert Smith, said that the final evidence did not support any of the claims or statements made by George Smith, including his original allegations that the payments constituted "hush money."

Jackie Sherrill and Texas A&M, as Sherrill predicted all along, had been vindicated.

However, he realized that as long as he remained the Aggie head coach, the NCAA, its investigators, and the leering press would always be standing in the shadows, constantly scrutinizing his every move, his every word. Even more importantly, they would be searching for ways to destroy a school and a football program that meant so much to him. His own image and reputation had taken a severe beating in the court of public opinion. He could not stand the thought of any potential spill-over, which was sure to come, tarnishing the image or reputation of Texas A&M.

He had made up his mind before the Hurricane Bowl with Alabama. It became official on December 13.

Jackie Sherrill submitted his resignation.

In a prepared statement, he said, because of my great love for this school and its people, I am removing myself from my position at Texas A&M. I have remained in my position because I felt it has been a period that has needed my complete interest and full cooperation due to the continuing national attention that has been paid to this matter. Now, with all this in mind, and with the best interest of Texas A&M upper-most in my thoughts, it is time for us to come to a mutual parting of the ways in order for everyone concerned to get a fresh start. Texas Aggies everywhere know of my great love and respect for Texas A&M. I consider my action now as a continuance of that love and respect for a great in-stitution and its people. I want to wish the very best for the entire Texas A&M athletic program and especially the best for the young men who have represented and will represent A&M on Kyle Field or wherever they may play.

Honest feelings?
Without a doubt.
The truth?
Definitely.

Those who knew Jackie Sherrill realized how much time he had devoted to Texas A&M, how he had taught the lessons of life, as well as football, to his players, the untold number of hours he had invested in his community on behalf of Texas A&M. His travels to Aggie clubs, both large and small, were legendary. Year after year, before the Texas game, Sherrill would climb high on the stack, wiring logs together for Bonfire. He had not missed a midnight yell practice since the day he had arrived at the university. He worked hard to develop and implement such modern, first-class athletic facilities as the 23,000-square-foot Na-tum A. Steed Physiology Research and Conditioning laboratory and the Colonel Frank Anderson Track and Field Complex.

Sherrill and his team both became regular visitors at children's hospitals in Houston and Dallas, giving away footballs and Aggie jack-ets, even during bowl week when time was a premium. Sherrill didn't mind. The game could wait. He and his team made time for the children. As the mother of one sick child said of Sherrill, with the demands placed on him in his job, I don't see how the man has the time to see and help the children, but he does. He is always there when he's needed.

Sean Page would never forget the day Jackie Sherrill came walking into practice late, wearing a clown costume. He had gone to see children in the hospital, had done his best to make them laugh, or at least smile, and brighten their day. He had lost track of time. The children may have laughed at the clown. The team didn't. Jackie Sherrill commanded re-spect regardless of the costume he might be wearing.

Early in his tenure at Texas A&M, Sherrill had developed a strong relationship and unwavering friendship with the son of A&M alumnus Jim Uptmore. Paul had Down Syndrome, and, like his father, he was de-voted to Aggie football. On game day at Kyle Field, win or lose, Sherrill would wrap a big, friendly arm around Paul's shoulders and usher him into the A&M locker room. After one major victory, the Coach handed the boy a football that had been autographed by the Aggie players.

Uptmore looked down at his son and asked, do you want Coach Sherrill to autograph the football, too?

No, sir, Paul said adamantly.

Why not?

Coach didn't play, he said.

Jackie Sherrill smiled. He appreciated the young man's honesty and understood his innocence. Coaches coached. Players played. That's the way it was supposed to be.

Sherrill had once told an Aggie Alumni Club in Houston that he might have to raise the ticket prices for the Arkansas game so that the band could spend the night in a motel instead of having to perform, then promptly turn around and take the long bus ride back home.

One man stood and asked, Coach, how much will it be to get them a night on the town?

Near as I can figure, Sherrill said, it'll take seven thousand dollars. Hell, the man said, let's don't mess with our tickets. Let's raise the mon-ey right here. I'll pledge the first thousand dollars.

Four minutes later, Sherrill had the entire seven thousand dollars pledged. The band would play in style and stay in style. Sherrill would have it no other way.

There was more to Texas A&M than football, and Sherrill embraced it all.

He was complex. He was complicated. He was tough. He had a soft heart. He hid his compassion behind a stern face and a private demean-or. He knew how to get things done.

In spite of the turmoil and trouble surrounding Jackie Sherrill, Texas A&M would miss him. As Royce Wisenbaker, Sr., a member of the board of regents said, we hate to see Sherrill go. He has been a great as-set to Texas A&M. I'm sure various and sundry things were done that he knew nothing about, but he's gentleman enough to stand up and take the punishment.

The players were stunned.

Said quarterback Bucky Richardson, I think Coach Sherrill was looking out for us and the school. He's that kind of guy and that kind of coach. He was doing it to protect us as much as he could.

Lineman Doug Williams pointed out, everyone is going to bring up the negatives and not the positives. When you look back at the positive things – how many people he has put in the pros, how many people he has helped find jobs after school, how he rebuilt the program and put the school on the map – you see how much Jackie Sherrill has done for Texas A&M. You add up all of the positives, and they outweigh the negatives by a long shot.

Dan Leyendecker was seated in the dressing room when Jackie Sherrill walked in and told the players of his decision long be-fore he sat down and met with a leering press that had made the journey to College Station so often to condemn him. Leyendecker knew about the controversy. He had read the headlines that denounced almost everyone associated with Texas A&M.

He knew Sherrill had done his best to keep the turmoil away from the field. Jackie Sherrill had never been one to saddle someone else with his own problems. He would take the bullet alone.

He's a good man, Leyendecker thought. He's a good leader. I would follow him anywhere.

So he did.

When Jackie Sherrill walked out, Dan Leyendecker walked out be-hind him.

Neither would be back.

Just before the great explosion downfield, the 12th man lines up its firing squad: Garry Sorrell (26), Kirk Pierce (10), Tommy Bolcerek (25), Trent Childress (17), Vince Palasota (1), and David Fronk (7).

Chapter 29

No one knew what to expect when the anxiety and unrest of a new year hovered tenuously above the Aggie football program. Texas A&M prevented a mutiny and mass exodus when they replaced Jackie Sherrill with R. C. Slocum, who understood the culture of the school and who had pieced together some of the most inventive, innovative defensive schemes in the country. With Slocum, A&M football was in good hands. He was profane in practice, soft-spoken and profound in public. He shunned the limelight, satisfied to coach without anyone looking over his shoulder or critiquing his every move. Sherrill had been center stage. Slocum would be just as content if no one ever raised the curtain. The only controversy trailing after R. C. Slocum came when he did or did not blitz on third down, and only the Aggie faithful cared about the aftermath of his decision. The leering press packed up and headed elsewhere. There was nothing else for them to criticize, condemn, or write about. Overnight, Texas A&M football had become a boring place to be.

The wins remained. R. C. Slocum made sure of it. At the moment, he was free of any rumors, gossip, or innuendo. Even the leering press missed Jackie Sherrill.

The 12th man kickoff team did not know what to expect.

The coach who had created the unit and never doubted its ability was gone.

The coach who had never quite trusted the 12th man was now running the show.

It would be, the team knew beyond a shadow of doubt, a long, strenuous, and unpredictable year.

The splintered gap between reality and paranoia was growing more narrow with each passing day. Sherrill had held a tight leash on his kickoff unit. Slocum had a short leash. Sherrill forgave them of an occasional mistake. They weren't so sure how Slocum might react. It was a new day with new rules and a new man in charge.

The year before, they had held teams to a mere 14.7 average per return. With Slocum, that might not be good enough. With Slocum, the 12th man had no idea what might be good enough.

Garry Sorrell said, we finally figured out we had a graduate assistant assigned to us, but we had to teach him how to coach us. He asked Bubba Hillje and me, what am I supposed to do. Some of these guys haven't even played football in two or three years, I don't know anything about teaching them how to shed blocks, hit, tackle, and I don't know a damn thing about the basics of kickoff coverage.

Don't worry, Hillje said. Here's what you do. Watch us. Keep notes on what we do and how we do it.

Is that all?

There's one more thing.

What's that?

Stay the hell out of our way.

Sorrell said, we knew what to do. We had played before. We still came early. We slugged it out before varsity arrived on the field. We worked on the scout team. We stayed late to practice kickoffs. Unfortunately, it was our lot to do pretty much everything on our own. We coached ourselves and, after awhile, we became damn good coaches.

R. C. Slocum immediately changed the 12th man's aggressive, attacking kickoff scheme – the one that had worked so well for so long.

For the first six years, the 12th man team lined up with wedge busters to clear out the blockers, alley guys to hold the containment, and ball guys search out whoever had the ball. They played with little regard for life or limb. For them, it was always a day of reckoning, and each of them had a definite assignment. They took it seriously.

Under Slocum, the scheme became passive and conservative. Each player was responsible for an alley, only five yards wide. Stick together. That was the plan. Stay together. Wait for the ball carrier to find you. If you attack too much and somebody makes a mistake, a seam can break open, and the ball carrier is gone.

Sure, there might be a few cracks from time to time, Sorrell said. But there was always somebody coming in to fill them. We watched out for each other. We trusted each other. We always knew where everybody was on the field. There might be only five left standing, but they played like eleven. That's why they call it a team. We were, however, Jackie Sherrill's team. We weren't his.

It didn't take Lyn McDonald long to understand the obstacles facing him. As a freshman, back in 1986, he walked on the football team as a better-than-average strong safety from Churchill High School in San Antonio who figured he had a better-than-average chance to make his mark on Kyle Field. He had already faced many of the top teams in Texas. He had squared off against a lot of the state's elite, heavily recruited athletes and, at best, knocked them on their respective asses or, at worst, held his own. At least, he did most of the time. He didn't win all of the battles. He seldom lost any of the wars.

After the first two weeks, Lyn McDonald discovered the vast chasm that separated high school football from college football.

College sports were a business, he said. Walk-ons weren't received with the kind of respect I had anticipated. We were maybe only a little better than the scum sticking like worn-out gum on the bottom of somebody's cleats. I thought Aggies would be out there embracing other Aggies the way it was on campus. I was wrong. I had been told that, unless you were a recruit with a scholarship, you would be treated by a different standard. I didn't believe it until I was confronted with it.

In practice, McDonald discovered the cold, hard truth in a hurry.

Hit.

Or be hit.

Fight.

Vince Palasota (1), Bubba Hillje (13, and Trent Childress (17) spearhead a unit of dedicated, all-volunteer, 12th man football players who give Aggie football everything they have on every play.

240

Or get whipped.

Come back.

Or go home.

And no one cared which was which.

After two weeks, McDonald said, I retired from college football.

He took up handball, won a national championship, and by the time he was a junior, Lyn McDonald began looking at the 12th man in a whole new light. They were held in awe, he said. They were respected on campus and around the country. By now, I wanted to wear that number twelve on my sleeve, too.

He walked down to Kyle Field with his roommate to try out. Jesse was a big guy, he said. He was 6-2, weighed at least 230 pounds, and looked like a linebacker.

Where did you play football, Jesse was asked.

Lubbock.

He didn't tell anybody that he hadn't played since the fifth grade.

No one asked.

Jesse made the first cut, but not the second.

When Lyn McDonald walked down that long, dark corridor and saw his name on the list after surviving the final series of cuts, it was, he said, the most exciting day of his life.

He promptly called his mother on the phone and told her the news.

She cried.

Danny Balcar (2) and Ronnie Glenn (9) cut sharply toward the blocker. Their plan is not that complicated. One takes out the blocker. One goes untouched toward the ball carrier. They have done it so many times in practice, they make the play on instinct. There was an unspoken form of communication among 12th man team members, and everyone understood.

John Bulovas had fallen into a rut. Three years of college. Three years of looking up one party and chasing down another. He had the grades to get into veterinarian school, but, he said, my life was on autopilot.

Going out for the 12th man changed all of that.

He had been a safety at West Orange Stark High School.

So had A&M's big-time cornerback, Kevin Smith.

We went out and ran together, Bulovas said. He was finishing the forty while I was still getting started. Funny. Forty yards didn't look that far. I was tired at twenty, out of breath at thirty, and running out of steam when I hit the 40-yard line. There was work to do. Spending three years of my life sitting in a classroom or looking for something else to drink at a party had taken a little of the life and most of the spring out of my legs.

Football wasn't as easy as it used to be.

On his first day of practice, John Bulovas was helping form a wall for a kickoff return, and he saw Trent Childress barrel down the field and knock some guy named Croaker into oblivion.

He was out cold.

It looked like a Billy Cannon hit, Bulovas said.

Childress was standing over him, eyes blazing, saying, you're not gonna take my position away from me today.

Croaker was simply wondering if someone was going to come and take him away.

In the locker room, Croaker was sitting on a bench, staring off into the far reaches of space.

You need a ride home, Bulovas asked him.

No, Croaker replied softly, my girl friend's gonna pick me up.

Who's that.

Croaker kept staring into a black abyss for a moment, then said, I don't remember her name.

Until that moment, John Bulovas said, I didn't realize how much abuse that people were willing to take just for the privilege of making their presence felt on the football field. Kyle Field was our Mecca. We spent all week trying to get there.

Brian Carpenter looked up when the door to his dorm room opened. John Roper was standing there, casting a very large shadow. In fact, the only thing larger than the shadow was the grin on his face.

I'm gone, Roper said.   He threw the key to the room on the bed.

Where?

Chicago.

Why?

I've just been drafted by the Bears. Roper's grinned broadened. Brian, he said, you can have everything in the room. I've already packed what I wanted.

Roper closed the door and left.

The waterbed wasn't bad. The bearskin rug was a little garish. The clothes certainly didn't fit Brian Carpenter.

It was, Carpenter knew, payback time.

He had been working throughout the semester as a bartender at the Mercury Bar, and a lot of scholarship players, Roper among them, wandered in from time to time, and Carpenter always poured their glasses full of booze.

He mixed their drinks exactly the way they liked them.

Plenty of liquor.

Plenty of ice.

And free.

John Roper hadn't forgotten.

Doug Lawson heard the hamstring pop before he felt it. We were running wind sprints, he said. I thought a bullet had hit me. Knocked him to the ground.

Didn't matter.

Doug Lawson had been knocked to the ground a lot.

He limped through the next week.

Nobody noticed.

Good.

Then, during a drill, rushing the punter at half speed, he was hammered by a blind-side block. When he stood up, his left shoulder was hanging at an odd angle from his body.

It was dislocated.

He could rotate his shoulder one way. It had no intention of moving the other. His hamstring began to tighten up.

In an instant, his life had gone from bad to worse.

I sat up for four days, he said. I couldn't lie down.

He stared into the darkness of night, and it grew darker. Sleep had traveled elsewhere.

Just how badly do you want this, he asked himself.

He waited for an answer.

The next afternoon he was back on the practice field.

You okay, John Bulovas asked.

Officially or unofficially.

Unofficially.

I hurt like hell, Lawson said.

And he would hurt worse before the day ended.

John Bulovas understood. Two weeks before the LSU game, he had caught his toe on the turf and tore the ACL in his knee.

He was a headhunter, although he had never been particularly fast, barely running the forty in 4.7.

He was confronted with two choices.

He could have surgery.

He could play with pain.

He did not want to give anyone a reason to cut him.

He gritted his teeth and played for the rest of the year without ever losing his position.

Billy Pickard saw him limping. You got a bad knee, he asked.

It's just strained.

You want us to have a look at it?

It's fine.

Bulovas grinned. Some moments in life only come around once, he told himself. This is mine. I'm not going to waste it.

A bad knee, he said, would be an easy thing for Pickard to waste.

Losing part of a fingernail in practice didn't sound like much of an injury, Lyn McDonald thought, and it hadn't been much to worry about until the doctor in the quack shack gave him a shot to kill the pain, grabbed a pair of pliers, and ripped the rest of the nail off his finger.

The shot hadn't worked.

The pain was excruciating.

The room became a blur.

It can't get much worse than this, McDonald told himself.

It did.

In practice, he slammed into Robert Wilson, a tough, powerful, 260-pound running back.

Lyn McDonald felt the impact.

He didn't remember the impact.

Where am I, he asked, and when did it turn night?

It's not night.

Then what are those stars doing up there?

McDonald stood up and shook his head.

You want to sit this one out, the coach asked.

Why?

You've got blood all over your face. The coach shrugged. Looks like the helmet cut the bridge of your nose, he said. Happens all the time.

I'm not gong out, McDonald said.

You ought to take a breather.

You may cut me, Lyn McDonald said, but not today.

For the 12th man, Cain Hall had always been the ultimate dining experience with a very exclusive clientele. As Bubba Hillje said, you could always tell how well the team was doing by the food Coach Sherrill had brought in. When we clinched a berth in the Cotton Bowl, he had lobster flown in from Maine. We all sat there and stared at it. None of us had ever seen lobster before, much less eaten it. We had no idea where the meat was and couldn't figure out how to get to it.

Crack the shell, somebody said.

With our heads?

They're used to it.

Cain Hall, according to Lyn McDonald, made the rigors of college football a little more acceptable. It had the best food on campus, he said. No. It may have had the best food in the state. You could eat as much as you wanted for as long as you wanted. Might as well. You'd probably throw up most of it after practice anyway.

The scholarship athletes ate free. During two-a-days in August, before classes began, the 12th man team ate free as well.

For Lyn McDonald, food had been scarce. He ate what he could afford, mostly spaghetti because a pot of it went a long way, or chicken pot pies because they were cheap. He would buy half a dozen hush puppies at Long John Silvers, then keep adding enough catsup until it made a decent meal. At the pizza parlor buffet, McDonald filled a trash bag with enough pizza rolls to smuggle out and last him a few days. Once a month, when a few dollars came from home, he would splurge and dine

R. C. Slocum became head coach of Texas A&M when Jackie Sherrill resigned, and the wins kept right on coming. The new coach, possessing one of the greatest and most innovative defensive minds in college football, built on the strong foundation that Sherrill had solidly left in place, and, in later years, Slocum would lead the Aggies to the Nokia Sugar Bowl.

at Schlotzsky's.

Now, he said, I was standing in line at Cain Hall, waiting to eat a steak filet, and the ladies were walking past us with bowls of fresh, peeled shrimp. Take all you want, they said. We don't want you boys to get hungry.

At Cain Hall, they never did.

R. C. Slocum brought Texas A&M a winning football team. No one had ever doubted otherwise. He had great talent and was acknowledged to be a great coach by everyone who worked with him or competed against him.

It was all about wins and losses.

R. C. Slocum would finish the year with eight wins.

Before the LSU game, Slocum told his players, all right, guys, before we go out there and play today, I have a song I want to play for you, and I want you to listen closely to the words.

Great, thought Garry Sorrell. Coach Sherrill had motivated us with music a lot of times, and they were always loud, hard-driving, blood-pumping, head-stomping songs guaranteed to have you running on high-octane adrenaline and ready to kill somebody by the time you hit the field.

Slocum reached over and placed a tape in the machine.

Out flowed the gentle, wistful, sentimental sounds of Whitney Houston, singing "One Moment in Time."

It was slow, Lyn McDonald said. It was a love song. It would have been great to play if we were getting ready to dance. I don't think LSU had come to dance. Whitney Houston drained away every ounce of adrenaline we had. But that was Slocum. He was a great coach. He generally lacked a little when it came to motivation.

Then again, maybe R. C. Slocum had pushed the right button after all. Who knew?

Despite the dreamy, sensual, romantic lyrics of Whitney Houston, Larry Horton ran the opening kickoff back for a touchdown, Texas A&M grabbed the early momentum, and Slocum did what Jackie Sherrill never been able to do. He beat LSU and beat the Tigers badly, winning the first game of the year, 38-16.

LSU's famed rowdy bunch was hanging over the walls, and security had to put a net over the top of the tunnel at halftime. Rene Casas said, the coaches told us to put on our helmets before we came out of the locker room. It could get a little dangerous. The LSU fans were throwing bottles and cans down on us, and by the time we reached the field, the net was covered and sagging with trash. I was afraid they were coming after us with their boiling pots of crawfish and blood sausage.

From the first minutes of the game, Lyn McDonald said, Billy Pickard was screaming every curse word he knew, and he knew a dictionary full of them. He was convinced that LSU was stealing our signals, and he almost tackled a referee to get his attention. Sometimes, Bill Pickard thought he ran the team. He even suggested the plays that Coach Slocum ought to run, and when they occasionally worked, you could hear his laughter echoing from one sideline to the other. Pickard was hard. Pickard knew football.

Doug Lawson broke past the wedge untouched, racing down the left sideline. The loose football had skimmed past the kick returner and was rolling crazily in front of him. It was almost within Lawson's reach. He could almost touch it.

Dammit, he said.

The ball bounced into the end zone.

LSU breathed a sigh of relief.

Lawson was heartsick. Maybe if his hamstring hadn't torn, he thought. Maybe if his dislocated shoulder hadn't been hanging at the wrong angle. Maybe if had cut another tenth off his forty time. Maybe if the ball had bounced right instead of left.

But that was football.

It was fraught with more maybes than anything else.

The Aggies lost to Washington, steamrolled their way to wins over TCU and Southern Mississippi, then braced themselves for the Red Raiders of Texas Tech. The game would be, as all games with Tech, a bitter brawl with no quarter and little mercy.

It had been a good day in practice for Bubba Hillje as A&M began to build a game plan for the Red Raiders. The Aggies were unveiling their latest in a long line of hot-shot running backs.

Keith McAfee and Randy Simmons took four reps.

Together, they barreled into the line of scrimmage four times.

Hillje stopped them for losses on all four carries.

In the film room, coaches turned off the lights and carefully watched the practice session. Over and over, frame-by-frame, they watched Hillje blast through and knock the hot-shot running backs to the ground.

None of them said a word.

The running backs might as well have stepped on a piece of bubble gum and tripped, Hillje said. It was as though I was the only one in the room who saw me make the tackles. I didn't expect to be glorified or even patted on the back. But I did think one of them might have the decency to mention my name.

On Wednesday before the game, Coach Bob Davie pulled Hillje off the field and told him, we have a backup inside linebacker who's hurt. I'm taking you to Lubbock and running you in his place against Texas Tech. Tomorrow after practice, you need to come up to the office and go over some game film. We'll discuss your assignments.

Well, Hillje thought, I guess Davie saw the film after all. Or maybe he was just desperate and reaching way down deep in the bottom of the barrel to find me.

The next afternoon, Hillje walked into the coach's office, still awash with sweat from practice and ready to learn whatever assignments Davie wanted to give him. Study all night if necessary. Whatever the coaches wanted him to do, Hillje would get it right.

Davie only smiled. No time for that, he said. But don't worry about it, Bubba. Practice has always been a little overrated anyway.

The Aggies dropped a heartbreaker to Texas Tech, 27-24, and the score could have easily been worse. The Red Raiders must have spent more time watching game film of the 12th man than any other team, Tommy Bolcerek said. They were ready for us. They brought a double team against me with the idea of kicking me off the field and leaving an opening up the sideline. The double team arrived a step late. I was able to split it and cause a pile up. I reached out and slowed the ball carrier down as he was making his move. Couldn't go straight. Had to find an alternate route. He cut one way. He should have cut the other. Bubba Hillje cleaned him up real good.

Texas A&M slipped past Houston and Baylor, blew out Rice, and welcomed a struggling and inexperienced SMU team back from the Death Penalty with a 61-14 win. Lyn McDonald had not played that much, but he was given his chance to go downfield against the Mustangs.

He said, I knocked down three guys at one time on one play. I had three years worth of hits bottled up inside of me.

As the season wore on, Garry Sorrell said, we began to see the handwriting on the wall, and we didn't like the message it was sending us. Coach Slocum had always been worried about the 12th man concept even when Coach Sherrill came up with the idea. Now, everything had changed. Even the practices were different. We felt as though he was waiting for us to fail just so he could pull the plug.

Once again, even after being saddled with a year on probation, Texas A&M had a conference championship squarely in its sights. Arkansas, as usual, loomed as the final and critical roadblock.

The Aggies had a bi-week to prepare for the Razorbacks, and practices had never been more vicious or brutal. Trent Childress said, Coach Slocum kept telling us, if you cover well and give us every damn thing you've got in practice, you'll be my kickoff team against Arkansas. However, if I don't see some improvement in your coverage during the next two weeks, I can guarantee that you'll be over there sitting on the bench when Arkansas comes to town.

His words did not make sense to Bubba Hillje. We had a better record against kickoffs than his varsity team did, Hillje said. I know. The first thing I did on Monday morning was head to the library and check the stats on the sports page of the *Eagle*. The varsity kickoff team may have been good, but it wasn't as good as we were.

For two weeks, Childress said, we covered well, gave Coach Slocum everything we had, and busted the heads of anybody crazy enough to run the ball back against us. Maroon. White. We loved those colors, but we left them tattered and torn on the practice field.

Practice was heightened. It had been ruthless. Now it was almost barbaric. Hillje said, we went live on every kickoff. Take somebody's head off or lose yours. Do the job or be banished to the bench. Slocum acted as though he were ready to cut anyone who slacked off. Hell, he might have been ready to cut us all. In my opinion, he was merely looking for a reason, any reason, and we refused to give him one. The kickoffs were furious and the collisions violent. It was rough on everybody.

One player blew out a knee.

Two others went down with injuries and had trouble getting back up. As Doug Lawson said, we knew we had to be able to suit up or we might as well leave for good. It was easier to endure the pain than endure the thought of leaving the team. So we bit a few bullets, buckled down, and practiced even harder. We were mad dogs all going after the same bone.

A walk-on linebacker was blocking on a running play, and he stormed into Hillje with an earthquake tackle fierce enough to rock the ground beneath their feet. Hillje said, when I got up and started jogging back up field, I tripped on the white yard-line stripe. I got up, hit the next one, and tripped again. Damn, I thought, those white stripes are a lot higher than they used to be.

The first two times Hillje tripped, the players laughed.

The third time he tripped, they laughed louder.

When he went down for the fourth time, someone yelled, hey, somebody better check Hillje. That boy's not quite right.

Concussions could do that to a player.

But rattling around in the far recesses of his mind, Bubba Hillje could hear the muffled, slurred words of R. C. Slocum saying, you're doing a pretty good job, men. Keep up the good work.

They did, all except Hillje.

Bubba Hillje was through for the day.

You can't play Arkansas if you can't spell it, Sorrell told him.

Rene Casas (9) puts the clamps on the Eric Metcalf, the elusive, speed-burning running back and kick returner for the University of Texas.

Texas A&M won the coin toss and deferred to the second half. Coach Slocum huddled with the 12th man and said, I've thought it over, and this is too big a game. I can't risk sending you boys on the field. We've got the Cotton Bowl at stake. I'm going to let the regular varsity team cover the kicks.

It was, Childress said, like a sucker punch in the gut. We had covered Jason Phillips of Houston like a blanket. We had shut down Tyrone Thurman of Texas Tech, holding him to less than fifteen yards every time he fielded a kickoff. The year before, he had led the nation in kickoff returns. Arkansas did not have a kick returner in the same class with Phillips and Thurman.

It didn't matter.

The 12th man team sat alone, no longer needed, no longer wanted, eased aside and exiled to the far end of the bench. They watched Arkansas slip past the Aggies, 23-22. We might have made a difference, Childress said. Probably not. But we'll never know.

The vision of cotton faded on the campus of College Station.

Bubba Hillje was furious. He had never missed a practice. He had sacrificed. He had been abused mentally and physically. And now the head coach, he said, had lied to him. Hillje struck back. He wasn't going to take it anymore.

He boycotted practice for three days.

What the hell?

When he did return to the field, Coach Kirk Doll asked him, where have you been, Bubba, taking a test?

Nope. I didn't feel like coming.

Well, the coach said, it looks to me that if you want to dance, you've got to pay the fiddler.

The way I look at it, coach, Hillje snapped, we've already paid the fiddler. Slocum owes us. We don't owe him a damn thing.

He feels differently.

He can afford to. Hillje could feel the tension knotting up the muscles in the back of his neck. He's the head coach. His word is law. He just didn't keep his word to us.

He had his reasons.

Hillje shrugged and walked away.

He had just as soon be arguing with a fence post.

After a brief and animated conversation with Doll, Coach Slocum headed across the field, yelling loudly and sternly, where's Hillje? Right here, coach.

What's this I hear about you not coming to practice just because you didn't happen to feel like it?

You heard right, coach. Hillje's face had reddened. You lied to us, he said, and you know it. You stood there, looked us in the eyes, and straight-up lied to us.

What do you mean?

You told us that if we worked hard, gave you our hearts and souls, and covered kickoffs live in practice, then you'd send us out against Arkansas, Hillje said. We did. And you never took us off the bench.

I did what I felt was best for the team.

We have a better average.

Slocum couldn't argue with that.

Coach, frankly I am sick and tired of getting kicked around like dogs, Hillje said. All we ask for is a chance. We deserve a chance. There are a few guys out here who hustle more, work harder, and are better than some of your scholarship players. They work their tails off, but they don't get a chance and never get a chance to play simply because they're walk-ons. Being a walk-on. That's like getting a death sentence, except there's no appeal.

Slocum was stunned. I didn't expect this of you, Bubba, he said.

Well coach, Hillje said over his shoulder as he stalked away, I didn't expect this of you either. You flat out lied to us, and I learned the first day I was in school at Texas A&M that Aggies don't lie, cheat, or steal. What part of that don't you understand?

Neither player nor coach had anything further to say.

The tempers had already said enough.

Bubba Hillje, Slocum knew, was a fine damn player.

R. C. Slocum, Hillje knew, was a fine damn coach.

At the moment, neither had anything good to say about the other.

Those bastards from Austin came to town for Thanksgiving, and long before the opening kick, war was declared. The Texas A&M football team, as was its tradition at home games, lined up across the field, faced the student section, and began singing the revered *Aggie War Hymn*.

The Longhorns lined up shoulder-to-shoulder and walked purposely across the field and stood eye-to-eye with the Aggies.

No respect.

They had just spit on tradition.

The Aggies were singing.

Texas, Lyn McDonald said, was talking trash.

The Aggies kept singing.

The trash, McDonald said, turned to garbage, and the garbage became a little too vile to swallow.

A little shoving. A little pushing. Then someone threw a punch, the skirmish became a battle, and the brawl spilled across the field. McDonald couldn't believe his eyes. Players were taking their helmets off, he said, and I thought that had to be the most stupid thing I had ever seen. If you want to fight, that's fine with me. I'll throw a few punches, and I'll take a few. No problem. I kept my helmet on. I didn't have much of a face, but I wanted to keep what was left of it.

Dennis Descant was a senior. He looked around and told himself, I'm gonna let these kids fight it out all they want, but I'm not about to do something foolish enough to get kicked out of my last game.

One of the 12th man players was grabbed by three Longhorns, dragged to the end zone and beaten without mercy.

No one forgot.

Descant said, we kicked off. The Texas running back brought it back about fifteen yards, and we leveled him. At the bottom of the pile, tempers were still burning hot. Fists were swinging, elbows being thrown, and I heard a great deal of cursing, and a little of it sounded a great deal like my voice.

Suddenly, one of our defensive linemen jerked me out of the pile. Leave that stuff to us, he said. I knew by the look on his face that Texas was in for a long and dangerous night.

The game began with a bang.

It ended with a whimper.

Those bastards from Austin had little left to say and nothing else

to fight about as they quietly loaded the bus and headed back home, cloaked by a 21-10 defeat. The string of consecutive A&M victories over the Longhorns had grown to six.

Ahead lay the Sun Bowl and a clash with, ironically enough, Jackie Sherrill's old school, Pittsburgh, and the *El Paso Times* wrote of 12th man kickoff team, using a headline that said: *This Aggie tradition really packs a wallop.* The article quoted Bubba Hillje as saying, we might only play one play all day, but there are bigger collisions and people flying around everywhere when we're out there.

Hillje had been foolishly optimistic about the team being on the field for one play.

As a 12th man unit, no one touched the field.

The Sun Bowl would rise and set without them.

Rene Casas said, it was my final game as a member of the 12th man team, and it was far more difficult than my last game in high school. At least, then, I had an outside chance to play football somewhere again. After leaving Texas A&M, I knew I wasn't going to the next level. This was it.

His career had already ended.

Rene Casas just didn't know it.

Brian Carpenter said, Coach Slocum didn't even bother to come tell us it was over. He sent a graduate assistant in to meet with us.

I hate to say it guys, the young coach said, but only one of you will be allowed to play today. The coaches have taken an informal poll and believe it should be Hillje.

Bubba Hillje shook his head. Go tell the coach to do strange things with himself, Hillje said. I'm not leaving the other guys. If they can't play, I don't play.

Carpenter told him, you gotta do it, Bubba.

It's your one chance to go out there and show them the difference between a real 12th man and a bunch of pretenders, Garry Sorrell said. If we can't kick Pittsburgh in the mouth, then you can do it for us. We're counting on you.

I never saw Bubba run as fast or as hard as he did that day, Carpenter said.

He played like a man possessed, Tommy Bolcerek said.

He was only one man, Sorrell said, but he was playing for all of us.

The Aggies lost, 31-28. In fact the Aggies had lost two in a row with the 12th man on the bench. Hard to explain, Sorrell said. Then again, maybe not.

Texas A&M kicked off five times against Pittsburgh, and the Aggies made four tackles.

Bubba Hillje made all four.

On one, he caused a fumble.

They found out who the 12th man really was, he said. A slow-footed Texas boy with a hard head. There were nine more just like me. Waiting. Just like E. King Gill had waited. His coach needed him. Our coach didn't need us.

When the final whistle blew, Hillje felt like crying.

It was over.

The glory had faded.

The 12th man team, he knew, might or might not go on.

But it would never again be the same.

The end was already in sight.

Bubba Hillje was selected as the lone member of the 12th man team to cover kickoffs in the Sun Bowl against Pittsburgh. An irate Bubba Hillje (13), representing his teammates, was a one-man wrecking crew. He made all four tackles on kickoffs.

The boys of another autumn gather to relive the glory days of the 12th man kickoff team: David Fry (in the cowboy hat). Kneeling on the front row, left to right, Garry Sorrell, Ronnie Glenn, and Kirk Pierce. Second row, left to right, David Coolidge, Scott Slater, Dan Leyendecker (with gig'em sign), Brian Edwards, Derek Naiser, Scott McClatchy (a trainer with the team), Tommy Bolcerek (in Aggie cap), Danny Balcar, Dennis Mudd, Warren Barhorst, Dean Berry, Trent Childress, John Bulovas, John Gregg, Vince Palasota, Brian Carpenter, Blake Dwoskin, and Sean Page. On the back row, left to right, Chris Massey, Roy Kokemoor, Mark Wurzbach, Bobby Bostic, Alec Cuellar, Bubba Hillje, Rene Casas (in white cap), Andy McDonald, Butch Motley, Dennis Descant, Spencer Baum, and Chad Adair.

Epilogue

It all came to an abrupt end on a sunny Saturday afternoon in 1990 when Texas Tech's Rodney Blackshear, with only eleven seconds remaining in the first half, returned a kickoff ninety-two yards for a touchdown.

The 12th man, as a unit, never left the bench again.

In reality, the 12th man kickoff team had already been watered down. Coach R. C. Slocum had sent in two of his scholarship athletes to play as safeties on the kickoff, and, unfortunately, neither of them caught Blackshear either.

Slocum said of the touchdown run, that kickoff return points out the problem we have with playing a team of walk-ons. Of course, he admitted, the regular kickoff team didn't cover very well that day either.

Slocum knew better than to openly defy a sacred A&M tradition. He came up with his own version of the team. He announced that he would choose one man from the 12th man unit to wear the cherished number twelve on his jersey sleeve and go downfield on kickoffs at both home and away games. When E. King Gill came out of the stands, he was only one guy, Slocum said. It wasn't eleven or twelve guys. It was only one. We are trying to maintain the true tradition of the 12th man. He will be with us every time we play. I think it will be in our best interest to do that.

The college game had changed, and Slocum felt obliged to change with it.

First the NCAA put the kickoff back five yards, Slocum said, and we were able to survive. Then the NCAA put the kickoff back another five yards, and the return game became an overnight offensive juggernaut. No longer were teams merely filling out their special teams with second and third team players. Now, they were sending the best they had onto the field. Kickoff return teams had All-Americans returning the ball and All-Americans blocking for them. We believed we it was vital for us to fight fire with fire.

The way it had been in the past, Slocum said, really put both of our kickoff teams at a disadvantage. The opposition had one kickoff team, and it was a polished unit. We had two. The 12th man didn't get to play in road games, and when we came home to play, they may not have covered a kick in two or three weeks. They were going against an offensive team that had been practicing on a regular basis. The 12th man was rusty. The same went for our regular kickoff team. By the time we traveled to a road game again, the varsity unit may not have seen any action in a couple of weeks, and it was rusty. Having two distinct and separate teams just made for a lot of inconsistency in an era when we could not afford any inconsistency. Wins or losses depended on how consistently we played, and wins and losses have always been important to Aggies.

Ironically, Slocum's son, Shawn, was working as the Aggies special teams coach when the action was taken. Shawn Slocum was a former 12th man team member who suffered a series of concussions that ended his playing career. He said, this was the most difficult decision my father ever had to make. We discussed it for days and long into the night before changing up the kickoff team. In reality, the final decision was not a critical reflection on the 12th man team. It was simply a move we were forced to make in order to further strengthen our varsity kick... The regular s... ...actice. It need... ...more in order to achieve its full potential. Road games wer... ...al, and varsity covered on the road. We did not want their lack of practice or playing time to cost us.

However, Jack Davis, a student, wrote a letter to the editor of the Battalion and pointed out, Coach Slocum says that having two kickoff teams is inefficient. I agree. But he got rid of the wrong one. We'll miss that special moment when ten crazy guys come jumping out on the field, waving those towels. But, hey, we'll win, won't we?

An era, as eras tend to do, had fallen by the wayside.

With the 12th man, the student body had a face on the field.

No.

It had ten faces.

Not helmets.

Not numbers.

Faces.

The faces were fading into the mist of a mystical time that was and would never be again.

The suicide squad had been shot down from within.

The mad dogs no longer had a bark.

The kamikazes had no place to crash and burn.

Those who had made a difference on the field would graduate and begin making a difference in society. The headhunters who fought, scratched, and clawed for everything they ever earned or were given on a football field left to become doctors and lawyers, veterinarians and dentists, teachers and coaches, engineers, executives, and entrepreneurs. They flew planes and ran restaurants. They caught crooks and interrogated the bad guys or built dams and buildings in Iraq and Afghanistan. They searched for oil in the sands of the Mid-East. They built the infrastructure of the world. For them, nothing had changed except the uniform.

They spun the world upside down on a football field.

Now they were helping make the world go round.

On a better day in an-

other time, not really so far away, they had all occupied special places of interest and importance on the sacred turf of Kyle Field.

They return today, the boys of another autumn, hoping that nothing has changed and knowing full well that everything has. Two decades or more are behind them. The eyes of maturity long for the days when a single kickoff – a single moment in time – was all that mattered to them. Life was as good then as the memories are now.

Sean Page points out, over twenty years have now passed, and time is a blur. I always take the same farm-to-market road 50 still in search of crop dusters and the very first moment when Kyle Field can be seen so far out on that horizon. I search for cotton now as I did when I was a mere pup. I search for a clear vision of where it all began.

My eyes wander briefly into the fields, which are a faint shade of green despite the drought conditions settling down upon the Brazos Valley. I catch a glimpse of an old farmer with his back to FM 50, his straw hat creased with sweat, clad in Wranglers, his boots straddling a row of crops. Robert Earl Keene's The Front Porch Song and the office Blackberry cannot compete for my attention as my concern and curiosity mount for the weathered figure standing alone beneath an unforgiving sun. As I pass, the old farmer slowly turns my way, revealing maroon "Texas Aggie" letters across the front of a T-shirt, a blending of cotton with layers dirt. From him, I see a "gig 'em," a wave, and, as I like to believe, a knowing smile.

I leave him farther back in my rearview mirror, a confident man like my father and Jackie Wayne Sherrill had been. For there is a spirit inside that old bull, a spirit that ne'er be told, a spirit we desperately hoped to capture in the development of this book. It is the Spirit of Aggieland.

In the distance, on around past the bend, a green and yellow fiberglass crop duster makes another pass across the crops that virtually

When Hurricane Katrina stormed across the Gulf and devastated the Louisiana coast, Bobby Bostic's home was ravaged by high winds and higher water. When he was finally able to trek through the ruin and floodwaters to reach his house, he was able to find and save his most prized possession, his 12th man jersey. It had withstood the storm and remained undamaged, not unlike the 12th man kickoff team during the Jackie Sherrill era of Texas A&M football.

surround me. Each fall, the cotton, now left behind by Stallings, Sherrill, and Slocum, still litters FM 50. In the distance, Kyle Field stands stall, far out upon the horizon, once beckoning the dreams of pups from Nowhere, Texas, who were just a little too short, a bit too small, or a step too slow.

On game day, the towels still wave in the stands. The Aggie Spirit remains strong through it all. The crowds are larger than ever.

But never again has Kyle Field exploded with the same wild, unmitigated fury and frenzy as it did when a bunch of unknown walk-ons from the backroads, crossroads, and freeways of Texas raced onto the field with a number twelve stitched on their jerseys.

They certainly didn't turn Texas A&M's football fortunes around.

Jackie Sherrill did.

And R. C. Slocum kept the momentum traveling full speed ahead.

But they were hustling, battling, and cheating impossible odds on every kickoff when A&M's meteoric rise to prominence happened. They saw it all and were an integral part of the football resurrection at Kyle Field. Dennis Descant once said, we all worked with a common purpose to share an uncommon tradition. Derek Naiser explained, when we ran off the field, little kids would look up at us like we were Roman gladiators. And Dennis Mudd explained, opposing players didn't quite understand why in the world people would volunteer their own time all week just to play football on Saturday.

They didn't understand what it meant to be an Aggie and represent Aggies all over the world.

The story of the 12th man kickoff team is one of personal triumph and occasional tragedy. Some memories and recollections have dimmed with the years. Others remain as vibrant as the day they

occurred. And the complexity of the truth lies deep within the woven layers of fact. Perception so often is founded on truth that has been colored by layers of high anxiety and high excitement that people recall or choose to recall. For them, life was at its pinnacle. They were playing football, college football, big-time football – Texas A&M football. The thrill of victory. And the agony that went with defeat. The truth for others may have suffered from the dismay of a few bad days, hard times, bruises, and disappointment. Neither is necessarily right, and neither is necessarily wrong. It just happens to be the way it is – and the way it was.

Jackie Sherrill reached into a bunch of unknowns and plucked a few who would forever form the backbone of a legacy.

He gave them a chance when no one else would.

And they were forever indebted.

None of them ever really knew Jackie Wayne Sherrill.

None of them ever had many, if any, conversations with their Head Coach. As one said, I can count every word I ever spoke to Coach Sherrill on one finger.

They feared him.

They respected him.

They became his disciples. He taught them the game. He taught them about life. He taught them how to be better than any of them thought they could be.

He made a difference.

Then.

And now.

Their day in the sun was a magical time, one trapped in a single moment of fate, time and circumstance.

They were the little engine that could in a world that said they couldn't.

They were the student body.

They were Texas A&M.

They were the 12th man.

The memories, when all is said and done, are not really about football, but about friendships gained during a time when the 12th man would not let each other fail. Remembering it all, left to right, are Chad Adair, Ronnie Glenn, and Garry Sorrell.

Where Are They Now?

Chad Adair, the first of the four-year members of the 12th man kickoff team, lives in Houston, Texas. He is director of operations for Sharps Compliance, Inc.

Cory Allen lives near Victoria, Texas. He is assistant general manager for the South Texas Electric Cooperative.

Tom Arthur lives in Houston, Texas. He serves as business manager for Gulf Energy, a chemical and fuel blend stock trading company.

Les Asel lives in Katy, Texas. He owns the Les Asel Construction Company and is a general contractor in the Houston metropolitan area.

Danny Balcar lives in Corinth, Texas. He is the Manager of Engineering Services for TEMSCO, located in Lewisville, Texas, and has obtained his Master's Degree in Business Administration.

Warren E. Barhorst lives in Houston, Texas. He owns Barhorst Insurance Group, LTD, which provides expert solutions for the insurance and financial needs of its clients. Securities are offered through Warren E. Barhorst as a Registered Representative of Nationwide Securities.

Spencer Baum, DDS, owns and operates the Baum Dental Clinic in Mineral Wells, Texas.

Dean Berry lives in Abilene. He and his brothers, Greg and Ray, work for the family business, BML, Inc., founded by his father, Powell, in 1981. BML is a crude oil marketing and gathering company that operates from Eastern New Mexico to the Fort Worth Basin.

Tom Bevans lives in College Station, Texas. He is a partner in the Risk Management & Security Consulting Firm of McConnor-Meade. The primary office is located in The Woodlands, near Houston.

Russ Birdwell, MD, lives in Garland, Texas. He is a general surgeon at Baylor Hospital in Dallas.

Tommy Bolcerek lives in Brenham, Texas. He serves as the Business Unit Manager for Small Parts and also manages the shipping department for MIC Group, a precision manufacturing facility.

Bobby Bostic lives in New Orleans, Louisiana. He works in industrial and equipment financing for Coactiv Capital Partners.

Jeff Boutwell supervised construction programs for parks througout Texas before going to Iraq with the U.S. Corps of Engineers and building wastewater plants for cities with a population of 40,000.

John Bulovas lives in The Woodlands, Texas. A DVM, he opened The Animal Hospital, a 6,500-square-foot free-standing facility, in 2006. It provides advanced veterinary medicine to dogs and cats, as well as routine boarding and grooming services.

Tom Bumgardner lives in Alpharetta, Georgia. He is president of a $100 million company, SIMOS Insourcing Solutions, which has more than six thousand employees. The firm provides engineering, management, and labor for such nationwide companies as Wal-Mart, Target, Home Depot, Yamaha, NIKE, and Williams Sonoma.

John Burnett is vice president of sales for Fox Sports Network in Dallas, Texas. FSN is a unit of the Fox Entertainment Group.

Dennis Burns is in the United Emirates, working for Lockheed Martin.

Brian Carpenter became a podiatrist after a podiatrist in College Station built a special boot to protect his ankle, injured when he was a member of the 12th man team. He is a Doctor of Podiatric Medicine at the North Central Texas Orthopaedics and Sports Medicine in Decatur, Texas. He also works with the Department of Orthopaedics at John Peter Smith Hospital in Fort Worth, Texas.

Rene Casas lives in his hometown of Freer, Texas. He, his father, and younger brother operate four companies: Freer Iron Works, Duval Lease Service, STX Process Equipment Company, with 175 employees in South Texas, and an Ace Hardware Store in Zapata, Texas.

Trent Childress lives in Temple, Texas, where he is vice president and general manager for Lock Joint Tube, a company that manufactures and processes steel tubing and sheet products. The firm has 102 employees and $38 million in annual sales.

Tom Christner coaches freshman football and teaches science at Augusta Middle School in Augusta, Kansas.

David Coolidge lives in Houston, Texas. He owns an energy commodity trading fund, specializing in natural gas, called Velite Capital Management. He launched the firm in 2006 with $22 million of assets under management and presently manages more than $750 million. He previously worked for Coastal Gas Marketing and Reliant Energy, then became a trading principal for AAA Capital Management.

Robert M. Crouch lives in Sunnyvale, Texas. He is owner and president of Crouch Construction, involved with commercial construction across the state of Texas and works with BioEnergy Partners LLC, producing renewable energy.

Alec Cuellar lives in San Antonio. He is a South Texas Region Application Engineer for Capital Machine Southwest, the nation's largest distributor of Fabrication Equipment and Robotic Welding.

Dennis Descant lives in West Houston. Professionally, he is a shareholder in Brady Chapman Holland & Associates, a Houston-based insurance agency. He manages the surety operations of the firm.

Blake Dwoskin lives in Houston as president and partner of Cayo LP. He has been involved with the marine construction industry since graduation from Texas A&M, working in Hawaii, Maryland, Florida, Texas, Wyoming, Arkansas, Louisiana, the Dominican Republic, Georgia, Kentucky, Illinois, Mississippi, and Guantanamo Bay. Projects have included demolition, reha-bilitation, and construction of wharfs, piers, dams, platforms, and pipelines on, in, or underwater.

Brian Edwards teaches social studies and serves as the head boys and girls golf coach for Dumas High School in Dumas, Texas. He and his wife also own a Tex-Mex restaurant in town called Chica Blanca.

David Fronk lives in Fort Worth, Texas. He is the regional sales manager for Cantex, Inc., which manufactures electrical conduits and fittings.

David Fry went back to school after recording a 0.0 grade point average during his first two semesters of playing on the 12th man team, raised his grades dramatically, and graduated from the Texas A&M College of Veterinary Medicine with a 3.48 GPA. He owns his own Equine Veterinary Practice – Fry Equine Health – in Marble Falls, Texas.

James Fuqua, the red pot who introduced Jackie Sherrill to Bonfire, owns and operates the U Lazy 2 Ranch and U Lazy 2 Cattle Company near Quanah, Texas. He is the fourth generation to operate the ranch, which was established in 1894. About 3,000 acres are devoted to cropland, but the majority of the ranch is a commercial Angus cattle operation. All beef are produced for the domestic high-end restaurant market, as well as to markets in Japan and South Korea.

Ronnie Glenn lives in West Houston and, since 1994, has been with Tri-anim Health Services, selling specialty anesthesia, critical care, and respiratory equipment and supplies.

John Gregg lives in Round Rock, Texas. He is a senior buyer for Golfsmith, International.

Charles "Bubba" Hillje, after graduation, received his wings at the Naval Aviator flight school in Pensacola, Florida. He flew the CH53-D Sea Stallion, a large transport helicopter. Presently, Hillje is first officer for UPS Airlines, having flown both domestically and internationally for the company.

Harold Huggins lives in San Antonio. He serves as a teacher and assistant football coach at Claudia Taylor "Lady Bird" Johnson High School.

Larry Johnson lives in Aledo, Texas. He is a manager for VersaCold Logistics, a company that offers refrigerated logistics services – storage and transportation – to the food industry.

David Joiner serves as Boys Athletic Coordinator and Head Football Coach for Magnolia West High School in Magnolia, Texas. His kickoff team still uses the same scheme developed for the 12th man unit.

Brian Katara lives in Sun Valley, Idaho. He is general manager for Davis Embroidary, an ad specialty company.

T. Douglas Lawson is president of Baylor Regional Medical Center at Grapevine, Texas. Several years ago, it was discovered that Lawson had Stage 4 Hodgkins Disease. He said, I dug down deep and practiced everything I had learned during my days on the 12th man team. I visualized getting rid of the cancer just as I visualized making a tackle. After chemo and radiation treatments, the cancer was gone, and Lawson spent the next decade building cancer programs at hospitals across the country.

Dan Leyendecker lives in Corpus Christie, Texas. He is president of LNV Engineering and a partner of the company, along with fellow 12th man kickoff team member, Derek Naiser, and another A&M graduate, Robert Viera. LNV Engineering is a 70-person firm with disciplines in Water, Wastewater, Transportation, Structural, Environmental, Architectural, and Surveying.

Ike Liles, who is a licensed engineer in Oklahoma and Texas, lives in Clyde, Texas. He is the distribution manager for the Abilene District of Texas for American Electric Power, a utility company that provides electric service to about five million customers across eleven states.

Corey Linscombe lives in Weatherford, Texas. He is an engineer and program manager for the F-22 Raptor, built by Lockheed Martin. The F-22 uses stealth technology and is considered a critical component of the U. S. strike force. Lockheed Martin also produces the F-16 and F-35 fighter aircrafts.

Paul Luedke is Traffic Operations Manager of HDR/WHM Transportation in Dallas, Texas.

Andy McDonald lives in Fredericksburg, Texas, and is president and co-owner of Sports Medicine & Physical Therapy of the Greater Texas Hill Country.

Lyn McDonald lives in San Antionio. He is the school psychologist with the Northeast School District and serves as head golf coach for Madison High School.

Bobby Middleton lives in Montgomery, Texas. He owns and operates R. Middleton Construction Company. He says of his years on the 12th man team, if it had not been for the grace and mercy of our Heavenly Father, I would not have played football or finished school.

Doug Middleton, lives in Brenham, Texas. He is the ingredient processing manager of Blue Bell Creameries in Brenham.

Larry "Butch" Motley lives just south of Azle, Texas. He is a Senior Project Engineer for Enbridge, a natural gas and oil company. He works in the natural gas gathering and processing division of the company, located in Springtown, Texas. He previously worked for Mid-Valley Pipeline and ConocoPhillips.

Dennis Mudd lives on a ten-acre farm in West Chambers County, Texas. For more than two decades, he has worked with Mobil Corporation, now ExxonMobil, which included a five-year family assignment in the Middle East. He has held multiple positions with the company but is presently Emergency Preparedness/Response and Security manager for the company's Baytown manufacturing complex.

Derek Naiser lives in San Antonio. He is one of three owners of LNV Engineering, a Civil/Structural/Transportation/Environmental/Surveying consulting firm with offices in Corpus Christi, San Antonio, and Austin. The company has grown from seven employees when it was established in 2000 to seventy.

Keith Newton is president and chief operating officer of Concentra, the nation's largest primary care provider for occupational health care with 320 locations in forty states. The company, with more than 150,000 employees, is centered on improving the quality of life by making health care accessible and affordable.

Sean Page lives in San Antonio. He is an attorney and partner with the law firm of Thornton, Biechlin, Segrato, Reynolds & Guerra, practicing civil litigation in San Antonio. The Thornton Law Firm is a Member of the International Society of Primerus Law Firms.

Vince Palasota lives in Denton, Texas, and is one of the owners of several companies. However, he spends the majority of his time as the Chief Executive Officer for Med Pharmex Animal Health. He also works with entrepreneurs to develop marketing strategies and business plans to help launch new products. He and his partners recently built a Christian orphanage in India to support more than 400 children left orphans by the Tsunami.

Tony Pollacia lives in Plano. He is vice president of field sales for the Rug Doctor in Dallas.

Kirk Pierce lives in Frisco, Texas. He works as a Hospitalist/Physician Assistant Mid-Level Practitioner in Denton, Texas.

Dan Pollard lives in San Antonio. He is vice president of corporate services, working as a commercial real estate broker for Jones Lang LaSalle America, Inc., which purchased The Staubach Company – Central Texas.

Tom Ray still lives on the old family ranch near Floresville. After fighting one drought too many, he turned his attention from ranching and bought the 43-year-old Wiatrek's Meat Market in nearby Poth.

Edward Silverman, DVM, owns and operates his own veterinarian service in San Antonio.

Scott Slater lives in Fort Worth. With seven years of experience in the global investment bank Morgan Stanley, he joined Developers Resources, LLC, a hospitality financier focused on the financing of developers of extended stay hotel sites around the United States. Slater previously served as an officer and Naval Aviator in the United States Marine Corps. He flew in Operation Southern Watch over Iraq and earned a single mission Air Medal for landing a jet aboard an aircraft carrier with a complete hydraulic failure and the jet's landing gear still in the "up" position.

Shawn Slocum is assistant special teams coach with the Green Bay Packers, and he also assists in coaching linebackers. Previously, he coached at Texas A&M, the University of Southern California, and the University of Mississippi. He was serving as special teams coach at Texas A&M when his father, R. C. Slocum, guided the Aggies to three straight Southwest Conference Championships.

Garry Sorrell lives in Lufkin, Texas. He is a Plant Manager for the Diboll Lumber Operation of Temple Inland, a manufacturing company strong in building products and containers. He is responsible for managing a top-quartile performing operation.

Barry Stevens is an agent for the Federal Bureau of Investigation, stationed in Dallas, Texas. He has worked with all branches of the military, conducting more than two hundred official interrogations of high-level Al Qaeda and Taliban leaders in Iraq and Afghanistan.

Rick Tankersley lives in McKinney, Texas. For almost two decades, he was named the top-performing sales person for Centex Homes. He won the top Dallas/Fort Worth Sales Person award so often, he stopped submitting his name. Tankersley is presently sales manager for a Centex Homes community in McKinney.

Mike Tolleson lives in Sunnyvale, Texas. While at Texas A&M, he began an operation he called the Free Pizza Club, offering students, for a ten-dollar membership, two pizzas for the price of one, a deal he had established with pizza parlors throughout College Station. He remained in the business after graduation, founding CiCi's Pizza.

Mark Wurzbach lives in Dallas, Texas. A twenty-year employee for Rockwell Automation, he serves as the Business Unit Manager for a company that manufactures Industrial Automation software solutions.